To my good and longtime f
Keith Harvey with best
regards, Jim "Rick" Rickleps
12-10-99

WHIRLYBIRDS

A History of the U.S. Helicopter Pioneers

WHIRLYBIRDS

A History of the U.S. Helicopter Pioneers

JAY P. SPENSER

University of Washington Press

SEATTLE AND LONDON

in association with

Museum of Flight

SEATTLE

To my brother,
Jonathan G. Spenser,
whose help made this book possible

Library of Congress Cataloging-in-Publication Data

Spenser, Jay P.
Whirlybirds : a history of the U.S. helicopter pioneers / Jay P. Spenser.
p. cm.
Includes bibliographical references (p.   ) and index.
ISBN 0-295-97699-3- (alk. paper)
1. Helicopters—United States—History.
2. Sikorsky, Igor Ivan, 1889–1972.
3. Piasecki, Frank N.
4. Young, Arthur M., 1905–   .
5. Hiller, Stanley.
TL716.S73   1998   97–45600
629.133'352'092273—DC21   CIP

Contents

Preface

Although the invention of the helicopter was a remarkable milestone, the crowning achievement in the quest for vertical flight was the greater task of placing this new machine into volume production. Only four people in the world—all of them in the United States—successfully met this enormous challenge before the close of the 1940s, that seminal decade in which humankind's ancient dream of practical vertical flight was at last realized.

Igor I. Sikorsky, Frank N. Piasecki, Arthur M. Young, and Stanley Hiller, Jr., the top-ranking U.S. helicopter pioneers, all developed working helicopters of their own before attempting volume manufacture. The four chose very different paths in their race to turn a novelty of the 1930s into the essential tool it is today. Different in most regards, highly independent by nature, they nevertheless shared a vision, resourcefulness, and the willingness to take extraordinary risks. In many ways they were cut from the same cloth as Wilbur and Orville Wright.

Getting into the helicopter business would never again be as challenging as it was for these men and their companies. By 1950, rotary-wing engineering had advanced to the point where most technological unknowns had been eliminated and there existed a small but growing market for commercial helicopters. Even more significant, the new decade brought the Korean War, which opened the floodgates to military funding for rotorcraft. Kaman, Hughes, and other latecomers to the U.S. helicopter manufacturing scene would find that far fewer challenges remained in this arena compared to those their predecessors had faced.

Throughout the 1930s and early 1940s, the helicopter was the unwanted stepchild of U.S. aviation. The nation's fixed-wing industry and its autogiro manufacturers both chose to ignore it. Had they joined forces in a cooperative effort to support helicopter development, the history of vertical flight would have unfolded far differently. Both camps might reasonably have been expected to pursue helicopter manufacture. They shared an understanding of aerodynamics, lightweight structures, and the mechanics of flight research and development. They also had production facilities readily adaptable to helicopter construction. If the fixed-wing industry had greater resources, the autogiro community made up for the lack through practical experience with rotors and rotary-wing phenomena.

Creating America's helicopter industry fell by default to a third camp: visionaries from all backgrounds who had the audacious dream of practical vertical flight. So daunting and arduous a task confronted them that, of several hundred U.S. helicopter efforts, just four succeeded.

As a young man before World War I, Igor Sikorsky—the patriarch of the vertical-flight industry—had built and flown the world's first multi-engine airplane. Between the wars he developed flying-boat airliners before returning to his helicopter experiments, interrupted in 1910. Sikorsky's stature as an aviation pioneer thus falls little short of that of the Wright brothers. Like Breguet in France, he spans fixed-wing and rotary-wing aviation, linking the "whirlybirds" to the "earlybirds."

Frank Piasecki grew up in Philadelphia, the center of U.S. autogiro manufacturing. Alone in that community, he willingly faced the fact that what the world really wanted was not the autogiro but the helicopter, with its true vertical flight capability. An audacious showman, he succeeded in becoming the world's supplier of big helicopters well before Sikorsky.

Arthur Young's invention of the Bell helicopter represents one chapter in his lifelong quest to reconcile mathematics, science, and fundamental philosophy in an integrated theory of the workings of the universe. An inventor-philosopher, Young embraced the helicopter challenge as a means to obtain greater insight into the laws governing the physical world.

Stanley Hiller, Jr., was first of all a businessman. Unlike America's other early helicopter builders, he always viewed vertical flight as a market opportunity as well as a technical challenge. As a result, his company was able to define and manufacture the first civil helicopter to truly meet the needs of the marketplace.

This business focus—a fundamental difference between Hiller and the other top-ranked

helicopter pioneers—helped him succeed despite seemingly overwhelming odds. Growing up on the West Coast, he lacked access to the knowledge of the East Coast rotary-wing community, upon which Piasecki, Young, and Sikorsky all drew. Alone of the four, he had neither military funding nor corporate support to help him achieve production. And he was the only one of them who chose to become a founding member of the American Helicopter Society when that organization formed in 1944 to represent the struggling vertical-flight industry.

Only Igor Sikorsky—the "old man" of the foursome—was not alive to help the author in his research for this book. Neither were Boris Labensky, the Gluhareff brothers, and many other members of Sikorsky's team. Like Igor himself, most of the key players in his camp had fled the Russian Revolution of 1917 and were of an earlier generation. Thus if the Sikorsky pages are perhaps less rich in behind-the-scenes detail, the author hopes that this failing will be forgiven in light of the lavish attention already paid to Sikorsky and his company by other writers.

In contrast to the fame Igor Sikorsky's great achievements have accorded him, the accomplishments of Frank Piasecki, Arthur Young, and Stanley Hiller have gone unappreciated. This book attempts to redress that oversight, a task aided considerably by the kind help provided by the pioneers themselves. In chronicling their activities this volume makes perhaps its greatest contribution.

It is rare that an author can fill a large gap in the existing body of flight literature. Rarer still is the opportunity to work closely with an industry's creators to uncover what *really* happened. Rarest of all is the chance to preserve for posterity events as entertaining as

those that follow. This volume is a true labor
of love. The author hopes that it is as much
fun to read as it was to research and write.

JAY P. SPENSER
Seattle, Washington
1997

Acknowledgments

The author is hugely indebted to top U.S. helicopter pioneers Frank N. Piasecki, the late Arthur M. Young, and Stanley Hiller, Jr., all of whom endured long interviews and endless follow-up questions with grace and generosity. Heartfelt gratitude also extends to Sergei Sikorsky, who so kindly labored on behalf of his famous father to ensure the accuracy of the pages devoted to the company that bears their name.

In the Piasecki/Vertol/Boeing camp, boundless gratitude goes to Thomas R. "Ren" Pierpoint, who heads a very long list of individuals donating time and energy to see this book realized. Ren grew up amid autogiros in the 1930s, flew and tested helicopters during World War II, then spent a career contributing to the success of Piasecki Helicopters (later Vertol and Boeing Helicopters).

The author is equally indebted to former P/V/B rotary-wing engineer John Schneider, whose career in vertical flight spanned four decades. John rigorously reviewed successive drafts of the entire manuscript, bringing to it his unique perspective as an industry insider and a noted aviation historian.

Other P/V/B insiders who participated in interviews or otherwise contributed are Lee Douglas, Mark Kirschner, Joe Mallen, Frank Mamrol, Kenneth Meenen, Donald N. Meyers, William B. Peck, W. Z. Stepniewski, Howard Stuverude, Tadeusz Tarczynski, Floss Piazza, and George Townson. Heartfelt thanks also to my friend and colleague Nicole Piasecki, her brother Frederick, and the rest of the Piasecki clan. Their help, as well as that of others not named for want of space, has greatly enriched this first-ever history of what is today Boeing Helicopters.

In the Bell camp, Bartram Kelley heads a long list of individuals to whom the author is grateful. Arthur Young's right hand at Gardenville and later director of engineering at Bell, Bart Kelley contributed enormously to this first full history of Bell Helicopter. No less helpful were key Bell figures Hans M. Weichsel, Jr., James Fuller, and the late Charles M. Seibel and Joseph Mashman—legends all in the helicopter industry. Gail Baird, Carl Harris, Robert Leder, Connie McConnell, and Dick Tipton also provided substantial assistance. Ron Foley in particular deserves heartfelt appreciation for the use of his personal collection of professional photography, much of which he shot himself.

The Hiller pages draw upon extensive primary research performed by the author for his previous work, *Vertical Challenge: The Hiller Aircraft Story* (University of Washington Press, 1992). Special thanks go to the Hiller Aviation Museum, as well as to Linda Bennett, Wayne Wiesner, and other individuals too numerous to name here who are properly acknowledged in that book's opening pages.

In addition to Sergei in the Sikorsky camp, sincere thanks go to Dr. Anne Millbrooke, former chief archivist of United Technologies Corporation, for her extraordinarily knowledgeable and generous help. Among the ranks of those who actually helped create Sikorsky history, the author is profoundly grateful to the late Ralph Alex, to Edward F. Katzenberger, Gary R. Kohler, Harold Lemont, Ralph Lightfoot, the late Charles Lester Morris, Edmund R. Vianney, and Dimitry "Jimmy" Viner.

The pages that follow also reflect the valuable contributions of Rhett Flater and Kim Smith at the American Helicopter Society; Peter Wright, former Flying Tiger, commercial helicopter pioneer, and current executive director of the superb new American Helicopter Museum and Education Center near Philadelphia; Michael Lombardi and Thomas Lubbesmeier, Boeing Historical Archives; Tudor Huddleston; the Library of Congress; Dr. F. Robert van der Linden and Donald S. Lopez of the National Air and Space Museum, Smithsonian Institution; Lisa and Brian McCarthy; the National Archives and Records Administration; Boeing Vice President Elizabeth F. Otis; Howard Fox and Tom Horne of the Seattle Public Library; U.S. Army Center of Military History; U.S. Army Aviation Museum; and Lt. General Bob Williams.

A special tribute goes to aviation artist Bart Hunt, whose talent gave *Whirlybirds* the best of covers. To Leila Charbonneau go my thanks for her editing. These acknowledgments would also not be complete without the expression of gratitude to Naomi B. Pascal, Nina McGuinness, Julidta Tarver, Marilyn Trueblood, Pamela Chaus, and others at the University of Washington Press for making publication of this seventh work of aviation history a productive and pleasurable association.

WHIRLYBIRDS

1 / The Beginnings of Vertical Flight

Sikorsky, Piasecki, Bell, and Hiller laid the cornerstones of an active U.S. helicopter industry that continues to meet much of the world's demand for rotorcraft. The four companies they founded were the first and only ones in the world to achieve volume helicopter manufacture before 1950. Three of them remain world-class helicopter builders as of this writing.

For all its American success, the helicopter was a European invention. Working prototypes flew on that continent during the 1930s. Interestingly, no one person, or even one group, invented this new form of flight. A much more difficult technology to realize than the airplane, the helicopter simply presented awe-inspiring challenges. Greater complexity, undiagnosed instability, countless vibrations and stresses, and phenomena ranging from gyroscopic precession to ground resonance ensured that no equivalent of the Wright brothers would usher the helicopter into being, complete and working. Instead it was a collaborative effort.

World War II preempted Europe's hopes of dominating the coming helicopter industry. Germany built several dozen helicopters of various types during the war, but those efforts did not amount to true volume production. Activity shifted across the Atlantic, where parallel if less promising lines of development had long been under way.

America's top pioneers were acquainted with some of Europe's successes in the field of vertical flight. This knowledge base provided Sikorsky, Piasecki, Young, and Hiller with conceptual and theoretical guidance, but little technical or practical help. Although these pioneers built upon essentially the same understanding of past efforts, they chose far different paths. Gamblers all, they drew different cards from a common deck.

The following survey describes the helicopter scene as these four pioneers perhaps knew it at the start of the 1940s. To help the reader interpret the main body of this volume, particular attention is paid to the emergence of key technological elements and rotor configurations.

The roots of helicopter flight stretch back before the dawn of human flight, to a dream that has long captivated the human spirit. The gyrations of falling zanonia seeds, whose pods have an elliptical wing to aid dissemination, may well have inspired the earliest helicopter musings. Screw jacks and artesian wells certainly planted such thoughts in the minds of classical observers, once they understood air to be a medium.

3

The drawings of Leonardo da Vinci include a craft lifted by a helical wing. A lack of power plants or airfoil knowledge doomed this Renaissance vehicle to failure, but the intention was clear. Frenchmen Launoy and Bienvenue invented a rotary-wing toy that took off and flew by its own power. Demonstrated to the Paris Science Academy in 1784, it resolved a philosophical debate over whether heavier-than-air devices fashioned by human hands could indeed fly under their own power.

Nineteenth-century efforts at steam-powered helicopter models gave way by the twentieth century to attempts to create full-size machines, most of which were completely unsuccessful. The first experiment to show promise took place in France in 1907 when Louis Breguet hovered his uncontrollable Breguet-Richet machine, guided—some say assisted—by four or more helpers grasping the bases of its outrigger rotors. Weeks later, Paul Cornu made history's first free helicopter flights with brief ascents in a tandem-rotor, open-framework machine he had fashioned.

At the close of 1906, diminutive Brazilian aeronaut Alberto Santos-Dumont (who constructed an unsuccessful helicopter in 1905) made Europe's first successful airplane flight to great public acclaim. The wave of enthusiasm for fixed-wing aviation he touched off increased to national fervor in 1908 when Wilbur Wright visited France to demonstrate his biplane. The Wright concept of control around all three axes revolutionized French aviation, which would outstrip American efforts and lead the world. By the time the world's first air meet, the Grande Semaine d'Aviation, was staged at Rheims late in 1909, it was clear that support for French helicopter development had, for the moment at least, vanished amid the enthusiasm for airplanes.

One of aviation's greatest pioneers was a witness to the doings of the French aviation community. Returning from Paris to his native Ukraine in 1909, Igor I. Sikorsky built two helicopters in 1909 and 1910. Test beds rather than true man-carrying vehicles, these unsuccessful efforts convinced him that helicopters—although possible—would have to await further advances in the art of aviation. Like Breguet before him, Sikorsky turned to a brilliant career in fixed-wing aviation. He would return to his dream of helicopter flight later in life.

Among a number of other Imperial Russian helicopter experimenters was a remarkable inventor named Boris N. Yuriev. Although Yuriev's modern-looking craft of 1912 was not successful, it was the first helicopter to feature a single main rotor with a small vertical anti-torque rotor on a tail boom, the configuration later adopted by Sikorsky, Bell, and almost all other helicopter builders.

Halted by World War I, helicopter development resumed with fervor in the postwar era. In America, manufacturer Émile Berliner built an 80-hp coaxial helicopter which his son Henry flew in 1920. A second Berliner "helicopter," misnamed because it could not hover, flew two years later.

The shining star of the early 1920s, however, was the brilliant Argentine engineer Marquis Raul Pateras de Pescara. Working in Spain and France, Pescara constructed a number of single-seat coaxial machines with counterrotating biplane rotors. Having successfully flown these unstable machines indoors in 1922, he later set an outdoor record by flying around a pole 500 meters (1,640 feet) distant and returning. By early 1924 he was able to remain in the air for ten minutes at a time.

More significant, Marquis Pescara invented a means of changing the pitch of succeeding

(*Top*) French pioneer Paul Cornu made limited flights in this tandem-rotor helicopter in 1907. Courtesy NASM/SI.

(*Bottom*) Igor Sikorsky and his first unsuccessful helicopter test rig, 1909. Courtesy NASM/SI.

(*Top*) The Berliner helicopter of 1922. Courtesy NASM/SI.

(*Bottom*) Argentine helicopter pioneer Raul de Pescara—developer of the cyclic control and autorotation—hovers indoors in France in 1922. Courtesy NASM/SI.

(*Top*) The de Bothezat helicopter flies in Ohio, 1923. Courtesy NASM/SI.

(*Bottom*) The unworkable Curtiss-Bleecker helicopter had an engine in the rotor hub and a propeller to turn each winglike blade. Courtesy NASM/SI.

blades as they rotated around the same point of the rotor disc. Pescara developed this "cyclic" pitch variation to produce additional thrust where needed to tilt his helicopter laterally. This invention of cyclic control—which enables helicopters to fly forward, backward, and side to side—represents a major milestone in helicopter technology.

Pescara made another significant contribution by solving a problem plaguing rotary-wing pioneers. It was commonly believed that if the engine quit, the wingless helicopter would inevitably plummet and crash. In an era of unreliable engines, the pressing issue of safety seemed insurmountable until Pescara developed the concept of autorotation. He theorized that the upward rush of air as the helicopter descended could be used to spin a freewheeling rotor, which could store kinetic energy like a flywheel. When the ground loomed near, the pilot had only to increase the rotor's pitch at the right time to trade this stored inertia for momentary lift and a soft landing.

Also in 1922, Russian mathematician and scientist George de Bothezat (who immigrated to the United States following the 1917 revolution) built a large four-rotor helicopter which the U.S. Army Air Service tested at McCook Field in Ohio. The cruciform machine demonstrated stable hover for over a minute, although an inability to control lateral drift forced landings when it approached trees and other obstacles. Unlike Pescara's helicopter, however, de Bothezat's effort did not advance the state of helicopter design.

Meanwhile, work had resumed in France where in 1920 Étienne Oehmichen flew a helicopter somewhat similar to Cornu's, although it required a cylindrical balloon above it to offset instability and insufficient engine power. Two years later, Oehmichen was able to dispense with the gasbag and fly free. In 1923 he made the first hovering flight of more than five minutes, and the next year he negotiated a one-kilometer course to set a distance record for helicopters.

In America, Virginian M. B. Bleeker, funded by Curtiss Aircraft, built an ungainly helicopter in 1926. Its four winglike rotor blades each sported a propeller turned by a complex series of chains and gears. Trailing strut-mounted control surfaces affixed to the blades provided control. Like de Bothezat's machine, the unsuccessful Curtiss-Bleeker was a technological dead end.

Dutchman A. G. von Baumhauer built a helicopter in 1925 that flew in a very limited fashion. Able to stay in the air only briefly, this unsuccessful machine had a single main rotor and a small vertical tail rotor to offset torque. It needed the weight of dangling chains at each corner to keep level. A separate engine powered the tail rotor, which operated independently of the main rotor.

Unnoticed at the end of the 1920s was the earliest work of American experimenter Arthur Young, whose pioneering model studies would lead to his development, under Bell Aircraft sponsorship, of the world's first commercial helicopter. Young's significant contributions to helicopter stability distinguish him from other early pioneers.

Building on Juan de la Cierva's invention of the autogiro and his many rotor patents, Europe had a commanding lead in helicopter development as the 1930s began. At the start of the decade, a coaxial helicopter built by d'Ascanio flew to a height of sixty feet in Italy. By mid-decade, Austrian-born Raoul Hafner flew the first combined cyclic-and-collective control system on an autogiro with articulated blades. Although this machine was not capa-

(*Top*) Dutchman A. G. von Baumhauer prepares to fly his helicopter in the latter 1920s. Courtesy NASM/SI.

(*Bottom*) Italy's d'Ascanio helicopter, 1930. Courtesy John Schneider.

(*Top*) A tandem-rotor Florine helicopter of the early 1930s. Courtesy John Schneider.

(*Bottom*) The world's first successful helicopter was this coaxial-rotor machine built by French pioneer Louis Breguet in the early 1930s. Courtesy NASM/SI.

(*Top*) Germany surpassed France with the Focke-Achgelis FA 61 on the eve of World War II, a conflict that shifted subsequent helicopter leadership to the United States. Courtesy NASM/SI.

(*Bottom*) Today largely forgotten, Germany's many wartime helicopter efforts—like this Doblhoff WN 342 pressure-jet prototype developed by Austrian Baron Friedrich von Doblhoff—did not culminate in volume manufacture. Courtesy NASM/SI.

ble of hovering, it marks a milestone in helicopter technology.

One interesting development effort of the early 1930s was a series of tandem-rotor helicopters built by Russian-born engineer Nicolas Florine in Belgium, one of which hovered at altitude for ten minutes. An even more significant effort then under way in France was the Breguet Gyroplane, a coaxial helicopter with counterrotating rotors. Returning to his lifelong fascination with helicopters, an older Louis Breguet oversaw but did not participate directly in the construction and testing of this compact single-seater.

The Gyroplane was badly damaged in a ground accident at the end of 1933. Rebuilt with extensive modifications and tested conservatively on the ground, it resumed flight tests in June 1935. Breguet then audaciously committed it to maneuvering, speed, altitude, and endurance requirements far in excess of anything so far accomplished by a helicopter.

The Breguet Gyroplane flew at 120 kilometers per hour (75 mph), climbed to an altitude of 158 meters (518 feet), and remained in the air for more than one hour during tests that concluded late in 1936. Arguably the world's first successful helicopter, this historic machine was badly damaged in June 1939 during autorotation tests. It was subsequently destroyed by Allied bombing of historic Villacoublay Airfield in 1943.

Despite these remarkable accomplishments, the Breguet was completely upstaged by another European helicopter that first flew in June 1936. Built in Germany by Professor Heinrich Focke in 1936, this single-seat helicopter looked much like an airplane (its body was, in fact, the fuselage of a Focke-Wulf FW 44 Stieglitz biplane). Instead of wings, it sported upward-angled outrigger pylons supporting lateral rotors. This helicopter was des- ignated the Fa 61 in 1937 when Focke joined Gerd Achgelis to form the Focke-Achgelis Flugzeugbau.

The Focke helicopter performed the first successful autorotation in history in May 1937. It outstripped the Breguet by flying to 2,100 meters (6,890 feet). In February 1938, it flew indoors in a famous demonstration in Berlin's huge Deutschlandhalle with famed woman test pilot Hanna Reitsch at the controls. Two months later, this machine flew to an airfield 230 kilometers (143 miles) distant. In January, it climbed to 3,427 meters (11,243 feet), dispelling lingering doubts about the performance potential of helicopters. Charles Lindbergh and Igor Sikorsky were among the visiting dignitaries to observe it.

The sensational use of this helicopter was not accidental, for the busy Nazi propaganda machine paraded the Fa 61 as an example of German technological superiority. As a result of this promotion, the Fa 61—two examples of which were built—stimulated a wave of renewed helicopter research around the world.

A multi-seat version of this helicopter, the Fa 223, was built in small numbers and used on a very limited basis during World War II. Accorded a low wartime priority in Germany, however, helicopter research ended with the collapse of the Third Reich in 1945. French efforts to perfect helicopters had been entirely preempted when the war began in the fall of 1939.

World War II thus translated the realization of a common vision to the United States. Not drawn into the conflict until December 1941, America had two extra years to pursue helicopter development. Backed by the powerful United Aircraft group, Igor Sikorsky put this time to productive use. Before the decade was out, helicopters of various sizes and configurations had been perfected and a vigorous, balanced manufacturing industry had sprung into being.

Military use was not the only motivation for America's ardent if belated pursuit of helicopters. Nearly all of an estimated three hundred U.S. helicopter projects during or just after the war—the vast majority of which failed before a prototype was constructed—originated in the pervasive cultural expecta-

tion that the near future would witness privately owned helicopters vying for space in American garages with family automobiles. In an increasingly urban society, helicopters were seen as an answer to clogged city streets. Aerial traffic, rooftop platforms, and rotary-wing bus lines were the stuff of such national daydreams.

Whether for civil or military use, the race for production helicopters was on.

2 / Sikorsky

Igor Ivanovich Sikorsky towers as the father of the helicopter.[1] Although he did not invent this new form of flight, his was the first company in the world to place helicopters into volume production and the only one to do so before the end of World War II. So unique was Igor Sikorsky that a quarter century after his death his personal stamp remains strong on the company bearing his name.

An aviation pioneer whose stature rivals that of the Wright brothers, Sikorsky was born in Kiev, Ukraine, in 1889. As a child he devoured books about the physical world and scientific discoveries. Two events were particularly formative during this period. The first was the publication of Jules Verne's *Clipper of the Clouds*, which Igor first read at the turn of the century. An imaginative tale of an aerial ship supported by dozens of vertical airscrews atop mastlike shafts, it captured his imagination. Later in life he recalled poring for weeks over the book's intriguing illustrations.

The second influential event was the rediscovery a few years before Sikorsky's birth of Leonardo da Vinci's lost notebooks. The widely reproduced illustrations of this Renaissance genius—particularly his sketches of man-powered flying machines and a helicopter-like mechanism—greatly impressed Sikorsky as a boy. At a young age he displayed a remarkable understanding of physical principles, which he demonstrated with enviable mechanical skill. He bought wire and wound armatures to make little electric motors and installed them in model trains of his own design. Batteries that he made out of glass jars powered this and other toys he created.

Sikorsky was fourteen when the Wright brothers flew on December 17, 1903. That year, following in the footsteps of his older brother Sergei, he entered the Imperial Russian Naval Academy at St. Petersburg. After three years of general studies, he resigned to pursue his evident interest in engineering. This new career began with three months of study in Paris, after which he returned home in 1907 to specialize in electrical engineering at the Polytechnic Institute of Kiev.

During a summer vacation with his father in the Bavarian Alps in 1908, nineteen-year-old Igor came across a newspaper account of Wilbur Wright's dramatic flying displays outside Paris (Orville had stayed home to sell a Wright Flyer to the U.S. Army). The account and accompanying illustrations thrilled Igor, who decided to build a flying machine of his own.

Traveling to Paris early in 1909, he soaked up all the supposition and knowledge—the latter in short supply—available from France's flying community, then the most active in the world. Against the advice of seasoned aviators who thought the airplane more promising, he embarked on the development of a small helicopter, which he constructed back in Kiev later that year. The platformlike machine, and a larger one built the following year, failed to achieve flight primarily because of insufficient engine power.

Considering the state of the art in aviation and power plants not advanced enough to warrant further helicopter attempts, Sikorsky turned to fixed-wing aircraft design. During the next three years he built several craft, in which he taught himself to fly, and he also joined the Russo-Baltic Wagon Company and moved to its new aviation division in St. Petersburg.

In the spring of 1913, Sikorsky won international fame with the first multi-engine aircraft ever to fly. With dual controls in an enclosed cockpit (forward of which was an observation balcony), and a passenger cabin with wicker seats, folding tables, and electric lights overhead, the Sikorsky *Grand* was remarkably advanced. That it came into being less than ten years after the Wright brothers built history's first airplane is truly remarkable. From 1913 to 1917, Sikorsky built seventy-two larger *Il'ya Muromets* four-engine biplanes, which served as bombers for Imperial Russia in World War I.

Fleeing the 1917 revolution, Sikorsky traveled from France to the United States, arriving in New York City in 1919. Unable to speak English, he was also penniless, having left behind the personal fortune he had made in his native land. Despite huge obstacles, he began a new career in aviation and within five years had built a large twin-engine biplane called the S-29A.

Noted air racer Roscoe Turner purchased the S-29A and was checked out in it by Sikorsky himself. Turner found the designer as impressive as his airplane, noting that he was one of the finest natural fliers and test pilots he had ever flown with. At that time, Sikorsky had probably logged more multi-engine flight time than any other human being.

In 1926, Sikorsky built the tri-motor S-35 in which French ace René Fonck hoped to win the Raymond Orteig Prize by flying nonstop from New York to Paris. Having survived a fiery crash on takeoff, which destroyed this aircraft, Fonck commissioned Sikorsky to build another. The project came to an early end, however, when Charles Lindbergh successfully flew a monoplane from New York to Paris in 1927.

Sikorsky's first real success in the United States was the S-38, a twin-engine boat-hulled amphibious machine combining high performance with superb handling. A third of more than one hundred S-38s constructed were delivered to Pan American Airways. Their success in commercial service won for Sikorsky the chance to build the much larger S-40 amphibian and its S-42 successors. Pan Am used these flying boats during the 1930s to provide pioneering "clipper" service to Latin America.

Started in 1923 on a chicken farm in Roosevelt, New York, where the S-29A was built in the open, the Sikorsky Manufacturing Company soon moved to an old wooden hangar on nearby Roosevelt Field. Later it occupied a small factory at College Point on Long Island, which because of the success of the S-38 it quickly outgrew. In 1929, Sikorsky relocated to Stratford, Connecticut, where the Housatonic River flows into Long Island Sound in southern New England. The new location provided sheltered waters for boat-hulled aircraft.

(*Top*) Born in the Ukraine in 1889, Igor Sikorsky in 1913 became the first person ever to build and fly a multi-engine airplane. Courtesy United Technologies Corporation.

(*Bottom*) Sikorsky stands before his first U.S. airplane, the s-29, which for want of funding was assembled outdoors. Courtesy UTC.

While still at College Point, Sikorsky had attracted the attention of the newly forming United Aircraft and Transport Corporation (UATC) in Hartford, Connecticut. The two key components of this powerful new corporate entity were Pratt & Whitney (makers of the radial engines powering Sikorsky's clippers) and Boeing Aircraft of Seattle, Washington. Other companies in the United fold included the Hamilton Standard Propeller Company; Boeing Air Transport, an airline subsidiary of the Seattle company; and aircraft builders Northrop, Stearman, and Chance Vought.[2] Sikorsky officially joined United Aircraft and Transport in July 1929, thereby beginning a long association the aviation pioneer would never regret.

Ironically, a national scandal coming to light early in 1934 dramatically reduced the size and power of United Aircraft and Transport. Centering on purported abuses by the Post Office Department and the airlines in awarding and executing commercial air mail contracts, the scandal precipitated a wrenching, if temporary, shake-up of the nation's air transport system. All contracts were canceled and the Army Air Corps briefly flew the mails until the Roosevelt administration relented. Luckily the national airways system carefully orchestrated by previous Postmaster General Walter Folger Brown emerged largely intact.

New Deal sentiment, however, had also prompted another response to the Air Mail Scandal. Congress believed that the Aviation Corporation (AVCO), the North American Aviation Corporation, the General Motors Corporation (then heavily involved in aviation), and UATC had entered the airline field to guarantee themselves a market for their products. The government contended that these four holding companies with their avi-ation manufacturing interests threatened to dominate the industry and stifle market entry by newcomers.

Although formal antitrust proceedings were not initiated, legislation having a similar effect was quickly enacted. The Air Mail Act of 1934 prohibited the awarding of air mail contracts to corporations that also built airplanes, effectively forcing UATC and the other three corporations to divest themselves of their aircraft manufacturing interests or risk bankruptcy.

This episode in American history remains controversial to this day. It can be argued that an oligopoly in a capital-intensive industry, regulated as it was by the government, did in fact operate in the public interest. Whatever the truth, the face of U.S. aviation profoundly changed in 1934.

Out of United Aircraft and Transport—the largest of the four holding companies—three separate corporations emerged: the Boeing Aircraft Company and its subsidiary, Wichita-based Stearman Aircraft; Chicago-based United Air Lines; and the United Aircraft Corporation, which no longer extended beyond Connecticut.

In the restructuring, United's corporate headquarters, Pratt & Whitney, Hamilton Standard, and Chance Vought all took up residence in adjoining buildings on a newly constructed 578-acre airfield in East Hartford. Sikorsky thus became the only component of United Aircraft not located on Rentschler Field, as the airport was christened in honor of Pratt & Whitney founder Frederick D. Rentschler.[3]

Assets of the new corporate entity had dropped by the end of 1934 from a predivestiture $26,360,000 to $7,133,155. Thanks primarily to demand for its superb engines and propellers, it remained financially strong despite the Great Depression, which had bottomed out. The year's net operating loss of some $27,000 was attributable to the one-time expense of reorganizing, and $7,533,662 in unfilled orders remained on the books. During 1934, moreover, Pratt & Whitney had introduced its highly reliable new Wasp and Wasp Junior radial engines, Hamilton Standard had brought a two-position controllable-pitch propeller to market offering improved performance over fixed-pitch propellers, and Sikorsky had begun S-42 deliveries to Pan Am at a selling price of $210,487 each.

United Aircraft's Sikorsky subsidiary in fact lost money building the clippers that established Pan American as the most glamorous airline in U.S. history. But Sikorsky management could hardly be blamed for the loss, for Pan Am's dynamic leader Juan Terry Trippe, in order to elicit a lower unit purchase price, had promised substantially larger clipper orders than he eventually placed. In losing money to Pan Am, Sikorsky would find itself in good company before the decade was out, for Trippe's use of the same tactic in buying Martin M-130 and Boeing 314 clippers worked great economic hardship on those companies (Martin, in fact, was forced for a time to declare bankruptcy). "It was not intended to be a nonprofit operation," Sikorsky said later with dry humor, "it just turned out that way."[4]

Sikorsky was not a businessman. Business for its own sake held no interest for him. It was best delegated, since it kept him from the development and engineering work he loved. Under the United Aircraft umbrella he happily relinquished direct administrative and managerial responsibility for the company he had founded.

What Sikorsky did not relinquish was personal involvement. His unique presence permeated the company that bore his name. If his adopted country was predicated on equality, he himself was perhaps the truest egalitarian, for he addressed his employees by name and he treated everyone with the same courteous deference. A man of great natural humility who genuinely cared about people, he made an art of listening. Contact with their famous boss left Sikorsky employees glowing with the awareness that a special honor had been bestowed on them. Above all, this old-world aviation genius was polite. "It was frequently observed," recalls rotary-wing engineer Harold E. Lemont, "that nobody ever walked through a door *after* Igor Sikorsky."[5]

Yet another change in Sikorsky's corporate standing came on June 29, 1935, when Pratt & Whitney, Hamilton Standard, Vought, and Sikorsky—individual companies which had been subsidiaries of the parent United Aircraft holding corporation—were made divisions of a single new company known as the United Aircraft Manufacturing Corporation (all stock of which was owned by the corporation). Assets at the end of 1935 were $10,445,017, liabilities $3,177,465, net profit for the year was $434,635, and unfilled orders had doubled to $15,804,052.

Sikorsky continued designing and building boat-hulled aircraft in moderate numbers, notably the twin-engine S-43 Baby Clipper amphibian of 1935 and the ocean-spanning VS-44A of 1942 (developed from the Navy-sponsored XPBS-1 of 1937). But the end of the great flying-boat era was on the horizon. In fact, by greatly accelerating transport plane development and prompting construction of land-plane facilities around the world, World War II would sound the death knell of this romantic chapter in aviation history. No

Sikorsky s-42 Clipper of Pan American Airways.
Courtesy UTC.

demand would exist for large flying-boat airliners in the postwar era.

In 1938, Sikorsky finally saw his opportunity to resume dedicated helicopter development. Not that he had ever really stopped working on his lifelong dream. Drawings accompanying patents he was awarded in the late 1920s and early 1930s clearly show that his thoughts were never far from vertical flight. One patent in particular (applied for June 27, 1931, and granted March 19, 1935) shows a craft incorporating virtually all the key features of the Sikorsky vs-300 helicopter of 1939.

The limitations in aviation and engine technologies which had forced Sikorsky to abandon his first efforts in 1909–10 had largely disappeared. Louis Breguet's success in France, and especially Heinrich Focke's in Germany, convinced him that production helicopters were now a possibility.

Ironically, the same lessening demand for flying boats that had given him the time for such a project now threatened to deny him the means, for also in the fateful year of 1938 he learned that Sikorsky Aircraft was to be shut down. It was a painful decision for the management of United Aircraft, which out of deference to the respected pioneer had delayed the action as long as possible, but the vast cost of running an unproductive factory and meeting its payroll left no alternative.

The news, delivered by United Vice President and Sikorsky General Manager Eugene E. Wilson, came as no surprise to Sikorsky. Hearing the other out, he played the ace up his sleeve with his usual eloquence. Asking only that he be allowed to retain his talented team, Sikorsky proposed developing a research helicopter to lay the groundwork for future helicopter production. He estimated that a prototype would cost no more than $30,000, and the potential rewards for success were great.

Wilson agreed immediately to Sikorsky's request to retain his talented team and granted permission for the group to begin work on a helicopter. It was understood that continuation of this program beyond the design phase would require United Aircraft management's ongoing approval. Since the helicopter had few if any champions among the ranks of United leadership—or among the aircraft industry as a whole—such approval was hardly a sure thing.

Thus Sikorsky came away from his meeting with Gene Wilson with a provisional go-ahead for an ambitious and technically demanding program. Others embarking on such a project might well have had second thoughts, but not Igor Sikorsky. The opportunity to pursue full-time a solution to the "vertical flight problem," as he called it, thrilled the forty-nine-year-old aviation pioneer.

"It was a wonderful chance to relive one's life all over again," he would say many years later. "It was a chance to design a new type of flying machine without really knowing how to design it; then to build it without really knowing how to build it; and then the chance to climb into the pilot's seat and try to test fly it, without ever having flown a helicopter before."[6]

Upon finishing the conceptual phase at the start of 1939, Sikorsky sent the following memorandum to United Aircraft Corporation vice president and board member Rensselaer W. Clark:

I am convinced of the importance of helicopter development and I wish to emphasize the extreme desirability of our continuing this work and completing the second phase of the project, which would be to construct a small, single seater [sic], experimental machine. The work could be done at a total cost of $20,000, this to include all draft work, labor and material, but would not include general overhead. We have an excellent opportunity for leadership in a new field which may have possibilities far in excess of what is attributed at present to this type of aircraft. The cost would be negligible, and patent protection could be created at present, while at a later date all the difficulties and expenses involved in entering a new field will increase considerably. . . . United would have a good chance to gain leadership in this new line in the United States, and possibly even outside the country. We must, however, take into consideration that interest in the direct lift aircraft, which has remained dormant for a reasonably long time, has obviously been aroused everywhere abroad, as well as in this country, and it is, therefore, extremely important that we do not lose time in this respect.[7]

Sikorsky realized that a worldwide race was under way to perfect a helicopter and bring it to market, but to his disappointment United seemed not to appreciate the need for quick action. In truth, it was hardly surprising that additional funding was slow in coming; construction and testing of a prototype helicopter would entail significant expenditures and would threaten to commit United Aircraft to a long-term and possibly unrewarding development effort. Although United traditionally devoted substantial resources to research and development (R&D), the corporation did not authorize highly speculative programs without due consideration. But deliberating the value of this helicopter program was challenging because

helicopters were an unknown quantity. Many high executives doubted their value or feasibility. They felt the corporation would do well to avoid them.

United Aircraft had little time to lose. Having abandoned dedicated helicopter development almost three decades before, Igor Sikorsky was returning to it late, for experimenters in Europe held a commanding lead. The race was on.

On February 17, 1939, an article in the *New York Times* caught Sikorsky's eye. President Franklin D. Roosevelt, it reported, had recommended that Congress appropriate funds, as described later in this section, for War Department use in fostering American rotary-wing development. In a memorandum dated February 21, 1939, Sikorsky informed Rensselaer Clark of this development, which promised military support for industry helicopter programs in the near future. In a concluding paragraph, which both importunes Clark and lays out a brilliant strategy for United Aircraft to follow, Sikorsky wrote:

It is most firmly recommended that the modest program of the helicopter development, including the construction of a single seater flying machine, should be approved. This would permit building and having a ship ready for test by the middle of summer. I believe it would be by far the best for us to carry out this preliminary work by ourselves, independently and with as little publicity as possible. A modest amount of success after the completion of the first ship would enhance our position in respect to obtaining an experimental order from the Government for the next ship, and would permit continuing the development of this most promising type of aircraft at Government expense.[8]

Still without a firm commitment from United Aircraft, Sikorsky tried a different tack in a proposal dated March 12, 1939, asking for $60,000 to carry his research helicopter through both construction and a test program. Perhaps because they found this lump-sum proposal more palatable than earlier requests which had not 'made the overall program cost clear, United chief executives at last gave their consent. The decision was more a measure of their faith in Sikorsky than their belief in the helicopter.

The Stratford helicopter team could now set about building an experimental research prototype, which they designated the vs-300. Standing for Vought-Sikorsky, the prefix (also applied to Sikorsky's last great flying boat, the vs-44a of 1942) reflected a 1938 consolidation of United Aircraft's Vought and Sikorsky divisions.

The physical relocation of Vought to Stratford was spurred by a growing military demand for engines and propellers on the eve of World War II. This move allowed Hamilton Standard to occupy Vought's old plant in East Hartford, while Pratt & Whitney absorbed the space vacated by the propeller division. Accomplished with a relatively small outlay for additional manufacturing facilities at the Stratford factory (necessary to accommodate both divisions), the move provided increased floor space for the engine and propeller divisions in East Hartford, and more efficient operation with lower overhead for the aircraft divisions (which had been jointly administered for some time in any case).

The vs-300 team under Sikorsky consisted of Michael and Serge Gluhareff, Boris P. "Bob" Labensky, Alexander Nikolsky, Nicholas Glad, Michael Buivid, Adolph Plenefisch, and various others as their skills

were needed. Igor *Alexis* Sikorsky—a younger cousin of the company founder whose scholarly demeanor earned him the nickname Professor—provided theoretical help with rotary-wing aerodynamics.

The Gluhareff brothers had fled Russia's 1917 revolution, and had joined Sikorsky's company in Long Island shortly after its founding. Their interest in aviation had its roots in glider experiments in Finland before World War I. Short and wiry, in love with airplanes and fast cars, Michael Gluhareff was a gifted engineer whose specialty was wings and airfoils, which he laid out with an artist's eye. As Sikorsky's right-hand man, he handled the bulk of the vs-300's detailed engineering. Serge Gluhareff, physically and temperamentally the opposite of his brother, was also a member of the engineering department, but his contributions to the helicopter project were more administrative in nature.

Bob Labensky, longtime head of the experimental shop, was a brilliant engineer whose conceptual abilities made him a key problem solver. A former officer in the Imperial Russian Navy, he had been with Sikorsky since the company's founding in 1923. Adolph Plenefisch would supervise the mechanical functioning of the new helicopter. Nick Glad—tall, aristocratic, and another former Russian naval officer—was a natural craftsman who could seemingly build anything. So could Michael Buivid, who had headed up the Sikorsky test shop.

Buivid and Labensky were the first to get their hands dirty. In 1938, well before work began on the actual helicopter, they constructed a test rig incorporating dynamic components proposed for the vs-300. The helicopter team used this wheeled rig—which was reminiscent of Sikorsky's helicopters of

The first Sikorsky factory in Stratford, Connecticut, site of vs-300 testing. Courtesy UTC.

Team members Michael Buivid, Sikorsky, Boris
Labensky, and Michael Gluhareff pose with
vs-300 cockpit trainer. Courtesy UTC.

1909–10—to develop lift and torque data, because small wind tunnel models had proved insufficient.

Since detailed design drawings were not required for a one-of-a-kind engineering improvisation, the design phase did not take long. The features, general dimensions, and overall configuration of the emerging helicopter had long since been worked out by Sikorsky himself. Construction of the vs-300 was therefore under way by March 1939 and progressed through the summer.

The experimental machine coming together featured welded steel-tube construction. Steel tubing offered strength, lightness, and easy access to internal components for rapid repair and modification. At the front was an open pilot's seat, which reminded Sikorsky of the exposed perches of his earliest flying machines of a quarter century earlier. Overhead, a three-bladed main rotor spanned 28 feet in diameter (later increased to 30), while the anti-torque rotor at the rear of the tail boom—a single-bladed unit balanced with a counterweight—had a radius of 40 inches. In addition to lateral main landing gear wheels, the craft had both a nose and a tail wheel.

Power was supplied by a Lycoming air-cooled aircraft engine rated at 75 hp. A transmission converted its maximum of over 2,000 RPM to the main rotor's rotational speed of slightly over 250 RPM. Reduction was achieved with automotive bevel gears and five V-belts, the latter to permit quick changes in the reduction ratio by substitution of different-size pulleys.

On September 14, 1939, the vs-300 was wheeled out to open ground behind the Vought-Sikorsky plant. Igor Sikorsky settled into the metal seat. As the engine idled and the rotor turned in flat pitch, he felt out the controls with the probing touch of the skilled test pilot he was. The stick shook as he held it. This shaking—the result of unbalanced rotor blades—grew much worse as he opened the throttle. Raising the collective lever, he gingerly lifted the novel craft a few inches off the ground (the limit of its tether cables) before settling immediately down again.

Sikorsky made several more such "flights" on this historic first day of testing. Very tricky controls and a lack of rotary-wing flight experience reinforced his natural caution, and he ended the session after a total of perhaps ten seconds in the air. Nevertheless he was thrilled and excited.

By November 1939, the vs-300, temporarily modified with a full-swivel main landing gear, was making sustained tethered flights. Controllability remained marginal, however, and stability was poor. A gust of wind was able to overturn the hovering craft during a hover test on December 11, 1939. Although the rotor blades were destroyed and the aircraft itself was badly damaged, the pilot—in this case, Serge Gluhareff—emerged shaken but unhurt.

Learning from the accident, film of which was studied, Sikorsky and his team rebuilt the vs-300 with extensive modification. The primary change was the removal of cyclic pitch control from the main rotor, which retained collective pitch control only.[9] The latter had worked well enough, but the former had failed entirely to provide directional control in flight; attempts to bank produced unwanted pitch changes and vice versa.

Sikorsky's decision to remove "azimuth control," as he called cyclic pitch, reflected his distinctive step-by-step approach to engineering. Cyclic problems held up testing so he turned to another means of achieving lateral control. Never one to run from engi-

(*Top*) Igor Sikorsky lifts the tethered vs-300 helicopter a few inches into the air for the first time, September 14, 1939. Courtesy UTC.

(*Bottom*) Wearing the perennial homburg, Sikorsky pilots the vs-300 in its second configuration in the spring of 1940. Courtesy UTC.

neering challenges, he fully intended to come back to cyclic pitch and make it work; but first he had to solve the problems of "vertical control."

It was a very different looking helicopter that took to the air on March 6, 1940. The most obvious change was the addition of two lateral booms stretching wide on either side of a new trusswork aft fuselage just forward of the tail rotor. Atop each of these outrigger pylons was a 40-inch-radius horizontal propeller whose blade pitch could be increased or decreased as needed to vary the downward thrust. These propellers, in other words, featured collective pitch control like the main rotor. Varying the lift of these units in unison served to tilt the helicopter's nose up or down for control on the pitch axis, whereas differential control of these rotors (increasing the lift of one while simultaneously decreasing that of the other) induced a lateral tilting moment for control around the roll axis.

The new control system still had problems, but at least the vs-300 could now dispense with tether cables and fly freely. This milestone was achieved May 13, 1940, and one week later the Sikorsky helicopter was publicly unveiled. "The invited guests looked on in amazement as Igor flew the vs-300 backwards, sideways, up and down, and even turned on a spot," wrote Sikorsky biographer Frank J. Delear. Following this display, Charles L. Morris, commissioner of aeronautics for the state of Connecticut, stepped forward and handed Sikorsky an envelope. "Mr. Sikorsky," he stated, "I am happy to present you with Connecticut helicopter license no. 1." It was the first helicopter license ever issued in the United States.[10]

Ironically, so enthusiastic were the onlookers about all the things a helicopter could do

that few noticed it had not flown forward any distance. The vs-300 in this second configuration flew well in any direction *except* forward. If coaxed to creep forward, it would balk and stop; if pushed to fly faster, it would become unstable, control effectiveness would diminish, and it would again stop.

"The trouble was that the thing really would fly nicely backwards but it just didn't want to go forwards," Sikorsky admitted a few years later. "Once in despair I even thought that, well, if this is the case, I will just turn the seat around and let her go backwards if that is what she wants to do." Eugene Wilson, by now president of United Aircraft, soon noticed this odd circumstance. "Mr. Sikorsky," the helicopter's inventor recalled being asked, "I have seen fine movies of your machine hovering . . . and flying sideways and backward; why haven't you made movies of [it] flying forward?" His answer: "Yes, Mr. Wilson, forward flight is a minor engineering problem we haven't solved yet."[11]

By July the vs-300's Lycoming engine had been replaced by a 90-hp Franklin. An increase in power was welcome, although there was little noticeable difference in the machine's performance. On July 18 the craft remained aloft for fifteen minutes in its longest flight so far. Six days later, it was flown for the first time by Captain H. Franklin Gregory, the experienced autogiro pilot entrusted with administering the fledgling helicopter program of the U.S. Army Air Forces.

As rotary-wing project officer at Wright Field in Dayton, Ohio, Frank Gregory had drafted technical specifications for an Army helicopter in 1939. This assignment reflected passage the previous year of the Dorsey Bill (H.R. 8143, Public Law 787), a forgotten piece of landmark legislation that helped shape the U.S. helicopter industry.

Ironically, the Dorsey Bill began life as special-interest legislation designed to promote autogiros, not helicopters. The Pitcairn and Kellett companies, which together formed America's failing autogiro industry, gave rise to this bill by petitioning Congressman Frank J. G. Dorsey for two favors: taxpayer subsidization of further autogiro development, and government intervention to see autogiros incorporated into widespread military use.

The U.S. armed services did not want autogiros, of course. They had evaluated this rotorcraft and had not found a role for it. The same was true of the civil market, which had little use for autogiros. Thus a declining autogiro industry in desperation sought Dorsey's support. Its diminishing hopes for volume production were squarely pinned on the Pennsylvania Democrat's evolving legislation.

To the dismay of his constituents, Dorsey presented a far different bill for ratification. As enacted into law June 30, 1938, the bill was evenhanded, broadly worded, and devoid of "pork." Embracing helicopters and other aircraft as well as autogiros, it authorized $2,000,000 "to remain available until expended for the purpose of rotary-wing and other aircraft research, development, procurement, experimentation, and operation for service testing." An initial appropriation of $300,000 followed in 1939.

Drawing on these funds, Frank Gregory opened an industrywide request for proposals (RFP) on April 15, 1940, for the U.S. Army's second helicopter.[12] Only four bids arrived, reflecting the "unwanted stepchild" status of helicopters within the broad United States aviation industry. On July 19—just five days before he flew the VS-300 in Stratford—Gregory had awarded this contract to Platt-LePage, a Philadelphia company already at work on a twin-lateral-rotor

machine the Army would call the XR-1.

Among the losing proposals was one prepared and submitted by Igor Sikorsky. Platt-LePage's entry had emerged the winner because it followed the side-by-side rotor configuration used successfully by Germany in the much-publicized Focke-Achgelis FA 61.

On August 9, 1940, the VS-300 flew about 250 yards and performed an aerial pickup for the first time. Four days later, it flew for National Geographic Society photographers at Bridgeport Airport. Demonstrations took a back seat to engineering work, however, because much remained to be done before the research craft's builders could feel satisfied.

Stability and controllability went hand in hand and remained major concerns of Sikorsky and his team. To address the inherent instability of helicopters, they went to work on controllability. The pilot must always be able to keep the machine under control. For added safety, Sikorsky designed the VS-300 with long moments of inertia so that it was well damped. By slowing the rate at which it would diverge from normal flight, he pushed it toward neutral stability. There would be no such thing as "hands off" flight in the Sikorsky prototype, but the pilot would at least have a bit of time to take corrective action.

Nevertheless, the VS-300 was high-spirited and demanding. Through much of its test program, it had a defiant streak and a mind of its own. Remarks made by Sikorsky at the First Annual Dinner of the newly formed American Helicopter Society, held at the Ambassador Hotel in New York City on October 7, 1944, are revealing in this regard.

"I can give up one more secret now which we withheld very carefully at that time," he said with typical humor, "namely, most of the early movies were made slow motion movies, and this was for two reasons: One was to extend the length of the flight for obvious reasons. The other—which was just as necessary—was that while the machine was stable in the air, yet it was to say, frankly, not too stable, and of course if you could see the movies at the natural speed, the audience might become frightened, while in slow motion it all looked very graceful and nice."[13]

One test resulted in a loss of control fifteen feet above the ground, followed by a very hard landing. To determine the value of viscous dampers in restricting extraneous rotor blade motion, the team had drained the oil out of the dampers to render them useless. The jolting conclusion to the flight quickly convinced everybody that the rotor blades indeed benefited from viscous damper snubbing.

On October 14, 1940, Igor Sikorsky was flying over Bridgeport Airport at 30 mph some twenty feet off the ground when the VS-300 rolled and slammed on its side into the ground. Unhurt, he climbed out as fellow team members ran up to survey the damage to the helicopter. It was immediately apparent that a supporting member had failed near a weld, allowing one of the tail outriggers to fold upward. With the drive belt loosened, the rotor atop the outrigger stopped developing thrust and the craft had rolled. The earlier hard landing had obviously damaged the structure and set the stage for a major accident caused by metal fatigue. That the outrigger had broken during attempted forward flight was not surprising. With its rotor then straining to maintain a tail-up attitude, it was under maximum stress.

Sikorsky knew why his ship was so unwilling to fly straight ahead: with forward airspeed, the downwash of the main rotor shifted aft to envelop the horizontal tail rotors. This downwash offset the extra lift they were called upon to generate in order to tilt the helicopter into the nose-down attitude needed for forward flight. When the machine started moving forward, a countering force came into play that worked to push the tail back down and halt the progress of the machine. Balancing these forces, a pilot could push the VS-300 into a balky, halting forward flight punctuated with unexpected stops, but it was not easy.

Before the crash, Sikorsky had already raised the rotors a bit on the existing outriggers, which he had also widened. These steps, taken to reduce downwash interference, worked little improvement. In a sense this accident (on the thirteen-month anniversary of the VS-300's first flight) was timely, for it provided an opportunity for more extensive modification than the team might have wished to undertake otherwise.

The VS-300 that emerged on Christmas Eve 1940 retained the same basic configuration, but its outriggers were now angled upward to lift the horizontal tail rotors out of the main rotor downwash. These rotors were also canted inward 18 degrees to improve lateral stability.

On January 10, 1941, the prototype remained aloft for 25 minutes. Good as this performance was, it fell considerably short of European accomplishments (the Breguet Gyroplane had flown more than an hour almost six years earlier). Still, constant refinement was clearly bearing fruit. By mid-January, for example, it was clear that the inclined tail rotors provided less control authority, so the amount of inward tilt was reduced to 7 degrees. Two months later, these rotors were raised 8 inches on their pylons to provide yet more clearance. The problem of main rotor downwash was proving difficult to avoid. This modification necessitated small V-braces at the tips of the outriggers to support the rotor shafts just below the blades.

(*Top*) Upward-angled rear outriggers reveal another vs-300 configuration by the spring of 1941. Courtesy UTC.

(*Bottom*) Sikorsky sets a world record by keeping the vs-300 aloft 1 hour and 32 minutes on May 6, 1941. Courtesy UTC.

The helicopter now flew well enough for its builders to contemplate breaking a record or two. Accordingly, on April 15, 1941, Sikorsky lifted the vs-300 into the air to establish an official American helicopter endurance record of 1 hour, 5 minutes, and 14.5 seconds. It was still 15 minutes short of the world's record of 1 hour, 20 minutes, 39 seconds, established in 1937 by the Focke-Achgelis helicopter in Germany.

On May 6, Igor Sikorsky again lifted the vs-300 into the air for what he assured reporters would be the most boring flight they had ever witnessed. When the hovering craft settled onto the grass after 1 hour, 32 minutes, and 26 seconds, an official world's record had indeed been set. Bringing this distinction to American shores signaled a much larger shift, for Igor Sikorsky had now taken the lead in worldwide helicopter development.

Between the two records, Sikorsky flew the vs-300 on rubber floats. With two of the sausage-shaped devices in place of the main wheels and a smaller one at the rear, plus a basketball and volleyball under the nose to ensure that the pilot stayed dry, he demonstrated the first operation of a helicopter off water in history. Here at last, the inventor observed with pride, was a vehicle that could land on virtually any surface provided there was clearance for the rotor blades. Also in April, a more powerful Franklin engine rated at a full 100 hp was installed. The craft's designation was officially amended to vs-300A to reflect that fact, although nobody bothered to use the suffix.

All this activity attracted important visitors. One was Arthur Raymond, chief designer of the legendary DC-3 airliner, who came all the way from California to determine if Douglas Aircraft should undertake helicopter development. Before leaving, he reportedly announced, "I'm going to go back and tell my board of directors that it's too complicated. We shouldn't get involved!"[14]

One visitor who strongly believed in helicopters was Charles Lindbergh, who observed the vs-300 on October 9, 1940. He eventually returned to fly the craft several times during March 1943. Royal Air Force Wing Commander Reginald A. C. Brie of the British Purchasing Commission visited January 20, 1942. This event set the stage for wartime British helicopter use. Beginning early in 1942, the Sikorsky team was also visited by U.S. Coast Guard Commanders William J. Kossler, Frank Erickson, and W. A. Burton, all of whom would play roles in the further development and service acceptance of Sikorsky helicopters.

Les Morris, the state aeronautics official who had awarded Sikorsky his helicopter license the previous year, joined Vought-Sikorsky's flight test department in March 1941. New demands on Sikorsky's time (the development of a two-seat military helicopter, as described below) required him to delegate the flying of the vs-300. Recalling Morris's interest and enthusiasm, Sikorsky offered him the opportunity to be the helicopter's new test pilot. Morris jumped at the chance. He made his first flight May 12, 1941, and immediately proved to be a valuable addition to the hardworking team.

About mid-June 1941, Sikorsky made the momentous decision to reintroduce cyclic pitch (azimuth) control to the main rotor. Many other problems associated with helicopter flight had been resolved and it was time to solve this one as well. Since cyclic pitch had not worked before, the designer decided to return to it in stages. Accordingly, the main rotor was reworked with a swashplate which rocked side to side for roll control only. Also, the collective pitch controls of the outrigger rotors were locked to work only in unison. They would continue to provide pitch control, but now that they were divested of differential action, they would no longer serve to roll the helicopter. The vertical tail rotor (which had long since gone to two blades) continued to provide yaw control. All three of these rotors were increased to a radius of 46 inches.

The vs-300 still exhibited less than satisfactory control. Testing continued into the summer when Sikorsky ordered yet another major configurational change. A tall pylon mounting a three-bladed horizontal rotor was added to the tail, and the cumbersome outriggers with their rotors were discarded. Less readily apparent, the entire rear fuselage was new. Where the previous one had been square, the new three-longeron (two on top and one at bottom) aft body was triangular in cross section.

Two rotors had not been needed for pitch control and had produced slight "Dutch roll" instability in any event. Worse still, they were still subject to main rotor downwash. When testing began August 11, 1941, the revised vs-300 showed that this last problem had been resolved. The new rotor was not ideal (it introduced a pitching moment during sideways flight), but the vs-300 flew considerably better.

On October 2, 1941, the vs-300 team had its first—and mercifully only—experience with a truly frightening rotary-wing phenomenon known as ground resonance. A landing on one spongy float initiated a destructive lateral oscillation during which it seemed as if the vs-300's rotor wanted to depart its fuselage. As helpers restrained the damaged machine, Les Morris cut power.

The vs-300 was repaired and back in the air a week later, this time with its tail rotor temporarily repositioned forward almost directly below the horizontal rotor. As a concession to its growing fame, the vs-300's forward fuselage was enclosed with silver-doped fabric, and a vertical sheet of silver fabric was laced into the tail boom. Despite the basketball still dangling from its chin like some lucky charm, the prototype looked more refined.

In this two-tail-rotor configuration, the vs-300 at last revealed why Sikorsky's full cyclic control of 1939 had not worked. The clue was a pitching moment associated with use of the craft's partial azimuth control: left and right cyclic input pitched the prototype instead of rolling it as expected. The culprit that had so long troubled the team turned out to be gyroscopic precession.

Just as a toy gyroscope translates a child's push 90 degrees, the vs-300's rotor—effectively a gyroscope—had offset pilot control inputs at right angles. That Sikorsky and his team had not even known to anticipate this phenomenon is an indication of how new the helicopter was. If there had been even one autogiro engineer on the team (or if one had visited from Philadelphia and observed their consternation), this problem might have been solved at the outset.

Reinstating full cyclic control in the vs-300, the team offset the helicopter's control linkages at the swashplate to eliminate the effects of precession. This simple fix would prove to be an effective solution to a very frustrating problem. Two years had passed since azimuth control had been abandoned. If the presence of gyroscopic precession had been recognized at that time, the vs-300 would not have had to undergo such extensive modification with additional outrigger-mounted control rotors. Myriad other day-to-day engineering challenges were also addressed in the

A detailed view of the rotor head shows cyclic control (side-to-side only) reintroduced to the VS-300 in mid-1941. Courtesy UTC.

intervening two years, of course, and one can only speculate how much sooner the VS-300 might have been perfected if this single problem had been solved.

"The Old Man's approach was cut-and-try with the testing of many modifications," said noted engineer Harold E. Lemont, who joined the VS-300 team late in the program. "A dozen or more major issues needed to be addressed in an orderly manner to avoid catastrophic results, only one of which was the gyroscopic problem. To say that it delayed us is quite beside the point; the key thing was to fix the stability and achieve controlled flight."[15]

On December 8, 1941, the day America entered World War II, the VS-300 flew in its fourth and final configuration. Now with full cyclic pitch control in its main rotor, it flew forward better than it hovered, a reversal of its earlier performance. Better blade damping solved this problem and within three weeks a breathtaking improvement in flight characteristics was realized. By the end of the year the machine flew perfectly. On the last day of 1941, the much-modified research prototype flew, in the words of Les Morris, "forward, backward, and sideways, and no wobble was discovered at any time."[16]

In March 1942, Morris received his commercial helicopter pilot rating. That same month, he was attempting to herd ducks at the request of promotion-minded movie photographers when a departing tail rotor gave him his closest call in the VS-300. The float-equipped helicopter slammed perfectly level into the Housatonic River, a lucky happenstance to which the test pilot attributes his survival, and the ensuing volcanic splash left him thoroughly chilled but unhurt.

"If it had occurred two seconds earlier,"

Morris wrote about the incident, "I would have landed among people on hard ground; fifty feet higher, I would probably have lost the ability to control the craft at all; fifty feet lower, I would have certainly dived head-on into the water instead of landing flat."[17]

In the face of such setbacks, the management of United Aircraft remained firmly committed to the helicopter program it had authorized. "I have frequently said that in my opinion there is no performance comparable with that of the Sikorsky group in pioneering new developments," Eugene Wilson wrote encouragingly to Igor Sikorsky in May 1942.[18]

In the middle of 1942, the craft's downward-angling silver nose was exchanged for a shorter, more photogenic bullet-shaped cockpit. Gone also was the basketball that had almost become a trademark. Having laid the technological basis for a working production helicopter by the end of 1941, the VS-300 spent the remainder of its active life in devising and evaluating options for use in helicopters of the future. By the time its career came to a close in the fall of 1943, this flying laboratory was going as fast as 80 mph.

Shortly after the VS-300 program began, Sikorsky had doubled his estimate of the cost of building and perfecting the machine to $60,000. This figure was well short of the mark: by his own accounting, that much had been spent by July 1, 1940, some seventeen months before the craft was perfected.[19] Had gyroscopic precession not gone undiagnosed, this target might have been met.

Still, United Aircraft's investment in the venture had been money well spent. "It is hard to recall any experimental device from which so much benefit has been had at so little cost," United's president Eugene E. Wilson wrote in December 1942 to C. J. McCarthy, his suc-

The vs-300 in its final configuration at the end of
1941. Courtesy utc.

cessor as general manager of the Vought-Sikorsky Division. By then, the Army was already evaluating its new Sikorsky R-4s.

On October 7, 1943, in a formal presentation including a farewell flight by Igor Sikorsky, the historic vs-300 was donated through Henry Ford to the Edison Institute Museum at Greenfield Village in Dearborn, Michigan. Sikorsky's good friend Charles Lindbergh, who had flown the craft on several occasions, was on hand for the ceremony. At the time of its retirement, the Sikorsky vs-300 had flown 102.5 hours. With this donation, a pioneering chapter in U.S. aviation came to a close.

At the end of 1940, the Army Air Forces (AAF) diverted $50,000—all that remained of the $300,000 in Dorsey Bill funds appropriated by Congress in 1939—from Platt-LePage to Vought-Sikorksy. Frank Gregory's enthusiasm for the vs-300, coupled with the AAF's prudent desire to have a fallback program should the Platt-LePage xr-1 fail, prompted this action. Would United Aircraft, the Army asked, apply this money toward developing a two-seat military helicopter?

Although the amount was clearly insufficient, United Aircraft's leaders agreed to the Army's request in a historic meeting on December 19, 1940, in Washington, D.C. A formal contract followed on January 10, 1941, restoring an opportunity Sikorsky had believed lost when Platt-LePage won the Army's primary helicopter contract.

As specified, the Sikorsky xr-4 (company designation vs-316) would be more than twice as heavy and have almost twice the power of the vs-300, upon which it would be based.[20] That the latter had not yet been perfected only added to the challenge. Sikorsky was committed to perfecting helicopter

technology to the point where a machine could be placed into volume production for active military service.

Ironically, receipt of the xr-4 contract fully vindicated Sikorsky's strategy of two years earlier. With military involvement avoided, and with little initial publicity, the vs-300 had been free to evolve as a company project. The "modest amount of success" to date (to again quote Sikorsky's farsighted memo of February 21, 1939) now opened the door at the right time for military support of subsequent Sikorsky helicopter efforts. If military support was counterproductive in developing this new technology, it was essential in its application.

Sikorsky's doubled work load had prompted him to hire Morris as test pilot of the vs-300, and new arrivals now filled out the engineering department, bringing enthusiasm and talent to the division's growing helicopter program. Chief among the latter was Ralph Alex, who became project engineer of the xr-4.

The xr-4 took shape in a Stratford hangar during the latter part of 1941. Its steel-tube skeleton featured three tail rotors like the vs-300: a vertical anti-torque rotor at the rear and two horizontal control rotors on aft-fuselage outriggers. When the single-seat research helicopter shed its extra tail rotors, so did the military prototype, to the relief of Frank Gregory, who had specified full cyclic control for the xr-4.

On January 14, 1942, two weeks after the vs-300 was at last perfected, the Sikorsky xr-4 (AAF serial no. 41-18874) made its first flight at Stratford, Connecticut. Prototype of the world's first mass-produced helicopter, the xr-4 ranks as the most significant rotary-wing aircraft in history, for it marks the earliest emergence of the practical helicopter. Fittingly, this XR-4 is preserved today in the collection of the Smithsonian Institution's National Air and Space Museum.

The Sikorsky XR-4 was powered by a seven-cylinder Warner R-500 Super Scarab radial engine rated at 165 hp (185 hp in production examples). Slab-sided for ease of construction, it carried a crew of two in side-by-side seating beneath an enlarged VS-300-type rotor 38 feet in diameter. Its looks suggested it had been built strictly for utility with little regard to aesthetics.

The craft was clearly underpowered, but that was easily fixed. So were cooling problems, which—coupled with the fact that the Franklin engine was required to run continuously at full power in flight—substantially reduced engine life.

In flight, the XR-4 picked up speed rapidly and effortlessly outpaced powerful automobiles. Like the VS-300, it had a top speed of about 80 mph. But scaling up that earlier prototype had also scaled up the rotor forces passed to the pilot through the cyclic stick. The XR-4 and its successors flew awkwardly, and control was rubbery rather than crisp. The stick shook hard and described constant small-diameter circles in the pilot's hand. The pilots initiated flight in more or less the right direction, constantly nudged the craft to do their bidding, then landed more or less where they wanted.

"The vibration characteristics of the XR-4 were really terrible," said Sikorsky engineer Ralph Lightfoot, designer of its rotor blades. "Many adjustments were made just by hit or by miss to get the blades to be balanced within a set so that the shake of the pilot's control stick would be tolerable; it was not good, but at least the pilot could stand it."[21]

The trouble clearly lay in the main rotor, where unanticipated extraneous movements of the blades caused dissymmetries of lift. This unwanted blade motion, whose cause was not then known, fed wobbling vibrations back down through the control linkages. The vibrations transmitted to the pilot's hand were caused by the difference in loads imposed on the rotor mast by the individual blades.

The Sikorsky team had done all it knew to ensure that the blades performed as expected. Conventional design was used to produce a structure that resisted deflection even though it was not entirely rigid. A symmetrical airfoil had been employed.[22] The blades had been placed on accurate scales to be sure that they weighed the same, and the entire rotor assembly had been placed on a teeter to be sure the longitudinal centers of gravity were equal.[23]

Sikorsky's first effort to diagnose what was going on in the rotor involved use of a long-handled bristle brush dipped in oil and carbon black and cautiously extended into the fast-spinning rotor of the XR-4, running on the ground. When there was a sharp thud punctuated with an oily spray, the helicopter was shut down and its rotor tips examined. Generally, not all three blades showed black stains, proving that they were not tracking on the same plane.

Under an accelerated wartime development program, the Army had ordered three YR-4As for initial evaluation, soon followed by twenty-seven improved YR-4Bs for service testing (after which the company would produce one hundred operational R-4Bs). The first of the preproduction machines coming off the line in 1942 also showed tracking problems. By this time, a somewhat more refined tracking diagnostic aid had been devised. A different colored chalk was liberally applied to each blade tip before the helicopter was run up, after which a sheet of canvas stretched

The Sikorsky XR-4, first prototype of the world's
first production helicopter. Courtesy UTC.

vertically on bungee cords in a pole frame-work was rolled carefully forward until con-tact was made. When it was pulled back, the cloth had documented in colored lines the tracking height of each blade.

At first it was thought that getting the blades to track together on the plane of rota-tion would solve the problem. Since the trail-ing edges of the R-4's rotor blades could be bent by hand, Sikorsky technicians experi-mented with bending them up or down like ground-adjustable trim tabs. Such tinkering did improve tracking, but getting the blades to track did not eliminate the vibration in flight.

The Sikorsky team had been treating the symptom and not the cause. They failed to realize that the blades had to do more than just weigh the same. Rotor blades subjected to aerodynamic and centrifugal forces also had to be dynamically balanced so that the inter-nal distribution of their weight was similar.[24] This had not been done on the VS-300, but that prototype was light enough that forces fed back through the stick were minimal. Its blades were also shorter, giving them greater resistance to torsional stress. Thus the seeds of trouble unsuspectingly sown in the VS-300 had not emerged until the design was scaled up.

To their credit, Sikorsky engineers soon determined the reason why each blade acted independently, twisting and flexing differ-ently in flight. Although built the same, weighing the same, and appearing identical to the naked eye, these blades had differing internal weight distributions. Care had been taken to match the longitudinal balance of each blade (locating their centers of gravity the same distance from the root to the tip), but *chordwise* balance (the side-to-side cen-ter of gravity located between the leading and trailing blade edges) had been ignored.

The chordwise balance of these early Sikor-sky rotor blades varied down the length of a single blade. It should ideally be located at the main spar, the internal structural member connecting the rotor blade to the hub. In that case, a blade (which is hinged at the hub) flap-ping in response to a gust of wind will not tend to twist. With the center of gravity *off* the spar, however, a twisting moment is intro-duced when the blade flaps (just as any load tilts when lifted off center).[25] In the R-4, these twisting moments worked to change the rotor blade's pitch from that selected by the pilot.

The pounding stick vibrations were worse on some machines than others. Because the R-4 was already a marginal performer, this problem often dictated whether a helicopter was flightworthy or not. "As we got into pro-duction," Lightfoot noted, "we built the YR-4 and we got some of them to work and some-times they didn't. One day it would work and another day it wouldn't."[26]

Wartime production schedules and lim-ited resources denied Sikorsky the opportu-nity to redesign these blades (perhaps even perfecting metal units whose weight distrib-ution could be more easily and precisely con-trolled). But three corrective steps were taken, which brought some measure of relief.

The first was instituting better weight con-trol during construction. Using standard auto-giro technology, Lightfoot had designed his blades around an extruded steel spar, forward of which was a spruce and mahogany leading edge (balsa was also used in these units). Air-plane-style wing ribs tapered aft of the spar to brass brackets supporting a wire trailing edge (it was these brackets that Sikorsky per-sonnel had bent by hand to adjust tracking). The entire structure was then covered with cotton fabric and doped; a brass frontal abrasion strip was applied to protect the leading edge; and then the whole unit was covered with a second layer of fabric and dope.

More care was now taken to make sure that the spar was perfectly straight. More important, spruce, balsa, and mahogany sections were all weighed and sorted into bins (some being heavier per given volume than others). By controlling the relative weight of woods used in construction, a more uniform chordwise weight distribution was achieved down the length of each blade.

The second corrective step was to establish a company policy requiring that rotor blades be used in matched sets. If an R-4 suffered damage to one blade, all three blades had to be replaced. The military was understandably not pleased with the lack of interchangeability, but there was no alternative.

The third measure was the most successful. Correctly analyzing the underlying cause of the rotor vibrations, Lightfoot addressed the problem of "torsional imbalance," as he called it, by placing a counterweight at the blade root. This weight corrected the overall chordwise blade imbalance at the hub, although it could not eliminate the effects of individual disparities in fore-and-aft center of gravity of different blade sections. When applied to an R-4's rotor blades, Lightfoot's weights noticeably lowered rotor vibrations in flight.

For operational use, this system was refined into a tube on a collar at the blade root. The tube could be angled forward or backward at 45 degrees, depending on whether fore or aft center-of-gravity correction was needed. Inside the tube was a weight on a threaded screw terminating in a little wing nut at the outer end. By turning the nut to move the weight in or out, the moment exerted by the weight—hence the degree of correction—was

adjusted. When positioned properly, the weight was locked in place and the tube sealed.

Lightfoot's invention worked well enough that Sikorsky R-4 blades could at last be interchanged. Sikorsky continued to require that matched sets of blades be used, however, to minimize vibration caused by any remaining imbalances.

These and later efforts to address rotor vibration were conducted in parallel with flight testing. They had not kept the XR-4 (and later the YR-4s) from accomplishing a great deal in the minimal time allotted by the Army during World War II. An indication of just how quickly the military expected its new helicopter came at the end of March 1942 in a telephone call from Lieutenant Colonel Frank Gregory. The recently promoted helicopter project officer informed Vought-Sikorsky that within a month the XR-4 had to perform a full spectrum of maneuvers, including flight at altitude, before military leaders at Stratford. Afterward, it was to be delivered by air to the Army Air Forces' Flight Test Center at Wright Field in Dayton, Ohio.

Gregory's call precipitated a drastic acceleration of the factory flight test program. Top priority was given to successfully performing an autorotation landing. Only with this milestone reached could the Sikorsky XR-4 safely be flown at altitude.

Autorotation to the ground is the maneuver that allows a helicopter to land safely in the event of an in-flight engine failure. Practiced by all helicopter pilots, it consists of placing the rotors (which automatically disengage from the drive shaft by means of a freewheeling clutch) in low pitch so that they windmill rapidly as the powerless craft

Wartime urgency spurred manufacture of the utilitarian R-4, which featured marginal performance at best. Courtesy UTC.

descends. Near the ground, the pilot pulls up on the collective pitch lever to trade the rotor's stored inertia for momentary lift. This maneuver must be performed at the right height if the helicopter is to land gently. Pull up either too soon or too late and the result is a crash.

No helicopter had ever been autorotated in the United States (the VS-300 was restricted to low-altitude testing). While the mechanics of autorotation flight were well known—this was, after all, how autogiros flew—the techniques for its employment in helicopter emergencies had yet to be worked out. With little to guide him, therefore, Les Morris approached the challenge cautiously on April 3, 1942, and made a successful autorotation landing from an altitude of 200 feet the following day.

On April 20, the XR-4 put on a magnificent display at Stratford Airport for military observers. It flew forward, backward, sideways, straight up to 500 feet, and back down to a hovering landing. It demonstrated an autorotation, then it flew flat-out at 82 mph. Finally, Morris put it into a climb and leveled off at 5,000 feet (clouds prevented him from going higher). He finished off with another autorotation to the ground. The test pilot emerged to find himself heartily congratulated by overwhelmingly enthusiastic United Aircraft and Army personnel.

"Despite its limitations, it was clear that our aircraft could be operated as it was," Morris wrote of this event. "And everyone was realizing that it was just a beginning, comparable perhaps to the automobile in 1910."[27]

The way was now clear for the first extended cross-country flight in U.S. helicopter history. The XR-4 took off on its historic 761-mile trip to Wright Field on May 13, 1942, with Morris at the controls. Taking the trip in more than a dozen leisurely stages, it arrived in Springfield, Ohio, five days later. Despite ominous thunderstorms over the sparsely populated Allegheny Mountains, the trip had been uneventful.

A support team followed in a car with a bright yellow circle painted on the roof to help Morris find it at planned rendezvous points. It met him now at Springfield, where the helicopter was cleaned and polished. Igor Sikorsky himself then climbed aboard to accompany Morris on the short final hop to Wright Field (today Wright-Patterson Air Force Base). Late in the afternoon of May 18, 1942, the record-setting flight ended with the official presentation of the XR-4 to the U.S. Army Air Forces.

Military evaluation of the Sikorsky R-4 was not without humorous moments, usually arising from this first-generation production helicopter's marginal performance. Early one morning later in the summer of 1942, Frank Gregory tested a YR-4A newly arrived at Wright Field. That afternoon, knowing that it was in flying condition, the AAF officer confidently ushered an important visiting official into the machine. This time, to Gregory's acute embarrassment, the helicopter proved unwilling to fly. Full throttle and desperate efforts on the controls succeeded only in extending the oleo struts; the tires themselves never left the ground.

The commander of the Army's helicopter program promptly placed an animated call to Vought-Sikorsky, and within hours Ralph Lightfoot found himself headed for Dayton to work with the squadron's engineering officer, Lieutenant Harold Hermes. With Lightfoot and Hermes aboard, the helicopter flew fine and hovered fully 1,600 feet above ground level. The explanation, Lightfoot realized, was a heat wave, which had ended just before his arrival. Gregory's failed attempt had taken place on a sweltering windless day when the flight ramp's black tarmac was extremely hot. The resulting high density altitude had exceeded the YR-4A's limited performance capability at gross weight.

On January 1, 1943, to make room for Vought, which was expanding greatly to produce thousands of Corsair fighter planes for the U.S. Navy, Sikorsky moved to a disused factory in nearby Bridgeport. The South Avenue plant, as it was called, had been occupied by a manufacturer of plumbing fixtures and was not on an airfield. But nearby was Seaside Park, a large expanse of beautiful parkland fronting Long Island Sound. Sikorsky received special wartime permission to operate its helicopters there (it would also perfect the process of dropping bombs weighing up to 500 pounds from YR-4B helicopters there).

Although the two divisions were once again separate (spelling an end to the "vs" designation prefix), Sikorsky kept one hangar at the former facility so that construction and testing of preproduction YR-4s could continue without interruption (production R-4Bs, however, would be built at Bridgeport). For the time being, Sikorsky helicopters could continue to use the wide marshy riverfront alongside the Vought factory, as well as the airport just across the street.

This arrangement led to unanticipated difficulties for two of Gregory's hot young Army helicopter pilots, Lieutenants Frank Peterson (later chief test pilot of Hiller Aircraft in California) and Harold Hermes. The two men changed into flying gear at Sikorsky's new South Avenue plant in Bridgeport and flew as directed to Stratford. There, to their dismay, they were detained by a Vought security man who demanded to know how they

had got past the guard post at the main gate. Explaining to him that they had flown over the gate and showing him the helicopter—now tucked into the Sikorsky hangar—failed to dispel his suspicions. Since they had left their identification in their uniforms in Bridgeport, the fliers were held incommunicado until members of the Sikorsky engineering staff finally came looking for them.

Another rotary-wing milestone took place with little ceremony on the Sikorsky Aircraft flight ramp at Bridgeport on July 3, 1943, when Lieutenant Colonel Gregory accepted formal delivery of the first YR-4A helicopter (AAF serial no. 42-107234). The XR-4 being strictly a test vehicle, this preproduction YR-4A (one of three slated for operational service evaluation) in many ways introduced the U.S. military services to helicopter use.

The U.S. Navy found itself under enormous congressional pressure during 1943 to initiate a helicopter program of its own. Strongly criticized by the Truman Committee for opposing this new form of flight despite a clear requirement for vertical-flight aircraft, the Navy issued development contracts in 1944 to the P-V Engineering Forum (later Piasecki Helicopter Corporation) and McDonnell Aircraft Corporation. These contracts would give rise to the successful Piasecki HRP series and the unsuccessful XHJD-1, respectively.

In the meantime the Navy turned to Sikorsky for smaller helicopters to make up for lost time. Accordingly, three of the Army's twenty-seven YR-4Bs were turned over to the Navy as the HNS-1 for initial evaluation. In 1944 the Navy would also get twenty production R-4Bs that had been built for the Army, plus a couple more manufactured from the outset as HNSs. Ironically, these production machines were available to the Navy thanks to the British, who had taken

The South Avenue plant in Bridgeport, to which Sikorsky Aircraft moved during World War II to make room for Vought Corsair production at Stratford. Courtesy UTC.

leadership in fostering R-4 production.

When RAF Wing Commander Reggie Brie visited Stratford at the end of January 1942 to observe the VS-300, he also saw the brand new XR-4, which had flown the previous week. Following a return visit by Brie in 1943, Sikorsky received an electrifying telegram from the British Ministry of Defense asking if it would entertain the idea of building 150 R-4s for Great Britain. Sikorsky, and the entire United Aircraft Corporation, found the idea very entertaining indeed.

In the dark early days of World War II, vast convoys crossed the North Atlantic bringing desperately needed fuel, supplies, aircraft, and equipment to beleaguered England. This vital lend-lease supply line so critical to Britain's survival was being severed by Nazi U-boat "wolf packs."[28] Since few aircraft carriers were available to provide aerial submarine patrols, British planners turned in desperation to the helicopter, the only aircraft capable of operating from the decks of cargo and noncarrier escort ships.

It was this large British commitment that truly convinced the skeptics, some of them in United Aircraft's top management, that the helicopter could be important in wartime military aviation. Consequently, initial blocks of British-ordered YR-4Bs and R-4Bs coming off the Bridgeport assembly line early in 1944 were turned back to the U.S. military services. Having jumped firmly on a bandwagon the British got rolling, these services now invoked priority.

The U.S. Coast Guard received the first of these redirected helicopters. Pioneering USCG use of this new form of flight would play an extremely significant role in the further development and employment of vertical-flight aviation. The British, meanwhile, eventually received forty-five R-4Bs late in 1944. By then

the U-boat menace was luckily declining, for the R-4 was unequal to landing on pitching decks at high sea. Consequently the British used the R-4B (designated Hoverfly Mk. 1) for training, air-sea rescue, and radar calibration.

In addition to the R-4, two other two-seat Sikorsky helicopter designs were produced during World War II. The first, the R-6, was basically the same size and weight as the R-4, which it was meant to replace. The second new type, the larger R-5, had enough power to promise real utility (in contrast to the R-4, which was so limited as to be suited only for training and observation).

Construction of both machines became possible on January 5, 1943, when Eugene Wilson authorized up to $135,000 for this purpose. United Aircraft's further support of Igor Sikorsky's work displayed both wisdom and courage, for neither the value of the helicopter nor the military's perception of a need for it had truly been proved at the start of 1943. Wilson's act increased the amount the corporation was gambling.

During his Connecticut visits to lay the groundwork for Britain's acquisition of R-4s, Wing Commander Brie had also expressed interest in a next-generation helicopter capable of carrying and dropping depth charges. This was the first military contemplation of helicopter use in antisubmarine warfare. Brie's insistence on maximum visibility gave rise to a greenhouse canopy with fore-and-aft seating and minimal framing to obstruct vision. Gross weight at 4,900 pounds was nearly double that of either the R-4 or R-6, and useful load was calculated at 1,500 pounds, then an enormous amount since previous helicopters had lifted little more than themselves and their crews.

Another member of the British Purchasing

Commission who exercised some influence over the new helicopter was Dr. J. A. J. Bennett, a patriarch of British rotary-wing development who in 1945 would develop the Fairey Gyrodyne helicopter in England. Bennett remained at Bridgeport as Britain's Resident Technical Officer at Sikorsky.

The R-5 started out to be all wood except for a steel-tube engine mount and aluminum cone landing gear. Wooden construction was complex, however, and when a widely anticipated shortage of strategic materials—aluminum in particular—failed to materialize, the R-5 was converted to all-metal construction. To save weight, the landing gear cones of production R-5s and R-6s were made of magnesium. The R-5 was carefully rounded because it had been determined that the R-4's square cabin spoiled much of its rotor's lift.

The heart of the new helicopter was the 450-hp Pratt & Whitney R-985, the air-cooled radial engine used in the Beechcraft Model 18 and the Vultee BT-13 basic trainer. The reliable R-985 also powered Vought's OS2U Kingfisher, a float-mounted Navy observation plane, which gave rise to an engineering shortcut. To save precious development time, R-5 project engineer W. E. Hunt incorporated the existing Kingfisher engine installation directly into the XR-5. But when it began ground tests in the summer of 1943, the engine overheated badly and whatever engineering time had been saved was now spent devising a lightweight cooling fan of sufficient capacity. The rotor pylon and tail boom were opened in order to aid airflow through the engine compartment.

Les Morris made the first flight of the XR-5 on August 18, 1943, initiating what soon proved to be a disappointing flight test program. From a control standpoint, the R-5 was markedly worse than the R-4. Further scaling up VS-300 technology to double the gross weight of the R-4 had aggravated problems arising from rotor blade imbalance. Lightfoot had not designed the R-5 rotor blades as he had those of the R-4 and R-6. He observed the XR-5 to have "very, very bad vibrations" which rendered the craft "very difficult to fly."[29] Consequently, the counterbalancing blade collar he had developed for the rotor of the R-4 and R-6 was also adapted for use on the R-5.

This troubled helicopter had an additional rotor problem. Having tested the R-5 rotor blade at Sikorsky's request, the National Advisory Committee for Aeronautics (predecessor to the National Aeronautics and Space Administration) announced that its aerodynamic center was at 23 percent mean aerodynamic chord (23 percent of the way back from the leading edge). Sikorsky had built the test blade with a 25 percent MAC spar, believing that to be the center of pressure. Accepting the NACA findings, Sikorsky redesigned the R-5 rotor blade to incorporate a spar at the 23 percent MAC location.

Once this was done it was clear that Sikorsky had been right all along. But it was now too late to switch back, for the new blade design had been locked in and production had commenced. The R-5s coming off the assembly line now had to have "pie plates" added to their rotors, with strong springs to pull the tail-heavy blades back into line. This quick-and-dirty fix took a further toll on handling qualities.

Because no interruption of wartime schedules was permitted, it was only after World War II ended that Sikorsky could correct these problems. Although wartime production was just sixty-five units, the troubled R-5 was able to evolve in 1946 into the

(*Top*) Sikorsky R-5s in production during World War II. Courtesy UTC.

(*Bottom*) The R-6 replaced the R-4. Shown here at Bridgeport, it became the first helicopter ever built on a moving assembly line when license built by Nash-Kelvinator in Detroit. Courtesy UTC.

excellent s-51, a four-seat helicopter which would find both military and commercial success.

In contrast to the all-new r-5, the Sikorsky r-6 was a revised and improved version of the r-4, with which it shared many dynamic components. This is not to say that the r-6 was not ambitious, for the trim machine—which underwent many design changes during development—emerged with major innovations as well as improvements suggested by initial evaluation of the r-4.

Immediately obvious was the r-6's streamlined fuselage for improved aerodynamic efficiency. Other changes included a vertically mounted engine[30] (a 225-hp Franklin) and unconventional construction. It was a "paper" helicopter in the sense that some of its non-structural skinning—notably around the rotor pylon—was made of resin-impregnated paper. The cockpit, moreover, was fiberglass. Design efforts to improve utility while keeping gross weight in line with that of the r-4 also dictated a magnesium tail cone and landing gear.

To maximize the productivity of its small new helicopter factory, Sikorsky had gone to vertical assembly. Upright orientation of fuselages offered several advantages: horizontal floorspace per helicopter was reduced, workers could do more of the work standing upright, and otherwise wasted ceiling space was put to use.

The xr-6 made its first flight October 15, 1943, and completed its factory test program in and around Bridgeport. Despite innovative vertical manufacture, however, the venerable South Avenue plant was too small to support three manufacturing programs at once, so it was arranged that Nash-Kelvinator, a Detroit manufacturer of automobiles and refrigerators, would produce the r-6

under a technical assistance contract. Whereas the r-4 had been built in place, the r-6 at Nash-Kelvinator was the first helicopter ever manufactured on a moving assembly line.

Efforts continued to improve rotor technology, since lack of dynamic blade balance remained the biggest problem with Sikorsky's wartime helicopters. The tedious sorting of woods by weight for blade construction took place in a loft of the Bridgeport plant, which had once been a brass foundry. The windows were kept closed in the summer in a vain effort to control humidity.

Operational experience had by now led to the internal insertion of fabric every few ribs, and to the drilling of a vent hole in each blade tip. These measures were taken to prevent a centrifugally induced flow of air through the blade during flight; such flow had produced enough pressure to explode the tips of a few r-4 rotor blades. No simple solution was found for another newly identified problem: the billowing and sagging of fabric between the ribs. But since only the aft portion of the rotor blade suffered distortion, Sikorsky engineers decided that no serious lift degradation was occurring.

Sikorsky soon sought to relieve itself of this burden by contracting with both a baby carriage company and a furniture company for blade construction. Results were unsatisfactory, however, and the helicopter manufacturer went back to making its own blades.

In 1943, Sikorsky enlisted the help of the Hamilton Standard Propeller Division, hoping that it would come up with a better blade and take over that part of the business. Hamilton Standard responded enthusiastically enough, building a whirl test rig on Rentschler Field and putting both time and money into the effort. Their team (including a young engineer named Charles Kaman, who would later found a rival Connecticut helicopter company) failed to develop a rotor blade that would hold together. Eventually they gave up. "Their blades were not at all like our blades," notes Lightfoot, "and neither were their methods of blade construction anything that would lend itself to our type of blade size and construction."[31]

However nagging, rotor blade troubles did not prevent United Aircraft's Sikorsky helicopters from seeing some wartime service, notably in the China-Burma-India theater of operations and in the Aleutians. Although haphazard and far from routine in nature, their World War II use in rescue work—particularly the lifesaving transport of wounded—foreshadowed a primary use of helicopters in future conflicts.

The lifesaving potential of vertical flight was demonstrated on November 29, 1945, when an oil barge broke adrift during a severe storm off Bridgeport, Connecticut, and was driven onto a reef. Two seamen were stranded aboard. Sikorsky pilots Jimmy Viner and Jackson Beighle flew from the nearby Sikorsky plant in an Army R-5 equipped with a rescue hoist developed by the Coast Guard. Fighting 60-mph winds, they hovered above high seas to retrieve the sailors one at a time. This rescue was the first of thousands to use the lifesaving Coast Guard invention.

With the end of World War II in 1945, Sikorsky Aircraft could make badly needed improvements to the R-5/HO2S series helicopter, long deferred by wartime production schedules. A complete redesign was effected, and an enlarged, vastly improved second-generation R-5 called the Sikorsky S-51 took to the air February 16, 1946.

Now entering the postwar era, Sikorsky Aircraft found itself free to pursue a special-ization formally acknowledged before the war's end: "A major effort of Sikorsky research and engineering staffs has been directed toward still larger types of helicopters for use by the Armed Forces," the United Aircraft Corporation informed its stockholders in the spring of 1945.[32] With some civil production as well, Sikorsky would successfully pursue large military helicopter production to the present day.

At war's end, Sikorsky was also in a race to bring to market the world's first civil helicopter. An accelerated certification program for the S-51 was launched, with the aim of winning the coveted first-ever government approval to sell helicopters to nonmilitary customers. Based on the prevalent expectation of a postwar aviation boom, Sikorsky had made wildly optimistic projections of S-51 sales to commercial operators. While company executives recognized that the S-51 was too big and—at $48,500—far too expensive for private owners, high hopes were held for a variety of commercial uses. Possibly thousands of sales were thought to hang in the balance, a bonanza waiting to be reaped by the first manufacturer to receive CAA production approval.

Although Bell won the race for certification within a few months, Sikorsky in August 1946 had the satisfaction of delivering the world's first commercial helicopter. The customer was Helicopter Air Transport, a short-lived training school based at Camden, New Jersey. Civil sales thereafter were disappointing, with scarcely more than a dozen S-51s selling over the next two years. Among these were the machines used by Los Angeles Airways, which initiated America's first scheduled helicopter air mail service in October 1947. For the moment, at least, the military looked to remain Sikorsky's primary customer.

When a barge became stranded during a storm on
Long Island Sound, Sikorsky Chief Test Pilot
Jimmy Viner responded to the emergency call for
help in a hoist-equipped R-5. Courtesy UTC.

But with war just ended and the Pentagon facing excessive peacetime aircraft inventories, military demand for s-51s was also low. Anxious to change that situation, Sikorsky at its own expense sent an s-51 and test pilots aboard the USS *Franklin Delano Roosevelt* to participate in an extended Navy Atlantic and Caribbean cruise beginning in February 1947. So well did the civil-registered s-51 helicopter perform—including six actual rescues—that Sikorsky secured immediate Navy contracts for HO3s helicopters for plane-guard duty.

In mid-1947, prospects also brightened on the Army front when the AAF took delivery of its first postwar helicopters, a small number of R-5Hs handed over to that service at the Bridgeport plant. These machines would be used in rescue operations.

In May 1948, United Aircraft's Chance Vought Division began a month-long move to an empty Navy-owned plant near Dallas, Texas. It made sense for Vought to be in an area conducive to the testing and flying of the jet aircraft it was developing for the Navy. Sikorsky elected to remain in Bridgeport rather than reclaim its former factory in Stratford.

Sikorsky had long realized that the military-inspired s-51, although fine technically, was too expensive for extensive use by civil operators. As a result, the company developed a smaller helicopter intended for both military and civilian use. The s-52 was a two-seat aircraft embodying the lessons learned with the R-4 and R-6. First flown during 1947, it completed a government certification program and was awarded the third approved certificate ever issued to a helicopter.

Perhaps as a result of Sikorsky's nightmarish problems with wooden rotor blades, the s-52 was the first production helicopter to feature all-metal rotor blades. It was not, however, the first helicopter to fly successfully with metal blades, a distinction that goes to the Hiller XH-44 prototype of 1944. The s-52 also featured a revised offset-hinge rotor head for improved controllability.

Sheet metal cabin panels and other parts for both the s-51 and s-52—as well as models to follow—were manufactured using a gigantic 5,000-ton Bliss hydraulic press purchased secondhand in 1947. Originally built in Brooklyn, the Bliss press weighed 450 tons and took ten freight cars to transport from Cleveland. Its acquisition expressed eloquently the company's belief that future helicopter demand would be strong enough to sustain a high volume of production.

The Sikorsky s-52 civil helicopter was publicly unveiled at the 1947 Easter Show at New York City's Radio City Music Hall. One of the highlights of that elaborately staged event, the somewhat dowdy looking two-seater appeared to fly through clouds across the proscenium arch to land center-stage in the middle of a springtime scene. Sadly, however, the audience's wild enthusiasm was not followed by noticeable public demand for the new machine.

In fact, the Sikorsky s-52 would run a distant third in civil and military sales behind the comparably sized Bell Model 47 and the Hiller 360, the fourth and last helicopter to receive CAA production certification during the 1940s. Sikorsky therefore enlarged the s-52, giving it two more seats and replacing its 178-hp Franklin engine with one of 245 hp. Thus propelled into a size and weight category where its only competition was the utterly unwanted Bell Model 42, the s-52-2 eventually found employment as the Marine Corps HO5S-1 and Army H-18. Its success at this juncture was not due to the s-52-2's

(Top) Intended for civil and light military use, the Sikorsky s-52 could not compete with the superior Bell 47 and Hiller 360. Courtesy UTC.

(Bottom) Despite poor performance and reliability, the s-52-2 entered production in the Korean War as the Army H-18 (shown here) and Marine Corps HO5S-1. Courtesy UTC.

intrinsic merit, however, but to the 1950 outbreak of war in Korea.

Several years earlier, Sikorsky had participated in a Navy competition for a new fleet utility helicopter. The company's entry—three of which were built—was the five-seat XHJS-1 (S-53) of 1948. Of basically the same configuration as the S-51, the new machine was fitted with a three-bladed all-metal folding rotor, a tail rotor raised above head height, and a hoist-equipped floor hatch for plane-guard duties. Power was supplied by a 500-hp Continental R-975 engine. First flown in 1948, the XHJS-1 participated in a fly-off against the competing tandem-overlapping-rotor Piasecki XHJP-1 at Naval Air Station Patuxent River, Maryland, in 1949. So resoundingly did the Piasecki machine—which would evolve into the HUP series—outperform the XHJS-1 that Sikorsky company literature to this day makes little or no mention of the S-53. The forgotten machine did have one abortive shot at glory when it was dispatched aboard a Navy carrier to perform a rescue on the Greenland ice cap, but legendary arctic flier Bernt Balchen got there first in a ski-equipped C-47.

Piasecki had earlier denied Sikorsky another contract when the Navy, perceiving the Connecticut manufacturer to be hard pressed to meet AAF helicopter orders, had ignored a wartime Sikorsky proposal and issued contracts to McDonnell and an unknown named Piasecki. The latter had led to the HRP-1 of 1947, history's first transport-sized production helicopter. Now with the fleet utility fly-off, Piasecki Helicopters of Morton, Pennsylvania, served fair notice to Sikorsky that it was a force to be reckoned with. The lesson was timely for Sikorsky, which would henceforth engage in head-on competition in the construction of large mil-

itary and civil helicopters with what is today Boeing Helicopters.

Having been bettered by the tandem-rotor Piasecki design, the Sikorsky company in 1949 initiated development of a tandem helicopter of its own called the S-54. The outbreak of war in Korea the following year led to this project being abandoned, but not before Engineering Manager Igor Sikorsky had determined to his own satisfaction that tandem helicopters do not enjoy an inherent advantage over single-rotor designs. During cruise, he concluded, the tail rotor of a single-rotor machine absorbed no more engine power than that lost by twin-rotor helicopters through rotor interference.

But even as the humiliating XHJS-1 defeat took place, another design was in the works that would firmly establish Sikorsky Aircraft as a world leader in the manufacture of large helicopters. This was the milestone S-55, a bulbous yet boxy ten-place helicopter of just adequate performance but featuring a new configuration to overcome an operational drawback of all Sikorsky's earlier rotorcraft.

This limitation was excessive load sensitivity, stemming from the basic intolerance of single-rotor helicopters to center-of-gravity (CG) shifts. When the engine and transmission are placed directly beneath the rotor, as in the S-51 and earlier company models, any crew, cargo, and fuel weights have to be located elsewhere, either forward or aft, where they exert longitudinal moments that displace the CG. This situation necessitated careful loading, since incorrect weight distribution quickly pushed the aircraft's balance point up to and beyond the helicopter's narrow CG range limits. As a result, it was a challenge for the operators of these helicopters to exploit their full lifting potential.

Piasecki helicopters with fore-and-aft rotors

(Top) Proposed as a Navy fleet utility helicopter, the Sikorsky s-53 lost out to the superior Piasecki HJP/HUP. Courtesy UTC.

(Bottom) A milestone in single-rotor helicopter design, the s-55 introduced an entirely new configuration that placed the variable loads (fuel and cargo) directly under the rotor. Courtesy UTC.

did not suffer this drawback. Even before the fly-off military competition in Maryland, it was evident to the Sikorsky design team that a solution had to be found if its products were to remain competitive.

Igor Sikorsky and the Gluhareff brothers solved the load sensitivity problem one afternoon around the dining room table at the Sikorsky home.[33] Their solution was to relocate the fixed weights of engine and transmission away from the CG, thereby opening the space beneath the rotor to variable loads where weight added would not tip the helicopter. The result was a new helicopter configuration.

The new design began when Igor himself drew a box as the ideal cargo compartment from the standpoint of functionality. He placed the rotor directly above so as to minimize the effect differing loads within that box would have on CG travel, and he located the fuel tank below the cargo compartment for the same reason. Now, regardless of load or fuel quantity, the helicopter's center of gravity would remain comfortably within limits.

An inspired aspect of this design was the relocation of the engine to the nose of the aircraft, where clamshell doors provided easy ground-level maintenance. The s-51's basic gearbox, divided into two stages to accommodate an angled transmission shaft, provided the new helicopter's gearbox. The s-51 rotor was also used, its new-generation rotor blades being extended to accommodate the extra lifting power of the new craft's 600-hp R-1340 radial engine (some versions would be powered by an 800-hp Wright R-1300). A two-pilot cockpit—essentially a fixed weight since there would always be two men in it—was placed above the engine. A tail boom—a strengthened s-51 boom—completed the design.

Laying out the new machine, whose design is best described as a rounded box, reportedly took four and a half hours. The next three weeks were then consumed preparing a proposal to submit to the military services. The fact that the U.S. Air Force (USAF) still had a last block of twenty-six unbuilt s-51s on order gave Sikorsky Aircraft an opportunity to sell its unsolicited product. If that service would let Sikorsky use the money for the twenty-six s-51s, the company proposed, it would give the Air Force ten cargo helicopters capable of doing the same amount of work. Anxious for greater utility, the Air Force agreed and a contract was issued.

On November 10, 1949, a few weeks after the company celebrated its tenth anniversary of helicopter pioneering, the ten-to-twelve place XH-19 (s-55) made its first flight. With the coming of the Korean War, the arrival of the new helicopter would prove timely and all the military services would line up to procure examples of their own. Navy HO4SS, Marine Corps HRSS, and British s-55s all flew in Korea, as did Army Field Forces H-19s, which arrived belatedly in 1953, shortly before war's end.

Before 1949 had ended, an initial order from the Army for s-52-2 helicopters added that service to the USAF, Navy, Marines, and Coast Guard as Sikorsky military customers. Four-place s-51s were still selling strongly, with the 200th delivered to the Navy in November. Civil and military s-51s had in fact logged 107,000 hours in the air during 1949—more than all other makes of helicopter combined—and had added to the grand total of eighty-eight lives saved by Sikorsky rotorcraft.

To commemorate these rescues and to honor the thirty-nine heroic pilots who had performed them, United Aircraft Corpora-

(*Top*) Despite its limited performance, the s‑55 was built in numbers and firmly established Sikorsky as a leading manufacturer of large helicopters. Courtesy UTC.

(*Bottom*) In 1955, Sikorsky occupied this plant in Stratford, Connecticut, which remains the company's home today. Courtesy UTC.

tion issued pins featuring its Sikorsky Division's "winged-S" logo with the word RESCUE at its base. Along with certificates, these commemorative pins were issued to rescuers and rescued alike. That helicopters were still the one branch of aviation that saved lives rather than taking them (a situation that would inevitably change) was to Igor Sikorsky a source of special pleasure and pride. His office contained scrapbooks with clippings and photographs documenting these rescues, the latest volumes of which always sat on his desk where he could look through them and show them to visitors.

When the entire helicopter industry won the Collier Trophy for 1950, Igor Sikorsky appeared at the White House as its representative. In a ceremony held in the fall of 1951, the pioneer accepted from President Harry Truman America's highest aviation honor on behalf of every helicopter manufacturer, proponent, and enthusiast in the country. If the recognition was gratifying, it was also premature, because the struggling industry was not yet on its feet.

It took the Korean War to bring the vertical flight industry to maturity. In the early 1950s, Sikorsky suddenly had more business than it could handle. To accommodate demand, 180,000 square feet of plant space were added in the spring of 1952, making Sikorsky's South Avenue plant at Bridgeport the largest factory in the world devoted exclusively to helicopter production.

During the three-year Korean conflict, the number of rescues performed by Sikorskys would top 10,000, by one Department of Defense estimate. Starting in June 1950, USAF, Navy, and Marine s-51s shouldered the load by themselves until the first Bell H-13s became operational early the following year. Even after the Bell and Hiller medical

evacuation helicopters arrived, the bigger Sikorskys continued to share the rescue load between the utility and transport missions they were designed for. More than the products of any other manufacturer, Sikorsky s-51s, s-52s, and s-55s had ushered in the era of widespread tactical helicopter use by war's end in 1953.

On the home front, the war delayed civil certification of the s-55, which Sikorsky hoped to sell as an airliner. CAA approval of the world's first transport helicopter was finally obtained March 25, 1952, in time for New York Airways to place cargo-carrying examples in service that October. On July 8, 1953, NYA inaugurated America's first scheduled commercial passenger helicopter service using five s-55 Skyvans configured to carry seven passengers, a flight attendant, and two pilots. Although noise and vibration levels were excessive from the passengers' standpoint, and the helicopters themselves were so expensive to operate that hefty government subsidies were required to make service viable, these s-55s nevertheless pioneered helicopter passenger travel in the United States. Long imagined to be a natural use for helicopters, scheduled passenger service was destined to prove a disappointing market indeed for helicopter manufacturers.

The previous May, an s-55 crashed when its tail rotor flew off at Los Angeles International Airport. The hapless aircraft spun straight down from 400 feet and was totally destroyed, although fortunately nobody aboard was killed. Sikorsky Service Manager Alan G. Day rushed to Los Angeles, where he determined that a spring lock had worked loose when the helicopter was flown across the country and had become dislodged from the tail rotor shaft. Back in Connecticut, the

(Top) First flown in March 1954, the prototype s-58 prepares to lift an underslung boat. Courtesy UTC.

(Bottom) Two piston-powered helicopters, a Marine Corps HR2S-1 (s-56) transport helicopter (foreground) and an Army H-34 (s-58) take flight over the Sikorsky ramp in the late 1950s. Courtesy UTC.

Sikorsky Division general manager, Benjamin L. Whelan (United Aircraft's former chief pilot, an "early bird" whom Orville Wright had taught to fly), announced immediate steps to prevent similar problems in other s-55s, which by that time had flown 18,000 hours in service without any such trouble.

In August 1952, two USAF s-55s garnered international acclaim by performing history's first transatlantic helicopter flight. Assigned to the Air Rescue Service, Military Air Transport Service, these machines arrived at the Paris Air Show where their crews were warmly greeted by Igor Sikorsky himself. With two brand new helicopters and a turbine conversion of a third then under development on the home front, the patriarch of American helicopter development could safely hint to fellow air show attendees that much would happen at Bridgeport in the coming months.

To accommodate all this activity, United Aircraft in 1953 purchased 720 acres at Stratford, Connecticut, and broke ground for a new Sikorsky plant, doubling the capacity of that division's Bridgeport facilities. By then, Sikorskys were being built elsewhere in the world too. Westland in Great Britain was the first to negotiate a license production agreement with the American manufacturer, arranging at the end of World War II to manufacture s-51s (Westland would build Sikorsky designs for a decade before introducing models of its own). In 1953, France's Société Nationale de Constructions Aéronautiques du Sud-Est (SNCASE) became Sikorsky's second foreign licensee, and newly reformed Mitsubishi Heavy Industries in Japan would become its third in 1954.

On December 18, 1953, the Sikorsky s-56 took to the air. Powered by two 2,100-hp Pratt & Whitney R-2800 radial engines in stub-mounted pods, and weighing 31,000 pounds fully loaded (four times as much as the s-55), the HR2S-1, as it was designated, had been sponsored by the Navy to address a Marine Corps requirement for an assault transport helicopter. The Army, which had shared in the development costs, would also operate the type as the H-37 Mojave. There was no doubt that the s-56 offered both performance and utility: late in 1956 it set a world speed record of 162 mph, and in normal operations it could carry thirty-six fully equipped troops or three jeeps. Even so, only 156 were built because it was too expensive to operate even by military standards. Hoping for a commercial market for the s-56, Sikorsky had proposed a thirty-to-thirty-five-passenger short-haul airliner version, but there were no takers.

By mid-1954, the seven-passenger s-55 was in scheduled commercial service with no less than five carriers: New York Airways, Los Angeles Airways, Sabena Belgian Airlines, National Airlines, and Mohawk Airlines (the last two would be particularly short-lived). On the military front s-55s were again in combat, this time with the Fleet Air Arm in support of Britain's military involvement in Malaya.

The U.S. Navy had briefly used the s-55 around 1950 to test antisubmarine warfare (ASW) equipment and develop appropriate tactics, but these Florida-based machines lacked sufficient power and performance to do the job. Accordingly, the Navy swapped machines with the Marines at Quantico, taking their tandem-rotor HRP-1s, which—stripped of fabric—offered somewhat better performance. Frustrated by the lack of instrument and automatic-pilot flight capabilities in both of these types, the Navy shifted interim ASW duties to the new Piasecki HUP utility series. Because this series was initially underpowered and plagued by engine troubles, it awarded a contract to Bell to develop the first helicopter specifically designed for ASW, the HSL-1.

It was obvious to Sikorsky Aircraft that it needed a better helicopter in order to secure and retain military business. That better machine—the legendary S-58—was even then emerging under Navy contract concurrently with the S-56 as the XHSS-1 antisubmarine helicopter. The first prototype of the workhorse S-58 series took to the air March 8, 1954. It was powered by a 1,525-hp Wright R-1820 Cyclone radial engine.

Basically an enlarged S-55 with twice the horsepower and a gross weight of 13,000 pounds, the S-58 featured a four-bladed rotor 56 feet in diameter. More streamlined and less boxy than the S-55, it had a revised three-wheel landing gear and a vertical tail fin mounting a horizontal stabilizer and a four-bladed all-metal anti-torque rotor. More capacious, the S-58 could accommodate eighteen passengers or eight stretcher cases. Used by all the American military services, it would be known as the HUS in non-ASW duties with the Navy and as the H-34 by the Army and Air Force. It would also find other military and civil applications around the globe. Among its commercial uses would be scheduled service as a twelve-passenger airliner by both Chicago Helicopter Airways and Sabena. Altogether some 1,887 S-58s would be built over fifteen years.

During 1955, Sikorsky gained 830,000 square feet of badly needed floor space when it occupied its new Stratford facility just north of the Merritt Parkway on the west bank of the scenic Housatonic River. Production of the S-55 and S-56 had moved to Stratford—with the first S-56s delivered late

Although he officially retired in 1957, Igor Sikorsky continued working at Stratford until his death in 1972 at the age of eighty-three. Courtesy UTC.

in the year—while S-58 production remained at Bridgeport. By year's end, this two-plant expansion had increased the size of Sikorsky's work force by a remarkable 60 percent, to 8,400.

Although military sales accounted for the lion's share of production, commercial sales of both S-55s and S-58s were strong. The former were used in mining and construction projects in the United States and Canada, and also in the oil industry to fly workers and supplies to and from offshore drill rigs along the continental shelf and in the Gulf of Mexico.

Further brightening prospects for sales of the new S-58 was a 1955 Navy announcement that the type had been cleared for standard instrument flight under the same rules as fixed-wing aircraft.[34] This first-ever helicopter approval for blind flying, extended to civil use by subsequent CAA approval, vastly enhanced the utility of military and civil s-58s.

The record one-thousandth s-55—whose production life finally seemed to be drawing to a close—was delivered in the fall of 1956. Throughout the following year, during which total employment would top 10,000, Sikorsky delivered s-58s to the Army, Navy, and Marine Corps and completed its first export models for French, West German, and Japanese military service.

With successes on all fronts, it was a proud Igor Sikorsky who bid official and formal—if not actual—farewell to the company he had started more than thirty years earlier. On May 25, 1957, the patriarch of the world's helicopter industry, and one of fixed-wing aviation's greatest pioneers, retired from his post as engineering manager. For the next fifteen years he kept an office and remained active as a consultant at the company that still bears his name today.

Igor Sikorsky died at the age of eighty-three on October 26, 1972. By then his adopted countrymen firmly believed he had invented the helicopter. It was a foregone conclusion that Americans would view him as vertical flight's sole developer. He was ideally cast for the part: entering his fifties when he set to work on the vs-300, humble, gentle, and paternal, he looked like the "father of the helicopter." Having first risen to the challenge of vertical flight in 1909, Sikorsky's eventual success decades later also held cultural appeal. In this example of American mythmaking, the idea that Sikorsky inventing the helicopter became an oft-quoted parable about the value of persistence in realizing one's lifelong dream.

Further driving Sikorsky's fame was the fact that no one person or group had invented the helicopter. Americans simply needed to attribute this new form of flight to someone specific. The Wrights had invented the airplane and Edison the lightbulb; in the case of the helicopter, who was more deserving of the honor than Igor Sikorsky? National pride was also at work, of course. Calling Sikorsky the inventor of the helicopter appropriated this new form of flight for America. It made the vs-300 the world's first successful helicopter, thereby stripping Europe of credit for its successful helicopters of the 1930s. In so doing, it fostered in America the assumption that the United States—the land where heavier-than-air aviation was born—led the world in all forms of flight.

Throughout the last three decades of his life, Sikorsky took great pains to give credit where it was due. He repeatedly observed that he had not built the first successful helicopter, nor had he invented the single-main-rotor-with-tail-rotor configuration that predominates today. His efforts fell on deaf ears, of course, dismissed by Americans as the self-effacing disclaimers of a man known for his humility. Had they known him better, they might have realized that he simply did not lie. False modesty was as alien to him as boastfulness. There is a difference between inventing and perfecting, and the elderly aviation pioneer was well content with the latter distinction.

Sikorsky's true contribution to rotary-wing flight was to place helicopters in volume production for the first time in history. A much more difficult challenge than just making a prototype fly, this singular achievement marks the greatest milestone in the history of vertical flight. By adapting this difficult technology to practice during World War II, Sikorsky turned an aeronautical novelty into a working aircraft. If any one person ushered in the helicopter, it was Igor Sikorsky.

About the time Sikorsky retired in 1957, United Aircraft initiated a major expansion of the Stratford facility, which was then barely two years old. Completed the following year, this expansion provided 503,000 square feet of added floor space for a new engineering wing with an adjoining experimental shop, plus slightly more space for aircraft production.

A reason for this expansion was to have sufficient plant space available for the forthcoming production of turbine-powered helicopters. Turbine propulsion promised to revolutionize the helicopter industry. In use since World War II, turbojet engines by 1957 were powering a wide array of military aircraft as well as the de Havilland Comet civil jetliner. Turboprop engines (turbojets whose extended shafts drove propellers through reduction gearing) had also recently entered military and commercial service, notably in the Lockheed C-130 transport and Vickers Viscount airliner.

Smaller, lighter, and more reliable than piston power plants, turboshaft engines—the helicopter's version of the turboprop—offered the industry greater thrust-to-weight ratios for impressive performance gains. Turbine helicopters had already been flown experimentally by 1957, by which time Sud-Aviation's Aloutte II—history's first production turbine helicopter—was entering production.[35]

Interested in turbine propulsion since the 1940s, Sikorsky first pursued turboshaft use in 1951 under U.S. Army contract. The resulting aircraft was the YH-18B, a modified S-52, which flew with a French-built Turbomeca Artouste I engine July 24, 1953. Further development of this research prototype produced the XH-39 (S-59), two of which took to the air the following year. Equipped with a more powerful Artouste II engine driving a fast-turning four-bladed rotor, and with retractable landing gear, the S-59 set a world helicopter speed record of 156 mph (251 km/h) August 29, 1954, and a world altitude record of 24,522 feet (7,474 m) the following October 17. Although the Connecticut manufacturer entertained hopes for the attractive four-place S-59, a market failed to develop to support production.

Sikorsky gained additional turbine experience with the experimental conversion, under Navy contract, of an S-58 to turbine power in 1958. This project initially seemed unpromising because the much lighter weight of the General Electric T58 power plant unbalanced the helicopter, but Sikorsky engineers arrived at an excellent solution: two T58s were employed instead of one, offering the felicitous advantages of a hefty power reserve and twin-engine reliability. To accommodate the new engines, the S-58's gearbox was beefed up and redesigned for 100:1 rather than 10:1 reduction, the latter requirement being met by the addition of another transmission stage.

Although this engineering was accomplished before the end of the 1950s, Sikorsky elected not to produce a turbine-powered S-58 until 1970. By that time, the craft incorporated newer Pratt & Whitney of Canada PT6-T-3 turboshafts sharing a common gearbox in a Twin-Pac installation. That same year, Sikorsky began marketing kits to convert tired 1,525-hp piston-engined S-58s into Twin-Pac S-58Ts whose 1,800 shp substantially improved both performance and reliability.

Despite this focus on turbine power, Sikorsky would develop one last piston helicopter

(*Top*) The YH-18B—a modified S-52 flown in 1953—was the first turbine-powered Sikorsky helicopter. Courtesy UTC.

(*Bottom*) The Sikorsky S-58T, a turbine conversion of the venerable S-58. Courtesy UTC.

before the 1950s were out. This was the s-60, an experimental flying crane. Design of this helicopter, borrowing heavily from the Army and Marine Corps' big s-56, was finished in 1958 and construction of a prototype immediately began using s-56 engines and dynamic components released for that purpose by the military. Instead of the s-56's capacious fuselage, the new machine had only a dorsal keel—in effect, a metal backbone—connecting the three-place cockpit to the tail.

Sikorsky was not the first manufacturer to attempt to realize the long-held vision of a flying crane. Aviation manufacturers beginning with Kellett during World War II had sought to create the "sky hook" that civil engineers had so long dreamed of. For Sikorsky, specializing in the construction of large military helicopters, it was a natural desire. It was also a cherished dream of founder Igor Sikorsky, who, though retired, would participate in its realization.

Among the many challenges confronting the Sikorsky team was devising a configuration that would facilitate precise handling of loads, which had to be slung under the main rotor well behind the pilot. Veteran company engineers were quick to recall that the luckless hoist-equipped Sikorsky xhjs-1 had failed in this regard a decade earlier, a factor contributing to the company's loss of the Navy utility helicopter competition of 1949.

This one aspect of the overall challenge—precision control in relation to loads on the ground—gave rise to Sikorsky's revolutionary idea of a helicopter with no central fuselage. The radical configuration permitted installation of a third aft-facing pilot's seat offering panoramic downward and rearward visibility. To facilitate the work of the third pilot/crane operator, Sikorsky designers provided a side-mounted control stick by which

the s-60 could be flown with fingertip pressure for maximum control with minimum fatigue. Tying into a company-developed automatic flight control system, this side-stick controller avoided bulky mechanical controls by letting the pilot fly the helicopter through its autopilot.

If this system seems to anticipate today's fly-by-wire technology, it must be observed that the idea was not new. Sikorsky engineers had borrowed it from the "formation sticks" found in some U.S. bombers produced late in World War II, notably the Consolidated b-24 Liberator. These fighter-grip autopilot controllers freed pilots from having to maintain tight formation by hand, an exhausting process in the notoriously ungainly Liberator.

The Sikorsky s-60 took to the air March 25, 1959. Weighing almost a thousand pounds less than the s-56 that inspired it, the crane's performance was impressive for a piston-powered helicopter. Cruise speed was 130 mph and useful load approached six tons. In hover, the copilot would face rearward and assume control to operate the hoist, a system that worked well.

Igor Sikorsky had the further idea of developing a family of modular units, or pods, whose specialized loads would vastly enhance the flying crane's already formidable utility. A Sikorsky sky crane would need only attach whatever pod was required for the mission— a hospital unit, a portable machine shop, an air-transportable radar station, replacement parts for vehicles or aircraft, or whatever— and fly off within minutes of a summons.

With this system in mind, Sikorsky requested that a platform suspended on cables be installed within the s-60's open structure to study the in-flight dynamics of cable suspension. He then invited Chief of Engineering for Operations John P. W. Vest, Chief

The s-60, a piston-powered flying crane derived
from the s-56, took to the air in 1959. Courtesy
UTC.

Engineer Ralph Lightfoot, and Project Engineer Charles Echeverria to accompany him on an unforgettable open-air excursion early in the test program.

"It was a breezy and somewhat nerve-tightening ride," writes Vest, a former Naval aviator,[36] "and I was still trying to loosen my grip on the bench—there was not even a lifeline around the platform—when without warning Igor unfastened his belt and stepped over to the edge for a closer look and feel of the suspending cable there. He then walked around the platform, inspecting all the cables as calmly as though he were on the ground."[37]

For Igor Sikorsky, that open-air ride—whose risks were arguably much smaller than many taken earlier in his career—was a rare opportunity to recapture some of the thrills he had known as a young man. His casual inspection of support cables that day in 1959 was typical of an aviation pioneer whose courage was deep and genuine. Occurring exactly half a century after his first attempts to build a helicopter, the flight beneath the s-60's huge 72-foot rotor must have given the visionary inventor particular pleasure.

The s-60 was not built as a production prototype, but as a proof-of-concept vehicle intended to lay the groundwork for a turbine-powered flying crane with performance no piston power plants—not even Pratt & Whitney's big radials—could provide. The Army was particularly taken with the prospect of turbine-powered flying cranes. But Sikorsky Company executives realized that Army interest alone was not enough for a viable flying-crane program; the Navy would have to be involved if a new turboshaft powerful enough for a flying crane was to be developed.

During the next year Sikorsky sent the s-60 on an extended tour to demonstrate the flying crane to the Navy as well as the Army.

Among its Naval appearances was use as a minesweeper during Navy trials in the Gulf of Mexico. This machine also lifted cargo from the holds of ships and transferred truck-size containers from dockside to the decks of moving freighters.

These displays were well received by Naval observers who saw in the flying crane a solution to the problem of combat resupply at sea. Conventional ship-to-ship transfers from supply vessels required fighting ships to stop dead in the water, where they were particularly vulnerable to attack, until transfer was completed and they could again develop maneuvering speed. The ability of flying cranes to supply moving vessels, demonstrated by the s-60, promised to close this window of vulnerability.

With Navy support thus enlisted, development of a turbine-powered successor to the s-60 was accelerated. To deal with the lack of a turboshaft engine of sufficient power, the Navy proposed adapting either of two power plants then under development: the General Electric T64 or the Pratt & Whitney JT12. For flying-crane use, these engines would need to be redesigned with an extended rear shaft.

The T64 was being developed for the Vought-Hiller-Ryan XC-142A, a vertical-takeoff-and-landing tilt-wing transport plane under development for all three military services. Turboprop use of the T64 on the XC-142A demanded a forward shaft, and General Electric, perceiving a limited market for flying cranes, was not interested in a companion rear-shaft version. Learning as much on a trip to Washington, D.C., Lightfoot returned to Stratford, where he gave the disappointing, if hardly surprising, news to H. M. "Jack" Horner, president of United Aircraft. "Okay," Horner reportedly replied without hesitation, "we'll build the crane with a JT12 with a rear drive."[38]

Horner's instant decision reflected a characteristic United Aircraft Corporation strength —the willingness to take risks in support of its divisions. This decision was a major commitment because the Pratt & Whitney JT12 was a straight turbojet designed to power air-breathing missiles. Adapting it for the Sikorsky flying crane would be expensive.

Horner called a meeting at the Hartford headquarters with Lightfoot, Barney Schmickrath of Pratt & Whitney, Dick Gamble of Hamilton Standard, and United Aircraft's Operating and Policy Committee. The result of this gathering was the formal go-ahead to develop what would be the 4,050-shp JFTD-12A turboshaft engine, two of which would power the coming s-64 Skycrane when it took to the air in 1962.

In parallel with the s-60, Sikorsky had proposed a junior flying crane called the Universal Tactical Vehicle (UTV). Essentially an s-61 reconfigured like a smaller s-60, it was intended for less demanding load-lifting. The Navy might well have bought the UTV if Boeing Vertol had not beat Sikorsky to the punch by selling the Navy its new Model 107, which entered service as the CH-46A Sea Knight.

Much was happening on the business front. On July 1, 1958, United Aircraft formed two new divisions: Missiles and Space Systems, reflecting growing American awareness of space following the Soviet launching of Sputnik late in 1957; and the new Norden Division, created by the acquisition of that company—famous for its World War II bombsight—whose headquarters were in nearby Stamford, Connecticut.

Later in 1958, United Aircraft spent $3,016,440 to acquire 43 percent of West Germany's Weser Flugzeugbau G.m.b.H., a step taken to increase its penetration of European markets. Weser would become the Vereinigte Flugzeugwerke (VFW) in 1963. Also in 1958, in response to unprecedented government funding for vertical-flight R&D, the Sikorsky Division expanded its research and development staff to address alternate approaches to VTOL. The year also brought CAA approval for civil use of new Sikorsky-developed automatic helicopter stabilization equipment. Common in helicopters today, such devices are now known as stability augmentation systems (SAS).

The most significant event at Stratford in 1958 was the flight on May 14 of the world's first boat-hulled helicopter. This was the single-turbine-engine Sikorsky s-62. Work on this aircraft had begun just eleven months earlier, after development had commenced on the larger twin-turbine s-61 described below. The s-62 nevertheless beat the s-61 into the air by ten months.

Accounting for the pace of development was U.S. Coast Guard interest in procuring a new search-and-rescue helicopter. Since the s-61 would be too large and expensive for that mission, the decision was made to develop a smaller single-engine machine about the size and weight of the proven s-55. Instead of having that older model's piston engine, the new helicopter would be powered by a 1,250-shp G.E. T58 weighing half as much and producing double the power. Because Bell and Kaman were known to be vying for the USCG contract, moreover, Sikorsky engineers dropped plans for an all-new vehicle in favor of a design reusing as much as possible of the now-aging s-55.

The s-62 employed the s-55's main and tail rotor heads and blades, its transmission with an extra stage for added reduction, shafting, flight controls, electrical and hydraulic systems, and assorted other components. In addition to reducing development time, this extensive commonality between designs meant that the s-62 could draw spares from s-55 stocks to save its operators money.

Despite this selling point, the USCG passed over the s-62 in favor of the newer T58-powered HU2K-1 (later redesignated UH-2A Seasprite) built by rival Connecticut manufacturer Kaman. However, when that company later experienced difficulties meeting its contractual obligations to the Navy, which had fostered HU2K development and whose requirements took priority, the USCG in 1962 returned to the Sikorsky fold and bought s-62s after all. Sikorsky delivered the first five of an eventual fifty-eight before the year was out.

The Coast Guard's about-face was welcome news to United Aircraft executives. It was the first hint of U.S. military interest in the s-62, in marked contrast to the strong demand enjoyed by the s-61. Commercial sales of the s-62 were far too few to recoup company investment in the program.

Destined to be used for many years, the Coast Guard's hardworking, faithful Sikorsky HH-52As would fly in the worst imaginable weather to save many thousands of lives. The USCG's first turbine helicopters, they reportedly rescued some 1,200 people when Hurricane Betsy slammed into New Orleans in 1965.

Meanwhile, the Sikorsky s-61B—first prototype of the larger twin-turbine series—had flown for the first time March 11, 1959.[39] Called the XHSS-2 Sea King by the Navy, this amphibious aircraft was powered by two 1,250-shp G.E. T58s turning a five-blade rotor that folded for shipboard compatibility. The main landing gear was retractable to allow it to alight on water on a seaworthy fuselage, drawing from Sikorsky's long experience with boat hulls.

To the Navy, the HSS-2 represented a quantum leap in utility and effectiveness. True all-weather capability, enhanced by Sikorsky's new stability augmentation system, significantly increased utility and operational flexibility, while twin turbines and a robust boat hull worked similar improvements in reliability and safety. Best of all, the HSS-2 had sufficient performance to conduct both sides of the ASW mission at once.

The Navy's current ASW helicopter, the piston-powered Sikorsky HSS-1, could be configured to search for submarines or to destroy them, but not both. That necessitated dispatching two-ship hunter-killer teams on antisubmarine sweeps. Offsetting the higher acquisition and operating costs of the new machine, therefore, was the ability of one HSS-2 to do what two HSS-1s had previously done. Here at last was the helicopter the Navy had long sought.

A Department of Defense directive dated September 18, 1962, soon placed all U.S. military aircraft under a single designation system. Because the USAF's category-series system was simpler than the Navy's cumbersome mission-manufacturer-number nomenclature, Air Force–style aircraft designations were adopted servicewide. At that time, the Navy HSS-2 (s-61) became the H-3, and the Coast Guard HU2S-1 (s-62) became the H-52 before it ever entered service. Under this system, a prefix denoting specific function appeared before H for helicopter (i.e., C for cargo/transport, H for search/rescue, M for missile-carrying, R for reconnaissance, S for antisubmarine, U for utility, V for VIP transport, and so on). Suffixes indicated successive production models.

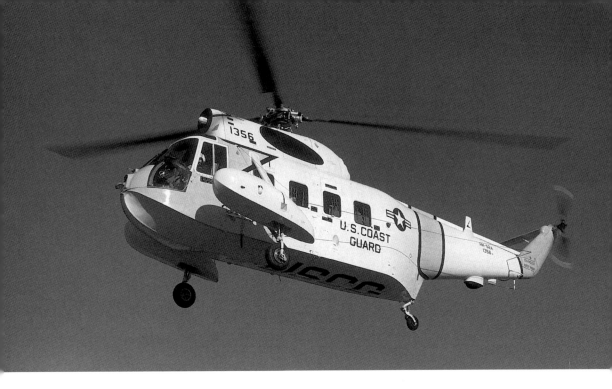

(*Top*) The Sikorsky s-62—the world's first boat-hulled helicopter—first flew in 1958 and earned fame in lifesaving duties as the U.S. Coast Guard's HH-52A. Courtesy UTC.

(*Bottom*) Water streaming from its tailwheel, the twin-turbine XHSS-2 Sea King (S-61B) demonstrates its seaworthiness. Courtesy UTC.

On the business front, the end of the 1950s witnessed a strong decline in Sikorsky factory production. One reason was the planned conversion from piston to turbine production. Another was an unexpected Defense Department austerity program coming at the worst possible time for Sikorsky. In just a few years, these causes conspired to lower total employment from an all-time peak of 11,000 to 7,900 by decade's end.

The end of the 1950s also saw the venerable s-55 finally phased out, although it would remain in licensed production abroad for a time. Just two other piston types remained on the assembly lines: the s-56 and the s-58. The former was being built at a reduced rate while the latter showed no sign of declining popularity.

Initial delivery to the Navy of its new HSS-2 Sea Kings began in 1961 with the flight of five across the United States. This event established a record for the fastest helicopter crossing of the continent: 17 hours flying time at an average speed of 150 mph. During that year and into the next, Sea Kings broke all five of the recognized helicopter world speed records, and became the first rotary-wing aircraft to exceed 200 mph in officially witnessed speed trials. On February 7, 1962, one Navy example established a world's record over a 12-mile straight-line course of 210.6 mph, bettering by 11 mph the previous record set by a Soviet Mil Mi-6.

By 1962 when the s-61 truly achieved volume production, the company's fortunes had reversed. Strong orders were on the books for both the Navy SH-3A Sea King (as the HSS-2 was redesignated) and the venerable s-58, including eighty-seven ordered by West Germany. Marine Corps s-58s, equipped with special armor protection developed by Sikorsky, were already in service in Vietnam

as the Kennedy administration commenced U.S. military involvement in that country.

The USAF began operating its s-61As in 1962, initiating development of a revised tricycle-gear model with rear-loading capability. Early that year, several s-61s had been delivered to the Marine Corps and Army for special use in Washington, D.C., as transports for the president and upper-level government officials. This highly visible use of Sikorskys continues to this day.

On the commercial front, the s-62 in 1960 became the first American-designed turbine helicopter granted FAA certification, while the s-61 received similar civil production approval at the end of 1961. Because Sikorsky Aircraft expected scheduled commercial service to be the primary market, commercial s-61s and s-62s were given stretched fuselages.

The first airliner model of the larger type was the s-61L, which despite its boat hull was not truly amphibious. For that, commercial operators flying regularly over water had to wait for the later s-61N, whose lateral floats indeed gave it amphibious capability. Commercial examples of the smaller s-62 were amphibious from the outset.

So taken was President Jack Horner with these new United Aircraft commercial products that he kept the original s-62 civil demonstrator as his personal helicopter. With soundproofing added overhead to reduce transmission noise, he used it to clinch sales of both series. Prospective customers visiting East Hartford were frequently whisked aboard for aerial tours by the chief executive, who glibly—if less than accurately—described the s-62 as a miniature version of the s-61.

Los Angeles Airways became the first scheduled commercial helicopter operator to place an order. It purchased two s-62s in

Marine Corps and Army s-61s were used for many years to transport the president of the United States and other high-level government officials. Courtesy UTC.

1959, followed by five s-61s in the early 1960s. LAA used the former to start the world's first scheduled turbine-helicopter passenger service December 21, 1960, and the latter to inaugurate the first twin-turbine service March 1, 1962. Ignoring the s-62, which was available sooner, Chicago Helicopter Airways and New York Airways both ordered s-61s equipped for twenty-five to twenty-eight passengers. As it turned out, CHA would never use its s-61s, because worsening financial woes in 1962 forced it to cancel the order.

From the outset, in fact, the helicopter carriers—as these rotary-wing airlines were known—showed a marked preference for the larger s-61 because it offered greater revenue-generating potential. By the end of the 1960s, s-61s would engage in scheduled passenger service in Australia, Europe, Italy, Great Britain, and Greenland. High operating costs and a poor safety record eventually put an end to such operations, except in those few markets where vertical-flight capability truly justified their use.

Fuji Airlines, a local-service carrier later absorbed by Japan Air Lines, was one of the few purchasers of the smaller s-62 airliner. The dozen-passenger single-engine transport had a forgettable career with one remarkable exception: San Francisco & Oakland Helicopter Airlines, a privately financed local-service carrier, for a time operated a fleet of s-62s in profitable unsubsidized service. Since America's three other helicopter carriers depended on heavy government subsidization to survive, SF&O's anomolous success was heartening news indeed to rotary-wing transport proponents.

Nonairline commercial s-62 use was fractionally broader. Okanagan Helicopters, a general operator based in British Columbia, put this type to a wide variety of uses in the wilds of Canada. Mitsubishi Heavy Industries—a Japanese license manufacturer of s-55s—was another customer, purchasing two in 1962 in anticipation of building both s-61s and s-62s for Pacific Rim markets. Early commercial use centered primarily on offshore oil rig support, where the s-61's turbine performance and boat hull gave it distinct advantages over earlier piston-powered types like the s-58. Petroleum Helicopters, Humble Oil and Refining, and the California Company were that industry's first s-62 operators.

Traditionally the largest single commercial helicopter market, the petroleum industry, like the military, would make far more extensive use of the s-61, particularly the amphibious s-61N, once they became available. Under contract, Okanagan used them to shuttle crews to and from offshore drilling platforms in Hudson Bay and off Canada's east coast. British-based Bristow Helicopters—destined to become the world's largest commercial helicopter operator—employed them off Malaysia, as did Brunei Shell. Bristow also flew s-61Ns in the North Sea, where KLM Nordzee Helikopters, Helikopter Service of Norway, and British Airways Helicopters also used them to support drilling platforms. Other early commercial s-61 operators included Court Line Aviation of South Africa and Construction Copters of North America. At the time of this writing, Greenland Airlines and British Helicopters still use s-61s, the latter to link Penzance and the Scilly Islands.

The high visibility of such use disguised the fact that commercial markets were extremely small and quickly saturated. Far more important to Sikorsky Aircraft's economic well-being were foreign military markets. The Indian Air Force was one of the first such cus-

This unusual view of a commercial S-61N, used by
the petroleum industry, shows the S-61's large rotor
to good advantage. Courtesy UTC.

tomers for Sikorsky turbine helicopters, purchasing two s-62s for high-altitude work in India's mountainous north. A great many other militaries worldwide would place these workhorse helicopters, primarily the s-61, in service in a variety of roles in the coming years. In 1962, for example, the Royal Canadian Navy and Japanese Maritime Self Defense Force initiated foreign use of s-61s in the antisubmarine role.

Still going strong in the early 1960s, the piston-powered s-58 remained Sikorsky's lower-cost alternative for customers who could not afford turbine power. Proof that s-58s could hold their own in the jet age came even as the new decade dawned: A Marine Corps HUS-1 launched a 12.5 foot, 570 pound Martin Bullpup radio-controlled missile in an experiment that was part of an interservice effort to add life-taking capabilities to the helicopter's well-proven lifesaving ability, an inevitable step that saddened Igor Sikorsky. At Sussex County Airport in Delaware, an H-34 made several midair pickups of packages descending by parachute; this series of experiments refined aerial recovery methods later used to retrieve spy satellite film containers. Also in 1960, an HUS-1 recovered Ham—the heroic chimpanzee who flew in space—from the Atlantic Ocean.

On May 9, 1962, the huge Sikorsky s-64 Skycrane made its first flight. Capable of lifting ten tons, topped by a six-bladed rotor 72 feet in diameter, the turbine-powered Skycrane bore a superficial resemblance to the earlier s-60 but in fact was an all-new design. Its fuselage—nothing more than a dorsal keel—was designed with careful attention to resonance so that it would be unresponsive to the forcing functions of the rotor system. This effort marked the first time Sikorsky engineers had consciously designed to elim-

inate vibration from the start rather than trying to cure it afterward with heavy vibration absorbers.

The s-64 came into being only with great difficulty. Since logistical support aircraft traditionally received low procurement priorities, the U.S. military was not able to support the s-64 as greatly as Sikorsky had hoped. Luckily, the West German Ministry of Defense had stepped in to fill this gap by contracting through Weser Flugzeugbau for two of the first three s-64s built. These German Skycranes were delivered early in 1963 while the third machine remained with Sikorsky as a demonstrator.

In 1963, Sikorsky won two more military turbine-helicopter contracts, bringing to five the number of defense production programs. That year also, the Air Force formally awarded a contract for a new version of the s-61 called the CH-3C. Given the company designation s-61R, this model was redesigned with a tricycle landing gear to accommodate a rear boarding ramp for cargo operations. This in turn required a rearward relocation of the helicopter's sponsons. The first CH-3C, as the USAF called it, flew in June and entered service the following year.

The other new Defense Department order of 1963 was for six Army s-64s. Designated CH-54A Tarhes, these first U.S. military Skycranes were procured for concept evaluation tests in conjunction with the Defense Department's upcoming industrywide heavy-lift helicopter (HLH) competition. By the time they were delivered late in 1964, the demands of escalating combat saw four of them diverted to Vietnam as described below.

On the commercial front, Pakistan International Airlines and British European Airways ordered s-61Ns in 1963. PIA used its s-61s to inaugurate scheduled service in

Although the Sikorsky s-64 Skycrane could lift ten tons, few would be built because of extremely high operating costs. Courtesy UTC.

November; in addition to reducing trips over the country's rugged eastern terrain from a full day to minutes, these machines spared the country the expense of constructing and maintaining airfields.

Most significant for the company's fortunes, 1963 also saw the start of prototype construction for the Marine Corps' new high-speed CH-53A (S-65) assault transport helicopter. Initiated by Navy contract the previous August, the S-65 combined a beefy fuselage of original design with G.E. T64 engines and proven S-64 dynamic components to create the largest production helicopter anywhere outside of the USSR. The S-65 also featured automatic main-rotor and tail folding for shipboard compatibility, and a watertight hull with flotation sponsons for safety, although this helicopter was not truly amphibious.

The first prototype flew October 14, 1964, and CH-53As entered operational fleet service the following year. With a crew of three, the aircraft could carry thirty-eight fully equipped troops at a top speed of almost 200 mph. Normal gross weight was 33,484 pounds, although an excellent power-to-weight ratio permitted operations at weights up to 42,000 pounds, as with a Skycrane. A wide rear ramp facilitated loading jeeps, 105 mm howitzers, or a wide variety of other cargoes in a compartment 30 feet long, 7.5 feet wide, and 6.5 feet high. Except for high purchase and operating costs, which limited the number that could be procured each fiscal year, this was the helicopter the Marines had long wanted.

The commercial S-61 received a boost in 1964 with airliner-version sales to Ansett-ANA, BEA, Greenlandair, Los Angeles Airways, San Francisco & Oakland, and Okanagan. By special agreement, three S-61Ns were also delivered to New York Airways for use at the New York World's Fair in 1964 and 1965. The utility of S-61L and N airliners in scheduled service increased dramatically in 1964 when they became the first turbine transport helicopters to be granted instrument flight certification by the FAA.

Production of the piston-powered S-58 finally ended in the fall of 1964 after 1,762 examples had been built. It would briefly resume the following year to fill Mutual Defense Assistance Pact (MDAP) orders for another 125 S-58s to be given by the Defense Department to foreign militaries. Also in 1964, another helicopter project was initiated with Defense Department acceptance of a Sikorsky proposal for a compound helicopter to serve as a stable, high-speed weapons platform for the Army's Advanced Aerial Fire Support System.

In 1965, the USCG announced its decision to procure 40 S-61Rs (HH-3Fs) for long-range search and rescue. That this largest Coast Guard helicopter would be based on the USAF's version of the versatile S-61 and not the Navy's (now possible under Kennedy-era Secretary of Defense Robert McNamara's unified procurement program) marked an interesting departure from past tradition. That year also, Sikorsky formally entered the space age as a subcontractor on the Titan III-C missile. Sikorsky would build the structures attaching new side boosters to the original Titan rocket.

Like other aerospace manufacturers, Sikorsky was now embarked on a path of greater international involvement. A 1965 agreement with Gruppo Fratelli Agusta authorized the Italian company—already a manufacturer of Bell helicopters under license—to construct Sikorsky S-61s. Additional European production (the assembly of

American-made parts to complete a key West German order for 133 S-65s) would be performed by newly merged VFW/Fokker starting in 1970.

Sikorsky helicopters set more official records in 1965, adding to an impressive list of rotary-wing achievements. In March, a Navy S-61 made the first nonstop unrefueled helicopter flight across the United States, flying 2,105 miles from San Diego, California, to Jacksonville, Florida. The next month, an Army S-64 set three altitude records, with loads of up to 11,000 pounds, in one day. In December, a USAF S-61R fitted with a refueling probe topped its tanks behind a Lockheed C-130F, marking the first time a helicopter refueled in flight from a fixed-wing tanker. This last success greatly expanded the utility of helicopters in military operations.

Forty years after Charles Lindbergh flew the Atlantic, two USAF HH-3ES (S-61Rs) used this range-extending capability to make lesser aviation history with nonstop transatlantic flights between New York and Paris, and New York and London. The 48th Aerospace Rescue and Recovery Squadron Jolly Green Giants had taken off from NAS Floyd Bennett and refueled from C-130 tankers four times.

On the research side, Sikorsky initiated a new R&D program in 1966 to evaluate coaxial counterrotating rotors. Called ABC for advancing blade concept, this military-funded program would retrace, slowly and at considerably greater expense, pioneering research in high-speed super-rigid rotors first pursued by Hiller Aircraft in 1946. Taking advantage of recently introduced composite construction techniques, the ABC rotor would in 1970 fly at 350 mph in the NASA/Ames Research Center wind tunnel, Moffett Field, Califor-

nia. A special research helicopter would be developed in the 1970s to test this and other rotors in flight, as described later.

Also in the 1960s, NASA's manned space-flight program made large turbine-powered Sikorsky production helicopters familiar sights to Americans through televised images of Navy HH-3s and HH-53s plucking Mercury, Gemini, and Apollo astronauts and spacecraft from the high seas.[40] Such use garnered welcome publicity for the Connecticut company; if its products looked low-tech compared to glamorous space hardware, they nonetheless were cast in the choicest of supporting roles.

The space program, of course, provided welcome relief from grittier, less comprehensible images of a war in which helicopters would star as never before or since. If another manufacturer's product—the ubiquitous Bell UH-1 Iroquois, or "Huey"—would become the archetypal image of the Vietnam conflict, larger Sikorsky and Boeing Vertol helicopters would also play major roles.

Supporting the 1st Air Cavalry Division, the four Army CH-54A Skycranes sent over in 1964 repaid their $4 million procurement cost several times over by picking up more than a hundred downed U.S. aircraft in eighteen months of service. The first Sikorsky S-65s (USMC CH-53As) arrived in Vietnam in January 1967, where they joined their close cousins in retrieving downed airplanes and helicopters. By the end of 1968, U.S. S-65s had reclaimed 816 crashed airframes, outstripping the S-64's end-of-year tally of 425.

Hundreds of American airmen downed well behind enemy lines were similarly rescued by Sikorskys. Of particular note in this regard were the exploits of the USAF's Aerospace Rescue and Recovery Service, whose CH-3C Jolly Green Giants routinely flew far

(*Top*) Operated by the U.S. Air Force, this HH-3E Jolly Green Giant features a rear loading ramp and an aerial-refueling boom. Courtesy UTC.

(*Bottom*) An HH-53B of the USAF's Aerospace Rescue and Recovery Service in flight. Courtesy UTC.

into North Vietnam to retrieve aircrew. The USAF took delivery of its S-65s under the designation HH-53B in 1967. Equipped with external rescue hoists, in-flight refueling booms, armor protection, and jettisonable external fuel tanks, these larger HH-53Bs significantly enhanced the ARRS's rescue capability.

Notable Navy employment of Sikorskys in Vietnam included the use of RH-3A minesweepers to clear Vietnamese ports and harbors of mines following the cessation of hostilities in 1973. Larger RH-53Ds, which would become the mainstay of Navy minesweeping, would enter service a little too late to participate in that conflict, but in time to clear mines from the Suez Canal in 1974.

Combat use focused attention industry-wide on the ability of helicopters to absorb damage ranging from small arms fire to anti-aircraft shells. An area of particular concern was the rotor blades, where undetected damage could cause a crash. Metal rotor blades—the industry standard—could take quite a bit of damage, even bullet holes, as long as this damage avoided the spar. If that key load-bearing structure was so much as nicked, however, blade life was compromised and a clock began ticking down to total failure. If the helicopter was hovering, the crew might survive; otherwise the results were sure to be fatal.

Sikorsky blades were particularly susceptible to rapid degradation following spar damage because they were built around aluminum spars. Under the dynamic stresses imposed by flight, even difficult-to-detect hairline cracks soon widened in the soft metal to precipitate total structural failure. This problem came to light even before America became embroiled in the Vietnam War.

The fatal crash of a commercial Sikorsky S-58 in Chicago first focused company attention on this critical issue. Shortly before the accident, the helicopter had experienced a quick start which compressed and slightly distorted the trailing edges of its rotor blades. Sikorsky had remanufactured these blades in Connecticut and returned them to the operator. Official investigation of the crash revealed that a rotor blade had come apart in flight because a fatigue point had been introduced into one blade spar. Whatever the cause, it had gone unnoticed during the remanufacturing process.

Engineer Harry Jensen came up with an ingenious system to detect imminent blade failure due to spar damage. Incorporated into all Sikorsky production helicopters, his solution was BIM (blade inspection method), which consisted of a visual indicator at each blade tip. If even a hairline crack had formed in the spar, the BIM indicator changed from white to red to alert operators to ground the helicopter until the blade could be changed.

The secret behind this seemingly miraculous diagnostic aid was air pressure. Jensen had conceived the brilliantly simple idea of pressurizing the hollow aluminum spars and placing gauges at their tips. If air seeped away through undetected cracks, a spring-loaded visual indicator would tilt into the red zone to indicate danger. A later version of this system saw a BIM indicator mounted on the instrument panel of the giant H-53 for in-flight blade integrity assurance.[41]

Rival manufacturer Boeing Vertol initially thought it did not need a system similar to Sikorsky's. Cracks developed and spread more slowly in the steel spars of their blades, giving mechanics the opportunity to detect them during routine inspections before the blades could fail in flight. However, the Vietnam War proved that Boeing Vertol H-46s and H-47s needed visual blade integrity indicators for greater safety in combat. This requirement presented B-V engineers with a problem: pressurization would distort the thin walls of their steel spars, particularly when the strong centrifugal forces encountered in flight further compressed the air at the blade tips. As a result, those engineers took the opposite approach and evacuated the sealed spars to create visual blade integrity indicators actuated by a failing vacuum.

A better solution was already on the horizon, of course, because the aviation industry was moving toward the use of lightweight composites. These nonmetallic structural materials would make possible a new generation of blades remarkably resistant to loss of structural integrity, regardless of the location of damage.

A peculiarly abrasive dust and sand encountered at dry Vietnamese airstrips presented U.S. helicopter builders with another headache. Kicked up by rotors during dry-season operations, this penetrating abrasive drastically shortened turbine engine life to strain supply lines and reduce both combat readiness and vehicle reliability. Sikorsky's answer, christened Engine Air Particle Separator (EAPS), consisted of a long intake plenum whose curving airflow threw dirt to the side to remove 96 percent of particulate contamination. Sikorsky's chief engineer Ralph Lightfoot traveled to Vietnam in mid-1967 to oversee EAPS installation and use. By the following spring, the device had saved an estimated $17 million in reduced S-64 and S-65 maintenance expenditures.

This war saw the U.S. Army for the first time completely dependent on rotary-wing aircraft for organic air support (i.e., provided by its own aircraft rather than those of other services). While helicopters did make possible highly effective air-mobility tactics, the Army had not willingly forsaken fixed-wing aircraft. Political considerations were responsible for what from a military standpoint was a questionable and crippling decision.

Even high-performance fixed-wing aircraft found North Vietnamese airspace inhospitable. More heavily defended than Germany during World War II, this combat theater took a heavy toll of aircraft of all types. Although helicopters proved more difficult to shoot down than anyone had expected, Army aviation losses were still far too high. Sikorsky and rotary-wing manufacturers strove feverishly to correct this situation by addressing unprecedented design survivability challenges.

One such effort, developed under military contract, was Sikorsky's Aerial Armored Reconnaissance Vehicle (AARV). The fuselage of this proposed armed helicopter was of steel armor topped by armored glass in a prismatic shape for maximum crew protection. The small AARV had a gross weight of 6,800 pounds and was expected to achieve high speeds because it was to make use of the ABC rotor described above. Ball and armor-piercing projectiles were fired at a full-scale AARV fuselage mockup but the project progressed no further, in part because the weight of such a helicopter would have denied it the maneuverability needed for combat survival.

Another Vietnam-inspired helicopter flew at Stratford in August 1970. Company-financed as a speculative venture, designed and built in just nine months, this was the Sikorsky S-67 Blackhawk (not to be confused with the S-70 Black Hawk of 1978). Born out of the lessons of modern warfare, this fast twin-engine machine—the prototype set a world speed record of 220.6 mph in December 1970—was offered to the military as a

The one-of-a-kind Sikorsky s-67 Blackhawk of
1970 was destroyed in a fatal crash. Courtesy UTC.

helicopter gunship. The Army awarded Sikorsky no less than four evaluation contracts for further study of this troubled helicopter, but a fatal crash put an end to the Blackhawk before production could begin.

The s-67's rapid development was achieved by combining proven s-61 components with a narrow low-drag fuselage featuring stub wings, an airplane-style tail, and speed brakes. This engineering shortcut had been an effective strategy a dozen years before when liberal borrowing from the s-55 had sped development of the s-62. But it failed this time, because Bell Helicopter Textron in Texas had used the same tactic to present the Army with a smaller, less costly, far more maneuverable gunship, the HueyCobra of the late 1960s. Had the Cobra not existed, the larger s-67 might well have played a role at the tail end of the Vietnam War.

Warfare brought booming business and high profits, but Vietnam was not Sikorsky's only source of government contracts. In November 1967 the company had reorganized into an Air Transportation Division and a Surface Transportation Division. Based at Sikorsky's Bridgeport facility, the latter was created especially to cater to the U.S. Department of Transportation (DOT). This nontraditional customer was beginning to contract with segments of the aviation industry for high-speed train development in an effort to wean America from near-total reliance on automobiles. For lack of public support and political will, the program was destined to fail despite ever more polluted air and congested roads.

In December 1967, the first of two three-car Sikorsky TurboTrains accelerated to 170 mph over a special high-speed track during a trial run between Trenton and New Brunswick, New Jersey. This was the highest speed ever attained by a U.S. passenger train. These MetroLiners, as the Sikorsky trains were christened, were initially leased to the DOT, which in 1968 placed them into scheduled passenger service between New York and Boston. Four more cars—two for each MetroLiner—were built at Bridgeport in 1971, increasing the capacity of both trains from 144 to 240 passengers each.

Decades of decline had left America's once-proud railroad infrastructure largely incapable of accommodating high-speed rail service. Sikorsky found another customer in Canada, however, and built five seven-car TurboTrains for service between Montreal and Toronto beginning in 1968. All Sikorsky TurboTrains were powered by PT6 gas turbine engines made by Pratt & Whitney of Canada.

As the 1960s drew to a close, the Air Transportation Division introduced new versions of existing Sikorsky helicopters to military and commercial use. The s-64E was a civil counterpart to the Army CH-54A, which entered commercial service in 1968. Leased from Sikorsky by Rowan Air Cranes, two s-64Es logged more than 800 flight hours in three months of intensive operations on Alaska's North Slope during 1969. By carrying over 24 million pounds of equipment—including complete drilling rigs specially designed for air transport—these machines reduced somewhat the total damage done to that region's slow-healing tundra environment.

The first sale of a commercial s-64 was not registered until three years later. The customer was the Erickson Air-Crane Company of Portland, Oregon. In addition to hauling trees for the Northwest timber industry, the company used this aircraft to haul cement during construction of the four-mile-long Chesapeake Bay Bridge in Maryland. It also flew to Europe to help build a new dike in Holland. Other projects facilitated by commercial Skycranes included positioning air-conditioning units atop a Pittsburgh automotive plant, where one s-64 accomplished in thirty hours what would otherwise have taken eight months; erecting utility towers; repositioning high school grandstands across a marshy football field; and transporting prefabricated structures ranging from bridges to houses.

By the early 1970s it was nonetheless clear that the s-64 Skycrane program was a financial flop bordering on the disastrous. The fault lay with Sikorsky and the UAC, who had both failed to assess civil and military requirements for such a vehicle. These mammoth machines were too expensive to see sustained commercial utilization, and too limited in utility to enjoy enduring military popularity.

When commercial Skycranes were busy working, they were worth their weight in gold. But profit-making commercial ventures were far too few, because smaller, less expensive helicopters could address most industry needs. Since idle s-64s threatened to bankrupt their operators in short order, Sikorsky found few takers.

The military was not willing to play its usual role of program savior to offset slack civil sales. Navy support for the H-54 evaporated in 1969 when a USN-fostered "growth-version" called the CH-54B took to the skies. Expected to double the A-model's load-carrying capability to 20 tons, this helicopter's actual lift performance of 12.5 tons fell far short of the mark. The 20-ton target represented the weight of a Polaris intercontinental ballistic missile. Strategic planners had looked to the Skycrane to fulfill the questionable aerial resupply mission of delivering fresh ICBMs to submarines.

The U.S. Army also had little use for the s-64 Skycrane. It had tested Igor Sikorsky's interchangeable multifunction pod concept during the Vietnam conflict and found it too cumbersome and expensive to support. The pods themselves created new and unwanted logistic problems and did not satisfactorily offset the substantial utility lost through the Skycrane's lack of an enclosed fuselage.

Army planners viewed each s-64 purchase as a lost opportunity to purchase many smaller helicopters. Numerical strength was more important than aerial crane capability in fulfilling the Army's mission of tactical capability across a broad front. One s-64 cost taxpayers as much as seven or eight versatile Bell UH-1s (the Huey had an exceptionally low unit price because of its record production), and each Skycrane cost much more to operate than smaller helicopters.

In 1971, Sikorsky test pilots used the CH-54B's improved performance to set eight more helicopter records, including a breathtaking altitude mark of 36,711 feet. But these accomplishments did little to hearten UAC executives who had invested so much in the unwanted Skycrane concept. The appearance of an improved s-65 with Skycrane-like performance further hastened the decline of the s-64.

That the military services preferred the new model to the s-64 became evident when it entered service in 1966. As the Navy's largest helicopter, the Sea Stallion combined excellent load-carrying capability with enclosed-fuselage utility. But the Navy found it still had a need for Skycrane capability after canceling its s-64 procurement in 1969, and contracted with Sikorsky in 1971 to initiate development of a three-engine s-65 expected to lift 16 tons. Designated CH-53E Super Stallion, it was in so many ways a new aircraft that it was eventually given the designation s-80. The s-65's already huge rotor was increased to 79 feet in diameter and given a seventh blade to accommodate the extra power generated by the s-80's third engine.

In response to the Civil Aeronautics Board's northeast corridor VTOL study of 1968, Sikorsky had completed design in 1969 of an even more radical s-65 development. Proposed as an eighty-six passenger short-haul intercity airliner and featuring the CH-53E's three engines, this aircraft was in fact a compound helicopter with stubby wings and propellers for airplanelike cruise, at 265 mph, between vertical takeoffs and landings.

To promote this new program, Sikorsky in 1970 flew a series of demonstrations in Europe and the United States to prove that large turbine rotorcraft could provide rapid short-haul service between urban centers. The demonstrator was a modified CH-53D converted several years earlier under NASA contract to become the prototype for a civil transport called the s-65C. Also known as the Ride Comfort Research Aircraft, and initially fitted with sixteen of a possible forty-two seats, this machine provided valuable data and was still in experimental use with the FAA twenty years later.

With Pan American World Airways as cosponsor, Sikorsky even submitted a proposal to the Department of Transportation to conduct joint service in a yearlong demonstration along the crowded Northeast corridor. The stated purpose was to confirm that "short-haul intercity helicopter service with present flight equipment is operationally and economically feasible, environmentally acceptable, and desirable from the public's viewpoint."[42]

As proposed, this commercial service would initially be conducted with modified s-65s

carrying forty-two passengers at a speed of 173 mph on routes of up to 225 miles. Such service, Sikorsky noted, would reduce travel time between city centers and alleviate growing congestion at major jetports. For future operations, Sikorsky pointed to its already-designed compound helicopter.

This burst of enthusiasm for commercial helicopter travel came at a time when Sikorsky s-61s were providing scheduled service with more than half a dozen carriers around the world. Sikorsky knew these operations to be marginal at best, however, and recognized that chances were slim that commercially viable intercity helicopter operations could be established during the 1970s.

In fact, apprehension rather than enthusiasm prompted Sikorsky to team up with Pan Am for a new attempt to establish broad civil-market demand for helicopter airliners. The American military involvement in Vietnam was coming to an end, and with it the boom in production all U.S. helicopter manufacturers had come to depend on. Postwar military inventories, moreover, would for a time be glutted with helicopters.

Removal of the last American troops from Vietnam in 1973 was joyous news to the nation as a whole. But for U.S. helicopter manufacturers it meant painful downsizing and massive layoffs (except at Bell in Texas, where a large military order from Iran provided sufficient business). In Sikorsky's case, this period saw sharply decreasing orders on the books through 1976, the production nadir. Sikorsky Aircraft built just nineteen helicopters during the entire year. Only the s-65 and s-61 remained in production, although additional plant space had been devoted since 1971 to remanufacturing s-58s as turbine-powered s-58Ts.

Precisely how bad a year 1976 was for the

Connecticut manufacturer is difficult to assess. United Technologies Corporation (United Aircraft Corporation's new name beginning in May 1975) maintains a policy of revealing only corporatewide financial figures. Gross earnings, net income, assets, unfilled orders, and other information are disclosed, but not once since the corporation formed in 1929 have these figures been broken down by division. Industry analysts and insiders have long characterized Sikorsky Aircraft as a chronic underperformer, however, with earnings rarely living up to expectations. Such reports are understandably difficult to verify.

Even during this 1976 low, Sikorsky's survival was never in question. UTC's deep pockets and a heartening array of promising programs ensured a quick return to former glory. Among these programs was the three-engined S-65 for the Navy and Marine Corps. First flown on March 1, 1974, it generated badly needed production volume as the CH-53E Super Stallion when placed in service at the end of 1980. Healthy growth in international markets also helped Sikorsky by increasing civil-market orders, although commercial sales alone could not support the company.

Significantly, Sikorsky had two all-new helicopters under development. The first was the company's entry for the Army's huge Utility Tactical Transport Aircraft System (UTTAS) competition. UTTAS sought to foster a new-generation helicopter to replace aging Bell UH-1s, Sikorsky H-3s, and other types then in U.S. and foreign arsenals. This milestone procurement promised multiservice production of more than three thousand helicopters over decades. The second program was the S-76. The sleek lines and high performance of this twelve-passenger commer-

cial helicopter confirmed that it was aimed at the lucrative petroleum-support and executive-transport markets. A military version was also planned.

Launching these two concurrent programs —one military-funded and the other company-financed—demanded a considerable investment by United Technologies, whose leaders clearly saw the need for a new, technologically advanced product line if Sikorsky were to remain competitive in an industry it had traditionally dominated.

The UTTAS competition narrowed in the summer of 1972 to Sikorsky and Boeing Vertol, at which time both companies received contracts for construction of three flying prototypes plus one ground-test example. On its own, Sikorsky constructed a fourth flying prototype to explore commercial prospects for the new machine. These military prototypes were then exhaustively evaluated before a final decision was made on which type to procure as the Army's versatile new combat-assault troop/utility transport helicopter.

Designated S-70 by its builder and YUH-60A Black Hawk by the Army, Sikorsky's entry took to the skies October 17, 1974. Long and sleek, its pronounced hump suggesting a fish more than a bird of prey, this new-generation rotorcraft could carry a fully equipped eleven-man infantry squad or substantial underslung loads.

The new machine drew heavily from the recent lessons of Vietnam to demonstrate extreme crashworthiness. The S-70's light-alloy and composite fuselage, forming an external shell around the cabin, absorbed impact, as did the rugged landing gear and collapsible energy-absorbing seat frames. So great was the structural integrity of the Black Hawk design that the engines and gearbox remained in place above the cabin even during 20 g impacts. Power was provided by two newly developed G.E. T700 turboshaft engines each rated at 1,560 shp. A common gearbox was limited to 2,828 shp.

The four-bladed rotor featured a high-lift asymmetrical airfoil and swept tips for reduced sensitivity to Mach effects. Constructed around titanium spars pressurized for integrity verification, these fully articulated blades consisted of a Nomex honeycomb core, a graphite root and trailing edge, and a plastic leading-edge counterweight, all encased in plastic skin with a titanium leading edge for abrasion protection. The tail rotor, employing the same airfoil section, also displayed Sikorsky innovation; it needed no lubrication, was much more reliable, featured just 10 percent as many parts as earlier units, and weighed just 20 percent as much. Even if this unit were shot off, the tail pylon offered sufficient stabilizer area to permit a controlled landing.

UTC's all-out effort to win the UTTAS competition showed clearly in the remarkable performance of the Black Hawk. Weighing over 16,000 pounds fully loaded, this rugged vehicle proved more than nimble enough to perform the terrain-hugging "nap-of-the-earth" operations the Army considered essential to combat survival. Advanced technology also answered the Army's desire that this machine be little more than half as expensive to operate as earlier helicopters of comparable size. In fact, the Sikorsky UH-60A fulfilled every military requirement but one.

The original procurement circular and subsequent development contracts specified that the UTTAS helicopter be air-transportable for greater operational flexibility. The helicopter was to fit whole inside a Lockheed C-130 Hercules transport plane. While the length and width of the C-130 cargo hold presented

no problems, Sikorsky engineers knew that they would have a difficult time conforming to the height constraints imposed by its low ceiling. The company chose to risk military displeasure by telling the Army it would just have to live with a helicopter that seven men could break down and load into a C-130 in two hours.

On December 23, 1976, official announcement was made that Sikorsky Aircraft had won the competition and would be supplying the Army's next-generation utility helicopter. Throughout the competition, Sikorsky personnel had not hesitated to take digs at archrival Boeing Vertol, which to meet UTTAS requirements had been forced to depart from its traditional tandem-rotor configuration, a fact liberally interpreted in Connecticut as vindication of the Sikorsky single-rotor approach to helicopter design. When an independent postprocurement technical analysis, conducted by the government's General Accounting Office, concluded that the YUH-61A's rotor and dynamic system were in fact superior to those of the YUH-60, such comments lessened markedly.

In 1977, Sikorsky won yet another production contract stemming from a major competition. Calling for construction of more than two hundred Navy helicopters, this was the LAMPS (Light Airborne Multi-Purpose System) Mk. III procurement. While it would build the LAMPS III vehicle, Sikorsky was a subcontractor rather than the prime contractor. Reflecting the increasing importance of electronics to aerial warfare, IBM's Federal Standards Division had bid and won; in turn, it had selected the Sikorsky S-70 as the platform for its integrated electronics in order to take advantage of lower unit costs accruing from mass production for the Army.

The sh-60b (h-60l) Seahawk, as Sikorsky's lamps III aircraft was christened, is most easily distinguished from its Army cousin by the forward relocation of its tail wheel. Less obvious to the observer are a rotor brake, automatic blade folding, a folding tail and stabilizer, and improved corrosion control for shipboard compatibility. This Seahawk today serves the Navy in an impressive variety of roles. Its primary missions of antisubmarine and antisurface-ship warfare require it to be fitted with combinations of surface surveillance radar, sonobuoys, magnetic anomaly detectors, homing torpedoes, antishipping missiles, and a vast array of other equipment. Since all this added capability demanded increases in both gross weight and engine power, development and production schedules kept the Seahawk from entering widespread fleet service until 1984.

Other s-70 users include the Coast Guard, which has a need for a limited number of hh-60j Jayhawks; the Customs Service, which has put its Black Hawks to hard use against aerial drug runners; the usaf, which operates hh-60d Night Hawks and mh-60g Pave Hawks; the military's Executive Flight Detachment near Washington, D.C., which transports key government figures including the President; and foreign countries including Australia, China, Japan, Spain, and Turkey.

In contrast to the s-70, Sikorsky's other new production program, the s-76, addressed the commercial market. The lean post-Vietnam years having driven home the dangers of relying too heavily on defense production, the company had at last brought a dedicated civil helicopter to market. All its previous commercial offerings had been converted from military types.

Announced during 1975 to permit heavy

yearlong promotion during America's 1976 bicentennial celebration, the first Sikorsky s-76—the model number was no coincidence—rolled out in January 1977. Recession and rising interest rates following the Arab oil embargo of 1973 had conspired to make it an inauspicious time to launch a new commercial venture, but utc executives were heartened to note eighty-seven firm orders already recorded in Sikorsky's books.

The helicopter itself was a masterpiece of styling, with racy lines and—depending on how it was configured—up to twelve seats. A familiar-looking rotor and tail, both scaled down from the s-70, suggested liberal borrowing of uttas-program advanced technology. The first flight of the s-76 took place March 13 at Palm Beach, Florida, where three prototypes logged more than 400 hours before the year was out. faa certification was granted in April 1978 and deliveries started early in 1979. By that time some 200 had been ordered.

Already home to utc subsidiary Pratt & Whitney's military power plant division, Palm Beach had been selected by Sikorsky as the venue for its lavish new corporate test center. There the company constructed what it claimed was the most modern, best-equipped rotary-wing test and commercial support center in the world. The scope of this facility underscored utc's determination to claim a larger share of the civil helicopter market.

There were also Sikorsky research programs. First of these was the Army-funded xh-59a (s-69), which was built for flight evaluation of the advancing blade concept rotor system described above. The first of two examples flew in the summer of 1973 but was damaged soon after. Following extensive

(*Top*) Capable and highly versatile, the Sikorsky s-70 Black Hawk is today widely used by U.S. and foreign military services. Courtesy UTC.

(*Bottom*) Redesigned for maritime use, the s-70 became the U.S. Navy's sH-60B Seahawk in 1977. Courtesy UTC.

The attractive, high-performance Sikorsky S-76 corporate helicopter overcame early reliability problems and today serves in a variety of civil and military roles. Courtesy UTC.

modification, the second s-69 flew in 1975 and continued in test for some years.

Another purely research-oriented program sponsored jointly by NASA and the Army gave Sikorsky two invaluable s-72 Rotor System Research Aircraft in 1976. Designed to test almost any rotor system in flight, these vehicles feature removable wings and pod-mounted jet engines which allow them to fly at a wide range of speeds even with rotor systems too small to lift the RSRAS off the ground by themselves. These vehicles can in fact fly with no rotor at all, although for initial testing they were rolled out with s-61 rotors. One of these machines was modified in 1984 for x-wing aircraft concept evaluation.

A more recent flight research effort began when the U.S. Army's Advanced Technical Laboratory selected Sikorsky early in 1981 as one of two companies to participate in its Advanced Composite Aircraft Program (ACAP). Sikorsky's ACAP effort, the s-75, used the dynamic system and rotor of the s-76, which it superficially resembled despite having fewer windows and a rudimentary fixed landing gear. Its Kevlar and graphite fuselage having displayed a 23 percent weight and 25 percent cost savings over conventional construction methods, the s-75 began flight evaluation trials in the summer of 1984.

At that time, Sikorsky was already an industry leader in the use of composites. The lower structural weights and superior resistance to vibratory fatigue of such materials had recently prompted the company to build a new 85,000 square foot composites facility in Tallassee, Alabama. By 1985, some 10,000 composite components a month were being manufactured, most under contract to other manufacturers. Ailerons and flaps for Cessna Citation business jets are one example of composite components produced there.

But problems and setbacks plagued the s-76 program. The worsening world economy hit the helicopter-dependent U.S. petroleum industry particularly hard, undercutting orders in that market for which the s-76 had been expressly designed. Other problems included the chronic service problems and less-than-sterling safety record of s-76s already in commercial service.

As demand fell from a 1980 high of 400 orders, the company undertook expensive in-service upgrades through factory kits provided to operators at no cost. Sikorsky also redesigned the s-76 with a beefier structure and more-powerful P&W of Canada PT6B-36 engines in place of its Allison 250-C30s. While much improved, the resulting s-76B—promoted as the s-76 Mark II—remained a weak seller as Sikorsky struggled to overcome the market coolness created by its teething troubles.

The s-76 has since vindicated itself in commercial and other services. Among the fastest of the world's lifesaving emergency medical service (EMS) machines, it has also won acclaim in the search-and-rescue (SAR) role. For example, Hong Kong Police s-76s, perhaps the most sophisticated SAR helicopters in service, have performed extraordinary rescues in the most extreme monsoon conditions.

To reduce losses on this program, Sikorsky Aircraft turned to the very market it had hoped to get away from. In 1982 it dispatched a militarized s-76, designated H-76 Eagle, on a demonstration tour to interest U.S. and foreign militaries and government agencies in the type. Fitted with a variety of armaments and armor, the H-76 Eagle filled out the bottom of the Sikorsky military products line as a lower-cost, less-capable alternative to the s-70 Black Hawk.

To prepare for heavy Black Hawk/Seahawk/CH-53E production schedules, meanwhile, United Technologies in 1977 initiated a five-year, $100 million modernization of Sikorsky manufacturing facilities. This program came just in time, for in February 1978 Sikorsky received a contract for 20 CH-53E Super Stallion Navy and Marine helicopters (the Navy would also procure the MH-53E Sea Dragon version with enlarged sponsons and other changes for airborne-mine countermeasure use). At the time of this 1978 contract, the Defense Department informed the builder that CH-53E production would run to about 100 units, twice as many as Sikorsky had anticipated.

This outcome was a mixed blessing. Feast-and-famine cycles are unwelcome in any industry, but aviation manufacture has been particularly prone to their negative effects. Having survived lean times in the mid- to latter 1970s when it built few helicopters, Sikorsky now found itself with the opposite problem. Too-rapid expansion brought production delays and spiraling costs from inefficient structuring, poor communications, and quality concerns arising from an undertrained work force. President Robert F. Daniell, who had come up through the engineering ranks, faced the task of confronting these problems and pushing Sikorsky back toward competitiveness.

Daniell's successor was thirty-year veteran engineer Robert Zincone. Named president in 1985, he quickly set a new course for the company by announcing the goal of becoming more than just a basic manufacturer of helicopters. "We want to be responsible for delivery of the wholly integrated system," he announced, "and are already moving in that direction."[43]

Behind these words lurked the clear lesson of LAMPS III: However good the helicopter might be, today's sophisticated combat environments frequently demand the installation of considerable interactive electronics equipment for mission capability and survivability. Rather than build a flying platform for IBM or others to equip, Sikorsky would develop and produce helicopters containing fully integrated electronics packages. In short, all military helicopters would emerge from the factory ready for specific military operations.

That same year, Sikorsky began work on two new contracts providing the company with its first full systems-integration experience. The first was the Navy's CV-Helo program, which saw a version of the S-70 (the SH-60F) selected to replace Sikorsky SH-3H Sea Kings for protection of battle group inner zones from submarines. As the prime contractor and systems integrator, Sikorsky in turn selected Teledyne Systems for electronic development support.

The second opportunity, won competitively, was a contract to build multimission Seahawk derivatives for the Australian Royal Navy. For this program, Sikorsky selected Rockwell Collins as the principal subcontractor. On the civil side, Sikorsky in 1985 created a company in Belgium to undertake European production and sales of the S-76.

In July 1987, Eugene Buckley succeeded Zincone to the presidency. Described as a "no-nonsense production man,"[44] Buckley believes in focusing on the central functions the company performs best, always keeping in mind the needs of the customer. One way he addresses global competitiveness is by furthering the industrywide trend of recent decades to move toward greater international cooperation. As of this writing, off-site manufacture or joint development agreements exist or are being discussed with companies

A military-funded XH-59/S-69 research helicopter
tests Sikorsky's advancing-blade concept (ABC)
coaxial rotor in the 1970s. Courtesy UTC.

in Brazil, Canada, France, Germany, Great Britain, Japan, South Korea, and Spain.

Early in 1991, Sikorsky and Boeing together won a key contract to build the next-generation Army light helicopter. This landmark procurement initially promised production of up to six thousand advanced military rotorcraft beginning in the 1990s. To share development costs and reduce risk—a necessity in aviation today—Sikorsky teamed with Boeing in June 1985 to bid for the LHX (later simply LH) contract. Putting aside their traditional rivalry, they had by 1988 designed an all-composite, tandem-seat military helicopter with a shrouded tail rotor set in a T-tail. This design features heavy internally housed armament, fly-by-light fiber-optic controls, and remarkable capabilities through extensive systems integration.

The Sikorsky-Boeing team was announced the winner of the LH contract early in 1991. Subsequently designated RAH-66 Comanche, this helicopter's development has been slowed by defense cutbacks but it has survived cancellation.

United Technologies revealed in early 1983 that its Sikorsky Aircraft Division had the previous year exceeded one billion dollars in sales for the first time in its history. Four years later, with military production high and new contracts won, that figure was $1.6 billion. With s-70 production alone scheduled to continue through the first decade of the next century, company fortunes seem assured for some time to come.

Ultimately, however, success depends on developing new products, and one is already on the horizon: the Sikorsky s-92 Helibus, a nineteen-seat commercial helicopter intended as a successor to the s-61. Two full-scale mockups were unveiled—one civil and the other military—at Heli-Expo '92, a vertical-flight industry trade show held in Las Vegas, Nevada. Formally launched at the Paris Air Show in 1995, the s-92 program is truly multinational, with risk-sharing partners in Japan, China, Spain, Taiwan, Brazil, and possibly Russia.

The s-92 combines UH-60 Black Hawk/SH-60 Seahawk systems and components with a larger fuselage. Scheduled to fly in 1998 and enter commercial service three years later, the s-92 is intended primarily for civil markets, although Sikorsky is also proposing a troop-transport version for the Marine Corps when that service finally retires its faithful CH-46s.

Like Boeing Heilcopters, Sikorsky Aircraft continues to depend heavily on U.S. and foreign military sales. Ongoing cutbacks in worldwide defense spending, increased competition from the European helicopter industry, and the prospect of additional competition with the manufacturers of the former Soviet Union all cloud Sikorsky Aircraft's prospects on the eve of the twenty-first century. Whatever the specific turn of events, the company that Igor Sikorsky founded in 1923—manufacturer two decades later of the world's first production helicopters—is likely to be around for many years to come.

3 / Piasecki, Vertol, and Boeing Helicopters

In France for the signing of the Treaty of Paris formally ending the American Revolutionary War, Benjamin Franklin witnessed the ascent of a Charles hydrogen balloon on the Champs de Mars on August 27, 1783. Following the event, an observer disparagingly dismissed the large unmanned balloon. Of what use was it? he demanded. "What is the use of a newborn babe?" replied Franklin.

His reply was prophetic. Barely two months later, a paper hot-air balloon built by the Montgolfier brothers carried people aloft for the first time in history. The age of human flight had dawned.

Two centuries later, Franklin's home city would itself be a unique center of aviation activity. The fertile Delaware River Valley surrounding twentieth-century Philadelphia boasted such heavier-than-air manufacturers as Huff-Daland/Keystone, Fleetwings, Hall Aluminum, Brewster, and Budd. Just across the state line in New Jersey were Luscombe, Chase, and the Eastern Division of General Motors. Following the valley the other direction into Delaware, one found Bellanca and Acquaflights. And in Philadelphia proper was the venerable Naval Aircraft Factory, which beginning in World War I built airplanes as well as the ill-fated dirigible *Shenandoah*.

But what truly distinguishes the Delaware Valley is its unique prominence in rotary-wing flight. To begin with, Philadelphia and its surroundings were home to the fascinating if short-lived American autogiro industry. Born in the late 1920s, active in the 1930s, and all but gone by the end of World War II, this ephemeral industry in its heyday gave Philadelphia a rotary-wing technology base and talent pool unique in the nation.

The region remains to this day the center of large, tandem-rotor helicopter manufacture. Philadelphian Frank Piasecki built America's second working helicopter during World War II. Out of the success of his diminutive PV-2 arose history's first volume producer of large helicopters, a company known variously as the Piasecki Helicopter Corporation, Vertol, Boeing Vertol, and today Boeing Helicopters. The pages that follow chronicle the story of Frank Piasecki and the company he created.

As the cradle of U.S. rotary-wing aviation, Philadelphia on the eve of World War II was the nation's clearinghouse for information on the subject. Igor Sikorsky himself would contribute to and draw from the resources of this region before successfully flying the VS-300 at the start of the 1940s.

Late in 1938 and 1939, he and other helicopter pioneers attended two profoundly significant symposia at Philadelphia's venerable Franklin Institute. Organized by the Institute of Aeronautical Sciences—predecessor of today's American Institute of Aeronautics and Astronautics—which cosponsored the events with the Franklin Institute, the now-forgotten Rotating Wing Aircraft Meetings offered a priceless forum for pooling knowledge and exchanging ideas. There would be a third and final rotary-wing gathering in New York City at the start of 1941.

These three gatherings were convened to advance both the autogiro and the helicopter. Since no helicopter industry existed, the autogiro community—represented by Harold Pitcairn, Wallace Kellett, Burke Wilford, Dick Prewitt, Laurence LePage, and Agnew Larson, among others—initially dominated the proceedings. At the first meeting, LePage (who in November 1938 formed a helicopter company with mechanical engineer Haviland Platt) showed movies of Germany's Focke-Achgelis Fa 61 helicopter, inspiration for the Platt-LePage XR-1 helicopter of 1941.

In addition to Sikorsky, two other men who would go down in history as early producers of helicopters were on hand. One was Pennsylvanian Arthur Young, whose decade of experimentation would culminate within five years in the Bell helicopter. The third architect of America's soon-to-emerge helicopter industry was a teenage engineering student named Frank Nicholas Piasecki. The local youth followed these proceedings with rapt interest.

Proponents of the sharply divided autogiro and helicopter camps set forth their views during these forums. There was universal agreement that the helicopter was enormously more complex than the autogiro, but heated differences emerged over whether the former was worth the cost and bother when the lat-ter could already do everything short of hover and fly vertically.

For all the enthusiasm it briefly commanded in the United States, the autogiro was not an American invention. Spaniard Juan de la Cierva had perfected this type of aircraft in the 1920s and had granted licenses for use of his patents and manufacture of his designs in the United States, England, and Germany. Also referred to as gyrocopters and gyro-planes, autogiros are incapable of hovering flight because their windmilling rotors provide only lift—like the wings of an airplane—rather than lift *and* thrust like the rotor of a true helicopter. Consequently, autogiros need airplane-style engines and propellers to provide thrust.

Pennsylvanian Harold Frederick Pitcairn had flown a Cierva autogiro—the first ever demonstrated in the United States—at Willow Grove, Pennsylvania, in 1928. With great enthusiasm, he settled on the autogiro as the vehicle that would realize his dreams of mass-produced aircraft as safe and easy to operate as cars. Accordingly, in 1929 he obtained American rights to Cierva's auto-giro patents and designs. In the belief that one autogiro company could not address the anticipated demand for personal flying machines, Pitcairn formed the Autogiro Company of America in Philadelphia as an administrative rather than a manufacturing entity. Its sole purpose was to create, through licensing, the formation of a full-fledged auto-giro industry in the United States.

Of the companies concluding manufacturing agreements with the ACA, two were located in the Philadelphia area: Pitcairn's own Pitcairn-Cierva Autogiro Company and the Kellett Aircraft Corporation, founded by former World War I flier-turned-industrialist Wallace W. Kellett. Despite Pitcairn's grand vision, these companies enjoyed only modest success in the manufacture of autogiros. Enthusiastic fellow experimenters Burke Wilford and Gerard Herrick found even less success, their efforts never leading to production.

The Buhl Aircraft Company of Detroit, Michigan, a well-known builder of fixed-wing aircraft, also negotiated a license with the Autogiro Company of America. Only one prototype of a two-seat four-bladed-rotor pusher autogiro, intended for aerial photography and observation, was built before the Great Depression forced Buhl to suspend aircraft manufacture in 1931.

A third autogiro manufacturer was incorporated in the Delaware Valley in the late 1920s, although not under the Pitcairn umbrella. E. Burke Wilford (who with Vincent Burnelli had built an aircraft for the Guggenheim Safe Airplane Contest in 1927) had traveled to Europe in 1928, where he obtained American rights to the 1926 gyroplane of Walter Rieseler, a Cierva licensee in Germany. Flown in Paoli, Pennsylvania, in August 1931,[1] the advanced Wilford Gyroplane featured partial cyclic control (roll only) and would later have helicopter-style full-azimuth cyclic control. Although his gyroplane was the first rotary-wing aircraft in the United States to fly successfully without wings (a feat Cierva had accomplished a year earlier in England), Wilford failed to bring his Gyroplane to the civil market. A 1937 attempt by his Pennsylvania Aircraft Syndicate to interest the Navy in a hybrid Consolidated N2Y/Wilford Gyroplane called the XOZ-1 was similarly unsuccessful.

About three hundred autogiros were built in America before it entered World War II. These rotorcraft flew approximately 100,000 hours with a poor safety record, but with only one reported death because landings took place at very slow speeds. Autogiros were flown by celebrity aviators and sportsmen pilots; they shuttled mail between the airport in Camden, New Jersey, and the roof of Philadelphia's main post office; they advertised Beechnut Gum and other products; they underwent military evaluation trials; and they appeared in Hollywood productions like the classic *It Happened One Night* (1934) with Clark Gable and Claudette Colbert. The only thing that autogiros did *not* do was catch on: they failed utterly to find a meaningful niche in aviation.

Even as autogiro production declined, an entirely new chapter in the annals of rotary-wing flight quietly began. The long-anticipated age of practical helicopters was dawning, in part thanks to the remarkable efforts of young autogiro engineer Frank Nicholas Piasecki (pronounced pie-SECK-ee).

Born October 24, 1919, in Philadelphia, Piasecki loved aviation from the time he was small. He had his first airplane ride at age seven when his father, Polish-born tailor Nikodem Piasecki, bought him a flight with a barnstormer. The ride thrilled the impressionable boy.

His awakening interest in flying machines focused on their construction, a lifelong fascination. Like so many youths growing up in the golden age of flight, Frank built models and pored over aviation magazines. He joined his high school Aero Club and soon became its president, a position that took him behind the scenes at many of the greater Philadelphia area's aircraft companies.

The firms that impressed Piasecki most were Pitcairn and Kellett, America's premier autogiro builders. In February 1936, at the age of seventeen he had a ride in a Kellett KD-1 piloted by test pilot Lou Leavitt, America's first licensed rotary-wing pilot. "With that

Looking much older than his twenty-three years, helicopter pioneer Frank Piasecki doffs his hat while flying his PV-2, the second successful U.S. helicopter. Courtesy John Schneider.

experience," Piasecki remembers, "my interest exploded into the desire to build my own design. The helicopter particularly appealed to me, vertical lift being the hot topic in aviation at that time."[2]

The wingless KD-1's ability to land in a moderate wind without rolling out particularly impressed Piasecki. In fact, as Pitcairn and Kellett so frequently observed in their product promotions, autogiros required remarkably short takeoff and landing rolls. They could stop in their own length when landing into the wind. Development by Pitcairn of the "jump takeoff" in the mid-1930s even allowed the autogiro to take off without a ground run. This was achieved by briefly diverting power to the rotor to bring it to an overspeed condition, after which collective pitch was applied. The craft then jumped like a bullfrog into the air and flew away.

But such refinements were to no avail; the world simply didn't want autogiros. What it wanted was true vertical flight capability. Although long anticipated, helicopters had defied easy realization because of their inherent complexity. Enormous work was required to go from the autogiro, a simple aircraft capable of near-vertical performance, to one truly capable of vertical takeoff and landing (VTOL) flight.

Perhaps for this reason these autogiro manufacturers only very late and grudgingly embarked on helicopter developments of their own, thus missing a golden opportunity. With extensive rotary-wing experience and proven hardware, they nevertheless let a substantial lead slip away.

The fixed-wing aircraft industry displayed a similar lack of enthusiasm. America's largest airplane builder, Curtiss Aircraft, had funded a major helicopter effort in the early 1930s. The two-seat Curtiss-Bleeker had four wing-like rotor blades turned by propellers mounted halfway out each blade from the hub. Failure of this costly program after three years of intensive effort hardened the belief among fixed-wing manufacturers that vertical flight offered few rewards.

Without leadership during the 1930s from either the autogiro or fixed-wing aircraft communities, realization of the dream of true vertical flight was pretty much up for grabs, and there was no shortage of takers. Helicopter experimenters ranged from backyard tinkerers to accomplished aeronautical engineers. Rather than just seeking to build a working helicopter, these experimenters embarked on the more tantalizing and difficult quest of perfecting vertical-flight technology to the point where helicopters could be manufactured. If helicopters were ever to make a profit for their inventors, they had to go from being an aerial novelty to being mass produced.

The rapid pace of technological advancement during flight's golden age set the stage for realization of this dream by the end of the 1930s. With a lead of several years over his competitors, Sikorsky went on to achieve true volume production of military helicopters during World War II. His was the only company in the world to do so. But since nobody knew just how big the emerging civil and military helicopter markets would be or what shape they would take, a new industry would doubtlessly coalesce over the next decade and it could be expected to have room for at least a few other companies. Profits remained to be made by others following in Sikorsky's footsteps.

This description perfectly fit young Frank Piasecki, who graduated from high school in 1936 and promptly joined Kellett. But his duties did not bring him in contact with auto-

Philadelphia's autogiro industry provided Piasecki with invaluable rotary-wing expertise. Simpler than helicopters, autogiros—like this Pitcairn PA-36—were incapable of hovering or vertical flight. Courtesy NASM/SI.

giros as he had hoped, for his job was to prepare the steel-tube frames of exercise bicycles for welding. However, he spent his lunch hours and other free moments on the flight line, where he added to his already substantial knowledge of mechanics.

On the job, the enthusiastic teenager performed every task given him in record time. So fast did he work that Kellett literally ran short of material. Piasecki was cutting lengths of steel tubing at a workbench one day when a foreman stopped by to commend him on his work. Gradually it dawned on him that he was being fired, not promoted. The shocked teenager realized he had worked himself out of a job.

Piasecki next worked for the Aero Service Corporation, a nearby aerial mapping company. There he learned the processes of mapping and soon was given the chance to fly as a cameraman. An opportunity to attend college had also arisen, however, prompting the young man to seek the advice of Aero Service President Virgil Kauffman. The latter considered the question at length before telling his employee to go to engineering school.

Nikodem and Emilia Piasecki accepted their son's announced intention to become an aeronautical engineer, although the former entertained high hopes that his musically gifted son would pursue a career as a violinist. Frank had played with several orchestras and he had even performed as a soloist. To his mother, the announcement came as no surprise. "Frank was never out on the street playing with the other boys," she remarked some years later. "He was always too busy in the cellar with his model airplanes or his cameras."[3]

There was never any doubt that he would have their approval, for the Piaseckis were a close and supportive family. Their Polish values stressing hard work would be an essential ingredient to his later success. Another was his enormous energy. This characteristic, which Piasecki jokingly attributes to "tough Slavic genes," is to many observers his most remarkable trait.

A close second in Piasecki's personal makeup is his legendary salesmanship, a talent stemming from sheer force of personality. "When I was in school I learned that I wasn't brilliant, but had a very persuasive manner," he once confided to a magazine writer.[4]

His extraordinary ability to motivate others sprang from boundless self-confidence. A showman who loved to dress elegantly, always meticulous in his grooming, he demanded notice and signed his name in bold letters with a flourish. Animated dark eyes flashed in a large round head, and when he smiled there was irresistible charm. The smile faded quickly, however, dispelled by chronic impatience with a world unable to move as rapidly as he did. Observers tempted over the years to dismiss him as an egotist failed to comprehend a basic truth: Frank Piasecki was in a hurry and could not be bothered with amenities.

The young man pursued three years of mechanical engineering studies at the Towne School of Engineering, University of Pennsylvania. Anxious to focus on flight, he transferred to New York University's Guggenheim School of Aeronautics to study aeronautical engineering. This school was headed by noted aircraft designer Dr. Alexander Klemin, who shared his student's fascination with vertical flight. But the single most valuable lesson Piasecki would learn from Klemin was about business rather than engineering.

Piasecki's reputation as a skilled model

maker accounted in part for his acceptance in the course, for Klemin frequently needed wind tunnel models built. He asked Piasecki to help meet this need, and the young man agreed to do so for 75 cents per hour. "When I presented my first bill," Piasecki recalled, "Dr. Klemin said, 'That's impossible; you couldn't possibly be so inefficient as to have spent this much time on doing these models.' With that, he wrote out a check for half the amount. When he needed another model built I again went down into the shop and got a lot of students together to build it, but this time I took the actual numbers and multiplied them by three. He went through the same routine, cutting my bill in half, and we were both satisfied."

During this period, Piasecki attended a graduate course in rotary-wing flight. The instructor was Kellett's chief engineer Dick Prewitt, who during World War II would design the flea-shaped Kellett xR-8, an experimental Army Air Forces helicopter with Flettner-style canted intermeshing rotors. This course heightened Piasecki's enthusiasm for helicopters and introduced him to the rotary-wing community.

Meanwhile, he had continued to work during his studies. Following brief stints with the Aero Service Corporation and the National Machine & Staple Company, and with his degree in hand, he now obtained a position as a junior engineer with Platt-LePage Aircraft of Eddystone, Pennsylvania.

Located on the banks of the Delaware River southwest of downtown Philadelphia, Platt-LePage was formed in 1938 by aeronautical engineer W. Laurence LePage and industrial designer Haviland Platt, the latter a brilliant mechanical engineer who had invented the first successful automatic transmission for cars. Germany's Focke-Achgelis Fa 61 heli-copter had inspired this company. After watching that aircraft fly in Berlin's Deutsch-landhalle in February 1938, LePage had returned to the United States to seek government support for a similar project.

Laurence LePage was well equipped to find that support. Tall, courteous, and well-spoken, the British-born engineer had worked for Pitcairn and Kellett, and with the Edward G. Budd Manufacturing Company, a large industrial concern with aviation interests. To cultivate support, he made many visits to Wright Field in Ohio, where his credentials, enthusiasm, and movies of the Fa 61 won him the chance to bid for a contract from the U.S. Army Air Forces.

Timing was in LePage's favor, for the AAF had recently obtained funds earmarked for helicopter development. Under the landmark Dorsey Bill of 1938, Congress had authorized $2 million for this purpose, of which $300,000 was appropriated the following year.

The Army's first helicopter—the de Both-ezat of 1922—had been a failure. Since that time, helicopters had indeed been built that truly flew. With substantial funding now available, expectations ran high that a working military helicopter would soon be realized. Of four companies submitting designs for consideration, only Platt-LePage's PL-3 incorporated the Fa 61's proven configuration. On July 19, 1940, therefore, Platt-LePage was awarded the contract and the PL-3—work on which had already begun with private financing—became the xR-1. The designation denoted "experimental, rotary-wing, first type."

As junior engineer on the xR-1 design team, Frank Piasecki initially drew uninspiring assignments like laying out floorboards and devising foot- and handholds. A related duty, however, provided invaluable training and began an association that would be essential to Piasecki's later success. This duty was to assist the chief designer, Elliot Daland.

The highly regarded senior engineer—who had worked at the Kellett, Pitcairn, and Wilford autogiro companies before coming to Platt-LePage—was blind in one eye and had extremely poor vision in the other. So limited was his eyesight that seeing or reading anything required him to peer from a distance of an inch or two through a jeweler's loupe hinged on eyeglass frames. Daland's ability to grasp complex drawings viewed one square inch at a time awed young Piasecki, who found in the older man a brilliant mentor. "I became his eyes, while he taught me all the things that his experience had given him,"[5] Piasecki said of Daland.

Daland's skill as a rotary-wing engineer was only part of his fascinating history. He had been a cofounder of Huff-Daland Aircraft, the Ogdensburg, New York, company that built the world's first crop dusters shortly after World War I. A subsidiary company, Huff-Daland Dusters, evolved directly into today's Delta Airlines. Relocating in 1925 to Bristol, Pennsylvania, Huff-Daland later became Keystone Aircraft, builder in 1932 of the B-6, the Army Air Corps' last lumbering biplane bomber in the World War I tradition.

The vehicle the Platt-LePage design team came up with was fairly large and had tandem seating for two. In overall appearance, it suggested a fixed-wing airplane despite two side-by-side rotors, an impression enhanced by its winglike support pylons. A conventional landing gear and an airplane-style tail heightened the effect.

Frank Piasecki had an early opportunity to see drawings of an "innovation" Laurence LePage had incorporated into the design of the XR-1. A 450-hp Pratt & Whitney R-985 radial engine buried in the fuselage supplied power to both rotors through a transmission. To this transmission LePage had added the equivalent of an automobile differential in the belief that differential power was needed when the aircraft turned.

Thinking it through, Piasecki realized that the initially appealing idea lacked merit and was dangerous. It would cause the banking helicopter to fall off to the outside of a turn, necessitating a quick reversal of the controls by the pilot to regain control. He stated his belief, summarizing his reasons, in a memorandum to President LePage.

Unknowingly, Piasecki had opened a can of worms. Pet theories can have a life of their own, particularly when they have been used as a selling point. The young engineer's efforts therefore won him only the opprobrium of those above him, and he found he was suddenly persona non grata. His memo was not answered and many company higher-ups stopped talking to him.

The first phase of the flight test program began in May 1941. This was a protracted period of refining, modifying, and debugging. Day after day of run-ups and adjustments finally gave way to hovering, and then to flights in ground effect. The only problem that failed to appear, in fact, was the potentially dangerous control reversal anticipated by Piasecki in his memo.

Over the weeks that followed, doubts assailed the young engineer as the XR-1 performed ever better low over the riverbank. Had he made a mistake, and had he needlessly damaged his career in the process? His quandary was not helped by the knowledge that, with war looming on the horizon, his draft board was waiting if Platt-LePage chose not to renew his aircraft-industry deferment.

Test pilot for the XR-1 was Lou Leavitt, the

former Kellett test pilot who had given Piasecki his first autogiro flight five years earlier. The young engineer pulled his friend aside and confided his concerns. Leavitt appeared to take little note, being overtly unconcerned.

The day arrived finally for a first test at altitude. With Captain Frank Gregory, the AAF helicopter project officer, and other dignitaries in attendance, the XR-1 was wheeled ceremoniously out and carefully checked over. Mechanics made last-minute adjustments and warmed it up. Piasecki stationed himself, as assigned, some distance down the riverbank to work a movie camera pointing at the craft's tail.

Leavitt lifted cleanly off the ground and took the XR-1 straight up about 300 feet. It was the first time the craft had been so high. Sunlight glinted off bare aluminum as Piasecki gazed in awe. Suddenly there came a loud *brupp-brupp* and the helicopter dropped to one side, then to the other. The wallowing and noise ended abruptly with a hard landing that stopped the rotors.

Some part of the helicopter has broken, Piasecki thought, running as fast as he could. The other observers had already clustered by the ship as he got there and Leavitt was climbing shakily from the cockpit. The test pilot ignored the insistent questions and looked around until he caught sight of Piasecki. Striding over, he shook the twenty-two-year-old engineer's hand. "Thanks, kid, for saving my life," he told him.[6]

Piasecki resigned from Platt-LePage that same day. Vindication meant little to him after the anguish he had endured. "It wasn't that I was *right*," he observes, "it was that nobody could be bothered to tell me whether I was right or wrong. I was treated like a child and tortured for three months."

Difficult as the experience was for Piasecki, it was formative. He learned not to doubt himself, not to defer automatically to age or reputation. The Platt-LePage association was a toughening process that cleared the way for Piasecki to pursue his long-standing desire to develop production helicopters. "It was no mere dream," he now comments. "It was total envelopment, a constant."

He next found employment with the Edward G. Budd Manufacturing Company in northeast Philadelphia, where he worked as an aerodynamicist on the Budd RB-1 Conestoga, a stainless-steel military cargo plane. With America already gearing up for the war in Europe, Budd—a general manufacturing company with many divisions—paid well; for Piasecki, it was a bread-and-butter job and a means to an end. He already had an idea how to begin accomplishing his goal of helicopter development.

Piasecki had begun telephoning former college classmates during 1940 to see if any were willing to get together evenings and weekends in a speculative engineering venture. It was not long before erstwhile schoolmates Harold Venzie, Donald Meyers, Walt Swartz, Frank Kozloski, Ken Meenen, and a few others had banded together in an after-hours venture known as the P-V Engineering Forum (the initials standing for Piasecki-Venzie, the latter individual having been Piasecki's closest friend at the University of Pennsylvania).

As announced by founder Piasecki, the purpose of the new organization was to pool the ideas and skills of its members in order to develop products for commercial exploitation. Everyone was invited at the outset to suggest anything from vacuum cleaners to washing machines, but it soon became clear that the others had little to suggest.

Piasecki heard them out before speaking. In

the absence of other ideas, he proposed that the team construct a helicopter. This ambitious goal stunned the group, but before long Frank's enthusiasm and persuasiveness had infected those around him. They would build and perfect a single-seat prototype that could be scaled up for production after World War II. Intended for personal use, it would serve as the aerial equivalent of a family car.

Like every helicopter pioneer before him, Piasecki had failed to appreciate the magnitude of the challenge. For him the commitment to vertical flight would last a lifetime. "Helicopters have taken so long," he would quip a half century later, "that we haven't yet got around to a second project."

Piasecki approached Elliot Daland and invited him to join the effort. The senior aeronautical engineer agreed, much to his junior colleague's relief. Since he was an aerodynamicist and Don Meyers a mechanical engineer, Piasecki considered it essential to have a dedicated "nuts-and-bolts" rotary-wing engineer involved. Daland, his first choice, would contribute greatly to the group's success.

In the engineering hierarchy thus formed, Piasecki exercised overall creative control. He consulted frequently throughout with Daland, whom he venerated. The two made an amusing contrast, Piasecki always neatly dressed and Daland in baggy old clothes with holes from his scattered pipe ash.

Meyers worked for both of them, relieving Daland of tasks made difficult or impossible by his near blindness. Meyers's training as a mechanical engineer proved critical in the design of both the transmission and rotor. Always on an even keel, so soft-spoken that his contributions were in danger of being overlooked, the young engineer who earned his degree in 1940 made the perfect foil to the ebullient Piasecki. Piasecki was the idea man

and Meyers the methodical engineer capable of interpreting and exploiting his concepts. Meyers would spend his entire career working for Piasecki, as would Ken Meenen, a young tool-and-die maker who had also studied engineering at the University of Pennsylvania.

The organization was further strengthened by Frank Kozloski, who, although trained as an engineer, supplied organizational help rather than contributing technically. Newly graduated lawyer Wesley R. Frysztacki provided part-time legal support. These men gambled their time and energies, sacrificing social outlets and sleep, and scraping up what little money they could to buy needed materials. If they failed, it would all be a waste.

Nobody knew what the profit-sharing arrangement would yield were they to succeed. The immediate technological goal of a working helicopter was so demanding as to push aside all such considerations. "There was a natural feeling that if we were successful in what we were trying to do," Piasecki states simply, "somehow the world would repay us."

In the summer of 1940 the P-V Engineering Forum set up shop at 1937 Callowhill Street, a vacant storefront rented to them by a carpenter who worked in the back. They chose the location because of its proximity to the main branch of Philadelphia's Public Library on Logan Square. In addition to research sources, the library offered restrooms to P-V members, whose crude headquarters lacked bathroom facilities.

The forum moved in the fall of 1941 to a new home behind the Venzie Construction Company on 27th Avenue in a commercial pocket of a residential section of Philadelphia. The Venzie company occupied brick-fronted row houses gutted and joined to make offices.

Trucks and equipment crowded the shabby back yard where Piasecki and his group had a few hundred square feet. There were no walls but at least there was a roof of sorts.

One corner of the forum's open space was enclosed to become the engineering office. Crowded with two or three drafting boards and a desk, it was cramped but provided more protection from the elements than the breezy "shop floor." Manning the drawing boards were two or three recent high school graduates who became the forum's first paid employees. Their part-time work paid twenty-five cents per hour. A low rate even by Depression standards, this sum was far from competitive now that Philadelphia boomed with wartime manufacture.

Although one of these teenagers, Frank Mamrol, had been offered sixty cents an hour by Cramp Shipyards, his love of aviation led him to interview for a job with P-V Engineering one Sunday. Piasecki, himself barely in his twenties, opened the door wearing elegant clothes and spats. He sat Mamrol down in Venzie Construction's front office and described the project. Mamrol accepted the position enthusiastically. Arriving for his first evening on the job, he was directed to the work area out back. He settled in happily and got right to work.

The forum's first helicopter proposal, the PV-1 of 1940, had not progressed beyond the drawings stage. The PV-1 was a single-seater with a main rotor but no tail rotor. Its tapering fuselage terminated in a right-angle deflector or "fan jet tail reactor" through which air was ducted to counteract main rotor torque (the force trying to spin the helicopter in opposition to the rotation of its rotor). There were good reasons for trying to get rid of the tail rotor. Tail rotors were giving the young helicopter industry fits; Igor

Sikorsky and his team had experienced serious problems with theirs. In any event, having something akin to a buzz saw mounted on the fuselage seemed unacceptably dangerous on a machine expected to take its place beside the family car.

Forcing air down the tapering tail cone, or plenum, by means of an engine-driven fan was clearly an alternative to be investigated. Unfortunately, calculations revealed that the 90-hp Franklin aircraft engine—the aviation power plant most readily available and lowest in cost—was simply not capable of powering both the rotor and the plenum fan. For the time, this promising concept—today termed NOTAR for "no-tail-rotor"—had to be shelved.

The PV-2 which followed featured a conventional tail rotor. Its design seemed agonizingly slow to Piasecki, who clearly perceived himself to be in a race. With several hundred helicopter efforts under way in the United States alone, he felt an urgency which he communicated to those around him. "He was a most unusual person, very much driven," Frank Mamrol recalls, "always urging us to work harder, get things done, be efficient and produce."[7]

Piasecki worked by gathering his team around the drafting tables for animated discussions. He displayed a comprehensive understanding of every aspect of the emerging helicopter. When the others went home at ten or eleven, Piasecki—who had already worked a full day at Budd—was still at work on the PV-2.

After a few months, the draftsmen's positions were upgraded to full-time to speed things up. Elliot Daland also went full-time. Independently wealthy, he could afford to leave his post as chief designer of Platt-LePage in favor of a more interesting, if physically less comfortable, challenge with P-V Engineering.

With drawings at last finished, the time had come to make a helicopter. If Piasecki wanted it built quickly, he also wanted it built cheaply, because P-V Engineering was operating on the thinnest of shoestrings (as Mamrol found out when one of his paychecks bounced). A step in the right direction was the forum's decision to "recycle" the fuselage of a Curtiss-Wright CW-1 Junior, a light two-seat airplane built more than a decade before. The welded steel-tube structure of a Junior was the right shape and sufficiently light to serve as the skeleton of a single-seat helicopter.

A search turned up a derelict airframe in a brewery in Pittsburgh. Piasecki bought it at scrap prices and hauled it back to Philadelphia on a rack he had improvised atop his old Ford. Back at P-V, the fuselage was cleaned, sandblasted, and reprimed. The Curtiss Junior airplane had an upward-angled tail, but for its new incarnation as a helicopter the tail boom had to be horizontal. Orienting it in this new position of course made the nose angle upward. The solution was to cut the nose off, leaving an integral tail and center section (the latter to house the engine and support the rotor pylon).

Next to arrive was a Franklin engine. Having failed to locate a used engine of the right weight and horsepower, P-V Engineering bought one of the last new units available before wartime priorities halted general civil sales. Franklins were notorious for rarely producing their full rated power even when new, Piasecki reflected, and the helicopter would in any event have enough gremlins to exorcise without taking a chance on using a secondhand power plant.

The time had come to hire a mechanic. Philomena Lalli, an Italian-American aircraft

factory worker in his mid-thirties, assumed this position as a full-time P-V employee. Their assignments finished, Mamrol and the other draftsmen became Lalli's assistants.

Working together, the three men fashioned a new forward fuselage out of steel tubing and welded it onto the Junior airframe. Next they constructed a rotor support pylon which was bolted into place. A landing gear was built but not yet installed. The helicopter went into a jig, which facilitated alignment and assembly of all controls and linkages. Sheet metal parts were fabricated.

The design of the PV-2 called for installing the engine directly below the rotor, facing upward with its crankshaft parallel to the rotor shaft. Modification of the Franklin for vertical operation required building a new oil sump at what had been the rear of the engine and was now its lowest point, revising the lubrication system, and relocating the magnetos with right-angle drives to keep the engine running in the event of an oil leak.

Because of his machine shop skills, Harold Venzie also worked on the helicopter at times. But it was as the project's master scrounger of parts that he contributed the most. Touring automobile junkyards, he came up with an oil scavenge pump from a Packard, which Mamrol adapted to pump oil from the Franklin's new sump back to the old one. Venzie also found a clutch from a junked Chevrolet, which allowed the engine to be started before the rotor was engaged.

To cool the engine buried in the fuselage, a fan had to be designed and built from scratch. It also served as the flywheel and starter; a cord on a grooved flange encircling it served as a pull starter. One last critical find by Venzie was a freewheeling clutch bought new from Studebaker, the first production automobile to offer overdrive. In the PV-2,

Piasecki, Vertol, and Boeing Helicopters 106

it would automatically disengage the rotor in the event of an engine failure, allowing autorotation to a safe landing.

These acquisitions helped in the absence of either military or corporate financing, neither of which Piasecki had at this early juncture. For the time being, all expenses were paid directly out of the pockets of members, none of whom—with the exception of Daland—had much, if any, extra money. In addition to picking through junkyards, P-V members became adept at enlisting free services. Given drawings and raw materials, for example, the University of Pennsylvania's mechanical engineering shop willingly provided finished parts, writing off the free machining as training exercises for its students.

In this way, a right-angle gearbox was fashioned and fitted to the engine shaft to drive the tail rotor. Above this unit was a universal joint, and above that sat the main transmission, whose function was to reduce high engine revolutions to the much slower rotor speed.

Remarkably, the transmission consisted of just two gears on parallel shafts with bearings at either end. A pinion gear with fifteen herringbone teeth transmitted power to a much larger gear with 101 teeth of matching pattern. Where standard automotive gears bought from a catalog sufficed elsewhere, the main gearbox demanded high quality custom-made gears. After the engine itself, these transmission gears represented the second greatest expense.

These gears were to be housed in a transmission case fashioned out of flattened sheet-metal cones welded at their bases to steel rings. Venzie scrounged scrap rings from a local ball-bearing manufacturer. When these rings proved not to be weldable, the PV-2 team just brazed the cones together. The resulting transmission case, although less robust than intended, proved adequate.

About the time the fuselage was completed and the engine installed, P-V Engineering had moved into more suitable quarters on Ridge Avenue in Roxborough, a section of northwest Philadelphia. The new facility—an automobile showroom closed for the duration of the war because of the suspension of automobile manufacture—offered a common area by the display windows out front, a shop floor in the back for helicopter assembly, and two offices. Piasecki took one for himself and used the other as a secure vault for PV-2 construction drawings.

Piasecki was aware that many other groups were developing helicopters. The perception that his team, which by now numbered upwards of twenty-five people, was in a race had only increased over the months, lending a heightened sense of urgency to the project. Since the PV-2 incorporated some new ideas, industrial espionage could not be ruled out.

It was the rotor blades of the helicopter now taking shape that embodied new thinking, because they were balanced dynamically rather than merely statically. Using stock autogiro blades would have been much easier than the route the team took; it would also have guaranteed failure. The success and significance of the PV-2 would in fact arise directly from an all-out effort to find, in Piasecki's own words, "the proper balance of the blades that would give stability under all flight and control conditions."[8]

Autogiro technology provided the basis for these blades. In materials and construction they were almost identical, aside from the issues of balance and the use of adhesives. Mamrol would build them under the guidance of Daland. The blades were built around a round steel-tube spar made up of two sections,

A lightweight structure is evident as the completed PV-2—which initially flew in this open configuration—is checked at the company's home in Roxborough, Pennsylvania. Courtesy John Schneider.

the inner portion having a diameter of 1.25 inches and the outer portion 1 inch. Welded together, they provided the structural basis for a slightly tapered rotor blade.

Where they were joined, however, the heat of welding had left a crook in the eleven-foot spars. Mamrol was dispatched to the Summerill Tube Company to have them straightened. There an old craftsman put the first of the three spars in a large hydraulic press and closed it. When he opened it, the ends of the rod bent upward fully thirty degrees. The metalworker repeated this process with the other spars, producing a similar deformity to the remaining two units.

Mamrol did not know that this excessive bending was a necessary first step in the straightening process. Dismayed over the seeming disaster, he watched the craftsman twirl the bent tubes, sight down their lengths, and calmly work them back into shape on his press. When he finished, each tube was perfectly straight down its entire length. The vastly relieved teenager brought the spars back to Roxborough.

Solid leading-edge blocks of aircraft-quality spruce were painstakingly routed to the contour of the spar and bonded in place with a newly developed inorganic glue. Gluing in fact represented a major advance over the autogiro industry's use of rivets and spot welding to anchor the surrounding blade structure onto the central steel spar. Those practices introduced stress points at which cracks would eventually begin. In contrast, gluing produced a uniform interface free of stress concentration points.

Mamrol used a jig-guided hand plane to cut a symmetrical airfoil contour into these blocks, an extremely time-consuming process followed by hand sanding to a smooth finish. Trailing edge ribs were fashioned out of bass-

wood and applied, and a 3/64-inch strip of aircraft-grade birch plywood, slipped into notches at the rear of the ribs, formed the trailing edge of each blade. The leading edges were then skinned with 3/16-inch birch ply extending aft of the spar to overlap the ribs. A brass strip was applied to the airfoil leading edge, and lead was inserted between the brass and the wood as needed to adjust for chordwise weight distribution. Next, trim weights were placed internally to achieve proper lengthwise balance. A teeter balance was used to ensure that all the blades weighed the same amount.

The three blades were then hung by their ends and set swinging. The one that swung the slowest had its internal trim weights moved inward toward the root, while the one that swung the fastest had its trim weights moved outward toward the tip. The process was like adjusting the speed of a metronome by moving its weight. Repeated swingings and readjustments at last produced blades that swung at the same rate.

Before this process of dynamic balancing, these blades had weighed the same but their centers of gravity had been different. They were only statically balanced and would have behaved differently in flight. Now that identical weights and centers of gravity had been attained, they were covered with balloon cloth and placed on a teeter balance, where they were doped and painted. The spray itself served as a last fine-tuning of static balance. When dry, they were ready for installation on the PV-2.

These units featured symmetrical airfoils even though asymmetrical profiles produce better lift. The reason was that lift generated by an airfoil moving through the air is concentrated at a point known as the center of lift. With most asymmetrical airfoils, this point shifts forward or backward as the airfoil's angle of attack changes relative to the airstream. In contrast, symmetrical airfoils have a stationary center of lift, which remains unaffected by changes in angle of attack. Not bothersome in fixed-wing aircraft, fore-and-aft center-of-lift travel is highly undesirable in a helicopter because its blades connect to the hub at a single point. This point is the spar around which each blade pivots in response to cyclic and collective control inputs by the pilot. If the center of lift shifts away from its desired location relative to the spar, a pitching moment is introduced; a forward shift noses the blade up, while a backward shift does the opposite.

These aerodynamic moments are translated down through the control linkages to the cyclic control stick as fatiguing vibration. Depending on its intensity, this feedback could range from merely bothersome to dangerous if it grew strong enough to wrest control from the pilot or cause vibration-induced structural failures. Use of a symmetrical airfoil sidestepped this problem.

The PV-2's designers did not stop there. They also positioned the chordwise center of gravity (CG) of the blades a small distance forward of the center of lift (CL) of the rotor blade, which was a quarter of the way back from the leading edge. With the CG just forward of the CL, Daland and Piasecki theorized, the blades would be self-centering. Should a stray gust of wind push one up, having its CG forward of the spar would cause the blade to pivot as it rose; this in turn would tilt its nose downward, introducing an automatic aerodynamic correction to bring it back into place.

Furthermore, the two men intentionally avoided the industry practice of using a metal bar forward of the spar to offset the normal tail heaviness of blades of conventional construction. They realized that centrifugal forces acting on whirling blades lent far greater importance to weight near the blade's tip than to weight near its root. As a result, they balanced the PV-2's rotor blades at the tip where mass was needed in any event to prevent coning, the tendency of lifting blades to bend upward. By eliminating balance weight near the root where it was ineffective, they reduced the overall weight of each blade, a savings that improved the performance of the helicopter.

Dynamically balanced blades, the PV-2's key innovation, were by no means its only novel feature. Another was a new approach to reducing or eliminating the destabilizing effect of blade flapping. This system consisted of blade restrainers that, functioning like cushioning springs, would arrest up-and-down flapping at the rotor head. Unique to the PV-2 was the use of Lord rubber shock mounts, cut in half, in place of springs.

Piasecki and his team were also proud of their simplified rotor hinge assembly. The key element here was placement of the blade pitch bearings between the horizontal pin at the hub and the vertical pin—the lead-lag hinge—just outboard.

Work continued, meanwhile, on the helicopter itself. The tail rotor shaft required a right-angle gearbox to connect to the tail rotor. Again demonstrating great ingenuity, the P-V team acquired an old outboard motor and salvaged its lower case, which proved ideal for this purpose. The two-bladed rotor featured birch plywood paddle-shaped airfoils mounted on steel-tube spars. Piano wire wound in loops held them in place while allowing them to change pitch as required for yaw control. This clever tension-torsion system eliminated the need for costly thrust bearings.

A wing tank from some light airplane was strapped onto the left side of the rotor pylon tubing to complete the helicopter. A temporary expedient which permitted initial testing, this ill-fitting tank would be replaced later by an internal one specifically constructed for the machine. The PV-2 was now finished.

The helicopter was run up with its rotor in flat pitch. Everything seemed to be working perfectly. After that, it was taken back inside and the weight and center of gravity were checked. Empty weight was a little over 700 pounds and gross weight was established at an even 1,000 pounds. The three-bladed rotor had a diameter of 25 feet. Overall length was 22 feet (with two blades folded), width was 8 feet, and height was 7 feet, 7 inches.

With the helicopter at last ready for the first tethered tests, its blades were folded and five men in coveralls pushed and towed the PV-2 down Ridge Avenue to a small vacant lot not far away. At the test site, they looped a borrowed clothesline connected to sandbags around the wheels to restrain the diminutive machine. Piasecki then climbed into the cockpit. Although he had logged fourteen hours of fixed-wing aircraft time in a Piper J-3 Cub, too little to earn a pilot's license, he was nevertheless elected test pilot.

Piasecki opened the throttle and began gingerly to explore the workings of the controls. Suddenly a gust of wind lifted the helicopter by its left side, putting tension on the restraining cord, which promptly broke. The PV-2 was now off the ground in free, unrestrained, and canted flight. Although thrown hard sideways, Piasecki had the presence of mind to shove the overhead control stick the other way, saving the PV-2 from being wrecked. It righted itself and settled back to earth with a jarring thud when its shaken pilot chopped the throttle.

The date was April 11, 1943. America's second successful helicopter had made its historic—utterly unintentional—first free flight. "It was that damned piece of tie-down rope," Piasecki later laughed. "I borrowed my mother's clothesline, and it was so old it was rotten."

Tethering was never tried again. The P-V team members physically held onto the landing gear legs as testing resumed that same spring day. Piasecki cautiously opened the throttle again and managed to hover less than a foot off the ground for several seconds. It was a promising start.

Neither this day's events nor those of the coming months ever drew more than a few curiosity seekers. Already accustomed to autogiros, Philadelphians seemed as a whole unimpressed by helicopters. Ironically, had they been in any other part of the United States, the P-V Engineering team would probably have attracted the attention necessary for enlisting financial support.

Not too many miles to the south, much was happening at Platt-LePage. In the spring of 1943, Captain Frank Gregory, the AAF helicopter project officer from Wright Field, had flown the XR-1 at 75 mph and performed a closed-circuit flight. Despite the infusion of hundreds of thousands of dollars in public and private monies, technical problems continued to plague this helicopter program.

In July 1943 the XR-1 crashed with James G. Ray at the controls. Although the machine was destroyed, the former Pitcairn test pilot emerged unhurt. A second ship, the XR-1A, assumed test duties when completed at the end of the year. It was flown to Wright Field for AAF evaluation but proved unsatisfactory in performance and handling, particularly during the transition from hover to forward flight. As a result, the AAF withdrew its support of Platt-LePage in April 1945.

Despite years of effort and lavish funding, this Army helicopter had failed. The abandoned XR-1A suffered from extreme longitudinal instability at transitional speeds. Fore-and-aft control stick input took much too long to produce noticeable pitch changes. The machine's hover performance was also deficient because of downwash impingement on the rotor pylons. Only at speeds above 50 mph when its airplane-style controls were fully effective did it fly at all well. Moreover, its excessive complexity, inadequate engine cooling, and narrow swashplate travel limits had made it a maintenance and rigging nightmare for Wright personnel.

Back in early 1943, the large XR-1 had looked promising and the tiny PV-2—if noticed at all—was the dark horse. Piasecki spent this period teaching himself to fly. The PV-2 dipped, bucked, shoved, and swung with a mind of its own until he mastered its controls and learned to correct for the wind. To those restraining the little machine, the PV-2 seemed a spirited creature.

After less than ten hours of testing, ground resonance reared its head and the behavior of the craft turned spooky. It began without any warning when Piasecki landed on one side and the helicopter rocked onto its other wheel. A lateral oscillation started, which grew in intensity until the blades tried to go one way and the fuselage another. Piasecki shut down and his assistants held on from the outside, but the eerie phenomenon had to run its course.

Piasecki later learned that the proper reaction would have been to open the throttle and take off again before the rocking became too violent. Only in this way could damage have been avoided. In those early days, however, ground resonance—aptly described by Piasecki as "like knowing the devil"[9]—remained largely a mystery.

A grim crew assessed the damage. Most obvious were the mangled rotor blades which had tried to wrap themselves around the hub. The Lord rubber shock mounts serving as centering springs had been ruined, and the wheel axles had been badly bent by the pounding.

Piasecki noted resignation on the faces of those around him. Despite a head wound and a badly bruised back, he was filled with resolve that the setback would not end what they had all worked so hard to achieve. He mobilized the crew to tow the damaged PV-2 back to the shop. There, Lalli assessed the blades and assured Piasecki that he could fix them.

Repairs took nearly a month, most of which was spent fixing and rebalancing the blades. Instead of making new rubber centering springs for the blades, a standard set of autogiro rotary-lag dampers was located and installed. The axles were straightened and the landing-gear struts were revised. Intended to absorb the force of hard landings, these spring struts had actually contributed to the development of ground resonance by pushing back against its oscillations. Thus they were redesigned as oil-filled units that provided damping without rebound.

So great was concern over ground resonance that ground-up cork was substituted for air in the PV-2's spongy Goodyear airwheels to reduce their tendency to bounce. Without air pressure to seat the tires on the wheels, they leaked. Wherever the PV-2 went from then on, a residue of cork marked its trail. These precautions were more than adequate, for ground resonance never manifested itself again.

During flight testing, the PV-2 demonstrated a top speed of about 90 mph and a cruise speed of 65 mph. The prototype was also extremely responsive. "It was very quick, the snappiest machine ever," Piasecki recalled. "You couldn't take as much time with it as you could on the controls of an airplane."

It was also fully controllable, confirming that sufficient travel had been designed into the swashplate. The craft's few controls consisted of an overhead cyclic stick for the right hand, rudder pedals for the feet, and a long-travel throttle for the left hand. A collective pitch lever was also mounted on the left, but it was left locked in an intermediate rotor pitch setting. Much like riding a bicycle entirely in middle gear, the helicopter was generally flown without touching the collective.

No standards for helicopter control systems existed in 1943, of course. Modern helicopters take off with a simultaneous increase in power and collective pitch to maintain a constant rotor RPM. Although more efficient, this system was never considered, because it demanded simultaneous coordination of cyclic, collective, throttle, and rudder pedal inputs. The general expectation that helicopters would be used as family conveyances led the Piasecki team to sacrifice some aerodynamic efficiency in favor of simplicity.

As a result, the PV-2's pilot controlled lift by throttle alone. To take off, he advanced it until the helicopter rose vertically, at which point he pushed the cyclic stick forward to initiate forward flight. The stick was then returned to neutral and the throttle retarded to cruise power. This control technique actually demanded the use of fewer controls than automobiles of the day.

Using the cyclic stick was intuitive. One merely tilted it in the direction one wished to go. The rudder pedals—so called even though helicopters achieve yaw control with a tail rotor rather than a rudder—took a bit more getting used to, although coordinating rudder and cyclic soon became second nature.

As fall approached, Piasecki felt the time had come to use the PV-2 to win the support needed to start a helicopter manufacturing company. Philadelphia being a tough town to impress when it came to rotary-wing aircraft, Piasecki enlisted the aid of Harry S. Pack, a young industrial designer with exceptional public relations instincts who was then working for Pennsylvania Central Airlines.

Pack arranged a public unveiling for the PV-2 at PCA's home base, Washington National Airport. Newly constructed on the Virginia side of the Potomac River minutes from downtown Washington, D.C., National Airport was closer still to the even newer Pentagon, just built to house the leadership of the nation's armed services.

Despite its focus on civil helicopters, P-V Engineering had observed how World War II had advanced military funding for aviation. For more than a year, Piasecki had devoted time to trying to interest the armed services in the PV-2. Capable of lifting just its own weight, however, this prototype offered no utility whatsoever. It seemed destined to be overlooked by both the civil and military markets.

It was Pack's job to change that situation. He visited Roxborough, where he cast a dubious eye on the craft he was to promote. It was a glamorless conceptual test bed. Its open-frame structure facilitated changes and repairs but did nothing to help its looks. Accordingly, Pack had the Piasecki team cosmetically revamp it for its official unveiling. They filled out its pylon and forward fuselage with sheet aluminum and red fiber, a lightweight insulating material. They also added a three-piece nose and a cockpit enclosure with a lightweight plexiglass windshield. A fabric-

The PV-2 hovers at the Roxborough facility with
an enclosed cockpit and maroon-and-silver paint
scheme. Courtesy John Schneider.

covered "discus" three feet in diameter was also fabricated and installed, with the purpose of smoothing out the airflow around the rotor head. The craft was then covered in balloon cloth, a fabric lighter than the standard Grade A cotton, and doped and painted.

For the paint scheme, Piasecki selected his favorite colors, silver and maroon. His instincts for showmanship led him to mount a bulb-type car horn on the left landing gear. He reasoned that using the horn in the air would help people view his helicopter as an aerial automobile, garnering attention and laughs in the displays to come.

Application was made to the Civil Aeronautics Authority, which awarded the PV-2 the number NX-37061 (the "x" denoted its experimental status). Painted on the tail cone just forward of the rotor, the number completed the prototype's metamorphosis. "It not only looks better," Piasecki happily informed Pack after a test hop, "it flies better."[10]

The P-V Engineering Forum had officially incorporated in the state of Pennsylvania in January 1943. Piasecki was president, Daland vice president and chief engineer, and Wesley Frysztacki secretary-treasurer. The size and assets of the group did not really warrant incorporation, but it provided valuable credibility.

The name was not changed even though "engineering forum" fell short of describing the company. The phrase "helicopter company" had been avoided because in 1943 the word "helicopter" was anathema to the financial community. Helicopter builders were considered crackpots, not businessmen to be taken seriously.

Soon after leaving college, Piasecki had briefly been engaged to a young Philadelphia woman. This relationship survived his all-consuming dedication to helicopters, only to end when his fiancée's father learned of his prospective son-in-law's activities. The engagement ring Piasecki had bought was summarily returned to him.

Frank still had the ring. With no one to give it to, he sold it and used the money to buy himself a black homburg and a stylish double-breasted business suit. Wearing them instead of a leather helmet, coveralls, and a flight jacket was another expression of Piasecki's showmanship. It was also reminiscent of Igor Sikorsky, who had worn a homburg while flying his VS-300.

Everything was ready for Harry Pack's first promotion, but how were they to get the PV-2 to Washington, D.C.? Flying it there was out of the question. The experimental ship was simply not up to it because nobody knew how long its transmission and other critical components would last. Flights were kept brief and cross-countries were avoided as a matter of policy. So conservative was the P-V team in this regard that pilot and rotorcraft had together logged just fifteen hours since the first flight a half year earlier. "We did that to spare our machine, not out of fear for the pilot," Piasecki explained. "We just didn't know how long the PV-2 would last."

A flatbed truck was the ideal way to transport the PV-2, but the team's financial resources were exhausted. That left towing the helicopter on its wheels behind a car, a poor alternative because the landing gear axles used bronze bushings instead of bearings. Still, the team had no choice.

The tail of the PV-2 helicopter was lashed to mechanic Bill Roach's blue Pontiac, and the party set off down U.S. Route 40 in two cars for the 135-mile trip to the nation's capital. A need to stop and cool the bearingless helicopter wheels dictated frequent stops and

For want of a truck, the PV-2 is towed on its landing gear to Washington, D.C. Courtesy John
Schneider.

forays in search of water. On one such search in a large field, Piasecki was charged by a bull. The party arrived intact at its destination, however, and the helicopter was checked and polished.

Pack had done his job well. A good-sized crowd gathered for the PV-2's demonstration at National Airport on October 20, 1943. Standing in a long line at the edge of the flight ramp were government officials and representatives of the various military services. They were there, Piasecki joked, "to collect their bets on whether I crack up."[11]

With great flair, a smiling Frank N. Piasecki made several individual flights during which, as one reporter observed, "the aircraft rose vertically, hovered a few feet off the ground, climbed higher, and turned in its own length. He then flew forward at a good speed, backed up, flew sideways and descended vertically to hover again and pose for pictures a few feet off the ground."[12]

Elliot Daland provided a running commentary on the technical merits of the PV-2. He emphasized that the diminutive craft was, as paraphrased by *Aviation* magazine, "free of vibration and flutter characteristics throughout [its] full operation range."[13] This claim impressed America's small helicopter community, for it contrasted markedly with the one other helicopter then available for comparison, the Sikorsky R-4, whose flight characteristics a Wright Field test pilot characterized as "palsied and wobbly."[14]

This command performance at National Airport turned out to be the most difficult flying Piasecki would ever do in the PV-2. A strong westerly wind cut across the roofs of the hangars. When he ascended it picked him up like an elevator, and throttling back did not help. So powerful was the updraft that Piasecki had to reduce collective pitch, some-

thing he ordinarily didn't bother with in flight. Those observing had no inkling that the day's flying was especially demanding, because Piasecki positively radiated confidence when he rejoined them on the ground.

Playing to a military audience, Piasecki and Daland stressed possible military applications of their technology. They downplayed the obvious civil-market appearance of the PV-2. "No claims are made that it is the answer for the 'man in the street'," *Aviation* informed its readers. "A larger model, said to have a payload of more than a ton and a range of some 400 miles, has already been designed."

In fact, P-V Engineering Forum had already roughed out the preliminary design of a large military machine in anticipation of an urgent Navy requirement for a helicopter program of its own. The Navy was currently the focus of public indignation, scathing press reports, and stinging criticism from the renowned Truman Committee over its steadfast, well-documented refusal to foster vertical flight. The source of this acute discomfort was a general public perception that if Navy leaders had acted with foresight, the service might already have helicopters to counteract the U-boat menace.

Late in 1943, marauding Nazi submarines were taking a huge toll on Allied shipping in the North Atlantic. Then at their most effective, Hitler's wolf packs threatened to choke off the Lend-Lease supply lines so vital to Great Britain's survival, and to America's ability to wage war in Europe. As a result, the issue of why the Navy lacked convoy patrol helicopters was political dynamite.

Desperate to save face and make up for lost time, the Navy in 1943 seized upon Piasecki's remarkable success. He already had a working helicopter, he was available unlike Sikorsky who had been "sewn up" by the Air

Corps, and he was in the area. Thus through the Coast Guard, to which the Navy had delegated conduct of its newly created helicopter program, America's senior service selected tiny P-V Engineering Forum to pull its chestnuts out of the fire. Although the odds against success were long, Piasecki would do precisely that.

Concluding the performance at National Airport, CAA inspector Paul Young presented Piasecki with the first helicopter license ever issued to someone who did not already have a fixed-wing aircraft license. Unfamiliar with helicopters, the official left it to the recipient to suggest a suitable flight test. Piasecki proposed and then flew a square pattern and landed in the same spot, keeping the PV-2's nose pointing in the same direction throughout the maneuver. Although he looked much older, Piasecki was four days short of his twenty-fourth birthday when he won this civil helicopter license, one of the first in the world.

Buoyed with success, the P-V team embarked the next day on selling the PV-2 and the technology it embodied to the civil market. Pack's ingenuity led the team to Seven Corners, then a rural township in northern Virginia west of the District of Columbia. Attired in his pinstripe suit, homburg, and bow tie, a dapper Frank Piasecki led newsreel cameras on a fictitious outing for a newsreel segment called *An Air Flivver in Every Garage*. An exercise in wish fulfillment, it showed an American stepping out of his house one Saturday morning for a round of golf. He opens his garage to reveal a helicopter, not a car, which he wheels out into the sunshine. After unfolding the rotor blades, he inserts his golf bag, takes off, pauses at a gas station to fill up, then flies to the golf course, where he lands and tees off.

Filming this brief sequence consumed two days. To begin with, the tiny PV-2 could hold *either* a pilot or a golf bag, but not both. Trick photography came to the rescue: after Piasecki had placed his clubs inside, the cameras were stopped and the bag was removed. Then they were turned on again to record Piasecki climbing in and taking off, the clubs seemingly still on board.

After this opening scene was shot, Piasecki landed and the helicopter was towed to the Texaco station selected to serve as a backdrop. Piasecki noted with growing apprehension the steel sign pole, trees, and other hazards to the main rotor, as well as a ring of white-painted logs that could catch the tail rotor in a landing.

Pack later admitted that it was the only filling station he could get permission to use: "The clear space was hardly larger than the helicopter's rotor. It was a dangerous place to land, but only our group knew how dangerous. The PV-2 was so low-powered that a single backfire from the engine as Frank was coming in or leaving would have meant a crash. But he was determined to make the flight."[15]

Standing just out of view of the cameras, Pack could help guide the helicopter to a safe landing with hand signals. With a dry mouth and pounding heart, Piasecki took off. "I'm risking the whole thing and taking chances," he said to himself. "I could crack up the machine, myself, and the whole damn gas station to boot."[16]

Vowing never again to perform such a dangerous stunt, Piasecki landed safely by the pumps. There he learned that one of the cameras had run out of film. Because of a standard agreement among newsreel photographers, moreover, none of the rest of the footage could be used. His vow notwithstanding, Piasecki had to perform the landing all over again.

Piasecki, Vertol, and Boeing Helicopters 118

After being filmed leaving the gas station, the PV-2 settled to earth and was towed to a golf course at Falls Church, Virginia. The cameras filmed a sunny fairway as Piasecki landed in the foreground and climbed out. More trick photography allowed the jauntily clad golfer to retrieve his bag from his personal helicopter and tee off.

An Air Flivver in Every Garage aired to substantial acclaim. With the popular newsreel feature being shown in movie theaters around the country, offers poured in from people eager to acquire the PV-2 and all rights to its postwar manufacture. The money was attractive, but Piasecki resisted these attempts to buy him out. He was not about to abandon his personal goal of civil helicopter manufacture.

He was, however, willing to postpone it. Sensing that a military market might be emerging, Piasecki refocused P-V Engineering solely on enlisting Pentagon support for a military helicopter program. This major shift in strategy late in 1943 made sense: the Navy's need for large helicopters promised heavy funding that could put the company in a strong position for the postwar manufacture of civil *and* military rotorcraft.

Publicity from the unveiling at National Airport and the newsreel had brought P-V Engineering to a new plateau. Although creating America's second successful helicopter would not bring anything like Sikorsky's fame, P-V Engineering was now an established entity.

With the display at National Airport, the company had begun a shift away from its dream of mass-produced aerial flivvers. Knowingly or not, Piasecki that day committed himself and his company to a new race against time in the military arena. His focus henceforth would be large transport helicopters

with fore-and-aft rotors. With this new chapter, the historic PV-2 would be all but forgotten. It would be flown only infrequently to commemorate anniversaries and company milestones. In one special flight, it also returned a favor to test pilot Lou Leavitt, who had given Piasecki his first rotary-wing ride more than a decade earlier. After flying the diminutive prototype, Piasecki noted with delight, "Leavitt said it was the best little aircraft he had ever flown; so light, so small, fitting like a glove—it was almost like a motorcycle of the air."[17]

Two decades later, on July 6, 1965, Piasecki donated this remarkable helicopter to the Smithsonian Institution in Washington, D.C., where it occupies a place of honor in the collection of the National Air and Space Museum as America's second successful helicopter. It is today on long-term loan to the American Helicopter Museum and Education Center near Philadelphia.

If ever somebody was in the right place at the right time, it was Frank Piasecki in the fall of 1943. He perceived in the Navy's desperate need for helicopters a once-in-a-lifetime opportunity. There was no question in his mind that he was in a race fraught with extraordinary technical challenges. Others might have hesitated, but not Piasecki, who possessed enormous energies. He would routinely work till ten at night and then socialize into the early hours of the morning. Driven and adept at driving those around him, he went through life in high gear.

It was fortunate for both Piasecki and the Navy that its leaders initially failed to realize how young the company president was. A leonine head, a mustache, and an undeniable presence made him seem considerably older than his twenty-four years. Only later, when called upon to intercede with Piasecki's draft board in the matter of a deferment, would chagrined military officials learn his true age.

Although an able engineer, Piasecki excelled in vision and salesmanship. Like most successful entrepreneurs, he never doubted his abilities and he exuded confidence. He was also capable of considerable charm when it served his purposes (Piasecki employees often joked that procurement officials received more pleasantries and small gifts than they did). Whereas Igor Sikorsky wore a Homburg in pictures and Stanley Hiller a bow tie, Piasecki frequently wore both, with spats and a red-lined evening cape for good measure. In the tradition of the grand showman, Piasecki was somehow larger than life.

These traits might have seemed theatrical affectations in another person, but in him they were totally in character. Inevitably, there were those who objected to his style or strong will, and perhaps looked invidiously upon his success, but Piasecki's ardent supporters at all times overwhelmingly outnumbered his detractors. Whatever one thought of the young helicopter pioneer, he commanded attention.

P-V's dealing with the Navy began with research-oriented studies and a contract—issued at the time of the Washington demonstration—for evaluating a PV-2 rotor in a NACA wind tunnel at Langley, Virginia. It was already clear to Piasecki that, despite external political pressure and the Navy's obvious need, there was little enthusiasm for helicopter development at high levels.

Loss of much of America's fleet during the Japanese attack on Pearl Harbor two years earlier had severely complicated the Navy's utterly unprecedented wartime expansion. Getting more ships, submarines, airplanes, armaments, trained personnel, and supplies already taxed that service's resources to the limit; getting into the helicopter business was something Navy leaders did not even want to think about.

"The Navy didn't want a damn helicopter at all in World War II," Piasecki recently recalled. "The reason was that technical experts in the Bureau of Aeronautics had this curve showing the bigger you made a helicopter, the heavier it would be until you got it so big you wouldn't be able to carry any payload. They were simply not interested in a helicopter capable of lifting less than a ton, yet they believed a machine capable of lifting anywhere near that much was impossible."

The Navy's misplaced faith in this specious weight-versus-payload curve explains why the Sikorsky R-4, though it proved that helicopters could indeed be manufactured in number, failed to sway Navy thinking. The fact that the Army machine could lift only its two-man crew (and just one person on hot days) consolidated the Navy's pessimism about vertical flight. If Sikorsky and the Army between them had managed to wring so little performance out of a little machine, what hope was there for a helicopter big enough to be of real fleet value? Perhaps someday helicopters might be capable of carrying both sonar and depth charges, and of shuttling troops and supplies, but that day looked far off to the Bureau of Aeronautics in 1943.

In contrast, Piasecki in 1943 saw no reason why large helicopters could not be built. Determined to exploit this business opportunity, he proposed to the Navy a large military helicopter capable of lifting 1,800 pounds or more. This was considerably larger than any helicopter in existence. The plan seemed impossibly audacious, particularly since P-V Engineering had no working capital, no real plant, no equipment, and only a handful of

A dapper Frank Piasecki poses in the PV-2, his right hand on the craft's overhead cyclic control stick. Courtesy John Schneider.

employees. However, P-V did have several strengths. Aside from talented team members and a proven technology base, the company possessed vision and the willingness to take risks.

As laid out by P-V, the Navy's first helicopter would have two rotors. Building a single-rotor machine capable of lifting such a load was then considered impossible. Before committing to any one configuration, Piasecki and his engineers reportedly conducted a series of comparative studies of the various options. The tandem configuration, whereby one rotor is placed behind the other, emerged as the most promising.

Piasecki knew of the work of early experimenters Cornu and Florine, who had each sought to develop a tandem-rotor helicopter. He shared their faith in the fore-and-aft configuration, even though it forsook the high-aspect-ratio benefits claimed for twin-lateral-rotor types like the FA 61 and XR-1. As Piasecki observed, the tandem configuration avoided the weight, additional downwash impedance, and aerodynamic drag penalties imposed by side-by-side rotors, which need cumbersome mounting pylons. In contrast, the fuselage of a tandem helicopter supports the rotors so that no pylons are required. Tandem helicopters also promised greater efficiency than single-rotor types like Sikorsky's machines. Because each main rotor spins the opposite way, no power-robbing tail rotor is required to counteract torque. Finally, a tandem helicopter can easily hover facing any direction because of its relative insensitivity to wind direction compared to single-rotor helicopters.

One other factor may perhaps have influenced Piasecki's selection of configurations. During his brief tenure at Platt-LePage, he had observed with great interest that the XR-1 flew better sideways than forward. With so little really known about helicopters in the early 1940s, such clues were useful.

Many experts asserted that tandem helicopters would suffer insoluble problems with shaft vibration, transmission weight, or rotor control. Aerodynamicist Alexander Klemin, Piasecki's former professor, further asserted that front rotor downwash would rob the rear rotor of efficiency, thereby destabilizing and endangering the entire craft.

To settle at least this last issue, Piasecki built a tandem-rotor model and tested it in a small wind tunnel at the University of Pennsylvania. Using the Schlieren process in which a bright light tracks airflow through the varying optical properties of different air pressures, he was relieved to confirm that front rotor flow washed downward at enough of an angle to leave the rear rotor in unaffected air.

All of this testing was accomplished rapidly and a formal proposal was quickly written. Piasecki raced this document to Washington, where he shared it with a lieutenant commander in the Bureau of Aeronautics. Not impressed, the officer showed Piasecki the Navy's infamous chart "proving" that such a helicopter could not be built. "I thought you knew that," was the expert's offhand comment.

Nevertheless, political realities had left the Navy no choice but to accept the proposal. On January 1, 1944, P-V Engineering received a major Navy contract calling for construction of the world's first transport helicopter. Company designation of this craft would be PV-3. To the Navy it would be known as the XHRP-X.[18]

Wild jubilation broke out when the news reached Roxborough. Ebullient P-V employees joked that the Navy had been so desperate for helicopters that all their boss had to do was walk in and say the word and a contract was stuffed into his hands. The contradictory joke also circulated that Navy procurement officials had been so harried and worn down by the indefatigable Piasecki that they had finally made the award just to get rid of him. This second theory probably held a grain of truth, for Piasecki had virtually camped at the Navy's door in his eagerness for its business.

As laid out, the ten-place machine had a long cylindrical body, the cabin of which offered an unprecedented 400 cubic feet of space. Almost 50 feet long, the XHRP-X (affectionately nicknamed *Dogship*) weighed some 5,000 pounds empty and less than 7,000 pounds fully loaded. Its light but strong tubular steel structure was to be filled out with wooden ribs and covered with fabric, although it would initially fly uncovered.

Behind the plexiglass at the front end of the machine was tandem seating with dual controls for a pilot and copilot.

A 450-hp Continental R-975 radial engine was housed amidships near a mix box. Shafts angling forward and aft from this transmission connected to additional reduction gearing below each rotor. The *Dogship* used some automotive gears in its transmission, an expedient that perhaps reflected failure by company engineers to appreciate the stresses these critical components would experience. The rotors themselves were scaled up almost exactly from the dynamically balanced rotor that had worked so well on the PV-2. Disk and power loadings were very low. While sensitive to even light breezes, the XHRP-X was controllable and relatively free of vibration.

This underpowered prototype relied on light structural weight and generous rotor area to lift promised loads. Performance gains through greater power could come later; for now, Piasecki realized, it was enough to have a machine that did what the Navy thought impossible. Unrefined and minimal, the XHRP-X was little more than a proof-of-concept vehicle. Like the PV-2, which had also been hastily built, the PV-3 validated Piasecki's conviction that availability was more important than refinement.

In January 1945, fast-growing P-V Engineering—now with eighty employees—moved to new quarters in Sharon Hill, Pennsylvania, still in the greater Philadelphia area. In miserably cold, wet weather, the helicopter team took up residence in a plant rented from a Navy-controlled facility. P-V's new home comprised a one-story building with a large shop floor and an engineering area big enough for perhaps twenty drafting tables. Although the building was not located on an airport, Piasecki had large hangar-type doors installed at the end facing a field suitable for limited helicopter flying.

Piasecki and his fast-working team completed the XHRP-X three months later. Despite the disruptions of moving, only thirteen months had elapsed since the Navy issued its contract. In view of the magnitude of the challenge, it was an amazing feat.

The XHRP-X's stated mission was to address a USCG requirement for a helicopter to perform maritime rescues from ships torpedoed within U.S. coastal waters. Since the vast majority of ships were sunk at sea, however, the Coast Guard was not the helicopter's logical customer. It was also evident that the war would be over before tandem-rotor helicopters were available for operational service. In fact, the Navy and Marines would eventually make greater use than the Coast Guard of production HRP-1s.

As the prototype neared completion and brief hovering run-ups were attempted, Piasecki enlisted the aid of autogiro pilot George Townson in case the XHRP-X's controls required more strength than a single pilot could supply. He described how he and Townson prepared for the first flight of any consequence:

> In order for us to develop pilot-copilot cockpit coordination before flying the *Dogship,* the Navy arranged for Commander Frank Erickson to take George and me into the U.S. Coast Guard Helicopter Training Squadron at Floyd Bennett Field in Brooklyn, New York. After a few days of Coast Guard training, each of us singularly learned to fly the Sikorsky R-4 two-seaters. We soon realized we could not fly together, though, since there was only one collective lever in the center. That would force one of us to operate the cyclic stick with his left

hand. Since neither George nor I could do this easily, we never really got cockpit-acquainted. This experience with the R-4s gave me an insight as to Sikorsky's poor cyclic control handling qualities as compared to our single-seat PV-2. In order to further increase his helicopter piloting time, I had George fly the PV-2 with which he became well-acquainted.[19]

On March 7, 1945, the *Dogship* was wheeled out for flight. It was devoid of fabric covering, its fuselage structure left open to facilitate last-minute checks and adjustments by mechanics. Then Piasecki and Townson climbed aboard and settled into the tandem seats, Frank in front and George behind. Piasecki preset the ratchet collective lever at what he guessed was the correct pitch setting. He then gingerly opened the throttle of his banana-shaped flying machine and it grew light on its tires. History's first large production rotorcraft—the progenitor of today's successful tandem-rotor Boeing helicopters—rose from the ground.

It required only a short hovering flight to show that the *Dogship* was out of balance and in need of rerigging. With so little then known about helicopters, the P-V team was not surprised. Its members anticipated that the flight test program would consist primarily of debugging and trial-and-error refinement.

If this initial flight lacked drama, not so one performed soon after before Captain Clayton "Spud" Marcy and other high-ranking Navy officers. This first public display had its heart-stopping moments when the XHRP-X unexpectedly pitched steeply upward at an angle of at least 45 degrees, then nosed downward at the same sickening angle. The tips of the rotor blades came within five feet of the ground during this wild ride, but fortunately did not strike it. Piasecki regained control and brought the prototype to a safe landing. What follows is his own account of the incident:

> When the Navy came to see the *Dogship* fly, I put George in the copilot seat behind me and told him to monitor the controls for me since I was pilot-in-command. We lifted off to an altitude of about 50 feet and crept forward. A west wind coming from our right did not feel strong but we were in the lee of the trees at Sharon Hill. When our flight path crossed above Elmwood Avenue, an east-west street, the wind added lift to the front rotor and we nosed upward even with the cyclic stick pushed full forward.
>
> We were at the apex when George abruptly closed the throttle. Fortunately, I was stronger than him and I punched it back open. We had drifted across the street in the meantime and now the rear rotor was getting the additional lift from the west wind while the front rotor was shielded by some more trees, causing the nose to point downward. It felt like we were almost perpendicular to the ground but actually it was quite a bit less. Once again George pulled the throttle closed, and once again I overpowered him to keep us in the air as I pulled the overhead cyclic stick full back. Somehow we leveled off long enough for me to land the machine with the throttle and the demonstration was over.[20]

A greatly sobered Townson quit on the spot. In contrast, Piasecki was unfazed by the flight, for he knew intuitively what was wrong with his machine and how to fix it. Rather than listen to Townson's parting advice to follow an extremely conservative test program, he was off and running before the Navy's observers had a chance to draw a shaky breath. There was a good reason for pressing on: competitors were sure to arise to bid for Navy helicopter funds, and the company could not afford to fall behind in its race to perfect its product.

Piasecki's fears were well founded. In May 1944, the Navy had awarded a second major helicopter contract to the McDonnell Aircraft Corporation in St. Louis, Missouri.[21] That group's twin-engine, twin-rotor XHJD-1 Whirlaway, ironically enough, would be a new incarnation of the Army's failed XR-1A upon which Frank had worked while at Platt-LePage. Shortly after the *Dogship* flew, the Army Air Forces had terminated support for that disappointing effort, hastening the demise of Platt-LePage. McDonnell, which had bought 51 percent of the company at the time the XR-1 first flew, then bought up what was left. In the process, it acquired Platt-LePage's preliminary engineering and design data on a twin-engine follow-on twice the size of the XR-1A.

When McDonnell decided to press forward with development of this machine, it knew better than to seek Army support. The AAF—by now thoroughly disenchanted with twin-lateral-rotor helicopters—had abandoned the Platt-LePage approach in favor of Igor Sikorsky's more successful single-rotor configuration. Consequently, the St. Louis company turned instead to the Navy, and there—despite McDonnell Aircraft's failure to achieve airplane production throughout the whole of World War II—it had an ally.

Founded by James McDonnell in July 1939, the company had yet to manufacture an airplane. Nevertheless, in the summer of 1943 the Navy had chosen it to develop America's first carrier-based jet fighter plane. The service clearly had faith in the unproven corporate entity, which enjoyed an insider status that few proven manufacturers could boast. McDonnell played upon that status, and upon the belief of the Navy's planners that it was unwise to have all their eggs in one basket, to snag this second wartime USN helicopter contract.

Like the XR-1, the McDonnell XHJD-1 Whirlaway employed the twin-lateral-rotor configuration first demonstrated by the Focke-Achgelis FA 61 in Germany a decade earlier. Two Pratt & Whitney R-985 radial engines were housed in nacelles halfway out each of its rotor outriggers. The weight of these power plants, combined with rotor lifting loads, caused a host of vibration problems including harmonic resonance that made life miserable for McDonnell's brightest engineers.

McDonnell took two years (twice as long as Piasecki) to design and build its prototype. While its engineers struggled to eliminate the XHJD-1's pylon vibrations, the Philadelphia team readied its tandem-rotor machine for production. So daunting were McDonnell's protracted developmental difficulties, and so great was Piasecki's lead, that the Navy had no choice but to cancel its fall-back program. Today the unsuccessful XHJD-1 Whirlaway survives together with the XHRP-X *Dogship* in the collection of the National Air and Space Museum. At the time of this writing, both await restoration.

At Sharon Hill, Frank Piasecki continued to be both president and test pilot. His early tests established that the *Dogship* lacked sufficient fore-and-aft controllability. Fears that excessive pitch changes might cause the machine to tumble end over end led him and his team to severely restrict differential collective control limits. The men had briefly considered relying on cyclic control alone for pitch control, but this concept had been rejected as unrealistic. When flight showed fears of excessive lift at either end of the *Dogship* to be exaggerated, the differential collective control limits were opened up until the prototype had adequate longitudinal control authority.

The *Dogship* was now safer in the air. But until such time as autorotations could be successfully demonstrated, flights at altitude were not a good idea. In fact, Piasecki would never autorotate the XHRP-X. With overrunning clutches in its rotor gearboxes, the helicopter was technically capable of giving its crew a safe autorotative descent in the event of an engine failure. However, in their haste to have a working demonstrator, the team had not interconnected the *Dogship*'s rotors to ensure identical freewheeling rates in unpowered flight. This failure may account for no autorotation ever being attempted in the helicopter.

The XHRP-X's flight test program consisted primarily of debugging, a process required by every first-generation helicopter production prototype. Blade damage resulting from engine surging was just one of a host of problems the team solved at a record clip, thanks to Piasecki's forceful leadership. Not surprising in view of this haste, the debugging process included more than the usual number of close calls and near disasters, any one of which might have ended the company.

One day, for example, the short shaft between the engine and the mix box failed and erupted from the fabric side of the helicopter. The heavy steel unit shot through the air just a few feet above the head of Elliot Daland. Had it hit the renowned engineer, the consequences would certainly have been fatal and the Navy's support for the program would likely have evaporated.

Other dangers lurked but never struck.

Piasecki, Vertol, and Boeing Helicopters 125

(*Top*) The Piasecki xhrp-x—first helicopter of the U.S. Navy—pitches dangerously upward in spring 1945 flight tests at the company's new home in Sharon Hill, Pennsylvania. Courtesy John Schneider.

(*Bottom*) The unsuccessful McDonnell xhjd-1 Whirlaway. Courtesy nasm/si.

Piasecki flew his prototype day and night, with much testing conducted at dusk and after dark when daytime winds had died down. The Sharon Hill factory bordered the Pennsylvania Railroad's main line, high above which were strung the high-voltage lines used by diesel-electric locomotives. Piasecki flew back and forth time after time, parallel to and just a few hundred feet from the wires. At other times he climbed directly toward them, and it seemed from the ground that he could not possibly clear them. Although Piasecki himself felt safe enough, his employees took a different view. They were quick to cite freak winds, nighttime disorientation, distractions, control failures, and many other possibilities. They also observed that their boss, although gifted, was not a professional pilot.

Aerial expressions of Piasecki's exuberant personality made them cringe, like the night the *Dogship*'s instrument panel lights failed to work. Piasecki scooped up a flashlight and took off anyway, flying with the light stuffed between his legs to shine on the panel's few gauges. Only extraordinarily good luck would carry the fledgling helicopter company through the tribulations of this difficult early period.

An electrical fire in the engine section came close to claiming the XHRP-X, which fortunately was on the ground at the time. It took several long minutes before a fire extinguisher could be used, because many fasteners retaining an access panel had to be unscrewed. Luckily, the ship was saved. The access panel was subsequently replaced by a door.

Another close call came when Piasecki transported a log by air to demonstrate lifting ability. The underslung load unexpectedly began to swing. Piasecki tried to correct and a serious pendular oscillation resulted. Despite the gyrations, he managed to jettison the log and land in one piece. "It was very hairy," conceded former Piasecki employee and close associate Kenneth Meenen, "Pi barely got out of that one by the skin of his teeth."[22]

Piasecki's closest shave in the *Dogship* may well have been the round trip made to the airfield at the Philadelphia Navy Yard. After successfully demonstrating the *Dogship* to a Navy captain, he decided to take the high-ranking visitor back to Mustin Field, where the latter's airplane was parked. The flight went well and the officer climbed into his plane glowing with enthusiasm for helicopters. He flew back to Washington never suspecting that a potentially devastating problem had arisen en route to the airstrip.

Told by his flight engineer that the *Dogship*'s mix box was running hot, Piasecki went aft to examine the unit. The transmission housing was so hot its paint had blistered. A dilemma confronted Piasecki: If he shut down and left the *Dogship* on the Navy's airfield, it would sit there through an unauthorized and protracted teardown and repair that would damage the confidence he had worked so hard to build; if he risked a quick flight back to the factory, it might fail en route, with catastrophic results.

Negative perceptions on the part of the Navy could mean waning confidence and eroding financial support. To Piasecki, that was a worse risk than the flight. He asked his flight engineer to stay behind but the latter insisted on riding along to monitor the gearbox in flight. "All right," Piasecki said, giving him money. "Then go to the PX and get me all the cold sodas and ice you can find."

Huddled in the fuselage, the two men bathed the unit in the icy liquid until it had cooled enough to touch. They next checked it out to the best of their ability. When everything seemed to be connected and working properly, they started up.

Just as Piasecki prepared to take off, an officer of low rank appeared and flagged them down. Piasecki thought that word of their troubles had got out and the man was there with a grounding order. As it turned out, the officer lived minutes from the plant and wanted to hitch an exotic ride home. Talking to him through the side window, Piasecki tried his best to dissuade the unwanted rider, but he insisted. The pilot had no choice but to relent.

That officer had a memorable ride. Piasecki barely lifted his helicopter from the pavement and immediately pushed the overhead cyclic stick forward, flying as low as he dared all the way to Sharon Hill. Barely clearing trees and rooftops, rising in response to obstructions before sinking again to hug the ground, he skimmed along at faster-than-highway speed. So low was he that he had to pull up slightly to clear the higher ground surrounding his factory. It literally rose to meet his wheels as the *Dogship* slid to a stop.

Nobody said anything until the exhilarated officer was finally escorted off the property. Everyone else knew that something was seriously wrong. The helicopter's rotors had strangely come to an almost instant stop as soon as power was cut. After waiting impatiently for the transmission to cool, the capable P-V team stayed long into the night tearing the unit down. Veteran employee Edward Keast will never forget what he saw.

"When we opened the mix box, we saw the gear teeth were almost completely worn down," Keast remembered. "There was so little left that they looked like weld marks. Those gears didn't look like they could carry any load at all; everybody wondered how the helicopter flew as long as it did."[23]

Part of the problem was that needle bearings had naively been used. These bearings had ground down to nothing, loosening the precise gear alignment. Needle bearings would not be used again by the helicopter industry, and Piasecki never again employed automotive gears. Production HRPs and their successors instead employed custom-designed and specially manufactured transmission components.

If there were dangers, there was also substantial humor in the new company. Extended-duration static testing of an XHRP rotor was a requirement of the Navy contract. Lacking a whirlstand or funds to build one, the company president improvised by rescuing an ancient flatbed White truck from a junkyard and adapting it. The venerable vehicle's solid-rubber tires made it a stable mount for the rotor.

Day after day the HRP rotor was run on this stationary platform. Unfortunately, the vehicle sat—whirling rotor and all—in full view of commuters taking the train in and out of Philadelphia. It was a public relations disaster.

"That's it?" many commuters asked, jumping to the wrong conclusion. "That's the Piasecki helicopter we've read about in the newspapers? It'll never get off the ground!"[24]

If Piasecki was unaware of this negative publicity, he fully appreciated the humor of another incident involving the truck. During a wintry New Year's night as heavy snow fell over Sharon Hill, employee Bill Roach sat morosely in the vehicle during an interminable rotor test. He was heavily bundled against the cold and, since it was the holiday season, he had brought along a bottle. It was not long before he drifted off to sleep. He awoke in alarm to find the truck rearing up

A confident Frank Piasecki poses in winter flying
gear with his XHRP-X. Courtesy John Schneider.

on its tires. Rising winds and the greater density of the cold night air had augmented the rotor's lift to raise the heavy vehicle. Roach's impassioned and highly subjective report of the flight—exaggerated by the consumption of alcohol—was the source of considerable mirth at the plant the next day.

Summer brought its share of amusing incidents. On hot days when the Sharon Hill plant's large hangar-style doors were opened for ventilation, engineers and other staff members enjoyed a mesmerizing view of the *Dogship* as Piasecki flew it around and around the grassy meadow. Noting a drop in the productivity of his workers, Piasecki repeatedly ordered the doors shut only to find them open again. Sweltering heat in the summer of 1945 frequently drove the employees to disobey. Determined to have his way, Piasecki had the doors spiked shut, and an unusual strike erupted. There was no protest of any sort and nobody picketed. Most of the staff simply picked up and went to the Garden State Racetrack in Camden, New Jersey, where they enjoyed a wonderful day.

Trying to test a large helicopter in a predominantly residential neighborhood also had its humorous moments. Piasecki had bought a vintage 1920s fire truck and installed radios to make it a mobile command post. Much to the ire of the surrounding community, company employees charged up and down the residential roads in this extraordinary conveyance, hotly pursuing an even more extraordinary one—the noisy XHRP-X. It did not help that Piasecki had ordered a truck horn installed in the *Dogship*. More than once he alarmed local residents by flying up behind their cars with an insistent *OOH-gah, OOH-gah*.

The dead-end public road running in front of the plant was a particular point of contention between P-V Engineering and the town of Sharon Hill. With no houses on it, this street struck Piasecki as a good helicopter test airstrip. To keep cars out, he had plant workers place a barricade at the entrance to the road whenever testing was in progress. When residents took exception to a public road being appropriated, a police car interrupted the *Dogship* development program and officers wrote out a citation. Piasecki and Daland were forced to appear before a magistrate and pay a fine.

Another very talented engineer at P-V Engineering was Donald Meyers, a classmate of Piasecki's at the University of Pennsylvania. Graduating with a degree in mechanical engineering in 1940, he had been a member of Piasecki's spare-time engineering forum and had participated in design of the PV-2. After it flew, he left his job with a locomotive parts company to become one of P-V's earliest full-time employees.

Meyers's grasp of complex mathematics made him invaluable to Piasecki, whose engineering was of a more intuitive and less rigorous sort. Frank thought up the ideas but it was Don who worked them out in full detail. Meyers balanced off Piasecki's energetic ebullience, which often benefited from the presence of a moderating influence. Despite their very different personalities—or perhaps because of them—the two men remain the closest of friends. At the time of this writing, they continue to work together in the vertical-flight field.

By war's end, the once skeletal *Dogship* had been covered with doped fabric that gave a more substantial if decidedly unmilitary look. Like the PV-2, it was maroon and silver. Piasecki also painted his name in flowing white letters on the helicopter's flanks. Below the rear rotor appeared the U.S. national insignia, the bureau number 37968, and the tiny word "Navy."

The impropriety of using a military-funded prototype as a flying billboard for self-promotion greatly offended the Navy. So too did the large disparity in size between the company's name and that of the sponsoring service. To be fair, the status of the prototype had never been defined. Despite its military markings and serial number, the PV-3 was by mutual agreement a technology demonstrator and a factory test bed. The follow-on XHRP-1 would be the Navy's first prototype.

These subtleties were lost on the Navy officer who pulled Piasecki aside. Having *both* names on the machine, he heatedly informed the company president, was intolerable. It could be interpreted, he explained, as military endorsement of a private company, something that clearly ran counter to Navy regulations.

"I'll have it fixed right away," Piasecki assured him.[25] True to his word, the next time the XHRP-X appeared before a large official assembly, the word "Navy" had been removed.

The end of World War II brought P-V Engineering face to face with an emerging crisis: the need for external financing. The Navy's lavish infusion of public monies had entirely covered previous operating and development costs. The XHRP-X helicopter had been built and the company had expanded several times on a "pay-as-you-go" basis with funds provided in advance. Employment at war's end stood at two hundred.

Business in the postwar era promised to be far different. The relative austerity of peace-time procurement dictated that future dealings with the Navy would be conducted on a fixed-price basis without advance payments, thus shifting to the company much of the financial burden of military helicopter programs beyond the HRP-1.

To meet this challenge, P-V Engineering had to convert itself into a viable manufacturing company. Besides financing, business functions had to be attended to, systems set up, and a cost-effective production capability achieved. Even the Navy doubted whether the young company—so recently an informal engineering forum—could make the transition.

The private sector also had reservations. Despite Piasecki's limited success with the PV-2 and PV-3 (XHRP-X), his military helicopter company struck financial analysts and potential investors as a poor second to Sikorsky Aircraft. Enjoying the support of wealthy United Aircraft, Sikorsky had by then built well over four hundred rotorcraft, though admittedly none had been more than a third the size of the *Dogship*. Diminishing Pentagon support, critics noted, might precipitate a failure of the Philadelphia company at any time.

Piasecki met this challenge with boundless energy and enthusiasm. His ability to sell himself and his company once again offset perceived negatives and melted reservations. As he had done with the Navy, he tirelessly canvassed the financial community for the funds, his jovial optimism betraying no hint that success was less than assured.

Among those who approached him was Laurance Rockefeller. The wealthy speculator knew of Piasecki through wartime duties as a reserve officer at the Navy's Bureau of Aeronautics. Soon after the war ended, Rockefeller visited Sharon Hill where Piasecki

Wearing maroon-and-silver doped fabric, the
Navy-funded XHRP-1—progenitor of thousands of
tandem helicopters to follow—looks decidedly
unmilitary. Courtesy John Schneider.

invited him for what Rockefeller assumed would be a conservative hop in the XHRP-X *Dogship*. As it turned out, the financier's introduction to helicopters was memorable:

> Piasecki gave [Rockefeller] a set of earphones and took off enthusiastically. He put the ship through every maneuver he knew and some he had been planning to try. There were no extra seats in the helicopter and Rockefeller crouched worriedly in the cabin, holding on as best he could while Piasecki discussed the excellent features of the tandem design at length. Finally, as the wind shrieked around the ship's flapping sides and every brace wire trembled, Piasecki shouted that they were going faster than a helicopter had ever gone before. "Anything else you want to see?" he asked. The answer is not recorded.[26]

Rockefeller agreed to back the company despite the nerve-racking ride, which he later described as "a tremendous thrill." He was a venture capitalist who specialized in funding for profit the commercial applications of new technologies. He had already used his considerable wealth and influence to finance aviation companies, including Platt-LePage and McDonnell Aircraft.[27]

In 1946, P-V Engineering Forum reorganized as the Piasecki Helicopter Corporation, with Frank Piasecki named president and chairman of the board of directors. To raise capital for this fledgling company, Rockefeller teamed up with A. Felix du Pont, Jr., of nearby Delaware. Each could well afford to take the risks accompanying speculation in emerging technologies. The investment group they put together—which included Harper Woodward, Nicholas Ludington, and Douglas Dillon—offered Piasecki Helicopters

a half million dollars. Not a great amount even then, it was sufficient to place Piasecki Helicopters on the new financial footing demanded by the Navy.

In return, the Rockefeller group wanted a controlling interest in the company. Although he understood their desire to protect their investment, Piasecki was extremely reluctant to grant the request. Only when forced to choose between losing control of his company or watching it fail did he concede. He and other original P-V members relinquished company shares to let the Rockefeller group have a 51 percent stake in the corporation. Formalizing this turn of events, Felix du Pont joined its board of directors in March 1947.

Even as the *Dogship* continued in tests, Piasecki employees were hard at work on its successor. Called the XHRP-1 by the Navy, the second machine was more a true military prototype and less a company demonstrator than its predecessor. It bore the unwieldy company designation SDTA, an acronym standing for Static-Dynamic Test Article. This title reflected Piasecki's observation that lashing a helicopter to the ground for static runs totaling 500 hours—as required by the Navy contract—poorly approximated the stresses, vibrations, and deflections of true flight. In place of these ground tests he requested and won from the Navy the right to fulfill this "static" testing requirement "dynamically" via actual flight.

The XHRP-1 incorporated all the lessons learned in building and flying the *Dogship*, including the need for a more powerful engine and coupled drive shafts. The 600-hp Pratt & Whitney R-1340 radial that was chosen would also power production HRPs. This bare-bones machine would log more than 1,000 hours of endurance and programmed

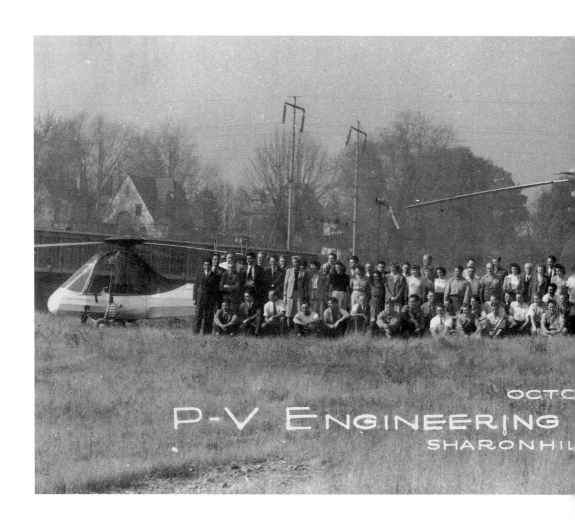

The P-V Engineering Forum's employees pose with their two working prototypes at Sharon Hill, fall 1945. Courtesy John Schneider.

945.

RUM, INCORPORATED
NNSYLVANIA

flight test time over a very cold winter without ever wearing a covering of doped fabric.

On the morning of Saturday, November 9, 1946, carefully guided by its builders and flight crew, the Piasecki XHRP-1 SDTA rolled through the shop doors for the first time. The uncovered framework of the helicopter scarcely vibrated as the engine started and the rotors began turning. With all proceeding smoothly, the crew concluded a battery of ground-resonance tests by early afternoon. One taste of that destructive phenomenon with the PV-2 had been more than enough for the Piasecki team. The lesson had been well learned and no hint of ground resonance was detected.

William G. Knapp, Piasecki's new chief test pilot, lifted the machine a foot off the ground to check the controls. A lieutenant commander in the U.S. Naval Reserve, Knapp had been the Navy's first rated helicopter pilot. He made several conservative hops, then relinquished the controls to Piasecki, who hovered for fifteen minutes while feeling out the controls. The team ended the day well satisfied with the performance of the prototype, whose flight one member enthusiastically described as "smooth as silk."[28]

More powerful and sophisticated than the *Dogship*, this helicopter had problems of its own. Before the interrelated rigging of its two rotor control systems was properly understood, it demanded that two people be at the controls for sheer strength. The collective pitch lever required roughly 30 pounds of upward force when in the down position, and just as much downward force when it was up. One pilot would therefore fly while the other held the collective lever until his arm ached, at which point they would swap duties. The throttle likewise demanded inordinate force, requiring both men to push in

unison with their left thumbs to change power settings.

Assisting Knapp in flight tests was Thomas R. "Ren" Pierpoint, another talented helicopter pilot with strong engineering credentials. In the vertical-flight field since 1938 (he started as a draftsman with the Pennsylvania Aircraft Syndicate, which tried to interest the Navy in Burke Wilford's XOZ-1 Gyroplane), Pierpoint went to Kellett in 1939, where he later became an autogiro/helicopter test engineer. He traded this post in 1942 for an AAF commission as a test pilot/design and development engineer with Colonel Frank Gregory's rotary-wing development organization at Wright Field. Four years later, these credentials earned him an offer of employment from Sikorsky. Pierpoint was on the verge of accepting when, through Burke Wilford, a similar offer came from Piasecki. A flight in the *Dogship* so impressed him that he immediately accepted, reporting for work in February 1946.

Flying the SDTA, the Navy and Army veterans took turns piloting or holding the collective while mechanical engineer Edward Ritti served as flight engineer. This three-man crew quickly developed a routine to deal with the new machine's idiosyncrasies. Ritti continuously checked the mixing gearbox, which would overheat with little warning and spew out hot lubricating oil. He also kept a close eye on the clutch, whose locking pins had a disconcerting habit of backing out, dumping the helicopter onto the ground, and torturing its suddenly disengaged engine.

The initial phase of the test program focused heavily on trial-and-error rotor control adjustments and stick force compensation, the latter achieved primarily with elastic bungee cords. These highly effective measures soon reaped dramatic improvements. The

(Top) The xhrp-1 sdta hovers in full sunshine the morning after its first flight. William Knapp and Thomas "Ren" Pierpoint are at the controls and flight engineer Edward Ritti perches in the aft fuselage. Courtesy Ren Pierpoint.

(Bottom) A second xhrp-1 flies at Sharon Hill. An unusual road sign reads "Danger, Helicopter Crossing, No Parking Between Signs." Courtesy John Schneider.

SDTA became, in the words of Ren Pierpoint, "a joy to fly, even in crosswind and downwind conditions not achievable in any other helicopter up to that time."[29]

Experiments determining the relation between rotor control settings brought memorable moments. On December 5, rear rotor pitch was increased 1.5 degrees above that of the front unit to gauge the effect on handling characteristics. The following month, as a brisk wind gusted across the flying field, Knapp and Pierpoint found out. What follows is excerpted from their report of January 30, 1947:

> Upon attaining the speed of approximately 35 mph at 100 feet altitude, a 90 degree turn was attempted downwind and diagonally back into the wind. As the ship turned, the nose went down and we began approaching the ground at a rather fast rate. Full aft stick did nothing to relieve this condition, and since we were losing altitude up collective pitch was attempted. No correcting effect resulted from this action either. By this time the ship was in a 20 to 30 degree nose-down attitude. Accordingly, down collective pitch was tried so that lift was lost and the ship settled quickly on an even keel longitudinally. Very slow forward flight was then used back to the landing area.[30]

Having come within inches of crashing, the SDTA bore out the aphorism that flying (particularly test duties) consists of hours of boredom punctuated by moments of stark terror. A more insidious hazard was cold weather, because to facilitate adjustment and modification the skeletal SDTA never had a fabric covering. Piasecki's insistence that this machine pile up hours in the air rather than in ground runs meant that much time was spent flying around simply to generate reliability data, disclose problems, and identify inadequate parts. However important, this requirement made life miserable for the twenty or so company employees who froze in the helicopter's open framework, force-cooled in the middle of winter by the downwash of two 41-foot rotors.

Pierpoint himself must have felt somewhat like the Flying Dutchman sailing endlessly under a curse. Logging over 150 hours in the machine during the winter of 1946–47, he flew on Thanksgiving, Christmas, and New Year's Day. The coming months would soon bring relief in the form of a well-deserved promotion to company service manager, a post Pierpoint would ably fill.

One more XHRP-1 took to the air, and went straight to the Navy for testing. A third example was to have been built, but Piasecki's decision to forgo ground static testing in favor of piling up flight hours on the first ship eliminated any need for it. The SDTA itself accumulated 1,150 hours in the air in a test program ending in the early spring of 1947 at Philadelphia International Airport. This hard-used test vehicle was then disassembled and its usable parts sent to the Navy to keep the second XHRP-1 airworthy. These two machines paved the way for production of the HRP-1, whose manufacture began in 1947 following June 1946 and April 1947 Navy orders for ten aircraft each.

Further brightening company prospects during 1946 were contracts for two entirely new helicopter programs. The first, designed by Piasecki engineers in answer to a 1945 Navy request for proposals for a fleet utility helicopter, gave rise to the XHJP-1 prototype, which in turn led to production of the Navy's HUP series and a smaller number of Army

H-25 Mules. The second contract of 1946 initiated development of a long-range AAF rescue helicopter designed to retrieve downed crews of that service's globe-spanning strategic bombers. Although it did not lead to production, this effort brought forth flying prototypes—the Piasecki YH-16s—larger than most aviation experts then thought possible.

Gross sales for 1946 totaled $1,148,689. Net profit after the heavy development costs were subtracted was $16,413. Although delivery of the first production helicopter was still the better part of a year away, its year-end backlog of orders totaled a healthy $4,769,807. Employment had more than doubled during 1946 to 450. Many skilled workers came from Kellett, which was then in decline.

By now outgrowing the leased Sharon Hill plant, Piasecki Helicopters cast about for larger quarters suitable for manufacture. None being found, the decision was made to build a factory on a 55-acre site in Delaware County, Pennsylvania, near the town of Morton. Only ten miles southwest of Philadelphia and adjacent to a branch of the Pennsylvania Railroad, it was an ideal location with ample room for helicopter testing and later expansion. A loan through the government's Reconstruction Finance Corporation financed the majority of the $500,000 cost of the land, building, and miscellaneous improvements. Half that much again would be spent on tooling and production equipment over the next several years.

The factory was constructed at one corner of the property, leaving a large central field for flying. Total floor space was 60,000 square feet (although another 18,000 square feet would soon be added). This facility, which marked PHC's emergence as a major force in the industry, was dedicated in an official ceremony May 20, 1947. President Piasecki's speech to some 700 employees, board members, and investors stressed his continuing belief that rotary-wing development was a race against time. "By building a better helicopter faster than the others," he told the enthusiastic audience, "we will continue to lead the industry in the transport helicopter field."[31]

Indeed, PHC's rapid pace of development and expansion was breathtaking. Throughout the late 1940s, the company would attain high public visibility through dramatic displays. In the spring of 1947, one XHRP-1 flown by Bill Knapp transported what its builders hailed as "the first military load of any significance,"[32] a jeep weighing more than a ton. Taking off with this underslung load, the Navy helicopter carried the vehicle past newsreel and press cameras to a safe landing nearby.

High-ranking Navy officials witnessing this display were as impressed with the pilot as with the helicopter itself. They convinced Knapp, a reserve officer, to return to active duty to assume a series of important rotary-wing assignments. In his stead, H. S. "Steve" Tremper became the company's chief test pilot. Hired by Knapp a few months earlier, Tremper was a former Coast Guard instructor pilot who had served under military helicopter pioneer Frank Erickson. He would build PHC's fast-growing flight department into one of the best in the business.

Fresh talent also filled out the ranks of the company's growing engineering department. One group in particular distinguished itself through invaluable support in stress and other engineering analysis functions. Al Flax, Ed Ryan, Lou Thompkins, Chuck Miller, and Hugh Mulvey provided hard answers for other company engineers who had been skating on the thin ice of guesswork.

The fast-growing Piasecki Helicopter Corporation
—at the time, the world's only producer of large
helicopters—occupied this newly constructed
facility in Morton, Pennsylvania, in 1947. Courtesy John Schneider.

The first shiny Piasecki HRP-1 Rescuer emerged from the factory in late summer 1947. The significance of this event is difficult to overstate. Seemingly overnight the available performance of production helicopters had more than doubled. Neither of the other two manufacturers worldwide then engaged in helicopter production offered anything like the cavernous HRP-1, whose utility—though small by today's capabilities —then set a standard the rest of the industry could not equal.

Production HRP-1s were covered with navy blue fabric that contributed to a top speed of 120 mph. In contrast, aerodynamic interference in forward flight had limited the uncovered SDTA to less than two-thirds that speed. The HRP-1s also sported a new horizontal stabilizer with twin vertical fins for greater stability about all three axes. The first three production machines featured bulbous cockpit glazing, giving them a caterpillar-like rounded nose; subsequent HRP-1s would revert to a flat profile, albeit less canted than that of the original XHRP-X.

On September 12, 1947, PHC delivered the first production HRP-1 to Naval Air Station Patuxent River in Maryland for evaluation by the Naval Air Test Center. During that same period an HRP-1 took General Alexander A. Vandegrift, the Marine Corps commander, on an inspection flight around his base at Quantico, Virginia. This helicopter also landed on the lawn of the Pentagon to give rides to Admiral A. M. Pride, then chief of the Bureau of Aeronautics, and other high-ranking Navy officials. Since BuAer was then housed across the Potomac River in temporary buildings on Washington's Mall, however, it was obvious that Piasecki's Pentagon stunt was not so much for the Navy's benefit as to impress the other services. Naval

leaders were not happy to see their helicopter company courting business from rival military services.

On October 31, the new helicopter had its operational debut when Piasecki delivered it to Captain Clayton C. Marcy, commander of VX-3 (soon to be redesignated HU-2) at NAS Lakehurst, New Jersey. While Piasecki remained on the ground to explain its capabilities to onlookers, Tremper hovered the helicopter forty feet in the air as five men clambered up a ladder suspended from its cargo door. In an emergency, Piasecki stated, ten men could be rescued in this manner at one time. He reminded the onlookers that his tandem helicopter could retrieve ten times as many people as the unit's one-at-a-time Sikorskys.

Six more HRP-1s were delivered to the Navy and one to the Marines before the end of 1947. By then, the first production example had performed the first real HRP-1 rescue by retrieving a downed pilot. Later in December, however, this machine was destroyed when its drive system failed during hover. The Piasecki company responded by identifying the cause and modifying other HRP-1s to ensure that this potentially fatal failure did not recur.

Scarcely two months later on February 25, 1948, test pilot Leland G. Felt was killed in the crash of the seventh production HRP-1. Jim Wells, his flight engineer, was badly injured but would recover. The craft appeared to be making a normal landing not far from the factory when it plunged to the ground. No cause was determined although eyewitness accounts ruled out pilot error.

Cool-headed, a veteran flier at twenty-nine, Bud Felt had been popular during his year with the company. His inexplicable death saddened and sobered everyone. Soon

Covered in dark blue doped fabric, the U.S.
Navy's first production Piasecki HRP-1 Rescuer
demonstrates its then-unique ability to retrieve
more than one person at a time. Courtesy John
Schneider.

afterward, two new test pilots joined the company to continue HRP-1 testing and help fly the three Piasecki XHJP-1 prototypes then being developed. The first of these new fliers was William H. Coffee, a former USCG helicopter instructor pilot who like Tremper had served under Erickson. The second was Jack L. Zimmerman, an AAF/USAF veteran and graduate of the Air Force Helicopter School at Freeman Field, Indiana. During World War II, Zimmerman had spent the better part of two years in an R-4 helicopter flying B-29 spare parts from supply ships to air bases on islands in the southwest Pacific. At war's end, he had conducted rescue missions in R-4B and R-6A helicopters while attached to the 6th Emergency Rescue Squadron on Okinawa.

In fact, Piasecki's flight department was rapidly becoming one of the best in the young industry. Among its fliers were Jim Ryan, who would loop the XHJP-1; Phil Camerano, cocky and scarcely over five feet tall, who would fly the huge XH-16; Leonard LaVassar, who would later be chief of flight test, a title he would hold for more than twenty years; and Marty Johnson, who with LaVassar would make the first flight of the YH-21A Work Horse.[33] The dangers faced by these pilots and others were considerable. Their contributions to the development of vertical flight should not be overlooked.

On October 14, 1947, Piasecki appeared before President Truman's Air Policy Commission, a body convened to recommend ways to improve and rationalize aviation in the United States. In his remarks to the commission, he urged the government to continue nurturing vertical flight. "Since current development costs are beyond the means of the industry," he said, "the government should not withdraw its sponsorship at this time, but should carefully plan additional expenditures in order to establish the industry and make it self-sufficient."[34]

With three companies then engaged in helicopter manufacture and others—notably Hiller, an entirely private venture—seemingly on the brink of production, Piasecki's argument rang hollow. America was experiencing an explosion of flight technologies from a war-fueled boom that had yet to moderate. That helicopters needed special financial consideration simply did not make sense. Even as Piasecki addressed the committee, the vigor of American aviation was driven home by Charles E. Yeager, who that same day shattered the sound barrier in the Bell X-1 rocket plane high above the California desert.

By then Bill Knapp—before his return to the Navy—had flown the first Piasecki XHJP-1 (company designation PD-14).[35] Fleet utility requirements dictated that the XHJP-1 be substantially smaller than the HRP-1 in order to be based on ships at sea. A key feature of its design was a high aft-fuselage pylon permitting closer spacing of the rotors by making them overlapping. This configuration allowed a shorter fuselage more at home on crowded decks. It also allowed the XHJP-1 to ride aircraft carrier elevators without folding its rotor blades, a time-saving advantage in operational service. Positioning the helicopter on the elevator was simple: its wheels had only to be placed on painted spotting marks, and its three-bladed 35-foot rotors aligned so that their tips cleared the rectangular cutout that the elevator occupied in the flight deck. Blade folding was provided for in the design, however, to allow the XHJP-1 to operate off cruisers with smaller decks.

In marked contrast to the HRP-1, the XHJP-1 featured an all-metal semi-monocoque fuselage. The pilot and copilot, moreover, sat side

The Piasecki xhjp-1 Retriever featured all-metal
construction, side-by-side pilot seating, and compact dimensions for Navy shipboard use. Courtesy
John Schneider.

by side for improved crew coordination. Behind them, an open cargo area provided ample room for six passengers.

The new helicopter employed the Continental R-975, which had also powered the *Dogship*. A version of the popular 450-hp Wright R-975, it had been uprated to 525 hp and modified by Continental to power Army tanks. The Navy had specified its use of Piasecki helicopters, reasoning that an engine able to power ground-based vehicles without overheating would also work in helicopters with their similar cooling problems.

Compared to the HRP-1, the XHJP-1 (proclaimed the world's fastest helicopter by its builder) flew almost like an interceptor. In unofficial speed trials at Morton, the first prototype attained 131 mph, to break the official world helicopter speed record then held by the Fairey Gyrodyne of Great Britain. The XHJP-1 climbed at 1,600 feet per minute in forward flight and 1,500 vertically. Perhaps reflecting the newness of helicopter technology, however, it was not an easy aircraft to fly.

During tests to explore the machine's ability to withstand g forces, Jim Ryan pulled out of progressively steeper dives to attain the required loads. On his third try he hauled hard back on the cyclic and the ship nosed to the vertical. The veteran pilot decided it was better to continue through a loop instead of releasing back pressure. Startled employees and Navy observers saw the XHJP complete a perfect loop, apparently the first ever executed by a helicopter. Analysis of flight data recorders aboard the fully instrumented XHJP-1 confirmed it had sustained greater flight loads than any other helicopter had been known to have endured, yet the prototype showed no structural damage. The company delivered the XHJP-1 to the Navy in March 1948, and

the second and third prototypes in December 1948 and February 1949.

Another overlapping-rotor machine flew in the area in 1948, the small JOV-3 built by the Philadelphia-based Helicopter Engineering and Research Corporation. A would-be manufacturer of private rotorcraft, HERC based this craft heavily on the Piasecki PV-11, a design whose development PHC had elected not to pursue. HERC's top three officers were former Piasecki employees D. K. "Gish" Jovanovich (president), Frank J. Kozloski (vice president), and George Townson (treasurer). When the four-seat JOV-3 failed to find a market, they sold it to McCulloch Motors. Similarly unsuccessful, McCulloch let the rights pass to Hughes, which would employ JOV-3 rotor technology in helicopters of its own.[36]

On July 31, 1948, in honor of its golden jubilee, New York City began a week-long celebration billed as the grandest aerial pageant in history. Hundreds of thousands of New Yorkers flocked to newly completed Idlewild Airport in Queens, then the biggest airfield in the world, which President Truman formally dedicated. When he finished, more than a thousand USAF aircraft—the greatest number of aircraft ever to fly together over the United States—passed in review in a flyby lasting thirty-five minutes.

Ironically, the crowds and press—clearly jaded by airplanes in the aftermath of the war—felt the helicopters had stolen the show. Sikorskys, the HERC JOV-3, the new Brantly, Bells, and Piaseckis participated in rescue demonstrations, carried air mail, and otherwise displayed the possibilities of vertical flight. The star of the show was an HRP-1 (referred to as a "Piasecki bent banana") that rescued six members of HU-2 sitting on the ground in a yellow life raft. The door of the

The McCulloch MC-4, a tandem-rotor personal helicopter employing Piasecki technology, reflects the once-prevalent expectation that a market for personal helicopters would emerge. Courtesy NASM/SI.

hovering helicopter was opened, a chain ladder was thrown out, all six sailors climbed
aboard at once, and off it flew to thunderous
applause.

That September, an HRP-1 performed an
assault demonstration for the crowds at the
22nd annual National Air Races in Cleveland. It flew in with an underslung 37 mm
antitank gun weighing 950 pounds, plus crew
and ammunition in its cabin. As it landed,
two combat-ready Marines jumped out, aimed
the weapon, and blew up a midfield target to
the delight of over a hundred thousand spectators. Military observers, however, were more
impressed by the craft's 420-mile trip from
Lakehurst to Cleveland via Harrisburg and
Pittsburgh. Made by Steve Tremper, this was
the first significant cross-country flight by a
large production helicopter.

Despite the favorable publicity, the Piasecki
HRP-1, like all first-generation helicopters,
suffered difficulties in day-to-day service. One
HRP-1 shed its plywood blade covers while
hovering 15 feet off the ground but settled to
a safe landing. Others suffered transmission
bearing and gear failures. Yet another experienced a cracked rotor hub, which nearly
failed in flight. These problems grounded the
entire fleet perhaps five times, sometimes for
months at a time.

Less serious was vibration, but even moderate levels loosened fasteners and seals,
shortened radio life, and often rendered com-
passes useless by making them precess endlessly. Although Piasecki products suffered
less from this problem than those of rival
manufacturer Sikorsky, vibratory and harmonic gremlins had to be exorcised here too.
Some HRP-1s—like Bureau Number
111816, which had performed at Idlewild—
demonstrated more in-flight vibration than
others. The worst of the company's produc-

tion Rescuers, Bureau Number 111816 defied
the rotor "fine-tuning" that had tamed its sib-
lings. Its instrument panel shook so badly in
flight that it was impossible to read. The
opposite was true of ship 812, which the
company's experienced rotary-wing pilots
proudly proclaimed the smoothest-flying helicopter in existence.

No two helicopters were alike, partly
because their 48-foot steel-tube fuselages were
too long to be built in rigid jigs. They were
assembled in articulated jigs using spring tension to maintain positioning as welded parts
cooled and contracted. Misalignments of the
structural members resulted from inevitable
differences in static tensions and compres-
sions. Another reason no two HRP-1s flew
identically was the lack of uniformity in the
rotor blades despite the dynamic balancing
described earlier, as well as in other dynamic
components of these first-generation rotorcraft.

Control force issues also demanded attention. One attempt to improve matters
involved installing a collective-pitch bungee
system. But instead of making things better,
this "fix" doubled static collective lever up-
loads to the weight of an average pilot. "The
figure of 150 to 175 pounds," reported Service
Manager Ren Pierpoint, "is an estimate based
on the fact that it requires the full strength
of two average men to reduce collective pitch
from 14 to 2 degrees in the static condition."[37]

The Piasecki HRP-1 ranks high among the
most significant first-generation production
helicopters. Whatever their limitations, these
rotorcraft represented a breathtaking leap
forward in vertical flight. For several years the
only large helicopters in existence, they compiled an impressive list of achievements.

In the spring of 1949, eight Marine Corps
HRP-1s carried troops and artillery in a pro-

foundly influential demonstration of aerial assault that would forever change the nature of modern warfare. Navy HRP-1s pioneered helicopter antisubmarine warfare techniques off Key West in 1951, locating and "sinking" a submarine in mock exercises for the first time in history. Other Navy HRP-1s were the first to engage in helicopter minesweeping in tests performed at Panama City in 1953. And Coast Guard HRP-1s performed history's first long-range helicopter rescues, including a dramatic lifesaving retrieval ninety miles out to sea.

The last of twenty HRP-1s rolled off the Piasecki production line before the end of 1948. During that year, the Piasecki Helicopter Corporation recorded nearly $3 million in total sales with after-tax profits of $65,657. On June 18 the company's prospects had brightened with receipt of a major USAF contract calling for development of a giant helicopter then known as the XR-16. This initial contract funded construction of a full-scale mockup of the huge rotorcraft.

Meantime, development was well under way of the company's second production tandem helicopter. The much-improved HRP-2 (PD-17) featured a streamlined metal fuselage offering better visibility for two pilots, who now sat side by side ahead of the front rotor. The most significant improvement was the HRP-2's all-metal stressed-skin construction. Compared to it, the HRP-1 (with or without its balloon-cloth covering) looked like a dinosaur.

In the spring of 1949, Lee Douglas arrived as Piasecki Helicopter Corporation's new chief engineer. A 1932 graduate of New York University's Guggenheim School of Aeronautics, Douglas had earlier worked for Seversky, Bell, Barkley-Grow, and Brewster. When poor management and militant

wartime labor disputes brought about this last company's decline, Douglas had moved to nearby Kellett, where he gained rotary-wing experience helping to develop the XR-10.

From the fixed-wing aviation industry, Douglas brought an extensive knowledge of all-metal aircraft construction, although he arrived too late to contribute much to the design of Piasecki's first metal helicopter. He also possessed managerial skills and knew how to run an efficient engineering department. Not long after his arrival, Piasecki field service personnel called on these latter abilities to help solve a chronic problem.

Stationed at military bases with helicopters already in service, these company technicians clamored insistently for adequate and timely support from the main plant. It had not been forthcoming because the company was too disorganized to provide quick, effective fixes. As a result, the operational readiness of HRP-1s was poor and Piasecki's unhappy military customers were rapidly becoming disenchanted. Ren Pierpoint arranged for Douglas to make a fact-finding trip to the Marine Corps base at Quantico. The chief engineer returned to PHC and promptly corrected the company's inattentiveness to the needs of its customers.

Meanwhile, the first HRP-2 was rapidly taking shape in the factory. It used the same engine and rotors as the HRP-1, but was slightly shorter and lighter. If its semi-monocoque fuselage had been built like that of an airplane, it would have been too heavy. The Piasecki team used a thinner skin and had the longitudinal members shaved down, as well as other extruded parts that could not be manufactured thinly enough.

Jim Ryan lifted the new Navy helicopter into the air for the first time October 29, 1949. While it was indeed better than the HRP-1,

(*Top*) For several years the only large helicopters in production, HRP-1s had a top speed of 120 mph and could lift large payloads. Courtesy Ren Pierpoint.

(*Bottom*) A streamlined "flying banana" takes to the air late in 1949. The aluminum-fuselage HRP-2 lacked power and only five were built. Courtesy John Schneider.

the fast pace of helicopter technology had already passed it by, and better helicopters could now be built. With a gross weight of 7,225 pounds, the HRP-2 was simply too light to offer much utility. Four more HRP-2s concluded HRP production the following year, bringing to twenty-four the number of -1s and -2s delivered to the military.

By then the Navy preferred the smaller XHJP-1, a machine better suited to fleet use than the HRP-2. But a hurdle remained before this smaller member of the Piasecki tandem family could enter production. Sikorsky Aircraft, like Piasecki, had been issued a contract to construct three prototypes of utility helicopters for the Navy. These two companies would compete for the final contract.

The Sikorsky XHJS-1 was a bigger five-place brother to the R-5, which it resembled in overall configuration except for a raised tail boom designed to get the rotor above head height. The XHJS-1's three-bladed folding rotor, which featured all-metal blades, was powered by the Continental R-975 engine like the XHJP-1 (this unit having been specified for both machines by the Navy).

Early in 1949, these two very different helicopters participated in a formal fly-off at NAS Patuxent River. To the delight of the Philadelphia contingent, the Piasecki routed the Sikorsky from the start. The other helicopter flew much slower and performed poorly. In a side-by-side simulated rescue, the tandem-rotor machine retrieved an "injured" sailor and returned him to the starting point so quickly that its pilot was able to shut down his helicopter and stretch out by it in languid repose, a spectator to the remainder of the event.

The Navy preferred the Piasecki machine's wide center-of-gravity range, which permitted people to move about and loads to be shifted in flight. By comparison, the single-rotor Sikorsky was intolerant of center-of-gravity shifts. The Piasecki XHJP-1 was also easier to service because its engine, cooling fan, cowling, oil system, and accessories could be lifted out as a single unit from a hatch in the rear fuselage.

But what really sold the Navy on the XHJP-1 was its ingenious rescue hoist. In flight, the copilot left his seat and folded it forward to clear the space above an electrically operated hatch. At the push of a button, the hatch dropped open to deploy a rescue sling connected to an overhead electric winch. This hatch was long enough to permit a standard Navy Stokes litter to lift horizontally into the helicopter, allowing better care of critically injured patients. Best of all, the XHJP-1 pilot could see the rescue in progress to keep his helicopter properly positioned as the hoist was used.

The XHJS-1 paled by comparison here as well. Balance considerations dictated that its hoist be located farther aft, in line with the rotor, thus depriving the pilot of a view and forcing him to rely on his crew for verbal instructions.

The XHJP-1 outperformed the XHJS-1 so resoundingly that Sikorsky company literature has avoided virtually all mention of the XHJS-1 ever since. Having rather smugly dismissed the Philadelphia corporation as an upstart, Sikorsky had suddenly been served notice that Piasecki was a force to be reckoned with. One of the vertical flight industry's longest rivalries began at this fly-off early in 1949. With Sikorsky even then unveiling its excellent S-55, the two firms were quickly squaring off head-to-head in the manufacture of large helicopters. The customers of both companies would benefit from this competition over the coming decades.

Piasecki, Vertol, and Boeing Helicopters 150

Despite its excellent showing, the Piasecki helicopter suffered developmental troubles. Early in 1948, the first XHJP-1 crashed while hovering when a forward rotor blade shed its entire wooden cover. The craft was extensively damaged but nobody was hurt. This incident prompted Piasecki to redouble its efforts to develop metal rotor blades, as Hiller and Sikorsky had already done. Work was progressing on this front in the early 1950s when the Navy forced Piasecki to contract with the Prewitt Aircraft Company of Clifton Heights, Pennsylvania, for metal blades.

At this time the HJP was redesignated HUP, a change reflecting the Navy's logical decision to denote the utility role for helicopters by the letter U rather than J.

Prewitt did indeed create bonded-steel rotor blades for the HUP-2. Designed by former Kellett chief engineer Richard Prewitt, these blades had been in development under Navy contracts since 1947. Unfortunately, they were poorly designed and caused unacceptable vibration levels on HUPS. A waste of public and Piasecki money, they were not used operationally.

HUP fuselages were built at Philadelphia International Airport, where Piasecki had rented two new hangars from the city. The HUP engineering team and test pilots were moved to that location, on whose flight ramps newly completed HUPS were tested. Dedicated as Plant 2 in October 1949, this airport facility raised total company floor space to an impressive 125,000 square feet.

Work was already under way on an autopilot for hands-off flying and hovering. An autopilot was considered essential for the HUP because the Navy badly wanted to be able to fly it in instrument conditions. Short-coupled and plagued with stability problems, HUPS were hard to fly (this notorious insta-bility contributed to Ryan's unintentional loop). The company had already experimented with a variety of horizontal, vertical, and canted tail surfaces, but these problems defied an adequate solution.

The company approached the requirement for stability augmentation by testing Sperry, Minneapolis Honeywell, and Lear autopilots in the XHJP-1. Performed by company and military test pilots in 1950, these flight tests were the first ever performed of an autopilot in a helicopter. Although success was obtained in forward flight, the units were unable to stabilize the helicopter during hover.

Some success was eventually obtained with the Sperry A-12 autopilot of World War II vintage, but it came too late for the HUP-1. As a result, the HUP-2 was the first production helicopter ever to feature an autopilot. Thus equipped, it dispensed with its predecessor's large tail surfaces. A number of crashes because of a severe hardover failure mode would lead to this autopilot being removed in operational service.

The HUP-1 Retriever entered full Navy service in January 1951, and the HUP-2 the following year. Chronic engine problems soon led to the loss at sea of more than ten helicopters, although fortunately without loss of life or even serious injury. That these losses were through no fault of the Piasecki Helicopter Corporation was no consolation, for they threatened the viability of the entire HUP program. The original Wright R-975 had been a fine engine; as modified and uprated by Continental, however, it was no longer trustworthy.

When the many fixes proposed by Continental failed to provide a cure, it fell to Commander Pete Brown, the talented aeronautical engineer-cum-helicopter pilot then heading BuAer's Helicopter Class Desk, to come up with a workable solution. Brown observed that the carrier-based HUPs had a crew of two, a pilot and a crew chief. These machines stood by to retrieve the crews of airplanes that ditched following failed arrested-landings. Since this "plane-guard" mission rarely called for more than two men to be plucked from the sea at one time, the helicopters were rarely being loaded to capacity.

Brown's idea was to lower the HUP's gross weight by 1,000 pounds and derate its engine by 100 hp. These operational limits were immediately placed in effect and losses subsided to acceptable levels, allowing HUPs to operate successfully for the next decade. During that period, the operating limits were gradually phased out as engine improvements were implemented.

HUPs rescued thousands of people in operational use, including more than 10,000 civilians in Colombia during U.S. Navy flood relief in the mid-1950s. Because tandem-rotor helicopters lack the sensitivity to wind direction that single-rotor types display, the HUP series further endeared itself to carrier skippers who could launch their Retrievers without turning their vessels into the wind.

In June 1954 the last of 339 production examples of this hardworking series was delivered. This successful production run, an impressive total for the day, had included an Army version of the HUP-2 known as the H-25A Mule, plus a limited number of fleet helicopters for the Canadian and French navies.[38]

On the last day of 1954 the vastly improved HUP-4 flew for the first time. This prototype featured the reliable 700-hp Wright R-1300. Its substantial power increase would be fully exploited the next year when a companion

development of an uprated transmission was completed. Had the HUP-4 been available sooner, it would have greatly extended the service life of the excellent HUP series. But the Navy canceled the whole program in frustration in 1955 and sponsored instead development of the HU2K-1 (UH-2) Sea-sprite, the Kaman company's first single-rotor helicopter.

Ironically, the revised HUP could have been available much sooner but for the actions of C. Hart Miller, PHC president from 1950 to 1953. The Rockefeller/du Pont faction had installed Miller, a former Martin and Republic senior executive, as executive vice president and general manager in 1949. The investors had then seen to it that he was elected to the board of directors and elevated to the presidency early the following year.

Hart Miller had impressive credentials as a former aeronautical engineer and pilot. He was amiable and well liked but his three years at Piasecki's helm frustrated everyone. In contrast to the previous leadership of Frank Piasecki, Miller's tenure was marked by a lack of direction. His well-meaning but misguided effort to hold down development costs explained PHC's slow response to HUP service troubles, prompting the needless cancellation of the program.

Miller had been installed as president at the annual stockholders' meeting March 20, 1950. At this same meeting, Frank Piasecki was elected board chairman and named chief of research and development. Other company officers on the board were Elliot Daland (vice president, R&D), Wesley R. Frysztacki (vice president and secretary), Harry Pack (vice president for public relations), and William Palmer, who served as the corporation's treasurer, controller, and assistant sec-

Chronic engine problems compromised the reliability of the otherwise excellent HUP-2. Courtesy
NASM/SI.

retary. In addition to Felix du Pont, outside directors were William B. Harding, Nicholas Ludington, and Harper Woodward.

The announcement of Frank Piasecki's new status suggested that the man who had previously done almost everything was now handing over the day-to-day administrative demands of running his company. Piasecki would focus on overall policy as board chairman, and on product development as executive vice president for R&D, this latter being the area of company activity that he loved best.

In truth, however, the financiers had imposed this restructuring on the founder against his will. The reason was simple: the Piasecki Helicopter Corporation was not well run. Its small size and lavish Navy funding had disguised this fact in the early days, as had the subsequent brisk growth. But by 1950 the company was far too large for any one person to run, especially one who liked to "wing it."

Having worked well in the days of the PV-2 and *Dogship*, this one-man show was strained to the limit as the company expanded beyond even Piasecki's enormous energies. His need to be everywhere and do everything lay at the heart of the company's current troubles. And perhaps because he put in so many hours himself, he tried to get his employees to do the same—for free. P-V employees had routinely donated their weekends to the company during World War II. That war and the company's informal days were now well past, yet the expectation of sacrificed evenings and weekends remained. One way Frank got more out of his people than they were paid for was to make many of them salaried rather than hourly employees in order to avoid having to pay overtime. Another tactic was to call major meetings at five o'clock to keep his professional staff from going home at quitting time. Morale problems, as well as more than

a few divorces and ongoing trouble with Philadelphia's powerful unions, were the outcome.

A schism thus emerged at the start of the 1950s. On one side was the industry pioneer whose vision, drive, and talent had positioned the organization as a premier manufacturer of helicopters. Starting a company and seeing it through its initial growth requires one set of abilities; running it after it has matured demands another. Few people are good at both. Frank Piasecki excelled at the former but did poorly at the latter. Hardcore business functions could not compete with the countless other demands on his time, all of which he found more interesting. As a result, matters had reached a point where even loyal supporters who considered him a near genius knew that something had to give.

On the other side of this schism was the financial group whose willingness to invest speculatively had saved the company from demise amid postwar defense cutbacks. Members of this group clearly perceived the threat that a lack of professional leadership posed to Piasecki Helicopters. Saving the company, they believed, demanded an immediate infusion of rigorous business discipline befitting PHC's newfound stature and responsibilities. Bringing Hart Miller on board and stripping Frank of all but two of his hats were efforts toward this end. There would also be others, as detailed below. In the meantime, a major new challenge had arisen that would forever change the vertical-flight industry.

In June 1950, war broke out in Korea. This three-year conflict had a profound effect on the four companies engaged in volume helicopter production. In the case of Piasecki, annual sales more than quadrupled to $26,366,852 for the year 1951, and within

Piasecki, Vertol, and Boeing Helicopters 154

two years had skyrocketed to $86,726,430. PHC's backlog of orders—the largest in the industry—rose from $60 million on the eve of war to hover around $150 million through most of the conflict. Net earnings in 1953 for the first time broke the million-dollar mark at $1,226,938.

This new plateau of economic activity also worked dramatic physical changes. A 220,000 square foot manufacturing building and a 36,000 square foot flight hangar were built in 1951 even as off-site leased space rose from 60,000 to 162,000 square feet. A warehouse in nearby Chester, Pennsylvania, further increased this total as Plant 5 the following year. Total acreage at Morton would rise from 54 to 88.5 before war's end. Having broken the 3,000 mark in 1952, employment reached nearly 5,000 by the end of the following year. The company had come a long way since the first flight of the PV-2 just ten years earlier.

Explosive wartime growth brought pandemonium in many quarters. To the acute embarrassment of Piasecki management, parts control became so poor that one too many HUP fuselages was manufactured. This unneeded shell hung from the factory ceiling for four years until the Navy finally bought it and used it to create a "new" helicopter out of two HUPs that had crashed.

On April 11, 1952, the YH-21 Work Horse —Piasecki's best helicopter yet—took to the air with Len LaVassar and Marty Johnson at the controls. Winner of a USAF competition for an arctic transport helicopter, the new craft looked almost like the HRP-2, but weighed 14,700 pounds fully loaded, more than twice the earlier machine.[39] A 1,425-hp Wright R-1820 engine (derated in early models to 1,150 hp) and a three-foot increase in rotor diameter to 44 feet gave it much better per-formance than the HRP-2. Structurally, it was a new aircraft.

The company had come up with a winner. The Work Horse could carry fourteen fully equipped troops or an equivalent weight of cargo. Features included a rescue hoist and inflatable donut-shaped floats around its wheels for landings even on marshy tundra. Winterized to support Distant Early Warning (DEW) Line radar stations far to the north, it was just the aircraft the Air Force had wanted. Extensive cold-weather testing was performed atop Mount Washington, the highest peak in New Hampshire's beautiful White Mountains, as well as in the climate hangar at Eglin Air Force Base.

Eighteen months after the H-21, the Piasecki YH-16 Transporter—the other new tandem machine ordered by the Air Force— took to the air at Philadelphia International Airport. On October 23, 1953, company personnel and military officials watched the majestic helicopter take off, hover, and fly forward and sideways during a successful twelve-minute maiden hop flown by Harold Peterson and Phil Camerano. "It was just like watching an ocean liner pick up and fly," recalled Ken Meenen.[40]

The Transporter was by far the largest helicopter then flown. It was 78 feet long and topped by two overlapping rotors each 82 feet in diameter. In-flight vibration was low and of a loping nature. Bonded and tapered all-metal rotor blades (built using a new company process) combined milled-aluminum skins, aluminum honeycomb filler, and a leading-edge balance weight that also served as a mechanical fastener for the skins.

A USAF requirement for a wide-ranging helicopter capable of rescuing downed strategic bomber crews had given rise to the new helicopter. The hefty fuel capacity required

Developed for the U.S. Air Force, the Piasecki
H-21 flies in April 1952. A growth version of the
HRP-2, which it resembled, the highly success-
ful H-21 combined higher power and increased
gross weight to offer real utility. Courtesy John
Schneider.

to meet its specified 1,400-mile range in part dictated its size. Without the extra fuel, the capacious aircraft also had possible military application as a large troop and cargo transport. With this alternate use in mind, the company announced that the Transporter could carry forty passengers or three light trucks loaded through its rear ramp.

These capabilities appealed to the U.S. Army, which saw in the H-16 an answer to several helicopter mission requirements of its own. It therefore joined the USAF in sponsoring further development of the YH-16 (the "Y" prefix denoted reclassification from experimental to service-test status). The helicopter's utility was limited, however, because it was underpowered despite two 1,650-hp Pratt & Whitney R-2180 radial engines. Like the *Dogship* before it, the YH-16 lifted as much as it did only because of very low disc loading that compromised other aspects of its performance. Greater power was clearly needed to realize the design's potential.

Turbine power provided the answer. Smaller, lighter, more powerful, and more reliable than piston power, turboshaft engines then promised to revolutionize the entire helicopter industry. Two 1,800-shp Allison T38 units were accordingly adapted to the Piasecki design to create the world's first twin-turbine helicopter. Designated YH-16A, this second aircraft took to the air in July 1955 with Harold Peterson and George Callaghan at the controls. When it set an unofficial speed record of 166 mph the following year, prospects for the H-16 program could not have looked brighter. Piasecki had met a challenge others had thought impossible (Sikorsky had declined to bid for this same USAF contract). In the process, the company had once again extended the technological boundaries of rotary-wing flight.

In December, the YH-16A broke apart in the air and crashed near the Delaware River, killing Peterson and Callaghan as they returned from a test flight in New Jersey. Investigators determined that the rear rotor shaft had failed, allowing the blades to desynchronize and wobble into the plane of those of the forward rotor. In fact, a frozen bearing in the test instrumentation had precipitated this failure by allowing a steel-tube standpipe, placed within the aluminum rotor shaft to guide wires from the instrumented blades, to undetectably inscribe a deepening groove within the shaft.

This tragic accident caused the H-16 program to be scrapped, preempting the sixty-nine-passenger YH-16B Turbotransporter (a conversion of the YH-16 then in progress), which would have flown with two 3,700-shp Allison T56 engines. It also preempted Frank Piasecki's vision of interchangeable underbody pods for the rapid transport of differing loads such as field operating rooms, communications centers, and mobile repair centers.[41] A tall stilt landing gear had already been designed to let the YH-16B accommodate such pods.

During the National Aircraft Show on September 4, 1953, meanwhile, USAF Captain Russell Dobyns set world helicopter speed and altitude records of 146.7 mph and 22,110 feet, respectively, at the controls of a standard H-21. Despite this success, teething troubles arose to delay full-scale H-21 production the following year.

In February 1954, all H-21s were grounded pending correction of potentially dangerous design flaws. Just as the first modified helicopter was readied for delivery that spring, a rotor blade failed during a test and the fleet was again grounded on May 18. Then the USAF decided that H-21 vibration levels

Dwarfing the HUP and H-21, the huge YH-16
Transporter dominates the company ramp at
Philadelphia International Airport. Courtesy John
Schneider.

were excessive, prompting deliveries to be deferred while this situation, too, could be remedied at company expense. Hundreds of Piasecki employees were laid off in June, and more still in October, before these technical difficulties were at last resolved.

Sales for 1954—the first full year of peacetime operation after the Korean War—dropped below $50 million, and employment stabilized at 3,500. Piasecki's manufacturing area nearly doubled that May with the lease of two newly renovated buildings in Ardmore, twelve miles from the Morton facility, early in May. Located on the former Autocar factory site, the two buildings were soon equipped with component construction tooling to reduce the amount of subcontracting. One result was that H-21 fuselages, formerly built by the Goodyear Aircraft Company, could now be manufactured in-house.

The painful process of reducing employment from wartime levels had been the task of Donovan R. Berlin, PHC's new chief executive. A 1921 Purdue University graduate in mechanical engineering, Berlin had begun his aviation career with the Army Air Corps' Engineering Division at McCook Field, Ohio. He left five years later to join Douglas, the first of his many posts in the fixed-wing aviation industry. These would include Northrop; Stearman; Curtiss-Wright,[42] where he designed the P-40 fighter plane of World War II fame; General Motors, which manufactured airplanes during the war; and McDonnell. It was at McDonnell, as senior vice president and general manager, that he came to the attention of Laurance Rockefeller.

Tall, domineering, and fond of wearing a cowboy hat and boots, Berlin was as forceful as Miller had been amiable. It was precisely this quality that prompted the Rockefeller and du Pont contingent to install him as pres-

ident January 1, 1953. Miller's concurrent demotion to vice president and general manager reflected the investors' realization that he had not been the right choice for chief executive after all.

In fact, the Rockefeller contingent consisted of financiers, not experts in business management. They had waited too long to take action to help the troubled Piasecki corporation, only to impose the wrong solution in 1950. They compounded their mistake by letting the leadership crisis continue under Miller. Problems with the H-21 program had finally brought matters to a head at the end of 1952.

Installing Berlin at the start of the new year was the idea of the Rockefeller group, but the timing was dictated by the U.S. Air Force, which had brought pressure to bear on the investment faction. Cold war tensions were running high as the presidency of Harry Truman drew to a close. Finishing the DEW Line, the nation's safeguard against surprise attack by Soviet aircraft and missiles, had top priority. To meet this strategic objective, the Air Force needed its H-21 Work Horse arctic helicopters on time and in serviceable condition.

The Pentagon had viewed the company's ongoing difficulties with considerable alarm. With so much at stake, Air Force leaders began pressuring the Rockefeller group to resolve the helicopter company's chronic leadership muddle. High drama ensued.

Berlin was recruited specifically to counter the equally forceful if very different Frank Piasecki. Piasecki had not confined himself to the board chairmanship and control of company R&D, as the investors had hoped. He continued to operate as he always had, inserting himself into all aspects of the corporation's running. With Berlin in the equation, the situation soon became so acrimonious that Piasecki was barred from the engineering department.

Coming just in time to preside over the layoff of more than a thousand employees, Berlin was not popular with the rank and file. He also alienated the engineers. But as the investors had hoped, Berlin made life so miserable for Piasecki that he departed the company in 1955.

With this parting of the ways, an era drew to a close. Gone from the Piasecki Helicopter Corporation was one of rotary-wing flight's great innovators, a first-rank pioneer nearly equal in stature to Igor Sikorsky. In one key area, his accomplishments stand alone. Nobody else, not even Sikorsky, had dared to think so *big* so early.

The Piasecki Helicopters era had begun closing early the preceding year when sixty-eight-year-old Elliot Daland resigned his directorship and retired from the company. The departure of the eminent senior engineer, whom Piasecki revered, had eroded Frank's base of support. Daland's absence left him outnumbered on the board, whose chairmanship Berlin assumed following Piasecki's departure.

Piasecki's decision to leave the company did not entirely end his involvement in vertical flight. Immediately upon leaving he created the Piasecki Aircraft Company. A number of PHC employees followed him to this new entity, the earliest meetings of which took place in the Piasecki home. This new company soon relocated at Philadelphia International Airport.

PIAC, as Piasecki called his new company, would focus on alternate VTOL concepts. Over the ensuing years it investigated a variety of ideas, including helicopter drones, flying jeeps in the Hiller Aircraft tradition, high-speed compound helicopters with ducted pusher propellers, and a combination helicopter-airship heavy-lift vehicle. PIAC came to be very much a family business. Frank had married forest-products heiress Vivian Weyerhaeuser. Three sons of the couple's seven children work for the small research-oriented company at the time of this writing. PIAC's home for many years has been in Eddystone, Pennsylvania, adjacent to Boeing Helicopters and near the site of the former Platt-LePage company. These facilities include space for manufacture, although only experimental prototypes and subcontracted parts made for other companies have been built there over the decades.

Ironically, an early PIAC project spelled the end of the Platt-LePage XR-1A. In 1947, Piasecki bought the wartime prototype for $1,500 from Helicopter Air Transport in Camden, New Jersey. He paid HAT founder and former P-L test pilot Lou Leavitt an additional $500 to fly the aircraft to Morton. When Piasecki left, the airframe followed him by truck to his new company, where it became the company-funded mockup of a vectoring-ducted-fan aircraft concept.

"There sat that old XR-1A gathering dust," recalled John Schneider, a longtime Boeing Helicopters engineer who worked briefly for PIAC, "so we cut the booms off, removed the engine, and *voilà!* We had the fuselage and tail of our Ring-Wing V/STOL. We had intended to put the XR-1A back together again, but somehow parts got lost or misplaced and it never happened."[43]

Had it not been seized upon as an expedient mockup for some forgotten project, the Platt-LePage XR-1A would probably have joined the Sikorsky XR-4, Piasecki PV-2 and XHRP-X *Dogship*, Bell Model 30, Hiller XH-44, Kellett XR-8, McDonnell XHJD-1, and other early helicopters in the unique collection of

Six original employees gather in April 1953 to celebrate the tenth anniversary of the PV-2's first flight. From left to right are Ken Meenen, Elliot Daland, Frank Piasecki, Don Meyers, Frank Mamrol, and Walter Swartz. Courtesy John Schneider.

the Smithsonian Institution's National Air and Space Museum. It was a sad end for the unsuccessful but historic prototype.

Almost on the day that Frank Piasecki and his allies departed Piasecki Helicopters, Don Berlin began transforming the company through sheer force of will and an infusion of new talent. Among those he brought in were Chief Development Engineer Thomas Peppler, Chief Project Engineer Richard Degen, and Vice President for Production Bill Davey. Giving his staff little time to reflect on all the recent changes, Berlin forged ahead in his ambition to take PHC to new heights. For all the friction between him and Frank Piasecki, he was an able leader who would lay the groundwork for the company's subsequent technical success by spearheading the development of its first turbine helicopter.

At the March 1956 annual meeting, Piasecki Helicopter Corporation stockholders voted to change the company's name to Vertol (derived from "vertical takeoff and landing"). The year ended with healthy net earnings of $3,437,563. Sales totaled $90,025,697, up 56 percent from the previous year's $57,690,074, in part thanks to the company's successful entry into export markets. The French government's initial order of fifty H-21s in 1956 was followed early in 1957 by a West German purchase of thirty-six (West Germany would also buy four VIP-configured V-44s in 1961). To encourage further export orders, Vertol appointed sales representatives in Europe, South America, South Africa, and the Far East.

The large French order, and two subsequent ones for an additional seventy H-21s, provided opportunity to conduct pioneering research on military helicopter operations. With the piston Work Horse nearing the end of its service life, company planners decided to find out just what the military needed in a next-generation helicopter. The question was pertinent since the company was poised at the threshold of the turbine era, and the inordinate development costs of entirely new turbine helicopters could make a wrong guess catastrophic.

It made sense to study H-21 use in combat. The single opportunity lay in Algeria, which France saw as more than just a colonial possession and was determined to retain. Loaded aboard a French aircraft carrier at Norfolk, Virginia, in May 1956, the first French H-21s had gone to Africa accompanied by Vertol's finest service technicians and instructor pilots. From the harbor at Algiers, these rotorcraft flew directly to the French Army air base at Sétif in northeastern Algeria. Training and combat duties commenced almost at once due to wartime urgency.

By the start of 1957, over twenty H-21 troop transports were performing history's first "vertical envelopment" combat operations from several bases in Algeria. This pioneering use of helicopters in the aerial-assault role preceded by almost a decade the U.S. Army's widespread employment of "air-mobility" tactics in Vietnam during the 1960s and early 1970s. These strikingly similar combat operations had common roots in the 1949 U.S. Marine Corps demonstration performed by eight Piasecki HRP-1s.

From the first Algerian helicopter missions in 1956 to the last in October 1959, from twenty to thirty Vertol people were on hand at all times to assist and observe. Service Manager Ren Pierpoint, along with Chief Service Pilot Bill Coffee and Chief Field Service Engineer Louis "Jack" Geier, compiled extensive statistics for stateside analysis, and made profuse notes on the technical and operational lessons learned by the French in the day-to-

This H-21, with West German markings, marks a 1957 foray into export sales by Vertol, the new name adopted by the company in 1956. Courtesy NASM/SI.

day use of Vertol helicopters. What emerged was a comprehensive understanding of the strengths and weaknesses of the H-21 Work Horse.

Algeria's hot, sandy environment challenged the Vertol service representatives with problems like severe rotor-blade leading-edge erosion, accelerated bearing wear, and seal failures. It also produced a mysterious condition termed "engine skip," a heart-stopping problem that also afflicted the Sikorsky H-34s operated by the French Air Force in western Algeria (the H-21 and H-34 used the same Wright R-1820 radial engine). Pierpoint described this phenomenon:

> Engine skip was a frightening experience, one I had on three separate occasions. I would be cruising serenely along when all of a sudden there was instant silence—no power at all. The rotor RPM would immediately decay and I would have to drop the collective even if I had no place to land. Then two or three seconds later there was a *blam* and the engine was running again as though nothing ever happened. To the best of our knowledge, we never lost an H-21 to engine skip, although we did bend rotor blades.[44]

On disassembly these engines yielded no clues, although most showed signs of having been overboosted by French pilots evading ground fire. The R-1820—famous as the power plant of the B-17, PBY, and some DC-3s—had been a highly reliable engine, but its adaptation to helicopter use had compromised its cooling efficiency, and Algeria's harsh conditions had taken a further toll. The Vertol people tinkered with the carburetor air ducting, mixture settings, magneto advancement and retardation, valve clearance adjust-

ment, and other components. They also worked with the French crews to modify their throttling and boost-setting procedures. Although the skip problem soon diminished to an acceptable level, its cause was never learned.

Largely through the efforts of Vice President for Engineering Lee Douglas, Vertol conducted a short-lived operations research program early in the Algerian campaign. Commandant Henri Boris, a former French resistance fighter and founder of pioneering European helicopter service Helicop-Air, convinced the French Defense Ministry to approve and support this exercise. It lasted less than a month and generated just two reports. At its conclusion in April 1957, it was recommended "that in mid-1958 development be started on a helicopter of 20,000 to 30,000 pound size as a replacement for the H-21."[45]

French helicopter operations in Algeria taught Vertol much about military helicopter requirements. From this data emerged specifications for a turbine-powered H-21 follow-on, designated as Model 107. With its preliminary design in hand, Vertol personnel briefed all branches of the U.S. military services on the new helicopter's features and capabilities. These included a rear loading ramp, added maneuverability, simplified maintenance, improved armor protection, and increased gunfire resistance. The Vertol briefings were well received because the armed services badly needed guidance on combat helicopter requirements. Rotary-wing technology had advanced too far for the limited lessons of the Korean War to be pertinent.

Even as its personnel labored in Algeria, Vertol had also conducted stateside research. Tom Peppler, chief of preliminary design, and other key engineers traveled to bases around the country to talk with military personnel of all levels about their desires in future transport helicopters. Although opinions varied widely, the consensus emerged that what was needed was the aerial equivalent of the standard Army two-and-a-half-ton truck. "Whatever the truck could carry or tow," observed historians David Anderton and Jay Miller, "the Army wanted to be able to put into a helicopter that could fly swiftly over swollen rivers, destroyed bridges, and/or impassable roads."[46]

Don Berlin was so sure that the new helicopter would be a winner that he authorized initial Model 107 development with company funds. To save money, the new turbine machine would borrow rotors and dynamic components from the H-21. This latter series enjoyed continued popularity, with Burma, Canada, Japan, Sweden, and the Soviet Union buying it. The H-21C would also be available to civil operators by the end of the 1950s, among them New York Airways, which in 1958 bought five improved fifteen-passenger Model 44Bs plus spares for $2 million.

On the business front, the Rockefeller investment group announced in the mid-1950s its intention to sell its Vertol holdings. The venture capitalists specialized in fostering the commercial application of new technologies, not managing up-and-running corporations. Vertol's gloomy near-term financial picture might also have influenced their decision. Earnings dropped as HUP manufacture declined and H-21 production ended. At the same time, the need to develop turbine helicopters and put new tooling in place for their manufacture promised a sharp rise in costs.

With the investment faction leaving just as Vertol entered dire financial straits, an infusion of new capital was desperately needed. The logical solution was to find support within the fixed-wing aviation industry. As a group, America's airplane manufacturers had emerged enormously powerful after World War II. The Korean War, the jet age, cold war tensions, and record domestic prosperity had subsequently maintained this economic vigor. Rival helicopter builders Bell and Sikorsky were already sheltered by the financial umbrella of this industry, an advantage Vertol was now anxious to share. Accordingly, Vertol board members approached the fixed-wing giants to explore merger prospects.

It appeared for a time that Northrop Aircraft (where Don Berlin had once worked and where Hart Miller was now a vice president) would be Vertol's new owner. As a condition to this merger, however, the California company stipulated that the two blocks of Vertol stock owned by the Rockefeller family group and the Piasecki Aircraft Corporation be placed into voting trusts. When the directors of Vertol and Northrop met to consummate the merger January 16, 1957, they found that the voting trust from Frank Piasecki's new company had not been executed. With action thus stalled, the merger was postponed. Barely a month later, Northrop had second thoughts and retracted the offer because, as phrased by one knowledgeable observer, "Vertol needed so damn much money to get going."[47]

Three years later, the Boeing Airplane Company succeeded where Northrop had failed. George Martin, George Schairer, Ed Wells, and other senior Boeing executives visited and thoroughly investigated the Philadelphia company before deciding in favor of acquisition. Vertol shareholders overwhelmingly approved (99.2 percent of the 80 percent who voted favored the merger) and the takeover took effect March 31, 1960. In the process, Boeing also acquired Vertol-affiliate Allied Research Associates of Boston, and subsidiary Canadian Vertol Aircraft of Arnprior, Ontario. Partly in recognition of the addition of helicopters to its product line, the Seattle-based organization renamed itself The Boeing Company on May 3, 1961.

The significance of this merger cannot be overstated. It brought about profound changes that would be essential to Vertol's survival. In a constructive clash of corporate philosophies, the Seattle giant imposed on the Vertol Division of Boeing—as the helicopter company became known—its own distinctive stamp in two primary areas.

The first was safety. Although it meant digging deep into its corporate pockets, Boeing immediately committed Vertol to a new level of product reliability. Fundamental design standards perfected in Boeing airplanes like the 707 jetliner were extended to embrace Vertol's tandem helicopters. The first was a "no-limited-life" design philosophy requiring the redesign or elimination of all components that could wear out during a helicopter's operational life, unless they were easily accessible for periodic inspection. Another was a "no-critical-failures" design philosophy that disallowed single-failure modes with catastrophic consequences; this fail-safe concept dictated backup systems and multiple structural-load paths.

Beyond corporate differences, the Boeing/Vertol merger underscored fundamental differences between the fixed-wing and rotary-wing industries. Boeing people were amazed by the relative austerity of all phases of Vertol activity, particularly R&D. They came to realize that the Philadelphia group had grown up doing a lot with very little, and they

expressed admiration that the helicopter company had done as much as it had.

For their part, Vertol engineers were happy to be able to achieve a new level of reliability and capability in their product line. Vertol had not been building helicopters on a shoestring by choice, and the sudden availability of greater resources revitalized the company on the exciting threshold of turbine production.

This 1960 merger also benefited the helicopter industry at large. In the critical area of reliability, for example, Boeing Vertol would lead the industry by producing the first and second safest military helicopters in history, the Army/USAF H-47 Chinook and the Navy/Marine Corps H-46 Sea Knight, respectively.

The second key area of change was production. Knowing how to design good helicopters does not mean a company knows how to build them efficiently and in large number. Whereas the administrators and engineers it had dispatched to Philadelphia had come from the Seattle area, Boeing's production people—who took a decidedly different approach to helicopter manufacture—came from the company's large Wichita division. The know-how of this talented team would make it possible for Boeing Vertol to achieve and sustain a production rate of thirty large helicopters a month during the Vietnam War.

Conceptual development of the Model 107 was of course under way at the time of the Northrop merger attempt. Vertol's stateside surveys and Algerian experience had been so well received by the Department of Defense that it asked the company to help write the U.S. government's own requirements for the next-generation military transport helicopter. In an effort led by Peppler and Pierpoint, Vertol wrote this document largely unaided. It thus found itself in the enviable if questionable position of tailoring military helicopter demands specifically to the machine it intended to build.

Yet another tandem helicopter program appeared on the horizon. It was learned at the start of 1957 that the Army wanted a platoon carrier, not just a squad carrier. Worries that Vertol would overextend itself trying to address this requirement for a bigger brother to the 107 helped Northrop decide to withdraw its acquisition bid. Ironically, that bigger helicopter would be the CH-47 Chinook, one of the most successful and enduring military helicopter programs in history.

But the Chinook's predecessor came first. The Model 107 design team included Carl Weiland and Bill Weller (project engineers), Tom Griffith (designer), Joe Mallen (chief aerodynamicist), Rens Swan (chief weight engineer), and Ken Grina (structures). Ren Pierpoint served as the program proposal director. The project had the enthusiastic and essential backing of Don Berlin, whose deep personal belief in the 107 program led him to gamble a million dollars on building a company-funded demonstrator based on the latest H-21 technology.

Made nearly three years before Boeing arrived to resolve Vertol's financial difficulties, this decision by Berlin displayed courage and foresight. The risky road to which he had committed Vertol would in fact be the company's salvation, poising it for enduring success in the turbine era.

Weller, Weiland, and their talented design team retained the tandem configuration to meet Model 107 operational requirements. Particularly favoring Vertol-style fore-and-aft rotors for this helicopter was military insistence on indiscriminate loadability. Troops in combat needed helicopters they could load

and fly without making painstaking weight-and-balance calculations. Here, tandem designs with their wide center-of-gravity range had an inherent advantage. Compact external dimensions, optimal utilization of internal spaces, a rear ramp, and low rotor downwash velocities near the ground also favored two rotors, which—borrowing from the HUP series—were overlapping on the 107.

The Army lent Vertol two 825-shp Lycoming T53 turboshaft engines for the company demonstrator. This civil aircraft, registration N74060, took to the air April 22, 1958. Ren Pierpoint and Bill Coffee flew it around much of the world on demonstration tours that served primarily to bolster internal morale and external perceptions of the beleaguered company. In London, this crew made headlines by landing in the Thames in front of Big Ben.

On June 26, 1958, Vertol received an Army order via the Navy for ten revised and improved Model 107s to be designated YHC-1AS. One day before this order was placed, the Army also issued an industrywide request for proposals for a "medium transport helicopter" larger than the 107. Bell, Kaman, McDonnell, Sikorsky, and Vertol all submitted proposals (limited to 125 pages at government request). Vertol was named the winner in March 1959. Shortly afterward, the YHC-1A order was reduced to three machines, the funds thus saved being diverted to the newer program.

Originally referred to as the 107-1, this new type became the Vertol Model 114 and the Army YHC-1B. A mockup and five prototypes were ordered in 1959, and another five machines—built to production standards and called HC-1Bs—were ordered in 1960. Having initiated this aircraft as chief of preliminary design, Peppler moved over to become

Introducing turboshaft power to tandem-rotor
helicopters, the Vertol 107 takes flight on April
22, 1958. Courtesy John Schneider.

program director. As he had done with the 107, Pierpoint guided the design review process to ensure that the new machine reflected everything learned by observing the French Army's use of helicopters in Algeria.

Models 107 and 114 differed primarily in size. Both featured external fuel tanks and watertight hulls for greater operational safety, and both had side-by-side turbine engines high in the aft fuselage. Company engineers, who knew what could be improved in the 107, made the newer machine better still. For example, conventional internal placement of the engines made servicing difficult, so the larger machine was designed with its engines mounted in external pods attached to the aft rotor pylon.

LaVassar made the first flight of both new turbine helicopters, testing the YHC-1A on August 27, 1959, and the YHC-1B on September 26, 1961. Between these events, Vertol was acquired by Boeing. It was this association that gave the Navy the confidence to select the further-improved and re-engined Model 107-II, which first flew on October 25, 1960, as the Marine Corps' new assault helicopter in February 1961. Briefly known as the HRB-1, this machine became the H-46 Sea Knight when the services adopted a unified system of aircraft nomenclature the following year.

Boeing Vertol agreed to a tight fixed-price contract of $295,000 per helicopter that it would soon regret. The CH-46A's first flight on October 16, 1962, revealed that the automatic blade-folding feature specified by the Navy for shipboard compatibility created high vibration levels, and Vertol engineers could not quickly cure the problem. World War II style accelerated development then being in effect, production overlapped development and helicopters were rolling off the assembly line before a fix had even been devised. Unable to deliver these machines, the company was forced to pay late penalties. It was a very stressful time at Boeing Vertol. With Vietnam on the horizon, the Navy finally relented and accepted the machines even though the blade-folding specification could not initially be met.

By 1962, Boeing Vertol had outgrown its home at Morton. Chosen for the expansion was a 290-acre site Vertol had earlier purchased along an industrial highway in Ridley Township, Pennsylvania, three miles west of Philadelphia International Airport. The heart of this complex had once been the Baldwin Locomotive Company. Tanks had also been built and tested there during World War I. If the disused facility itself was a bargain, any savings realized were more than offset by the huge sums of money Boeing subsequently poured into new plant facilities and equipment. After the relocation, Morton was left with little more than machine-shop functions during most of the Vietnam War.

The CH-46 Sea Knight entered service in 1964 as the basic USMC troop helicopter. The Navy also procured UH-46s for shuttling supplies and personnel between ships at sea. A major Navy complaint was the need to cycle these CH-46s stateside for periodic replacement of their metal rotor blades, whose life was limited by corrosion caused by the salt-water environment.

The CH-46s initially earned a poor reputation in Vietnam. They were suspected of structural weakness in the aft fuselage. A number of crashes were incorrectly attributed to this purported failing. Bill Peck and Harry Spatzer, two of the company's most talented engineers, plus support personnel were dispatched to Southeast Asia to troubleshoot. Their investigation of crashed machines

(*Top*) By the early 1960s, Boeing Vertol had outgrown its Morton plant, which may scarcely be recognized as the same facility pictured previously in this section. Courtesy John Schneider.

(*Bottom*) The Boeing Vertol CH-46 Sea Knight (Model 107) became the Marine Corps' standard troop carrier in the early 1960s. Courtesy John Schneider.

revealed that the broken aft fuselages were a coincidental symptom of other failures. One had resulted from torsional stresses induced by the catastrophic failure of a rotor blade hit by antiaircraft fire; another was caused by a main landing gear failure that initiated severe ground resonance; yet a third tail had come off when a rear rotor tangled with jungle during an attempt to land in a small clearing.

Peck and Spatzer further determined that the Marines were not properly equipped to maintain the CH-46 in Vietnam. Poor maintenance was the result. The peculiar dust in that environment—a ferruginous soil of decomposed rock called laterite—presented further operational challenges by severely eroding turbine engines.

Marine Corps flight crews in Vietnam continued to focus on the CH-46's supposedly weak rear fuselage. So shaken was their trust in the helicopter that the aft end of every CH-46 in service had to be replaced with a stronger unit. At considerable expense, these helicopters were modified at the Navy's Subic Bay depot in the Philippines. Stateside machines were similarly modified.

Boeing Vertol manufactured more than 650 H-46s before production ended in 1971, including models for Canada (CH-113), Burma, Japan, and Sweden. Since then, the company has fulfilled successive contracts to upgrade and modernize the hard-used world fleet. A civil Model 107-II, certificated by the Federal Aviation Administration in 1962, was also marketed. Manufacture for Pacific Basin military and civil markets was licensed to Kawasaki Heavy Industries in Japan in 1961.

Although the Model 107 failed to vindicate Berlin's vision of broad commercial applications, it has had some notable nonmilitary use. Among the earliest civil users was New York Airways, a helicopter airline then operating in conjunction with Pan American World Airways. A former NYA Model 107 operated at the time of this writing by Columbia Helicopters has accumulated more than 50,000 flight hours. Industry observers claim it to be the world's high-time helicopter.

Having ably led the company, Berlin had by now left Boeing Vertol because of Boeing's desire to install its own people. The best of Berlin's successors in the 1960s were finance man Bob Tharrington and engineer Howard Stuverude, exceptional executives who were popular and worked well with the Philadelphia crowd. Such would not always be the case with the leaders and engineers Boeing imposed on its new division, a number of whom were clearly not top-quality people. Even among those who were, many viewed their tenure in the East as a stepping stone to advance their West Coast careers. Derisively called "tree-huggers" by the Philadelphia crowd, these individuals made little effort to learn about helicopters and clearly could not wait to return to the Great Northwest, or Midwest in the case of Boeing Wichita personnel. Their presence took a toll on morale: it seemed Boeing leadership in Seattle did not adequately value the abilities, experience, and knowledge of the engineers and executives who had been with the Philadelphia company since the Piasecki days.

As a result, Boeing Vertol did not have one of its own people at the helm until Joe Mallen was appointed division president in 1980. An extremely capable MIT-trained engineer who first worked for Piasecki as a summer intern in 1948, Mallen had been program manager under Peppler for the B- and C-model Chinooks. A popular and able leader, he was succeeded in 1987 by Boeing-Wichita executive Don Chesnut, and Seattle veterans Ed

Renouard in 1990 and Denton Hanford in 1993. In 1996, another Philadelphia veteran, Jim Morris, was named to head Boeing Helicopters.

If any one helicopter made Boeing Vertol famous, it was the Chinook. In 1962 the YHC-1B and HC-1B prototypes were respectively redesignated YCH-47A and CH-47A, at which time—following the Army practice of naming its aircraft after Indian tribes—the Chinook name was first applied. Production pressures accelerated quickly because the Vietnam War was gearing up, allowing the first CH-47As to arrive in Southeast Asia late in 1965. They acquitted themselves well in combat from the outset, unlike the Marine Corps CH-46s. The Chinooks also retrieved more than 10,000 downed aircraft and helicopters, the majority from behind enemy lines. The value of the aircraft they recovered more than repaid the entire costs of the H-47 development program.

As the 1970s began, all was far from well with The Boeing Company. The end of lucrative NASA funding for the Apollo Program (Boeing had built the Saturn V moon booster's first stage and the Lunar Rover vehicle used in the later moon missions), stagnant domestic sales (not a single American carrier purchased a Boeing jetliner during all of 1970), cancellation by Congress of Boeing's SST program early in 1971, and a recessionary national economy together conspired to reduce total company employment from a peak of 142,400 in 1968 to only 56,300 just three years later. So dire was this downsizing, and so disastrous its effects on Seattle, that a billboard with grim humor asked the last person leaving the city to turn out the lights.

Fortunately for its corporate parent, Boeing Vertol across the continent was even then enjoying record prosperity. The Vietnam War had pushed Vertol employment above 13,000, an all-time company high, and thirty large helicopters were rolling off the assembly lines each month. Suddenly Boeing's most profitable division, it was in a position to help its Seattle parent make the transition to leaner, more efficient operations under the brilliant leadership of Thornton "T" Wilson. This traumatic process and sales of the new 747 jumbo jet helped Boeing return to robust economic health later in the decade.

By then, ironically enough, Boeing Vertol was in deep trouble. Completion in 1971 of CH-46 production had cut the division's helicopter output in half, and the end of U.S. military involvement in Southeast Asia two years later reduced CH-47 production from fifteen Chinooks per month to just one or two. As T. Wilson had so recently done in Seattle, Boeing Vertol President Howard Stuverude in Philadelphia drastically pared his division to just 4,000 employees in a short span of time. This painful downsizing was not the only change. Stuverude also consolidated operations in the Ridley Park area and sold the Morton plant—once the proud new home of Piasecki Helicopters—to the Ford Motor Company.

With 90 percent of its business gone, Boeing Vertol now struggled to survive on just twelve to eighteen helicopter deliveries per year. It naturally looked to commercial markets to offset this lost defense spending. The abysmal track record of large helicopters in commercial service—in particular, Sikorsky's staggering losses trying to foster rotary-wing airliner use—did not bode well for this venture, but Boeing Vertol was desperate for new business.

The result of this effort was the Model 234 Commercial Chinook, an extensively rede-

The CH-46/Model 107 also enjoyed strong export
sales, as this Swedish Navy example illustrates.
Courtesy John Schneider.

(Top) An Army requirement for a helicopter bigger than the Model 107 gave rise to the Boeing Vertol Model 114, which flew in Vietnam as the CH-47 Chinook. Courtesy John Schneider.

(Bottom) At the peak of Vietnam War production, Boeing Vertol was producing fifteen Chinook helicopters a month. Courtesy John Schneider.

signed helicopter airliner with rear loading stairs and 747 comfort. That twin-aisle jetliner's sidewalls, windows, overhead baggage compartments, and outboard seats (two on each side of the aisle) happened to fit perfectly into the single-aisle Chinook, saving development costs. A major hurdle in certifying this civil variant was vibration, for Chinooks simply shook too hard for passenger service.[48] Ken Grina, one of the company's most talented engineers and later vice president for engineering, successfully led a drive to reduce in-flight vibrations to a satisfactory level. This goal was achieved at great effort by building and isolating a second fuselage within the outer fuselage.

British Airways Helicopters wanted Chinooks for commercial service in support of British oil rigs in the North Sea. With promises of substantial orders from BAH, Boeing Vertol sought and received FAA certification in 1980. To this day, the Chinook remains the only large helicopter ever certified for sale on the civil market. A minimum of eighteen Model 234s needed to be sold for this program to pay for itself, but just then oil drilling declined precipitously, dashing company hopes for strong sales. BAH purchased six machines and Norway's Helikopter Service A/S another two. A couple more 234s were leased to an oil company for use in Alaska.

In desperation Boeing Vertol looked to logging companies, but these operators have always preferred to make do with used equipment. Construction Helicopters (later Columbia Helicopters) in Oregon, the largest civil user of Chinooks in the United States, bought two of its machines from British Airways. In more recent times, the 234 has been demonstrated in China as Boeing explores the possibility of its manufacture there under license. This lack of success confirmed what the industry already knew: demand for civil helicopters, particularly large ones, was too small to support a company. Whatever the consequences, Boeing Vertol's existence remained firmly tied to military markets.

Boeing built 732 military Chinooks (345 AS, 108 BS, and 270 CS) for the U.S. Army, and export versions for some 17 foreign operators including Great Britain, Australia, Canada, Italy, and Japan. These last two countries built Chinooks under license. Starting in 1980, more than 400 older Army airframes were rebuilt as CH-47DS. This new-generation Chinook evolved as a CILOP ("conversion in lieu of procurement"), making it in many ways a new aircraft. The D model's performance bears this out: with a maximum gross weight of 50,000 pounds, it can carry external loads of up to 26,000 pounds (more than double the 12,000 pound load of the A model). It also features lower operating costs and greater reliability, maintainability, and survivability than its predecessors, and it has provision for aerial refueling. A Japanese-assembled version built from components manufactured in the United States and Japan is called the CH-47J.

Yet another conversion of earlier models is producing a small number of MH-47E Chinooks for clandestine operations with the U.S. Special Operations Command. This long-range Chinook relies on sophisticated electronics and extensive cockpit integration to accomplish its covert mission. Its crews can fly at low level, day or night in almost any weather, through all types of terrain. The first production example was delivered in September 1993, and plans call for the delivery of twenty-four more through the following year.

The CH-47D Chinook competes with the Sikorsky CH-53E Super Stallion. America's

(Top) The versatile Chinook has filled many roles, like this heavily armed Vietnam-era ACH-47. Courtesy John Schneider.

(Bottom) The Boeing XCH-62—the largest and most powerful U.S. helicopter of all—was completed but did not fly before the heavy-lift helicopter (HLH) program was canceled in 1975. Courtesy John Schneider.

two largest helicopters, these machines reflect the very different design philosophies of their builders. The CH-53E is designed for performance at all costs. It can lift a slightly greater load than the more conservative CH-47D, but it needs three engines to the Boeing's two and is consequently more expensive to operate. Moreover, the single-rotor Sikorsky machine features an extremely high disc loading and heavy vibration levels, whereas the CH-47D features lower, more forgiving disc loadings. The CH-53 also relies on otherwise-composite blades with metal spars, despite the susceptibility of such spars to catastrophic failure when damaged. The Chinook, in contrast, has had failure-resistant fiberglass blades since the mid-1970s. Thus the safety record of the Sikorsky compares poorly to that of the Boeing.

The longevity of the Chinook bridged three decades during which Boeing Helicopters failed to place a single new design into production. However, the company's fortunes finally took a turn for the better when traditional rivals Boeing and Sikorsky jointly won the Army's light-helicopter (LH) contract.

The result was the RAH-66 Comanche, a stealthy, armed reconnaissance two-seater that is the centerpiece of the U.S. Army's aviation modernization plan. First flown on January 4, 1995, the Comanche is scheduled to enter service in the opening years of the twenty-first century

Another new source of production is the V-22 Osprey tiltrotor, which Boeing developed jointly with Bell. Evolving from the earlier Bell XV-3 and XV-15 experimental tiltrotors, the V-22 was developed as an assault transport for the U.S. Marine Corps. It will perform duties for all four U.S. armed services, including combat search and rescue, fleet logistics support, and special warfare

operations. In June 1996, the U.S. Naval Air Systems Command (NAVAIR) awarded the Bell Boeing Tiltrotor Team a $1.385 billion low rate initial production (LRIP) contract.

One noteworthy program early in these unproductive decades was the XCH-62, a tandem-rotor flying crane Boeing Vertol built in the mid-1970s under Peppler's leadership. Intended to address a military requirement for a heavy-lift helicopter (HLH), the XHC-62 placed ambitious technological demands on its builder. The first fly-by-wire helicopter program, the HLH's control technology was successfully tested on a Chinook variant called the Model 347.[49]

Boeing Vertol developed and built all the dynamic components for this advanced machine, including a remarkable rotor with four wide-chord blades. It also constructed an aerodynamically clean fuselage of bonded aluminum. At this late juncture, the U.S. government handed Boeing Vertol a heartbreaking setback by canceling the HLH program before the nearly completed aircraft could fly in 1975. So deeply did Boeing Vertol believe in its XCH-62 that, at considerable expense, it stored and maintained all the components for years in the vain hope the program would be reactivated. This remarkable prototype—the most brawny rotorcraft built in the United States—survives today in the collection of the Army Aviation Museum at Fort Rucker, Alabama.

Far more damaging to the company's fortunes was the loss of the lucrative Utility Tactical Transport Aircraft System (UTTAS) competition to archrival Sikorsky. Because the UTTAS was to be a single-rotor helicopter, President Stuverude named Vice President/Assistant General Manager Chuck Ellis (the only senior engineer on staff with significant single-rotor experience) as program manager. Jack Diamond was project engineer. These men and their team came up with the YUH-61, a rakish and rugged helicopter that proved remarkably reliable even in prototype form.

Sikorsky and Boeing Vertol engineers had both struggled to make their competing UTTAS prototypes capable of fitting into the cargo bay of a C-130, an initial program requirement. The two designs were consequently both topped by very low rotors that produced severe in-flight vibrations. The Sikorsky team elected almost immediately to ignore the C-130 loadability requirement by increasing the fuselage-to-rotor gap of their YUH-60. The Boeing Vertol team adhered rigorously to this unrealistic requirement long after it should have done the same.

Every time the blades of the YUH-61's bearingless, semi-rigid rotor passed low over its fuselage, the crew received another hard shake. The cumulative result was suggestive of a jackhammer. Chuck Ellis tried every trick he knew, including pendulum absorbers, but the troubling vibration remained at an unacceptable level. The problem defied solution as the team struggled to qualify the helicopter for competition.

With time slipping away, Stuverude handed the company-owned prototype to Ken Grina, who in turn enlisted the help of Joe Mallen. The two eventually solved the problem late in 1976 by unbolting the short rotor shaft and installing a longer one. With adequate spacing now between the blades and the fuselage, the jarring pounding disappeared. By then it was too late; the milestone UTTAS contract had been awarded to Sikorsky.

Ironically, the YUH-61's vibration problem could have been solved sooner but for the dogged determination of one key program engineer to meet every stated military specifi-

cation, including loadability aboard a C-130 without disassembly. Having lost UTTAS, Boeing Vertol also lost the Navy's second Light Airborne Multi-Purpose System (LAMPS) procurement. It made economic sense for that service to order a version of Sikorsky's UTTAS helicopter—the SH-60 Seahawk—to take advantage of unit cost savings stemming from high-volume production.

The Boeing Vertol YUH-61A, as it became known, was in some respects a better machine than the Sikorsky helicopter that today enjoys wide use. The dynamic system that Boeing Vertol engineers designed for it was deemed superior by a postprocurement assessment performed by the General Accounting Office. Among the advanced technology incorporated into the losing UTTAS entry was a hingeless rotor system borrowed from the Messerschmitt-Bölkow-Blohm BO 105, a West German twin-engine light helicopter.

Boeing, which held minority ownership of the MBB company, was extremely impressed with the exceptional safety and utility of this European helicopter, which Boeing engineers had helped create. Having already decided to certify and sell it in the United States, Boeing had its Vertol engineers stretch the helicopter and add air conditioning and other systems to make it more marketable. Unfortunately, currency fluctuations drove the price of the BO 105 up to $700,000, severely limiting sales and acceptance in the marketplace. For better or worse, the Philadelphia company's fortunes remained tied to military production.

The HLH, UTTAS, and LAMPS losses painfully underscored Boeing Vertol's inability from the 1960s through the 1980s to sell its programs to the military. In contrast, Sikorsky was adept at marketing and promotion,

The Boeing YUH-61 competed to become the military's successor to the Bell Huey, but rival Sikorsky won the landmark UTTAS competition in 1976. Courtesy John Schneider.

and Bell was better still. Here was where Frank Piasecki was most gravely missed, for Boeing Vertol seemed no longer to possess its founder's talent for snagging contracts. Also departing during this period were able marketers Bill Coffee, Harry Pack, Steve Tremper, and Ren Pierpont.

Pursuing new business, Boeing Vertol also participated in light rail development. This foray into surface transportation began in 1970, amid the economic woes Boeing was then suffering in Seattle. Although the Department of Defense had severely reduced its spending, federal money was available from the Department of Transportation, which had a grand vision of U.S. cities served and linked by modern, efficient trains. As envisioned by DOT planners, these trains were to combine turbine power, advanced aerodynamics, and lightweight structures— all the specialties of the U.S. aviation industry.

The Vertol Division led Boeing's effort to court this DOT business. Under this program, Vertol developed the U.S. Standard Light Rail Vehicle, an articulated self-propelled train car intended for use in major American metropolitan areas. San Francisco and Boston bought the Boeing Vertol trains, but nobody else did. Other cities instead pressured the federal government for the money, professing a desire to select their own transportation options. In this way, a worthy program devolved into political battles of will that ended a notable effort to wean America from its excessive dependence on the automobile.

Boeing lost hundreds of millions of dollars in its foray into light rail. So did Sikorsky, builder of the Washington–New York–Boston corridor's speedy MetroLiners. General Electric at Erie, Pennsylvania, also lost a great deal of money, and Budd—a neighbor of Vertol's

in Philadelphia—was driven out of business by the high-speed rail program. Boeing's reaction was to forsake diversification and concentrate on its unrivaled strengths in commercial and military aircraft manufacture.

Boeing Vertol was officially renamed Boeing Helicopters in 1988. A leader in composite structures, this company manufactures wing leading edges and assorted parts for all Boeing jetliners, including the new 777. Its 290,000 square foot Composite Manufacturing Facility, which produces advanced helicopter assemblies and fiberglass rotor blades, plays a major role in fabricating the Bell-Boeing V-22 Osprey tiltrotor.

During the 1980s, Boeing Helicopters developed the world's largest all-composite helicopter, the tandem-rotor Model 360. First flown in 1987, the 360—thanks in part to its sleek, lightweight structure—has attained a level-flight speed of 214 knots (246 mph). Only the high cost of composite construction keeps Boeing from pursuing Model 360 production at the time of this writing.

The company's administrative and manufacturing site at Ridley Township today covers 355 acres and boasts 3.5 million square feet of covered manufacturing space. This complex includes the division's headquarters, a whirl tower, a wind tunnel, and a variety of laboratories whose functions reflect the importance of total systems integration in military helicopter design today.

Success has many measures. If Boeing Helicopters is judged on the merit and quality of its products, it ranks as one of the most successful helicopter companies in history. Like its parent company in Seattle, it sets industry standards for safety and dependability.

If the ultimate measure is economic, Boeing's helicopter division has done less well,[50] and senior Boeing executives in Seattle may

After decades of tandem-helicopter manufacture, the Philadelphia company's future on the eve
of the twenty-first century rests, in part, on a
single-rotor machine. The RAH-66 Comanche
armed-reconnaissance helicopter has been jointly
developed for the U.S. Army by traditional rivals
Sikorsky Aircraft and Boeing Helicopters. Courtesy Boeing.

well be forgiven for sometimes wondering if acquiring the company in 1960 was a wise move. Enormously costly to produce and support, large helicopters find few operators in the civil marketplace. As military transports, moreover, they traditionally garner lower procurement priorities and funding levels than other classes of military aircraft.

More than a half-century after its humble beginnings as the P-V Engineering Forum of 1940, the company that Frank Piasecki founded remains the world's only original producer of tandem-rotor aircraft. Having built more than 2,500 rotorcraft to the configuration first conceived by France's Paul Cornu in 1907, what is today "Boeing Phila-delphia" will play a major role in the production of rotorcraft well into the twenty-first century.

On the eve of this new millennium, Boeing is forsaking the tandem-rotor configuration that has defined Piasecki/Vertol/Boeing helicopters for more than half a century. Future manufacture will center around the single-rotor Boeing/Sikorsky RAH-66 Comanche helicopter and the twin-lateral-rotor Bell/Boeing V-22 Osprey tiltrotor. Nevertheless, modernization programs should ensure that Boeing tandem-rotor helicopters remain in first-line U.S. military service at least through the opening decades of the coming century.

4 / Bell Helicopter

America's third successful helicopter was the first of three Model 30 research prototypes created by Pennsylvanian Arthur M. Young under Bell Aircraft sponsorship during World War II. Based on Young's pioneering research dating back to the late 1920s, these prototypes gave rise to the Bell Model 47 of 1946, the world's first commercial helicopter.

Arthur Young was born in Paris on November 3, 1905. A long way from the family home in Pennsylvania, France was nonetheless a natural place to find the Young family, since the boy's parents shared a love of art (Arthur's father, a landscape painter, had met his wife when she was a student in his art class at the Philadelphia Academy). As a small boy back in Pennsylvania, Arthur made cranes, sailboats, and other toys that demonstrated an inventive nature, discipline, and manual ability. His wide-ranging interests soon led him to construct radio receivers and transmitters fashioned with hand-wound wire coils, and to countless other projects.

By the time he entered Princeton, Young harbored a strong desire to pursue an understanding of the universe. Unraveling its mysteries through the reconciliation of science, mathematics, and philosophy became the focus of his life. Graduating in 1927, he cast about for a project to serve as an instrument

of learning. It had to be demanding and complex enough that the discipline and focus of solving it would reveal clues to fundamental laws governing the world around him. In this way and for this express purpose, Arthur Young tackled the problem of the helicopter.

Short on funds, Young moved into the local community hall where he constructed a wind tunnel and began experimenting. Since every child in the neighborhood seemed to show up to watch these unpromising efforts, Young soon discontinued. He also traveled periodically to scour the libraries of Philadelphia, Detroit, New York, Washington, D.C., or other centers for new ideas on projects and avenues to pursue.

The nature of his next challenge became clear on a trip to Washington with its Library of Congress and U.S. Patent Office. He came across a small book by Anton Flettner, who had invented a boat which, propelled by rotating cylinders, had crossed the Atlantic in 1927. The book included a picture of a large windmill with small propellers—windmills themselves—at the tips of its blades. The illustration gave Young the idea of using a similar system to power the rotor of a helicopter.

Lindbergh had only just crossed the Atlantic the year before. Fixed-wing aviation was still in its exuberant youth in the 1920s, and anybody then working on helicopters ran the risk of being labeled eccentric or worse. Still, the challenge intrigued Young because it promised significant complexities. Late in November 1928, therefore, he returned to Pennsylvania from Washington, D.C., resolved to tackle the problem of vertical flight.

In this way, Arthur M. Young embarked on a lifelong path of discovery through experimentation and observation. An original thinker, deeply philosophical, highly self-disciplined and individualistic, he now had precisely the sort of project he required to help him formulate, in his own words, "a synthesis of science and fundamental philosophy."[1] Truly remarkable helicopter achievements—including pioneering studies of rotor stability—would result from this twenty-year effort, one chapter in a greater pilgrimage of discovery.

Young's first model was six feet in diameter and built of balsa and tissue paper. Powered by rubber bands wound behind two propellers, it remained aloft ten seconds. Since model airplanes of comparable weight and power stayed aloft much longer, it was obvious to him that helicopters needed more power than fixed-wing aircraft. To learn more, he realized, he would have to construct far more sophisticated models driven by electric motors.

A modest inheritance gave Young independent if limited means to pursue research. Accordingly, he built a small workshop in the stable of his parents' home in Radnor in 1931; there, he constructed the first of a great many models and a whirling arm for testing propellers. Bartram Kelley, a boyhood friend some years Young's junior, helped him with these initial experiments.

One significant difference between Young and other helicopter experimenters was his reliance on the construction and testing of models. The reason was partly financial—full-scale helicopters were much more costly—and partly that models were more quickly built, tested, modified, and if necessary discarded. In this approach, his lack of formal engineering training was an advantage; engineers tend to work from existing theory and be bound by its limitations. Young's empirical approach revealed underlying principles that had yet to find their way into the body of rotary-wing literature.

Developing flying helicopters in miniature was no easy task. Since gear and bearing alignment was critical, the inventor spent much of his time achieving the necessary precision. To do this, Young made his own gears and bearings. Before the end of 1931, he had completed an electrically powered model with propellers at its blade tips to turn the rotor. It operated well enough, but was unsatisfactory as a proof-of-concept device because it failed to simulate the high stresses of a full-scale helicopter.

In 1933, Young decided to construct an intermediate machine using a 20-hp outboard motor to turn a rotor fully ten feet in diameter. Although much more time-consuming and costly to build than its predecessors, this larger model would realistically simulate the stresses experienced by the dynamic components of a full-scale helicopter. But before its flight characteristics could be evaluated, Young had to confront the challenge of making it hold together.

"The stresses were even larger than I had anticipated," he recorded in his journal. "On the first test the propeller blades broke off. The stress induced by rotating the small propellers at 4,000 RPM and at the same time having to reverse the direction of their rotation as the big rotor turned 400 times per minute was too much."[2]

(Top) Arthur Young contemplates the first Bell helicopter prototype in 1943. Courtesy Bell Helicopter Textron.

(Bottom) Unlike other helicopter pioneers, Young spent years working with models that gave him a unique understanding of rotor dynamics. Courtesy Bell.

Strengthening the blades caused the shafts to fail during another test. The third time around, Young built the blades of forged magnesium alloy and contoured them with a profiling machine of his own construction. He made the shafts out of nickel vanadium steel. The model held together until he tried an overspeed test with the helicopter blades in flat pitch so as not to generate lift. "This time," he noted, "it blew up with a vengeance."[3]

Although quickly summarized, these efforts—which never brought Young to his goal of evaluating helicopter flight characteristics—took place over five years. He had married in 1933, and three years later the couple moved to a farm he bought in Paoli, Pennsylvania. His helicopter research was relocated to the property's big barn, which had not even been reshingled since its erection in 1792. Young's first act was to rebuild the structure to provide him with an enclosed space 35 feet wide, 48 feet long, and 16 feet high in which to construct and fly helicopter models.

Late in 1938, Young attended the first Rotating Wing Aircraft Meeting at Philadelphia's Franklin Institute, an event organized by Burke Wilford. At that historic gathering, Igor Sikorsky stated his conviction that the most promising helicopter configuration was a single main rotor whose torque was offset by a small vertical tail rotor. Although Sikorsky had yet to begin construction of his vs-300 prototype, Young found the pioneer's argument persuasive.

Sikorsky's reliance on this configuration—which the vs-300 would vindicate three years later after flying in other configurations—was challenged at the meeting by autogiro engineer Laurence LePage. He considered Heinrich Focke's two-lateral-rotor approach far more promising. How could a tail rotor be expected to work, LePage demanded, when it sought to correct a couple with a force?

This question—paraphrased in layman's terms as *how can a twist be corrected with a pull?*—confounded the forum's attendees. Basic physics, engineers in the crowd knew, held that countering main rotor torque with a vertical tail rotor should propel the craft sideways. In fact, such movement does occur in tail-rotor helicopters, but intuitive corrective action—a slight bank to arrest lateral drift—is so easily taken that pilots are not even aware of the phenomenon. It is revealing of how little was known about helicopters in 1938 that nobody could come up with this answer to LePage's question.

From Young's point of view, a far more significant event at this meeting was the paper read by mechanical engineer Haviland Platt. Platt argued that articulated rotors—those with blades hinged at the hub—would be more stable in flight because their hinges would allow the helicopter to swing beneath its rotor without tilting the rotor itself. "This was the argument given in *Le Vol Vertical*, a French text," Arthur Young later wrote, "but it was not until I heard it from Platt that I questioned it."[4]

Like Platt, the autogiro community and most helicopter experimenters believed hinges to be the answer to the vexing problem of helicopter instability. When vertical air currents—updrafts and downdrafts—hit the rotor blades, they transmitted tilting forces to the helicopter through its rotor shaft. Hinges at or near the hub, it was widely believed, would permit these blades to flap up and down in response to such deflections without tilting the entire helicopter.

If hinges were thought to reduce instability, one type in particular, the delta-three hinge, was expected to create stability. Support for this hinge was ardent at the forum, its many proponents claiming that it would introduce automatic aerodynamic corrections to counter random upward and downward blade deflections. On the surface, the theory seemed to make sense: set 45 degrees to the blade rather than forming a right angle to it, the delta-three hinge would automatically impart a nose-down tilt to rising blades and a nose-up tilt to dropping blades, thus making them aerodynamically self-centering.

Young felt intuitively that hinges, even of the delta-three variety, would not in themselves produce stability. Platt's assurances that they would, and Sikorsky's argument for the single-main-rotor-with-tail-rotor configuration, together set the Pennsylvanian on a new course of empirical studies at the end of 1938.

That meant abandoning the unpromising 20-hp blade-tip-propeller helicopter. If it was daunting to start over almost from scratch, Young could at least reuse his handmade bearings and gears. The machine with the propellers on the tips of its blades had also given him valuable experience in designing strong structures and computing stress loads.

As 1939 began, Young initiated a new series of experiments with simple one-sixth-scale models whose five-foot rotors were turned by electric motors salvaged from vacuum cleaners. The speed with which these tests now progressed showed Young that working on a larger scale had been counterproductive; discoveries made with the big model had taken longer and cost more money.

With these new models he evaluated a variety of rotor configurations. Whether their blades were fixed or hinged made no differ-ence—all displayed a chronic lack of stability. Once in the air, the models dipped and raced in widening swings until they tipped over and crashed. Here was the classic hovering instability that, together with the gremlin of vibration, so clearly explained the chronic lack of success bedeviling early helicopter pioneers.

"Many earlier helicopters had received backing only to crash on their trial run," Young noted. "The backers then pulled out and the project collapsed. I felt you had to have the crackups before the initial flight, because the crackups were teaching you something."[5]

Young now sought a more effective mechanism for making helicopters stable. To avoid unproductive avenues of investigation, he decided to try to identify those variables truly important to stability so that he could concentrate on them and ignore the rest. It was in the course of this research in his rebuilt barn that he came to examine the phenomenon of "rotor following" and made a discovery that threw existing helicopter theory out the window.

Young had discovered that rotors—even those with hinged blades—follow their masts to new orientations far more quickly than was generally believed. The accepted theory, an intuitive guess which had found its way into the literature of the day, was that rotors acting as gyroscopes would initially resist shifts in orientation. If the rotor shaft tilted, the whirling blades of the rotor would hold their previous orientation before slowly coming around to perpendicular rotation around the mast in its new position.

Films made by Young of a bench-mounted helicopter model belied this theory. As he tilted the model, its articulated rotor spinning at high speed, the blades followed with little or no perceptible lag. By extension, Young reasoned that the reverse was also true: deflections originating in the rotor were translated to the shaft—and thus to the helicopter itself—much too quickly for hinges to have an opportunity to screen out destabilizing blade motions.

What was needed, Young concluded, was a way to decouple the rotor from the mast. If the rotor plane could be made to lag behind when the mast shifted, instead of remaining aggressively perpendicular to it, substantial gains in stability would result. Accordingly, the inventor set out to increase the following time of the rotor.

As so often happens with discovery, the solution came fairly quickly once the proper question was asked. In December 1939 the inventor hit upon the idea of using a stabilizer bar set transversely to the rotor blades. Later patented as the Bell "fly bar," this device would be at the heart of the remarkably successful Bell Model 47 helicopter.

With small weights at its tips, Young's stabilizer bar was set at 90 degrees to the blades, where it was free to teeter. A control linkage connected it to the blades, allowing it to change their pitch and thus modify their lift. When the rotor tilted, this bar—acting like a gyroscope—retained its previous orientation for a time, appearing to seesaw once per revolution as it struggled to describe the old plane of orientation even as the helicopter's rotor assumed a new one. The bar automatically imparted cyclic corrections to the rotor, prompting it to retain its previous orientation. Rotor following time was increased, and gusts and other extraneous influences on the rotor—formerly highly destabilizing—were rendered innocuous.

The increase in lag time was truly dramatic. Movies of Young tilting a model fitted with his new stabilizer bar show the rotor spinning in its previous orientation for a very long time before gradually coming around to its shaft's new angle. When tested in flight, Young's bar produced similarly dramatic results. "With the addition of this device," the inventor stated, "the model performed remarkably, showing great stability. In a few days I was flying the helicopter in the barn. I could even hover it motionless."[6]

On the eve of inventing the fly bar, Young had attended the 1939 Rotating Wing Aircraft Meeting, which again was held at the Franklin Institute. By late 1939 he knew more about rotor dynamics than any other person. Certainly no one else in the world had given so much consideration to the issue of rotor stability.

On the afternoon of November 29, 1939, the event's opening session, Young delivered the paper "A New Parameter of Lifting Rotors." In it he traced his findings to date, stopping short only of describing the decoupling bar he already envisioned (the device had still to be tested and a patent applied for). Since Young's talk refuted hinges as an approach to rotor stability just when other autogiro and helicopter developers were pinning their hopes on them, this historic presentation exerted less influence that it deserved.

Back in Paoli, Young by early 1940 was actually flying his stabilizer bar on a model helicopter with coaxial rotors. The top rotor spun at high speed to provide lift. Below it, turning more slowly in the opposite direction, was an anti-torque rotor whose broad vanes—angled downward to prevent them from striking the blades—reduced the model's tendency to spin in flight. When the air was still, this model would climb straight up two hundred feet (that being the length of its power cord).

It flew very well on windy days too, although Young—with no control other than lift—had no way to prevent the wind from carrying it sideways.

Young's next step was to construct a fully controllable model. With that in hand, he could approach aircraft manufacturers about producing full-size helicopters (he had no interest in forming a company of his own to undertake manufacture). Recalling Sikorsky's persuasive arguments at the 1938 Rotating Wing Aircraft Meeting, Young built this demonstration model to the single-main-rotor-with-vertical-tail-rotor formula.

At that time in Connecticut, Sikorsky was busy taming and refining his VS-300 prototype. He doubtless would have been shocked to learn of Young's success with models, which are far less stable than full-size machines. These two towering figures in helicopter development had approached the issue from diametrically opposite directions. Of America's first-rank rotary-wing pioneers, Young had paid the most attention to the workings of the rotor itself, and Sikorsky the least.

Young's demonstration model was a masterpiece of compact precision engineering. Clad in Bakelite and painted bright red, the cylindrical craft looked like a submarine topped by a five-foot-diameter two-bladed rotor. Since there was no way to achieve remote control with the stabilizer bar fitted, he had substituted a flywheel above the rotor to perform the same function. A vertically mounted electric motor in the fuselage drove the main rotor through reduction gearing. Ringing its shaft in the wide pylon atop the fuselage were four vertical solenoids to provide lateral rotor control. A separate electric motor in the nose drove the tail rotor through a long shaft.

One example of Young's genius was his use of a gyroscope in the nose to coordinate the output of the two electric motors to ensure precise directional control. If the helicopter's nose tried to swing left or right, the gyro would precess; this would alter the voltage flowing to the tail rotor's motor, increasing or decreasing its power as required to maintain a constant heading.

A wire connected the helicopter to a box worn around Young's neck. With a joystick and other controls, he maneuvered it around the barn, then out the door and back. Later, he filmed it being put through its paces outdoors in strong gusty winds.

By the third and last Rotating Wing Aircraft Meeting, held in New York late in January 1941, Young must have seemed like a wizard to his fellow attendees. He began his talk by flying simple rubber band-powered models made of aluminum cigar tubes to illustrate aspects of rotary-wing stability. A first model with the rotor on top illustrated his contention that helicopters are inherently *unstable*. He next flew a model with a rotor at bottom to demonstrate that placing the center of lift *below* the center of gravity produces some stability in upright flight; this stability lasts until, inevitably, the craft finally tips over and propels itself into the ground. Finally, he flew a third model—with rotors at each end thrusting in the same direction—to illustrate the one formula for total inherent stability: having the center of lift right at the center of gravity. This toy flew beautifully in the large auditorium.

Young was not proposing that helicopters be designed with rotors around their middles. He hoped to show that the vehicle whose development was then being pursued around the world was not stable, and to suggest that methods were needed to achieve that stabil-

Young flies his model helicopter by remote control early in 1941. Courtesy Bell.

ity. His fellow attendees might have expected the presentation to end at that point, but the inventor went on to reveal that he had come up with a way to do precisely that. Without further ado, he showed a movie of the remote-controlled model.

On the screen that evening, America's assembled rotary-wing fraternity saw Young's model fly with a stability even full-size machines had never demonstrated. More than a few noted experimenters must have felt profound shock, particularly those whose faith in the delta hinge as an approach to stability had been shattered. First to speak was Igor Sikorsky, who with characteristic humility politely offered Young his heartfelt congratulations. If Arthur Young had perhaps been viewed by some as an outsider at earlier meetings, he was now fully accepted as one of America's premier helicopter pioneers.

With this film and the model itself, Young began early in 1941 to try to interest private industry in his helicopter. He quickly found that the fixed-wing aircraft industry as a whole had little interest in helicopters, however well perfected. Brewster Aircraft near Philadelphia was a rare exception, its executives making an offer to develop Young's helicopter in a highly secretive program. The dealings of this company struck Young as less than reassuring, however, and the proposed program itself remained ambiguous despite his efforts to elicit answers. He decided to continue looking.

He also hoped to interest the U.S. military in his helicopter. He demonstrated his model at the Philadelphia Navy Yard early in 1941, and was told that the Navy had no interest in helicopters. He next traveled to Ohio to try the Army Air Corps at Wright Field. Captain H. Franklin Gregory, the flight development center's rotary-wing project officer,

had the previous year awarded a contract to Platt-LePage to develop the XR-1 military helicopter, and at the start of 1941 had issued a second contract to Sikorsky for the XR-4.

Gregory told Young that he would issue a research contract funding detailed evaluation of the latter's stabilizer bar. At that time, however, Gregory's attention was focused on the Platt-LePage helicopter, which was just days away from flying for the first time. Perhaps also because America's rush to gird itself for war preempted minor projects, the promised contract failed to materialize.

When both the XR-1 and XR-4 subsequently had stability and control problems, it was too late for the Army to avail itself of Young's direct services. By then he had found industry support.

Dr. John Sharp, a friend of Young's, had occasion to visit the Bell Aircraft Corporation in upstate New York. There he casually mentioned Young's remote-controlled helicopter to an engineer named Jack Strickler, who in turn mentioned it to company founder Lawrence D. Bell.

Neither an engineer nor a great businessman, Larry Bell was a gifted salesman with the remarkable ability to inspire others. Born in 1894 in Mentone, Indiana, the youngest of ten children, Bell moved with his family to California at the age of thirteen. Upon graduation from high school, he worked as an aircraft mechanic for his aviator brother, Grover E. Bell, and legendary stunt flier Lincoln Beachy. Grover's death in a crash July 4, 1913, and Beachy's the following year, were severe blows to Larry though he never lost his love of aviation. He learned to fly in 1928.

Bell went to work for the tiny Martin Company in Los Angeles, where his organizational skills, salesmanship, and hard work won him the title of superintendent before his twenty-first birthday. By then, he had already hired Donald Douglas fresh out of the Massachusetts Institute of Technology as the company's first professional engineer. Having orchestrated Martin's move in 1917 to Cleveland, Ohio, and risen to the posts of vice president and general manager, he felt it was time he had a share in the ownership of the company he had helped build. When Glenn L. Martin disagreed, Bell—still in his twenties—left in 1925. Jobs in aviation were scarce, however, and he sold machine tools for several years.

Returning to aviation in 1928, Bell joined Consolidated Aircraft in Buffalo, New York, where he became vice president and general manager. Recently formed by Major Reuben H. Fleet, a former Army flier-turned-procurement officer to whom Bell had previously sold Martin airplanes, Consolidated specialized in the manufacture of large flying boats for the U.S. Navy. Buffalo's harsh winters prompted the company to move to San Diego in 1935, where flying boats could be tested the year round.

Larry Bell stayed behind because this move presented him with the long-awaited chance to enter aviation manufacture for himself. Although the Depression made financing very difficult, Bell and other would-be officers of the new company—including brilliant aircraft designer Robert J. Woods—succeeded in forming the Bell Aircraft Company in 1935.

Bell Aircraft's first airplane, the YFM-1 of 1937, was an all-metal twin-engine fighter plane. Among its features were pusher propellers to make room for a manned gun blister in its wings. Hailed as a war-winning weapon, the YFM-1—soon revised with a tricycle landing gear as the YFM-1A—was in fact hopelessly ill-suited to the realities of the emerging war. The unwieldy craft could not have survived against either Germany's Messerschmitt BF 109 or Japan's Mitsubishi Zero, but its popularity in the prewar press won Bell the chance to build a better fighter plane using the winning single-seat, single-engine formula.

Bell thus joined Lockheed and Curtiss (the latter also located in Buffalo) as a primary producer of Army fighter planes at the time of America's entry into World War II. During this conflict, Bell produced some 12,900 P-39s and P-63s (the latter a much-improved development of the former), more than half of which went to the Soviet Union under Lend-Lease. Bell also built 663 B-29 Superfortress bombers under license to Boeing at a huge government-owned facility in Marietta, Georgia. The mother ship that would carry Chuck Yeager and the Bell X-1 aloft to break the sound barrier in 1947 was in fact a Bell-built B-29.

Before the first P-39 rolled down the assembly line, Larry Bell was already looking ahead to the postwar era. Peace could not come quickly enough for the nation, yet when it did a vast and growing work force at Bell would find itself out of work. The responsibility for providing employment into the postwar era weighed heavily on Bell, who cared deeply about people.

Larry Bell strongly shared the prevailing belief that the postwar era would see personal flying machines used as aerial automobiles. Based on his boundless enthusiasm for aviation, bolstered by the accelerating pace of technological advancement, Bell's sanguine if inaccurate vision of things to come included a starring role for the helicopter in both private and commercial service.

Through Strickler and Sharpe, Bell invited Arthur Young to visit Buffalo and demon-

Larry Bell sponsored Arthur Young's work because he believed that a market would emerge for privately owned helicopters after World War II. Courtesy Bell.

strate his model helicopter. The inventor did so on September 3, 1941, flying the model on the Bell factory floor between assembly lines of Airacobra fighters under construction. Off giving a VIP tour, Bell himself had his first glimpse of Young's accomplishments as he led several important visitors by.

Bell and Young liked each other from the start. The agreement they reached called for the inventor to assign his patents to Bell Aircraft. In return, the company would underwrite development of two full-scale research prototypes. Young insisted on two as protection against program cancellation in the event one should crash. Bell agreed to assign the skilled workers needed by Young, who further stipulated that Bartram Kelley should be hired as his assistant. For his part, Bell named only one additional requirement: the second

prototype was to be a two-seater so that he could ride in a helicopter.

Trained in mathematics and physics at Harvard University, Bart Kelley had grown up in Radnor, Pennsylvania, where he had met Young when he was five and the latter nine. In 1931, Kelley had interrupted his university studies to help Young with his first electrically powered model helicopter, the rotor of which was turned by propellers at its blade tips. During this apprenticeship, he learned about aerodynamics and aeronautical theory from his self-taught friend. His own growing fascination with helicopters had led him to assist Young again some years later, and at this juncture to leave a comfortable teaching post for the unknown challenges of the fledgling Bell helicopter program.

Although perhaps lacking Young's creative genius, Kelley was brilliant in his own right. Whereas Young would soon depart Bell and divorce himself from vertical flight, Kelley remained with the company for decades. He moved with the company to Texas in the early 1950s and rose to become senior vice president in charge of engineering for Bell Helicopter.

On November 24, 1941, Young and Kelley arrived at Bell's busy Elmwood Avenue plant in Buffalo, New York, for their first day of work.[7] The two friends signed in and soon found themselves seated in the office of Robert J. Woods. Gracious and amiable, Bell's noted chief engineer nevertheless had little time for helicopters. His new charges could not help but feel they were somewhat of a burden to the busy designer of Bell's warplanes.

Less than two weeks before Pearl Harbor plunged America into World War II, a major expansion of facilities was well along at Bell Aircraft. Young and Kelley felt overlooked and unwanted in the bustling plant. So great was their initial confusion and uncertainty that both men wondered if there was any real hope of building helicopters as agreed. They had no idea how to do things through channels and no one seemed to have time to teach them, but they soon managed to set up a shop in the middle of the factory. In line with wartime security requirements, Bell designated this minimal facility Gyro Test in a vain attempt to disguise its real purpose.

"It was a very feeble shop," Bart Kelley recalls. "We weren't doing anything, we weren't building anything real. I remember doing a lot of calculating while we were sitting there, extrapolating performance, trying to figure how big the rotor should be and how fast it should turn; that sort of thing."[8]

"When I arrived at Bell," Young adds, "I thought there would be engineers and experts on many subjects; that we'd immediately start building a full-scale helicopter after I told them how big it would be. But nothing happened. They were all too busy with war contracts following December 7."[9]

Nevertheless, two major milestones were met and passed in Gyro Test. First, Young developed a model capable of being scaled up into a manned prototype (the flywheel-stabilized model he had brought with him was not suited to this purpose). Second, he demonstrated to Bell that helicopters could indeed make safe autorotation landings.

With safety a deep personal concern since the death of his brother, Larry Bell had demanded proof that helicopters could land safely if their engines failed. If not, he had no wish to proceed with Young's development. Turning as always to models to settle the issue, Young built a simple one that descended from the plant's thirty-foot ceiling, its freewheeling rotor spinning like a pinwheel, and landed so softly that it did not crack the raw

egg that was its payload. Bell was so pleased with the demonstration that he released $250,000 in funding that he had been holding up.

This money was originally earmarked for making drawings, a fact Young and Kelley had learned when a carpenter showed up at Gyro Test to begin sawing down its walls. When the perplexed occupants asked why, the worker replied that the area was being enlarged to accommodate twenty-four drafting tables. This reply illustrated for Young the incompatibility of embarking on rotary-wing development in a fixed-wing aircraft factory. Building on forty years of experience, airplanes could be completely designed before a prototype was built, but helicopter technology was only then emerging.

Precision components like rotors, linkages, transmissions, and shafts required manufacturing drawings beforehand, but not the rest of the machine. The project would be doomed if an attempt to draw everything was made at the outset. Young needed to approach development from the opposite direction. To him it made sense to hand build Bell's two research prototypes from scratch, freely improvising and modifying without consulting time-consuming drawings fraught with unanticipated mistakes. These machines would be research ships, not production prototypes. Even after they were tested and refined, there would be no need for full drawings because they themselves were not to be mass-produced. Experience gained with them would be the basis for helicopters to be marketed. That would be the time for complete drawings.

Bell's corporate culture was so stifling to Young that he came close to quitting. The technical challenges were enormous enough. "I went over to my temporary shop in the factory, mocked up an engine and, twenty feet away, a tail rotor," he wrote. "How would I ever fill the space between with actual machinery that would lift 2,000 pounds into the air?"[10]

Even working on the intricate model from which full-size prototypes were to be built was a challenge. "I often had to work the moonlight shift from 12:00 midnight to 8.00 A.M.," Young later recalled, "because machine equipment was occupied during the day. I upset the payroll people because I was going in and out of the factory in quite an irregular fashion and I got the time clock all mixed up."[11]

To speed things up, Young bought his own lathe, vise, and drill press when all attempts to order them through channels failed. These nonstandard items confounded the company's inventory process, costing Bell more in paperwork and lost productivity than it would have spent providing the equipment.

By April 1942, an engine had arrived. A month earlier, Young and his small group had completed detail design of a full-scale rotor hub. Most of the parts needed to make a helicopter did not then exist, however, and there was a long way to go in a short time if he was to succeed.

Young took long weekends back in Paoli to think things through. Gradually a possible solution emerged: He would relocate his development effort away from the main plant, gathering a team in an environment furthering experimental work by providing direct communication and easy cooperation between members. He issued a memorandum to that effect back in Buffalo. When it failed to produce any results, he engaged the services of a real estate agent who quickly located an empty Chrysler automobile dealership. Although small, the facility offered Young precisely what he needed.

Young's relocation to Gardenville in the spring of 1942 was barely noticed at the main plant. Bell was busy building the top-secret XP-59A, America's first jet plane; testing a midget wooden fighter plane, the XP-77; setting up a separate ordnance division in Burlington, Vermont, to produce machine gun mounts and power-operated bomber turrets; preparing to open its own aircraft modification center; and running a P-39 maintenance training program. When in 1940 it had become evident that the Buffalo plant could not accommodate a wartime expansion, Bell had initiated construction of a new government-financed $8.5 million factory at Niagara Falls Airport in nearby Wheatfield, New York.

In contrast to the main plant, Young's little Chrysler agency—shut down by a wartime halt to automobile manufacture—was a haven of tranquillity. Set in rural surroundings at the intersection of Union and Lesser Roads in Gardenville, New York, ten miles east of Buffalo, it offered a large backyard suitable for run-ups, with a small meadow beyond big enough for limited flying.

Inside, a well-heated showroom suitable for offices fronted a somewhat drafty garage area just big enough for construction of two or three small helicopters. The showroom was divided with partitions into an administrative office, a machine shop, a drafting area called the paper shop, a woodworking area, and a model shop.

The Gardenville team initially numbered about fifteen. Over the three years this facility was active, the work force never exceeded thirty-two. Young directed operations, ably assisted by Kelley and Tom Harriman, a young Bell employee selected by Young to join the team. A year later came Charles Seibel, the group's first formally trained aeronautical engineer.

Danny McVey, John Pozda, and Pete Allen—three of Bell Aircraft's finest master machinists—made whatever metal parts and components were needed in the machine shop. Tom Darner, who had made blades for Young's helicopter models in Pennsylvania, and two professional woodworkers constructed full-scale rotor blades in the woodshop. Chief Draftsman Ed Cook, a former member of the New York Yankees baseball team, headed the paper shop. One of his junior draftsmen was Willard "Red" Russert; another was Jack Buyers, who would later be project engineer of the Bell UH-1 Iroquois, or Huey.

The Gardenville group over time also included Percy Waller, Butch Luke, Karl Camp, Harry Finnegan, and Frank H. "Bud" Kelley. Bart and Bud Kelley—not related— were two of six Gardenville members who would learn to fly the team's first helicopter.

Without the help he had expected from Bell's professional engineers, Young scaled up his remote-control model as a point of departure for design of a full-size machine. The rotor and other dynamic components of the Bell Model 30, as the prototype taking shape was designated, were those of Young's model but considerably refined and six times larger.

The body of the Model 30 was fashioned by hand around a center section of welded steel tubing housing the engine mount and main rotor pylon. Plywood and sheet metal were used extensively elsewhere in the aircraft. The magnesium tail boom was the only major component not built in Gardenville; of semi-monocoque construction, it was manufactured at the main plant in Buffalo.

The Model 30's rotor blades were of laminated spruce with a metal insert in the leading edge and balsa behind for chordwise balance. This construction produced fairly uniform fore-and-aft weight distribution across the ten-inch chord of the blade. The initial NACA 0012 symmetrical airfoil was later superseded by a NACA 2312 profile for greater lifting efficiency, even though the latter was more difficult to produce.

The transmission employed a double planetary gear with free-floating pinions. Of two transmission ratios built, 9:1 and 10.5:1, the former proved optimal. An initial problem of high engine wear and shortened life, attributable to this unit, would be solved over time by better alignment of gears and bearings.

Six months after work began at Gardenville, the helicopter was ready. On December 18, 1942, a bitterly cold day, the yellow machine was rolled out of the shop on a dolly. A skid landing gear of four 12-foot duralumin tubes—much too wide to fit through the door—was attached outside as snow swirled down. Huge icicles hanging from the building's roof framed the scene as a bottle of champagne was broken over the prototype, which was christened *Genevieve*.

The gear attachment and ceremony had taken so long that the by-then-frozen 160-hp Franklin engine refused to start. Part of the problem was the lack of a clutch, which required the machine's builders to spin the 32-foot-diameter rotor by hand in order to take sufficient strain off the engine for it to start. The wide skids were therefore taken off again and Bart Kelley's car was used to tow the craft back indoors. Perhaps because of the ignominious occasion, the name *Genevieve* did not stick. The first Bell helicopter would simply be known as Model 30 or, to distinguish it from its two successors, Ship 1.

Adding a second battery to the power cart solved the cold-weather starting problem. Run-ups and tethered tests began with Young himself at the controls. Raising the machine

Bartram Kelley (left) helps Young insert the rotor
mast and transmission gearing into the Bell Model
30 as construction proceeds, October 1942. Courtesy Bell.

a foot or two off the ground and feeling out its controls, he logged about eight hours in the machine. One problem emerged right away: in winds of twenty miles per hour or so, the machine severely shook its pilot on his wooden bench seat.

At this promising juncture, a visit by Bell's chief test pilot brought the project's first major setback. Just before the year was out, Robert Stanley—soon to be the company's chief engineer—visited Gardenville. He had heard that the Bell helicopter was ready to fly. Although he lacked rotary-wing experience, he felt that he should be the first to fly this machine. Stanley gingerly hovered, feeling out the craft's controls. To the dismay of the Gardenville team, the test pilot lost control as a pilot-induced oscillation developed. A particularly violent buck tossed him upward into the rotor, which shot him sideways into a snowbank. Miraculously, his injuries were confined to a broken arm.

Lying on his back on a desk in the office where the others had carried him, Stanley telephoned Larry Bell. "I'm sorry," he told the company president miserably, "but I've delayed your helicopter a little."[12]

Bob Stanley returned within days to flying fighter planes, but the helicopter he left behind was not so lucky. Its tail had broken off. Since there was no time to have another made at the main factory, an unattractive but functional truss of welded steel tubing was substituted. This utilitarian tail anticipated the steel-tube tails that would distinguish Bell's production helicopters for years to come.

Testing of the repaired machine was now turned over to Floyd W. Carlson, a junior member of Bell's flight test department. Although flying fighters hardly prepared him for rotary-wing experience, Carlson quickly mastered the craft's controls and was soon hovering in place without difficulty. Methodical to the point of stubbornness, he proved ideally suited to the often repetitive demands of testing a new type of aircraft.

Although not an engineer, Carlson spent long hours with Young, Kelley, and others going over drawings. He asked countless questions. When Buffalo's notorious weather ruled out flying, his interest kept him on the job when other test pilots would have taken the day off with a clear conscience. Carlson's contribution to the eventual success of the program would be significant.

Bob Stanley's needless accident made Young extra conservative, despite his new test pilot's obvious skill. He did not allow the helicopter to fly free of its tethers until June 26, 1943, when Carlson took it slowly around the meadow behind the dealership. This historic occasion established the Bell prototype as America's third successful helicopter.

That it was the third and not the second was purely a matter of circumstance. Stanley's crash at the end of 1942 substantially delayed the Gardenville effort, whereas an equally unexpected event on the outskirts of Philadelphia—ironically, at another converted automobile dealership also closed for the duration—had greatly accelerated the test program of the Piasecki PV-2. Although begun after Bell's, that machine flew on March 11, 1943, when a tether snapped during Frank Piasecki's first attempt to hover. Fittingly, both the original Bell Model 30 and the Piasecki PV-2 are preserved in the collection of the National Air and Space Museum in Washington, D.C.

Initial testing showed the Bell prototype to be too stable, a problem that would have

Pilot Floyd Carlson familiarizes himself with the
tethered Model 30 behind the Gardenville facility. Courtesy Bell.

evoked the envy of Igor Sikorsky. Moreover, rotor forces tended to rock the stabilizer bar around, requiring Carlson to make corrections with the cyclic control stick. To solve the former problem, Young made the bar follow the mast a bit more quickly. To correct the latter, he installed automotive shock absorbers to provide damping on the bar.

Although at least a half dozen control systems were tried, the one the team settled on consisted of a cyclic control stick topped by a motorcycle-style twist-grip throttle, and a "pump handle" collective lever coming out of the left side of the instrument panel. Moving the cyclic stick forward, backward, or to the side moved the helicopter accordingly through cyclic pitch variations of the main rotor; raising or lowering the collective lever increased or decreased lift by changing overall rotor blade pitch; and moving the collective side to side changed the blade pitch of the tail rotor for yaw control.

This approach differed from the control system perfected by Sikorsky, which was soon universally adopted. The Gardenville team knew of the Sikorsky arrangement, but shied away from it because of Larry Bell's insistence that Bell helicopters not have airplane-style "rudder" pedals. They were to have as much commonality with automobiles as possible.

The same hard vibration that had first occurred during static hovering in winds of twenty or more miles per hour now appeared in flight. This phenomenon—called "two-per-rev" vibration because the machine shook twice during each rotor revolution—is characteristic of rotors having two blades. Sikorsky encountered it in August 1941 when he tried a two-bladed rotor on his VS-300; two-per-rev vibration prompted a hasty return to three blades.

Floyd Carlson crept around the meadow in the Model 30 no faster than a man could run. On the assurances of newly arrived team member Charles Seibel, whose wind tunnel analysis indicated that the phenomenon would abate as speed increased, he did fly successfully through the severe shaking to smooth cruise at higher speed. Although Seibel's prediction proved accurate, the intensity of the interim vibration was great enough that Young called a halt to flying until a fix could be found.

Born in Iowa and raised in Wichita, Kansas, Charlie Seibel came to Bell with a master's degree in aeronautical engineering from the California Institute of Technology. While there, he learned of the Bell program when told that another Cal Tech graduate—Bob Stanley—had broken his arm flying a helicopter. During a visit to California, Stanley himself hired the young engineer when he mentioned that helicopter theory was the subject of his thesis.

Bart Kelley soon revealed the specific cause of the two-per-rev problem in a brilliant mathematical analysis of the phenomenon. He had already applied his remarkable intellect to finding a mathematical explanation for the workings of the Young stabilizer bar, and he would soon be granted valuable patents stemming from pioneering analyses of rotor shaft vibrations. The solution to the two-per-rev problem came not from Kelley, however, or from Seibel or Young. The Model 30's pilot made this contribution to the program.

Carlson suggested that a brace fitted above the rotor hub might solve the vibration by providing chordwise stiffening of the blades. Only nineteen days after flying had been interrupted, the Model 30 was back in the air fitted with a "Swedish yoke" (this name a humorous reference to the test pilot's ancestry). With the two-per-rev problem now

Work proceeds in the converted Gardenville automobile dealership that was home to Bell's helicopter team. Two Model 30s are visible, Ship 2 in the foreground and Ship 1 behind. Courtesy Bell.

cured, speeds of up to 70 mph were routinely attained. The yoke, a stopgap measure, was needed only until stiffer rotor components could be designed and installed.

The test pilot's solution illustrates a unique characteristic of Gardenville, which was a nucleus of creation in the truest sense. When the team conferred mornings in the showroom or retired to lunch at Schmaltz's, a roadhouse diagonally across from the Gardenville facility, Young would put out what others called "the problem of the day" for all to consider. Every team member was invited to contribute to its solution.

Nobody solved more helicopter challenges than Young himself, of course. A true inventor, he mulled problems over every waking moment and his subconscious carried on while he slept. He often awoke with the answer. Even the commute to Gardenville and back—a ride shared with Bart Kelley because of wartime gasoline rationing—was productively spent (regular hours were worked at Gardenville, which had a time clock like the main plant).

At this juncture, the fuselage and tail boom were covered and the entire helicopter was given an attractive dark blue paint scheme with yellow trim. A large windshield was fitted, wheels were substituted for the cumbersome skids, and an experimental civil registration number (NX-41867) was painted on its flanks. The Model 30 now looked more like a personal helicopter than an engineering prototype.

Having outgrown the tiny meadow behind the plant, the helicopter was towed by car to Military Road Airfield, a small private airstrip near the river on Buffalo's west side. Flying tests immediately revealed that much less power was needed in forward flight than in hover; the team had known this would be the case, but it had not appreciated to what degree. Carlson was embarrassed to find himself flying higher than the surrounding trees without meaning to.

The time had come to perform an autorotation to the ground, a necessary milestone if flights at altitude were to be performed. While the theory was well known and Young's model had successfully autorotated in Gyro Test eighteen months earlier, a power-off landing in the full-scale Model 30 carried an element of risk.

These tests were flown early in September 1943 at Gardenville Airport, a grass airfield much nearer the converted Chrysler agency. Without hesitating, Carlson performed a first autorotation, which was completely successful. The rollout was long because he had landed with considerable forward airspeed arrested only by a mild flare. The test pilot then flew a second autorotation, this time flaring more sharply before touching down, but the rollout was still longer than desirable in an emergency landing. Determined to kill off his forward airspeed, he attempted a third autorotation with an even more pronounced flare.

The instant it touched down, the helicopter split in two, slewed to the left, and came to a stop on its right side as parts rained down all around. Horrified observers came running from all directions to find Carlson miraculously unscratched. Dejected, they began to salvage what they could.

The tail boom and rotor blades had been destroyed and the machine looked ready for the scrap pile. But a postcrash survey showed the dynamic components to be relatively undamaged, and it soon became clear that the faithful Model 30 could be rebuilt. In a meeting held on the spot, Young and his team decided to finish up Ship 2, then almost ready.

Inventor Arthur Young (center) walks Ship 1 out
of the workshop. This first Model 30 has been
revised with stiffened rotor components, a wheeled
landing gear, and fabric covering painted dark blue
with yellow trim. Courtesy Bell.

to fly, and let it take over the test program.

The immediate cause of Ship 1's crash was the failure of a bottom bolt attaching the tail boom to the fuselage, but the accident had happened so quickly that nobody was sure why. Young's insistence that movies be made of testing now paid dividends, for the film revealed that the landing gear design was at fault. Too large and set too far aft, the tail wheel had hit first during Carlson's third autorotation; the upward load it imposed on the tail far exceeded structural design limits, and the boom had gone up into the main rotor. A need for dynamic stops on the rotor was also highlighted, as was the desirability of raising the tail rotor for ground clearance during autorotative landings.

The second Bell Model 30, also painted blue, was rolled out late in September 1943. This trim machine—employing all-metal semi-monocoque construction—would have been finished sooner except for the Bell company's insistence that its lines suggest a P-39 Airacobra. "A designer struggled with the idea for over a year," stated Young, "and when it was finally wheeled out, we found that two people couldn't get in because it was too streamlined. The cockpit, of course, had to be widened which took more time."[13]

Not willing to wait for Bell to produce more drawings, issue approvals, and finally construct parts, Young asked a friend who was a New York City architect-turned-interior designer to come up with a pleasing redesign. The result was the bulbous enclosed cabin which Ship 2 retained throughout its test career (unlike the much-modified first prototype, this aircraft was not altered over the course of its operational life).

This helicopter (NX-41868) featured rudder pedals and a single collective lever between the seats. At Carlson's insistence, a second lever was added at left after he nearly suffered several mishaps from having to grip the cyclic stick with his left hand while flying from the left seat. This machine also had a much lighter tail rotor than Ship 1, whose massively overengineered lobster-claw blade mounts exacted a needless weight penalty at the end of a long moment arm. Finally, Ship 2 had a clutch permitting engine start without first spinning the rotor by hand (although a ground technician had to flip a locking toggle before the helicopter flew away).

On September 10, 1943, two weeks before the new prototype flew, Larry Bell confirmed at an executive staff meeting his intent to pursue helicopter production in the postwar era. "We are in that business and we are in it to stay," he stated adamantly. His belief in a vast potential market for personal helicopters prompted him to add, "We believe that it is one of the great things of the future—one of the world's greatest future industries."[14]

Despite his busy schedule, Bell came to Gardenville once a week or so. He was fascinated by the helicopter and, though he disliked traveling in aircraft, he was eager to ride in Ship 2. "Man wants to fly like a bird," he frequently said, "not like a bat out of hell."[15]

Bell got his ride—the first of many—in the spring of 1944. The experience convinced him that it was time to publicize his helicopter, and soon a two-page feature appeared in the local Sunday newspaper. The road by the Gardenville facility was suddenly jammed with onlookers, a fact that surprised Young because passing traffic had never before paid much attention to the team's activities.

Doing what the Focke-Achgelis FA 61 had done in Germany six years earlier, Ship 2 made the Western Hemisphere's first indoor helicopter flight May 10, 1944. Performing for the region's Civil Air Patrol in Buffalo's 65th

Armory, Floyd Carlson put on a spectacular display of stability and precision control beneath the sixty-foot roof of the structure's drill hall. The helicopter even dipped its nose in graceful salute to CAP's national commander, Colonel Earle L. Johnson.

Fully rebuilt, the first Bell Model 30 emerged that spring to resume test flight duties. Now painted yellow overall and rechristened Ship 1A, the historic prototype incorporated a revised landing gear and a raised tail rotor on an upward-canted shaft extending from the new magnesium semi-monocoque tail boom. Contributing to Bell's ongoing promotion, this machine starred at a Fourth of July celebration in Buffalo's Civic Stadium in 1944. Some 42,000 of the area's war workers, returned veterans, and their families cheered when Carlson concluded his virtuoso performance by placing the left front wheel of the helicopter right into Arthur Young's outstretched hand.

Shortly afterward, a flight of Sikorsky HOS-1 production helicopters under the command of U.S. Coast Guard Commander Frank A. Erickson dropped in for a visit at Gardenville. In return for trying his hand at the new Bell machine, Erickson—one of the most influential early proponents of military helicopter use—allowed Carlson to fly the Sikorsky product. Arthur Young and Bart Kelley also got rides in the machine, which was the Navy's version of the Army R-6.

"I noticed right away that the pilot appeared to be working much harder during hover than Floyd Carlson had to work in ours," Kelley observed. "It was very obvious that there was a difference in hovering stability."[16]

This reciprocal inspection left Young and his team convinced that the Sikorsky helicopter was a good machine but it certainly did not fly as well as a Bell. Since the R-6 had no

equivalent of Young's stabilizer bar to introduce some stability, its pilots had to make constant corrections to keep it going where they wanted.

The Army had in fact expressed interest in Bell's program, even assigning the designation XR-12 to the Model 30. Refusing to depart from his development program's commercial focus, however, Larry Bell informed the military that the company planned to achieve civil certification of a helicopter before entertaining sales to the military services.

Early in 1944, the Gardenville team decided to build a third helicopter to incorporate the best of both predecessors and dispense with much that was wrong with them. Since enough surplus materials were available to support much of the construction, they were able to keep this third machine—not called for in Young's original agreement with Bell—a secret for some time. Progress on this illegal aircraft was slow because, without official blessing, it had to be built as time and supplies allowed. Word inevitably leaked out, however, leading to a distressed telephone call from a main plant executive assigned to oversee the Gardenville effort.

"I told him we needed it as a flying test bed," recalls Bart Kelley who took the call, "that it would be valuable in helping the production people make their larger helicopter. He finally said it would be okay for research, but if we planned to develop it as a product, Bell management wanted no part of it."[17]

Ship 3, NX-41860, was designed to perform as well as Young and his people knew how to make it. Looks were ignored and function dictated design. The open-frame three-seater had an uncovered tail boom and nothing around the cockpit. The instrument panel had been reduced to a thin vertical box so as not to detract from visibility. Flown on April 25,

(Top) Featuring an enclosed cockpit with seating for two, the second Model 30 flew in September 1943 and made this indoor demonstration at a Buffalo armory in May 1944. Courtesy Bell.

(Bottom) Carlson flies Ship 1, again rebuilt following a crash and painted yellow, in the spring of 1944. Courtesy Bell.

Gardenville team members pile aboard the third and last Model 30 to test its weight-lifting capability. Joe Mashman is at the controls and Young stands facing the camera. Courtesy Bell.

1945, it proved to be the best of the three prototypes.

A little-known fourth research helicopter was also constructed. Used to evaluate the coaxial configuration employed successfully by Breguet in France and Hiller in California, a single-seat prototype with two counterrotating rotors on a common shaft briefly took flight. "With a torque corrected by a torque, it was much more precise in hover than a tail-rotor machine," said Young, the only one to fly it. "It was just like standing on the floor; you could move it an inch or a half inch or whatever you wanted."[18]

The coaxial helicopter was set aside a couple of days into testing when the transmission gears were found to be badly gouged. Although he had learned what he needed from this unusual prototype, Young was later distressed to find that it had been unceremoniously taken away and junked. Larry Bell did not want any such distractions from Young's primary helicopter effort.

Much had happened in the meantime. On January 5, 1945, Bell's chief test pilot Jack Woolams—who succeeded Bob Stanley after the latter became chief engineer—was forced to bail out of a stricken YP-59 jet fighter. Bouncing off its wing, Woolams struck the tail and suffered a four-inch gash above his left temple despite his crash helmet. When he pulled his ripcord, the jolt of the opening parachute plucked his winter flying boots—and with them his shoes—from his feet.

Descending more than ten thousand feet, Woolams landed backward in deep snow and was pulled along at thirty miles per hour until he managed to release his chute. Not seeing a sign of life, he started walking on his freezing feet, frequently falling, until at last he sighted a house. It turned out to be deserted for the winter, as was a second he came to.

At last he arrived at the farmhouse of Lloyd Rockwood near Lockport, New York.

The snowbound family could not drive the injured flier to a hospital, nor could a Bell ambulance summoned by telephone make it all the way to him. The main plant therefore called Gardenville and Floyd Carlson took off immediately in Ship 2. Covering twenty miles at top speed to where the ambulance had stalled, Carlson picked up Dr. Thomas C. Marriott and continued to the house. Another Bell test pilot buzzed it in a Bell P-63 Kingcobra to help identify the location.

Carlson reached it in just five minutes and set down on snow the farmer had packed down according to telephoned instructions. The doctor's quick arrival spared Woolams— who suffered from frostbite, shock, and loss of blood—the loss of any toes. Rather than remove him by helicopter, the plant physician attended to his patient on the spot until the ambulance arrived behind a snowplow three hours later.

In addition to generating national publicity, this rescue boosted morale at Bell Aircraft. With war in Europe winding down, it was only a matter of time until military contracts would be canceled and thousands of employees laid off. Whereas nobody at Bell but Larry Bell had believed in the helicopter before, this event won many sudden converts who now looked to it to provide work in the postwar era.

Woolams had not actually been carried to safety by a Bell helicopter. That distinction would belong to Wallace Gillson and Arthur Johnson, ice fishermen from Olean, New York, who were stranded several miles out on Lake Erie in March 1945. Two other members of their fishing expedition had made their way to safety when the thawing ice began breaking up, but this hapless pair had wandered too far out and were trapped. Unable to rescue them, the Coast Guard called Bell, and Carlson came to the rescue again.

He began by taking Ship 2's doors off. Helped by Gardenville mechanic Harry Finnegan, he determined a fuel load and center-of-gravity location that would make it possible to pick up a man in a hover without settling. When he could successfully lift Finnegan out of a field without touching his tires, Carlson then retrieved the two fishermen one at a time. Having by then spent twenty-one hours marooned on thin ice, huddled on a dropped raft, the men didn't argue when the test pilot refused to let them bring their fish with them.

Also early in 1945, Joseph Mashman arrived at Gardenville as Bell's second full-time test pilot. Trained as a civil engineer, the native Chicagoan had been a civilian flight instructor for the Navy before joining Bell in 1943. His remarkable flying abilities took him from production test duties into the elite ranks of experimental flying, where he flew everything from the miniature XP-77 to the twin-jet YP-59. It had been Mashman who had buzzed the farmhouse in a P-63 to guide Carlson to Jack Woolams.

When volunteers were solicited to test fly helicopters, Mashman jumped at what he considered an exciting chance to do a new kind of flying. To his surprise, he won by default; not a single other Bell test pilot believed enough in the future of rotary-wing flight to volunteer.

A compact man, animated and extroverted, Mashman had that rarest of gifts, exceptional even among top pilots. He got every ounce of performance out of a machine, including sports cars, motorcycles, and speedboats (all of which he owned). Despite a spin to the

ground following a tail rotor failure on one of his first flights, he embraced helicopters with enthusiasm and soon flew the Model 30 as skillfully as he had his fighter planes.

The difference between Mashman and Carlson in the air was striking. One day as both machines flew at the same time, Larry Bell pointed to the one swooping and maneuvering with poetic grace and asserted, "That's the man I want to demonstrate my helicopter!"[19]

Yet from a test flying standpoint, Mashman was less successful than Carlson. "Joe was a perfectly wonderful pilot, a miracle man," Young noted, "but for testing an experimental ship you don't want a pilot who's so good he can cover all the faults of the machine. Floyd Carlson would say when things were wrong and I could see when he was having trouble."[20]

It was Joe Mashman who gave Larry Bell his first flight in Bell Model 30 Ship 3 in the spring of 1945. The company president was so impressed with the performance of this machine that he ordered key executives, and even members of Bell Aircraft's board of directors, to go to Gardenville and ride in it. The helicopter is the future of the company, he asserted at a board meeting, and he expected them to get a feel for it.

Looking like an early Bell production helicopter with its bubble removed, and entirely lacking a floor, Ship 3 made flying about as exciting as it could be. In the words of Arthur Young, riding in it was "like sitting in a chair and flying about through space." And Bart Kelley commented: "If your shoe became unlaced and fell, you lost it forever." The Bell executives and board members dutifully reported to Gardenville and took their rides. "I never demonstrated the helicopter to so many scared people," Mashman concluded.[21]

The exercise had been well worth it. Bell alone among the leadership of his company had believed in the helicopter, but support for rotary-wing flight began to percolate elsewhere at high levels. It was long overdue. Larry Bell's vision and determination had given Young the support needed to bring the company to the brink of production.

By the spring of 1945, the helicopter program had clearly outgrown the tiny auto dealership that had been its home for three years. With declining military production opening up space at Bell's large new Wheatfield plant on Niagara Falls Airport, the Gardenville crew was relocated there June 24, 1945. Team members were ambivalent to say the least, and for Young it came as a "great blow."[22] Gardenville had been a true nucleus of creation. However much sense the move made, it marked the end of an era of unique creation.

Among the earliest visitors at Gardenville had been Igor Sikorsky, whom Larry Bell brought by in 1942 to see the first Model 30 under construction. One of the last before the move was Vice President Harry Truman on the eve of ascending to the presidency. As a senator, Truman had done much to promote military helicopter development. After the relocation from Gardenville, the Bell helicopter program's growing recognition also brought VIPs to the Wheatfield plant's flight ramp, including Lieutenant General James H. "Jimmy" Doolittle; Jean Blériot, son of famous French aviation pioneer Louis Blériot; New York Governor Thomas E. Dewey; and New York City's popular Mayor Fiorello La-Guardia, who had piloted bombers during World War I.

Stanley Hiller, Jr., a tall, slender, twenty-year-old Californian, also came to see the Bell machine. Having created the first successful helicopter ever built west of the Mississippi River, Hiller would within a few years provide Bell with head-to-head competition in the light helicopter market. Mashman recalls his first meeting with the West Coast rotary-wing pioneer:

Larry Bell used to bring people out for me to demonstrate the helicopter to all the time. One day he brought up this young man whom I recognized as Stan Hiller. Larry said, "Joe, why don't you give this young man a helicopter ride?" Which I did, and a couple of days later, I found out that Larry had agreed to sell Stan a set of our rotor blades. At that time, Stan only had the coaxial machine but he was interested in developing a helicopter like ours. So shortly after that, Larry Bell came out to our hangar—as he did almost every day to see how we were doing, he being the only executive who had any interest in the helicopter—and I said, "Larry, I understand that you sold Stan Hiller a set of rotor blades and he's using them to put himself in competition with us?" Bell just smiled and said, "Joe, if you and my helicopter division are as good as I think you are, competition is only going to make you better."[23]

With characteristic largesse, Larry Bell worked to foster an entire civil helicopter industry, not merely his own company. A misplaced faith in a personal-use market too vast for one manufacturer partly accounted for his unstinting efforts. Bell was an ardent exponent of free enterprise; he knew the value of competition in making good companies better. His generosity would be fully vindicated by an intense if amicable rivalry between Bell and Hiller, which for two decades resulted in better products at lower prices for customers worldwide.

Application of successful Model 30 technology would initially be realized in the unsuccessful Bell Model 42 five-seat helicopter. Bell had intended from the outset that Young and his team confine themselves to research and leave production design to Bell Aircraft's aeronautical engineers. On the surface, this plan made sense: the company knew the ropes and had a complete—if greatly reduced at war's end—design and production infrastructure in place. The flaw in the plan, one all too evident to the Gardenville crowd, was once again the vast gulf between fixed-wing and rotary-wing aviation.

Bell engineers showed up at Gardenville well before it closed down to familiarize themselves with rotary-wing flight. They then returned to the main plant where, while Young's team was building and refining Ship 3, they designed a large helicopter along lines reportedly suggested by a market survey. The resulting Model 42 of 1945 looked like a luxury sedan, an impression enhanced by chrome-plated hubcaps, a plush interior, and other automotive appointments. This resemblance was no accident, for Bell had commissioned premier industrial designer Raymond Loewy's Detroit firm to come up with lines and a paint scheme in tune with the tastes of the nation's car buyers.

Powered by a Pratt & Whitney R-985 radial engine rated at 450 hp, the Model 42 was designed to have a gross weight of 5,100 pounds, a cruise speed of 100 mph, and a range of 300 miles. Its rotor—faithfully scaled up from that of the Model 30—had a diameter of 47.5 feet. The new machine looked like a sure winner in Bell's promotional literature, which blithely overlooked a production cost ten times that of the average luxury automobile.

Rollout of the first of three Model 42 prototypes in 1945 brought a rude awakening to Project Engineer Robert Wolf and his design team. The new machine was so riddled with mistakes and bugs that it simply did not work. The first hint of what was to come occurred at the official unveiling. As others toasted the machine with champagne, Young wandered over because the angle of the rotor blades looked wrong to his experienced eye. Reaching inside, he raised the collective lever and the blades went flat: the controls were connected backwards.

"They'd looked down their noses at our Gardenville team," Mashman recalled of the in-house engineers, "in particular at Art Young and Bart Kelley because they weren't aeronautical engineers. So they had said to Larry Bell, 'Let us do it right.'"[24]

An exasperated company president had to turn the Model 42 over to Young to fix. Getting the machine to fly was no easy task, and even then the problems were not over. The Model 42's unboosted controls were so heavy that it took two men to fly it. Pilot Carlson would tilt his head in the direction he wanted to go, and Copilot Mashman would lend his strength on the cyclic stick.

"The Model 42 was almost Floyd's and my demise at Bell," recalls Mashman. "We had just taken off on a test flight in the number one aircraft and were hovering about four feet off the ground, when all of a sudden the entire rotor disintegrated; it just shattered and we dropped like a rock. Had it happened a few minutes later we wouldn't have survived."[25]

Young himself had a close call some months later as he labored to improve one of the troubled prototypes. To locate the source of bothersome vibrations, he clung to its uncowled side to observe its dynamic components during flight. As Mashman taxied around a

With five seats and plush interior appointments, the unsuccessful Bell Model 42 reflected Larry Bell's misplaced belief in a market for aerial automobiles. Courtesy Bell.

hangar for takeoff, a strong gust of wind caught them broadside. The earlier problem of high stick forces had been addressed by increasing the mechanical advantage of the stick and reducing control travel. As a result, Mashman found he lacked sufficient control to keep the helicopter upright. The Model 42 rolled over and demolished itself, but Young—who was on the high side of the ship—was able to jump to safety. He spent the next hour searching the wreckage for his favorite fountain pen.

A third Model 42 prototype was fully instrumented, lashed down, and run at full power in a standard 100-hour ground running test. Less than twenty hours into the test, observers were dismayed to see its tail boom bend and break off. Coming on top of earlier events, this vibratory fatigue failure sealed the fate of Bell's aerial family car. Chastened aeronautical engineers at Wheatfield abandoned helicopters to return with relief to fixed-wing aviation.

Young and his team were already working on a smaller production helicopter of their own. Larry Bell had been so impressed with Model 30 Ship 3 that he decided to have the Gardenville veterans make production drawings for a commercial helicopter along similar lines. "I really exerted myself to get everything just right," Young later wrote. "Mast, hub, blade grips, bar control system, transmission with ground gears; all were done over to incorporate our experience and the opportunity to use forgings and take advantage of mass production."[26]

On Larry Bell's order, the new Model 47 was also given a Detroit beauty treatment like the Model 42 before it. An industrial designer used to fleshing out cars came to Buffalo and worked with Young to enhance the basic dimensions of the two-seater. "We struggled with a design for the 47," remembers Young. "I never really liked it but it was the best we could do."[27]

The inventor had a simpler vision of the form his machine should take. Since every pound detracted from performance and utility, why not leave the Model 47 uncovered, adding only a cockpit enclosure? For the enclosure, Young envisioned a full plastic bubble. No such canopy had been made before and for help Young turned to Joe Parrish, a friend from Philadelphia whom he had hired as part of the drafting department at Gardenville. Parrish's job had been to write a helicopter manual, but his real interest and expertise lay in the field of plastics. He now proposed heating a large plexiglass sheet in a furnace, laying it on a framework over a source of compressed air, and restraining it at the edges with a template.

Where not restrained, the sheet inflated into a spherical bubble with a square base. When trimmed of excess material, it tapered perfectly into the helicopter's fuselage. It was then a simple matter to cut doors into its sides. To Young's delight, bubble enclosures formed in this manner were free of optical distortions.

Nobody expected that this feature would soon become the trademark of the Bell Model 47 production helicopter. It was devised merely as a low-cost high-visibility expedient for a stripped-down alternate commercial version of the helicopter. Sales of this utility version were expected to be secondary to those of the coupe-body machine, which was clearly aimed at the private-ownership market.

The first Bell Model 47 rolled out December 8, 1945, less than six months after Young and his crew arrived at Wheatfield. This bubble-canopy machine was the first of ten assembled by hand from production parts before a true production line was set up. Reportedly the first Bell aircraft ever completed on schedule, it initiated a tradition of on-time helicopter delivery that would contrast sharply with the company's chronic history of late airplane deliveries.

Government certification for production was the next major hurdle to be passed. Bell gave top priority to an accelerated program with the Civil Aeronautics Authority. Sikorsky was pursuing commercial certification of its s-51 and s-52 helicopters in Connecticut. Those machines had been developed under military contract whereas Bell's Model 47 was designed from the outset as a commercial vehicle. Larry Bell was therefore especially anxious that his company obtain the world's first approved type certificate ever awarded a helicopter. It was a race that Bell was destined to win.

Raymond Malloy, chief CAA test pilot, came to Bell and learned how to fly a helicopter under Floyd Carlson. Since no helicopter had ever been certificated, the process threatened to be long and expensive. Success was not a foregone conclusion. How could the CAA—predecessor to today's Federal Aviation Administration—evaluate and deem safe a new type of aircraft? What guidelines were to be used?

In a display of government-industry cooperation, the CAA assigned its best people to the project, including the head of its flight standards division. This group began by providing Bell with its regulations and guidelines governing fixed-wing aircraft certification, and asked the manufacturer to devise a parallel program for helicopters incorporating the same philosophy. Carlson did so with the able help of Gardenville veteran Charlie Seibel, who—after a brief stint under Bob Stanley in the fixed-wing flight test department—had

returned to helicopter work as a stress engineer for the Model 42.

The primary obstacle to helicopter certification was that helicopters lacked stick forces in the fixed-wing sense. Without "stick-free" or hands-off stability, the control-force-per-speed gradient which is the basis for airplane testing was lacking. Arthur Young came to the rescue with "irreversible controls," a mechanical system to filter out rotor feedback. The result was a somewhat jerky control feel enough like an airplane's to be acceptable to the CAA.

"CAA cooperation couldn't have been better," Carlson stated of this effort.[28] The only disappointment was the government's insistence on complete overhaul after every twenty-five hours of flight. This conservative safety measure was not very practical, but Bell conceded that it was probably wise in view of the primitive state of helicopter technology. Time between dynamic-system overhauls would doubtless be extended and operating costs reduced as experience was gained; in the meantime, it was enough to get Bell into production.

On March 8, 1946, in anticipation of certification, the Bell Model 47 received the first commercial license awarded a helicopter. The appropriate registration number NC1H—for American, Commercial, First Helicopter—was affixed to the production prototype. A far more historic, if less celebrated, event came two months later with the Award of Approved Type Certificate (Helicopter) Number One on May 8, 1946. This date truly marks the birth of the commercial helicopter industry.

"The only way we can sell the helicopter is to have the courage to build some," Larry Bell stressed during meetings. With certification in hand, he went before his board of directors to request a go-ahead for large-scale production. "They gave us everything," he reported afterward with pride. "We asked for 500 helicopters, expecting approval for something less; we got the works."[29]

This endorsement reflected Bell's overriding conviction and singular influence, then buoyed by the euphoria of a postwar aviation boom yet to go bust. So sure was Bell that he immediately ordered 500 Franklin engines so as to be prepared for a massive demand for his helicopters.

Promotion of Models 42 and 47 began at the National Aircraft Show of 1947, a popular forum held at a disused aircraft factory in Cleveland, Ohio, during November 1946. Three Bell helicopters stole the show in the company's *Utility Unlimited* exhibit. One was a Model 42. Another was a Model 47B with automotive styling. The third was a fabric-covered "utility" model with military insignia and a bubble canopy (the XR-13, the U.S. Army's first Bell helicopter, due to be delivered the following month). Three more 47s stationed outside gave rides to VIPs and potential buyers, and rushed to the roof of Cleveland's main post office commemorative helicopter air mail pieces sent by novelty-seeking attendees.

The Model 42 was popular with families who lined up to sit in its plush seats, but the large machine failed to attract a single buyer. Larry Bell noted wryly that his displayed helicopters were like elephants at the zoo: people came to look at them, not buy them. Offsetting this disappointment was the sale of twenty-seven two-seat Model 47s at an aggregate total of $675,000 to customers in the United States, Canada, and Sweden. That every buyer was a commercial operator confirmed the nature of the emerging market for civil helicopters.

Central Helicopters of Yakima, Washington, was the largest purchaser with an order for nine coupe-body Bells for agricultural use. Of the two versions of the Model 47, however, the bubble-canopied utility two-seater consistently drew greater interest. "People swarmed all over the open bubble job," remembers Arthur Young.[30]

With production of the world's first civil helicopter now under way, Bell quickly refocused its sales efforts toward commercial use. A minuscule military market had also emerged—by the end of 1946, the company had helicopter contracts with the Army Air Forces, Army Ground Forces, and U.S. Navy—and it would soon expand greatly with the 1950 outbreak of war in Korea. So successful was the Bell Model 47 that within a decade it firmly established itself as the world's archetypal light piston helicopter.

This success would not come soon enough or be large enough to spare Bell Aircraft a difficult transition to a peacetime world. From a peak of $317 million in 1944, Bell's business shrank to a postwar nadir of $11 million in 1946. Bell employment also plunged, from a wartime peak of almost 48,000 to just under 3,000, and it continued to decline. Earnings disappeared and substantial amounts of red ink showed on the company's financial statements. Its only fixed-wing business was the construction of supersonic test aircraft built for the NACA and USAAF's joint high-speed research program. However glamorous the work, and however exciting Captain Chuck Yeager's shattering of the sound barrier in a Bell X-1 in the fall of 1947, building few-of-a-kind research planes did not offset the loss of volume production.

Tantalizing visions of large-volume mass production had prompted Larry Bell to fund Young's pioneering work. But all twenty-

Floyd Carlson holds his hands off the controls to
demonstrate the stability of the Bell Model 47,
which on March 8, 1946, became the first civil
helicopter licensed for manufacture. Courtesy Bell.

seven helicopter sales at Cleveland had been placed by commercial operators hoping to eke out a living with vertical flight. Absent from the list of customers were private buyers intent on using helicopters as aerial automobiles.

Other aviation industry executives— notably Leston Faneuf, Larry's assistant and Bell Aircraft secretary—were far less optimistic about prospects for a personal helicopter market. Their skepticism was now bolstered by signs that the postwar aviation boom was not living up to expectations. That all orders were commercial in nature might simply have reflected Bell Aircraft's inability to get the price of its helicopter down. At $25,000 the two-seat 47B (the 47A designation was shared by the USAAF YH-13 and the USN HTL-2) cost three times as much as a four-seat airplane and fully ten times as much as many luxury cars, and even at that price Bell was losing money with each helicopter sold.

By 1947, company executives saw considerable evidence that more than price was at issue. It seemed likely that demand for home-based rotorcraft might not exist in the United States. This disheartening realization prompted Bell Aircraft to reevaluate its marketing strategy. Just in time, the company shifted from a nonexistent personal market toward the embryonic commercial market. It was a painful adjustment for Larry Bell because it gave formal recognition to a distressing fact: the total number of potential civil helicopter buyers was a minute fraction of the vast pool previously envisioned. Bell Aircraft would now have to shoulder the burden of nurturing viable commercial markets *without* sufficient production volume to defray the high costs entailed.

As a businessman, Bell knew that enter-prising companies often fail when attempting to introduce new technologies, their resources consumed in defining and demonstrating commercial applications for their products. Despite this danger, his commitment to vertical flight never wavered because of a deep personal responsibility he felt toward his workers.

The closing at war's end of his government-owned B-29 bomber plant at Marietta, Georgia, had sickened him. He had vowed that his remaining employees would not suffer abrupt dismissal if he could help it. Yet demand had evaporated for the piston-powered fighter planes that had made Bell famous. And although the company had built America's first jet airplane in 1942, it was not among the manufacturers selected in the postwar era by the Army Air Forces—which became the U.S. Air Force in September 1947—to carry it into the jet age. Bell did have a joint AAF/NACA contract calling for supersonic research airplane development, but this glamorous program held no potential for volume production. For better or worse, Larry Bell saw helicopters as the one hope for keeping his company a viable airframe manufacturer.

It was hardly a propitious time to assume the ambitious task of convincing people to buy helicopters. That meant getting out in the field and demonstrating the benefits of vertical flight to prospective customers. And that, in turn, required costly research, experimentation, and the development and manufacture of ancillary equipment like hoppers and spray bars for agricultural use. With helicopters so new, the company had anticipated that it would have to teach people to fly them. Therefore, it established a flight training school July 1, 1946.

Larry Bell had little support for helicopters on his own board of directors. It was a testament to his persuasiveness, determination, and stature that the Model 47B had even entered production. The battle was far from won. Slow sales and the need for inordinate outlays soon prompted new debates among board members.

There was some good news. Bell had received orders for evaluation quantities of the Model 47 from the Army Ground Forces, Army Air Forces, and Navy before the end of 1946. Any or all of those services might place production orders for the Bell two-seater. Because of these orders, the first production Bell helicopter ironically did not go to a civil customer but to the AAF, which accepted the Bell XR-13—a stock Model 47 in military paint—on the last day of 1946.

Another bit of welcome news was the receipt at the National Aircraft Show of an order for three Model 47Bs from AB Hans Osterman of Stockholm. This first European sale marked the beginning of a strong international marketing program at Bell, and sales personnel were soon traveling the world in search of new business.

When Bell announced its first five helicopter dealerships early in 1947, Osterman's Aero made the list. The four other Model 47B dealers were Central Aircraft of Yakima, Washington (the first dealership); Southern Arizona Airlines of Tucson, Arizona (who got the first civil Model 47); the John Fabick Tractor Company of St. Louis, Missouri; and Skyways Services of Winnipeg, Manitoba. All five operators were helicopter customers who had opted to become franchised sales outlets in order to purchase their own helicopters at the 20 percent discount Bell offered dealers as a network-building incentive.

As it turned out, the earliest viable commercial market application was agricultural rather than training or general charter

use. Aerial application—crop dusting and spraying—accounted for the bulk of Bell helicopter sales in the late 1940s even though agricultural operators rarely purchased more than one or a few helicopters each. Collectively, they supplied Bell with enough business to scrape by.

For this market segment, the company developed the 47B-2 and B-3 utility models, which came equipped for crop spraying and crop dusting, respectively. These models lacked the full automotive styling of the standard B-1. On June 18, 1947, the B-3 received the first Civil Aeronautics Administration airworthiness certificate ever issued to a dedicated agricultural aircraft, either fixed or rotary wing.

To sell the 47B-3, Bell had to prove that fertilizer and insecticide application was substantially more efficient by helicopter than by airplane. Helicopters, the company pointed out, could go lower and slower with greater control. The swirling downwash from their rotors coated the undersides of leaves as well as the tops. So confident was the company that it staged a demonstration without performing a trial run.

Carrying 400 pounds of dust in two electrically operated hoppers attached to its fuselage, a Bell Model 47B-3 flew slowly at leaftop height over a 40-acre potato field in New York State. Company officials and some 2,000 regional farmers watched with approval until they began noticing puzzling dots of soil on each plant after the helicopter had passed. Closer inspection revealed that the low-and-slow dusting had uprooted every single plant, efficiently wiping out the entire crop. This botched demonstration was a major setback for Bell, whose officials would see humor in the event only years later.

Agricultural use also accounted for the

(Top) Bell's first commercial offering, the Model 47B-1, featured automotive styling and side-by-side seating for two. Courtesy NASM/SI.

(Bottom) Earliest commercial uses of Bell helicopters were primarily agricultural. This 47B-3's side-mounted hoppers are filled in preparation for crop dusting. Courtesy NASM/SI.

A 47B at the company's Niagara Falls plant displays the full-bubble canopy, a Bell innovation. Courtesy NASM/SI.

majority of Bell's initial international sales. Foreign purchasers included pioneering commercial operators in Sweden, Canada, Argentina, and Great Britain. On September 25, 1947, a Model 47 became the first helicopter to cross the English Channel when Bell's first British distributor, Irvin-Bell Helicopter Sales, sent it on an extended sales demonstration through Belgium, Holland, and Switzerland. This effort successfully snared other European customers for Bell.

Basic product improvement received high priority. Before the year was out a newer model had completed CAA certification and entered service with pioneering southern California operator Armstrong-Flint Helicopters. This was the Bell Model 47D (there was no 47C), which offered improved performance and a 100-pound increase in gross weight to 2,200 pounds. Top speed was 92 mph, cruise at 75 percent power was 85 mph, and useful load was 718 pounds.

This machine was basically a civil version of the Army H-13B. Its design benefited greatly from the exhaustive evaluation the Army had performed of its YH-13s (as it redesignated its YR-13s). In 1948, the H-13B became the first light helicopter to enter regular Army service. It also entered Navy service that year as the HTL-2.

The commercial 47D featured a functional two-piece bubble canopy, the upper half removable for fair weather flying. This arrangement provided much better visibility than afforded by the 47B-1's coupe body. In fact, the 47 series dispensed entirely with the Detroit-style car body. No longer bearing any resemblance to an automobile, the world's first commercial helicopter turned its back on the personal-use market.

Young and his team had fought hard to eliminate the automotive styling. They also wanted to dispense with the doped fabric encasing the Bell's tail boom. In addition to improving performance, leaving the boom exposed would reduce the helicopter's tendency to weather-vane when hovering in a crosswind. But Larry Bell detested the skeletal look of exposed steel tubing. He made sure his helicopters left the factory fully covered. Bell operators in the field, however, were often quick to strip the fabric.

Late in 1947, Arthur Young left the Bell Aircraft Corporation to return to Paoli, Pennsylvania. His desire to reconcile science, mathematics, and fundamental philosophy had brought him to Bell six years earlier; the helicopter challenge now met, his quest for insight into the workings of the universe was drawing him away from Bell. The parting of the ways between Arthur and Larry was completely amicable, and the inventor remained available to the company on a consulting basis.

One reason that civil helicopters sold poorly in the late 1940s was that people did not yet know how to use them. Another was a widespread public wariness toward rotary-wing vehicles. Airplanes were widely accepted, but not helicopters. The public regarded them at best as a risky military vehicle. At least airplanes had wings to hold them up.

On December 21, 1947, a Bell 47B belonging to the *Oregon Journal* was hovering 400 feet above a golf course when it suddenly plunged to the ground and burst into flames, killing the newspaper's associate publisher and a prominent Portland businessman. This crash occurred just 200 yards from the businessman's home at the edge of the course, as guests watched in horror from the veranda.

Helicopter program manager David G. Forman rushed a team of technical experts to the crash site. Neither he nor official CAA investigators found any signs of a mechanical failure to account for the accident, which was formally attributed to pilot error. But the event attracted widespread press attention, which took its toll on the already fragile reputation of the helicopter. Bell met this challenge with an active public-relations program depicting the Model 47, and all helicopters, as safe and fun conveyances. This campaign gave rise to carefully orchestrated and highly imaginative publicity stunts.

On July 25, 1947, a coupe-cabin Bell dropped into the parking lot of a new branch of the Manufacturers & Traders Trust Company of Buffalo, New York. The pilot emerged, casually made a deposit, and flew off. Covered by reporters and photographers, this staged event generated publicity for both the helicopter's builder and the bank. Lingering public fascination with the personal-helicopter myth was what made this stunt "newsworthy." Bell would continue to exploit the mystique of casual helicopter-as-aerial-automobile use as a captivating way of communicating the versatility and safety of its products.

Another promotion some weeks later saw 106-year-old Civil War veteran James A. Hard flying over his Rochester, New York, home in a Bell 47B. Landing unfazed, Hard delighted the crowd—and BAC executives— by declaring that helicopters were "a lot of fun and a fine method of getting around."[31]

But the majority of favorable publicity came at no cost to Bell, for scarcely a week went by that some Model 47 was not involved in an adventure ranging from the whimsical to the dramatic. A pregnant woman in a snowbound farmhouse was flown to a hospital to deliver her baby. Three fishermen were retrieved from an ice floe.[32] And Brown University football coach "Rip" Engle rented a 47B from New England Helicopter to analyze his team's weaknesses by observing scrimmages from above.

One dramatic event occurred in Bell Aircraft's backyard in the spring of 1950. A suicidal woman threw herself into the Niagara River, only to change her mind. She spent the night desperately clinging to tiny Goat Island at the brink of Niagara Falls. Bell pilots Owen Q. Niehaus and Joe Cannon took off to rescue her, but tricky winds and the woman's weight caused the float-equipped helicopter to flip completely over. The raging current lodged the aircraft against the island and the veteran pilots found themselves stranded with the woman they had come to save. Another helicopter was dispatched from Niagara Falls Airport, flown by William J. Gallagher and George White. Wary of downdrafts and other hazards, they lowered a strong rope that was made fast between the helicopter and the riverbank. A rescue was then effected by boat.

The most remarkable early demonstration of the Bell 47's capabilities, a vast dam construction project in the wilds of Canada, also received publicity. Dave Forman returned from a visit north with enthusiastic reports of the many duties being performed by a dozen Model 47s. His boss listened attentively to descriptions of narrow canyons and tiny landing platforms wedged against hilltops. "Do it up in a report, Dave," Larry Bell reportedly replied. "We'll turn it into a series of ads."[33]

If civil sales remained slow, things were not much better on the military front. Orders arrived in trickles, but Larry Bell was convinced that his helicopter, despite its small size and limited utility, had a meaningful role to play for America's armed services. It had pleased him when on April 11, 1947, Bell Aircraft established an industry record by delivering no fewer than thirteen military helicopters in one day, nine to the U.S. Army and four to the U.S. Navy. But with America busily reducing its World War II arsenal in the late 1940s, volume military production promised to remain elusive for some time.

It was obvious that the Navy would never be a big user of 47s. Except for training, that service had no need of light helicopters. Although the Army had a broad list of uses including tactical duties then being performed by liaison or "grasshopper" planes, another year would pass before it finished evaluating its YR-13s and was ready to order an operational version. There was some question whether Bell Aircraft would still be in the helicopter business by then.

At the close of 1947, Larry Bell and his staff reviewed their first full year of helicopter sales. Progress had been substantial—nearly one hundred 47Bs had been delivered around the world—but the company's financial performance was written in red ink. Employment had dropped by a third during the year to 2,022, and more layoffs would be necessary. Time was running out.

By the time the first production Bell helicopter left its factory, the company had invested almost $5 million of its own resources. More money was being lost with each Model 47 delivered. Getting set up to manufacture commercial helicopters clearly took extraordinary commitment. Had Larry Bell and his board known how great the cost would be, the company might never have entered the helicopter field. But the company president was determined to make a success of the program.

In addition to financial stresses, the year 1947 saw a battle for control of Bell Aircraft. A group headed by Jackson Martindell waged a proxy fight to take over the company, an effort that was narrowly defeated. To forestall other such attempts, Larry Bell let control of his company pass to the Equity Corporation of New York, an investment company headed by David Milton. Equity acquired slightly more than half of Bell Aircraft's stock.

The company did enjoy one bright moment during this difficult year. On October 14, 1947, USAF Captain Charles E. "Chuck" Yeager shattered the sound barrier in the rocket-powered Bell XS-1 (later redesignated X-1) research plane high above the California desert. This achievement—which the Air Force initially kept secret—marked one of the proudest moments of Larry Bell's life. Bell, Yeager, and John Stack of NACA together received the Collier Trophy, America's highest aviation award, on December 17, 1948.[34]

The year 1948 marked the nadir of Bell Aircraft's fortunes, although there were a few positive developments. The Argentine Navy purchased a half dozen improved 47Ds. Other South American countries also placed orders, many the result of an extended demonstration tour by Joe Mashman. Sent to Argentina in 1947 to instruct pilots for Bell's first customer on the continent, Trabajos Aéreos y Representaciones SA (TAYR), the irrepressible Mashman delayed his return until 1948. His yearlong adventure was so effective that Brazil, Chile, Paraguay, and Peru soon became Bell users.

Overall, however, sales were lower than in 1947. Despite the efforts of Mashman, Leonard LaVassar (who later became chief test pilot for Piasecki Helicopters), and other members of Bell's talented sales force, ground was being lost. The agricultural market, which had heretofore sustained Bell's production,

An industry record is set April 11, 1947, when Bell
delivers thirteen helicopters—nine Army YR-13s
and four Navy HTLs—in one day. Courtesy Bell.

was becoming saturated. Bell had to open other commercial market segments or go out of the helicopter business.

But what other uses of light helicopters could generate sufficient production volumes? A commercial operation performed by short-lived New Jersey operator Helicopter Air Transport provided an answer. Sponsored by a geophysical company, HAT had dispatched a 47B to Louisiana, where it conducted the first helicopter oil exploration survey in history. Representatives of the larger U.S. and Latin American oil companies observed with great interest as this machine flew over possible oil fields with gravity meters installed. The instrument readings thus generated were precisely plotted via radio fixes.

The helicopter promised to be invaluable to the hugely profitable petroleum industry. Quick to perceive the potential, the Bell company loaded a Model 47 aboard a DC-3 at Niagara Falls Airport on March 2, 1949, and flew it to Guatemala City. Upon arrival, Joe Mashman—now on his second Latin American tour—and service representative William J. Diehl assembled the helicopter. Mashman flew Ohio Oil Company geologist Paul L. Henderson over the jungles of Central Guatemala on a month-long geophysical survey that could not have been effectively accomplished any other way.

But Larry Bell knew that demonstrations alone would not bring viable markets into being. He made up his mind to create the world's first commercial helicopter operation dedicated to oil industry support. At that time, Bell was in the process of forming the Bell Aircraft Supply Corporation (BASCO), a wholly owned subsidiary, to provide Bell's West Coast customers with better sales and service. BASCO would be headquartered in Burbank, California, and key BAC executives would do double duty as its top officers.

That state's vast Central Valley was already the nation's leading center of helicopter dusting and spraying. The movie industry to the south also needed helicopters, which proved to be excellent aerial camera platforms. Pacific Gas & Electric, the giant utility with headquarters in San Francisco, was beginning to use Bells for power-line patrol and snow-pack surveys in mountainous regions.

BASCO presented Larry Bell with a ready-made opportunity to set up the for-profit petroleum venture he envisioned. Shortly before its incorporation on May 13, 1949, BASCO was revised to include an Oil Exploration Division headquartered at Lafayette, Louisiana. Given four 47D helicopters, four pilots, and four mechanics, and grubstaked by its parent company with a quarter of a million dollars, this pioneering operation made its services available to oil companies along the Gulf Coast and elsewhere.

BASCO's Louisiana branch proved profitable from the start. That news pleased Larry Bell and his nervous board of directors. But operating its own products for commercial gain left Bell Aircraft highly vulnerable should a would-be competitor one day file an antitrust charge against the helicopter manufacturer. That could get Bell into hot water with the U.S. government. The potential discomfort was great enough that when a group of oil men offered to buy the operation, the company readily agreed.

Thus began one of the great civil helicopter success stories, Petroleum Bell Helicopters. Following the acquisition of some non-Bell machines, this company became simply Petroleum Helicopters, Inc. Today it is one of the largest operators of civil helicopters in the world.

Another bit of good news arrived September 27, 1948, with the announcement of an Air Force contract for a new helicopter designated the XH-15 (Model 54), making it the third active helicopter program at Bell. The second program had already produced the Model 48, an all-metal transport helicopter series sponsored by the Air Force for Army use. The R-12 (redesignated H-12 late in 1948) was fitted with a scaled-up Model 47 rotor powered by a 550-hp Pratt & Whitney R-1340 engine. The design borrowed heavily from the unsuccessful Model 42 civil helicopter, and Bell's three Model 42 prototypes all flew extensively in support of its accelerated development.

Delivered to the USAF in May 1948, the first of two XR-12 prototypes was immediately returned to Bell under bailment for research and testing. It had five seats; an XH-12B and ten preproduction YH-12Bs built the following year would have eight seats, and production H-12Bs were to have ten.

Employment at the end of 1948 stood at just 1,861. In four short years, 24 of every 25 jobs at Bell had disappeared. But the company's demoralized work force would shrink no further. Sales for 1948 totaled $15,329,230, and a loss was reported of $347,122. As if to show that the worst was indeed past, the company on the last day of the year received a $7,575,072 contract from Boeing in Seattle to build engine nacelles for the advanced B-47 jet bomber. Within a year, this lucrative subcontracting swelled to over $10 million per year. A contract received from Convair on April 17, to manufacture the same twin-jet nacelles for its giant B-36 Peacemaker intercontinental bomber, was worth an equivalent amount.

Larry Bell was now steering his company on a firm course of diversification. In September 1948, Bell Aircraft purchased the Cleveland-based W. J. Schoenberger Company, a manufacturer of precision valves and fittings serving the gas-turbine, appliance, and air-conditioning industries. The following year, it acquired two companies from First York Corporation through an exchange of stock: the American Wheelabrator and Equipment Corporation of Mishawaka, Indiana,[35] and Baker Refrigeration with facilities in South Windham, Maine, and Omaha, Nebraska.

Although most of Bell's business remained missiles and supersonic research planes, the company felt it needed more products for civil consumption than just helicopters. Early in 1948 it introduced the Bell Prime Mover, a motorized half-ton wheelbarrow designed for construction use.

By the fall of 1948, Bell felt that its commercial helicopter was well-enough established to support a price increase. Anxious to recoup some of what had been invested in his vertical-flight program, Larry Bell raised the price of the 47D utility helicopter from $25,000 to $39,500. In an announcement to the press, he cited rising production costs and the expense of "developing and approving all types of accessory equipment" as key factors. "For example," he said, "we have had to design dusting and spraying equipment for agricultural use. . . . We have had to go even further, spending large sums proving the helicopter's superiority in pest control over many types of diversified crops."[36]

Bell Aircraft could institute this sobering price increase because it held a worldwide monopoly in light civil helicopters. The higher price would dissuade some would-be purchasers, but many more would bite the bullet and pay. In the absence of marketplace alternatives, Bell would come out ahead.

No sooner had it taken this action, how-

The Bell YH-12 (Model 48) troop carrier of 1948
was not produced in quantity. Courtesy NASM/SI.

ever, than the Model 47's first and—as it turned out—only serious competitor received CAA certification and reached the marketplace. The Hiller 360, a new light helicopter of roughly equivalent size, weight, power, and performance—destined to give the 47 a run for its money for the next two decades—offered several key improvements. It featured advanced semi-monocoque construction, it had three seats, and the patented Rotormatic paddles between its blades made it the first helicopter to offer "hands-off" stability.

The Hiller 360 was the creation of helicopter pioneer Stanley Hiller, Jr., in Palo Alto, California. It sold for $20,000, half as much as the 47D at its new price. Bell's monopoly had been completely shattered, and with it the company's hopes of a quick return to profitability.

Faced with such stiff competition, Bell reduced the price of its 47D to $23,500 the following spring. It was also forced to copy the Hiller 360's most popular feature and add a third seat. The result was the vastly improved 47D-1 unveiled April 1, 1949. Despite the lower price, the D-1 was so good that it would remain in production for four years. Its extra utility would see it used as the H-13D and HTL-3 and -4, and with a revised transmission as the H-13E and HTL-5.

Getting the Model 47 to lift three people instead of two could clearly be done, since the Hiller 360—powered by the same 178-hp Franklin engine as the two-seat 47D—flew very well that way. Bell engineers met the challenge by shaving 150 pounds off the D's empty weight of 1,530 pounds. A one-piece bubble, lightweight skids instead of wheels (a first for production helicopters), and an exposed tail boom accounted for most of the savings. These changes bore the personal stamp of Arthur Young, who suggested them

all. But Bell engineers did not stop there; they also substituted a modified Franklin engine uprated to 200 hp. In addition to letting the D-1 heft 40 percent more payload than the 47D, this improvement worked a doubling of the hover ceiling to 10,000 feet.

On March 24, 1949, the USAF XH-12—still on bailment to Bell—set an unofficial speed record of 133.9 miles per hour with chief test pilot Owen Niehaus and test pilot Bill Gallagher at the controls. Starting with two-mile level approaches to develop maximum speed and ensure accuracy, they made two passes in opposite directions over the 5,000-foot runway at Niagara Falls Airport. To the immense delight of onlookers, it was announced that the veteran pilots had broken the unofficial speed record of 131 mph recently set by the Piasecki XHJP-1. The Navy and Piasecki, who had loudly proclaimed their fleet utility prototype to be the world's fastest helicopter, only grudgingly ceded this title to the Air Force and Bell.

On June 13, Local 501 of the United Auto Workers initiated a nineteen-week strike at Bell Aircraft. The union's action greatly hurt Larry Bell, who felt as ever a responsibility to provide his workers with a continuing livelihood. World War II had placed enormous demands on the company president, but he refused to rest in its aftermath. Against the advice of his doctors, he perennially worked long hours pursuing his vision of new roles for his company, helicopter manufacture being chief among them. He was convinced that Bell Aircraft—or what was left of it—was a family brought close together by shared adversity. The strike, coming just as the corporation was getting back onto its feet, belied that belief.

Not until October 17 did the rank and file return to work after an agreement was finally

Revised with lightweight skids, an exposed tail
boom, and greater engine power, the Bell 47D-1
of 1949 featured improved performance despite a
third seat. Courtesy NASM/SI.

reached. In the meantime, Bell and his senior executives had availed themselves of an advantage that managements of other strike-bound companies would certainly have envied. They came and went by helicopter, flying unhindered over the heads of the picketers who blocked the company's gates.

Bell Aircraft nonetheless reversed its losing trend during 1949 and by year's end was solidly in the black. Although the strike had lowered total sales to $11,829,475, nearly $4 million below the 1948 level, the company recorded a $204,142 profit. The Schoenberger and BASCO subsidiaries spearheaded this return to profitability, which was buoyed by a $32 million backlog of orders. But this companywide backlog included few civil orders; the commercial helicopter market seemed to be drying up. Employment, which had dipped below 1,900 at the start of 1949, stood at 4,119 as the decade drew to a close.

In January 1950, Bell Aircraft founded the Erie Insurance Company, attesting to Bell's commitment to active leadership in fostering vertical flight. Created specifically to engage in helicopter hull insurance and underwriting, this wholly owned subsidiary solved a chronic problem for operators of Bell and other commercial helicopters. They had found little understanding among insurance providers of the needs, hazards, and realities of their profession.

A couple of months later, Bell Aircraft sold off the Prime Mover product line to a company in Iowa. Like Grumman's aluminum canoes, the motorized wheelbarrow and other nonaviation Bell products had helped sustain employment while the company struggled through difficult times and the vicissitudes of military procurement.

Helicopters remained Bell's real civil product. By early 1950 the company had sold about 200 machines when the commercial market collapsed. Since the few military Model 47s sold were performing well in operational service, and with some 300 crated Franklin engines still cluttering up his Wheatfield plant, Larry Bell decided to press for large-scale Army procurement of the humble Model 47.

Bell Aircraft spent millions of dollars performing helicopter demonstrations around the country. Consummate salesman Joe Mashman took part in this all-out hard sell, taking Army officers—with wives and children if available—for rides whenever possible. Whatever the ethics of this practice and however it might be viewed today, that was what it took for Bell to stay in the helicopter business in 1950.

Larry Bell's own dealings with the Army brought him into regular contact with Army Field Forces Commander Jacob L. Devers, whom one knowledgeable observer called "perhaps the most ardent supporter of helicopters in any of the three services."[37] The company president informed the highly regarded general that Bell Aircraft had no interest in building military helicopters a few at a time. If the Army wanted to make widespread use of his company's product, it would have to order a hundred or more at a time.

Devers was inclined to agree, but his was not the only voice, and industry leaders certainly had no business giving ultimatums to the collective leadership of any of the nation's armed services. When the Army's "top brass" balked, Bell simply smiled and waited for his idea of selling the Model 47 directly to the troops to bear fruit. He was astute enough to realize that once introduced to Bell helicopters, midlevel commanders and soldiers in the field would clamor for vertical flight.

Trying to convince the Army to buy more

helicopters had its humorous moments. Bell, Mashman, and newly hired demonstration pilot-cum-sales engineer Hans Weichsel together flew to Fort Monroe, Virginia, in a Bell 47 fresh off the assembly line. There, Bell and Mashman entered the headquarters to ask the general commanding the base to try out their helicopter. Weichsel stayed outside with the machine. As he guarded it, a little girl with a lollipop approached. Fascinated by the machine, she made a pest of herself. When Weichsel tried to discourage her from getting the gooey lollipop on the plexiglass and seats, however, he received a withering blast of imperious authority. Here, clearly, was the daughter of the commanding general.

In a flash of inspiration, he promised the girl a ride if she would get her father to take one first. Just then, Bell and Mashman came out of the building. Larry Bell's name had failed to open doors and they had been turned away. Bell—his ulcer acting up—grumbled, "Let's go get a milkshake."[38] Just then, out came the girl towing her high-ranking father. She dragged him over to the Bell helicopter for the promised ride. By the time the Bell team headed home later in the day, the general and his little girl were ardent supporters of Army use of Bell helicopters.

With its attention so heavily focused on the Army, Bell Aircraft was caught by surprise when the Navy announced June 13, 1950, that BAC had won an industrywide competition to build the world's first dedicated anti-submarine-warfare (ASW) helicopter. The result would be the HSL (Model 61), a large all-metal aircraft powered by a 1,900-hp Pratt & Whitney R-2800 radial engine and topped by two two-blade, stabilizer-bar-equipped rotors each 51.5 feet in diameter. The HSL's fore-and-aft layout mimicked the tandem-rotor configuration pioneered by Frank

Piasecki, although the HSL was distinctly less pleasing to look at than any Piasecki product. As specified, it would weigh 26,500 pounds fully loaded, placing Bell alongside Piasecki and Sikorsky as a manufacturer of large helicopters. The Navy entertained high hopes for this machine.

Less than two weeks after the HSL contract was announced, war broke out in Korea. America's three-year participation in the ensuing United Nations police action profoundly altered the climate for the U.S. helicopter industry. It would never again be so hard to sell helicopters, because Korea integrated them into the mainstream of American military tactics. Saving lives was the primary role played by vertical flight in Korea. As the number of soldiers rescued by helicopter soared into the many thousands, the public began to view them with newfound appreciation.

So great was the need for helicopters in the Korean War, and so valuable their participation, that the door was thrown open for volume production. Larry Bell would at last see his stockpile of Franklins used up, and quickly. Ordered for the personal-helicopter market that never materialized, these power plants—the component of helicopter manufacture requiring the longest lead time—expedited the fulfillment of Bell's Korean War orders.[39] "The best mistake I ever made," was how Bell enthusiastically described his fast-vanishing mountain of crated engines.[40]

If saving lives was the helicopter's present military mission, the possibility of using them offensively was already being discussed among manufacturers and military men. Early in the Korean War, Weichsel had occasion to demonstrate Bell's first "armed" helicopter to the U.S. Marine Corps at Quantico, Virginia. It was nothing more than a stock Bell HTL with a bazooka strapped onto it, but wartime priorities had diverted live munitions to Korea and no shells for the weapon were to be found anywhere on base. Displaying great resourcefulness, Weichsel offered a half case of scotch for each live bazooka shell rounded up by noon the following day. A good supply of ammunition materialized in short order.

Korea's impact on Bell was huge. In 1951, the company reported an after-taxes income of $1,827,369 on gross sales and income from subsidiaries of $82,371,336. Employment, which numbered 6,800 at the start of the year, zoomed to 11,500 by December 31, and unfilled orders reached $370 million. In 1952, earnings were $3,043,441 on sales and income of $129,514,375, employment reached 14,550, and the backlog hovered near its wartime peak of $450 million. Although the war ended in the middle of 1953, BAC recorded further increases for the year as a whole. The net income for 1953 was $3,465,423, gross sales/subsidiary income $146,929,791, and employment 16,627. Only during two years of World War II had Bell done better.

At that juncture, Bell Aircraft consisted of twenty-two separate facilities in four states. With floor space of 2,875,464 square feet, it once again ranked as a major component in the U.S. aviation industry. By now Bell's business fell into three main camps: electronics, rocket motors, and missiles; major bomber assemblies as a subcontractor to other manufacturers; and military and commercial helicopters. This last area—termed a company program since the Gardenville days—was belatedly elevated to a BAC division on January 7, 1951.

Company treasurer Harvey Gaylord was promoted to vice president and named Helicopter Division general manager. A Prince-ton man and stockbroker who joined Bell Aircraft in 1942, Gaylord had no engineering or manufacturing experience, but he was an able administrator who listened well and knew how to pick good people. The success his division would enjoy came about partly because he trusted his able staff and knew when to stay out of the way.

Within months, Gaylord and his Helicopter Division had vacated the Wheatfield plant at Niagara Falls Airport. Their departure reflected Larry Bell's conviction that vertical flight could not develop in the shadow of Bell Aircraft's other activities. "I want an organization that thinks helicopters morning, noon, and night," he explained to his board. "We have a great variety of projects in Buffalo. The staff doesn't have time to give more than a lick and a promise to the helicopter."[41]

On the weekend of March 3–4, 1951, almost the entire Helicopter Division moved to a two-story building in Kenmore, New York. Built for the Curtiss Airplane Company during World War II, its 38,000 square feet provided ample space for the division's administrative, engineering, contractual, sales, service, spare parts, and other departments. Only the construction of Bell 47s was left behind at Niagara Falls. The former Curtiss facility included a 375,000-square-foot manufacturing building, however, and Larry Bell was already arranging to move helicopter production there.

But Kenmore was to be merely an interim venue for the Helicopter Division. On January 30, 1951, Larry Bell had selected a 55-acre site near Fort Worth, Texas, to be the permanent home. The government-owned B-29 plant that BAC had operated during World War II in Marietta, Georgia, had left Bell favorably impressed with the South and its people. He had also been taken with the warmth, forthright demeanor, and pioneering spirit exhibited by Texans. The logical choice was the Dallas–Fort Worth area, a major transcontinental airline hub. That advantage would facilitate business travel and encourage visits by would-be helicopter customers. Fort Worth was also one of the homes of Convair, for which Bell was then building jet pods.

The Bell site on the outskirts of Fort Worth had open cattle land with railroad lines at the rear and a lightly traveled eight-lane highway at the front. Since only some 150 families lived in the entire region, helicopters could be flown with little worry of complaint. And the winters there—or for that matter, almost anywhere—were considerably milder than in snowy Buffalo, New York.

Bell Aircraft purchased this tract of land on March 22 at $1,000 per acre. On May 21, ground was broken in an official ceremony for a two-story 40,000-square-foot administration building fronting a 165,000-square-foot factory 500 feet long by 320 feet wide. The new factory also featured a helipad, a first for Texas. Total cost was $7 million. It would have been higher but for the U.S. Navy. Then committed to Bell as the manufacturer of its new ASW helicopter, that service provided much of the equipment needed to get HSL production under way.

On February 23, meanwhile, Bell Aircraft leased a disused aircraft factory fourteen miles to the northwest in the town of Saginaw, Texas. This government-owned facility had been the home of Globe Aircraft, which had built AT-10 trainers under license during World War II, and Swift light planes of its own design just afterward. Using the Globe plant as a local base of operations, Harvey Gaylord initiated the orderly transfer of Helicopter Division facilities and personnel to Texas. Helping him were special assistant Edwin J. Ducayet, Jr., an MIT-trained engineer with a gift for administration, and James C. Fuller, a former Fort Worth newspaperman hired by Larry Bell to handle public relations.

Although a small quantity of helicopters was assembled at Kenmore, the bulk of production had remained at Wheatfield instead of being transferred to the former Curtiss factory. Under Gaylord's direction, it all came south by train to Globe at Fort Worth. The move went remarkably smoothly, civil and military customers experiencing no disruptions in delivery or support of their helicopters. A total of 388 Bell helicopters had been built in New York State.

One of Fuller's assignments was to send Larry Bell weekly reports and aerial photographs documenting all progress in construction. Another assignment was to produce a movie showing Buffalo-area workers what they could expect if they moved to Texas. Fuller's film showed lakes and beautiful countryside, but it also paraphrased President Truman: if you can't stand heat, don't come. In the end, three hundred families followed their employer to Fort Worth and none later opted to return north. The majority of the work force, however, was drawn from the greater Dallas–Fort Worth region. Their remarkable warmth and friendliness characterize Bell Helicopter Textron to this day.

Larry Bell visited his new plant before it was finished. "There was a parking lot at one end and a landing field at the other," he later told his biographer. "When I got down there, they told me they planned to build the helicopters in a line headed toward the parking lot, then turn them around and bring them down the road to the airport. I told them: 'What the hell's the sense of that? Why don't

(Top) Bell Aircraft vice president Harvey Gaylord breaks ground in Texas for a factory dedicated to helicopters, May 21, 1951. At left stands Amon Carter, publisher of the *Fort Worth Star Telegram*. Courtesy Bell.

(Bottom) This heavily retouched photograph shows the newly completed Bell Helicopter plant in 1952. Subsequent construction has since quadrupled the size of this facility. Courtesy Bell.

you turn the line around and have them come out where they belong?' And that's the way it is now."[42]

Construction progressed quickly and on December 3, 1951, less than seven months after ground was broken, E. J. "Duke" Ducayet became the partly finished facility's first occupant. Without ceremony, the slender forty-three-year-old engineer threaded his way through the construction rubble, personal trappings under his arm, and found a place to sit. Finding it again on successive mornings proved to be a challenge until he learned to follow a cord. "I would come to work each morning and start looking for my desk," Ducayet later recalled. "Second shift construction workers would move it each night as work progressed on the administration building. And I had one telephone with about 50 yards of wire so the phone could follow my desk around."[43]

A proud new era thus began for Bell Helicopter, as Bell Aircraft's young vertical-flight division was informally named. Of the many advantages this dynamic organization counted, the greatest was the extraordinary enthusiasm of its dedicated work force. Despite a few conspicuous failures in the coming years, theirs was perhaps the most gratifying success story in the history of vertical flight.

Unfortunately, one conspicuous Bell failure was the tandem-rotor HSL then being developed for the Navy. Of all the roles helicopters would play in support of America's senior service, none was deemed so important as antisubmarine warfare. It was seen as a crucial deterrent to "sneak attacks" by an estimated 350 to 375 Soviet submarines. The HSL's relatively lavish budget confirmed that ASW had the highest priority. Having helped fund the construction of Bell Helicopter's new

home, this one program was now paying the plant's overhead expenses.

The largest production helicopter to date, the Bell HSL was designed around AN/SOS-4A dipping sonar equipment, which added 603 pounds to the empty weight of each airframe. As formulated by Pentagon planners, hunter-killer HSL teams would fly patrols lasting up to three and a half hours. The hunter version would carry two pilots and two sonar operators, while the killer would have one pilot and one sonar operator. The weight thus saved would allow this latter model to carry two Mark 43 acoustic torpedoes to home in on submerged submarines, and Fairchild Petrel missiles to combat those caught on the surface.

Bell's Niagara Frontier Division was already at work developing an autopilot for the HSL. Described in company literature as "far superior to human coordination for flight operations in turbulent weather where pinpoint accuracy is required,"[44] this unit would add to the stability already provided by the stabilizer bar on the craft's high-inertia foldable rotor.

Three XHSL-1 prototypes were constructed at Bell Helicopter. The first left the factory main gate at 8:48 A.M. on March 3, 1953. It was towed seven and a half miles to Fort Worth's new Amon Carter Airfield because the Navy was interested in evaluating its "roadability" (a strange requirement for a helicopter). The following day, chief test pilot Floyd Carlson and Joe Dunne, another veteran Bell test pilot, lifted the ungainly machine from the ground for the first time.

From the outset, the HSL series proved disappointing. Underpowered and slow, its interior noise levels were so high that the sonar could not be used effectively. Furthermore, its controls were so heavy that maneuverability suffered. The Navy received its first production HSL-1 in the fall of 1953. Six months later, one successfully flew 1,465 miles from Fort Worth to Patuxent, Maryland, for trials at the Naval Air Test Center on June 17, 1954.

An eight-day Atlantic cruise beginning February 25, 1955, provided the first opportunity to evaluate its suitability for Naval operations. Taken aboard the Navy carrier USS *Kula Gulf* amid a 50-ship task force, three HSLs hunted USN submarines doubling for their Soviet counterparts. These machines flew in winds reaching 50 knots above 30-foot waves that lashed the task force. Mashman, Carlson, Bart Kelley, and eight other Bell employees accompanied the HSLs as observers. So rough was the sea that Mashman awoke one night to find that the ship's gyrations had "walked" his cot out his stateroom door and down the ship's narrow corridor.

On the plus side, the HSLs demonstrated stability as a sonar platform, the ability to operate in rough weather, and ease of shipboard handling. Even in driving rain atop the pitching deck, little trouble was experienced positioning them or bringing them up and down the carrier's two elevators. But these advantages did not offset their considerable shortcomings.

In addition to the performance limitations and excessive interior noise, Navy personnel objected to the length of the new helicopter, which obstructed too much of the flight deck. They also stated that it took too long to unfold the rotor blades for deployment. Upon completion of the maneuvers, the *Kula Gulf* passed twenty miles off the Virginia Capes to allow the three HSLs to fly back to the Naval Air Test Center at NAS Patuxent River.

One month after this cruise, a hovering HSL-1 crashed when its forward rotor struck an obstruction at Hurst Heliport. The machine burst into flames. Bell employee Frank "Chick" LaJudice, then supervising flight operations, jumped into a jeep and raced to the scene. Mechanic Harry J. Campbell also reached the scene at that time. Seeing Navy Lieutenant Robert Edwards rolling from the wreckage, his clothes afire, the men pulled him to safety as other Bell employees arrived. Leaving him in their care, they tried in vain to rescue the craft's other occupant, Lieutenant W. A. Suker.

Edwards had been the Bureau of Aeronautics' Resident Representative (BARR) to Bell for two years. Although not based at Bell, Suker—a helicopter project officer with BuAer and father of four—was well known to company officials at Fort Worth. The tragedy came as a great blow. Added to the list of difficulties that had plagued the program, it helped seal the fate of the only tandem-rotor helicopter ever produced in the United States by a company other than Piasecki/ Vertol/ Boeing Helicopters in Philadelphia.

Bell had orders for ninety-six HSL-1s for the USN and eighteen more for Britain's Royal Navy. So unsatisfactory did the world's first dedicated ASW helicopter prove to be, however, that production ended after only fifty were built. Most were immediately mothballed upon receipt.

On a Friday afternoon at 4:30, Jim Fuller heard the clatter of the Telex machine. The incoming message brought official notification of U.S. Navy termination of the HSL program. Fuller and James F. Atkins, the company comptroller, were the only people still manning the front office. They immediately summoned their fellow executives back from their weekends to begin the grim duty of laying off employees.

By then, Bell's H-12 program had been over for a few years. Despite the success of eleven YH-12 service test aircraft, this intermediate-size transport helicopter (which weighed only a quarter as much as the HSL) had not been ordered into production by the Army on whose behalf the Air Force had procured it. The reason for its demise was the success of the Sikorsky H-19 of 1949, a slightly larger machine offering considerably more utility than the H-12.

Yet another disappointing military program was the USAF's XH-15 high-performance two-seater of 1948. Powered by a supercharged 275-hp Continental XO-470 power plant, this souped-up "hotrod" cousin to the Model 47 suffered from chronic troubles that greatly extended its flight test program. They would eventually cause the XH-15 to be canceled, but not before Test Pilot Elton J. Smith made the longest autorotation ever performed up to that time. Following a climb to high altitude in the spring of 1953, Smith was forced by severe engine surge to chop the throttle at 16,000 feet. It took the powerless helicopter more than ten minutes to spiral down to a safe deadstick landing on the factory ramp.

In fact, only one Bell military helicopter program during the Korean War years would not be classed a failure. The lowly Model 47, as the Army H-13 and Marine Corps HTL, played a starring role in Korea. Together with Hillers and larger Sikorskys, the Bells lowered the combat death rate to 2 percent, less than half the World War II level. Of almost 20,000 U.S., British, French, South Korean, Benelux, Thai, Ethiopian, Turkish, Greek, and other troops evacuated by helicopters during this conflict, 85 percent—well over 15,000 people—were carried to safety by Bells.

So great was the Bell helicopter's contribution to the Korean War that it inspired *Battle Circus* (1953), a forgettable motion picture starring Humphrey Bogart and June Allyson. Centered around a Mobile Army Surgical Hospital (MASH) unit near the front, this film was so cliché ridden that it did little to capture the imagination.

One new employee hired in October 1952 needed no Hollywood fluff to convince him of the lifesaving value of Bell helicopters. Nineteen-year-old Fort Worth native Vernie L. Collins, a painter at the Globe plant helicopter finishing department, lost part of his right arm during bloody fighting in Korea's infamous Punchbowl sector the year before. Ironically, he was at his job for a week before he realized his new employer had built the Marine Corps HTL-4 that had evacuated him.

About the time Collins arrived, Bell Helicopter was commended by the city of Fort Worth for its sensitivity to the needs of the disabled. More than 15 percent of Bell's work force was physically or mentally impaired, a statistic that reflected active hiring policies instituted by Larry Bell and Harvey Gaylord, who shared a strong dedication to helping the handicapped.

Larry Bell looked to his company to benefit the local communities. In a manner that was patriarchal but not patrician, he felt responsibility for the well-being of his new employees, their families, and all the region's inhabitants. The degree of his concern became clear as Jim Fuller drove him from the airport to the plant. Reflecting on the increased traffic his plant generated on the highway fronting the main gate, Bell told Fuller that he would not be able to stand it if Bell Helicopter caused even one fatality. As a direct result of this sentiment, new employ-

(*Top*) The unsuccessful Bell HSL-1 was the world's first helicopter designed from the outset for anti-submarine warfare. Courtesy Bell.

(*Bottom*) Developed for the U.S. Air Force, the trouble-plagued XH-15 (Model 54) was a high-performance cousin of the Model 47. Courtesy NASM/SI.

ees were required to sign statements promising never to exceed local speed limits. They were also made to display stickers to that effect on their car windows.

Bell Helicopter really got on its feet in 1952, the year it occupied its new permanent home north of Fort Worth. It began this pivotal year with just 256 employees in the unfinished factory, whose idle fabrication area served as a staff cafeteria. Twelve months later, it was a bustling factory with 2,600 workers. Model 47 production had been transferred there from Globe during May, leaving that alternate facility with B-36 and B-47 jet pod construction. It also served as the division's civil and military helicopter training center. Additional equipment and tooling installed during the year brought the new plant's value to $17 million.

In numbers produced—although not in airframe weight—Bell led the vertical-flight industry. The Fort Worth division had rolled out substantially more rotorcraft in 1952 than Sikorsky, Piasecki, Hiller, or newcomer Kaman—sixty-seven in December alone—and it had somehow never missed a delivery schedule despite its move and the wartime production pressures. At the end of the year, the Pentagon released information that made the holiday season more joyous: the number of soldiers evacuated by Bell helicopters in Korea had topped 12,000.

Perhaps the most memorable event of 1952 was an official world helicopter distance record established September 17, 1952, by test pilot Elton Smith (some eight months before the record 16,000-foot autorotation described above). In an overloaded Bell 47D-1 nicknamed *Longhorn*, equipped with two candy bars, a sandwich, a half gallon of water, and 187 gallons of gas (six times its normal supply), Smith departed the Texas division flight line before dawn and flew 1,217 miles nonstop to land on the front lawn of Bell Aircraft Corporation headquarters in Niagara Falls at 6:38 P.M. eastern time. President Larry Bell stepped forward to greet the pilot with a warm handshake as the helicopter's rotor wound down.

Smith, who had flown fifty-six bomber missions in the Mediterranean theater during World War II, had enjoyed clear sailing during the trip, except over the Ozarks where thunderstorms forced a detour. "When I arrived," he informed reporters, "I had enough gas left to go another four hours, and I used only two quarts of oil on the trip."[45]

Smith's *Longhorn*, N167B, was not a new helicopter. Built five years earlier as a 47B, it had been upgraded to D-1 standard. By the time of this flight, it had already logged almost 400 hours in the air. Although its radio had failed early in the trip, the *Longhorn* itself had functioned flawlessly during its twelve hours aloft. The Texas–New York flight easily shattered a record set six years earlier by Air Force Major F. T. Cashman, who flew a Sikorsky S-51 nonstop from Wright Field in Ohio to Boston's Logan International Airport.

On April 10, 1953, Bell delivered its 1,000th Model 47. Built less than seven years after Bell helicopter production began, this machine went to Wiggins Airways of Norwood, Massachusetts, which a half-dozen years earlier had purchased the 57th Model 47. Among those on hand to celebrate this company milestone were the nine members of Arthur Young's original Gardenville team who still worked for Bell Helicopter: Joe Mashman, Bart Kelley, Bud Kelley (no relation), Floyd Carlson, Percy Waller, Jack Buyers, Tom Harriman, "Butch" Luke, and Karl Camp.

By far the most significant event of 1953

(*Top*) Larry Bell congratulates Elton Smith at the conclusion of the test pilot's record-setting 1,217-mile nonstop flight from Fort Worth to Niagara Falls in Bell 47D-1 *Longhorn* on September 17, 1952. Courtesy Bell.

(*Bottom*) Gardenville veterans Joe Mashman, Floyd Carlson, Percy Waller, Bart Kelley, and Jack Buyers pose on April 10, 1953, with the 1,000th helicopter produced by Bell. Courtesy Bell.

Introduced in 1953, the rugged Model 47G—
Bell's finest piston helicopter—was versatile, capable, and reliable. Courtesy NASM/SI.

was the May 20 unveiling at Fort Worth of the Bell Model 47G. Powered by the same 200-hp Franklin as the 47D-1, the G offered fundamental rotor blade and control system improvements. It could be distinguished from the D-1 by twin fuel tanks, a ventral fin forward of the tail rotor, and an elevator. Linked directly to the cyclic stick, this movable control surface on the tail boom widened the Model 47's narrow center-of-gravity range by 40 percent, answering a long-standing request by commercial operators for wider CG limits.

Located farther forward than the old fuel tank, the two 20-gallon tanks placed the fuel at the helicopter's center of gravity to eliminate a shift in CG as fuel burned off. Their greater capacity gave the new 47G more range than earlier models. Maximum speed was 90 mph, cruise speed 77 mph, and gross weight 2,350 pounds. The Army's initial version of the 47G was the H-13G and the Navy's the HTL-6.

In June 1953, Larry Bell made a 12,000-mile tour of the Far East that included a visit to operational helicopter units in Korea. That undeclared war was all but over when the industry leader realized a long-standing desire to see the front lines (something he had not been able to do in the two world wars). Declining health made this inspection tour an ordeal. Bell looked ill and complained of chest pains, but he persevered. "I had dinner in a mess hall with 20,000 airmen," he remarked afterward, "and I remember the time when I personally knew every man in the Air Corps."[46]

Other Bell people also visited Korea. One was E. J. Ducayet, who coordinated H-13 spares support from there. Others were Bell's service and technical representatives. Rotary-wing technology was so new that the Army had not known how much support it would

need, but Bell had the foresight to send many more people than had been officially requested. They proved invaluable in keeping the underpowered little Bells operating in Korea's demanding environment.

On July 17, 1953, Bell delivered a 47G to Rod Moore's Aviation Service in Corpus Christi, the first commercial helicopter service in Texas. As it had done with Petroleum Bell Helicopters, the manufacturer went the extra mile to get Moore started. A Bell pilot and a service representative were assigned to the company to help launch its operations, and Bell's public relations firm, which was already serving Petroleum Bell Helicopters at no cost to that company, was brought in to help this new operator sell its services. With all this assistance, Moore's 47G was soon gainfully employed shuttling men and equipment around Gulf Coast oil fields.

Joe Mashman and other company pilots continued to demonstrate Bells around the country. Since 1951, they had had at their disposal a series of company helicopters painted gloss white with blue trim. These demonstration ships were nicknamed *Snow White*, an unofficial title that threatened trouble with Walt Disney Studios in California. By the time a new 47G joined the team early in 1954, a deal had been worked out with the Disney people and the helicopter sported a studio-supplied decal of the cartoon character. In return for permission to use the name and image, the Bell Helicopter Division sent Walt Disney a model of the ship to display on his desk.

From the start of production through 1953, Bell had delivered only 277 commercial Model 47s. Because of the Korean War, it had produced 938 H-13s. With that conflict over, the stage was set for the commercial side of production to boom. Three key elements were in place that had been lacking before the war: newfound awareness of the capability of helicopters; a large pool of trained pilots and mechanics, most of whom had chosen to return to civilian life; and expanded production capacity. The time was right for civil sales to catch up with military sales.

Bell Aircraft as a whole came out of Korea much enlarged. In marked contrast to its fortunes at the end of World War II, it would briefly continue to grow. By July 1954 the company had gained two more facilities in New York State, giving Bell's Niagara Frontier Division a total of nine sites. Between electronics, propulsion, and new high-speed research planes, the division boasted an impressive backlog of business, largely because Bell Aircraft had emerged as a key builder of U.S. guided missiles like the GAM-63 Rascal. No other company in the nation could build missiles from scratch, including guidance systems and rocket engines. Bell thus became a major cold-war arms supplier.

Although this newfound status promised to regularize the feast-and-famine production cycles that had plagued the company, Larry Bell continued to pursue his program of diversification. In December 1954 this effort saw the Hydraulic Research and Development Company of Burbank, California, brought under the Bell umbrella, bringing to five the number of BAC's wholly owned subsidiaries.

The continuing USAF/NACA high-speed research program also generated business. Late in 1953, Chuck Yeager had flown the Bell X-1A at 1,650 mph or 2.5 times the speed of sound. Earlier in the year, however, a Douglas airplane became the first to reach Mach 2. It was the first suggestion that Bell Aircraft's leadership in the design and construction of maximum-performance aircraft was beginning to erode. Had Bell kept abreast

of the decade's explosive technological growth, it would have reserved for itself a starring role in the U.S. manned space program. For whatever reason, it faltered in the late 1950s, surrendering this opportunity largely to North American Aviation. Employment at Bell's Niagara-Frontier Division declined from 16,000 in 1957 to just 3,000 by the start of the 1960s.

In April 1954, Bell's manufacture of jet pods for the ten-engine Convair B-36 finally came to an end. This lost production volume at Globe was soon offset by a Boeing order placed two weeks earlier for manufacture of inboard and outboard nacelles for the Strategic Air Command's B-52 bomber. Two new Bell helicopter models were also announced during the year, the 47G-1 and 47H. Both differed from previous 47s in having aluminum tail booms of semi-monocoque construction. "I don't want to see the sun set through that damn tail boom one more day,"[47] Larry Bell told Bell engineers and executives during a periodic inspection of the flight line at Fort Worth. Both new models showed that his vehement words had been taken to heart.

The 47H Bellairus, built at Globe, was in fact styled under Bell's personal supervision. This helicopter packaged the engine, dynamic components, and systems of the standard G model in a sleeker body whose cabin had been widened to 60 inches. The extra space permitted the installation of three automotive-quality seats and substantial soundproofing. The 47H also featured a roomy baggage compartment. Streamlining reportedly added 20 percent to this new model's speed, and subtracted a like percentage from fuel consumption at cruise speed.

The Model 47G-1 (soon redesignated the 47J Ranger) was a stretched H model with a single pilot's seat ahead of bench seating for three passengers. Like the 47H, the J model was intended primarily for the executive transport market.

Looking substantially more modern than the popular 47G, these new models appeared to employ full semi-monocoque or "stressed-skin" construction, as did the competing Hiller UH-12 helicopter. However, only the tail cones of the 47H and J used stressed-skin construction; disguised with sheet metal, their fuselages retained their steel-tube structures.

Now assistant director of contracts, Joe Mashman had a hand in defining these new helicopters, which were based largely on market research he had conducted. In the latter part of 1954, the Model H and J prototypes were dispatched on an extensive "market reaction" tour that failed to turn up much evidence of the enthusiasm Mashman's study had predicted.

Meantime, the Model 47G, with its girder tail, continued to sell briskly. Commercial sales for 1954 ran 20 percent above the previous year's record level, assuring Bell of another banner year, and they would be 30 percent higher still the following year. Export sales, including those to foreign military services, now accounted for seven of ten 47G commercial deliveries.

These successes were marred by a helicopter crash in October 1954, Bell's first since moving to Texas three years earlier. Company flight instructor Roger Kaadtmann and Philip Shrock, pilot for Safety Copters Inc., were killed just hours after the Dallas-based commercial operation accepted a new 47G in official ceremonies at the Globe plant. A postcrash fire made it impossible for investigators to determine what had gone wrong.

With 20,000 test, demonstration, and other flights logged without incident (the HSL-1 crash described above would not occur for another five months), Bell had good reason to believe in the safety of the Model 47 series. This tragedy prompted Chief Test Pilot Floyd Carlson to redouble his efforts in a personal crusade for safety. Carlson—famous as one of the world's first helicopter pilots—had a personal stake in the issue. He had lost his brother Milton to the similarly mysterious crash of one of the first ten Model 47s near Buffalo eight years earlier.

In this crusade, Carlson had the unswerving commitment of fellow Gardenville veteran Bart Kelley, who was fast rising to head Bell Helicopter's engineering department. Between them, they pushed Bell to extraordinary lengths in the pursuit of safety. Fortunately, they were supported by an enlightened management that saw the wisdom of investing in this critical area.

An uncompromising commitment to safety was just one of countless contributions Bart Kelley made to Bell Helicopter. "Bart had the gift of stimulating new developments and bringing out the best in us," observes helicopter pioneer Jan Drees, who left his native Holland to come to work for Bell. "From engineering, to the laboratories, to flight test, and manufacturing, Bart was very well-liked and highly regarded throughout the company. He was an excellent leader who helped keep Bell Helicopter lean and competitive."[48]

On October 1, 1954, Larry Bell had stepped down as general manager of Bell Aircraft, although he remained president. Bell had held both posts since founding his company in 1935. He announced that his decision "was made in view of the increasing diversification of Bell Aircraft and the company's growing responsibilities to the nation's defense."[49] Worsening health prompted this shift, however, for Bell suffered from hypertensive cardiovascular disease.

Board members elected Leston P. Faneuf to be the new general manager. Faneuf retained his duties as treasurer but relinquished the title of corporate secretary to comptroller William P. Gisel. Both he and Gisel had been with the company since 1942.

Larry Bell had a special fondness for the Bell Model 47H Bellairus, in many ways the helicopter he had long wanted to build. As a result, the first production example was diverted to Niagara Falls for his personal use early in 1955. In April two Model 47Hs were lent to the Atomic Energy Commission for use at its proving grounds at Yucca Flats, Nevada. In those less-enlightened times, the machines were used to speed VIPs to ground zero to observe the aftermath of aboveground nuclear bomb tests. The second official commercial delivery of a Model H was to Colombian President Gustavo Rojas Pinilla in June 1955. But the public never cared as much for the H, which sold modestly. Customers continued to prefer the less expensive and more utilitarian 47G.

Bell engineers had already come up with an improved version called the 47G-2 Trooper. Produced for many years, this superb helicopter was the definitive Bell piston helicopter. The G-2 was also Bell's first light helicopter not powered by the Franklin (Aircooled Motors) 6v4 engine. Franklins rarely delivered their full rated power, and their reliability left something to be desired. Their high-maintenance design was out of date. As a result, Bell engineers were delighted to replace them with newly developed Lycoming VO-435 power plants.

The Lycoming VO-435 considerably improved the performance of Bell's light helicopters. Rated at 260 hp, it had to be derated because the Model 47's transmission could not accept more than 200 hp. The substitution was nevertheless well worthwhile. As engine power fell off at altitude due to thinning air, the new engine's unused capability could be progressively called upon to maintain full power to a greater height.

Tests performed in 1954 of the prototype Model 47J Ranger had shown this four-seater to be excessively underpowered with the Franklin engine. The new executive model needed more than 200 hp at sea level. It was therefore withheld from the marketplace until a higher-power gearbox could be perfected and certified for use with the Lycoming engine. Ranger deliveries were accordingly delayed until 1956.

By April 1955, Bell Helicopter had received commercial orders worth more than a quarter million dollars for the Lycoming-powered Model 47G-2 Trooper. Its vastly improved high-altitude, hot-weather performance kept it much in demand with commercial operators. Because military use took priority, however, commercial deliveries were delayed until early the following year. Fenwick SA, Bell's French dealer, received the first 47G-2 in 1956, followed by two each to Canada's Spartan Air Service and Aero Copters of Seattle.

Under the designation H-13H (soon revised to OH-13H Sioux), two G-2s had begun Army trials at Fort Rucker, Alabama, early in 1955. Based on this evaluation, the service placed an order for an initial twenty-one H-13Hs in July. These helicopters were equipped with dual controls, radios, winterization kits, litters, and night-flying equipment. They introduced all-metal rotor blades of a type developed jointly by Bell at Fort Worth and the USAF's Wright Air Development Center in Ohio. Lighter and stronger than wood, these fully interchangeable units eliminated the previous need for matched blade sets.

The G-2 and all other Bell 47s got "power steering" in 1955. Introduced on the 47H, this hydraulic control boost added a feeling of smooth precision to the cyclic stick. Hydraulic boost was not essential for control and was not a critical system. If it failed in flight, the jerky irreversible control system developed by Arthur Young remained as a backup.

By mid-decade, some 125 companies or individuals were operating fleets of from one to thirty helicopters. Business was booming at Bell's Helicopter Division, where total sales for the year reached $48 million. Commercial sales were up 24 percent over the previous year, which had itself seen a 15 percent gain over 1953. Much of this boom resulted from successful company efforts to lower the extremely high operating costs of early Bells; by 1955 they were half the 1950 level.

During the year, the Helicopter Division embarked on a $415,000 facility expansion that covered construction of a transmission test building at Globe, the addition of control towers at both facilities, and rotor whirl-stand improvement. A further $600,000 was allocated for an additional 40,000 square feet of manufacturing floor space, bringing the total investment to nearly $16 million and total floor space to more than 625,000 square feet.

It was at this time, with expansion afoot and 47G-2 production just getting into full swing, that the Navy canceled the luckless HSL. Loss of the major Defense Department program had a profound effect on Bell. With it went the opportunity to enter the arena of large helicopter manufacture. Had the HSL met the Navy's requirements, Bell Helicopter might have joined Piasecki and Sikorsky as an established manufacturer of large rotorcraft. Writing off its heavy investment in the failed program, the Navy went knocking at Sikorsky's door to buy S-58s for interim ASW until a dedicated, turbine-powered submarine hunter-killer could be procured.

For five years, the Navy had carried Bell Aircraft's Helicopter Division with lavish infusions of public money that largely funded the facilities in Fort Worth and heavily subsidized the Model 47 program. Now with this funding abruptly gone, Bell awoke to find itself with only one viable helicopter program and a host of newfound challenges.

"Bell Helicopter grew up when the HSL was canceled," Jim Fuller recalled. "We'd been doing fine with the Navy carrying us. With the cancellation, we suddenly had to learn how to make the Model 47 both better and cheaper, and we had to learn how to merchandise it more effectively. Fortunately, we had just come up with the Lycoming-powered 47G-2. It really made Bell Helicopter."[50]

One way to market this helicopter was through publicity. Unlike earlier Model 47s, the G-2 gave commercial users the all-around capability they had long wanted. Since this new machine would first be delivered to the Army, Bell decided to whet the appetite of civil helicopter operators through a series of performance demonstrations. Fully a year before it hit the civil market in June 1956, a 47G-2 with two people aboard landed atop the 15,771-foot summit of Mont Blanc, the highest peak in the Alps. Mounts Whitney and Rainier in North America were soon also conquered by the G-2 or its military counterpart, the H-13H.

This program continued through October 1958, when Bell received a tip from an Army public information officer. An H-23 was scheduled to claim Pike's Peak, whose summit had yet to be visited by a helicopter. That Army helicopter was a military version of the Hiller UH-12 series, which offered slightly better performance per given horsepower than the Bell 47. The rival machine's altitude capability in particular had cost Bell sales ever since a dramatic 1949 occurrence in California's High Sierra, when a Hiller had succeeded in rescuing an injured boy after a Bell had failed.

When the H-23 approached Pike's Peak on the last day of October 1958, escorted by a camera ship, its crew was consternated to find a Bell already occupying the rocky summit. Such horseplay reflected the healthy competition between Bell and Hiller.

Another way to sell more helicopters was to nurture markets, and here Bell led the industry. It had already set up, demonstrated, and spun off what was by now the largest rotary-wing operation in the United States, Petroleum Helicopters, Inc. Senior Helicopter Division executives toured the world, visiting existing Bell users to ask how else they might use the Model 47 to increase their profits. This tactic paid off in follow-on orders that successfully offset declines in new business.

In March 1955, Bell Aircraft formed the Bell Exploration and Development Corporation with offices in Fort Worth and Glendale. The purpose of this wholly owned division, headed by Harvey Gaylord, was to interest the mining industry in hunting for uranium by air. Bell 47G N940B was fitted out as an aerial prospector with a scintillometer in the cabin and a portable diamond-tipped drill on its landing skid. However, this experiment did not match the success of Bell's petroleum-industry effort.

At 4:00 P.M. September 3, 1956, a Bell H-13H landed after remaining aloft 57 hours

and 50 minutes, setting an unofficial world endurance record at the conclusion of that year's National Aircraft Show in Oklahoma City. The old record had been doubled, yet Army officials announced that the helicopter could have flown another 50 hours without landing. Six Army fliers had taken turns at the controls, periodically hovering low over the ground to take on fuel and trade places.

The next day, Joe Mashman, now Bell's assistant contracts manager, and service representative Joe Beebe departed in the factory-fresh Model 47J *Silver Hummingbird* on a grueling Latin American tour. In eighty-three days of hard use, this Ranger faithfully carried the two men some 17,000 miles through Central and South America.

Mashman demonstrated the company's new four-seater in Mexico, Guatemala, El Salvador, Nicaragua, Costa Rica, Panama, Colombia, Ecuador, Peru, Chile, Argentina, Uruguay, Paraguay, Brazil, and Venezuela. Keeping to a tight schedule, he several times had to fly twenty or more miles out to sea to avoid bad weather. He also skimmed impenetrable jungles, brushing their green canopies with his skids, and hedge-hopped 5,000-foot mountain peaks while remaining in sight of the ground in heavy overcast. The altitude performance of the Lycoming-powered 47J— only the second Ranger off the assembly line—was ably demonstrated when Mashman topped 17,000 feet while crossing the Andes at Christo Pass. Twelve weeks after setting out, the pair concluded this remarkable tour with a well-practiced flight display at Caracas. Afterward, Mashman and Beebe delivered their faithful mount to Aerotécnica, a commercial charter operation serving the oil rigs of Lake Maracaibo.

A key purpose of the tour was to dispel mis-

The four-seat Bell Model 47J. Courtesy NASM/SI.

conceptions about high operating costs, poor performance, and lack of dependability of helicopters. The *Silver Hummingbird* had done this. Its 250 hours aloft had been trouble-free and it had required only 40 hours of routine maintenance on the ground. Extra spark plugs, ignition points, and a fan belt had not been needed, although they were used for added safety before crossing the Andes. "We proved without a doubt that the helicopter has come of age and can perform a wide variety of useful services for business and industry," an elated Mashman announced upon his return to Fort Worth.[51]

Compared to fixed-wing aircraft, nevertheless, helicopters still required a disheartening amount of maintenance downtime that added to their operating costs and limited their appeal. The entire industry was at work trying to find solutions.

Late in 1954, the Army had issued a contract to Bell to maintain seventy of its H-13s in a new way called "inspect-and-repair-as-necessary" (IRAN). Nine H-13BS, CS, DS, ES, and even a few GS went to Fort Worth each month under this pilot program, which the Army had recently adopted as a lower-cost alternative to completely tearing down each H-13 after 600 flight hours. At the same time, Bell upgraded its older Army models with skids instead of wheels, and made other improvements.

That helped the taxpayer but not the commercial operator. Both benefited greatly, however, from an extension in the recommended time between overhauls from 600 to 1,200 hours, announced by Bell at the beginning of 1958. This authorization meant that 47Gs and G-2s could be flown the equivalent of four times around the world at the equator between major servicings. A similar extension announced in the spring of 1960 helped the operators of the hundred or so 47Js then in service.

When a blue and white 47J whisked Dwight Eisenhower from the White House lawn to Camp David on July 13, 1957, he became the first U.S. president to fly in a helicopter. After spending a relaxing weekend at his "remote command post" in the Maryland mountains two hours away, he returned the same way. Chipper and smiling, Eisenhower—a licensed fixed-wing pilot—proclaimed this helicopter flight "the smoothest ride I ever had in my life."[52] This 47J, one of two Rangers that began a long tradition of presidential helicopters, is today preserved in the collection of the National Air and Space Museum, Smithsonian Institution.

Other Rangers patrolled highways and waterways for the New York City Police Department, shuttled executives in scheduled service between Northrop's three aircraft plants, patrolled ice floes for the Canadian Department of Transportation, and otherwise earned their keep worldwide. All in all, though, commercial sales of the Ranger were disappointing, and the 47J program would not have paid for itself had not the Navy ordered a version designated the HUL for instrument training and general utility use.

Eisenhower's use of Bell light helicopters showered the company with free publicity. More came unexpectedly from Hollywood, which discovered the photogenic Bells. Behind the camera since the late 1940s, Model 47s were now called upon to perform in front of them. There were movie roles, of course, but television was the principal forum for this newfound popularity.

It all began when DesiLu Productions needed a helicopter for the conclusion of a segment of *I Love Lucy*. Having literally missed the boat in one episode, comedienne Lucille Ball catches an ocean liner to Europe by snagging a ride on a helicopter. Pleased at the opportunity to bring its product before millions of viewers, Bell provided the Model 47 at no cost. Unknown to Bell, its helicopter would soon be the star of a hit television series.

Impressed with both the Model 47 and its cooperative builder, DesiLu owners Ball and Desi Arnaz cast about for a way to cash in on the newness and dynamism of light helicopters. What they came up with was *Whirlybirds*, a half-hour television series about two daring commercial helicopter operators in southern California. With this concept in mind, they visited Public Relations Director Jim Fuller in Fort Worth.

Bell's PR chief, who had helped the couple before, saw at once the potential of the series they outlined. Fuller assured them that Bell would provide helicopters and pilots for as long as DesiLu needed them. A veteran of international sales tours, Fuller knew a unique opportunity when he saw it. If the series failed to enter production, he reasoned, Bell would be out only the costs of supporting production for one episode. If it succeeded, the advertising and public relations rewards would be enormous.

Returning to Hollywood, Ball and Arnaz hired Kenneth Tobey and Craig Hill to play the helicopter jockeys in a pilot episode. If the show achieved production, Tobey and Hill were to have relinquished their leather A-2 jackets, khaki baseball caps, and Ray-Ban sunglasses to other actors. So well was the pilot episode received, however, that Tobey and Hill remained the leads. But the real star of *Whirlybirds* was N975B, a Bell Model 47G-2 that stole the show in every episode. It would be joined by a 47J in later episodes. Veteran

helicopter pilots Earl Gilbreath and Rod Parker did all the flying, doubling for the stars in long shots.

A syndicated series, *Whirlybirds* premiered in Omaha early in 1957, and within weeks had been bought by 115 stations across America. Tobey, Hill, and Executive Producer Arnaz were on hand for its Fort Worth premiere, which Bell employees celebrated outside of the plant.

Enormously popular, *Whirlybirds* introduced as many as 25 million people each week to all the capabilities of helicopters. Actual uses of rotary-wing aircraft were authentically depicted, thanks to Fuller, who carefully reviewed each script for technical accuracy.

Ninety-one episodes were completed before *Whirlybirds* went off the air after three seasons. Not particularly significant in the annals of television, the show was profoundly important to vertical flight. It consolidated the Model 47G's position as the nation's archetypal light helicopter, making rotary-wing flight familiar to Americans who rarely saw a real helicopter. With *Whirlybirds*, the Model 47 joined the cultural mainstream. A decade later, its position in American popular culture would be secured by the long-running television series M*A*S*H, in which Bell 47Gs doubled for the 47Bs and Ds that saved so many lives during the Korean War.

Final proof that the Bell 47 had achieved a unique status came with the March 1984 acquisition of an early model by the Museum of Modern Art in New York City. Suspended in flight above the entrance to the museum's Architecture and Design Wing, this venerable machine—a resplendent example of technological sculpture—is as much a work of art as it is an aircraft.

Subsequent models in the 47 series (notably the G-4 and G-5) featured more power, supercharging, and extensive weight reduction. The 5,800th and last of this famous series, a 47G-3B2A, rolled off the Fort Worth assembly line February 14, 1974. Model 47 license production by Mitsui in Japan ended the next year after 423 examples. In Italy, Agusta suspended manufacture in 1978 after delivering 762 units. Manufacture of 236 Model 47s had ended in England long before in 1959.

By the time Bell's piston-helicopter era drew to a close, of course, the Fort Worth company was already well established as a manufacturer of turbine-powered rotorcraft. Bell's first turbine helicopter, the XH-13F, took to the sky on October 20, 1954, with test pilot Bill Quinlan at the controls. Project engineer for this joint Army/USAF research program was J. R. "Bob" Duppstadt.

A French 280-shp Turbomeca Artouste I turboshaft engine powered the XH-13F. It weighed so little that it had to be mounted behind the helicopter's fuel tanks and rotor mast for weight-and-balance reasons. The light weight of turbines made them ideal for helicopters, whose performance had long been constrained by the low power-to-weight ratios of piston engines. Turbine power also promised greater reliability and lower maintenance costs. Their drawbacks were higher fuel consumption and a significantly higher purchase price. The latter would limit civil-market sales far more than those to the military. Putting a premium on performance and having public funds at their disposal, the world's armed services wholeheartedly embraced turbine power.

Pleased with the prototype during its Phase I (factory) testing, Quinlan called the XH-13F the "smoothest Model 47 ever built."[53] At the start of April 1955, the prototype was handed over to USAF Major Jones P. Seigler and First

Lieutenant Donald A. Wooley. The two officers, attached to Edwards Air Force Base in California, conducted the Phase II test program at Fort Worth to ensure good coordination with Bell.

On February 23, Bell had been selected from a field of eight manufacturers as winner of an industrywide competition to build the Army its next-generation medical evacuation helicopter. This USAF-administered contract called for construction of a single-rotor helicopter capable of carrying 800 pounds of payload, climbing at 1,500 feet per minute, cruising at 115 mph, and hovering at 6,000 feet in 95 degree (Fahrenheit) weather. Design gross weight was initially held to around 5,000 pounds, the maximum permissible weight of Army aircraft. But this limitation soon went by the wayside, to the relief of Bell engineers.

Other requirements further shaped the XH-40. It had to accommodate litters mounted crosswise in an enclosed cabin so injured soldiers could be treated in flight. It had to use the newly developed Lycoming XT53 turboshaft engine. It had to be narrow and low enough to fit in the cargo bay of a Lockheed C-130 Hercules transport plane. It had to have metal blades, be capable of instrument flight, have boosted controls, require less maintenance, and be more reliable than earlier helicopters. No loading restrictions were permitted; GIs had to have the flexibility to fly with anything they could get through the helicopter's doors.

To this formula, Bell's talented engineers added wide aluminum-tube skids to help the helicopter "cling" on rugged terrain, and an improved two-bladed semi-rigid rotor using Bell's recently developed underslung-feathering-axis hub. They also kept the cabin small to prevent excessive and out-of-balance loading, the single greatest cause of helicopter accidents. However, anticipating an increase in available engine power and Army desire to use the H-40 for other missions (notably troop transport), Bell also proposed an alternate configuration with a wider, roomier cabin. The military services initially showed no interest in this proposed alternate version.

The result was the XH-40 Iroquois, Bell Model 204.[54] Later redesignated HU-1 (these initials inspiring the nickname Huey) and further revised to UH-1, it was destined to become synonymous with America's military involvement in Southeast Asia. Bell employees sensed that the silver prototype was a winner but had no inkling of the huge success this program would enjoy, or of the profound changes it would work on Bell Helicopter in Fort Worth. Some 16,000 military and civil derivatives of the XH-40 would be built over three decades—twice as many helicopters as had ever flown by 1956.

The XH-40 was Bell Helicopter's first native-Texan product (previous Bell rotorcraft had at least been initiated in New York State). Project engineer for this program was Karl Camp, a Gardenville veteran. Ahead of schedule just sixteen months after work began, the XH-40 flew on October 22, 1956, with chief pilot Floyd Carlson and project engineer Jack Buyers at the controls. Carlson proclaimed it "the smoothest-handling new helicopter I ever climbed into."[55]

Two days earlier the XH-40 had hovered for the first time. Many employees had come to the plant with their families that Saturday to enjoy the spectacle. Just as the successful test ended, excitement gave way to sadness as word circulated that Lawrence D. Bell had died in Buffalo at the age of sixty-two.

In a forty-four-year career in aviation that took him from wood-and-fabric biplanes to rocket-powered Mach-2 research planes, Larry Bell had known no greater challenge than establishing his company as a manufacturer of helicopters. The Helicopter Division in Fort Worth was his legacy. Seeing it profitable and self-sufficient had fulfilled a dream the industry pioneer had long held.

Despite the cancellation of the HSL, Bell Aircraft's Fort Worth division had never done better. Sales for 1956 were $8 million higher than those of the previous year. At $56 million, they accounted for fully a quarter of BAC's total reported sales of $216,033,290.

So important had the Helicopter Division become that BAC stockholders voted on July 31 to make it a separate corporation. Assets totaling $23.7 million were accordingly transferred to the new entity. On January 1, 1957, six years after the move to Texas, the Bell Aircraft Helicopter Division officially became the Bell Helicopter Corporation. At this juncture, it employed 3,500 people in two plants plus a leased warehouse, a building in Hurst, and a records-storage site in Dallas.

Harvey Gaylord, formerly general manager, retained his duties but assumed the title of president. Edwin Ducayet, still his right-hand man, became executive vice president. Elevated to vice president were Bart Kelley, engineering; Roy Coleman, manufacturing; and G. B. Clark, sales. Jim Fuller was named assistant vice president for public relations.

Under Ducayet, a new department called Special Services was created to assist the Bell Helicopter Service Department with product support. Gifted with forward-thinking management, Bell had sent service personnel into the field with its civil and military helicopters from the earliest days. More company money had been spent by the Engineering Department correcting the defects identified by

The turbine-powered Bell XH-40 (Model 204) hovers on October 22, 1956. Redesignated UH-1 Iroquois and nicknamed *Huey*, this versatile helicopter would pioneer "airmobility" tactics employed by the U.S. Army in Vietnam. Courtesy Bell.

these "service reps." Cost or complexity might well have dissuaded other companies, but Bell remained steadfast. The reputation for industry leadership in customer support thus built would pay off over the years in increased business.

In the reshuffling, Joe Mashman became director of sales planning and Hans Weichsel assumed the post of contracts manager. Weichsel's team stressed customer support above all in administering Bell Helicopter's military business. For continuity from the perspective of the armed services, a single person was assigned to conduct all dealings with each military branch. Ironically, when the Army established the world's largest helicopter training facility at Mineral Wells, Texas, just west of Fort Worth, it selected Hiller H-23s over Bell H-13s for primary flight training.

Bell had talented people. One example was Joseph S. Dunne, who headed Sales Engineering under Weichsel. A fighter pilot early in World War II, Joe Dunne had volunteered for more duty and had been assigned to the Army Air Forces' first helicopter training class at Freeman Field, Indiana, in 1943. Joining Bell in the late 1940s as a test pilot, Dunne—who held an aeronautical engineering degree—soon proved to be an able administrator. It was he who had led BASCO's pioneering oil-industry support division in 1949.

The Army ordered more than 100 piston helicopters from Bell during 1956. Other groups within that service had also placed an assortment of research-and-development contracts. One issued in November 1956 from the Army Transportation Command asked Bell to evaluate the feasibility of "flying cranes" capable of carrying 16 tons. Such R&D contracts paid little (this flying-crane study netted just $57,719), but occasionally they generated new production or licensable commercial applications. By and large, however, they did little more than keep people busy.

Since the popular Model 47 could not remain in production forever, the H-40 program was of paramount importance for the Fort Worth company. Experimental Project Manager Martin "Marty" Vale had overseen the initial development of the Model 204 (XH-40). Now that it was in the air he expected to be reassigned to other experimental efforts, but Gaylord ordered him to stay on as H-40 project manager. Gaylord took this unusual step to ensure continuity and to maintain the accelerated development program's momentum.

Two other prototypes followed the first into the air early in 1957. The Air Force got XH-40 no. 2 in the spring, flying it to Edwards AFB aboard a C-130 for Phase II flight testing preempted in Fort Worth by bad weather. The Army got ship no. 3. It arrived at Fort Rucker, Alabama, aboard a USAF C-124 just in time to be featured in an Army aviation symposium. By then, six YH-40 service-test helicopters were under construction.

Receipt of three more military contracts brightened Bell's July 4th celebration in 1957. The first was for more H-40s, the second for forty-two Army H-13Hs, and the third for three HUL-1s (47Js) procured for the Brazilian Navy with Mutual Defense Assistance Pact (MDAP) funds. Meanwhile, the civil-market 47J received CAA approval for a gross weight increase from 2,565 to 2,800 pounds, boosting its payload by 40 percent to 1,182 pounds. Even with this greater utility, the Ranger sold poorly.

Bell and its military customers were in a race to prove their H-40 and get it into production. The program was threatened by the limited scope of the medevac requirement that had brought it into being. The H-40 was well suited for other military missions, some of which promised high production volume, but other manufacturers were already angling to address those requirements. To be produced in large number, the H-40 would have to sell itself as an in-service alternative to competitor aircraft, and time for that was running out.

Phase II testing took less than a year instead of the scheduled two. In September 1957, the H-40 program status shifted from experimental to production. Project engineer Jack Buyers, who had previously worked under chief experimental project engineer Robert Lichten, now reported to W. P. "Bud" Rollings, chief production project engineer. The H-40 program had cost American taxpayers a little over $13 million, 65 percent of it for the accelerated flight testing of the experimental prototypes.

The helicopter's design contributed to a rapid Phase II test program. Its high power-to-weight ratio provided a fast climb and rapid acceleration, dynamic stability was excellent, and hovering ability was all that had been hoped for. Mechanics approved of the XH-40's ease of maintenance, and pilots fell in love with its functional cockpit layout and superb handling characteristics.

Turbine power made a world of difference. Developed by Dr. Anselm Franz, Austrian-born designer of the engines powering the World War II Messerschmitt ME 262 jet fighter, the Avco-Lycoming XT53 was a compact turboshaft producing almost 700 shp. Originally conceived as a 400-shp engine, it would evolve over the years to produce 2,000. It was more reliable, much smaller, and weighed half as much as a piston engine of equivalent power.

Delivery of the 2,000th Model 47 took place on December 11, 1957. Senate Majority Leader Lyndon B. Johnson—a Bell supporter who had frequently flown with Mashman—cut the ribbon at the Fort Worth plant ceremony.

Joining the XH-40s in the air during 1958 were eighteen YH-40 service test aircraft. These went to a half-dozen different test agencies. That summer, for example, YH-40 no. 6 went by C-124 to Eglin AFB for tests at temperatures as low as 65 degrees below zero Fahrenheit in the USAF's "climate hangar." Even in that profligate era, only the military could have conceived of conducting extreme cold-weather tests in Florida during the summer! Among the remaining YH-40s, ship no. 5 underwent USAF Phase IV tests at Edwards before being turned over to the Army; ship no. 7 participated in hot-weather tests in Yuma, Arizona; and ships no. 8 and no. 9 went to Fort Rucker, where one flew 1,000 hours in less than five months.

Throughout this program, Bell had performed fixes and changes amazingly fast. Even a sharp projection on which an officer tore his uniform was immediately corrected. By the time the HU-1A (as the first production model was known) entered production early in 1959, 91 percent of the changes requested by the Army had already been made.

For Huey production, Bell successfully incorporated thousands of changes and refinements during "shipbreaks," the pauses between contracted production runs. The Huey improved at an amazing pace because Bell actively solicited input from all quarters rather than waiting for "engineering change proposals" to find their way through military channels. Because ECPs could take years to filter through the maze of bureaucracy, Bell sidestepped the process.

HU-1AS first entered operational service late in 1959 with the 101st Airborne at Fort Campbell, Kentucky, and the 82nd Airborne at Fort Lewis, Washington. Although ostensibly for medical evacuation, these 770-shp helicopters performed so well—Army rotorcraft had previously been piston types—that they were assigned other duties.

They were put to work developing the "airmobility concept" that had consumed Army strategists since the Marine Corps's historic first demonstration of "vertical assault" tactics a decade earlier. Facilitating this conversion from strictly lifesaving use was modification by Bell under Army contract of an HU-1A to carry six French-made ss-II missiles. This missile-equipped Huey was flown to Alabama in 1959 for use by the Army Rocket and Guided Missile Agency at Redstone Arsenal and the Army Aviation Center at Fort Rucker. There it pioneered "fire suppression," a capability essential for tactical combat vehicles. So completely had the Huey left the medevac role behind that Bell installed plasma-bag hooks in only the first hundred of the 173 HU-1AS built.

The HU-1B—redesignated UH-1B two years later—succeeded the A model into production in 1961. Although they were not requested by the military, Bell provided this model with hardpoints that it passed off as jack points and c-130 tie-down reinforcements. If the Huey was to be a weapon of war, it would need hardpoints for mounting external stores and ordnance.

With substantially more horsepower and a 1,300-pound gross weight increase over the A model, the UH-1B needed more rotor blade area. Bell engineers had already increased rotor blade length to accommodate weight growth during Huey development. As a result the 44-foot-diameter, 300-RPM rotor was already excessively noisy because of transonic airflow at the blade tips. Anxious not to worsen the noise problem, the engineers left the diameter alone but increased lifting area by widening the blade chord 40 percent from 15 to 21 inches. The composition of this blade was also changed to incorporate a honeycomb core.

The B model would see remarkable design growth during its four-year production. Power output would rise from 960 shp to 1,100 shp. The extra power, higher payload, and hardpoints allowed Bell to develop UH-1B "strapon" armament kits under an Army program called HOT SHOT. Loaded with machine guns, grenade launchers, and 2.75-inch rockets, these UH-1BS—called Hogs by their crews—served in Vietnam as close-support gunships in the absence of dedicated attack helicopters.

In combat, the UH-1B displayed a remarkable resistance to gunfire. Although Huey losses would be high throughout the Southeast Asian conflict, overall survivability of the UH-1 series was deemed acceptable by policy makers in Washington, D.C. A total of 1,033 UH-1BS were produced through 1965, all but six going to the Army.

The follow-on UH-1C, which remained in production for two years, featured longer range and greater speed for escort and utility duties. A revised Model 540 "door hinge" rotor, first used on the very last B models, contributed to this model's increased performance.

Developed with independent research and development (IR&D) military funds, the door hinge rotor reduced two-per-rev vibrations and aerodynamic drag. The performance improvements realized from this thinner, wider rotor head added to Bell's backlog of orders, since it narrowly averted an Army purchase of Kaman HU-2KS on performance grounds. The door hinge rotor would also be used on the Cobra with notable success.

The true evolutionary jump in capability came with the UH-1D (Model 205), which entered service in 1963. Based on Bell's alternate XH-40 proposal with its larger cabin, the D was a different bird dedicated to carrying a dozen soldiers. Troop transport was the military mission that promised the greatest production volume; as such, it was the focus of Vertol, Kaman, and several other companies. With its proven S-58 cargo helicopter still in large-scale production, Sikorsky in particular felt confident of supplying the Army's troop carriers as the 1960s began. Nobody there or anywhere else in the industry imagined that Bell would vie for this Army business with an enlarged version of the Huey.

Competition between Bell and Sikorsky for these lucrative defense contracts had been intense. One example was an early-1960s Army fly-off competition near Garmisch in the Bavarian Alps. Popular with U.S. Army forces in West Germany, Garmisch was a natural European venue for a comparative evaluation between the prototype UH-1D and S-58 troop ships. The Sikorsky delegation was confident. Since its helicopter was much larger, it could obviously lift more. Because of a loophole in the test regulations granting each company's test pilot discretionary permission to exceed normal gross weight limits, however, the irrepressible Bell contingent had a surprise up its sleeve.

Shortly before the competition, Bell Helicopter called Dr. Anselm Franz, asking him to lend it an uprated T53 turboshaft running on Avco-Lycoming's test bench in Connecticut. Air-shipped to Garmisch, this unflown engine was hastily installed in the Huey, whose design permitted one-hour engine changes, just in time for the test.

Simulating wartime use under difficult conditions, these two helicopters were to lift people and a substantial load—in this case, beer barrels—to a military outpost high in the majestic Alps. At the last minute the Sikorsky team upped the ante, suggesting that each helicopter carry more people. To their surprise, the Bell team agreed and further proposed that an extra keg of beer be added. Stunned, the Connecticut people agreed. Was it mere bravado on Bell's part, or could the trim little helicopter from Texas truly heft such a load? Two very different sounds broke the Alpine serenity, one the throaty clatter of a piston engine and the other the futuristic whine of a turbine.

With Mashman at the controls, the sleek Huey lifted into the sky far more quickly than the lumbering S-58. It quickly outpaced its larger rival, leaving it far behind as it climbed strongly away. When the outdated Sikorsky finally arrived at the lofty outpost, its demoralized crew found a beer fest in full swing.

Had the UH-1's rapid development proceeded at a more normal pace, Sikorsky would probably have won the Army transport-helicopter contracts. American servicemen would have had only the lumbering Sikorsky S-58. Instead, they also had the speedy UH-1D. The difference between these helicopters was like night and day. The Army would elect not to take the H-34—as it designated the S-58—to war with it in Vietnam, although the Marines did.

Army personnel in January 1960 reviewed a mockup of the thirteen-seat Bell Model 205 "squad-carrier" that combined a UH-1B nose and tail with a roomier cabin accommodating a fully equipped squad. Based on this review, Bell revised the design and the Army accepted it that spring as the HU-1D.[56] The first flight of the YHU-1D took place August 16, 1961, and deliveries began two years later. Going to war with the 1st Air Cavalry Division, the UH-1D became the workhorse of airmobility.

A 1,400-shp T53 incorporated into UH-1C and D production created the M and H series, respectively. Over 2,500 UH-1Ds were built when the further uprated engine became available, and some 5,000 more UH-1Hs were built before production ended in 1976. By then all D models had been upgraded to H (a simple process, as the newer engine was identical in size to the old one).

There had been no alternative but to increase rotor size for the Model 205. A 48-foot rotor substantially improved performance but was also noisier, making the UH-1D/H pound-for-pound the noisiest helicopter anywhere. The Huey's noise projected forward, moreover, giving ample notice of its impending arrival. Combat pilots became adept at availing themselves of any and all topographical cover.

As wartime production geared up in the early 1960s, other manufacturers brought pressure on Bell to license them for Huey production. Lobbying hard for the business, the congressional representatives of these rivals were only too happy to pursue the idea. After all, one company could not meet the Army's demands all by itself, could it? But Bell believed it could and—traditionally well represented on Capitol Hill—it successfully resisted all such efforts.

With fighting escalating in Vietnam, Bell increased Huey production to 20 per month by early 1963. At that juncture, the Pentagon demanded 60 per month, a challenge Bell met by mid-decade, although such a production rate was unprecedented in the vertical-flight industry. Yet before company executives

could savor their accomplishment, the Army demanded that production increase to 157 units per month. Bell met *this* challenge by the end of 1966, only to be ordered by the Pentagon to sharply cut back production as quickly as it could. Production exceeded 160 units per month at the start of 1967, and again in midyear, before the flow was stemmed. In 1973, as America curtailed military involvement in Southeast Asia, Huey production stabilized at 10 per month.

In the spring of 1968, Bell celebrated the delivery of its 10,000th helicopter. The 12,000th Bell helicopter (an AH-1G Huey-Cobra) and the 4,000th standard Huey were delivered within a week of each other in March 1969. The 13,000th company rotorcraft came before the end of that year, and the 20,000th in 1974.

Bell's unprecedented volume of manufacture staggered the entire industry. To put its phenomenal wartime production achievements in perspective, it might be noted that 10 helicopters per month—one-sixteenth the wartime peak—had been considered a respectable production rate for helicopters by pre-Vietnam and pre-Huey standards. So great was this volume of manufacture that it carried the growing company's entire overhead much the way the hapless HSL-1 had in the 1950s.

The largest single Huey order—for 501 UH-1Bs and 1,614 Ds, announced by the Army Aviation Materiel Command in St. Louis on June 30, 1966—was valued at $249,457,443. Just four years earlier, Bell's total sales had been $150 million ($90 million military and $60 million civil). In 1967, by way of contrast, Bell's military sales alone reached $1.79 billion, while civil sales rose to $385 million (driven by the introduction of a commercial version of the UH-1). A secondary production spike in 1969, caused in part by the AH-1 HueyCobra, produced Bell's record year for Vietnam War military sales: $1.81 billion in 1970. Thereafter, Bell's military business declined rapidly to hover below $300 million by mid-decade.

The war put a great strain on Bell's production capacity at Plant 1 in Fort Worth and Plant 2 (Globe) in Saginaw. At the end of the 1950s, the latter's administrative building had been razed as part of a company modernization program. Having lost its home, Bell's Service Training School had moved temporarily onto the factory floor, which then stood almost empty following the consolidation of Model 47 production at the main plant. When the war in Southeast Asia reclaimed Globe's production space, the training school moved elsewhere on the 157-acre site. In May 1966, a newly constructed production flight area, hangar, and office building opened at Globe.

Other new facilities were built during this period. One was the 51,000-square-foot Engineering and Research Building which opened at the main plant in 1964. Another was the Transmission and Gear Facility, Plant 5, which in 1967 began a growing Bell presence in the town of Grand Prairie. Also in 1967, a 93,600-square-foot office structure opened at Fort Worth. That same year, Bell's experimental flight activity shifted from Greater Southwest International Airport in Fort Worth to a 54-acre site at Arlington Municipal Airport. The 80,000-square-foot complex included a two-story flight test engineering building, an adjoining hangar, a control tower, a vibration test building, and ramp facilities. Anticipating future additions, Bell also purchased 74 acres adjoining the airport site.

Bell's expansion had been moderate considering the period's record level of military and civil sales. In general, the company favored making do with what it already had or taking over existing structures. In 1963, for example, it added 86,999 square feet of floor space to the main factory and 45,000 feet to its Richland Hills warehouse. Four years later, it opened the Bell Overhaul and Modification Center—for refurbishing combat-damaged helicopters—in buildings the U.S. Air Force had vacated in Amarillo. Bell's restraint with regard to expansion reflected the personal beliefs of Edwin Ducayet, who—war notwithstanding—was ever loath to invest in new buildings.

Despite building 14,000 helicopters during this undeclared war, the company never missed a single delivery deadline or exceeded contracted costs by more than 2 percent. With justifiable pride, company officials observed that Bell hadn't delivered a helicopter late since November 1956.

While the Army was by far the largest user of Hueys, other armed services around the world also embraced the UH-1. To meet a USMC Assault Support Helicopter (ASH) requirement, the Navy in 1962 ordered a quantity of UH-1Es, which were essentially B models modified with personnel hoists and rotor brakes for shipboard compatibility. Hiller Aircraft had developed an excellent turbine helicopter tailored to ASH requirements, which the Huey did not entirely meet, but the Navy opted for the UH-1E to take advantage of volume-manufacture economies: seemingly endless Army production orders had by then driven UH-1 unit costs down to just $114,000 plus government-furnished engines and equipment.

The Huey became a tri-service helicopter June 7, 1963, when the USAF procured UH-1Fs for use by Strategic Air Command units

Two UH-1B gunships roll out on target to suppress
enemy fire in the Vietnam War, during which Bell
Helicopter manufactured an astounding 14,000
helicopters. Courtesy Ron Foley.

in support of widely dispersed intercontinental ballistic missile (ICBM) silos. The Air Force also bought TH-IFS for instrument flight training. Foreign military services around the world adopted versions of the Huey, beginning with the Royal Australian Air Force, the Swedish Army and Air Force, and all three Italian armed services.

The 1960s saw profound changes at Bell. The decade began with an industry milestone as a Bell became the first helicopter in history to log 10,000 flight hours. First used by Helicopter Air Service to shuttle air mail around Chicago, this 47D now earned its keep in Colombia with Helicol, the South American subsidiary of Pennsylvania-based Keystone Helicopters. On the business front, Harvey Gaylord succeeded Leston Faneuf as president of Bell Aircraft in January 1960. Faneuf remained chairman of the BAC board and executive committee. Gaylord retained the presidency of Bell Helicopter, whose day-to-day running he delegated to Edwin Ducayet.

On June 10, 1960, the Equity Corporation and other Bell stockholders meeting at Buffalo approved the sale of Bell Aircraft's defense businesses to Textron Incorporated of Providence, Rhode Island. A price of $22 million was agreed to with the huge corporation, which boasted 22 major divisions, 90 plants, and more than 30,000 employees. Under the terms of this agreement, effective July 2, Bell Helicopter, Niagara-Frontier, and Hydraulic Research and Manufacturing became components of a wholly owned Textron subsidiary called Bell Aerospace Corporation. This acquisition further saw the former Niagara-Frontier Division renamed Bell Aerosystems and the Bell Helicopter Corporation renamed the Bell Helicopter Company. Sixteen years later, it would be renamed Bell Helicopter Textron.

Left with five industrial-products subsidiaries acquired in Larry Bell's diversification drive, Bell Aircraft renamed itself Bell Intercontinental Corporation and moved to Mishawaka, Indiana, the home of its Wheelabrator subsidiary. Textron's Bell Aerospace remained in New York State, where it had begun a quarter century earlier.

Textron Chairman Royal Little made it clear throughout the acquisition that he anticipated no change in management or operations at Bell Helicopter. During a spring visit to Texas accompanied by Textron President Rupert C. Thompson and Vice President G. W. Miller, he also made known his desire that Textron's new helicopter company operate autonomously. Initial wariness at Fort Worth soon subsided as it became clear Textron intended to honor its pledge.

With transfer of ownership to Textron, Gaylord left Bell Helicopter to take up challenging duties as president, treasurer, and chief executive officer of Bell Intercontinental. Long groomed as his successor, Ducayet took over the helm at Fort Worth. The Ducayet years would be marked by singular engineering excellence, as "Duke" for all his other skills was an engineer first. He was all over the plant, drawing his own curves as tests progressed and sniffing out production problems. It was during his tenure that the Huey evolved and the HueyCobra and JetRanger came into being.

A successful line of civil Hueys began with the Model 204B which Bell unveiled in September 1960 at the National Business Aircraft Association show in Los Angeles. The ten-seat, blue and white commercial helicopter prototype toured the United States and Canada before making its European debut at the 1961 Paris Air Show. There it was cosponsored by Costruzioni Aeronautiche Giovanni Agusta,[57] which would manufacture 204Bs for European markets.

Following Federal Aviation Administration certification April 5, 1963, the first 204B was sent to Mitsui and Company in Japan, Bell's Far East licensee. Like Milan-based Agusta, Mitsui would build, market, and support 204Bs in its part of the world. The days were gone when Bell had to show operators how to use its products: a ready market, although a limited one, existed worldwide.

The 204B outperformed piston helicopters like the ponderous Sikorsky s-58, and it offered better economics and reliability than Sikorsky's turbine s-61 and s-62. "This ship will do things—fly at speeds and altitudes and carry loads—that no other helicopter in its class has ever done," enthused Dwayne K. Jose, manager of commercial sales in Fort Worth. "It is the long-awaited breakthrough in performance and economy for commercial operators."[58]

Named commercial sales chief in the spring of 1960, Dwayne Kendall Jose was a thirty-five-year-old veteran flier with 3,500 fixed-wing hours accumulated in World War II, Korea, and selling Cessnas as that company's eastern sales manager. He was destined to play a starring role in the development of another hugely successful company helicopter, the Bell Model 206 JetRanger of 1966. What the Model 47 was to light piston helicopters, the JetRanger—joined in the mid-1970s by the stretched LongRanger—would be to light turbine helicopters. This ubiquitous Bell would dominate the civil market, establishing itself as the "generic" light turbine helicopter.

The JetRanger had its roots in the Army's major Light Observation Helicopter (LOH) program. Initiated at the beginning of the 1960s, this landmark procurement called for a new-generation helicopter powered by the Allison T63, a compact turboshaft engine whose development the Army had sponsored specifically for this purpose. Because that service lacked a mechanism for direct aircraft procurement, the LOH competition was administered on the Army's behalf by the Navy.

The LOH program, promising the production of thousands of helicopters, caught the eye of the entire U.S. aviation industry. Aware for some time that such a program was on the horizon and hungry for volume business, America's airframe manufacturers responded enthusiastically when the Navy solicited industrywide bids in the fall of 1960. By January 1961, no less than twelve companies—some of which had never built a helicopter—submitted seventeen design proposals for consideration by the two services.

Later in 1961, the Navy proclaimed Hiller Aircraft in California the winner on technical grounds. Bell was still in the running, though, because the Army, in a decision based on operational considerations, selected both Bell and Hiller. It appeared that prototypes of both models would be built for competitive "fly-off" evaluation, with the LOH production contract going to the winner.

In July, Bell President Ducayet announced the formation of an LOH team at the Bell plant in Fort Worth. Reporting to Executive Vice President Atkins, this team comprised three branches, each headed by a Bell vice president. LOH Engineering, directed by Bart Kelley, included engineering coordinator Bob Lichten and project engineer J. R. Mertens. LOH Contracts, the second branch, was the responsibility of Hans Weichsel who was assisted by C. R. Rudning and C. E. McGuire. Roy Coleman headed the third branch, LOH

Manufacturing, which included Huey project manager Marty Vale and P. M. Dodson. These team members retained their normal company responsibilities despite the new duties.

Termed the "project group method" by Bell, this enlightened system in many ways anticipated the design-build teams that today find favor in the aerospace industry. Employed with great success in the XH-40 program, this approach promised to increase Bell's competitiveness. It was only a matter of time until the venerable Model 47 fell out of production, ending Bell's traditional dominance of the light military helicopter market. Winning the LOH competition meant more than just military sales. The potential volume of Army production of this new machine was so great as to virtually guarantee the winner a preemptive share of the civil market as well. "We cannot over-emphasize [the] importance of the Model 206 observation project to maintain our dominant position in the light helicopter business," Ducayet stated when he announced his team in July 1961.[59]

Bell's competitive energies were focused squarely on besting Hiller, whose Model 1100 was favored to win the competition. A long-time supplier of Army light helicopters, Hiller Aircraft had lost many key contracts to Bell over recent years. Its Model 12E—widely regarded as superior to the Model 47G—was also nearing the end of its production life. With no equivalent of Bell's lucrative Huey program to carry it forward into the turbine era, Hiller had more at stake even than Bell. The Fort Worth company viewed the LOH competition in terms of market share, whereas the Palo Alto firm saw it as a matter of survival.

In their wildest imaginings, Bell's top executives could not have anticipated the bizarre

turn that the LOH procurement took late in 1961. When Bell and Hiller received $5.8 million contracts calling for construction of five prototypes each, designated OH-4 and OH-5 respectively, so did a third company whose proposed helicopter had already been eliminated during initial military review.

The unexpected reversal brought the Aircraft Division of the Hughes Tool Company into the competition. Its lightweight helicopter, the OH-6, appeared to have little chance of winning because it failed to meet fundamental Army requirements for its LOH. The OH-6 was physically too small and too light to hold all the equipment specified by the contract, and it was topped by a low-inertia rotor that compromised its safety in combat. Moreover, it was relatively flimsy, having been built to civil-certification standards instead of the more-rugged military standards to which the Bell and Hiller machines had been designed.

The Army dropped the "mil. spec." requirement, opening the competition to civil-certified helicopters. This decision to change the ground rules well into the procurement process worried Bell. In fact, there was good reason for concern, for the LOH program had been subverted. Determined to establish himself as a manufacturer of aircraft, Howard Hughes—sole heir to the Hughes Tool Company fortune—had embarked on an unethical and highly destructive effort to corner the light-turbine-helicopter market. His subversion is today well documented.[60]

All three companies built and flew their prototypes, which the Army evaluated at Fort Rucker. Despite its shortcomings, the Hughes OH-6 emerged victorious and Hughes was awarded the lucrative LOH contract in May 1965. From Bell's perspective, the loss was not entirely unexpected; had the Hughes

OH-6 not claimed the prize, the excellent Hiller OH-5—clearly the best machine—most likely would have won.

Howard Hughes had grossly underbid to secure the contract. His small Aircraft Division (not to be confused with Hughes Aircraft, with which it shared quarters in southern California) was not equipped to undertake volume manufacture. With the Vietnam War escalating, the Army was in urgent need of LOHs. These factors combined to give rise to a congressional investigation. At its conclusion in 1967, the government forced the Army to solicit a new round of LOH bids from industry.

Unexpectedly, Fairchild Hiller declined to participate in this second round, even though it had a commercial version of its OH-5, the FH-1100, in production. This turn of events provided Bell with a golden opportunity. Needing no urging, it signed a contract in 1968 for 2,200 OH-58 helicopters to be delivered through 1972. That same year, Bell received a contract to supply the Navy with OH-57s—as that service designated the Model 206—for training use.

The OH-58 and OH-57 differed from the OH-4 of a few years earlier. Following the 1965 loss to Hughes, Atkins had assigned Dwayne Jose and his fifteen-person commercial sales department the task of adapting the OH-4 to civil use. Bell Helicopter was then stretched to the limit meeting the Army's demand for Hueys in Vietnam, however, and it was also racing to develop a dedicated gunship called the HueyCobra. As a result, Jose's task lacked a realistic budget or meaningful priority.

Atkins expected Jose to confine himself to low-cost fixes like bulged doors and other small modifications. But bulging the doors would leave two of the three rear-seat passengers sitting partly out of the narrow helicopter, protected only by curved plexiglass. Bell's commercial sales chief knew that this arrangement would be unacceptable to the corporate executives who Bell hoped would buy and use the helicopter. Nor was there any room for baggage.

Two industrial design firms were then under contract to Bell on other commercial projects. Jose enlisted their services, hiding his costs within existing purchase orders. The result of this bootlegged assistance was a three-view drawing for a pleasing helicopter. Its stepped nose gave it a familial resemblance to the larger Huey. Jose was satisfied except for the issue of baggage space, which he recognized was critical to commercial acceptance. On a large drawing of the proposed design, therefore, he personally drew a new rear fuselage line. Although he eliminated the racy teardrop taper suggested by the industrial designers, the resulting helicopter was, if anything, cuter. It looked *right*.

By the time Jose ordered a full-scale wooden mockup built, the secret was out. He and Paul Kesling, project engineer for the commercialized OH-4, were summoned to the front office for a showdown with Atkins. They showed him what they had done. "What in hell is that?" the normally reserved executive vice president reportedly demanded. "That's not what I told you to do! I told you to bulge the doors." To this Jose replied matter-of-factly: "There is no way we can be successful doing what you want us to do."[61]

Because the dynamic components and primary structure of the OH-4 had been left untouched, Jose and Kesling explained, the new fuselage was truly cost effective. It promised to reap benefits disproportionate to the investment. Although not an engineer, Atkins perceived the potential of the new design and backed his sales chief.

Jose's covert efforts had given Bell a turbine helicopter that would repeat the success of the piston-powered Model 47. Drawing inspiration from the popular name of the 47J Ranger, President Ducayet named the commercial machine the JetRanger. Rolled out January 10, 1966, the first Model 206A entered a trouble-free flight test program. Bell's only concern was an initial lack of reliability caused by teething troubles with the Allison 250-C20 turboshaft engine. This problem prompted frequent trips by Bart Kelley and his staff to the Allison company in Detroit.

The JetRanger won FAA certification October 20, 1966, and the first two examples were delivered January 13, 1967, during the annual meeting of the Helicopter Association of America. The recipients were the Hollymatic Corporation of Park Forest, Illinois, and the National Helicopter Service and Engineering Company of Van Nuys, California.

It was this much-revised helicopter, then, that the Army procured during its second round of LOH bidding in March 1968. That service took delivery of its first Bell OH-58A Kiowa on May 23, 1969, and deployed this type to combat units in Vietnam before the year was out. There, the nimble helicopter acquitted itself well, relieving Hueys of stopgap service they had not been designed to perform. While a limited number of Hughes OH-6s had reached Vietnam, it was not until the late arrival of the OH-58 that the Army finally had enough observation helicopters.

Several thousand OH-58s had been built by the early 1980s, when the Army Helicopter Improvement Program (AHIP) gave this type of helicopter a new lease on life. In 1984, AHIP funding gave rise to five prototypes of a much-improved model called the OH-58D

Advanced Scout (Model 406). Distinguished by a new four-bladed rotor, a globe-shaped gunsight mounted above its rotor, engine exhaust infrared suppressors, and other modifications, this enhanced-capability helicopter met or exceeded all performance requirements in Army tests. As a result, Bell received a $223 million OH-58D production contract in October 1985.

Bell delivered the 1,000th commercial JetRanger in March 1973, the 2,000th in July 1976, and the 4,000th in February 1988. This last helicopter was built in Canada, where all commercial 206 production moved during 1986. This transfer—the wisdom of which is open to question—had its roots in the Canadian government's selection of Bell Helicopter Textron to help it foster an indigenous helicopter industry. Under the terms of a formal agreement, civil JetRanger and LongRanger production was relocated to a Bell facility at Mirabel near Montreal, whereas military production remained in Fort Worth. The Texas assembly lines would soon be even quieter as other Bell helicopter programs were transferred to Canada before the decade was out.

About the time the seven-seat 206L was introduced in the mid-1970s, the improved 206B five-seater was also brought to market. In the late 1970s, Bell and Collins Radio Group together developed and certified an instrument-flight avionics package giving these helicopters single-pilot IFR capability in non-icing conditions. Formerly limited to visual-flight-rule (VFR) operations, the JetRanger/LongRanger series now offered commercial operators greater utility.

Two record flights of the early 1980s demonstrate the capabilities of these two models. On September 30, 1982, Ross Perot, Jr., and Jay Coburn became the first people

(*Top*) Introduced in the 1960s, the Bell 206 JetRanger remains the world's most popular light turbine helicopter. Courtesy NASM/SI.

(*Bottom*) Bell's OH-58D (Model 406) Advanced Scout has been the Army's primary observation helicopter since its introduction in the 1980s. Courtesy Ron Foley.

in history to fly around the world by helicopter. The son of the Texas billionaire and his Vietnam-veteran instructor copilot had departed Dallas in their Bell LongRanger II *Spirit of Texas* on September 1. The following July 22, moreover, an Australian adventurer named Dick Smith completed a solo flight around the world in a JetRanger III.

Other light turbine helicopters have come and gone but the JetRanger series remains perennially popular. No other light turbine helicopter has been able to match its low purchase and operating costs, or a worldwide support base that combines the type's ubiquity with Bell's industry-leading customer service. The 206B and 206L also share the lowest accident rate of any U.S. civil aircraft except corporate jets and commercial jetliners. The Model 206 series reportedly has the lowest accident rate of any single-engine aircraft of any kind.

Bell's JetRanger family ranks as one of the most significant helicopter series of all time. Three decades after the LOH procurement that inspired it, the JetRanger family continues to dominate the low-end turbine rotorcraft market. No other helicopters in its class have ever challenged its ascendancy. JetRangers, civil and military, promise to remain in production longer even than their piston-powered predecessor, the Model 47.

Another Bell helicopter was also destined for production during the Vietnam War. This was the AH-1 HueyCobra, a dedicated gunship consisting of a narrow two-man fuselage wrapped around the Huey's proven dynamic components. So radically different did this lethal machine appear that helicopter pilots, the press, and the general public considered it a completely different machine. Not Bell and the Army, though, as indicated by the H-1 designation it shared with the standard Huey. Only the prefix was different: A for attack instead of U for utility.

Long interested in the possibilities of armed helicopters, the company in June 1962 showed the Army a mockup of a sleek attack helicopter called the Model D255 Iroquois Warrior. This proposed gunship combined a Huey rotor and dynamics with a narrow fuselage of great aerodynamic cleanness. It featured retractable skids and a stepped canopy in which the pilot sat behind the gunner, whose cockpit offered unobstructed visibility. The full-scale mockup of this ground-support aircraft was soon revised to feature an unstepped canopy, after which Bell dispatched it by truck to different Army bases. Although Army field commanders and pilots were extremely interested, the service's leaders rejected the D255 because it exceeded the limits set on Army aviation when interservice roles and responsibilities were defined at Key West, Florida, in 1948 (see pages 384–85).

Secretary of Defense Robert McNamara's perception that Army aviation was inadequate to the nation's defense needs was even then loosening those constraints on Army aviation. At McNamara's instigation, the Army convened a review panel called the Tactical Military Requirements Board. Made up of general officers and prominent civilians, this influential board was known informally as the Howze Board after its chairman, General Hamilton Howze, who was perhaps the Army's most effective proponent of air power. In a final report dated August 30, 1962, the Howze Board endorsed the establishment of "air cavalry combat brigades"[62] and called for procurement of suitable helicopters. In so doing, it helped clear the way for the Army to acquire the attack helicopters it had wanted ever since Bell mounted a bazooka on an H-13 a decade earlier.

America's military involvement in Vietnam was even then shifting from advisory status to open conflict. A rash of helicopter casualties resulting from Viet Cong ground fire prompted the United States in September 1962 to abandon a policy of not firing until fired upon. That month, rocket-equipped Bell HU-1AS were used offensively for the first time. Declared or not, it was a shooting war and Bell knew the Army needed helicopters more lethal than the Huey.

Showing the glamorous D255 mockup to the Army was phase one of a calculated three-phase Bell strategy. The second phase was to develop and prove its attack helicopter concept in a low-cost company program making use of available piston-helicopter technology. Phase three would be to encourage the Army to combine the two ingredients for the helicopter it wanted. This strategy promised to work where a direct all-or-nothing *ab initio* proposal might not.

Begun in December 1962, this second phase produced the Model 207 Sioux Scout, which married the dynamic components of a Bell 47G-3 to the center section, skids, and tail boom of a 47J. The Sioux Scout's entirely new cockpit featured stepped tandem seating for two under a common canopy, much as had the revised D255 Iroquois Warrior. Equipped with a remotely sighted chin turret developed speculatively by the Emerson Electric Company of St. Louis, this helicopter could be flown from either seat. A floor-mounted gunsight in its snug forward cockpit left no room for conventional controls, so the gunner was provided with a sidestick controller on the right side for three-axis control (rotating the grip about its vertical axis provided yaw control). On the left side of the gunner's cockpit was a miniature collective lever with a conventional twist-grip throttle. Using these

controls precisely was a challenge, but they were adequate.

Test pilot Al Averill flew the company-funded Model 207, civil registration N73927, in late June 1963. Following testing at Fort Worth, it toured several Army installations before being handed over to an operational helicopter unit at Fort Benning, Georgia. This evaluation concluded in January 1964 with high marks for Bell's proof-of-concept demonstrator. It was criticized only for its lack of turbine performance or commonality with the UH-1.

Following the Howze Board's findings, the Army issued a request for proposals (RFP) from industry for what it termed an Advanced Aerial Fire Support System (AAFSS) in July 1964. Because the D255 was too heavy to make optimal use of the UH-1's T53 engine, Bell engineers hastened to come up with a smaller design that could effectively use the Huey engine. The result was the Bell Model D262.

Eleven other companies also submitted AAFSS proposals. When the two finalists were announced by the Department of Defense early in 1965, Bell's D262 was not among them. Sikorsky and Lockheed had been selected to compete for the AAFSS contract. Based on the rigid-rotor technology demonstrated by its experimental CL-475 helicopter, Lockheed ultimately won this competition. So demanding were AAFSS program requirements, however, that the resulting AH-56 Cheyenne—an ambitious rotorcraft with wings and a pusher propeller —was an expensive failure. The Lockheed AH-56 program was canceled in 1972.

Aware from the outset that the AAFSS program might take years to produce operational attack helicopters, Bell Helicopter anticipated an urgent military requirement for an interim attack helicopter. Shortly after the AAFSS RFP was issued, President Ducayet authorized preliminary design work to begin on a UH-1-based gunship designated Model 209.

After Bell's AAFSS proposal was rejected early in 1965, Ducayet convened a management meeting on March 5 with some of Bell's top engineers and managers. Present were Jim Atkins, Bart Kelley, Charlie Seibel, Bob Lichten, Hans Weichsel, Phil Norwine, Bob Duppstadt, and Cliff Kalista. When this meeting ended some six hours later, Ducayet had committed his company to building and flying the Model 209 by September 1, 1965. Duke was betting his career on the move, but he had been to Vietnam and felt strongly that such a helicopter was needed.

Unlike all other Bells—including the UH-1, which had been designed for medical evacuation—the 209 was an offensive weapon dedicated from the outset to taking lives. Reflecting this menacing role, it was christened the *Cobra*. Inspiration for the nickname had not come from Bell's P-39 Airacobra fighter plane of World War II fame, as might be supposed, but from Cobra Platoon, the nickname of the 3rd Platoon of the 114th Airmobile Company, a colorful unit that operated heavily armed UH-1Bs. Returning from a 1964 tour of Army installations in Vietnam, Weichsel brought word of this unit, and the name Cobra stuck. When Ham Howze retired from a thirty-nine-year Army career and joined Bell in June 1965, he suggested an embellishment to the name that the Army later officially adopted: HueyCobra.

Ducayet wanted the HueyCobra to weigh no more than 5,100 pounds empty, for high performance even with heavy weapon loads. He wanted it to fly faster than 200 mph, since the Army's AAFSS competition had empha-sized high dash speeds. But he also wanted the helicopter in less than six months. This seemingly impossible demand stemmed from his realization that Bell would need a flying, nearly production-ready helicopter if the Army were to have any luck adopting the type.

The reason was strictly political. Bell already had so much wartime business that howls of protest were sure to greet the unveiling of the Model 209. Opposition would be fierce to Bell getting yet another major production contract as rival rotary-wing manufacturers invoked the aid of their congressional representatives. The closer Bell's attack helicopter was to entering production, therefore, the more leverage the Army could exert to get approval for a purchase. In the meantime, even the Army was to be kept in the dark as to what Bell was working on.

With so much riding on fast results, Ducayet selected veteran rotary-wing engineer Charlie Seibel to head the "company-confidential" Cobra program. It would prove a wise decision. As part of Arthur Young's original Gardenville team during World War II, Seibel had helped Bell Aircraft get into the helicopter business. He had left for a time to start his own company, which Cessna had later purchased. After Cessna got out of the helicopter business, Charlie had come back to Bell. His experience had given him an approach to design and troubleshooting that was pragmatic and "hands-on," traits that would prove crucial to the success of the project.

Seibel was given a budget of $1 million drawn from Huey program IR&D funds.[63] He asked to build two prototypes in case one was damaged, but Ducayet declined, observing that the loss of even one machine would bring the unsanctioned program to light, thus ending it. Seibel soon realized that having only one prototype was an advantage: it obviated having to make intermediate drawings or log differences between prototypes. The single 209 could be built, modified, and refined by hand, then used as a pattern for the rapid preparation of construction drawings.

Taking up residence in Bell's Hangar 45, which belonged to the Experimental Department, the Cobra team consisted of no less than forty-two engineers, as well as draftsmen, machinists, and shop personnel all working together. Shop superintendent Red Woodall built walls to enclose the group in a secure "green room," Bell's prototype for the STEAM (streamline techniques for engineering and manufacturing) Rooms the company would later employ on other programs. In many ways, the green room was an aircraft company in miniature. It was characterized by ready communication between disciplines, something valuable that had been lost when aviation became big business.

Getting his team to believe that their prototype would actually fly in September was a challenge for Seibel. Only when the skeptical engineers saw parts drawn a day earlier being mounted on the skeletal prototype did they come to share Seibel's confidence.

However, Kelley and Ducayet were less than pleased with the external appearance of the evolving gunship. It looked neither menacing nor fast. They turned to Jan Drees for help. One of Europe's outstanding rotary-wing designers, Drees was the developer of the remarkable Kolibrie ramjet helicopter, a small number of which had been produced in his native Holland.

Deciding to immigrate to the United States in the late 1950s, Drees had written to several U.S. helicopter firms to explore possibilities for employment. His letter to Bell happened to arrive just before Bart Kelley's trip to Italy to meet with helicopter builder Corrado Agusta. Always on the lookout for top talent, Kelley had juggled his itinerary to meet with Drees and recruit him for Bell before the competition scooped him up. The Dutchman had arrived in February 1959 as a senior research engineer.

"I looked up from my work," Drees recalls, "and there were Bell's president and engineering vice president standing before my desk. They ordered me to drop everything, go straight to Hangar 45, and stay there until the Cobra had new lines."[64]

Drees convinced Seibel and his team that large plexiglass canopy panels, recessed engine inlets, and a rimmed pylon to streamline the rotor mast and controls would make the new helicopter both faster and faster looking. The HueyCobra's revised lines did the trick. Rakish and menacing, it looked like it was going 200 mph standing still. Its newfound visual appeal would play a critical role in its adoption by the Army.

Although nominally a member of the Huey family, the Cobra looked so different from the standard UH-1 as to seem virtually a new helicopter. Built around UH-1C dynamic components, its fuselage was only three feet wide. The forward fuselage was flush-riveted and radio antennas were "buried" in nonmetallic areas for maximum aerodynamic cleanness. Another distinctive feature of the prototype was stub wings, whose purpose was to provide hardpoints for attaching external armament stores. The simplified Model 540 door-hinge rotor head topped the craft. It lacked the Huey's stabilizer bar. To save weight and reduce drag, the Cobra would rely on a stability augmentation system.

An escalating Vietnam War brought new

Developed in secrecy, the Bell AH-1 HueyCobra
(Model 209) combined the Huey's proven
dynamic system and components with a new fuselage dedicated to attack. A twin-engine version for
the Marine Corps, designated AH-1T, is illustrated here. Courtesy Ron Foley.

pressures on the Army to find a better armed helicopter than the UH-1B. Colonel Harry L. Bush of the U.S. Army Aviation Materiel Command in St. Louis was charged with selecting an "interim" gunship for use until the Cheyenne—then believed viable but years away from service—could become operational. On August 18, 1965, Bell Helicopters proposed to the Bush Board that the Army use the Model 209 Cobra.

That same day, the Cobra prototype was completed except for the installation of cockpit glass, a paint job, and rotor blades. With these details attended to, Bill Quinlan—who in 1962 succeeded Elton Smith as Bell's chief experimental test pilot—flew this helicopter, N209J, on September 7 at Amon Carter Field. A week or so later, its existence was made public.

A problem came to light at the outset of flight testing. The Cobra suffered from terrible lateral vibrations. It shook like mad because the inertia of the very narrow fuselage was so low. A couple of hundred pounds of lead had to be added to the wing stubs whenever the helicopter was demonstrated. This tip ballast tamed the vibrations but at the expense of maneuverability and overall performance.

"The engineers tell me it will take six months to solve this problem," Program Manager Ed Sargent complained to Seibel. "They say the ship will have to be fully instrumented and flown for three months, after which they'll need a couple more months to figure out what's causing the problem."

With the Cobra due at Edwards Air Force base in three months, Seibel knew another approach was needed. His apprenticeship with Arthur Young now stood him in good stead. "We don't have to figure out what's causing the problem," Seibel observed calmly,

"we only have to figure out how to fix it."[65]

Seibel and a few dynamicists under Drees worked late into the night, poring over the results of each day's flying. Measurements revealed that large oscillatory forces were entering the fuselage through the control system. This clue led Seibel to try a variety of solutions until he hit upon the cure: reversing the cyclic control linkages top and bottom, so that the vertical push rods moved in the direction opposite to their previous travel. This change—the single meaningful revision the Cobra would require during its rapid development—was made September 19, 1965. With the problem solved, the prototype six days later set an official world's speed record in its class of 200 mph.

The HueyCobra was an instant hit as it made the rounds of Army installations. Part of the credit went to Joe Mashman. Having obtained a dead spectacle cobra from Fort Worth's Forest Park Zoo, the veteran test pilot had taken it to a taxidermist, who converted it into the world's most unusual collective stick cover. This startling trophy—sure to appeal to military men if not the public at large—helped make the sale.

The Bush Board had come up with four other contenders for the Army's interim gunship until the Cheyenne was ready: the Kaman UH-2 Seasprite, the Sikorsky H-3 Sea King, the Boeing Vertol CH-47 Chinook, and an experimental compound helicopter called the Piasecki 16H. None provided meaningful competition for the HueyCobra; nevertheless, it was announced that a fly-off competition was to be held.

The Army now found itself in a quandary, because it desperately needed the HueyCobra. The heavily armed UH-1B Hog was not fast or agile enough for the gunship role, it lacked sufficient armor to protect its crew, and it was too slow to escort the UH-1D troop carrier. Yet the Transportation Corps within the Army Materiel Command strenuously opposed granting another major production contract to Bell. The Fort Worth manufacturer already had too great a share of the Vietnam War pie, Congress and the aviation industry contended. The political pressures they brought to bear hardened the resolve of certain Army leaders to kill Bell's HueyCobra at all costs.

The Pentagon seemed certain to decide against the AH-1, and then help came from an unexpected quarter. Because the reinlistment rate of Army aviators was dropping and pilots were already in short supply, the service found itself needing, in the succinct words of Hans Weichsel, "a sexy-looking helicopter to entice helicopter crews to reinlist."[66] This perceived requirement for a new and more exotic helicopter to support recruitment in fact tipped the scales in favor of HueyCobra production.

Bell received a contract in April 1966 for the first AH-1G HueyCobras. On June 2, 1967, the Army released $84 million toward the purchase of 530 HueyCobras, the first of which reached Vietnam two months later. This order was the first of many volume purchases by the Army and the Marine Corps, which would operate twin-engine HueyCobras. The success of the AH-1 series in Vietnam and afterward is well documented.

By the time the vastly more costly AAFSS program ended in August 1972, Bell had delivered 1,126 HueyCobras. It had also developed the Model 309 KingCobra, which weighed 40 percent more and was considerably more lethal. The Army declined to buy the KingCobra, however, and it did not enter production. Whereas the AH-1 program took sixteen months from contract to combat,

Lockheed's troubled Cheyenne effort would last eight years and never achieve production. Upon the Cheyenne's demise, the Army in 1972 revised its gunship requirement to reflect the lessons of Vietnam and initiate a new procurement called the Advanced Attack Helicopter (AAH) program. Bell entered a Model 409 (YAH-63), but the contract went to Hughes. Plagued with technical problems and cost overruns, the Hughes AH-64 Apache program took ten and a half years to attain production. The HueyCobra, meantime, soldiered faithfully on.

The AH-1's development cost of $1,040,000 was so close to Ducayet's million-dollar limit that Bell's management later asked Seibel how he had kept such close tabs on his funds. His answer startled them: "I didn't," he replied, "time was so short I never gave the budget a thought."[67] Remaining in production long after the rest of the Huey military line and generating more than $3 billion in orders, the AH-1's development would have been a bargain at several times the amount invested in it.

Much had been happening at Bell against the backdrop of UH-1, JetRanger, and AH-1 production, of course. On the technical front, the company had announced in January 1962 its development of MW RAILS (Microwave Remote Area Instrument Landing Sensor), an integrated system permitting zero-ceiling, zero-visibility operations "even when the ducks are grounded."[68] Using RAILS, a helicopter pilot could navigate through total darkness or fog and land within 25 feet of a predetermined point he could not even see. The Army Signal Corps thoroughly evaluated RAILS under realistic conditions at its Electronic Proving Grounds at Fort Huachuca, Arizona.

In 1966, Bell successfully demonstrated a three-bladed rotor developed under contract to NASA for spacecraft recovery. It also perfected and successfully tested a unique radar antenna built into the leading edge of a rotor blade.

On April 15, 1969, the Bell Model 533, the fourth YH-40 extensively modified with wings terminating in jet engines, attained a speed of 316 mph in level flight. Lou Hartwig and Bill Quinlan set this unofficial rotorcraft speed record as part of a research program sponsored by the Army Aviation Laboratory (AVLABS).

Early the following decade, Jan Drees invented a remarkable system for eliminating the two-per-revolution vibrations so characteristic of two-bladed rotors. Announced in November 1972 as a significant breakthrough, this was Bell's patented "nodamatic" system. It used two horizontal "nodal beams" attached to each side of the base of the rotor pylon. Vertical rotor forces would shake and flex these members in flight, but Drees designed them so that they would be still at certain points called nodes.

Much like fishing rods being shaken at their midpoints, the shafts of which seem to vibrate around fixed points, Dree's two horizontal beams each had two stationary nodes. The Dutch designer's brilliantly simple idea was to suspend the entire fuselage at these four vibrationless points. The Nodamatic system proved to be highly successful at screening out rotor vibrations, producing a smoother, less fatiguing ride. In addition to using it on the 206 and 206L, Bell incorporated it into all its two-bladed helicopters, notably the 214 and 222.

Early in 1963, Bell Helicopter was incorporated into Fort Worth. For a dozen years, the company had been *near* the city but not *in* it. During that time, it had contributed heavily to the prosperity to the region. Bell believed it was already doing enough for Fort Worth, but the city government, enticed by prospects of additional tax revenue, had long disagreed. It annexed the Bell factory in March. If fighting city hall was a lost cause, Bell at least had the satisfaction of forcing Fort Worth to provide water, sewage, fire, and other services the company had previously supplied for itself.

The fall of 1963 brought a change of military cognizance. Navy Bureau of Aeronautics representatives, who had previously been the Pentagon's liaison with Bell, turned their duties over to Army officers in an elaborate ceremony reflecting the rising importance of Army aviation. That same day, Bell set a carefully staged record for the helicopter industry by delivering no less than thirty-nine rotorcraft at one time.

Meanwhile, Bell's civil product line had expanded since the introduction of the Model 204B in 1960. Eight years later, Bell began deliveries of the fifteen-passenger 205A, a commercial version of its UH-1H squad carrier. In 1970, it delivered to Mack Trucks, Inc., a civil version of the twin-engine UH-1N, which all three U.S. services and Canada had already ordered. Powered by a Pratt & Whitney of Canada PT6 Twin-Pac, this was the Model 212, America's first midsize, twin-engine commercial helicopter.

Engineering groundwork for the Model 212 had been laid by the Model 208, which flew in April 1965. Basically a UH-1D modified with Continental XT67-T-1 twin engines coupled to a single transmission, the 208 was developed with company funds using a Huey provided by the Army and experimental 1,400-shp engines provided by Continental. The installation increased safety, since the

Introduced in 1970, the Bell 212—a civil version
of the UH-IN Huey—was sold to commercial
operators as a fifteen-passenger executive and utility transport. Courtesy NASM/SI.

helicopter could fly on one engine, but the engines proved less than ideal. As a result, the Model 208 had been shelved.

Helped by the introduction of the improved JetRanger II in 1971, Bell's commercial business hit new heights in 1972. The month of February brought 105 firm orders valued at $23 million. But the big news on the commercial front was the announcement by Congressman Jim Wright three days before Christmas that Iran had purchased 202 twin-engine AH-1J SeaCobras and 287 new Model 214As. Totaling more than $500 million, it was the largest helicopter order ever placed by a foreign government.

The ultimate development of Huey technology, the sixteen-place Model 214A was 80 percent stronger than the standard UH-1. It was essentially a small flying crane, and had been derived from Bell's experimental Model 211 Tug of 1968. Instead of the 1,400-shp T53, the 214A was powered by Lycoming's larger 2,950-shp T55, derated to 2,050 shp. This additional power, which dictated a larger rotor with blades 33 inches wide, led to nicknames like Super Iroquois, HueyPlus, and Big Lifter, but none of these names stuck. The transmission developed for the 214 helicopter was also used in the AH-1J, which had been adapted to employ coupled PT6 Twin-Pac engines.

Iran had for years been eyed by Bell as a natural market. Twice the size of Texas, with rugged desert and mountain terrain, it had a very real requirement for high-performance rotorcraft. The huge 1972 sale reflected years of groundwork laid by Jim Atkins, who succeeded Ed Ducayet to Bell's presidency December 13, 1971, when Ducayet became chairman of the board.

Atkins was a money man rather than an engineer. Unlike his predecessor, he was a "high roller" who spent lavishly on company facilities. Under his leadership, a paint shop, an engineering test and evaluation center, a machining center, a service department building, and additional technical and manufacturing facilities all sprang up. Under Atkins also, the LongRanger received its go-ahead in 1973 and the Bell 222—a racy ten-seat executive helicopter with retractable wheels—was initiated the following year.

Ducayet had not seen the value of his second-in-command's many trips to Iran to cultivate business. Both before and after his elevation to board chairman, he had suggested that Atkins dispense with this effort altogether. Luckily, Atkins had persisted. The timing of Iran's decision could not have been better for Bell. This half-billion-dollar order, the first installment in a program that would see a small helicopter industry established within that country under the name Bell Helicopter International, came just in time to spare Bell the pain of declining Vietnam War production. Bell had nearly failed after World War II, but it was in fine shape now.

In contrast, Sikorsky and Boeing Vertol would both teeter on the brink of insolvency after Vietnam. They laid off thousands of workers and survived only through the deep pockets and abiding faith of their corporate parents. Both these helicopter manufacturers looked enviously at Bell as it made the transition to peacetime production with hardly a twinge.

At the end of the 1970s, Bell flew the Model 412. A 212 revised with a quieter four-bladed rotor, the 412 marked an emerging trend at Bell of offering civil and military customers a choice of rotor configurations. A refined version of this utility helicopter, which is capable of lifting four tons, would be

(Top) Bell Helicopter Textron president James F. Atkins stands before commercial helicopters manufactured in Fort Worth during the 1970s. From left to right are a 206L LongRanger, a 222, and a 212. Courtesy Ron Foley.

(Bottom) Introduced at the end of the 1970s, the Bell 412 combines a four-bladed rotor with Huey technology. Courtesy Ron Foley.

license built by the Nurtanio Indonesian Aircraft Industry beginning in the mid-1980s. In 1989, Bell transferred production of this helicopter to its Canadian plant, where Model 212 production had gone the previous year.

Back in Texas, meanwhile, Bell had revised the military 214A for the civil market as the 214B, a model Iran also purchased before its fundamentalist revolution. With further refinement and the substitution of two G.E. T700 advanced-technology turbines rated at 3,250 hp, this aircraft became the Model 214ST Super Transport, Bell's best performer. The 214ST's ability to carry close to 8,000 pounds of cargo at high speed has made it the preferred crew mover/utility helicopter for offshore oil rig support by the petroleum industry.

With the 214ST, Huey-era technology reached its zenith. Over a span of two decades, this famous line had seen aircraft gross weights increase from 7,200 pounds to 16,500 pounds and capacities rise from seven to nineteen people. Although the 214ST retains strong commercial appeal, however, the military has since moved on to a newer-technology helicopter.

Ironically, the Bell 214ST—nicknamed Tug—gave rise to the Sikorsky Black Hawk by inspiring the Utility Tactical Transport Aircraft System (UTTAS) procurement of the early 1970s. Bell submitted two UTTAS proposals, one of which was accepted by the Army along with a Sikorsky proposal. Both types were to be developed for fly-off competition until Bell was dropped and Boeing Vertol was substituted to vie for the contract. Sikorsky ultimately won with the UH-60 Black Hawk, providing a successor to the Huey. Concurrently, in the Advanced Attack Helicopter (AAH) competition described earlier, the Army bypassed Bell's YH-63 in favor of the Hughes AH-64 Apache.

Although the reasons for these Army decisions are not known, it should be noted that Bell's loss of these two programs coincided with its receipt of the lucrative Iranian business. Anxious to maintain a diverse production base, the Pentagon may well have steered the AAH and UTTAS contracts away from Bell toward companies in greater need of production volume.

Bell and Sikorsky were both selected to participate in the Advanced Composite Aircraft Program (ACAP), which the Army initiated in August 1979. The goals of this research program are a 17 percent weight reduction and a 22 percent decrease in cost. Bell's ACAP effort produced a flying prototype called the D292. Employing Model 222 components, this prototype made its first hovering flight at the end of August 1985.

The Model 222 series would also help prove out Bell's Model 680 Research Rotor, a composite and bearingless four-bladed rotor that is significantly lighter than other rotors and has half the number of parts. Flown on a 222 utility/executive helicopter, the 680 reportedly gave "a jet-smooth ride with appreciably lower sound levels."[69] Bell subsequently entered into a joint agreement with Dornier G.m.b.H. in Germany to further develop the 680 concept.

In April 1983, Bell and Boeing Vertol jointly received a Naval Air Systems Command contract for preliminary design of a Joint Services Advanced Vertical Lift (JVX) program aircraft. Based heavily on earlier Bell VTOL efforts, this design evolved into the V-22 Osprey.

With risk-sharing a popular trend in the aerospace industry today, it is not surprising that Bell would join forces with McDonnell Douglas in 1986 to submit a proposal in the Army's landmark Light Helicopter (LH) com-

(Top) In 1986, Bell began transfer of civil helicopter production to its facility in Mirabel, near Montreal, Canada. Bell continues to build military versions of many of the same helicopters in Fort Worth. Courtesy Ron Foley.

(Bottom) Bell 214ST "Tugs"—like these Royal Thai Navy examples—can transport almost 8,000 pounds of payload at high speed, making them Bell's most capable helicopter type. Courtesy Ron Foley.

(*Top*) Today, Bell has a vigorous, highly competitive product line that includes the Model 430. Unveiled early in 1996, this fast executive/utility transport is a derivative of the 222 of 1979. Courtesy Ron Foley.

(*Bottom*) Introduced at the start of 1995, the Model 407 is a roomier and more capable successor to Bell's own Model 206 JetRanger/LongRanger series, from which it is derived. Courtesy Ron Foley.

Building on decades of Bell tiltrotor work, the
v-22 Osprey has been jointly developed by Bell
Helicopter Textron and Boeing Helicopters. It
combines vertical flight capability with faster-
than-helicopter speeds for Marine Corps vertical-
assault and Army special-operations use. Courtesy
Boeing.

petition two years later. However, this contract was awarded to the rival Boeing/Sikorsky team in 1991.

On July 20, 1983, L. M. "Jack" Horner was appointed president of Bell Helicopter Textron, succeeding Jim Atkins, who followed Edwin Ducayet to the board chairmanship. The son of H. M. "Jack" Horner, who long headed United Technologies, the parent corporation of Sikorsky Aircraft, Horner presided over a company becoming increasingly international. In turn, he was succeeded to the presidency by Webb F. Joiner in 1991.

On January 1, 1997, Terry Stinson arrived from Textron's Rhode Island headquarters to become president and chief operating officer, and Webb Joiner ascended to the chairmanship of Bell's board. Stinson—a former F-16 pilot and member of the pioneering Stinson aviation family—was subsequently promoted to president/chief executive officer in October 1997. Among his first acts at Bell was to learn to fly his company's rotary-wing products.

Bell Helicopter is today an increasingly international company. In addition to authorizing Indonesian and Canadian production, Bell also licensed helicopter production in Korea and airframe assembly in Norway and Argentina in recent years. License production of certain models continues at the time of this writing in Italy and Japan.

At Bell's Quebec facility, starting in the 1990s, an improved Bell 222 has been produced as the Bell 230. This beautiful machine has in turn been stretched, given more power, and fitted with a four-bladed, all-composite,

bearingless and hingeless rotor to create the Bell 430, which was officially unveiled in Singapore at the Asian Aerospace '96 airshow early in 1996. Demonstrating the capabilities of this new model, a 430 with two crew members set an around-the-world speed record in 1996, leaving England on August 17 and landing there again seventeen days later.

Bell Helicopter Textron introduced another helicopter program in Las Vegas, Nevada, in January 1995 at that year's Heli-Expo industry trade show. The Model 407, as it is called, is Bell's replacement for its reliable but aging Model 206 JetRanger, LongRanger, and TwinRanger. The derivative 407 family features a four-bladed rotor, a wider cabin, and greater engine power. It will be produced in Mirabel alongside the 206 until production of the latter comes to an end.

At the time of this writing, another new Bell helicopter is being considered. Designated the Bell 442, this medium helicopter is intended to replace the Model 412. International partners are being sought to share in its development.

Altogether, more than 32,000 Bell helicopters have been delivered worldwide, a record unmatched in the annals of vertical flight. More than 9,000 of these machines went to civil operators, a proud achievement for the company that brought the first civil helicopter to market in 1946. If its first half-century of helicopter production is any measure, Bell Helicopter Textron will remain a powerful force in the helicopter field for decades to come.

5 / Hiller Aircraft

Before the eventful 1940s came to a close, a small northern California company called Hiller Aircraft joined Sikorsky, Piasecki, and Bell as the decade's fourth volume manufacturer of helicopters. By doing so, Hiller laid the last cornerstone in America's coalescing vertical flight industry. This success would produce a healthy balance, with Sikorsky and Piasecki competing in large helicopter manufacture and Bell and Hiller going head-to-head in the production of smaller machines.

Also known at times as United Helicopters and Hiller Helicopters, this company in 1944 flew the first successful helicopter designed and built west of the Mississippi River. Following the construction and evaluation of an unprecedented array of prototypes, it brought to market the world's first truly stable helicopter. Certification of the Hiller 360 in 1948 won for Hiller the third license ever issued for the manufacture of civil helicopters.

In contrast to the products of the other pioneering companies, the three-seat Hiller 360—also called UH-12, or simply Model 12—was a wholly private venture. This light commercial helicopter belies the oft-repeated misconception that military spending fostered all helicopter development. Sikorsky and Piasecki's first production helicopters were indeed directly sponsored by the military, and Bell's commercial Model 47—built during World War II with profits from that company's lucrative military contracts—enjoyed at least indirect military support. Not so the first Hiller machine, which achieved production without either military funding or support from a wealthy corporation.

Hiller Aircraft faced enormous challenges beyond the daunting technical difficulties. The company was in the "wrong place at the wrong time,"[1] located south of San Francisco at least 2,500 miles from Philadelphia and other East Coast centers of helicopter development. Even Wright Field at Dayton, Ohio, was 2,000 miles distant. Moreover, company founder Stanley Hiller, Jr., started later. Alone of America's four helicopter pioneers, he took up the challenge of rotary-wing flight *after* the 1940s had already begun. By the time his Hiller 360 reached market late in 1948, the long-heralded postwar aviation boom had already gone bust the preceding year, and the private capital on which Hiller relied exclusively was exceedingly difficult to obtain.

Igor Sikorsky, Frank Piasecki, and Arthur Young had all attended Philadelphia's Rotating Wing Aircraft Meetings in the late 1930s. In contrast, Stanley Hiller—then entering his teen years—had not even known of these seminal East Coast forums for the exchange of rotary-wing knowledge. This relative isolation explains in part the unparalleled flowering of creativity and unique contributions for which his company would be known.

Stanley Hiller, Jr., first became intrigued by helicopters early in 1941 while still in high school. Researching this new form of flight in his free time over the next year, he gathered what little information San Francisco's public libraries, its technical bookstores, and the region's universities could provide. Like the articles in the mechanics and aviation magazines he had grown up reading—most of which predicted that Americans would soon fly their own personal helicopters—what he found generally ranged from historical to fanciful in focus; little of a technical nature was to be had.

Everywhere he looked, Hiller found clippings on Igor I. Sikorsky and the experimental vs-300 helicopter he completed in 1939. Photographs showed an elderly inventor, attired in overcoat and homburg, hovering his much-modified test bed at his Vought-Sikorsky plant in Stratford, Connecticut. Although of minimal technical help, these clippings firmed the young Californian's resolve to develop and market small helicopters of his own.

The odds against success were long, but Hiller was uniquely qualified. His great-grandfather settled in California in 1849, establishing a tradition of hardy self-reliance that Hiller's father, Stanley Hiller, Sr., brought to another frontier as a noted inventor and one of northern California's pioneer aviators.

Born November 15, 1924, Stanley Hiller, Jr., learned to use tools at an early age in his father's well-equipped workshop. Although he definitely possessed a mechanical aptitude,

the younger Hiller decided early in life that business was his calling. He was intrigued by business and perceived it to be a valuable tool for change. This decision stemmed in large measure from observing his father working with his business partner, Joe Coney. Although the former had the ideas, it was the latter who devised ways to apply them and reap their benefits.

In 1937, having lost a model airplane made of balsa wood and tissue to a crash, the young Hiller salvaged its little gasoline engine and put it in a model race car of his own design. Because demand quickly outstripped his ability to build others for his friends, and then for their friends, in 1940 he founded Hiller Industries to undertake large-scale assembly-line manufacture. The Hiller Comet was soon in national distribution.

To form sleek metal bodies for his racers, Hiller and his father together invented a method of die-casting nonferrous metals like aluminum. With the coming of World War II, Hiller Industries used this new process to make airframe parts—the first aircraft components so manufactured—for military aircraft rolling off West Coast assembly lines. Hiller's c-47 window frames were stronger and lighter than the steel units Douglas had used earlier for such applications.

Alone of the top four American helicopter pioneers, Hiller would rise to become a senior U.S. industrialist and the country's premier fixer of ailing corporations. But that success lay far in the future when vertical flight first caught Hiller's eye as a promising business venture on the eve of World War II.

In the months preceding America's entry into that war, Stanley Hiller began devoting his time to the preliminary design of a helicopter. To refine his ideas, he built models and dropped them off tall buildings after first stationing friends with cameras at window on different floors to photograph the models on their way down. Another substitute for a wind tunnel was Hiller's Buick convertible, which, modified with a test stand for models, simulated low-speed flight with some degree of success.

When after six months the preliminary design was finished, Hiller left both the University of California and Hiller Industries in order to form Hiller Aircraft. His first employee was Harold Sigler, a naval architect who had worked for Hiller Industries. Forty-ish, wiry, a fine draftsman and self-taught maritime engineer who worked quickly and often intuitively, Sigler set about producing a detailed design for the helicopter. "He was an extraordinary talent," Stanley Hiller later recalled, "a brilliant man in his field."[2]

Two other remarkable individuals filled out the ranks of Hiller Aircraft in 1942. The first was Jack Galliano, sixtyish, a true crafts-man in the old-world tradition. Galliano could form perfect compound curves in metal with nothing more than a hammer and a bag of sand. The second was Bert Cann, a burly welder in his mid-thirties whose skills had been honed in the Kaiser Shipyards of Richmond, California. Both men were jacks-of-all-trades who could build almost anything. Galliano in particular was a genius at machining parts from scratch.

If lack of aviation expertise hindered the small company, it also helped. Having no contact with the East Coast rotary wing community, and without any aeronautical engineers participating in the design, Hiller Aircraft was free to pursue fresh and unconventional approaches to the problems of helicopter flight.

When these men set to work in Galliano's automobile repair garage in Oakland, California, it was one of those rare instances of four people with precisely the right skills coming together. The small facility offered an unusual obstacle to the workers in the form of midget man-carrying race cars which Galliano built to supplement his income. Luckily the garage also had a machine shop with an antiquated lathe, drill press, milling machine, and other vintage equipment driven by belts from shafts spinning overhead. In this humble setting, work began in December 1942 on a machine very different from other successful helicopters developed in the United States.

Called the XH-44 Hiller-Copter (the designation denoted "experimental Hiller" and the year it would fly), the unusual craft taking shape featured two opposite-turning rotors on the same central shaft. It would in fact be the first successful helicopter whose rotors were "rigid," meaning that the blades were not hinged at the hub as was universally the case with rotary wing craft of that era; and it would also be the first successful helicopter to employ rotor blades of all-metal construction.

The idea of hinged, limp, overly flexible rotors such as were used on autogiros and other helicopters had not appealed to Hiller, who from the outset considered them a potential source of trouble. In a departure from accepted standards, he and Harold Sigler settled on totally rigid all-metal rotors because they promised higher speeds and permitted closer spacing between the rotor heads. Since these new rotors were subject to higher flight loads than conventional rotors, Sigler performed stress calculations, which, in retrospect, were extremely rudimentary and failed to take into account vibratory loads. The resulting helicopter nevertheless emerged very strong, its rotors up to the job.

Stanley Hiller, Jr., tries out the controls of his
uncompleted helicopter. Courtesy Hiller Aviation
Museum.

A twin-rotor coaxial machine then appeared to be more efficient than single-rotor designs requiring tail rotors to offset torque, the force trying to spin them in the direction opposite to the rotation of their own rotors. Tail rotors, Hiller knew, consumed 15 percent or more of the power generated by the engine—power that might otherwise help lift and propel the helicopter. Coaxial helicopters, in contrast, need no tail rotor because each main rotor cancels out the torque of the other.

A coaxial configuration also permitted a more compact design. With no tail rotor there was no need for a long tail boom, thereby offsetting to a degree the extra weight of two rotors. Control was simplified because all linkages and lines were clustered in the center. And a coaxial configuration avoided the tendency of single-rotor helicopters to roll during high-speed flight. A rotor's advancing blades combine their rotational speed with the helicopter's forward airspeed to produce increased lift on one side of the rotor; the retreating blades, in contrast, subtract their rotational speed from the helicopter's forward airspeed and produce less lift. The resulting asymmetrical lift at high speed produces a roll force that increases with forward airspeed. Coaxial helicopters whose rotors turn simultaneously in opposite directions, in contrast, present an equal number of advancing and retreating blades on each side, thereby neatly avoiding the problem.

Most important, the Hiller team settled on the coaxial configuration because it was different. Hiller's business instincts told him that unless the public could readily discern something new in his helicopter, his little company would fail to emerge from Igor Sikorsky's shadow.

Hiller's determination not to follow in Sikorsky's footsteps was clearly vindicated by the low-slung craft whose light tubular framework Bert Cann welded together. Countering general ideas of how a helicopter should look, it was a blunt-nosed teardrop that ended rakishly in a spike instead of an extended tail boom.

Because of the war, Hiller's group was forced to make fairleads, turnbuckles, and other items that would otherwise have been available off the shelf at the local airport. A more crippling shortage by far was the lack of a power plant, wartime priorities having reserved light plane engines for other uses. No engine meant no helicopter, and that would soon spell the end of the young company whose means were stretched to the limit.

In an effort to resolve this problem, Stanley Hiller made several trips to Wright Field in Ohio in the spring of 1943 to meet with Colonel Frank Gregory, head of the U.S. Army Air Forces' fledgling helicopter program. Although impressed with the slender six-footer who knew so much about helicopters, Gregory was steadfast in his refusal to help Hiller obtain an engine. Still, these trips were not entirely wasted, for the Californian got to see at close range the Army's first YR-4s, as the Sikorsky VS-316 was designated in military service. The world's first production helicopter, the R-4 was the first complete helicopter Stan Hiller had ever seen.

Hiller also traveled to Washington, D.C. Wartime priorities being in effect, he spent the three-day train trip standing or sitting on his suitcase, carefully guarding the quarter-scale one-hundred-pound model of the XH-44's coaxial rotor system he had brought along. Wind, rain, a wartime lack of public transportation, and startled looks greeted him as he made the rounds of what turned out

A proud team poses with the completed xh-44 late
in 1943. Left to right: Jack Galliano and son Jack
Jr., Harold Sigler, Stan Hiller, Bert Cann, and a
painter hired to apply finishing touches. Courtesy
Hiller.

to be disinterested agencies in the nation's capital.

In fact, it took several trips and months of rejection before Hiller finally found an office of the War Production Board interested in his efforts. A. W. Lewis, head of the Aircraft Priorities Division, thought enough of the XH-44 to arrange a meeting for Hiller with some of the National Advisory Committee for Aeronautics' rotary-wing experts. With Lewis's help the necessary priorities were eventually granted and Hiller Aircraft was free to purchase a 90-hp Franklin air-cooled engine.

The XH-44 was finished late in 1943. With it fastened firmly to the floor of Jack Galliano's shop in Oakland, which Hiller Aircraft had rented, Stan Hiller climbed aboard for the first static run. After the rotors had come up to speed, he pulled the collective lever to apply pitch to the blades. With an explosion of glass, the XH-44 sucked in all the building's skylights. Dramatic proof indeed that the Hiller-Copter was ready and eager to fly.

At that time Hiller Aircraft was close to going broke. Hiring a professional test pilot was out of the question even if one with rotary-wing experience could be found. Hiller was the only member of the company with any training—he had learned to fly fixed-wing aircraft in the mid-1930s—but it scarcely prepared him to fly the XH-44, particularly since his father's 1929 Stinson bore no similarity to his team's untried one-of-a-kind contraption. But the pragmatic company president rose to this challenge as he had to all the others. "It seemed to all of us," he later observed, "that if we could build it we could fly it."[3]

Cooling problems, trouble aligning the reduction gears, and other difficulties delayed the first attempt at tethered flight until early 1944. On this less-than-auspicious occasion, the yellow machine lifted off the ground, settled laterally, and rolled over with a loud bang as the blade tips struck the ground. A single restraining cable attached to the underside of the machine precipitated the accident, but the underlying problem was that the pilot had to teach himself to fly helicopters during the course of testing.

Ironically, had the Hiller team used rotors of conventional construction (hinged blades made of wooden ribs over steel tubing, all covered with doped fabric), the crash would have deformed the hinges and shattered the blades. Lacking money for all-new rotors, Hiller Aircraft would have been out of business. But the XH-44's ambitious rigid rotor with all-metal blades saved the day; however badly twisted they looked, damage was confined to the tips. Just enough money remained from sale of Hiller's model race car business to effect repairs and try again.

With a better restraint system consisting of three long cables attached to the XH-44's landing gear struts, tethered tests resumed in Memorial Stadium at the University of California's Berkeley campus. The stadium provided shelter from the wind and, with its gates locked, relief from the huge crowds invariably attracted by the novel helicopter. After much tinkering and having learned to control his machine, Hiller performed its first free flight on July 4, 1944.

No surging crowd, no throng of reporters, no emergency vehicles were on hand to mark the moment when Hiller, casually attired in a T-shirt, lifted the XH-44 into a hover, flew slowly forward, and then brought his yellow teardrop around in a wide circle to land where he had started. History had been made: the XH-44 was at once the first helicopter ever built and flown in the western United States,

Hiller runs up the finished XH-44. A moment later
he applied pitch to the rotor of the restrained helicopter, and inadvertently sucked the skylights
from the ceiling. Courtesy Hiller.

Ahead of its time, the XH-44 was the first successful
helicopter to fly with all-metal rotor blades. Courtesy Hiller.

and the first successful coaxial helicopter outside Europe.

Upon landing, Hiller looked up to the bleachers only to see one seat perplexingly empty. Just then Carolyn Balsdon's head popped up; the lovely young woman whom Hiller would marry in 1946 had not wanted to watch what promised to be an accident. Without brakes and with no directional control over his helicopter when not in the air, Hiller had rolled to a stop dangerously close to the stadium's goal posts. From the bleachers it had looked as if the whirling rotors would surely strike them.

In its second free flight, the XH-44 stayed in the air for five minutes. Hiller's own perception of this flight was that it was almost as if a switch had been thrown, transforming the helicopter from a monster to an aircraft in which he could do no wrong. Thus encouraged, he decided to climb out of ground effect and treat the stadium like a race track. The successful new helicopter was now off and running.

Hiller traveled east again armed with films of the Hiller-Copter in flight to show Lewis and the NACA's helicopter board. They arranged for him to see the Sikorsky HNS (the Navy designation of the R-4) then under development, as the guest of Coast Guard Commander Frank A. Erickson at New York's Floyd Bennett Field. The experience left Hiller all the more convinced of the merits of his team's machine. Returning home, he resumed flight tests in Memorial Stadium and in rural areas of nearby Contra Costa County. Lewis and a prestigious entourage later made a pilgrimage to the San Francisco area specifically to observe these tests firsthand.

The Hiller-Copter was first demonstrated publicly on August 30, 1944, at Beach Street and Marina Boulevard in San Francisco. Several hundred spectators, including government and military observers, watched as the pilot rose vertically in a stiff breeze to put the yellow craft through its paces. Adept by now in the intricate art of flying a helicopter, Hiller demonstrated circles, spun about the XH-44's vertical axis, moved forward and back, side to side, and otherwise thrilled the crowd before descending to settle gently on Marina Green. Cameras clicked and people cheered as he climbed out, but the international publicity and acclaim that followed did little to improve Hiller Aircraft's financial footing.

In a demonstration at the Claremont Country Club the next day, Hiller placed one tire squarely on a handkerchief spiked to the grass to demonstrate the precision possible in landing his machine. Soon afterward, he flew at Richmond Shipyard No. 3 to show the craft to wealthy shipbuilder and aviation enthusiast Henry J. Kaiser. Following a further demonstration in October 1944, during which the industrialist himself hovered the XH-44, Kaiser reportedly climbed out of the machine and exclaimed, "This is marvelous! We want to close the deal."[4]

Kaiser had earlier obtained support from the War Production Board for an unsuccessful helicopter development program pursued at Fleetwings, an aircraft company he owned in Bristol, Pennsylvania. Acquiring rights to Hiller's remarkable helicopter presented Kaiser with an opportunity to save face, as well as a chance to again pursue his dream of an aircraft for every American household, then a popular vision of what the near future would hold.

Kaiser insisted that Hiller move to the Fleetwings factory in Pennsylvania—formerly the manufacturing site of the Army's lumbering Keystone bombers—but Hiller and company steadfastly refused to leave the San Francisco Bay area. In the end, Kaiser relented and an agreement was reached whereby Hiller Aircraft became the Hiller-Copter Division of Kaiser Cargo.

Tests of the xh-44 meanwhile revealed that the Hiller team's original control input estimates were low. Travel of the swashplate—the collar controlling the rotor heads—was consequently opened up to improve the prototype's handling. And controllable the Hiller-Copter was, the minimal flex in its robust rotors giving maneuvers a uniquely crisp feel akin to wires under tension or a tightly wound spring. Tricky and demanding, the machine's flying characteristics nevertheless proved straightforward—until, that is, the time came to perform tests of autorotation.

As stated earlier, autorotation to the ground is the maneuver that allows a helicopter to land safely in the event of an engine failure. Practiced by helicopter pilots, it consists of placing the windmilling rotors in low pitch so that they spin rapidly as the powerless craft descends. Near the ground, the pilot pulls up on the collective pitch lever to trade the rotor's stored inertia for momentary lift. This maneuver must be performed at the right height if the helicopter is to land gently.

For his autorotation test, Hiller selected a small private airstrip in the Sacramento Valley. The plan called for him to climb several hundred feet and, from a semihover, reduce power and rotor pitch while initiating a fairly steep dive. This test approached autorotation in the most dangerous way possible, with a realistic simulation to the ground instead of at high altitude with a descent to a predetermined level. By simulating an engine failure beginning with both minimum altitude and airspeed, Hiller unknowingly placed himself

squarely in the middle of what aerodynamicists call the "dead man's curve," that infamous corner of the flight envelope where luck can quickly run out.

Halfway into the maneuver the aircraft began to twist wildly. Hiller corrected with opposite "rudder," and the rotation suddenly increased. With options rapidly running out and nothing left to lose, he tried reverse rudder—a control input that ordinarily would have accelerated the spin—and to his disbelief the xh-44 instantly stopped turning. Bringing in collective pitch and full power just before hitting the ground suddenly reversed the controls again, but Hiller stabilized just in time to make a passable landing.

He later learned that this unsuspected characteristic of coaxial helicopters, a lurking danger waiting to strike, was rumored to have caused French pioneer Louis Breguet's coaxial helicopter to crash during an autorotation test in France in 1939. The pilot, who was not hurt, had reportedly failed to recognize that control reversal was to blame, and thus the cause was never published to warn later experimenters.

There would be other close calls for the xh-44. The dream of rooftop landings made the company's temporary quarters in Berkeley a tempting target. Late one afternoon after the day's regular flying was finished, a roof landing was staged so that publicity photographs could be taken illustrating this dramatic use of helicopters. The roof itself was less than ideal. Because it presented a slight incline at the touchdown point, two Hiller engineers were stationed at either side of the landing zone to secure the machine as it came to rest.

Hiller touched down between two skylights. Leaving the rotors turning, he stepped away from the machine as planned. Suddenly he realized his employees could not

The cockpit of the XH-44. Courtesy Hiller.

hold the XH-44, which began rolling inexorably toward the edge of the roof. He scrambled aboard and threw on full power just as the machine slid off the edge three stories above the ground. His rotors approaching the vertical, Hiller shot across a parking lot, barely cleared a fence, and sailed over a row of houses before bringing the helicopter safely to a hover a full block away. Less than two minutes later, a somewhat shaken but unhurt founder-cum-president-cum-test-pilot landed normally on his helipad in the company lot and strolled away.

On another occasion, failure of the main gearbox instantly stopped the spinning rotors, but as luck would have it, the XH-44 was just moments away from what turned out to be a very jarring landing. Had the gearbox failed at altitude, the outcome would certainly have been fatal.

With so much work invested in the bright yellow Hiller-Copter and so many memorable experiences with it, Hiller and his team could not help occasionally anthropomorphizing a bit: the helicopter seemed to forgive its builders their inexperience and repay their enthusiasm with loyalty. In personality, the single-seater combined the faithfulness of a family dog with the mettle of a thoroughbred horse. This experimental prototype had long since become more than just a machine to those who built it.

The versatile XH-44 was also an ideal test bed because it was designed to be easily modified. An accessible steel-tube structure facilitated refinements and experimentation. The rotor assembly could be tilted forward and aft, the gap between the blades adjusted, and the swashplate changed to permit a full regimen of configurational studies. After flying for almost a year with completely rigid rotors, the XH-44 was modified in the spring of 1945 to incorporate teetering rigid rotors to reduce the jarring bumps felt while operating in ground effect. The machine's 90-hp Franklin was also exchanged for a 125-hp four-cylinder Lycoming for improved performance, a change marked by the amended designation XH-44A.

The historic Hiller-Copter was retired at the end of 1945 and donated in 1953 to the Smithsonian Institution in Washington, D.C. Displayed there since the National Air and Space Museum opened during the nation's bicentennial celebration in 1976, it has since returned "home" on long-term loan to the new Hiller Aviation Museum in San Carlos, California.

By the mid-1940s, a dozen more people had joined the staff of Hiller Aircraft, including draftsmen and engineers from the Kaiser Shipyards in Richmond, California. One nonengineer from Kaiser was Bob Chambers, who became Hiller's chief financial officer. Another, this one not from Kaiser, was Edward Bennett, who as a civilian instructor had trained Army pilots during the war. Bennett was hired as a test pilot, but he lacked rotary-wing experience and Hiller was testing the company's single flyable helicopter. He quickly assumed charge of the company's experimental shop, however, when it was realized that he possessed mechanical skills bordering on genius. Give Ed Bennett a crude sketch and he would construct whatever was needed in short order.

Work had begun in October 1944 on three Hiller X-2-235s, two-place metal-clad successors to the XH-44, each powered by a 235-hp Lycoming engine. Whereas the XH-44 was the world's first successful rigid-rotor helicopter, the X-2-235 featured super-rigid rotors. This unprecedented degree of rigidity was provided to ensure that the opposite-

(Top) The bright yellow XH-44—the first successful U.S. helicopter built and flown west of the Mississippi River—had a coaxial configuration with counter-rotating rotors. Courtesy Hiller.

(Bottom) The three Hiller X-2-235s had super-rigid rotors designed expressly for high-speed flight. A proposed development of this helicopter was to have featured stub wings, retractable wheels, and a pusher propeller. Courtesy Hiller.

turning rotors would never touch during even the most violent maneuvering. As built, in fact, the blades could support a person standing at the tip without noticeable deflection. Ground tests of the first example began in the summer of 1945 at the Old Berkeley Armory.

Although no specific military requirement yet existed for such a machine, the x-2-235 was intended primarily for U.S. Navy use in the light utility, observation, and training roles. The Navy did not actually order the type, but it did procure the third uncompleted x-2-235 under the designation UH-1X, for evaluation in NACA wind tunnels at Langley Field, Virginia. Vibration problems curtailed these tests for fear of damaging the wind tunnel, but not before results vindicated the Hiller group's belief that super-rigid coaxial rotors were a valid approach to very high-speed helicopter flight.

The UH-1X, Hiller's first military contract, clearly ran counter to normal aircraft engineering, but then the team building it had experience only in designing ships, bridges, and similar beefy structures. The lack of even a single aeronautical engineer on Hiller's payroll to introduce that field's antipathy to heavy structures was, ironically, an advantage in the uncharted terrain being explored.

As a result of the NACA tests, Hiller initiated redesign of the x-2-235 to incorporate three-bladed coaxial rotors augmented by an aft-thrusting rear propeller. The reworked craft was obviously geared to flight at speeds substantially higher than those attained by existing helicopters. Main wheels retracting into sleek wing stubs further confirmed this supposition. Meanwhile, the x-2-235s themselves had now progressed to tethered flight.

Late in 1944 the Office of Naval Research (ONR) had awarded Hiller a contract calling for development of a small tethered helicopter platform. This military contract—the company's second—specified a compact machine that would raise an emergency transmitter antenna some 300 feet into the air, that being the length of the tether.

In response, Hiller developed a tiny single-rotor machine called the Sky Hook. Disassembled, it fit into a tube just three feet long and six inches thick for easy stowage in life rafts. Power was supplied by a 1.1-hp gasoline engine. Torque compensation was ignored for the sake of simplicity; in flight, the Sky Hook's body rotated freely under its rotor, its spin retarded somewhat by aerodynamic vanes.

The Navy evaluated Sky Hook in the fall of 1945, but with World War II now over, the project ended even though the model performed well in wind conditions unfavorable to balloons or kites. The Hiller Sky Hook was the first American gasoline-powered model helicopter ever to fly successfully.

A parting of the ways between Hiller and Henry Kaiser some months later interrupted these projects. Precipitating the split was a carefully prepared Hiller Aircraft Division proposal calling for the expenditure of a million dollars, this being the amount Hiller calculated was needed to achieve helicopter production. Refusing to commit to so large an expenditure, Kaiser offered only to continue funding Hiller Aircraft at current levels.

It was clear to Stan Hiller that helicopter manufacture would not be achieved anytime soon if his company remained within the Kaiser sphere. Accordingly, he declined the offer, and the association of these two men came to an amicable end. Leaving the comfort of the vast Kaiser organization of course halted the regular influx of money to which Hiller Aircraft had been accustomed for a year.

New financing was the immediate concern. It took two forms, interim or "bridge" financing and, beyond that, a great deal more to cover design, development, and certification of a new helicopter, plus tooling for its production. But money was just part of the challenge confronting Hiller, who faced other pressing concerns.

He also had to transform his organization from a division into a self-sustaining company. That meant dealing with tax matters, legal counsel, employment procedures, and a host of other functions formerly provided under the Kaiser umbrella. Only with a credible corporate structure could Hiller go after long-term financing, and only with structure and financing in place could he get his credit references in proper shape to engage in business.

But the challenges did not end there. The busy company president found he had still more hats to wear in an ever-expanding spectrum of duties. There was the need to talk to colleges, employment bureaus, and other institutions to get the personnel he needed. Just joining the corporate world entailed community activities and a host of other involvements. The cumulative demands were so great that Hiller soon understood why good division chiefs and general managers do not always make good chief executive officers.

If his role was changing, Hiller relished the challenges and felt more than equal to them. Earlier experience running Hiller Industries now stood him in good stead, as had his observations from within the Kaiser organization. A greater asset still was Hiller's belief in himself and his implicit faith in his ability to create a successful company. He sensed strongly, moreover, that the time was right to pursue his dream of helicopter manufac-

ture. At this juncture, his capacity for bold yet realistic planning was critical to survival.

From approximately eighteen employees— the high point under Kaiser—the company shrank to nine people. Among them was Warren Galliano, son of original XH-44 team member Jack Galliano, who had retired. What was left from the Kaiser association, plus a $50,000 line of credit with the Bank of America, which knew Hiller from his earlier successes, bought critical time during which Hiller reformed his company to continue operating under the new name, United Helicopters.

With a revised version of the plan earlier presented to Henry Kaiser, Hiller began courting the East and West Coast financial communities in quest of one million dollars in development funds. Investment banks and other conventional sources of capital were no help. These institutions noted cautiously that the major aircraft manufacturers were for the most part ignoring helicopter development. What did these corporations know about rotary-wing flight that made them shy away? These financial analysts also wondered why Stanley Hiller, Jr., and the renowned Henry Kaiser had chosen to end their mutual association: had the latter decided that helicopter production—a questionable business venture at best—was simply too risky?

It was indeed hard to argue that 1946 was the time to jump into helicopter production. Hiller persevered, nevertheless, eventually locating a small securities firm right in his own backyard willing to grant start-up monies even though it had yet to back a successful company. Capital Securities of Oakland, California, in fact subscribed more than $900,000 over four months to United Helicopters, which also raised funds directly through continuing imaginative promotion of its products. These efforts were critical to staying in business.

Having moved into an old warehouse in Oakland in the fall of 1945, the company returned briefly to the Berkeley Armory, where it remained until May 1946, when it moved into the old Federal Telegraph Building in Palo Alto, directly across the street from the entrance to Stanford University. In the meantime, two new lines of helicopter development had begun.

The first was the company's first single-rotor helicopter, an open-frame single-seater called the J-5. Known informally as the "jet-torque helicopter," the novel craft relied on air ducted through a narrowing tail cone to counter torque, thereby eliminating the need for a tail rotor. Not having a tail rotor was a worthwhile goal: beyond siphoning off engine power and generating drag in forward flight, tail rotors were giving the young helicopter industry fits because of often-tragic failures of their wooden blades and long transmission shafts.

Designed as a test bed rather than a production prototype, the J-5 had a single 32-foot-diameter main rotor, which was tilted by direct cyclic control. Lacking collective, its laminated wood blades—designed and built at Hiller—were fixed in pitch so that throttle alone determined the amount of lift generated (limiting the craft's efficiency much as a single gear ratio limits that of a bicycle). Despite the lack of pitch control, the J-5 could safely be autorotated in the event of an engine failure by diving and flaring at the right time. A vertically mounted 90-hp Franklin engine supplied power.

Starting in the fall of 1945, Ed Bennett built the J-5 from scratch except for its rotor blades. In his late thirties, well liked and capable, Bennett improvised as he went, with only

occasional questions for the engineering staff. By sparing the company the laborious process of working up detailed design drawings, he had the J-5 ready for testing in the University of California Memorial Stadium in March 1946. Bennett himself performed the first tethered flights in this machine.

The J-5 featured an engine-driven ducted fan that moved air aft through a tapering plenum. Most of this air was exhausted to the right to offset torque, but an adjustable outlet on the other side permitted proportionately more or less air to be ducted to the left to rotate the aircraft as desired about the yaw axis.

Company hopes for the jet-torque concept were high, for it promised a cleaner, less complex machine. Better still, the single-main-rotor-with-no-tail-rotor configuration was one nobody else had used, and having a unique helicopter was a strong plus on the business front, where product differentiation is a powerful marketing tool.

Page Mill Road, a dirt road in a remote stretch of Stanford University's vast landholdings, was the site of flight tests commencing in the spring of 1946.[5] Concrete pads—all that remained of temporary wartime buildings—provided debris-free aprons for the exhaustive evaluations. Tests validated the general concept but were otherwise disappointing. The J-5's yaw control response was unacceptably slow, primarily because of engine power limitations. The stability of the machine also left much to be desired, not surprising since the J-5 lacked any mechanism to produce stability.

Simply stated, the J-5 was ahead of its time. The state of the art in power plant technology was not advanced enough in 1946 to warrant intensive development of the no-tail-rotor concept. Igor Sikorsky and Frank

Piasecki (unbeknownst to Hiller) had each considered this approach and rejected it without building prototypes; to Hiller, therefore, falls the distinction of building the first such machine.

A two-seat follow-on called the J-10 was already under construction with an eye toward ease of manufacture. Although the J-10 was never flown, two more single-rotor, single-seat prototypes would be tested. Both featured conventional tail rotors and collective pitch, and both were known variously as UH-5s (denoting United Helicopters' fifth design) or NC-5s, the prefix humorously denoting "no control" because these machines lacked stability. The NC-5 designation would later also be applied retroactively to the J-5.

The second line of development began late in the fall of 1945 with a U.S. Navy industrywide request for proposals for development of a ship-based light transport helicopter. The Hiller team responded in its first-ever bid to develop an entire military aircraft with a 450-hp five-place coaxial helicopter called the HO-346. Failing to win this contract, United Helicopters made this effort the basis of design for a much smaller two-place personal machine.

The result was the UH-4 Commuter, an aluminum and plexiglass teardrop of remarkable simplicity and startling beauty. As its name implied, it was intended strictly for private use. However novel the idea of home-based flying machines might seem today, it enjoyed wide acceptance at the time the Commuter came into being. All the elements seemed to be in place to realize the dream of an aircraft in every garage.

"We all truly believed that," Stanley Hiller recalls. "I remember listening to Igor Sikorsky in some of his speeches talking about helicopters in every backyard. We believed it;

that's why we sized and shaped the Commuters as a personal device."[6]

Automobiles having so profoundly altered society, America had come during the 1930s to expect aircraft to work similar changes to everyday life. Witnessing aviation's exuberant adolescence, a Depression-ridden United States embraced flight—mankind's oldest dream and a strong metaphor for freedom—as proof positive of better times to come. Realization of this appealing vision seemed imminent as America emerged from World War II.

This expectation ended when the long-anticipated postwar aviation boom went bust by mid-1947, a catastrophic year for "general aviation" as all nonmilitary and nonairline flying is termed. For the time being, it seemed, flying machines would stay at the airport rather than be based at home.

The Commuter's specifications called for a cruise speed of 90 to 100 miles per hour, a range of 150 miles, and a rate of climb of 500 feet per minute. Large enough to accommodate two people seated side by side as well as their suitcases, its cabin offered phenomenal visibility. A horizontally mounted 125-hp Lycoming drove its counterrotating teetering rotors through a two-stage five-gear transmission incorporating a clutch for automatic engagement of the rotor upon starting.

Considerably refined over the company's earlier efforts, the UH-4 Commuter's all-metal rotor blades tapered in both thickness and planform. Two versions of this blade were constructed, the first built around a hollow tapered tube running from root to tip. The second employed a heavy mandrel extending a third of the way out from the root, onto which aluminum stringers continuing the length of the blade were bonded. The entire airfoil assembly was then covered with riveted

Hiller hovers the single-rotor J-5 in the spring of
1946. Development of the no-tail-rotor concept
was soon shelved because of insufficient engine
power. Courtesy Hiller.

aluminum skin with magnesium trailing edges.

This latter unit, the last of five metal blade types built by Hiller, was the first blade in the industry to rely on chemical bonding—in effect, gluing. Unique at the time of Hiller's pioneering efforts, rigid and bonded metal rotor blades would be adopted industrywide decades later.

The first UH-4 was already undergoing final assembly at the time of the move to temporary quarters in Palo Alto. Minus its cabin enclosure, this aircraft began ground testing at a site provided by Stanford University. It flew for the first time one bright morning in July 1946. Because Stanley Hiller was by now an old hand at flying coaxial helicopters, he dispensed with restraining cables.

Toward the end of a long first day of testing, the open-frame Commuter was being evaluated in a nose-heavy condition with Shop Superintendent Smith D. Pettit accompanying Hiller as observer. As the control stick stop was round, Hiller found that he could not move the stick left or right at its full-aft position. Unable to counter a rapid side-to-side oscillation that developed, he was powerless to prevent the experimental prototype from slamming sideways into the ground. Fortunately, neither the UH-4's occupants nor any ground personnel were seriously injured.

This helicopter—the company's fifth to fly—looked worse than it actually was, for the blades had absorbed much of the impact. It was quickly rebuilt with a squared stick stop, and testing was resumed later that summer. It was joined by UH-4 no. 2 late in 1946 and UH-4 no. 3 the following spring. In contrast to the first example, these later machines featured fully enclosed cabins.

With new financing now flowing in, Stan Hiller traveled around the United States to talk with people involved in the rotary-wing industries. "You couldn't wait for people to come to you," he explained later. "You had to go to where you heard there were good people."[7]

One of the company president's first stops was the Kellett Aircraft Corporation of Upper Darby, Pennsylvania. A well-known manufacturer of autogiros, Kellett was in marked decline despite government sponsorship of several developments. There, Hiller found a core of engineers keenly interested in his work. All expressed amazement at how much had been accomplished by Hiller's West Coast group in relative isolation and without government support.

First to leave Kellett and join United Helicopters was Wayne Wiesner, a soft-spoken expert in rotary-wing flight with an inquiring mind, who replaced Harold Sigler as chief engineer. The latter became overall head of engineering with troubleshooting responsibilities more to his liking than making day-to-day engineering decisions, which was Wiesner's strong suit. Wiesner's initial duties were in the area of structural engineering. These changes brought peace of mind to Hiller, who realized his operation had been skating on thin ice for some time because of rotor blade loads and other potentially hazardous phenomena not fully understood before.

Other Kellett personnel joining Hiller in the fall of 1946 were top dynamics/structural engineer Robert Wagner, design/weights engineer James Rigby, and noted structural/design engineer Webb Scheutzow. From Sikorsky came engineer Harold E. "Hal" Lemont, Jr., who had participated in the closing stages of Igor Sikorsky's VS-300 program. Joe Stuart III, Robert Hurda, Dick Carlson,

Don Jacoby, and Robert Anderson were a few more of the new faces at Hiller who would later be honored for significant contributions to helicopter and vertical-flight technology. One much later arrival of note would be Dr. J. A. J. Bennett (no relation to Edward Bennett) who would come all the way from England, where he was a towering figure in that country's rotary-wing development.

On the suggestion of United Helicopters board member Francis Callery, Hiller also hired Frank Coffyn, who was then working for Liquidometer, an instrument company in the East. The last surviving member of the Wright brothers' original demonstration team, Coffyn was also the third licensed civil helicopter pilot in the United States. Tall, handsome, charismatic, married many times —nobody at Hiller knew for certain how many—the elderly "early bird" divided his time between promotional and research duties, taking frequent breaks to regale those around him with entertaining stories about the Wrights and flying's earliest days.

Also in 1946, a professional test pilot arrived to free Hiller for the full-time demands of running a growing company. Although at twenty-two scarcely older than his boss, Frank W. "Pete" Peterson was nevertheless uniquely qualified. When World War II interrupted his electrical engineering studies at Texas A&M University, he volunteered for flight training with the Army Air Forces. By 1943 he was test-flying fighters, bombers, trainers, and even captured enemy machines at Wright Field in Ohio. While there, he learned to fly helicopters under Colonel Frank Gregory and was assigned to be service test pilot for the Sikorsky R-4. By the end of the war, Peterson had amassed hundreds of hours of helicopter time. Coincidentally, it was Frank Peterson who had taught

Frank Coffyn to fly a helicopter.

The infusion of so much new talent could not help but add tremendous vigor to an already exciting environment. Fresh, dynamic, yet small enough to grant significant responsibility to those willing to shoulder it, United Helicopters soon built a reputation that drew top people. The opportunity to work on rotary-wing flight, and enviable living conditions in the Santa Clara Valley, were strong inducements to East Coast engineers to come west. Being the only rotary-wing company on the West Coast also gave United its choice of graduates of Stanford University and California Polytechnic who wanted more out of a job than a desk amid a sea of others, as offered by the fixed-wing aircraft giants.

Hiller himself consciously shaped the environment his stellar staff found so stimulating and conducive to creative effort. He learned to match people to jobs, assigning projects in such a way that employees would adopt them as their own. Tasks formulated by Hiller offered *real* challenges and satisfactions, and paid huge dividends in morale and productivity.

The top man always sets the tone. The tone Hiller set was one of honorable dealings, respectful attention to those around him, and extremely hard work in pursuit of a shared vision of vertical flight. It was this tantalizing vision that made the struggling Hiller company an exciting place to work.

The United Helicopters UH-4 Commuter helicopter was publicly unveiled at the San Francisco Presidio on March 18, 1947, before a large crowd that included Army officers, civic leaders, and West Coast businessmen. There the trim craft demonstrated precision takeoffs and landings, and a variety of maneuvers. Particularly impressive was its ability to leap into the air, rotate on its vertical axis, and skim off in any direction while climbing and accelerating.

For building the world's first successful two-place coaxial helicopter, the company received top honors at the World Inventors Exposition in Los Angeles in July 1947, winning over Preston Tucker, who came in second with his Tucker Torpedo automobile. By this time, however, Hiller had given up any plans for production of the Commuter. It was a difficult decision, for the trim UH-4 was a personal favorite, but by now it was clear that the age of personal helicopters was not at hand, nor even around the corner. Instead, United Helicopters announced its decision to proceed with a versatile working helicopter intended for commercial and agricultural use.

A fundamental breakthrough in helicopter control had by now brightened prospects for such a machine. Pilot Frank Peterson had established that the hovering stability of the first two NC-5s (the J-5 and its conventional successor) left much to be desired. Although equipped with collective pitch and a tail rotor, NC-5 no. 2 (also called the UH-5A) proved tricky and overly sensitive, particularly in the roll axis. The lack of stability was highlighted when the machine, which flew in the fall of 1946, crashed while hovering at Palo Alto Airport and suffered damage to its rotor blades. Despite Peterson's best efforts, it turned over and the blades whittled themselves down to a fraction of their original length with a buzz-saw clatter.

The dejected test pilot perched on the wreckage while others began collecting pieces. Hiller and other members of the team—coats on, hands in pockets against the cold day—gathered around what had been a flyable helicopter moments before. An earnest discussion ensued as a solution was sought to the crippling stability problem. Having heard of the airfoil "paddles" Hiller had drawn in 1940 as a means of aerodynamically boosting the main rotor controls, engineer Joe Stuart interjected this concept into the conversation. Excitement dispelled the gloom as the solution fell into place surprisingly quickly. In perhaps a minute and a half, a totally new and truly revolutionary control system had been conceived.

The answer was an aerodynamic cyclic control consisting of airfoil-shaped paddles mounted on the rotor head at right angles to the blades. With this fundamentally new approach to helicopter control and stabilization, the pilot does not control the heavy rotor system directly; his cyclic stick moves the paddles, which in turn adjust the main rotor. The new system promised positive dynamic stability, light control forces, and freedom from the fatiguing vibration passed down other helicopters' control sticks.

Ed Bennett worked all that night and by morning had an aerodynamic cyclic control flying in quarter-scale on one of his experimental shop's electrically powered models. This model showed astounding stability. Excitement remained high as Bennett set about rebuilding the J-5 into a test bed for what was christened the Hiller "Rotormatic" cyclic control. The craft was ready for testing in short order.

Flown in the spring of 1947, the NC-5 no. 3 (UH-5B) was far more stable than any helicopter flown up to that time. Frank Peterson, in fact, found the trim single-seater *too* stable, a complaint easily addressed by increasing the size and decreasing the weight of the paddles. In a no-wind situation, the machine could be lifted from the ground, hovered for an extended period, and landed again without the pilot having to touch the overhead

(*Top*) The first Hiller UH-4 commuter takes flight in July 1946. An uncontrolled lateral oscillation caused this machine to crash moments after this photograph was taken, but neither Hiller nor his passenger was hurt. Courtesy Hiller.

(Bottom) A newly manufactured UH-4 graces the parking lot of United Helicopters' temporary Palo Alto home. Hiller operated under this interim name from 1946 to 1951. Courtesy Hiller.

cyclic stick. Such a feat was unthinkable in a Bell or a Sikorsky. To illustrate this unprecedented stability, the company released photographs of the craft hovering with only piled sandbags in the pilot's seat.

In another dramatic demonstration of its capabilities, Peterson would hover several feet off the ground with his hands outstretched to show he was not touching the controls. Bennett would then approach, grasp the tire of the little machine, and give it a violent shove to induce a wild pendular swing. Witnessing the demonstration, *Aviation Week* editor Scholer Bangs noted with amazement that "within three quickly diminishing oscillations the 'copter restores to its hovering attitude."[8]

The NC-5 no. 3, or UH-5B, is in fact profoundly significant as history's first truly stable helicopter. The demon of helicopter instability that had so long bedeviled experimenters—which Arthur Young had at least tamed in the Bell 47—was now fully exorcised. Today all but forgotten, the extraordinary UH-5B survives in the collection of the Hiller Museum south of San Francisco.

This helicopter's stability wasn't all that impressed Bangs. "Hiller and his group individually work prodigious hours," he observed, "and with zealot enthusiasm shed titles to become errand boys and janitors when indicated. [Treasurer] Henry L. McIntyre . . . and Langhorne Washburn, operations manager, told this writer separately that [United Helicopters'] spirit is such that no work is contracted outside the organization if the job—no matter how small or large—possibly can be done by a company worker or executive during or after regular working hours."[9]

About this time, Frank Peterson took time off from flight-test duties to get married. Not long after he and the new Mrs. Peterson set off on a honeymoon camping trip along California's Russian River, a unique opportunity arose for Hiller to demonstrate the NC-5 to giant Convair in San Diego. Unfortunately, the demonstration had to take place the following day. Accordingly, the helicopter with support crew was hurriedly dispatched by truck to drive south all night, and official help was enlisted to locate the Petersons. Within hours, the stunned newlyweds were rousted from their appreciation of nature and each other by the California Highway Patrol.

"We got him on an airplane and sent him all the way down to San Diego," Hiller recalls with a smile, "and he made a nice demonstration the next morning, his wife absolutely enraged."[10]

On another occasion, aviation reporter William Flynn and photographer Bob Campbell of the *San Francisco Chronicle* visited Palo Alto to see the stable helicopter they had heard so much about. Stanley Hiller greeted them cordially in his office.

"Have you ever flown a plane?" Hiller inquired of Campbell. The photographer admitted that he had not. "Fine,"[11] the company president replied. Ground school concluded, Hiller led them to the "flying field"—a small parking area perhaps big enough for thirty cars—just outside the door. A light wind was blowing as mechanic Tex Swanson started the NC-5's engine, warming it as the rotors swished over his head. Campbell, a veteran of Iwo Jima, gulped and let himself be strapped into the single seat at the front of the open framework. He listened as the controls were explained to him: stick over his right shoulder, rudder bar under his feet, and throttle and collective levers below his left hand.

With Swanson standing by the aft fuselage

Invention of the Hiller Rotormatic control system creates the world's first truly stable helicopter. Other helicopter builders of the period could not have hovered their machines with sandbags substituted for the pilot. Courtesy Hiller.

and Peterson to Campbell's right, Hiller took up his station at the photographer's left to give instructions. Under his tutelage, the novice pilot levitated the craft into the air. Hiller dismissed his subordinates early in the session, and then himself walked away after just sixteen minutes, leaving Campbell successfully compensating for the wind while maintaining position above the ground. Since hovering a helicopter is demanding at the best of times, Flynn's article might well have been disbelieved had it found its way to the Bell and Sikorsky plants back east.

The invention of the Hiller Rotormatic stability and control system worked a profound change on Hiller's thinking about what sort of helicopter to manufacture. Rotormatic paddles could be adapted to any configuration, but installing them between the rotors of a coaxial helicopter promised an unwieldy rotor system. To verify this, the first UH-4 Commuter was reworked with three aerodynamic paddles between its rotors. The modified UH-4 displayed an instant and breathtaking improvement in stability, but its rotor assembly had indeed become excessively complex. United Helicopters' first production helicopter would therefore feature a single main rotor and tail rotor like the Bell and Sikorsky machines.

This decision presented a problem. Having obtained financing by selling investors on the idea of an obviously different coaxial configuration, Hiller now had to undo that allegiance and gain their support for a more conventional machine. He invited them to make up their own minds at the Redwood City High School football field. Some four thousand investors watched the UH-4 Commuter and NC-5 being put through their paces while the company president discussed their relative merits and disadvantages. When

the demonstration ended, Hiller had virtually unanimous support for the single-main-rotor-with-tail-rotor approach.

Eight helicopters in fourteen different configurations had been tested over almost four years to arrive at this juncture. No other manufacturer could begin to demonstrate such a lineup of experimental prototypes giving expression to so much creativity and variety. With a production configuration at last selected and development of a new prototype under way, Hiller in 1947 purchased a 61-acre tract of land on the outskirts of Palo Alto and set about building a long-needed permanent base of operations. All the elements were finally in place to realize the long-held dream of production.

In July 1947, development began on a production prototype known as the Hiller 360. Also called the Model UH-12 when introduced late in 1948, and later simply the Model 12, this helicopter would enjoy the longest production life of any rotorcraft.[12] Although never as familiar to the public as the archetypal Bell 47, the Hiller 12's sterling qualities in commercial and military service nevertheless earned it an enviable place in aviation history. The Hiller 12E of 1959, the most widely produced model in the UH-12 series, is universally hailed as the finest piston helicopter ever built.

By the end of 1947, a mockup had been constructed of the rotorcraft that Hiller Aircraft—still doing business under the interim name United Helicopters—planned to build for the civil market. Studying a full-size mockup of the new Model 360, however, Hiller and his team realized that its conventional seating arrangement was undesirable. From the perspective of a commercial operator, the two-place machine was a single-seater because the pilot always occupied one seat. Room for *two* passengers plus pilot, company personnel foresaw, offered vastly more utility at minimum added expense.

Two-person survey teams, businessmen conferring en route to meetings, sightseeing couples—the list of possible charter opportunities lost to operators of two-seat helicopters was a long one. Before it ever flew, therefore, Hiller engineers configured the 360 as a three-place machine. There had been three-seat aircraft before the 360, but none had placed all the occupants side by side. The revised configuration thus marked a new paradigm in aviation.

This design feature suggests a key difference between Hiller and the other three pioneering companies: Hiller Aircraft was "business driven." In contrast, Sikorsky, Piasecki, and Bell were "engineering driven" in the sense that technology predominantly dictated their business decisions. It was enough in the 1940s, those manufacturers believed, to come up with a working helicopter. Hiller thought differently, as evidenced by his startling variety of prototype experimentation, and by the three-seat configuration of the 360. Here was a helicopter company that considered the needs of the marketplace from the outset.

As a result of this business focus, the Hiller 360 proved to be the first civil helicopter suited to the emerging commercial market. It rewarded its developer with more pre-Korean War civil helicopter sales than were logged by all other manufacturers combined. As impressive as that statement sounds, it must be remembered that only three other companies were engaged in volume production during this period, and one of them, Piasecki Helicopters, built military machines exclusively.

Bell Aircraft failed to match the early commercial success of the Hiller 360 because its

Model 47 had only two seats. The Sikorsky s-51 had more, but this converted military machine was too expensive to operate in commercial use. Despite the claims of its manufacturer, the heavy s-51 achieved a consistent record of driving commercial users out of business. The ungainly Sikorsky s-52, initially offered as a two-seater, was likewise a commercial flop.

It was the business-driven Hiller 360 that first brought a viable balance of utility and operating costs to market. Similar to the Bell 47 in most respects, the 360's most significant difference was its third seat. Why did the Bell have just two seats for the first two and a half years of its production? Because fixed-wing aviation provided helicopter developers with ready-made paradigms, and light planes typically had two seats. Arthur Young and Bell's engineering-driven helicopter program—perhaps too preoccupied with technical challenges to pay attention to the needs of the end user—never thought to question this standard.

As it went together, the Hiller 360 simply looked right. Poised on its tricycle landing gear like some elegant piece of technological sculpture, the prototype gleamed from the nose of its low-slung silver fuselage to the tip of its rakish tail. The shine came from stressed-skin construction like that of modern airliners. In contrast, the Bell 47's welded steel tube structure harkened back to the era of fabric-covered airplanes like the Piper Cub.

The new Hiller was similar overall to the better-known Bell 47. Both were built to the single-rotor configuration and powered by the same engine. Both weighed about the same, had similar overall dimensions, and offered fairly comparable performance.[13] But from a technological standpoint the Hiller

360 was superior: Rotormatic paddles made it so stable that it could be trimmed for extended "hands off" cruise. In contrast, the Bell—the next most stable helicopter then in existence—could not be flown for more than a few seconds with hands and feet off the controls. In addition to modern all-metal semi-monocoque construction, the 360 required less maintenance, boasted a greater useful load, and cost less to purchase and operate than the Bell.

Efforts to reduce construction time, save weight, improve accessibility, and minimize maintenance requirements were evident throughout the Hiller 360. The power train was streamlined by designing the rotor head, transmission, and vertically mounted 160-hp Aircooled Motors (Franklin) engine into one integral unit that could be lifted out by removing six bolts. The transmission—which would suffer "teething troubles" in early service—was a single-stage unit providing a 9.17 to 1 reduction with just six gears, a quarter as many as were required by the two-stage Bell transmission. Instead of thrust bearings where the blades met the rotor hub, Hiller employed tension-torsion bars made up of forty-three parallel pieces of steel. These maintenance-free, low-cost items held the blades yet twisted to allow them to change pitch.

Another new feature was the Hiller's overhead stick, which connected directly to the paddle linkages. Eliminating almost all the control pulleys, rods, and cams found in other helicopter control systems, the overhead stick enhanced safety because—in contrast to helicopters in which the main rotor control linkages are buried in the airframe—one could verify visually during preflight inspection that everything was properly connected.

Finally, the Hiller 360 employed a bladder-type fuel cell buried in its fuselage pan under a protective stainless steel deck. This system was more complex and costly than the Bell gravity-fed system with its external fuel supply, but it was safer. In a crash, the Bell's tank or tanks could rip loose and enter the plexiglass cockpit bubble.

The single retrograde step in the 360's design was the use of wooden blades on its teetering rotor. Helicopter pioneers Arthur Young and Charles Seibel had developed these blades for use on the Bell Model 47. Made of laminated spruce with laminated balsa trailing edges, reinforced internally with stainless steel straps anchored by retaining pins at the hub, the blades were covered in fiberglass and their leading edges were protected with stainless steel.

In the tradition of Hiller's coaxial prototypes, the 360 was to have had metal rotor blades. The Universal Helicopter Corporation of Buffalo, New York, a company formed in 1946 expressly to manufacture blades for rotorcraft manufacturers, had been contracted to develop metal blades for Hiller. At the eleventh hour, these units were determined not to be fatigue resistant. With production imminent and lacking funds to develop new blades from scratch, Hiller obtained rotor blades from Bell Aircraft's supplier, the Parsons Corporation's Aircraft Division in Traverse City, Michigan.

Eight years later, with the introduction of the H-23D in 1957, Hiller Aircraft would finally return to the all-metal rotor blades it had pioneered. In contrast, the 360's tail rotor was all-metal from the start, a substantial improvement over Bell's wooden tail rotor, which frequently suffered damage from stones kicked up by main rotor downwash.

Painted yellow, the Hiller 360X (x for experimental) took to the air November 11, 1947, at 5:20 P.M. Thanks to 150 hours of

The Hiller 360x *Yellow Peril* takes to the air early
in 1948. Courtesy Hiller.

exhaustive flight testing by Peterson in the UH-5B, this occasion brought no surprises. The new machine's cabin was fully enclosed like that of an automobile, reflecting a continuing belief in the prospect of a personal helicopter market. Its color and lines, likened by one employee to "a yellow overstuffed dragonfly," earned it the unflattering nickname *Yellow Peril*. This machine was demonstrated to the U.S. Army and Navy before being unveiled to the public on December 11, 1947.

Hiller's new helicopter quickly became the focus of media attention, in part because its announced price of under $20,000—lower than that of any other helicopter—promised to hasten acceptance of light commercial helicopters. Published descriptions of the aircraft stressed unheard-of stability and controllability. Spring-balanced and self-centering in flight, the overhead stick required a mere fifteen-ounce fingertip pressure to produce the desired control response. The centering springs also served to provide artificial control feel, needed because the pilot did not directly control the main rotor.

Since the rotors passed through 180 degrees of travel before paddle input was fully translated to the main rotor, a slight but unobtrusive control lag was perceptible. This lag served to screen out unintentional control inputs, including violent jolts. Although the 360x responded well to sustained inputs, its stick could be moved briefly in straight lines or through complete circles without any rotor reaction. In contrast to the few other helicopters then in production, moreover, the new helicopter's stick transmitted no bothersome feedback forces from the main rotor.

Where other manufacturers faced the gloomy prospect of heavier controls as they designed larger machines, Hiller Rotormatic forces were entirely a function of the size of the paddles and the mechanical advantage designed into their linkages. The paddles offered light forces regardless of the size of the helicopter. Boosted controls, such as had been used in fixed-wing aircraft since World War II, would be the route other manufacturers would take to address the problem of heavy controls, and the perfection of stability augmentation systems would eventually let them close the gap in stability. For some years to come, however, the Hiller Model 12 (as the 360 would come to be known) would continue to do things that helicopters built by other companies simply could not.

Skepticism among these other manufacturers was laid to rest at the Institute of Aeronautical Sciences Annual Meeting, convened in New York City at the start of 1948. During the rotary-wing session of January 26, Hiller showed movies illustrating the unique characteristics of his Model 360, after which Joe Stuart presented a technical paper titled "The Helicopter Rotor Control." These efforts ended doubts about the effectiveness of the poorly understood Rotormatic system, which had been a hotly debated issue.

Hiller moved his company into its brand new home at 1350 Willow Road on April 3, 1948. Stockholders attending the annual meeting were on hand for dedication ceremonies, which included a performance by the 360x. An ideal site, the Willow Road property combined highway and rail-spur access (the latter never used by Hiller) with verdant surroundings flat enough to permit light airplane operations. With a concrete apron at the rear of the factory serving as a flight line, the facility suggested an airport although the unique capabilities of the helicopter rendered the construction of a runway unnecessary.

A 1948 aerial view shows Stanley Hiller's new factory at 1350 Willow Road, Palo Alto, California. Courtesy Hiller.

New aircraft types are required to run the gauntlet of government certification before they may enter production. To speed up this time-consuming process, construction of three additional preproduction 360s was initiated before the move to Willow Road. One of these new machines underwent static testing in which its airframe was stretched, twisted, and otherwise battered. The two others joined the original 360x in flight trials.

In contrast to the 360x *Yellow Peril*, these new machines had just a windscreen to which a top panel and side doors could be added for operation in inclement weather. Having at last perceived that his product would sell to commercial operators rather than private owners for whom a helicopter would be analogous to a car, Hiller had dispensed with the enclosed cabin. The uprated 178-hp engine was also left uncovered, thereby improving cooling and saving additional weight.

On October 14, 1948, the Civil Aeronautics Administration (predecessor of today's Federal Aviation Administration) issued production certificate 6-H-1, denoting the first helicopter to receive a certificate in the CAA's sixth region. In a ceremony held at San Francisco's Marina District, where Hiller had unveiled the XH-44 four years earlier, a CAA representative painted 6-H-1 on the hovering prototype, replacing the word Experimental.

Hiller thus became the third company (after Bell and Sikorsky) to receive approval to produce commercial helicopters. Significantly, in the course of certification the CAA had determined that the 360 possessed positive dynamic stability, in contrast to the Bell and Sikorsky machines, which—although controllable—were not completely stable.

The way was now clear to market the Hiller 360, which was offered at $19,995. At the time, the competing Bell 47D listed for nearly twice as much, its price having recently jumped from $25,000 to $39,500. With its light-helicopter monopoly now shattered, however, Bell was forced to drop its price to $23,500 in order to retain market share and remain in production.

The value of free-market competition could not have been more eloquently demonstrated. Intense if amicable rivalry between Hiller and larger, better-financed Bell would shape both companies, improving their products and services to the benefit of civil and military customers alike.

Bell's initial price of $25,000 had in fact dictated the price of the Hiller 360. Unlike his competitors, who first developed helicopters and only then set about trying to sell them, Hiller's business perspective had led him to design from the outset toward a target price 20 percent lower than the competition's. This marketing strategy placed severe constraints on Model 360 production costs, thus explaining the helicopter's overhead control stick and other expense-reducing design features.

To bring the 360 successfully to market, Hiller needed to control his company's mounting expenses, find adequate financing, and accomplish key goals like acquiring tooling and lining up suppliers. Time and money were both running out. With the receipt of government certification of the 360, therefore, the company assigned production contracts to more than a hundred subcontractors (most of them on the West Coast) who would initially build some 70 percent of the helicopter.

The reason was that external suppliers worked off their own capital to develop the contracted parts. Hiller's heavy use of sup-

The flightline demonstrates a variety of experimentation unmatched by other helicopter companies in the 1940s. Courtesy Hiller.

Hiller employees pose with the Hiller 360 on October 14, 1948, the day the company's Model 360 helicopter was awarded CAA production certification. Courtesy Hiller.

pliers therefore off-loaded onto external vendors some of the financial burden of getting his helicopter into production. This strategy also avoided capital outlays for additional tooling, equipment, and staffing at his own plant. Later, as capital became available to acquire additional tooling, total production costs could be reduced by dispensing with most subcontracting.

By the end of 1947, all thoughts of production looked decidedly premature to Hiller. Funds raised earlier were running out just when badly needed manufacturing equipment and parts were drastically increasing the company's expenses. With capital still not available from conventional sources, Hiller turned again to Capital Securities only to find that the venture capital group was almost out of business.

Refusing to concede defeat so close to production, the Hiller team proposed to assist that ailing organization's securities sales force. Before this joint effort could gear up, however, several hundred thousand dollars of desperately needed bridge financing had to be found. In these very rough times, Hiller, company officers Henry McIntyre and A. W. B. Vincent, and board member Francis Callery together provided this money in a demonstration of faith in their new helicopter. Without it, the Hiller 360 would not have achieved production.

Visitors to that year's California State Fair were startled to see gleaming Hiller helicopters displayed between the usual milking machines and hay balers. In the infield of a racetrack, these working machines gave convincing demonstrations of "air farming," a term coined by the company to describe such activities as dusting, spraying, and fruit drying. Similar active promotion throughout the state accomplished three goals: it gener-

ated an awareness of the company's new product, it provided advance orders for production examples, and it sold a great deal of common stock. All told, more than $1.5 million in production financing was successfully raised.

An unusual flight early in 1949 dramatically focused national attention on the new helicopter. Widely published air-to-air photographs showed a Hiller 360 cruising at 2,500 feet over San Francisco Bay with nobody aboard; closer inspection revealed two goggled and parachuted figures clinging to its sides aft of the empty cockpit. The figures were Stan Hiller and Lang Washburn. With weights in the front to make it nose-heavy, the 360 took off and climbed to altitude. As planned, Washburn crawled far back along the fuselage pan while Hiller trimmed the craft to maintain level flight. Hiller then abandoned the cockpit and moved back along the other side of the helicopter while Washburn came partway forward again to maintain trim. There the men stayed while the 360 cruised serenely along from south of Moffett Field to San Carlos, a distance of a dozen miles. It could have flown on until its fuel was exhausted but the point had been made; the Hiller 360 had extraordinary stability. No other helicopter in existence in 1949 could have flown this demonstration.

Also early that year, a preproduction 360 undertook America's first civil transcontinental helicopter flight.[14] The roundabout three-month tour—flown primarily by chief test pilot Frank Peterson—covered some 5,200 miles and included demonstrations at more than 450 centers across the United States. The helicopter took this arduous journey completely in stride as it lined up distributors, generated advance sales, and even performed a rescue along the way. Hiller

Hiller becomes the fourth and last company in the world to achieve volume helicopter production in the seminal 1940s. Courtesy Hiller.

A Hiller 360 crop duster demonstrates "air farming." Courtesy Hiller.

The first civil helicopter to cross the United States
lands at the foot of Wall Street in April 1949. Flying the last leg of this tour, Stanley Hiller, Jr., is
at the controls. Courtesy Hiller.

himself—taking over in New Jersey to fly the last leg—piloted the gleaming machine into Manhattan and landed at the foot of Wall Street on April 12, 1949.

The irony of this achievement was not lost on the New York financial community, which had chosen not to invest in Hiller's company. The record-setting helicopter became the gleaming centerpiece of a lavish event hosted by United Helicopters in the grand ballroom of the Waldorf Astoria. Although many prominent financiers attended, neither the event nor the transcontinental flight succeeded in enlisting the support of the East Coast financial community.

Hiller 360 production began early in 1949. The historic first commercial delivery took place on March 1, when B. F. Hodges of Walnut Grove, California, accepted one of the preproduction 360s for dusting and spraying in the Sacramento Valley. Deliveries of assembly-line machines commenced in May. Although the list price for the Hiller was $19,995, it was offered to dealers for just $16,000. This financial incentive of course prompted most early customers to proclaim themselves dealers, thereby building up United Helicopters' roster of distributorships.

If even $16,000 was more than the average private flier could afford to pay (by comparison, a new 1949 Beechcraft Bonanza four-seat airplane cost half as much), it was substantially less than the cost of any other helicopter and well within reach of even modestly funded commercial operators. Orders for the 360 soon sustained a production rate of three per week, less than half the factory's maximum production rate of one per day.

California, a huge agricultural producer, soon boasted more Hiller helicopters than any other state. Hiller 360s—also referred to by their builder as UH-12-360s or simply UH-12s—would soon find their way to other states, as well as Puerto Rico and Hawaii (the latter still a territory). In New York, a float-mounted Hiller 360 whisked Port Authority personnel from downtown Manhattan to outlying port facilities; another 360 flew scenic tours through the Grand Canyon; and yet another surveyed cane fields for a sugar company in Hawaii.

At this juncture, Stanley Hiller's role changed again. Having built a corporate structure, won certification, and commenced production, he now faced the even more difficult challenge of making his company profitable. Entrepreneurs in every industry had accomplished more or less what Hiller had done, only to fail at the day-to-day running of their companies. Drawing from experience gained running Hiller Industries a decade earlier, and fascinated with all aspects of business, Hiller successfully made this transition.

A single fateful event boosted Hiller sales more than any calculated promotion. On Sunday, July 31, 1949, twelve-year-old Terence Hallinan was thrown from a horse and knocked unconscious in the High Sierra of Yosemite National Park. It took the park's doctor eleven hours on horseback from the nearest road to reach him at Benson Lake, a body of water 8,100 feet above sea level. His examination in the remote wilderness disclosed that "Kayo," as the boy was nicknamed, had suffered a skull fracture and could not be brought out by horse or on foot. The boy would remain unconscious for three days.

A Navy plan to employ a tandem-rotor Piasecki fell by the wayside when the military services realized than none of their helicopters could in fact effect such a rescue. The Air Force considered using an amphibious

Grumman SA-16A Albatross twin-engine aircraft on the water despite Benson Lake's small size. High winds and rarefied air made getting to the craterlike lake risky enough; the greater challenge lay in taking off again with the boy aboard and climbing 2,000 feet almost vertically to clear the more than 10,000-foot surrounding peaks. But a human life was at stake and every effort had to be made.

Two days after the accident, having stripped his Bell 47 helicopter of every possible ounce of removable weight, Fresno-based helicopter pilot Knute Flint climbed to 8,000 feet before severe mountain downdrafts forced him to abandon his attempt. A former Army major and noted flier who had demonstrated the Sikorsky R-4 in China during the war, Flint was everybody's popular hero. His test flight proved, however, that the Bell lacked sufficient performance to take off at 8,000 feet with any added load.

Upon landing, a glum Knute Flint categorically informed the waiting crowd that neither a helicopter nor any other type of aircraft could land at Benson Lake. His description of "high, perpendicular cliffs surrounding the lake" also prompted the Air Force to abandon its unworkable Albatross rescue plan.[15] For the moment, at least, it seemed that Kayo Hallinan's only hope for rescue had failed.

New help, though, was on the way from Palo Alto. At the urging of test pilot Jay Demming, a standard Hiller 360 (UH-12) helicopter was pulled from the production line and trucked to Yosemite. At 8:00 A.M. on the day following Flint's attempt, the Hiller team arrived at the White Wolf Ranger Station, where Chief Ranger Oscar Sedergren escorted them to the end of a mountain road. On this improvised landing field, they assembled the Hiller 360 in just thirty minutes.

Members of the press had been camping out at White Wolf Lodge at the base of the 22-mile trail climbing to Benson Lake. By now cynical about aerial rescue efforts, they nevertheless found their hopes bolstered by the matter-of-fact approach of this new group with the shiny little helicopter. They gathered to watch as Demming made two test hops.

The former military test pilot decided to try again at first light when the air was still. Slightly built, disarmingly boyish with a baseball cap and an easy grin, he hardly fit the image of the dauntless rescue pilot. Nor did his elegant helicopter look capable of succeeding where even the nation's military services had failed. Nevertheless, few people at White Wolf Lodge slept much before Demming's appointed 4:20 A.M. takeoff time.

With stars showing in a pale sky scarcely bright enough to see by, Jay Demming climbed aboard the open craft wearing a heavy jacket and gloves against the rotor downwash. He climbed strongly away and the Hiller's echoing beat soon faded in the towering hills. By radio, those gathered at the takeoff site learned that he had landed successfully on the lake's narrow beach thirty-six minutes later. With young Hallinan strapped securely beside him, Demming was back less than an hour after his departure. "This is nifty!"[16] reporters heard the now-conscious youth exclaim as he was bundled into a waiting ambulance.

Demming's Yosemite rescue provided for the first time a dramatic comparison of the Hiller 360 (UH-12) with the Bell Model 47. It had a strong effect on company sales, beginning with an immediate surge of orders from previously undecided customers, many of them foreign. Because of the Palo Alto group's pioneering cultivation of export markets, international sales became so brisk that by the early 1950s UH-12s were being used in

Canada, England, France, Italy, Switzerland, Belgium, Mexico, Guatemala, Venezuela, Brazil, Indochina, Pakistan, the Philippines, Egypt, Thailand, and Madagascar. Hiller's sales, in fact, accounted for more than half the world's then very meager consumption of commercial helicopters.

The point must be made that although widespread, such use represented a small market indeed. In sharp contrast to popular expectations, rotary-wing flight was finding anything but universal acceptance. In the 1940s, in fact, Hiller's company had lost money with each helicopter it sold, and it had not been alone. Still, the narrow commercial market widened slightly with every Bell, Sikorsky, and Hiller delivered, and financial success was not far off.

Henry J. Timken of the Timken Roller Bearing Company of Canton, Ohio, visited both Bell and Hiller in 1949, bringing with him a metallurgist and his personal pilot. Himself a pilot and aviation pioneer, Timken bought a Hiller 360 on the basis of his careful on-site evaluations. So did John Crummy, founder of the Food Machinery Company (FMC). After turning FMC over to his son-in-law, the adventurous businessman flew across Africa in his Hiller 360 *Congo Wasp* in the first crossing of that continent by helicopter.

Aggressively marketing Hiller 360s throughout Europe, Helicop-Air of Paris quickly became the new helicopter's leading foreign sales agent. In late May 1949, two months before the Yosemite rescue, Helicop-Air sold two Hiller 360s to the French government for use in that country's losing war to retain Indochina as a territorial possession. Helicopter rescues during World War II had been irregular and few in number. These two French Hillers therefore share the distinction of performing history's first routine helicopter evacuations of wounded under combat conditions.

Two courageous individuals, Lieutenant A. Santini and Captain Valérie André, gained international prominence in the French Army's Helicopter Rescue Section. The former was its daring leader, the latter a combat surgeon dedicated to saving lives. Not content merely to treat those patients brought to her, Captain André (who later became the first woman general in the French Army) parachuted down to help wounded soldiers. While this dramatic approach saved lives, it meant that the wounded had to be treated on the spot rather than in well-equipped operating rooms. When the first Hiller helicopters arrived, Dr. André herself used them to perform countless daring rescues—at times up to seven a day—often under enemy fire.

Back at Palo Alto, an improved 360 called the Model 12A (UH-12A) received supplemental certification on May 8, 1950, and immediately entered production. It featured new rotor blades and a gross weight increase from 2,247 pounds to 2,400 pounds. Altogether, 194 UH-12s and UH-12As would be built before production ended in favor of improved models.

Then on June 25, 1950, North Korea invaded South Korea and America suddenly found itself at war for the second time in less than five years. Already an operator of Bell helicopters, the U.S. Army turned also to Hiller to meet an expanding need for rotorcraft. For the next three years, military rather than civil requirements would shape the Palo Alto company's fortunes.

In late September 1950, Army Field Forces Major John Oswalt accepted delivery at Palo Alto of the Army's first Hiller YH-23 (serial no. 50-1254). Essentially a stock Model 12A

(Top) Hiller test pilot James Meade contemplates another mode of transportation in Pakistan's Sind Desert, where 360s combated hordes of locusts. Courtesy Hiller.

(Bottom) Adventurous U.S. businessman John Crummy performs the first crossing of the African continent by helicopter in this Hiller 360 named *Congo Wasp*. Courtesy Hiller.

equipped with military radios and enclosed litter carriers, this "air ambulance" was shipped by air to Fort Bragg, North Carolina, for accelerated evaluation owing to wartime urgency. Its success prompted production orders totaling 105 H-23As at the end of 1950.

The Navy also had evaluated a Hiller 12A (BuNo. 125532) at NAS Patuxent River and, favorably impressed, had placed an order for sixteen trainer versions designated HTE-1. Because of the war effort, the Navy deferred to the Army, and many HTE-1s were converted right on the assembly line into H-23As. Except for floor-mounted control sticks, the Navy's HTE-1 and the Army's H-23A were basically stock Hiller 12As in military paint, powered by the same 178-hp engine as their civil counterparts. Once their initial teething troubles were resolved, these machines would prove economical and reliable in stateside training use.

The same could not be said of the H-23As shipped directly to Korea in the opening days of 1951. Too lightly constructed for front-line use under adverse combat conditions, and lacking sufficient power to do all that was expected of them after being overloaded with heavy radios and other military equipment, these first-generation 360s were found wanting in both performance and dependability. A lack of adequate field support compounded the problem, for technical and service representatives (the term for factory support personnel) and spare parts were in decidedly short supply.

"We were naive," Hiller later observed of his company's failure to provide adequate field support. "We didn't understand at first why we had only one tech rep in Korea and Bell had a slew of them. They knew that to maintain those ships they would have to have good tech reps with lots of spare parts. The Army didn't know it but Bell knew it and was able to talk them into it; we didn't know it and therefore couldn't talk them into it."[17]

Although H-23As saved hundreds of lives, their availability rate was significantly lower than that of the workhorse Bell H-13B. In performance, both aircraft—and all helicopters of that era—left something to be desired. None could be expected to maintain altitude on hot days when overloaded with a pilot, two wounded soldiers, and military equipment. If the Hiller team had been able to have another year of production experience before war broke out, the majority of these technical problems might well have been avoided. In the urgency of war, however, the company directed all its energies toward immediate improvement in two areas.

First, the availability of spare parts and other logistics support was upgraded, and additional factory representatives were trained and sent to Korea. Second, Hiller assigned top priority to developing a second-generation helicopter incorporating the hard-won lessons of battle. To facilitate this process, the company sought and received interservice agreement on changes to be specified for the new helicopter during a three-day Army/Navy/USAF engineering conference hosted in Palo Alto in April 1951.

A fifth American helicopter company joined Sikorsky, Bell, Piasecki, and Hiller in meeting the wartime needs for military helicopters. Kaman Helicopters in Connecticut was now building intermediate-size machines with intermeshing rotors as developed by Flettner in Germany during World War II. As the war geared up, the need for a six-to-eight passenger helicopter with internal litter-carrying ability became clear to all five companies.

(Top) Major John Oswalt (center) and Lieutenant Wayne Eggart (left) accept delivery of the Army's first Hiller helicopter from Stanley Hiller, Jr., in September 1950. Courtesy Hiller.

(Bottom) The success of the YH-23 in accelerated Army tests led to an order for 105 Hiller H-23As, some of which are shown here. Courtesy Hiller.

Hiller responded in 1951 by proposing the Model 720, which combined—as its name implied—the dynamic components of two 360s in a new body. This unusual approach was rejected because the Army doubted the company's ability to sustain a new line of production and still meet existing orders, and also because the proposal came at a time when H-23As in Korea were plagued with maintenance problems.

At the start of 1951, the factory at Palo Alto had converted entirely to military production with commercial orders deferred because of the national emergency. New hirings (needed to support a production rate of one helicopter per day, the maximum then possible) now necessitated acquisition of a second facility two miles north in nearby Redwood City, to which many company functions and personnel were transferred.

By now, the company was used to being called "Hiller Helicopters" by the public at large. Either "Hiller Aircraft" or "United Helicopters" was correct but not this appealingly alliterative alternative. By 1950, therefore, the huge lettering "United Helicopters, Inc." on the Palo Alto factory had given way to "Hiller Helicopters," a change unanimously endorsed at the Fifth Annual Stockholders Meeting of March 9, 1951. This meeting showed just how far the company had come: a rented circus tent was now required to accommodate some 5,800 stockholders.

At this same 1951 stockholders meeting, Hiller received approval for a major expansion of the Palo Alto facility to be financed by a $2.5 million debenture issue arranged through Charles Blyth & Company. Construction began with a ceremonial ground breaking near the existing factory on June 13, 1951.

In July a greatly improved second-generation military helicopter prototype was lashed to the ground at Palo Alto and was run for one hundred hours at full power. It passed this test with flying colors, as it did a series of drops to test the two new landing gears replacing the 360's original "tricycle" gear, four wheels for the Navy HTE-2 and maintenance-free skids for the Army H-23B (as introduced on the Bell Model 47D).

With a more powerful Franklin engine uprated to an even 200 hp, the new Hiller offered improved performance despite the hundred-pound increase in gross weight necessitated by its beefier structure. By September 1951 the H-23B was in flight test; two months later the first production B models were accepted by the Army.

Two pieces of stateside news, meanwhile, offset to a degree the daunting reports of Hiller helicopter troubles in Korea. First, the Army announced in September that H-23As operating in the United States had achieved a remarkable 95 percent reliability rate. In contrast to the Korean machines, however, these stateside Hillers enjoyed ample spares and were operated within their design gross weight limits. The second bit of good news concerned Operation Southern Pine, a three-week military exercise held in October 1951 at Fort Bragg, North Carolina, in which Hiller H-23As participated. This operation brilliantly validated the concept of helicopter support of military ground forces. Coupled with the real-life lessons learned in Korea, Southern Pine worked a profound change upon the Army by hastening its adoption of helicopters in a variety of tactical roles.

Then there was the splendid record of the 30th Engineer Base Topographic Battalion, which from 1950 through 1955 conducted summer expeditions to Alaska to map that territory (Alaska would become a state in

Introduced in 1952, the Hiller H-23B featured a
more robust structure, increased power, a skid
landing gear, and floor-mounted control sticks.
Courtesy Hiller.

1959). Based at Crissy Field at San Francisco's Presidio in the shadow of the Golden Gate Bridge, the 30th Topographic Battalion's aviation detachment initially operated Bell H-13s, which they traded after one year for Hiller H-23As. Using these aircraft and the newer B models, which began arriving in 1952, the 30th covered vast stretches of virgin wilderness. By 1954, the 30th Engineer Group (as it was redesignated) had standardized on Hiller H-23Bs because of their ruggedness and safety. From April through September of that year, its pilots logged some 8,000 accident-free flight hours with forty-four H-23Bs.

Shortly before the 1951 expedition, 30th Battalion pilot George Brockway established an interesting if unofficial record in a civil 360 fitted with H-23A-style floor-mounted control sticks. Accompanied by Hiller Test Pilot Jim Meade, Captain Brockway took off from San Francisco on a routine training flight and trimmed for a 60-mph cruise. On impulse, he decided to see how long the Hiller would fly along by itself. To their amazement, neither man had to touch the cyclic, collective, rudder pedals, or throttle for over two hours.

On the engineering front, Hiller undertook pioneering rotor-tip damper research under Air Force contract AF 33(600)-29488 at the start of the 1950s. Housed in the blades to control an articulated tip was a harmonic aerodynamic damper, devised by Hiller engineers to flatten out the undulating track of deflection-prone helicopter rotor blades. Reducing blade-bending stresses would produce a smoother ride. The advanced concept of tracking the rotor blade tips onto an even plane was far ahead of its time; NASA and the helicopter industry would return to it almost forty years later.

A mistake costing Hiller Helicopters its second largest military customer shook the company early in 1952, shortly before the Hiller H-23B entered service. As it expanded, the company's ranks had been augmented by senior staff arriving from declining segments of the fixed-wing industry. Several executives newly arrived from Convair (the interim name of Consolidated-Vultee Aircraft, today General Dynamics) took it upon themselves to try to dictate terms and conditions to the U.S. Navy—with disastrous results.

There were perhaps occasions during World War II when giant companies like the San Diego-based Convair—builder of the B-24 Liberator heavy bomber—could get away with high-handed and dictatorial behavior. For a small, fledgling company to presume to tell Uncle Sam where to get off, though, was a far different matter. Even with the Korean War in full swing in the early 1950s, excess aircraft production capacity remained from World War II. In short, the Navy could—and did—go elsewhere for its light helicopters after buying thirty-five HTE-2s. Twenty more of this model were built with U.S. Mutual Defense Assistance Program (MDAP) funds early in 1953 for use by the British Royal Navy, which designated the type HT.1.

This costly error, for which Stanley Hiller assumed ultimate responsibility, precipitated a major board-level confrontation that forced resignation of most of the Convair contingent. Despite its president's efforts at fence-mending with the Navy, it would be ten more years before the company received mainstream Navy support for a production contract. In between, Hiller's only Navy contracts would be issued by the Office of Naval Research and the Bureau of Aeronautics' power plant division. However interesting, these research-oriented projects would not generate volume production.

In March 1952, lessening military demands permitted the resumption of commercial production with deliveries to begin in June. The bulk of backlogged civil orders, however, would not be addressed until after hostilities ceased in July 1953. Customers who had patiently waited for up to three years for their Hillers were now rewarded with the greatly improved UH-12B, a civil version of the Army H-23B. The new commercial helicopter—offering a fully enclosed cabin, electric trim, and a skid landing gear—sold for $36,400. Good as it was, the best was yet to come in the UH-12 commercial helicopter series.

Newer Hillers, meanwhile, were evacuating wounded in Indochina. Having received four H-23As early in 1952, the French Army's rescue squadron now received three H-23Bs in March 1953. With enough power to really perform in Vietnam's hot climate, the B model—proclaimed a "veritable little miracle" by Dr. Valérie André—was a substantial improvement over the earlier machines.[18]

Of 273 B models procured in 1951, roughly half were shipped to Korea. The remainder stayed stateside to join the Army's new Primary Helicopter School. In all, 453 H-23B/HTE-2/UH-12B series helicopters would be produced between 1952 and 1955. The 500th Hiller production helicopter—a milestone celebrated in September 1953—was, appropriately enough, a U.S. Army H-23B, for the Army was still Hiller's biggest customer. By now, military Hillers also flew with the British Royal Navy, French Air Force, and Swiss Army. Holland, Canada, and Thailand's air and police forces would also soon fly H-23s.

Carrying dogs to locate buried survivors, Swiss H-23Bs rescued avalanche victims in the Alps following heavy snowstorms in January 1954. In the same part of the world some

months later, U.S. Army light helicopters plucked flood victims from Bavarian rooftops. The number of helicopter rescues worldwide had in fact risen to the point where they no longer necessarily generated newspaper headlines. The novelty, it seemed, was wearing off.

How had Korea affected Hiller Helicopters? The impact on the company is perhaps best illustrated by the increase in annual gross sales: The total for 1949—the first full year of sales—was $557,000. That figure rose to $1,262,000 in 1950 when war broke out, then jumped fivefold to $6,657,000 the following year. In 1952 it reached $14,399,000—fully twenty-five times the volume of just four years earlier.

Profitability during this period was limited by the heavy expenditures needed to support the high production rate. By the end of 1953, the company's total plant space had reached 146,000 square feet and employment stood at 550. A healthy net income after taxes of $247,637 reflected in part the resumption of commercial production during 1953. Civil Model 12 sales had already climbed to 20 percent of the company's total business by the end of that year, marking steady growth in the commercial sector.

After the high-level wartime production, total sales dipped to a little over $6 million in 1954 before climbing steadily again to more than $16 million by 1959. In 1950s dollars, this level of sales meant that Hiller had outgrown the "small business" label that had hindered its earlier military procurement efforts. Pentagon perceptions proved difficult to change, however, and Hiller Helicopters was still vastly smaller than fixed-wing giants such as Boeing, Convair, Douglas, Lockheed, or McDonnell.

A new executive vice president and general manager arrived in 1954 to help Stanley

An HTE-2 of the British Royal Navy. Courtesy
Hiller.

Hiller achieve this peacetime growth. Edward T. Bolton brought considerable management skills honed during years of singular service with airlines around the world. The British-born executive, who was also named a director of the company, replaced William C. Jordan, the former Curtiss-Wright Corporation head, who vacated the post after one year.

In September 1953, Hiller Helicopters acquired production rights to the Doman LZ-5, a six-to-eight passenger helicopter combining German Flettner patents with inventor Glidden Doman's own advanced semi-rigid, four-bladed rotor. The Army had shown an interest in Doman's work. A proposed Army version of the craft, the Doman YH-31, had already flown April 17, 1953.

Hiller was pleased with the prospect of producing the Doman LZ-5 because he realized that his company would always be at a disadvantage competing head-to-head against Bell, which enjoyed greater funding and acceptance. It made sense to develop new products not directly competitive with Bell. Between the three-seat Bells and Hillers and the much bigger Sikorskys and Piaseckis, there was a gap in the helicopter market only partly addressed by Kaman. Doman's promising design was the right size to fill it.

A shift in post-Korea Army priorities, however, put an end to the project. The Doman YH-31 was shelved before it could enter production in Palo Alto. An improved Doman-Fleet LZ-5-2 subsequently flew in Canada. Briefly considered by the Army, it was dropped in 1957 because the newer Bell XH-40 (later redesignated UH-1 Iroquois) showed greater promise.

Far less conventional helicopters would take to the sky over Palo Alto in the 1950s. Powered by ramjets mounted at the tips of their rotor blades, these Hiller HJ-1 Hornets would be built in two generations, one civil and the other military. Both were proof-of-concept vehicles for an ambitious company program whose ultimate goal was the production of tip-powered flying-crane helicopters of enormous size and capability.

This major Hiller effort had its beginnings in 1945, when Stanley Hiller performed his earliest experiments in a radically different approach to helicopter flight. Called "tip propulsion," this research-and-development program sought to power helicopters from the tips of their rotor blades. It was inspired by failings Hiller saw in existing helicopters.

A conventional helicopter produces power in its fuselage, passes it through a heavy transmission, then sends it through shafting to a rotor head, which turns the blades by their roots. Some engine power is diverted to the tail rotor to offset torque, the tendency of a helicopter to revolve opposite to the spin it gives its main rotor.

The complexity of this roundabout approach bothered Hiller. For example, it achieves flight with power produced by an easily overheated engine buried in the fuselage, far away from the lifting surfaces where the power is needed. Conventional helicopters also need transmissions to change their high-RPM engine power into low-RPM power at the rotor.

Tip propulsion promised significant benefits. Because the rotor of a tip-powered helicopter spins itself instead of being turned from below, torque is eliminated. So is the need for a tail rotor, the elimination of which saves weight, reduces complexity, and allows all the power the engine develops to go toward generating lift and thrust in the main rotor. Moreover, tip-powered helicopters do not require transmissions or vibration-prone drive shafts, thus allowing further reductions in acquisition and operating costs, weight, and maintenance requirements.

Hiller's vision of tip-power flying cranes would come very close to succeeding in the early 1960s, when the company won an industrywide competition to develop an enormous military helicopter powered by turbojet engines at its rotor tips. Although this and other Hiller flying-crane efforts were never constructed for want of adequate support, the program would nevertheless realize noteworthy goals. Other companies worldwide would pursue the tip-power concept, but none would rival the collective achievements of Hiller Aircraft in this field of study.

The U.S. Army, a logical user of large rotorcraft, had shown an early interest in tip-powered helicopters. In 1946 it issued the first military contract for such a vehicle to Kellett Aircraft. Financial difficulties forced Kellett to sell this program to Hughes Aircraft a few years later. The result was the Hughes XH-17, a stilt-legged flying crane with a 130-foot-diameter rotor. Compressed air from jet engines was ducted through hollow rotor blades and out cornering nozzles in what was termed a "cold-cycle pressure-jet rotor." The XH-17 proved badly underpowered when finally flown in 1952.

Hiller and his team had already studied and rejected cold-cycle systems as inefficient. In 1949 the company built and tested the Hiller Powerblade, the world's first hot-cycle pressure-jet rotor. Hot exhaust gases ducted through various Powerblades produced greater efficiency, which was further boosted by the use of "tip burning," a term describing the combustion of fuel at the blade's exhaust nozzle. However, even this arrangement yielded substantially less propulsive efficiency than was obtainable by mounting jet engines

right at the rotor blade tips. In 1950, therefore, Hiller abandoned the pressure-jet approach to tip propulsion and dedicated his company to experimentation with tip-mounted engines.

Over the next fifteen years, Hiller actively pursued the construction of tip-powered flying cranes with a variety of jet engines at their blade tips. In 1951, the company offered the Army a midsize flying crane called the "Aerial Carryall" or "Flying Truck." It also responded to a Navy request for an aerial-resupply helicopter with the huge "Class HC Heavy Lifter," a collapsible flying crane of tubular construction. Neither of these efforts reached the prototype stage.

The Army requested a design study for a flying crane with a 200-foot rotor in the mid-1950s. Hiller's response was BARC, an acronym for Besson's Aerial Railhead Crane. Named for Major General Frank S. Besson, chief of the Army Transportation Corps, this proposal similarly failed to find support. Neither did a series of parametric studies for a variety of tip-engined flying cranes that Hiller prepared in response to a 1955 military request.

By decade's end, it appeared that Hiller's continuing tip-propulsion efforts might at last pay off. Prompted by this promising body of exhaustive research, including thousands of hours of tip-powered rotor testing on Hiller whirlstands, the Army solicited industry bids for a tip-turbine-powered flying crane in the Hiller mold. Clearly favored to win a contract, Hiller teamed with Continental, manufacturer of the J69 turbojet engine. Although the Hiller-Continental team won the initial contract, funding for this Army program was cut in the early 1960s before a prototype was produced.

Company hopes for giant tip-powered heli-

Tested in 1949, the Hiller Powerblade was the world's first hot-cycle pressure-jet rotor. Hot gases were ducted through the blade to make the rotor spin. Courtesy Hiller.

(*Top*) As this model suggests, Hiller proposed a variety of "flying cranes" powered by jet engines at their rotor tips. Although the company pursued this promising concept for fifteen years, no tip-jet flying cranes were built. Courtesy Hiller.

(*Bottom*) Although the Hiller HJ-1 Hornet of 1951 was designed for personal use, it was never marketed. Courtesy Hiller.

copters revived briefly in 1965 when the National Aeronautics and Space Administration considered sponsoring a Hiller flying crane to recover Saturn V moon booster first stages during Project Apollo. Aerial recovery of this spent first stage, which weighed up to 400 tons, dictated that the Hiller/NASA recovery vehicle be the largest aircraft of any kind yet proposed. The resulting design featured a gross weight of about a million pounds and a rotor more than 300 feet in diameter. Powered by two or more jet engines per blade, this rotor would have turned at 60 RPM, presenting the illusion of slow motion to observers below.

As laid out, the Hiller/NASA flying crane would loiter at 10,000 feet some 475 miles downrange from Cape Kennedy. Sighting the moon booster descending by parachute, it would use special recovery gear to snag the spent rocket and winch it securely in. If the first pass was unsuccessful, sufficient time would remain for two more attempts before the booster was too near the ocean's surface for another try.

Expensive as such a helicopter would have been, the huge aircraft would have paid for itself with the first several recoveries. But long-range planning for the nation's space program was beginning to favor the concept of a reusable space shuttle over single-use rockets, and this recovery helicopter was not funded.

Although Hiller never realized the long-held dream of flying crane production for want of government sponsorship, this program did have conspicuous successes. The comprehensive body of research it generated has paved the way for such helicopters to be built in the future, eliminating every real or imagined obstacle to their construction. This program also fostered the development of two generations of the Hiller HJ-1 Hornet, mentioned above.

The first of these generations began with the construction of three HJ-1s in Palo Alto in 1950. Just seven feet high, weighing 900 pounds fully loaded, and topped with 23-foot-diameter rotors, these machines were far less complex than conventional helicopters. Only their Rotormatic paddles revealed them to be Hiller machines. Frank Peterson flew the first Hiller HJ-1 Hornet on a hot August day in 1950.

The HJ-1 Hornet generated substantial public interest when unveiled by Hiller in February 1951. At that time it was announced that the company might offer them for sale at less than $5,000 each. Here at last was an affordable flying machine that a private owner could keep in his garage. Its top speed was 80 mph, cruise was 70 mph, the service ceiling was 11,000 feet, and the initial rate of climb was a sprightly 1,100 fpm. The little helicopter's only drawback was range: a fully loaded HJ-1 could travel only a little under forty miles.

The HJ-1 was surprisingly stable for so small a helicopter because of its Rotormatic paddles and high-inertia rotor. The docile manners, however, ended at autorotation, an unpowered descent to landing that helicopter pilots practice in order to be able to respond in case of engine failure. Autorotation involves a controlled descent with the rotor in low pitch to keep it spinning. Near the ground, the pilot increases blade pitch to trade stored rotational energy for momentary lift. A soft landing results if the maneuver is performed properly.

Whereas conventional helicopters autorotate at a sobering 1,800 feet per minute or so, the Hiller Hornet plummeted at a terrifying 3,000 fpm because the gaping mouths of its dead ramjets retarded rotor windmilling. Hiller's aeronautical engineers christened this aerodynamic braking "cold drag." Nonetheless, however slowly it turned during autorotation, the rotor—with the weight of ramjets at its tips—had *plenty* of accumulated kinetic energy left to trade for lift when the time came. One merely needed skill, nerve, and fast reflexes to know when to haul up on the collective lever.

Hiller Test Pilot Bruce Jones was the first person to autorotate a tip-powered helicopter. Ground observers stood aghast as he hurtled downward in the HJ-1, came to a radical flare in the nick of time, and settled to the ground. With a mix of relief and anger, Hiller's nonpilot contracts manager ran up to the Hornet, shouting that the craft was not insured.

"Listen," the pilot replied hotly, steadying himself on rubbery legs. "I'm lucky to be alive! The aircraft was falling at 3,000 feet a minute and I was falling at 2,000, and I barely caught up with the controls to land the damn thing!"[19]

Jones, a veteran World War II flier and a former Bell helicopter demonstration pilot, soon became the undisputed master of Hornet autorotations. An argument arose on the Hiller flight line one summer day in 1951 over what accuracy, if any, was possible during "deadstick" landings. Jones settled the issue once and for all by autorotating from 3,000 feet to land within 50 feet of dead center of the Hiller apron.

With no torque to counter, the Hornet dispensed with a tail rotor in favor of a simple airplane-style rudder canted to take advantage of rotor downwash. Pedals were likewise eliminated; side-to-side movement of the collective lever worked the rudder to provide yaw control. An overhead cyclic stick provided lateral and longitudinal control as in

the early model 360s. On the touchy subject of noise, Hiller publicity releases optimistically stated that "the Hornet's sound range compares favorably with that of a conventional-powered [sic] helicopter."[20]

The idea of a low-cost flying machine that could actually fit into a garage briefly rekindled America's cherished dream of privately owned flying machines akin to personal automobiles. The Hornet certainly accommodated such daydreams, having just two controls (cyclic and collective-cum-rudder) and fewer items on its instrument panel than the dashboard of the average car (tachometer, fuel flow gauge, airspeed indicator, altimeter, and starter button).

Unfortunately for this last gasp of the romantic vision of personal flying machines, the Korean War preempted plans to market the HJ-1. Viewing its rapidly expanding backlog of military helicopter orders, and an uncertain public demand for the HJ-1, Hiller Helicopters announced in September 1951 that plans for marketing a civil version of the Hornet had been indefinitely deferred.

Early in 1952, Hiller approached the Navy about authorizing construction of an evaluation quantity of Hornets. The proposal was accepted because it was felt that a revised Hornet might meet a Marine Corps requirement for an ultralight flying vehicle. By summer a fixed-price contract had been negotiated for delivery of five units, three to go to the Navy as the HOE-1. Impressed by the simplicity of the original HJ-1, the Army asked to take the remaining two under the designation YH-32. At the end of 1954, Army officials ordered a dozen more Hornets, and Hiller's own test and demonstration requirements brought the grand total of second-generation Hornets to twenty-five, including the three ULV gunships described below. This evaluation quantity of HOES and YH-32s marked the first production of tip-jet-powered helicopters in history, and the first procurement of such vehicles by U.S. military services.

Coming only a year after the rift between the Navy and Hiller, the order for HOE-1s seemed to belie hard feelings on the part of Navy procurement officials. This small order for test and evaluation machines, however, was approved by the Office of Naval Research. When it came to the acquisition of operational aircraft, the Navy's grudge against Hiller was still in place.

Although the new military helicopter shared the name and designation of the three original HJ-1 Hornets, it was in fact an all-new machine with no commonality. Instead of wheels, it had lightweight skids. Gone too was the rudder worked by moving the collective lever side to side; the new HJ-1 had rudder pedals controlling a tiny single-blade tail rotor (these were reinstated for commonality with other military helicopters). While not needed to offset torque, the tail rotor—which furnished crisper yaw control than was provided by the earlier Hornet's rudder—helped during autorotation and permitted rapid sideways flight as required by increasingly stringent military control requirements.

The HOE/H-32 was a trim machine with perky lines that might just as easily have sprung from Walt Disney's drawing board as from the Hiller team's. In fact, it was designed by both Bob Anderson and the vice president of engineering, James B. Edwards, who had come to Hiller in January 1952 from Douglas Aircraft where he had been project engineer on the famous DC-4 and DC-6 airliners (Edwards would return to Douglas late in 1953 to fulfill the same function on the DC-7).

Unfortunately, as often happens with military involvement in a previously private venture, the HJ-1 suffered a growth in size and weight. A larger cockpit, fiberglass body and tail boom (the first structural use of fiberglass in aircraft construction), and other changes raised the empty weight from the original Hornet's 356 pounds to 536 pounds, and the gross weight climbed to 1,080 pounds. As a result, the service ceiling fell drastically from 11,000 to 6,900 feet. Even with fifty-two gallons of fuel, the craft's range shrank from forty to twenty-eight miles, its maximum powered endurance at economy cruise being roughly thirty minutes.

The decreased performance frustrated the Hiller team, which felt that the HJ-1 had evolved away from the original concept of a truly simple helicopter. Worse still, the joint military program was worked over and over by the Army and Navy with so many extra-contractual changes that—including the dual certification programs described below—it eventually consumed more than a million dollars of Hiller resources.

The first of the HOE/H-32 series flew in September 1953, with deliveries to commence the following spring. The services did not receive them until the end of 1954, however, because these machines had been procured on a "certification specification" basis rather than on the standard "mil. spec." basis, and civil certification of the helicopter and its engine would take time, as both were new to the experience of the CAA.

The 8RJ2B ramjet engine was a refined and uprated version of the unit Hiller had developed in 1949. Now eight inches in diameter and weighing 12.7 pounds, it produced the equivalent of 45 horsepower. Manufactured by Ryan in San Diego under license from Hiller, the 8RJ2B was made out of Inconel X,

Three Hiller HOE-1 ramjet-powered helicopters fly
at Palo Alto in 1954. Courtesy Hiller.

a high-nickel alloy also used in the Mach 6 North American x-15 research plane owing to its lightness and great resistance to heat. Because Inconel x corrodes on contact with lead—then commonly found in automotive gasoline, which was a likely fuel for this engine—the engine's interior was coated with a protective ceramic material.

By August, the 8RJ2B had logged 559 hours in the air, 2,104 hours on the whirlstand, and 1,545 hours in free airstream static tests. Its early teething troubles had been completely solved, even the once nagging problem of flameouts. If flameouts should occur, the engine now reignited itself so quickly that the pilot never perceived the problem. Another selling point was the remarkable portability and simplicity of the 8RJ2B. An untrained person could change a Hiller Hornet's engine in just three minutes with nothing more than a screwdriver.

Ramjet testing on the ground included static duration runs, which were a sore point with residents of Belle Haven and East Palo Alto. One test in March 1953 lasted 200 hours, while another the following February ran for 150 hours. At night when all was otherwise still, moreover, an inversion would often form over the entire San Francisco Bay area, causing the *bam-bam-bam* of the whirling ramjets to skip over much of the local area and bounce squarely into the fashionable Atherton and Menlo Park neighborhoods. Needless to say, it was not welcome. Nor could the company president himself escape it; the disagreeable noise often greeted Stan Hiller when he returned home to Atherton at night.

Harried residents telephoning the plant at Palo Alto to complain often found sympathetic listeners there, many of whom yielded to the temptation to suggest that the sound

"must be coming from the Navy at Moffett Field."[21] Fortunately, the problem was significantly reduced in the spring of 1954 by construction of a circular barrier eighteen feet high and forty feet in diameter, which was designed to muffle jet engine noise. Since the structure could not entirely encircle the facility without depriving it of sufficient air, however, the side facing the bay was left open. The necessity of building the barrier hinted at the seriousness of the tip-engine noise problem; in a world increasingly sensitive to aircraft noise, the issue was a significant obstacle to realizing Hiller Helicopters' vision of tip-turbine flying cranes.

During the last days of ramjet certification in 1954, several overspeed runs were conducted on the whirlstand. At peak RPM, when the tip jet was subjected to as much as 14,000 Gs (boosting its "weight" to some 178,000 pounds), supporting bolts sheared and the 8RJ2B shot away through protective walls, acoustical barriers, and property fences before coming to rest some 500 feet from the test site. The test stand also departed the area, flying off toward San Francisco Bay. It was later recovered from nearby mud flats. The only known structural failure of a Hiller tip-power rotor, this test far exceeded expectations and overwhelmingly satisfied the stringent certification requirements.

On October 28, 1954, the CAA awarded Hiller's 8RJ2B engine Type Certificate No. 280, officially approving it for commercial production and sale should Hiller so desire. Truly pioneering developments in power plant technology would soon overshadow this unit, which would be forgotten as Hiller moved beyond the ramjet in its tip-propulsion program (the subsequent power plant research lies beyond the scope of this book). As the first American-designed and manu-

factured jet engine to be approved for commercial sale, nevertheless, the Hiller 8RJ2B represents a milestone in U.S. aviation history.

Unfortunately, parallel certification for the
Hornet helicopter was not granted. The reason was the cold drag problem associated
with autorotation, described above for the
earlier HJ-1. The new military Hornets
descended steeply at almost 3,500 fpm, but
their massive rotors stored so much energy
that landings were simple after one became
accustomed—if one ever could—to the high
sink rate. Hiller test pilot and marketing
executive Robert Boughton found that
whereas one would begin to flare fifty to sixty
feet above the ground in a normal helicopter,
the Hornet demanded that one begin pulling
up on the collective a full two to three hundred feet off the ground. Enough inertia was
stored in the tip engines to permit the pilot
to touch down, rise into the air again, and
land a second time.

A solution to the unacceptably high sink
rate was proposed to the military during development of the H-32 and HOE. The company
suggested that the flameholders in the mouths
of the ramjets be modified to function like
controllable shutters. During autorotation,
they could simply rotate shut to close off airflow through the engine and greatly reduce
cold drag.

Flameouts had by now been all but eliminated. Even if one engine failed, the Hornet
could be flown some distance to a safe landing, although it could not maintain altitude.
An automatic low-fuel power reduction further enhanced safety by alerting the pilot to
land while sufficient fuel remained to do so
under power. Still, with range so limited and
the possibility of fuel starvation so great,
flameholder shutters were clearly a desirable
feature.

The military declined because its strict
acceptance standards made no provision for
such devices. Without them, the Hornet's
autorotation proved unacceptable to the CAA,
which otherwise found the diminutive craft
satisfactory. Civil certification was accordingly denied. Failure to achieve this production license removed any possibility of
Hornets reaching the private market, although it is doubtful that Hiller would have
chosen to market a civil version in any event.

What was it like to fly the Hiller HOE-1/
YH-32? Start-up was easy if not instanta-
neous, since a small electric motor first had
to spin the rotor up to 150 RPM, or a third its
operating speed. Fuel pressure was then built
up, fuel flow valves were opened, and the
starter button was depressed to fire a spark
plug in each ramjet. Ninety seconds later, the
Hornet's rotor reached 450–500 RPM and
away it flew. Pilots who had the chance to try
it out reported generally pleasant and forgiving characteristics.

A mini-gunship version of the Hornet
would mark a major milestone in the rebirth
of Army aviation. With Key West constraints
on that service's aerial capabilities easing,
Hiller in 1955 received the first U.S. contract
ever issued for an armed military helicopter.
Today largely forgotten, this rotorcraft—a
last incarnation of the HOE/H-32 Hornet
series—was the Hiller YH-32A ULV.

Because it was "stripped to the bare essen-
tials," the ULV (ultralight vehicle) was nicknamed *Sally Rand* after the fan dancer whose
nude performances had enlivened Chicago's
Century of Progress Exhibition in 1933.
Three YH-32As were built and tested in 1957
at Fort Rucker, Alabama, where they successfully carried and employed combinations
of rockets, wire-guided missiles, a 75 mm
recoilless cannon, land mine detectors, and

The Army's first contract for armed helicopters
produced three Hiller YH-32A ULVS (ultralight
vehicles) in 1955. Courtesy Hiller.

other equipment. The new craft featured twin tails to accommodate the recoilless cannons, which discharge gases rearward to counteract recoil. Simplicity dictated a return to canted rudders instead of a tail rotor. This helicopter was intended to travel with Army troops in a tarpaulin-covered trailer that housed spare parts, refueling equipment, and ordnance. With its side panels folded down, the trailer also served as the ULV's launch platform.

Under a separate contract, a modified *Sally Rand* was tested at an abandoned airstrip in central California to determine its vulnerability to enemy action. Although diminutive dimensions made it a difficult target to hit, the craft's size and limited range clearly rendered it unsuitable for operational use. As a proof-of-concept vehicle, however, the YH-32A ULV was successful; it laid groundwork for the U.S. Army's heavy commitment to helicopter firepower during the Vietnam War.

The final phase of the Hiller tip-powered helicopter program would involve the whirl testing of actual turbojet engines. By the early 1960s a unit small enough for such research had become available. Developed by the Williams Research Corporation in Michigan as a power plant for military target drones, this was the tiny WR2-1. Just 15 inches long and 10 inches in diameter, this Williams turbojet—the ancestor of today's cruise missile engines—weighed 23 pounds and generated 83 pounds of static thrust.

Eager to study turbine-engine suitability to rotor tip use, Hiller contacted Williams and an agreement was concluded in the fall of 1961. By the following February, the first turbojet ever mounted on a rotor blade was being whirled at Palo Alto. These whirlstand tests began quite conservatively because small-diameter rotors subject tip engines to far greater gyroscopic forces than large ones do. Nevertheless, the unmodified Williams WR2-1 ran without difficulty at 140 Gs, and Hiller engineers determined that little would have to be changed for it to operate at 1,200 Gs. This promising line of research came to an end with the termination of Hiller's flying-crane program.

During its life, Hiller Aircraft distinguished itself as the most creative component of the U.S. vertical-flight industry. The tip-powered helicopter was just one aspect of a spectrum of programs that would see the development and testing of flying platforms, tilt-wing VTOL cargo planes, and single-seat minihelicopters that could be assembled in minutes and flown by novices. Also investigated were serious proposals for flying jeeps, flying submarines, and wingless battlefield-resupply planes designed to hug the ground at Mach 1 and land in their own length.

After November 1, 1955, much of this remarkable flowering of creativity would come not from the main plant at Willow Road, but from a new facility to the east across the factory's main parking lot. This was the Hiller Advanced Research Division (ARD), the vertical-flight industry's first "skunk works" in the tradition made famous by Lockheed.

Staffed with the company's most innovative and talented engineers, the ARD was essentially an aircraft company in miniature. It was fully equipped with offices for scientists and engineers, a laboratory, an experimental fabrication shop, a drafting room, and assorted support facilities. Its occupants were afforded the freedom to think along unconventional lines and discuss ideas too readily dismissed elsewhere.

(*Top*) A Williams jet engine is whirled at Palo Alto in 1962. Courtesy Hiller.

(*Bottom*) Hiller tip-propulsion research included the testing of Hornet-based autogiros. This example flies with the power of hydrogen-peroxide tip jets that gave it true vertical-flight capability. Courtesy Hiller.

A key observation by Stanley Hiller had given rise to the Advanced Research Division. "We found that we couldn't mix our very talented engineers with our regular engineering department," he later explained, "so we gave them a separate building, separate funding, separate management. The extremely talented people there came up with the weirdest wonders."[22]

Administrative head of the ARD was retired Major General Frank A. Heileman, a mechanical engineer and veteran of World War I who had already proved valuable as a company director. Beneath him were such brilliant minds as Gerhard J. Sissingh, in charge of "aerophysics"; Elbert R. Sargent, chief of propulsion; and F. David Schnebly, head of Operations Research. Responsible for realizing the ideas of these individuals and their staffs in three-dimensional test devices was longtime Hiller employee Edward Bennett, now in charge of the ARD's fully equipped shop. The prototypes and experimental rigs built by Bennett and his group were often tested outdoors in the ARD's courtyard, which by careful design was screened from possible observation.

Away from the day-to-day obligations, frustrations, and interruptions of life in the hectic main plant, ARD personnel were free to explore all manner of intriguing pursuits, the most unusual of which may have been anti-gravitational studies, which remain classified at the time of this writing. "We had some major projects running through there," Hiller recalls, "perhaps not major in dollars but certainly in what they might lead to in the future."[23]

For all its engineering talent, the ARD had been created strictly for business reasons. Recognizing research and development as a major company product in its own right,

Hiller had formed the ARD expressly to streamline his firm's R&D and upgrade its quality. This business judgment proved sound: by 1957 the ARD was performing highly classified work for no less than five branches of the Navy, two of the Air Force, and six of its best customer, the U.S. Army.

On the west side of the main plant, meanwhile, the world's first transport-size VTOL aircraft was taking shape. The Hiller X-18 tilt-wing research plane would fly at Edwards Air Force Base in 1959. It would inspire the Vought-Hiller-Ryan XC-142A tilt-wing transport plane of the early 1960s. Both these aircraft lie beyond the scope of this volume.

With so much nonhelicopter work going on in Palo Alto, the company formally changed its name back to Hiller Aircraft Corporation on July 10, 1958. In March, Hiller had acquired the California-based Adhesive Engineering Company, a leading American producer of structural bonding materials for aircraft and missiles. On November 30, 1960, Stanley Hiller arranged for his company to join the much larger Electric Autolite Company. Heretofore a major supplier to Chrysler, Electric Autolite would soon sell its automotive interests to Ford and restructure under the new name ELTRA.

After fifteen years of growth without external corporate support, a new era thus began for the Palo Alto manufacturer. The merger was favorable in that it preserved Hiller company autonomy while providing access to much additional capital. Hiller, who became a major stockholder and board member of ELTRA, had not arranged the merger out of necessity; the Palo Alto company had been profitable right up to the merger. Rather, he had perceived a need to shift his company to a higher economic plateau.

Without the economic muscle provided by

the merger, the time would soon have arrived when Hiller Aircraft would have faced the choice of either scaling back its commitment to research and development or ending its trend of profitability and increasing return to shareholders. Willing to do neither, Hiller had found a third solution that poised his company for an ambitious new level of effectiveness as an aviation manufacturer.

By the end of the 1950s, Hiller Aircraft had built a remarkable variety of flying machines that included flying platforms, tilt-wing turboprops, and ramjet helicopters. For all its interest in alternative approaches to vertical flight, however, conventional helicopters remained the company's bread and butter. In designing these, Chief Engineer Robert Wagner and his engineering division at the main plant would show the ARD that they could be creative too.

Work began late in 1954 on a new helicopter in response to a Navy contract calling for development of a one-man escape-and-rescue vehicle for use by the Marine Corps. Of some thirty responses to an industrywide request for proposals the preceding year, Hiller in California and Gyrodyne in New York produced winning entries and were awarded development contracts.

Hiller's entry, the XROE-1 Rotorcycle, made its first flight in November 1956. Looking more like an insect than a helicopter and weighing just 290 pounds, the Rotorcycle was developed specifically for rescue, escape and evasion, and "small unit tactical missions."[24] The XROE-1 climbed at 825 feet per minute and cruised for 45 minutes at more than 50 mph. Power was supplied by a four-cylinder two-cycle Nelson engine rated at 45 hp. The primary evaluator of this minimal flying machine was Richard L. Peck, then Hiller Aircraft's chief test pilot.

During the Korean War, a fighter pilot downed behind enemy lines in rugged country had no helicopters available to pick him up before his position was overrun by enemy forces. A Hiller Rotorcycle, packed in collapsed form into a streamlined container just two feet in diameter, could be parachuted to the downed flier who, without tools, could assemble it in five minutes and fly off to safety. Fighter aircraft would provide top cover to the Rotorcycle if necessary; fighters could also deliver them to downed pilots, as Rotorcycle containers were designed to be carried on underwing bomb racks or even in place of wingtip fuel tanks.

Amazing as it sounds, the precision-engineered Rotorcycle could indeed be readied for flight in just minutes. Its assembly required only the insertion of a few quick-release pins. As for flying, the XROE-1 proved remarkably stable despite its size because it featured Hiller's Rotormatic cyclic. The servo-rotor paddles were rigged to accommodate the exaggerated control inputs of inexperienced pilots, although a quick readjustment on the ground could provide seasoned pilots with crisper control response.

The Navy procured five YROE-1s (the "Y" prefix denoting service test status) for evaluation beginning in late 1958, and the Hiller company built additional Rotorcycles of its own to use as demonstrators for potential foreign sales. Dick Peck flew an ROE-1 through the Alps on a European promotional tour, which led to limited Rotorcycle production under license in West Germany. Despite the success of the machine in testing by the Marines, however, the Rotorcycle was assigned too low a procurement priority to generate volume production contracts. The few examples of this trim little machine that today survive are a fascinating tribute to the

The Hiller YROE-1 Rotorcycle was a quickly assembled Navy escape vehicle that could be parachuted to downed U.S. pilots. Courtesy Hiller.

ability of their manufacturer to rise to challenges of all sizes.

Against the busy backdrop of Hornets, Rotorcycles, VTOL experiments, and ARD projects, Hiller consistently gave top priority to improving successive versions of the UH-12 series. The quality of the production aircraft rolling off the Palo Alto assembly lines bore proof that Hiller's facilities and engineering abilities were second to none, yet the best was still to come.

Army H-23BS already in service were supplemented beginning in late 1955 by the first Hiller H-23CS, a substantially revised version featuring a rounder canopy for more room and better visibility, especially downward where the metal fuselage lip had been replaced with more plexiglass. Other changes included a redesigned instrument panel a third smaller than that of previous models, and a new carburetor which reduced pilot workload by automatically adjusting the fuel-air mixture according to altitude. Canada received H-23CS in 1956, the same year Hiller brought to market a commercial version called the 12-C.

On April 3, 1956, the new Hiller H-23D flew for the first time. Largely unheralded in the annals of rotary-wing flight, this event marks a new plateau in piston-powered helicopter technology. Constant refinement of the UH-12 series, bolstered by a massive company commitment to produce the finest possible product, brought about a true quantum leap in helicopter technology.

More than just a refinement of earlier models, the revised UH-12D embodied every "wish-list" improvement its design team had come up with during years of effort, testing, and operational analysis. Backed by a management willing to shoulder high develop-

ment costs in order to "do it right," and further subsidized by Army funding, the new helicopter boasted several major innovations and countless lesser refinements. The first of the late-generation Hillers, the UH-12D would bring reciprocating-engine helicopter technology to its zenith.

To begin with, the new H-23D was designed to fly 1,000 hours between transmission and drive-train overhauls. All helicopters then in existence required frequent major overhauls of these areas, thus greatly increasing their operating costs. The earlier Hiller H-23C, by way of comparison, could operate only some 300 hours between dynamic-system overhauls.

When a Hiller study showed that it should be possible to design gears, bearings, and lubrication systems in such a way as to reach this 1,000-hour mark, the Army immediately offered developmental support. As the largest operator of helicopters in the world, it perceived huge potential savings in the program which, if successful, would put pressure on the rest of the industry to follow suit. At the same time that the Army ordered its first H-23C (serial no. 55-4060), therefore, it also ordered two H-23D prototypes (serial nos. 55-4061 and 55-4062). The success of these evaluation aircraft in meeting the manufacturer's claims led to three orders in 1957 and 1958 totaling almost $16 million for 316 aircraft at an average cost of $50,000 per aircraft plus spare parts.

The Hiller H-23D incorporated all that had been learned over seven years with some 900 helicopters already produced at Palo Alto. Obvious external differences between the D and preceding models were all-metal rotor blades; a lightweight skid landing gear; and the relocation of its tail rotor to the left side, with a concomitant relocation to the right of

(*Top*) The Hiller Model 12-C of 1956. Courtesy Hiller.

(*Bottom*) A quantum leap in rotary-wing technology, the Hiller H-23D (UH-12D) was designed to fly 1,000 hours between transmission and drivetrain overhauls. Courtesy Hiller.

the horizontal stabilizer, to eliminate a harmonic vibration in earlier Hillers known as "tail-boom buzz."

Almost every major system was revised in this helicopter. Power was supplied by a new 250-hp Lycoming VO-435 engine topped by a new unlimited-life transmission that, despite its smaller size, could accept 40 percent more power than the unit it replaced. A revised engine mount permitted the engine to be removed independently of the transmission and rotor. Gross weight was increased by 200 pounds to 2,700 pounds, while top speed was increased to 95 mph.

The first production H-23Ds reached the Army in December 1957. Most went directly to the Army's Primary Helicopter School, which had relocated in July 1956 to Camp Wolters in Mineral Wells, Texas, from San Marcos, Texas. Beginning with 120 H-23Ds, Camp Wolters continued to grow as helicopters became ever more central to Army aviation. Altogether some 600 Hiller H-23s would eventually accumulate in excess of three million flight hours at this training base. These Hiller Ravens—as the Army christened the H-23 in 1957—represented the largest concentration of helicopters anywhere in the world.

By 1958, reinvestment in state-of-the-art machine tools and other equipment permitted production of fully 80 percent of the H-23D helicopter right at Palo Alto. Even the optically perfect windshield was now made in-house. This marked increase in on-site fabrication resulted in a higher profit margin than had been possible with the heavily subcontracted early models.

Although granted a production certificate on December 23, 1957, the Model 12D (a civil counterpart to the H-23D) was not marketed. Instead, Hiller kept the commercial

12-C in production until ready to unveil an even better version known in prototype form as the H-23D-1. The now-classic Hiller Model 12E was introduced September 23, 1958, and certified January 6, 1959. It would remain in production well into the 1980s (most recently by the Rogerson-Hiller corporation in Washington State).

"Stan Hiller's 12E is the best lightweight three-place helicopter ever built," asserts Delford M. Smith,[25] whose Oregon helicopter operation has evolved over the years into Evergreen International Aviation, one of the world's largest all-service aviation companies. Smith logged thousands of hours in 12Es in agricultural, forestry, and construction duties, flying out to oil rigs, and even savings lives on occasion. "Frequently when a person's life was hanging in the balance," states Smith, himself a winner of the helicopter industry's Fred Feinberg Award for a heroic rescue, "the 12E was an angel of mercy."[26]

To the original 360's stability and maneuverability, the 12-B's ruggedness, and the 12D's reduced maintenance, the E model now added the final ingredient necessary for lasting commercial success: remarkable performance for a piston-powered helicopter. With a 305-hp Lycoming VO-540 engine, the Model 12E could routinely haul underslung loads weighing a full thousand pounds. Top speed was 96 mph, cruise 90 mph, and gross weight was 2,750 pounds.

The 12E was a commercial bonanza for Hiller. More of this version would be sold than all other civil models combined. This robust aircraft always did more, if anything, than the factory specifications called for. "The 12E was the Cadillac of the industry," remembers former Hiller employee Everett L. "Curly" Barrick. "It was hell-for-stout, a work-

Eleven Hiller employees weighing a total of 1,822 pounds hover aboard the Hiller UH-12D-1, prototype of the Hiller 12E series. Left to right: secretary-treasurer Jim Dresher, director of flight test Phil Johnston, engineering staff assistant Bud Cheney, vice president John Chadwick, flight test engineer Bob Jensen, Navy representative Lt. Cdr. Jack Caldwell, test pilot Dick Peck, project engineer Herb Mosely, assistant chief engineer (administrative) Bill Callery, marketing vice president Bill Vincent, and test pilot Larry Lape. Courtesy Hiller.

Considered the finest piston-powered helicopter
ever built, the rugged Hiller 12E could routinely
lift 1,000-pound underslung loads. Courtesy Hiller.

horse—hand-finished, and every one off the assembly line had a personal touch."[27]

Hiller publicity photographs showed 12ES carrying huge utility poles, steel pipes, and other loads. When so laden, "the machine could shake your teeth out," recalls Del Smith, "but it got the job done and it would fly anywhere under all kinds of weather conditions. It gave us the capacity to develop year round work, which is what we needed to make our business viable."[28]

Taking advantage of the extra lifting capacity, Hiller in 1960 introduced a four-seat "station wagon" version of the 12E called the E4. The seating configuration of the E4 copied that of the Bell 47J, a 1956 all-metal executive version of the venerable Model 47. A 25-inch extension to the standard 12E's forward fuselage provided space for a separate pilot's seat ahead of bench seating for three passengers. The basic airframe was otherwise unchanged except for a revised tail featuring an inverted-Vee tailplane. Kits were available from the factory to convert standard 12ES to E4S. Both versions featured such refinements to the Hiller line as dual carburetors, optional high-compression pistons that developed 340 hp, and optional superchargers that maintained full-rated horsepower all the way up to 20,000 feet.

An extensive enlargement of Hiller's domestic and Canadian sales organization was instituted at the start of 1959 to support these new machines. Closing out a busy decade, Hiller Aircraft recorded sales of $16,211,624 in 1959. This brisk volume of business marked a 23 percent increase over the preceding year, although net income after taxes at $305,903 was slightly lower than for 1958 due to heavy write-offs of aircraft development costs. All of the company's $1.6 million long-term debt had been converted to capital stock or retired, however, and shareholders' equity rose by $1.32 to $9.61 per share. "We are confident the company's position in the industry was materially improved," President Stanley Hiller, Jr., observed at a New York news conference in March 1960, "and that the future years will benefit from the heavy expenditures charged against 1959 profits."[29]

If Hiller Aircraft's helicopter production and VTOL work was well known, not so a wide variety of interesting lesser efforts that were overshadowed by the major programs. Hiller at the end of 1959 acquired North and Central American sales rights to the Bölkow BO 102 Heli-Trainer, a West German helicopter training aid providing students with realistic control movement and response. Essentially a captive helicopter, the trainer was topped by a small rotor powered by a 40-hp engine. Another effort—this one developed in-house—was a self-propelled warehouse pallet called the GEM-JAK; a commercial spinoff of recent ground-effect machine (GEM) studies sponsored by the Army through the ONR, the GEM-JAK supported very heavy loads on a cushion of air. Yet other little-known company products ranged in size from knee-pad navigation plotters for fighter pilots to large ground-based radar antenna arrays.

A dramatic mountain rescue—more than twice as high as the Sierra Nevada rescue eleven years earlier which had helped sales of the original Model 360—gave an unexpected boost to the Hiller 12E in the spring of 1960. On the weekend of May 21–22, Link Luckett, operator of a helicopter charter service in Anchorage, Alaska, successfully rescued two mountain climbers, one with a broken leg, from the 18,000-foot level of Mount McKinley. This was the highest altitude helicopter rescue in history, and Luck-

In 1960, Hiller Aircraft introduced a four-seat
version of the 12E called the E4, which the Army
ordered as the OH-23F. Courtesy Hiller.

ett's six landings over two days were also the highest landings and takeoffs to date by *any* type of aircraft, by a margin of almost three thousand feet.

In addition to demonstrating the remarkable performance of the 12E, Luckett's widely hailed rescue drove home the fact that for once commercial operators had beat the military to the punch. The Army had yet to add this latest Hiller to its inventory. Perhaps to disguise this fact, there would be no H-23E; the Army's first large order for 12Es in 1961 carried the designation OH-23G (the "O" suffix reflecting reclassification of the H-23 series as observation helicopters). The four-seat E4, thirty-three of which were eventually ordered, was further designated the OH-23F.

As a private venture, Hiller built and demonstrated an instrument trainer version of the OH-23F in 1962 under the designation TH-23F. It had a new rotor system (the rotor described below) and three seats arranged to permit the simultaneous training of two students. One student flew from the front right seat, with the instructor sitting to his left, and another student observed from a central seat behind the two. When time came to swap positions, the right seat slid back to facilitate changing places.

The Canadian Army's twenty-two CH-112s (12Es) entering service in 1961 proved so well-adapted to the rugged far north that Canada's Air Force also bought three CH-112s. Great Britain's Royal Navy, pleased with the HTE-2s it had received ten years earlier, found that the fourteen 12Es it bought in 1962 demonstrated an availability rate surpassing that of all its other helicopters, not to mention many of the fleet's fixed-wing aircraft.

On October 31, 1963, a Hiller OH-23G set a half dozen world records at Edwards Air Force Base in California. Piloted by Army Captain Bertram G. Leach, this helicopter flew as fast as 123.67 mph in multiple speed runs across desert sands. Before the day was over, six official rotorcraft speed records had been set in two weight classes on three straight and closed-circuit courses. Four were entirely new records, whereas two others had been claimed two years earlier by Bell test pilots Lou Hartwig and Al Averill in Bell 47Js. The Hiller OH-23G handily beat their respective speed records of 104.61 mph and 107.08 mph by an impressive 15 percent margin.

Despite its excellence, the H-23 series was inevitably nearing the end of its life. Military sales were becoming ever more difficult for Hiller because Bell Helicopter, now with many government contracts to subsidize its operations, could undersell Hiller. A mid-1950s contract for a medium-size helicopter initially called the XH-40 would alone eventually carry virtually all of Bell's overhead; redesignated the HU-1, then UH-1 Iroquois, this was the ubiquitous "Huey" of Vietnam War fame.

"The only way we stayed in competition," Hiller later observed, "was to prove with the Army's own figures that the H-23s cost less to operate over a period of time; to show that ours was a lower total-cost program despite higher initial cost."[30]

For a time, the Army adopted a "directed procurement" specifying purchase of fixed quantities of trainers from both Bell and Hiller, an arrangement that continued until 1967, when its final order for OH-23s was placed. Altogether some 1,693 H-23s were built by Hiller for the U.S. Army over a span of almost two decades. Another eighty-six had been built for foreign governments under the terms of the Mutual Defense Assistance Program (MDAP).

If H-23 production was nearing an end, a large new military program was now on the horizon. In October 1960, the Navy—on behalf of the Army—solicited design proposals for a new-generation turbine-powered light observation helicopter. The potential volume of military sales of this new machine was so great as to virtually guarantee the winner a preemptive share of the emerging civil market as well. The LOH competition—which was shaping up to be perhaps the biggest military helicopter contract ever issued—received top priority at Palo Alto, where Hiller engineers threw themselves into the design of an advanced new helicopter.

Anticipating this program, Hiller had for several years been sending engineers like Wayne Wiesner and Bud Cheney on extended tours of military bases to discuss requirements with hundreds of military personnel. By the time design work began in earnest, Hiller felt it knew what the Army wanted better than the Army did.

A radically different rotor developed for Hiller's LOH prototype was tested in 1961 on the H-23D-2, a second 12E prototype that had been set aside for this purpose. Lacking the distinctive Rotormatic paddles that had been the trademark of every other Hiller helicopter ever produced, the "L" rotor combined a Hamilton Standard stability augmentation system and new wide-chord rotor blades with high lift and inertia that permitted a gross weight increase to a hefty 3,100 pounds. Constructed of stainless steel with weight-saving metal honeycomb trailing edges, these long-life blades gave a smoother ride, more solid control feel, and superior autorotation characteristics. The L rotor was offered commercially in 1963

on the Hiller 12E as the 12E-L.

In 1964, the 12E-L became the Hiller L3, and the E4 with the new rotor became the L4. Supercharged versions of each, the SL3 (a military version of which was proposed to the Royal Australian Air Force) and SL4, were available in 1965, the final year of helicopter production in Palo Alto.

In 1962, Hiller had concluded an agreement with Pratt & Whitney of Canada for development of a Model 12 powered by a 500-shp PT6 turboshaft engine. This contract produced a single prototype designated the JL5. Another turbine installation was available from Soloy Conversions Ltd. of Chehalis, Washington. The UH12-J3 (a conversion of the standard 12E or E4) incorporated an Allison 250-C20B turboshaft power plant weighing 158 pounds and producing 420 shp. The Soloy conversion had in fact been developed by Hiller Aircraft, but the company had decided not to market it.

For operators desiring additional performance but unable to afford turbine power, Hiller also offered its customers the option of a turbocharged Lycoming piston engine. The turbo, which greatly increased altitude performance, paid for itself when a heavy load, altitude, and hot weather conspired to make life miserable for operators of helicopters with normally aspirated engines.

In March 1983, twenty-four years after it was built, a turbocharged Hiller 12E set a phenomenal altitude record of 27,900 feet. Flown by Terry Clark, an experienced pilot who had commanded helicopter gunships in Vietnam, the vintage Hiller demonstrated sustained cruise to capture official world class and U.S. national records for piston helicopters. His helicopter was the prototype for a commercially marketed turbocharger retrofit intended to boost the performance of working Hillers.

Substitution of the high-inertia "L" rotor developed for Hiller's light observation helicopter gave rise to the 12E-L of 1964, which lacked Rotormatic paddles. Similarly, the E4 with this new rotor became the L4 shown here. Courtesy Hiller.

This Phoenix Conversion, as it is known, was developed by Calvin Hunt and is marketed by Craig Helicopters of Colorado.

There is an odd phenomenon in helicopter flight whereby the floor beneath one's seat appears to shrink as one climbs higher. Five miles up, Clark's perch offered little more psychological support than a postage stamp. He later characterized this unusual flight as "harder than any mission I ever flew in Vietnam."[31]

The stability augmentation system (SAS) required in Hillers with the L rotor worked well, but its complexity and expense were simply not justified in a helicopter already as good as the 12E. Future production of this helicopter series—which would shift over the years to other companies and locations— would concentrate on the standard 12E with Rotormatic paddles reinstated.

Had the Army been receptive, Hiller might have built an odd-looking turbine-powered light helicopter called the CAMEL (Collapsible Airborne Military Equipment Lifter). Conceived in 1959, the Model 1091 was about the size of an H-23 but 400 pounds lighter. Its high back and open frame accommodated loads of all sizes and shapes weighing up to 1,500 pounds. Power was to be supplied by either a 250-shp Allison T63 or a 430-shp Boeing T60 turboshaft engine.

A full-size nonflying mockup was constructed in 1960 (under new model number 1094). It had a Hiller YH-32 Hornet windshield and overhead stick, the dynamic components (rotors, shafts, transmission, and controls) and tail boom of an H-23D, and the Rotorcycle's collapsibility. Six folded CAMELS could fit into the hold of a Lockheed C-130 at one time. The helicopter could be assembled by two men in six minutes. A civil version of the CAMEL (the acronym now

reworded to Civil Aerial Multi-Purpose Equipment Lifter) was also proposed, but the program ended before construction of a flying prototype because of a decided lack of Army interest.

A major new development effort took to the air July 14, 1961. Designated the Hiller Model Ten99, this six-place all-purpose helicopter was powered by a 500-shp Pratt & Whitney PT6 turboshaft engine flat-rated to 350 shp. No larger than the three-seat Hiller 12E, the Ten99 could in just minutes be smaller still for easy transport by cargo plane: the landing skids folded up and the tail cone came off with the removal of just a couple of bolts. With understandable pride, therefore, a Hiller promotional publication described the new machine as "the smallest big helicopter flying."[32]

With a gross weight of 3,500 pounds and a payload of more than a thousand pounds, the Ten99 was indeed a "big" helicopter in terms of utility. Wide side doors and clamshell rear doors greatly facilitated loading the boxy aircraft's capacious 100-cubic-foot cargo hold. Engine, transmission, and shafting, moreover, all sat atop the fuselage under a domed cowling instead of invading the interior space as was universally the case with small helicopters. Although the Ten99 first flew with Rotormatic paddles, an L rotor was soon fitted for improved performance.

The Ten99 was developed in anticipation of a major Marine Corps requirement for an assault support helicopter (ASH), to be procured by the Navy, from whom the Marines received their aircraft. Designed around the specified PT6 engine, the vehicle Hiller engineers came up with was ideally sized to address the mission of getting Marines and their equipment into tight corners rapidly and with great flexibility.

Despite war paint and dramatic promotional photographs showing the Ten99 in action, however, the single prototype (civil registration N3776G) would remain a company demonstrator for want of a buyer. The Bell Helicopter Company had convinced the Navy to buy a version of the UH-1 Iroquois as its new assault support helicopter. Accordingly, the Marine Corps would soon be flying Hueys along with the Army and the Air Force.

The fact that the larger Huey was initially not eligible to compete in the ASH procurement had not stopped Bell, which led the industry in its ability to sell programs to the military services. Believing it had a good vehicle for the assault support role, it first talked the Navy into waiving the requirement for use of the PT6 engine, this unit being too small to power the UH-1. Bell had then argued that volume production of the Huey—which promised to be built in greater numbers than any helicopter before in history—would bring prices down to acceptable levels despite the Huey's larger size. The opportunity to get extra carrying capacity at no extra purchase cost appealed to Navy procurement officials, who happily awarded the ASH contract to Bell.

Failure of the Hiller Ten99 to win this military contract placed its builder in a bind. Although business was booming and profitability continued to climb, Hiller Aircraft had failed to achieve volume production of any new product since the introduction of the UH-12 series in the late 1940s. Although 12E orders currently constituted the largest peacetime backlog in the company's history, Hiller employees knew only too well that new sources of production would have to be found soon or the company would not be able to continue.

Hiller had invested a great deal in the Ten99, which (like the inexpensive CAMEL before it) was financed entirely with company funds. After the UH-12 series itself, in fact, the Ten99 helicopter had been the most expensive program yet pursued by Hiller Aircraft. The lack of military support dealt the company a double blow, since it also undermined plans to bring an executive transport version of the Ten99 to the civil market. With club seating for four in an elegantly appointed interior separate from the cockpit, the civil Ten99—complete with a folding work table to serve as a desk—had promised the privacy and utility of a small office.

For Hiller Aircraft to survive, new sources of production were clearly needed. The failure of the Ten99—even by today's standards an excellent helicopter—underscored the realization that time was growing short. However successful the company's R&D programs, and however well its new prototypes flew, these things could not carry the company without a healthy base of volume manufacture.

Fortunately, if the early 1960s brought great challenge, they also offered unprecedented opportunity because of the enormous potential of the Army's expected requirement for light observation helicopters. Now on the horizon, this competition was tailor-made for the Hiller team, whose long experience building light helicopters for the Army gave it a clear edge over much of the rest of the aviation industry.

Therefore, although a lot of money had gone into the Ten99, much more still was now allocated to the Palo Alto team's entry for the landmark LOH competition. Behind the confident determination of Hiller's talented engineering staff, driving them to new heights, lay the knowledge that—like it or

Although its overall dimensions were comparable to those of a light helicopter, the Ten99 offered twice the passenger capacity, two-and-a-half times the usable cargo volume, and nearly double the payload. Courtesy Hiller.

not—the very existence of Hiller Aircraft might depend on the success of the trim turbine helicopter now taking shape on their drawing boards.

Much was happening on the business front. By early 1964, it was obvious that Hiller Aircraft's association with ELTRA had become less desirable. That organization had evolved into a holding company with too many divisions in different fields all competing for its resources. It was evident to Stanley Hiller, moreover, that ELTRA would eventually be for sale.

Hiller needed to reposition his company. He discounted joining forces with Douglas, Lockheed, or any other aerospace giants because their sheer size would threaten to deny Hiller Aircraft any measure of control over its own destiny.

Instead, Hiller settled upon Fairchild Stratos, the name since 1961 of the venerable Fairchild Engine and Airplane Company of Hagerstown, Maryland. It fit the bill nicely and—currently undervalued following years of lackluster management—it presented an opportunity. In addition to providing economic prowess, the association promised healthy diversification. In an arrangement proposed by Hiller, Fairchild bought the Palo Alto company from ELTRA on May 5, 1964.

During the negotiations, Hiller had begun purchasing stock with his own money to became the second largest Fairchild shareholder after Sherman Fairchild himself. He now took up duties as executive vice president and board member of the combined company. Ed Bolton remained in Palo Alto as general manager of Fairchild's new Hiller Aircraft Division.

The restructured Maryland-based aircraft company further moved to acquire Republic

Aviation on Long Island, New York. For continued product recognition, it had been decided during negotiations with Fairchild that the Hiller name would be retained. Accordingly, a now much-enlarged Fairchild Stratos officially became the Fairchild Hiller Corporation in November 1964.

The future looked promising for the combined company. This amalgamation placed the Hiller component in a position of newfound strength across a broad spectrum of the industry as a manufacturer of both rotary-wing and fixed-wing aircraft. Already in the air, the Hiller OH-5A prototype appeared likely to win the LOH competition. Demand for Model UH-12 commercial helicopters ran at record levels, and current military contracts—even though the Army's Raven was nearing the end of its production life—gave Hiller its largest peacetime H-23 backlog in the history of the company.

On the Fairchild side, there was license production of the Fokker F-27 Friendship turboprop airliner and of Fairchild Hiller's stretched FH-227 version. The company was also gearing up to build under license the Swiss-designed Turbo-Porter, a single-turbine-engine short-takeoff-and-landing (STOL) aircraft.

With the further acquisition of Republic Aviation, Fairchild Hiller gained F-105 Thunderchief support contracts, the construction of F-4 Phantom II empennages as a subcontractor to McDonnell, and a variety of promising research programs. Through the acquisition of Republic, Fairchild Hiller also gained one-third ownership of Fokker in Holland.

Hiller began transferring production from Palo Alto to Hagerstown in 1965. Consolidating manufacture under one roof rather than operating two plants at lower capacity yielded a more competitive cost factor and made good business sense. "A difficult decision even to think about, let alone make," as Hiller described it in 1967, this transfer was nevertheless essential and unavoidable.[33] Plans called for R&D engineering activities alone to remain at the Willow Road complex. At this juncture, therefore, most of Hiller Aircraft's work force either had to relocate to Maryland or leave the company. Many long-time employees opted to retire in northern California.

Ironically, combining with Fairchild had hardly lessened the singular importance to company fortunes of the LOH competition. Before acquiring Hiller, Fairchild Stratos had been plagued with excess plant capacity and a paucity of aircraft production; the company as a whole now looked eagerly to its new Hiller Aircraft Division for needed business.

Winning the LOH competition in fact remained critical to the survival of the Hiller division. With nothing comparable to Bell's Huey program to carry its overhead and maintain its financial health, it badly needed LOH production to remain competitive. Were Fairchild Hiller to lose, and were it to try without military funding to sell its new helicopter on the civil market, it would find it impossible to compete on a cost basis for very long with whichever company had won.

Fortunately, Fairchild Hiller's LOH entry had already been adjudged the winner of the competition's rigorous technical evaluation, which was conducted by the Navy at the request of the Army. The Army itself preferred the Hiller, which alone of several helicopters being considered truly met that service's demanding operational requirements. At the close of 1964, therefore, the graceful Fairchild Hiller OH-5A seemed sure to become America's premier light turbine helicopter.

But Fairchild Hiller was not destined to win the LOH competition. In a fascinating instance of a procurement gone awry, this milestone vertical flight decision would fall prey to the unethical scheme of Howard Hughes, Jr., a bedridden eccentric high atop a Las Vegas casino.

Howard Hughes was, of course, sole heir to the Hughes Tool Company fortune. The Texas-based company—manufacturer of a drill bit that had revolutionized the petroleum industry—provided its owner with access to more than a billion dollars to pursue his long-standing interests, filmmaking and aviation. Although the society-page glamour lingered on, the Howard Hughes of the 1960s was a far different person. No longer seen in public, he ran his business empire from his bed in a self-imposed exile that masked a progressive deterioration of both his physical and mental health.

When the light observation helicopter (LOH) competition was announced in October 1960, Hughes saw in it a golden opportunity not to be missed. The LOH program promised to generate the biggest helicopter contract yet issued by the U.S. government, one bringing such a great volume of military production as to also guarantee the winner a preemptive share of the emerging civil market for light turbine helicopters.

For Hughes, the LOH offered a last chance to establish himself in the cherished role of aircraft builder. He had long coveted such a role, but his earlier attempts to gain a foothold in the industry with aircraft such as the Hughes H-4 *Spruce Goose* had been notably unsuccessful. So poor was the wartime performance of Hughes Aircraft, in fact, that the Senate's renowned Truman Committee[34] had in 1947 investigated that company's singularly unproductive use of public funds.

In his determination to win the LOH competition, Hughes corrupted the procurement process using weapons of subversion alliteratively summarized by one observer as "babes, booze, and bribes."[35] Today well documented, in part by a 1967 congressional investigation into the billionaire's bizarre actions, this high-stakes theft brought havoc to the formerly stable helicopter industry.

In January 1961, twelve manufacturers—some of whom had never before built a helicopter—submitted seventeen LOH design proposals. Because the Army lacked a mechanism for directly procuring military airplanes, the Navy was overseeing the procurement. After performing a rigorous technical evaluation of the proposals, the Navy pronounced the Fairchild Hiller OH-5A the winner because its "design was the only one acceptable from a technical viewpoint." The Army, in a decision based on operational considerations, selected both Hiller's and Bell's proposals.[36] Hiller to date had built 60 percent of the Army's light helicopters, and Bell the remaining 40 percent in addition to larger types.[37] In accordance with established Army practice, these experienced rivals would receive contracts for the construction of actual prototypes.

Howard Hughes's bid had come not from Hughes Aircraft but from the Hughes Tool Company's Aircraft Division, which confusingly was collocated with that much larger company at Culver City, California. At that time, the Aircraft Division built only the Hughes 269 piston helicopter, a tiny two-seater then being evaluated by the Army as the TH-55A.[38] Having operated at a loss since its recent formation, the Aircraft Division was not capable of volume manufacture and was not seen as a serious manufacturer by the rest of the helicopter industry.

His proposal rejected, Howard Hughes was firmly out of the running. Refusing to concede defeat, and heedless of the destructive consequences of the actions to follow, Hughes embarked on a covert campaign to place his Aircraft Division back into contention. Ultimately, aided by high-ranking accomplices within the Army, he would indeed claim for his company the coveted LOH production.

At his instigation, the prototype selection process was revised. In an unprecedented and highly abnormal situation, three helicopter types rather than the usual two were now to be constructed and tested. On November 13, 1961, the Army awarded contracts for five each Bell OH-4As (serial nos. 62-4201/4205), Hiller OH-5As (62-4206/4210), and Hughes OH-6As (62-4211/4215). All three types were to be powered by the Allison T63 turboshaft engine, which had been developed under Army auspices specifically for such use.

The first Hiller OH-5A (company Model FH-1100) flew on January 26, 1963. From the start, this sleek turbine-powered thoroughbred looked and acted like a winner. Buoyed by that machine's first-place selection, Hiller was fully confident that it had the best machine. Unlike the Hughes OH-6A's hinged civil-type doors, the OH-5A featured sliding rear doors that could be opened in flight. Less obvious to the eye but more important, it had Hiller's high-inertia L rotor and an impact-absorbing skid landing gear. Mounted on longitudinal torque tubes, these skids would help spare the helicopter and its occupants by deforming in a hard landing or crash.

As testing began, Hiller could only hope that the Army appreciated these safety features and truly understood what was desirable in the multipurpose light observation role. The presence of the third helicopter in the competition was worrisome, but the Hiller was a more desirable machine from the Army's standpoint than the Hughes, let alone the Bell.

Army planners determined in 1964 that the initial LOH order would specify the construction of 1,000 helicopters to be delivered over three years. Although no formal announcement was made, the Bell entry had by then been eliminated, dismissed as the "highest in cost and lowest in military capability."[39] By all rights, the contract now belonged to the Hiller machine.

Except for its high-inertia rotor, the Bell OH-4A had little to recommend it. A narrow fuselage made largely of plexiglass favored the observation role, but lacked sufficient interior flexibility for the general utility use that the Army had also specified for the LOH, which was to be a multi-role vehicle. Realizing its error, Bell would soon combine the OH-4A's rotor and systems with a more sensible fuselage to create the famous JetRanger series.

The Hughes OH-6A was smaller, lighter, and faster than Hiller's or Bell's machine. Overall, the Army liked its diminutive size, although one general who was a rated helicopter pilot noted that the OH-6A was "very light and probably would not stand up to service usage."[40] Lieutenant Colonel Samuel R. Boyer, the Army's liaison to the Navy during selection of the LOH, also voiced concerns about the "thin-gauge materials on the aircraft, the very lightweight approach taken."[41] The OH-6A was so lightly built, in fact, that the Army had to reclassify the competition from military specifications to less stringent FAA certification standards in order for it to qualify. Bell and Hiller, in contrast, had designed to rugged military specifications from the outset.

Because the OH-6A employed a lightweight rotor, it had poor autorotative characteristics and was somewhat less safe than its competitors. As stated by Colonel Boyer, "the Navy dropped the Hughes entry out . . . because of the autorotative characteristics of the Hughes machine. It is a low inertia rotor system, and it has autorotative characteristics—I am a helicopter pilot myself—that I don't like. You come down like a streamlined brick."[42]

Aggravating both these problems, the Army, having opted for the lightest vehicle, then proceeded to demand that the gross vehicular weight be upped to allow it to perform its stated missions. Hughes complied with an increase from 2,100 to 2,400 pounds. The Army then asked for 2,700 pounds (by way of comparison, the Hiller OH-5A's gross weight was 2,750 pounds) for additional equipment needed to increase utility to the level of the Bell and Hiller helicopters. The FAA refused further certification on the grounds of safety. Referring to the Hughes OH-6A, FAA flight test specialist Donald Armstrong told congressional investigators, "we have data to show it cannot be certified at that weight. . . . It would be at the expense of compliance with present civil airworthiness requirements in both controllability and, I believe, performance."[43]

Although smaller, the Hughes OH-6A was roughly as costly to produce as the Hiller OH-5A and slightly less expensive than Bell's OH-4A. Minus engine, radios, and other government-furnished equipment, that meant a price of almost $30,000 per aircraft. Howard Hughes sat in bed agonizing endlessly over how much to bid per helicopter to win the fixed-price Army contract. He knew that the Army had already eliminated the Bell entry, although that fact had yet to be made public. Hiller was the competitor to beat, and Hughes was obsessed with doing so. Because he himself planned to resort to unscrupulous measures to secure the contract, he perhaps mistakenly convinced himself his competitors would do the same.

In the end, desperate to win the competition, Howard Hughes bid an absurdly low $19,860 per helicopter. In so doing, he embarked on an ill-advised and highly unethical "buy-out," a term denoting winning a contract through false low pricing. Typically in a buy-out scheme, once the other contenders have been eliminated, the winning company—having established itself as the sole supplier—raises its price to the government to recoup its initial losses and subsequently reap additional profits at public expense.

Subversion of the LOH procurement had been possible because of the disorganized state of Army aviation. Further evidence of confusion within that service was now at hand. Failing to question the patently unreasonable price, the Army awarded the LOH contract to the Aircraft Division of the Hughes Tool Company on May 26, 1965. Hughes had now committed himself to building 714 helicopters at an estimated loss per machine of $11,000, representing a personal loss to him of almost $8 million. The Army's first installment of its order called for 88 machines.

Because U.S. involvement in Vietnam was escalating rapidly, meanwhile, the Army placed a separate order for 121 more OH-6s to be produced concurrently with the original 88 machines. Eager to recoup, Howard Hughes raised his price for these additional helicopters—which were not part of the order for 714—to $55,927 each, a stunning price increase of 282 percent. Desperate attempts by a now-alarmed Army to negotiate with its sole supplier brought the price down to $49,500 (still almost $30,000 more per aircraft than before), which was as far as Hughes was willing to come down.

The Army agreed and asked Congress for supplemental funds to purchase additional Hughes helicopters. So great was congressional consternation over the price disparity, however, that the Army immediately tried to withdraw its request, but it was too late to avoid acute embarrassment. Congressman L. Mendel Rivers, chairman of the House Armed Services Committee, had already directed his Subcommittee for Special Investigations to conduct a formal inquiry. Much of the information presented here came to light during this investigation, which at its conclusion in 1967 focused withering criticism on the Army for its mishandling of the procurement process.

A clause in the original LOH contract permitted the Army to order up to half again more helicopters at the original price, should it so desire. With American lives being lost in Vietnam for want of light turbine helicopters, this option was fully invoked for 357 more Hughes OH-6As. Howard Hughes now stood to lose half again as much as he had anticipated.

Meanwhile, production at Culver City was in serious trouble. Disorganized, badly structured, and woefully unprepared for mass production, Hughes Tool Company's Aircraft Division was turning out a mere trickle of Army helicopters instead of the stream so urgently needed. Hughes had committed his company to delivering 88 OH-6As in fiscal year 1965, 168 in 1966, and 458 in 1967, making the total of 714. He was hardly off to an auspicious start: by the end of FY 1965, his company had delivered 12 helicopters.

"There wasn't a blessed thing going on when we sent our people out [to Culver City] and they took pictures of . . . what should have been the production line," observed Congressman Porter Hardy, Jr., the subcommittee chairman. "And anybody with two grains of sense examining those pictures would have known it was impossible for this delivery schedule to be met."[44]

To Hughes's dismay, having exercised its option for more helicopters under the old price, the Army—at the insistence of Congress—canceled its order for 121 additional OH-6As and went elsewhere to buy its helicopters. This about-face astounded military and industry observers alike. By long tradition, once a manufacturer became the supplier of an article of military equipment, whatever it might be, it would remain the supplier as long as the military continued to use that item. Initially unwilling to depart from this sacrosanct if unofficial policy, the Army only with great reluctance yielded to intense congressional pressure to do so.

Fairchild Hiller, meanwhile, had tooling in place to produce new LOHs because it had decided to bring a civil version of the OH-5A to market. Granted FAA certification on July 20, 1964, and rolled out on June 3, 1966, the Fairchild Hiller FH-1100 was the first American light turbine helicopter to reach the commercial marketplace. The OH-5A's chances of winning this new round of bidding were excellent and its price was highly competitive. Relocating helicopter production from Palo Alto to the Hagerstown factory, where there were other assembly lines to defray overhead costs, meant that the OH-5A now cost about $4,000 less per example manufactured than would otherwise have been the case.

Texas-based Bell Helicopters was the competitor to beat this time. It was also bringing a civil version of its LOH entry—revised with a new fuselage—to market as the Bell Model 206 JetRanger. With tooling already in place, it would be a simple matter for Bell to turn out militarized JetRangers. As a result, the company needed no encouragement to jump at this unprecedented second chance for the LOH business.

Ironically, with everything to gain and nothing to lose, the Fairchild Hiller Corporation declined to bid this second time around. The reason lies in differences between Fairchild Hiller's president Edward G. Uhl and the executive vice president Stanley Hiller. Disagreement between the two men—the latter also the company's second largest stockholder—centered on two issues: how to deal with the military, and whether to continue commercial production.

It had been agreed during Fairchild Hiller's formation that Edward Uhl would concentrate on the internal running of the company while Stanley Hiller would attend to external affairs, an arrangement summarized at the time by the informal titles "Mr. Inside" and "Mr. Outside." One of Hiller's first tasks in the latter role was to convince Pentagon officials that troubled Republic Aviation— whose F-105 Thunderchief then had a poor operational record—would, under Fairchild Hiller management, again be a credible supplier of military aircraft.

That Uhl had long-standing difficulties dealing with the military was a matter of record. In contrast, Hiller was highly regarded for his business skills and broad knowledge. As the LOH competition had geared up, in fact, Secretary of Defense Robert McNamara had asked the pioneering helicopter builder to serve as assistant secretary of defense for logistics and procurement. Fearing a possible conflict of interest, Hiller had declined this post.

Although the Fairchild Hiller FH-1100 did not
win the Army's light observation helicopter competition, this superb rotorcraft became the first U.S.
light turbine civil helicopter. Courtesy Hiller.

The industry pioneer's hard-won experience in procurement matters was sorely needed at Fairchild Hiller. Ironically, it was Uhl who harbored ill feelings toward the U.S. Army for permitting Howard Hughes to snatch the LOH contract away from his company. Not shared by Hiller, Uhl's antipathy toward that armed service ran counter to his otherwise strong preference for military production over civil, for he believed that Fairchild Hiller should get out of building commercial aircraft altogether.

Hiller disagreed strongly on both counts. Already looking forward to the second chance to build LOHs that he now saw must inevitably come, Hiller also perceived many commercial opportunities for the company. However, his attempts to work toward these goals were repeatedly blunted by the company president's apparent disinclination. Sherman Fairchild, who might have acted to resolve this stalemate, sadly chose not to involve himself in the direct running of the company.

With other challenges and business interests to pursue, Stanley Hiller decided that one year of frustration with little to show for the effort was enough. Furthermore, the Hiller family missed the West Coast and felt it was time to return. Accordingly, Hiller prepared to move back to California with his wife and two growing boys.

He took satisfaction in surveying the company he was leaving behind. With the Fairchild association, Hiller Aircraft now enjoyed a new plateau of capability and unprecedented opportunities. Better still, a healthy mix of products and customer bases had been achieved. Corporate diversity was in fact one of three elements Hiller had worked to put in place, in addition to meeting his responsibility to his shareholders and establishing lines of development to provide

for the future well-being of the company. Even with the end of the line in sight for the Model 12E and OH-23G, the Palo Alto company had brought to Fairchild a huge backlog of more than 600 orders for those piston helicopters.

And three Hiller projects were under way at Fairchild to provide for future business. The first was a new tip-propulsion effort involving the mounting of Williams turbojets on an L rotor-equipped HOE-1 Hornet, a test program Hiller had recently proposed to the Navy. Its favorable reception there suggested that Hiller's tip-turbine flying crane program was still alive. The second was Hiller scientist Gerhard Sissingh's "desensitized rotor," a possible next-generation approach to high-speed helicopter flight. The third, of course, was the OH-5/FH-1100, for Hiller knew that it was just a question of time before the Army—under pressure from Congress—solicited a new round of LOH bidding.

In Stanley Hiller's considered judgment, the time had come to move on, and he expected the company to continue to support these three efforts in his absence. "It seemed we had done everything we wanted," he said of his company and its activities. "While we hadn't succeeded in some projects, we had built up the company and made our stockholders a good return."[45]

Thus, at the age of forty, a stage in life often bringing change, Stanley Hiller turned his energies to new directions. He would subsequently attain unmatched success as America's premier fixer of troubled corporations, an entrepreneurial course he had never consciously planned. It just seemed to turn out that way, supported by the genius for business that had served him so well in the past.

What has Stanley Hiller done since leaving the field of vertical flight? He has achieved an unbroken record of successful corporate turnarounds. The corporations he has revitalized are all leaders of their respective industries, with annual sales ranging from hundreds of millions of dollars up into billions. Most are Fortune 500 companies. All had suffered from the common malady of years of indifferent or poor management. Without divisive restructurings, Hiller—as chairman of the board or chief executive officer—and a few key associates restore those businesses to solid financial health before moving on to repeat the process at other troubled companies.

These turnarounds are performed amicably and at the request of the ailing companies' boards of directors. Moreover, Hiller demands no payment unless he succeeds, and he spurns the "golden parachutes" often accorded top executives as protection against failure. In an era marked by liquidations, work-force decimation, and other manipulative strategies too often intent upon looting, he engages only in constructive rebuilding and growth. He is philosophically opposed to participating in hostile takeovers or situations involving excess debt leverage, and he eschews "quick-fix" measures that produce short-term profits at the expense of long-term health and growth-generating capital investment.

The list of companies Hiller has helped includes such industry giants as Baker International, Reed Tool, Bekins, and York International. "It's not any one million-dollar fix," he says simply of his methods. "It's a whole bunch of thousand-dollar fixes."[46]

In a twist of fate that holds elements of poetic justice, Hiller engineered the acquisition of an ailing Hughes Tool Company in 1987, years after Howard Hughes's death. As the retired chairman of Baker International, an oil-tool industry giant he helped shape, Hiller orchestrated the successful merger of

the two companies into a profitable new corporate entity known as Baker-Hughes, with Baker management in full control.

In the latter 1960s, this career change meant that the Army's request for new LOH bids arrived in Stanley Hiller's absence. Left to his own devices in Hagerstown, President Edward Uhl, still angry over the Army's mishandling of the first round of bidding, resolved never to do business with that branch of the military. Despite impassioned urgings from his staff, Uhl steadfastly refused to participate in this second round of procurement.

Chief financial officer and second-in-command James T. Dresher, formerly a vice president of Hiller Aircraft, on his own initiative worked up a proposal for a last minute submittal, should Uhl be persuaded to relent. Dresher argued that there was nothing to lose and everything to gain in submitting it. As the deadline approached, however, it became ever more certain that the contest would be between Bell and Hughes alone. Fairchild Hiller would not participate.

In Las Vegas, meanwhile, Howard Hughes now faced the fact that in 1968 he was losing a whopping $62,000 on every helicopter he was compelled to build. Production speed-up costs, unrealistic manufacture estimates, and his decision to underbid in the first place accounted for this unbelievable total. The only good news for Hughes—something that appalled Congress—was the Army's curious failure to specify or even provide for late charges in the LOH contract.

Trapped in a dilemma, Hughes once again agonized over how much to bid per helicopter. Too high a price this time around would lose him the Army's business, and with it any hope of recovering part of his lost millions (Hughes no longer entertained hopes of easy profit). Bidding low enough to be certain of winning, on the other hand, would obligate him to extremely long-term production at an untenable loss. And the Hughes Tool Company—that seemingly inexhaustible money machine—was now hard pressed to support his escalating deficits.

Chronically unable to make decisions and quick to blame others, the former billionaire now railed at his employees as he vacillated right up to the deadline. At the eleventh hour he entered a bid of $59,700 per OH-6 helicopter, only to learn on March 10, 1968, that Bell had underbid him to land a $123 million contract for 2,200 LOHs (designated OH-58 in Vietnam service).

Ironically, the bid sitting on Jim Dresher's desk in Hagerstown was lower than either Bell's or Hughes's. Had it been submitted, the OH-5 and its FH-1100 civilian counterpart would have been built in the thousands rather than the hundreds. But for this costly mistake, the Fairchild Hiller Corporation of Hagerstown, Maryland, might still be in business today.

Two more years would pass before the Hughes Tool Company's Aircraft Division completed its existing military contracts. Thereafter, Hughes could only confront a shocking truth: his unscrupulous attempt to corner the light-turbine helicopter market had reduced his personal fortune by $90 million. Only his standing as a public figure, and the fact that he had lost rather than profited, spared him prosecution.

In all probability, Hughes never gave much thought to the destructive consequences of his scheme gone sour. Uncounted lives were lost because U.S. forces in Vietnam failed to receive their desperately needed LOHs. The Army, which engaged in direct aircraft procurement for the first time since 1942 to purchase the OH-6, lost credibility badly needed

for future programs. And Hiller Aircraft no longer existed as a distinct corporate entity. The Willow Road plant closed in February 1966.

The first company ever formed expressly to manufacture helicopters, Hiller Aircraft was a true industry pioneer. Isolated, denied the advantages accorded America's other helicopter pioneers, it nevertheless flourished, sparked by the philosophy of its founder and by the exuberant force of sheer creativity. It was never a large company. At its peak in the early 1960s, the Hiller payroll numbered only some 2,000 employees. But without question it was the most creative component of the U.S. vertical-flight industry.

During its remarkable twenty-five years, the company ushered into being all-metal rotor blades and many other significant technologies, some of which have since become the industry standard. It also laid down a prodigious body of empirical data to aid future generations of VTOL researchers. From flying platforms to tilt-wing transports, and flying cranes to flying submarines, Hiller performed some of the most original work in the industry.

Hiller is best remembered, of course, for helicopters. In production longer than any other rotorcraft, most recently by Rogerson-Hiller in Washington State, the Hiller Model 12 is widely hailed as the finest piston-powered helicopter of all. Countless pilots learned to fly in these forgiving workhorses, in part because the U.S. Army bought more Model 12s than Bell 47s. Hillers have done every type of work in all climate conditions around the globe. During the 1940s they flew the world's first routine medical evacuations under combat conditions, in the 1950s they saved thousands of lives in Korea, and today they still perform dramatic rescues from time to time. For those who either flew or were saved by the trusty, paddle-equipped machines, their builder is missed; the vertical-flight industry was much the richer for the presence of Hiller Aircraft.

Fortunately, the tangible legacy of Hiller Aircraft survives. Whether from a sense of history, or from the memory of adventures shared and challenges conquered, Stanley Hiller over the years carefully preserved prototypes and production examples of his company's aircraft, engines, and other products. This unique collection—which includes examples of nearly every model built by Hiller and his company—today shares a 50,000-square-foot museum with other aircraft, artifacts, and exhibits relating to the region's rich history. Located at San Carlos Airport in San Mateo County, the Hiller Aviation Museum bears witness to a remarkable chapter in the history of vertical flight that began in a rented repair shop just a few miles away.

6 / Summary: The First Fifty Years

The helicopter was a hard technology to perfect and the road to practical vertical flight was arduous. By comparison, aviation experimenters of an earlier generation faced fewer challenges in the development of fixed-wing aviation. But something central to the human spirit drove the pioneers of vertical flight to pursue the helicopter with the same relentless determination Wilbur and Orville Wright displayed at Kitty Hawk in 1903.

This book has traced the successes of Igor Sikorsky, Arthur Young, Frank Piasecki, and Stanley Hiller, Jr., America's first-rank pioneers. In so doing, it refutes the popular misconception that Sikorsky invented the helicopter. He did not perfect his VS-300, America's first successful helicopter, until late in 1941. In Europe, a helicopter of French pioneer Louis Breguet successfully flew a half dozen years earlier, followed shortly by Heinrich Focke's FA 61 (Sikorsky observed this latter helicopter in 1938, two years before his VS-300 flew untethered).

The outbreak of war in 1939 ended Europe's dominance of helicopter flight, preempting European hopes for a starring role in the rotary-wing industry to come. At peace for another two years, the United States took up where Europe left off, to realize the long-standing dream of practical vertical flight.

But it would be unfair to suggest that America merely availed itself of European technology. This country's successes were largely the result of parallel but unrelated helicopter programs.

The helicopter's reduction to practice was more challenging—and is historically more significant —than its invention. It was not enough merely to create prototypes that with tinkering and fine-tuning would fly. To be of value, this technology had to be tamed and refined sufficiently for helicopters to be manufactured in number.

Therefore, the challenges faced by Sikorsky, Piasecki, Young, and Hiller were far more demanding than any faced by Breguet or Focke. Of the four American pioneers, Sikorsky knew and cared least about the workings of the rotor itself. But for this lack of familiarity with rotor phenomena, the VS-300 test program might have concluded a year earlier, making U.S. helicopters available sooner to play a more significant role in World War II.

Mathematician-philosopher Arthur Young was a fascinating counterpoint to Sikorsky. By the start of the 1940s, Young knew more about rotors and their workings than any other human being. Alone among America's top pioneers, he worked in model form to develop a workable helicopter before ever building a full-size machine.

Frank Piasecki was the helicopter inventor in a hurry. The only top-ranked pioneer with direct ties to the autogiro industry, he thought *big*. His efforts gave the world the only enduring manufacture of helicopters not built to the single-main-rotor formula.

Stanley Hiller—the businessman of this elite group—was the only pioneer to succeed in the absence of either military or corporate support. Piasecki had the former, Young the latter, and Sikorsky both. From the earliest days onward, Hiller's company distinguished itself through extraordinary creativity.

The success of these four men ensured the United States of dominance in the field of helicopter manufacture for a half century. As of this writing in the mid-1990s, however, Europe is making strides to try to reclaim the helicopter as its own. With its increasingly multinational and government-subsidized aerospace industry, Europe in recent years has eroded America's traditional helicopter dominance. European manufacturers today build superb light and medium helicopters that claim a growing share of the world market. The United States retains its lead in the manufacture of large transport rotorcraft, although Russia's experienced industry may arise to claim much of this market in the future.

Today the helicopter is a mature technology. Gains remain to be made—notably, improvements in turbine engines, and greater use of lightweight composite materials—but these are evolutionary, not revolutionary, in nature. The science of rotary-wing aviation is fully understood; the unknowns that plagued the industry pioneers are all but gone.

Although military requirements nurtured the helicopter and continue to shape it to this day, the focus of military applications has shifted from improving the helicopter itself to enhancing its mission capabilities through integrated avionics. Members of the Sikorsky Black Hawk/Seahawk helicopter family, for example, are seen by Pentagon planners as platforms distinguished almost entirely by the capabilities of the black boxes they carry. Improvements in military helicopters may depend more on upgraded electronics, software, and armament than on changes to the helicopter itself.

For all its technological success, the helicopter industry has failed to meet its greatest challenge: to get production and operating costs down. Despite exhaustive efforts over the decades to make rotorcraft of all sizes affordable, this technology has stubbornly remained costly.

Cost is also the reason why the vertical-flight industry has not progressed significantly beyond helicopters in a half century of trying. A VTOL airplane—whether in civil airline or military transport service—will spend more than 90 percent of its time in cruise, during which its vertical-flight capability contributes nothing but dead weight. This means that VTOL transports cannot compete with conventional aircraft, except where vertical-flight capability is truly needed.

The helicopter is the bargain-basement VTOL vehicle. It is cheaper to operate than other vertical-flight machines. Even so, only where fixed-wing aircraft and other forms of transportation have not provided viable alternatives has it won acceptance. Reflecting the "niche" status of the helicopter, the world's vertical-flight industry also remains small.

Can a VTOL transport be built whose economics would not place operators at a competitive disadvantage? Probably not. Hybrid aircraft—part helicopter and part airplane—are not as good at either role as aircraft dedicated to specific functions. Yet two factors continue to drive nonhelicopter VTOL development. One is the cruise inefficiency of helicopters, particularly in missions demanding long range and high speed. The other is the growing congestion of airports and the likelihood that not many new ones will be built.

As the infrastructures of major metropolitan regions approach saturation, the economics may at last be propitious for VTOL transports capable of efficient, airplane-style cruise. These aircraft will be pressurized for comfort much like today's commuter airliners, which they will resemble in size.

During the 1930s it was widely expected that fixed-wing or autogiro companies would pioneer the helicopter. In fact, neither of these industries truly championed vertical flight, which emerged with little help. United Aircraft did not believe in the helicopter; it believed in Igor Sikorsky, whose experiments it funded. Likewise, Larry Bell funded Arthur Young, who had to move to an abandoned automobile dealership to perfect a helicopter that Bell's own company did not believe in. Thus when VTOL transports are built, the pioneers may not come from the helicopter companies as might seem logical, but from unexpected quarters.

Despite the size of this volume, space has precluded detailed coverage of Kaman, Hughes, and other U.S. companies, or the fascinating helicopter programs of France, Italy, the former Soviet Union, and elsewhere. The author hopes that others will follow his lead and provide detailed case studies of vertical-flight companies beyond the four that are within the scope of this book.

Appendix A / Early Military Helicopter Use

In the United States, military requirements have shaped the helicopter and the industry created to manufacture it. To provide a fuller understanding of this industry, this appendix examines the specific involvement in vertical flight of all the U.S. armed services except the Air Force, which has had little need of helicopters.

Air forces and navies have requirements for helicopters, but armies benefit the most from vertical-flight capability. They rely on helicopters much as they once relied on horses. The helicopter's ability to transcend natural and man-made barriers, its speed advantage over land vehicles, and the many roles it can play in tactical warfare render it an essential tool to conventional land forces. No modern army can afford to be without vertical flight, which has profoundly altered battlefield operations.

U.S. ARMY

With so much to gain, the U.S. Army sponsored America's first serious attempt to build a working helicopter shortly after World War I. The Army Air Service's Engineering Division,[1] at McCook Field in Dayton, Ohio, constructed a large open-frame helicopter designed by Dr. George de Bothezat, who, like Igor Sikorsky, had fled the Russian Revolu-

tion. Constructed at McCook Field in 1917, this helicopter featured four six-bladed rotors each 22 feet in diameter. Differentially increasing or decreasing the pitch of each rotor's blades was to provide control.

On December 18, 1922, Major Thurman H. Bane, chief of the Engineering Division, lifted the cumbersome machine into the air for the first time. "The movement was graceful and there was no noise of friction in any part of the mechanism," reported one eyewitness. "The craft began to move, slowly, ever slowly. Then inch by inch it lifted itself, strained and shook and lifted higher. It was free. Up off the ground, one foot, two feet, three feet and then the height of a man, and for one minute and forty-two seconds it remained there. The Army's helicopter had flown."[2]

The machine hovered with impressive stability, but Bane could not prevent the wind from moving him laterally. He gently set the machine down, concluding history's first officially observed helicopter flight of more than one minute. After several more hovering flights in 1923, including one on April 17 in which four men clung to its structure, the machine was retired. Although unsuccessful, de Bothezat's rotorcraft of 1922 is significant as America's first dedicated attempt to construct a man-carrying helicopter. It is preserved—disassembled and as

Only marginally controllable, the de Bothezat
helicopter hovers at McCook Field, Dayton, Ohio,
in December 1922. Courtesy NASM/SI.

yet unrestored—in the collection of the National Air and Space Museum, Smithsonian Institution.

The Army's second helicopter effort was the Platt-LePage XR-1 program already described in this book, funded by the Dorsey Bill of 1938, which empowered the secretary of war to allocate helicopter development funds among various military services and federal agencies. The big winner was the U.S. Army, within which the Air Corps, Cavalry, Field Artillery, Coast Artillery, Infantry, Signal Corps, Medical Corps, Office of the Quartermaster General, and National Guard all qualified for Dorsey funds. Dorsey monies were also available to the Navy's Bureau of Aeronautics and Office of the Chief of Naval Operations; the Marine Corps, which obtained its aircraft through the Navy; the Coast Guard within the Treasury Department; the National Advisory Committee for Aeronautics; the Post Office Department; the Department of Agriculture's Bureau of Entomology and Plant Quarantine, Bureau of Biological Survey, and Forest Service; the Department of the Interior's National Park Service; and the Department of Commerce's Bureau of Air Commerce.

Under the terms of the legislation, civil agencies were encouraged to apply for funds for planning and experimentation with existing rotorcraft. In 1938 that meant autogiros. The Department of Agriculture had obvious uses for rotary-wing flight, such as combating locusts and other insect pests with greater precision than was possible with airplanes. The Interior Department required patrol and utility aircraft capable of operating without airports. The Post Office Department hoped to speed the nation's flow of mail through rotary-wing flight.

While civil agencies were to use Dorsey money for planning and evaluation using existing rotorcraft, the legislation specified a more difficult task for the military: the armed services were to foster technological development, particularly that of the helicopter. "The sum of $600,000," the bill directed, "is to be taken by the Secretary of War from this appropriation and used exclusively in the placing of contracts for the construction of improved and experimental types of rotary-wing and other aircraft by private industry."[3]

The Engineering Division of the Army Air Corps (formerly Army Air Service) showed immediate interest in the bill's intriguing if imprecise challenge. Concerned that the phrase "and other aircraft" opened the way for the funds to be diverted, the small nucleus of rotary-wing proponents at Wright Field petitioned actively for the opportunity.

Although the Navy had been invited to participate, it did not share the Army's enthusiasm for helicopters. Committed to fixed-wing aviation (like carrier-based fighters and shore-based patrol bombers) and to blimps, the Navy wanted nothing to do with autogiros or helicopters. Since it had its own cabinet-level leadership, it did not report to the secretary of war and was thus able to avoid much of the pressure placed on the Army to embrace rotary-wing flight. This disinterest was formalized in a 1939 interservice meeting, at which an agreement was signed designating the Army Air Corps the military branch to pursue rotary-wing development.

Also in 1939, an initial $300,000 in Dorsey funds—a considerable sum by prewar standards—was appropriated by Congress for the placement of industry contracts. Overseeing the disbursement was Captain H. Franklin Gregory,[4] an enthusiastic autogiro pilot recently appointed helicopter project officer at Wright Field.

Frank Gregory knew that autogiros were less complex than helicopters, and that recent advances—notably the "jump" takeoff—had further narrowed the performance gap between the two. Although Philadelphia's autogiro builders were adept at ignoring the limitations of their vehicles, Gregory saw clearly that autogiros could never fulfill military missions demanding true vertical-flight capability. Whatever expense and difficulty their development entailed, helicopters had a reason for being.

Gregory further noted that prototype helicopters were flying in France and Germany, thus demonstrating that aviation technologies were sufficiently advanced to promise success where de Bothezat had found only failure a generation earlier. He concluded that developing a production military helicopter in cooperation with American industry—as stipulated by the Dorsey Bill—was the optimal use for the substantial funds at his disposal.

Gregory initiated the Army's quest for a working helicopter by issuing AAF Circular 40-260 in the fall of 1939. Distributed to the aviation industry at large, this statement of the Army's requirements for a helicopter specified performance parameters and two seats. Thereafter the circular departed from standard practice by leaving dimensions, weights, and even configuration up to manufacturers to propose. Helicopters involved too many unknowns for the military's technical advisers to pronounce a specific approach.

Opened to bids on April 15, 1940, this competition generated only four proposals from industry. Two were immediately discounted since they were for autogiros instead of helicopters, narrowing the field to Sikorsky and Platt-LePage. Because the latter's proposal embodied the German Focke-Achgelis FA

61's proven twin-lateral-rotor configuration, Platt-LePage was granted a contract on July 19, 1940, to build the Army its helicopter. The company was already building a prototype under private sponsorship at the time. Its XR-1 flew tethered in May 1941, but chronic technical problems plagued the prototype and it crashed in 1943. Flights resumed later in the year with the XR-1A, which was nearing completion when the first machine crashed. This second and last Platt-LePage helicopter featured a revised cockpit and wartime Army camouflage paint.

In 1944, Platt-LePage proposed a new helicopter with twice the power of the XR-1A, but the Army—disenchanted with the company's poor performance—went elsewhere to fulfill a requirement for a large transport machine. Full cancellation of the XR-1A program followed in the spring of 1945 because Platt-LePage had failed by that late date to provide service-test helicopters to the Army. It was an ignominious end for the company once expected to produce America's first operational helicopters.

Belatedly in World War II, autogiro manufacturers Kellett and Pitcairn pursued helicopter development. Had either company done so five years earlier, it might have dominated the emerging helicopter industry. Having built working autogiros, both companies were halfway to success, whereas Sikorsky and other pioneers—with the notable exception of autogiro engineer Frank Piasecki—had to start almost from scratch.

Pitcairn's growing troubles led to its reorganization as the Pitcairn-Larson Autogiro Company in 1940. Soon afterward it became the AGA Aviation Corporation, and then the G&A Aircraft Company. It was acquired by Firestone in 1943. As that company's G&A Division, it developed a small heli-

(*Top*) Built during World War II, the Platt-LePage XR-1A copied the twin-lateral-rotor configuration of the Focke-Achgelis FA 61. Courtesy. NASM/SI.

(*Bottom*) The Kellett XR-8, 1945. Courtesy NASM/SI.

copter called the XR-9, which it delivered to Wright Field in 1946. It and an enlarged version called the XR-14 failed to hold military interest. The pioneering autogiro company then made an abortive effort to market a two-seat civil version of this helicopter before finally going out of business in 1948.

Kellett was slightly more successful. It built and flew the U.S. Army's XR-8 helicopter in 1945. Looking like a flea topped by canted side-by-side rotors with intermeshing blades, it was the first U.S. helicopter to employ the "synchropter" configuration developed by Anton Flettner in Germany shortly before the war—a configuration employed in some two dozen wartime Luftwaffe helicopters. The XR-8 today survives in the collection of the National Air and Space Museum.

In 1945, the Army Air Forces issued a follow-on contract to Kellett for a larger synchropter. The result was the XR-10 of 1947, an ambitious all-metal, twin-engine machine with a gross weight of 13,500 pounds—almost three times that of the AAF's next largest helicopter, the Sikorsky R-5. A fatal crash—the pilot became entangled in the rotors as he sought to parachute to safety—ended the XR-10 program in 1948.

This loss was a further blow to Kellett. Directed by trustees since declaring bankruptcy in October 1946, the company had depended on XR-10 sales to the Army or Navy to escape its financial woes. With that program dead, Kellett was forced to sell a highly experimental flying crane project to Hughes Aircraft late in 1948. Purchased by Howard Hughes, the turbojet-powered XH-17 proved unsuccessful when flown under U.S. Air Force sponsorship in 1952.

The USAF sponsored another giant helicopter concurrently with the Hughes XH-17: the Piasecki XH-16. Initiated years earlier as a long-range rescue vehicle for retrieval of downed globe-spanning strategic bomber crews, the mammoth helicopter—its fuselage as large as that of a four-engine Douglas DC-4 airliner—first flew in October 1953. There followed a turbine version known as the YH-16A Turbo-Transporter that handled and performed well, proving the feasibility of very large helicopters. After attaining 166 mph and flying well above 20,000 feet, it was destroyed in a December 1956 crash caused by some test instrumentation equipment fitted to it. The Army had joined the Air Force in supporting the program because of this helicopter's ability to transport forty passengers or three jeeps. Because of the crash, the H-16 did not enter production.

Overshadowing all other wartime efforts was the success of Vought-Sikorsky Aircraft in Connecticut. This pioneering firm emerged from World War II as the military's sole supplier of production helicopters, and indeed the world's only volume manufacturer. Military support began with the diversion of $50,000 of Dorsey Bill money from Platt-LePage to initiate development of the VS-316, a two-seat AAF version of the company-financed VS-300. A contract was signed January 10, 1941, and the XR-4—as it was designated by the AAF—flew for the first time January 14, 1942. On May 17, Gregory flew it to Wright Field, where it was formally accepted on May 30. On hand to greet the machine were Orville Wright, Henry Ford, and Igor Sikorsky.

Initial experience with the XR-4 gave rise to three YR-4A service-test machines incorporating a slightly larger rotor, more power, and other refinements. Flown in May 1943, this version was followed by the YR-4B, which made provision for either a 300-pound external bomb load or a litter. Before service tri-

(Top) The Firestone XR-9, 1946. Courtesy   (Bottom) The Kellett XR-10, 1947. Courtesy
NASM/SI.   NASM/SI.

als were completed, production of more than 100 R-4Bs began in April 1944. The AAF received 55 of these, the British 52, and the Navy 23.

Tests revealed the new helicopter to be badly underpowered. One Coast Guard aviator observed that "under ideal conditions of wind and temperature, it could get off the ground with a pilot and one passenger; on a hot day with no wind and full throttle, it would roar and strain and beat the air a few feet above the ground [before] settling to the earth in defeat."[5]

Despite successful deck-landing demonstrations performed by Gregory on the merchant tanker ss *Bunker Hill* and the Army troopship *James Parker*, the Sikorsky was clearly not up to the mission of convoy patrol and defense on the high seas as envisioned by its proponents. The AAF and the British—the two biggest operators of R-4s—would therefore consign the majority of these machines to training, coastal patrol, radar calibration, and other less demanding duties. Production ceased before the end of 1944.

This historic helicopter nevertheless had opportunities to show what it could do. The U.S. Coast Guard pushed its Navy-supplied HNS-1s hard as it pioneered lifesaving techniques and equipment (described later in this appendix). The Army sent some thirty R-4s to perform rescue and evacuation duties in the China-Burma-India theater of operations, for cold-weather tests in Alaska,[6] and to transfer aircraft parts from offshore "floating aircraft repair stations" to B-29 bombers based on Guam.

America's first wartime helicopter rescue was reportedly performed by Army Lieutenant Carter Harmon, who retrieved—one at a time—a downed American liaison pilot and three British infantrymen stranded in Japanese-occupied Burma. But such rescues were too few and sporadic in nature to be viewed as organized combat evacuations.[7]

To obtain greater utility in a helicopter, a contract was initiated in January 1943 for a substantially larger two-seater called the XR-5. Powered by a 450-hp Pratt & Whitney R-985 radial engine, it made its first flight in August 1943. But only with the cessation of hostilities could Sikorsky finally work the bugs out of this promising but troubled machine, turning it into the fine S-51 five-seat military/commercial series helicopter. So extensive was this process that the AAF did not receive its first postwar R-5Fs (S-51s) until mid-1947.

Meantime, a companion program was under way to provide the military with the performance that the R-4 should have offered. Of basically the same dimensions and incorporating the same rotor, the Sikorsky R-6 had a more powerful engine, a new transmission, and a streamlined fuselage. Although it also suffered teething and vibratory troubles, it was numerically the most successful of Sikorsky's wartime helicopters. Produced under license by Nash-Kelvinator of Detroit, the R-6 saw limited operational use, primarily in China.

Special mention must be made of the Propeller Laboratory, a component part of Wright Field's vast wartime air development complex. Much of Gregory's team fell administratively under this organization, whose leader was D. Adam Dickey, a civil servant. A capable administrator and an authority on helicopters, Dickey and his small staff turned the Propeller Laboratory into the nucleus of U.S. government vertical-flight research, far outstripping the National Advisory Committee for Aeronautics—America's traditional source for government-funded aviation research and development—in this area.

With the NACA then concentrating on supersonic flight, helicopters would have received short shrift had it not been for the advocacy of the Propeller Laboratory.

Although this laboratory focused primarily on Sikorsky helicopters during World War II, one of its first major rotor tests involved the 32-foot 9-inch, two-bladed, teetering rotor of the Bell Model 30, the ancestor of the postwar Model 47 civil helicopter. Conducted in the spring of 1945, this test began with calibration studies to quantify the rotor's thrust, torque, and blade deflection. It also recorded vibratory stresses at various RPMs and blade pitches. Then the Bell rotor was whirled to destruction, reaching a speed of 570 RPM and producing more than 5,000 pounds of thrust before failing. Bell helicopter developers Arthur Young and Bartram Kelley observed with interest as Second Lieutenant Thomas R. Pierpoint ran the test. After leaving the military, "Ren" Pierpoint—a member before the war of Philadelphia's autogiro community—would subsequently play a major role in the success of Piasecki Helicopters.

NATIONAL SECURITY ACT OF 1947

A major restructuring of America's military establishment in the postwar era significantly altered the course of helicopter development. Under the National Security Act of 1947, the Army Air Forces became the new and independent United States Air Force. A revised aircraft nomenclature system was adopted, under which the designator for helicopters—which had been R for rotorcraft—appropriately became H. Overnight the Sikorsky R-5 became the H-5, the Bell R-13 became the H-13, and so on.

This shift left the Army with no aviation capability other than liaison planes. Senior Army commanders were nevertheless relieved by the departure of the "fly boys," for the AAF had emerged from World War II so powerful that it threatened to usurp the ground forces's traditional dominance.

A "good riddance" attitude toward aviation prevailed among the Army's top leadership for some time. In marked contrast, midlevel field commanders confronting the realities of warfare began pressing for the tactical air power they viewed as essential for a modern army. Unarmed low-powered light aircraft (as provided for under the 1942 organic aviation agreement) were useless in the ground support, battlefield resupply, and troop transport roles.

A formal definition of the missions and responsibilities of the various military services came April 21, 1948, in the form of the Key West Accord. This document extended the 1942 agreement, limiting the postwar Army to unarmed light aircraft with gross weights of 5,000 pounds or less. For air support beyond the capability of these machines, the Army was instructed to call upon the Air Force.

Unfortunately, the USAF was rarely there when the Army needed it. A postwar focus on supersonic jet interceptors and long-range strategic bombers left that service poorly equipped to provide tactical ground support. And the Air Force was not particularly well disposed to providing air cover for the Army.

Forgotten amid the politics was one of World War II's clearest lessons: close air support works best when controlled directly by field commanders. If it must be requested from elsewhere, the response is inevitably less satisfactory; more than one battle has been lost to second-guessing by air commanders unacquainted with real battlefield conditions.

If the Navy could have a full air force, Army field commanders wondered, why were the nation's ground forces denied tactical and logistical aircraft? The Air Force was certainly not to blame; it had not drafted the Key West Accord alone.

In fact, the Army was at fault for failing to stand up for itself at Key West. Having absolved themselves of dealing with air power at this key juncture, top Army commanders had deferred to Air Force leaders, who naturally staked as broad a claim for their service as possible. If the Army had addressed the issue, and realistically assessed future aviation requirements, the Air Force could not have made such a proprietary claim on aviation.

The Air Force all but preempted a meaningful aviation program for the Army. The outdated 1942 organic aviation agreement making light "grasshopper" airplanes available to ground commanders was extended by default. Although these unrealistic restrictions eased over time—a process hastened by the Korean, Algerian, and Vietnam Wars— they significantly retarded the development of vertical-flight aviation in the United States.

The USAF found it had little use for helicopters except in peripheral rescue and VIP transport roles. It is perhaps worth noting, however, that two USAF Air Rescue Service/ Military Air Transport Command Sikorsky H-19s accomplished the first nonstop transatlantic helicopter crossing in August 1952, setting official records during the 4,000-mile flight.

THE U.S. ARMY IN KOREA (1950–53)

The Army Ground Forces ordered thirteen Bell helicopters early in 1946, eighteen months before the restructuring described above. This order followed closely CAA certification of the Bell Model 47, history's first

commercial helicopter. Certification—or government production approval—made the new two-seat light commercial helicopter available to the AGF through a process known as "off-the-shelf procurement."[8]

The Army Air Forces, unlike the AGF, showed no interest in Bell's product. Its larger Sikorsky R-4s and R-6s were already too small for AAF procurement officials, who worked to obtain larger helicopters (a process that would continue after the USAAF became the USAF). With a gross weight barely over two thousand pounds, the Bell machine seemed best suited to Ground Forces use under the Organic Aviation agreement of 1942. Accordingly, it joined the ranks of AGF liaison and light utility planes.

The Bell XR-13 was accepted by the Army on the last day of 1946. This machine entered a six-month service-test program conducted by the Aircraft Service Test Section of Army Field Forces Board No. 1 at Fort Bragg, North Carolina, to assess its applicability to Army functions. Artillery fire adjustment, reconnaissance, evacuation of wounded, aerial photography, wire laying, short-range resupply, and VIP transport were among the many roles studied.

Here was the Army's new mechanized mule. Its ability to fly rapidly over obstacles and land virtually anywhere endeared it to every field commander. If the Navy had no need for light helicopters except for training, not so the Army, where a broad variety of uses existed—including those then addressed by liaison or "grasshopper" planes.

On January 6, 1947, the first two YR-13AS left Bell's Niagara plant in a Fairchild C-82 Packet for cold-weather tests in Alaska. Nine more were accepted April 11 to participate in cold-weather testing in Wisconsin and hot-weather desert studies in Arizona. Ten of them joined the 82nd Airborne Division at Fort Bragg and the 2nd Infantry Division at Fort Lewis, Washington, for wide-ranging operational service trials.

The first H-13Bs—an improved model incorporating lessons learned from those tests—arrived in 1948. The Army's first production Bell helicopters, they participated in summer testing in the thin air of Colorado's Rocky Mountains. Their poor altitude performance also prompted Army officials to evaluate a Sikorsky S-52 (modified with a 245-hp engine) and a prototype Bell 47D, both lent by their manufacturers in hopes of promoting sales. Under military contract, moreover, Bell undertook development of a high-altitude light helicopter designated XH-15. Flown in 1950, it did not enter production because substantial improvements in altitude performance were by then anticipated in later-model H-13s.

Overall, the Bell helicopter proved remarkably successful despite the fragility, anemic performance, and high maintenance demands displayed by all first-generation helicopters. So effortlessly did it integrate itself into Army operations that the Infantry, Artillery, Medical Corps, Signal Corps, Engineers, and Armored Cavalry all expressed a strong interest in using it for one purpose or another. Particularly striking was the helicopter's superiority in rescue and evacuation, the mission used to justify the Army's early procurements.

The first AGF helicopter pilots were trained late in 1945 under an informal agreement with the AAF. Selected from among the former's experienced fixed-wing liaison pilots, these fliers trained in Sikorsky R-4s and R-6s at Scott Field, Illinois, and Sheppard Field, Texas. This intraservice training ended a year later when Bell Aircraft took over pilot

and mechanic training under an AGF contract. Bell's month-long flight training classes at Niagara Falls ran every two weeks from March 3 through May 12, 1947. The company also instituted maintenance courses beginning at Fort Bragg on March 1 and at Fort Sill in April.

Later in 1947 the AAF resumed responsibility for primary helicopter flight training of AGF pilots at its Helicopter School in San Marcos, Texas. The first class convened in September with four Ground Forces students flying the YR-13. Formal AGF advanced tactical training began in October 1948 by the Air Training Department of the Artillery School at Fort Sill, Oklahoma, already the site of advanced fixed-wing liaison pilot training.

Fort Sill, the Army's "finishing school" for helicopter pilots, by the end of 1952 boasted fifty H-13B, C, and D helicopters, which saw hard use in a rigorous five-week course that made Army pilots the best trained in the world. Included in the curriculum were more than fifty hours of rough-terrain landings, supply drops, specialized autorotations, evacuations, visual night operations, aerial application, and so on.

Before the end of the 1940s, Army planners were already looking to large helicopters for troop and supply transport use, including machines as large as the Piasecki XH-16 and the Hughes XH-17, neither of which would achieve production. But political factors, formalized at Key West in the 5,000 pound gross weight restriction, still precluded Army use of transport helicopters.

On the eve of another war just five years after the end of World War II, the Army had 1,186 fixed-wing aircraft and fewer than a hundred helicopters. In addition to Bell H-13s, it boasted a few Sikorsky H-18s (S-52s), a poor helicopter that would not enjoy wide

Cumbersome and lacking utility, the Sikorsky
H-18 was overshadowed by the Army's two other
first-generation light helicopters. Courtesy UTC.

production. Acquisition of the first Sikorsky H-18 in 1949 offered further proof that the Army's helicopter program lagged behind those of America's other military services, for by then the USAF, USN, USMC, and USCG were all experienced Sikorsky operators.

On June 25, 1950, North Korea invaded South Korea and America found itself at war again. The U.S. Army immediately began operations there with fixed-wing aircraft like the Stinson L-5 and the North American L-17, the former a World War II liaison plane and the latter a general aviation four-seater minimally suited to military use. It was immediately obvious that helicopters were in far too short supply.

A USAF H-5 reportedly performed the first helicopter evacuation of wounded in July 1950. Improvised evacuations by Marine Corps HO3S-1 (H-5) helicopters belonging to observation squadron VMO-6 took place August 4, 1950. The Air Force, Navy, and Marines soon had a larger and more versatile helicopter at their disposal: the H-19/ HO4S/HRS, as the Sikorsky S-55 was variously designated. Arriving in June 1951, S-55s performed transport and rescue duties although their large size made them uneconomical for the routine evacuation of combat casualties.

Before 1950 ended, the Army had performed its first air evacuation with a Bell H-13B. In the opening weeks of 1951, litter-equipped Bell H-13s and—in smaller numbers —Hiller H-23AS were routinely removing wounded from combat zones to Mobile Army Surgical Hospital (MASH) units for lifesaving medical treatment. Each MASH unit had a helicopter detachment assigned to it comprising four helicopters, four pilots, and four mechanics. Indicative of the hazards of this new form of combat flying, every pilot of the Army's 2nd Helicopter Detachment earned a Distinguished Flying Cross within the first two weeks of operational flying.

Ironically, although the Army was the service with the greatest need for transport helicopters, it was denied Sikorsky H-19s of its own until the war was all but over. Because of Key West restrictions, this service had to make do with light helicopters that lacked the logistical support capability of larger types. For this reason, U.S. Army operations in Korea more closely resembled those of World War II than those to come in Vietnam.

To offset the crippling lack of larger helicopters, additional airplanes capable of short and rough-field operations were pressed into service. In the spring of 1951 came the Cessna L-19 Bird Dog, a two-place tandem version of that company's rugged civil Model 180. Toward the end of 1952, there arrived the de Havilland L-20 Beaver, a capacious Canadian-built "bush" airplane capable of carrying heavy loads. But these fixed-wing types could not counter the lack of troop and transport helicopters in Korea's rugged terrain.

This point was driven home in 1952 when a lone Bell H-13 spent five days shuttling twenty-nine soldiers and 20,300 pounds of supplies and equipment to the top of Korean Hill 1304. The 65th Engineers needed the materials to help the 25th Infantry dig in after that unit received orders to hold the strategic hill from advancing enemy forces. Observing this historic first Army helicopter airlift, one field officer noted in disgust that it was crazy "to send a sedan to do the job of a truck."[9]

Only by late 1951 had Key West restrictions finally eased sufficiently for the Army to get helicopters weighing over 5,000 pounds. The first of an initial order for ninety-seven H-19s was delivered before the end of the year and began an accelerated service-test program.

A Bell H-13 delivers a wounded soldier to a MASH
unit. Use of light helicopters for air evacuation
cut the Korean War fatality rate by more than half
compared to that of World War II. Courtesy Bell.

The USAF now also began procuring Piasecki H-21s and H-25s for Army use (the latter a version of the Navy's HUP-1), but unlike the Sikorsky these tandem-rotor transports—both of which saw service elsewhere in Korea—would not become operational with the Army before hostilities ended in mid-1953.

Sikorsky H-19s of the Army's pioneering 6th Transport Helicopter Company arrived in Korea in January 1953 and flew their first combat mission in April. H-19s of both the 6th and 13th THCs participated in Operation Little Switch, a repatriation of sick and wounded United Nations troops that began before the war ended. Fourteen of these transport helicopters also took part in Operation Sky Hook in support of the 25th Infantry Division, carrying more than a half million pounds of supplies in just three days.

Although their late arrival denied them a significant role in Korea, these H-19s demonstrated conclusively the value of large helicopters to Army tactical operations. As it turned out, however, the evacuation of wounded soldiers by Bell and Hiller light helicopters would remain the U.S. Army's single meaningful use of rotary-wing aviation in that conflict.

More than any other factor, the helicopter reduced the death rate from battlefield injuries in Korea to the lowest point in the history of warfare, a rate less than half that suffered by wounded American troops in World War II. In some cases, pilots even administered plasma in flight by squeezing a pressure bulb connected to a bottle suspended in the cabin. This practice—one of many shock trauma innovations to emerge during the war—was developed by personnel of the 2nd Helicopter Detachment.

When peace was declared July 27, 1953, the Army had about 1,000 helicopters, mostly training and evacuation types. Bell and Hiller machines (the former also used in this role by the Marines) evacuated more than 20,000 American, South Korean, British, French, Ethiopian, Benelux, Greek, Thai, and Turkish troops during the war.

Army Lieutenant Joseph Bowler flew 824 seriously wounded soldiers to field hospitals in 482 missions. Lieutenant William P. Brake later bettered this score with 900 evacuations during 545 missions. Married, the father of three, Brake—a flight engineer on Navy PBYs during World War II—had switched services in order to fly in Korea. "There's a lot of satisfaction in bringing wounded men back," he stated in 1953. "Most evacuation trips took about thirty minutes from the time the men were hit until they were in the hospital. The same trip by ambulance would sometimes take four hours, which could mean the difference between life and death."[10]

Among his toughest missions were six night flights placing extraordinary demands on his knowledge of the rugged Korean countryside, culminating in landings made by jeep headlights or flashlight. His closest call came when incorrect map coordinates took him two miles behind enemy lines. There he evaded withering small arms fire by ducking behind a riverbank and skimming away at zero altitude. The dangers Brake faced were not unique: U.S. and foreign pilots participating in the multinational police action pushed the newly perfected helicopter to its limits.

On the home front, the Army Field Forces had established its first helicopter transport companies in 1951. It used them in full-scale training operations at Fort Bragg, North Carolina, the following year. Troops, equipment, and supplies were carried by new Army H-19s. These exercises marked the first time

Soldiers in a jeep communicate by radio with a
litter-equipped H-23C during 1956 summer maneuvers at Fort Ord, California. Courtesy Hiller.

Army H-19s provided the capability to transport
troops, equipment, and supplies. Courtesy UTC.

the U.S. Army had full helicopter tactical support.

In 1952, the Army used the Korean War's loosening of Key West constraints to adopt a twelve-battalion helicopter program. This blueprint called for three battalions each of heavy and medium cargo helicopters of five- and three-ton capacities, respectively, plus six battalions of light cargo machines with a capacity of one and a half tons. Although Key West still imposed some gross weight limits, restricted operating radii, and prohibited the arming of Army helicopters, implementation of this program was a major step in the development of "airmobility." Applied exhaustively in Vietnam, this tactical philosophy of the U.S. Army drew directly from French Army experience in Algeria in the latter 1950s, as reported at the end of this appendix.

U.S. NAVY

Having evaluated a few autogiros during the 1930s, the Navy developed an active disinterest in rotary-wing flight lasting well into the 1940s. Although authorized to pursue rotary-wing development by the Dorsey Bill, it divested itself of all such responsibilities in the 1939 interservice meeting described above, in which the Army Air Forces was designated to pursue such activities.

Congress had appropriated just $300,000 of the $2 million authorized by the legislation, a sum Navy leaders argued was too small to sponsor full-scale development by both services. In any event, it made sense for the Army to take the lead because it had both need of helicopters and some previous experience in their development. Thus, only months before the outbreak of war in Europe, Navy leaders absolved themselves of rotary-

wing involvement in a decision they would soon regret.

To be fair, the Navy had little time for the sort of program specified by the Dorsey Bill. Retarded by years of financial austerity between the wars, it faced massive efforts to catch up with the fascist powers. Building new ships, training crews, and converting its carrier air arm from antiquated biplanes to modern monoplanes were the Navy's priorities.

Japan's surprise attack on Pearl Harbor on December 7, 1941, placed extraordinary additional demands on the Navy. Much of the Pacific Fleet had been sunk or damaged by this attack, which catapulted America into World War II. A massive shipbuilding and repair effort would be required. Fortunately, the fleet's aircraft carriers had been spared because they were away on maneuvers during the attack.

The Navy's long-standing commitment to lighter-than-air flight also prompted it to reject the helicopter. Having given up dirigibles after the USS *Akron* and *Macon* crashed, in 1933 and 1935 respectively, it nevertheless remained fully committed to nonrigid airships, or blimps, for coastal patrol. In 1937, the Navy became the world's only operator of an LTA fleet. By World War II, Navy blimps were a common sight over major U.S. seaports. This fleet—the largest ever assembled—grew to 167 blimps during the war.

With global war came mounting pressure to protect American shipping, particularly convoys carrying desperately needed fuel and supplies to Great Britain under Lend-Lease. In 1942, the mounting toll of tonnage sunk by German submarines threatened to choke this lifeline unless an answer could be found to the U-boat menace. Particularly dangerous was the central North Atlantic, a region more than 500 miles across that lay beyond the extended ranges of shore-based American and British patrol planes. Far out at sea, Germany's "wolf packs" roamed with impunity.

What was needed was an aircraft capable of detecting and perhaps even attacking enemy submarines. Since aircraft carriers were too few in number to escort every convoy, it had to be an aircraft without need of a carrier. Ideally, it would operate from the decks of the cargo vessels themselves.

Blimps were not the answer. Although these machines patrolled far out over shipping lanes in search of U-boats, they could not accompany convoys across the open Atlantic. Only the helicopter filled the bill. Thus the concept of ship-based rotorcraft arose to acutely embarrass Navy leaders, who suddenly found themselves having to explain why they had actively and repeatedly resisted helicopter sponsorship. The Army had helicopters; it had even demonstrated their ability to operate off ships. So why did the Navy not even have a helicopter program? With so many lives and so much tonnage being lost, there was simply no answer Navy leaders could give that would satisfy Congress and the American public.

At the urging of Vice Admiral R. R. Waesche, commandant of the Coast Guard, Admiral Ernest J. King, commander in chief of the U.S. Fleet and chief of naval operations (CNO), issued a directive dated February 15, 1943, to the chief of the Bureau of Aeronautics calling for creation of a U.S. Navy helicopter program. BuAer was to undertake tests to determine the practical value of helicopters in convoy defense. This directive went on to state that convoy patrol helicopters, to be effective, must have a four-hour fuel supply, be capable of instrument flight, carry life rafts, and mount radios with a 100-mile range. Such performance, of course, far

exceeded the capability of helicopters in 1943.

However valid the CNO's views, this statement served only to forestall rapid action because the program called for aircraft not yet in existence. Since military helicopter development was the exclusive responsibility of the Army Air Forces, the Navy had again postponed dealing with the issue.

But whether helicopters were yet suited to sea duty was not the issue. The American public wanted to know whether the Navy was willing to help solve a problem that threatened ultimate Allied victory and the very survival of America's chief ally. It seemed all too clear that the Navy's belated Helicopter Program was more concerned with self-protection than protecting Atlantic convoys.

On April 21, 1943, the chief of Naval press relations, Captain Leland P. Lovett, speaking before members of the National Newspaper Promotion Association in New York City, described how the U.S. Navy was using helicopters to combat U-boats on North Atlantic sea lanes. Unfortunately for Lovett and his service, it came to light that the Navy had no ship-based helicopters in operation at sea anywhere in the world.

What at first seemed an embarrassing gaffe took on more ominous shadings the next day when the Truman Committee released a report criticizing the Navy for failing to embrace helicopters. Since this damning document had been shown to the Navy before being made public, speculation arose as to whether Lovett's misleading statements had originated at a higher level in a misguided attempt at damage control. Far from defusing congressional criticism, the incident added to the Navy's acute embarrassment.

In his nationally syndicated column of May 13, 1943, Drew Pearson speculated that Captain Lovett was perhaps "pulling the chestnuts out of the fire for his superior officers who bungled the helicopter program." The widely read columnist wrote that "[the] inside fact is that the Navy not only has not done anything about helicopters until the last few days, but actually has been opposing them despite appeals from the Maritime Commission, the Coast Guard, and to some extent from the Army that helicopters are the only way to lick the submarine."

Pearson laid much of the blame for the Navy's failure on Captain Morton K. Fleming of the Bureau of Aeronautics, an officer reportedly opposed to Naval helicopter use. "Supposed to be the Navy's rotary-wing expert," Pearson said of him, "he has consistently pooh-poohed the idea."

Whatever the merits of this allegation, BuAer had indeed been opposing helicopter use. Operations at sea demanded performance and ruggedness, qualities not yet demonstrated by rotorcraft of any kind. The Army's limited success with the Sikorsky R-4 had done nothing to reverse the Navy's perceptions of the limitations of vertical-flight technology.

The Navy's antipathy toward helicopters was rooted in two questionable beliefs then held by its policy makers. The first was that only large helicopters could be of value to the Navy, a view stemming from the logical identification of antisubmarine warfare and aerial resupply as the primary roles vertical flight might play in fleet service. The former mission required heavy depth charges and heavy sonar equipment. The latter, which promised to turn many smaller vessels into helicopter carriers, dictated sufficient capacity and performance to allow cargo to be delivered and people to be shuttled.

The second misconception was that as heli-copters grew in size their weight would increase to the point where large machines would be unable to carry any payload. BuAer technical experts during the war swore that a mathematical curve "proved" such to be the case. This supposition, which was quickly disproved in the postwar era, explains why the AAF's two-seat R-4 had failed to alter Navy thinking in 1943: too small to be useful as anything but a trainer, even the R-4 was hard pressed to carry anything more than its crew.

Under pressure, the Navy now hastened to place orders for R-4s with Vought-Sikorsky. It was a humbling about-face for the service, an operator of fixed-wing Sikorskys since 1927 and Voughts even longer. Just two years earlier, BuAer had rebuffed Igor Sikorsky when he came to Washington, D.C., seeking Navy support for his helicopter work. Diplomatic as always, Sikorsky now went out of his way not to remind Navy officials of their recent humiliation.

On October 16, 1943, Commander Frank A. Erickson of the U.S. Coast Guard officially accepted delivery of the Navy's first Sikorsky HNS-1 (YR-4A ser. no. 11). That the Coast Guard received this first wartime Navy helicopter and many others to follow was a political fluke resulting from the Navy's dilemma. Normally part of the Treasury Department, the USCG had been temporarily reassigned to the Navy Department on November 1, 1941, to facilitate wartime coordination between its coastal activities and those of the Navy farther out to sea. That it was—at least for the moment—part of the Navy presented a safe if inglorious course for Naval leaders through perilous political waters.

This course was to make the subordinate Coast Guard responsible for bringing the helicopter into operational maritime use, an action the USCG had itself proposed the previous year. Admiral King did precisely this when he established the Navy helicopter program. In contrast to the Navy, the USCG was keenly interested in helicopters and had plans for their employment. If it succeeded in introducing helicopters into regular shipboard service, the entire Navy could bask in the shared glow of success. But if helicopters proved incapable of lending useful service, as Navy technical experts predicted, the USCG would shoulder the blame.

This cynical ploy fooled no one, least of all Congress. It was adopted nonetheless. For its part, the visionary and enthusiastic Coast Guard was more than willing to accept the risk if that was what it took to acquire helicopters.

In May 1943, meanwhile, AAF Colonel Frank Gregory performed the first shipboard helicopter landings in history. Despite mast cables and other hazards, he set the float-equipped Sikorsky XR-4 down on the SS *Bunker Hill* in Long Island Sound off Stratford, Connecticut, some two dozen times under a variety of wind conditions and ship speeds. The irony that an Army pilot in an Army helicopter had been the first to fly from the deck of a ship was not lost on official observers.

Faced with mounting congressional displeasure, scathing press coverage, and growing public indignation, King also enlisted the help of the British, who were staunch advocates of maritime helicopter use. The Anglo-British program announced May 4, 1943, would be supervised by the Bureau of Aeronautics as it called on the Coast Guard to carry the American share of the joint effort.

Admiral King further established the Combined Board for the Evaluation of the Helicopter in Anti-Submarine Warfare. Comprised of Navy, Coast Guard, and British officers, and chaired by the CNO himself, this board convened for the first time May 18, 1943. Expanded in August to include a civilian representative of the War Shipping Administration (WSA), and in September to include one from the NACA, its recommendations would help shape the U.S. Navy's adoption of vertical flight.

Among the board's first actions was to order construction in the summer of 1943 of helicopter landing platforms aboard two vessels: the *Governor Cobb*, which WSA had turned over to the Coast Guard for use as an escort cutter, and the British merchant vessel *Daghestan*, an American-built cargo ship supplied to Great Britain under Lend-Lease.

During the last week of November 1943, Coast Guard and British pilots made 328 landings on the *Daghestan* in Long Island Sound (166 performed by the former and 162 by the latter). On January 6, 1944, a critical phase of evaluation began when two Sikorsky HNS (YR-4B) helicopters of the so-called British Helicopter Service Trial Unit went to sea aboard this vessel amid a fifty-ship convoy bound for England.

The *Daghestan* was hardly an ideal vessel for this trial, even modified with a 50-by-96-foot helipad over its stern. According to Admiral J. F. Farley, who would succeed Vice Admiral Waesche as commandant of the Coast Guard, the 10,000 ton vessel (loaded with 8,000 tons of grain) "had a tendency to excessive roll and yaw due to her deep loading with no cargo between decks, never throughout the voyage rolling less than ten degrees from port to starboard and back to port in a period of ten seconds. Under the worst conditions, the roll increased to forty-five degrees each way."[11]

Why this ship was selected by Admiral King's board is difficult to comprehend, since it needlessly aggravated the effects of rough seas and bad weather. These conditions so greatly hampered the Sikorskys that only two half-hour flights were effected during the sixteen-day voyage, one by a Coast Guard pilot on January 16 and the other by an RAF pilot the following day.

The experiment fully vindicated the Navy contention that use on the high seas exceeded the abilities of the Sikorsky HNS, then the only operational helicopter. Although weight had been kept to a minimum by flying with no radio, one seat empty, and only 20 gallons of fuel, these machines lacked sufficient power and controllability to follow the motions of a pitching deck. Made athwartships into the wind which was on the beam, the landings had been controlled crashes luckily accomplished without damage. But although the HNS itself proved unsuitable for antisubmarine use, wartime urgency led the board to strongly endorse further helicopter development.

Late in 1943, the Navy joined the AAF in sponsoring the Sikorsky R-6 program. The XR-6 prototype, which first flew October 15, became in Navy service the HOS-1. This trouble-plagued machine gave the Navy its first real experience with helicopters. This service also placed an order for fifty larger R-5s under the designation HO2S-1, but that machine's extensive development difficulties saw this order subsequently reduced to two. However, postwar versions of the craft would lend vital service to the Navy in the plane-guard and search-and-rescue roles, as depicted in the excellent film *The Bridges at Toko-Ri* (1955).

Early in 1944, the Navy, through the Coast Guard, at last initiated development of helicopters of its own. The two very different programs it funded were similar only in a common requirement for a minimum payload of 1,800 pounds, reflecting the Navy's need for large helicopters. That both designs would exceed this requirement with useful loads of over 2,500 pounds must have shocked Navy technical experts, prompting an overdue reevaluation of the potential of military helicopters.

The first of these programs was initiated with the P-V Engineering Forum, whose single-seat PV-2 of 1943 was the second successful helicopter to fly in America. The Navy contract via the Coast Guard in February 1944 called for development of a helicopter to address the USCG's "urgent . . . need for at-sea rescue of torpedoed shipping crews along the U.S. east coast."[12] That the helicopter specified was larger than the Coast Guard required for rescue use, and that it was in fact being built for Navy use, was evident to all.

The result was the XHRP-X (denoting experimental/helicopter/transport category/Piasecki). The highly unusual "x" suffix in place of the traditional "1" served to heighten the experimental status of the project. This odd designation—reflecting a conspicuous lack of faith on the part of the Navy that production would ensue—was clearly intended to soften criticism of future failure by suggesting a research rather than a production focus to the program.

But the Navy had failed to take into account Frank Piasecki, an optimist who knew how to think big and make things happen. Just twenty-five years old at the time, Piasecki built and flew the XHRP-X *Dogship* in March 1945, only fourteen months after receiving the contract. An improved XHRP-1—not the first prototype as its designation would normally suggest—flew in November 1946, and delivery of twenty production HRP-1 helicopters began the following September. These first-generation tandem-rotor helicopters could lift two and a half times the payload of any other helicopter, making them the world's first transport rotorcraft. Despite their limitations, they would see innovative and historically significant use with the Navy, Marine Corps, and Coast Guard over the following half dozen years.

Clearly, Piasecki had pulled the Navy's chestnuts out of the fire. In return, he received lavish funding enabling him to develop manufacturing facilities and enter production. This success was all the more critical to the Navy because the development of its second wartime helicopter project, the McDonnell XHJD-1 Whirlaway, was not proceeding well. Powered by two 450-hp Pratt & Whitney R-985 Wasp Juniors, this hefty prototype—which flew at gross weights exceeding 12,000 pounds—was plagued by severe vibrations aggravated by the incurable flexing of the pylons supporting its engines and intermeshing 46-foot rotors. As a result, the Navy canceled this program in 1950.

In the postwar era, the Navy would phase out its first-generation HNS and HOS helicopters in favor of the HO3S (Sikorsky S-51), a much-improved and enlarged version of the wartime R-5/HO2S. The HO3S would go to sea on carriers, battleships, and cruisers. For still smaller helicopters, the Navy acquired Bell Model 47s (called HTLs in Navy service) beginning in 1947, Hiller 360s/UH-12s (HTEs) in 1950, and Kaman K-225s (HTKs)[13] in 1951. All developed as commercial helicopters and certificated by the CAA, these types were available to the Navy through simple off-the-shelf procurement.

Now that it had a broad array of helicopters, the Navy found vertical flight a supremely useful tool. Its value during rescues was obvious. Whereas ditched pilots previously had to wait for a destroyer to pick them up, they could now expect to be back aboard their carriers within minutes, sometimes without getting wet.

Helicopters assumed other functions previously handled by destroyers—such as delivering mail and transferring personnel—at a considerable savings in time and fuel. In wartime operations, task force security no longer had to be compromised by the diversion of destroyers from normal screening duties.

Another role for helicopters was observation and scouting, particularly for submarines. Such flights could be made from a variety of vessels, reserving aircraft carrier catapults for other uses, especially in bad conditions. Ship-to-ship and ship-to-shore liaison was yet another use, as was providing aerial support during landings of shipborne U.S. Marine Corps troops.

In February 1946, Coast Guard Lieutenant Walter C. Bolton and an HNS-1 from the USCG air station at Floyd Bennett Field accompanied the USS Midway—then the largest carrier in existence—on an arctic cruise designated Operation Frostbite. The first helicopter ever to go to sea on an aircraft carrier (though not the first to land on one), this HNS had the advantages of wind over the bows providing excellent translation lift, high air densities from the cold weather, and the huge ship's ample deck space. When three Midway aircraft ditched early on, nevertheless, the Navy used escorting vessels to recover their crews.

As this experiment suggests, Navy acceptance of helicopters remained slow. But that reluctance finally gave way after a four-seat Sikorsky S-51 in a factory paint scheme and

A naval aviator is plucked from the ocean by a
Piasecki HUP moments after ditching his Grumman Avenger. Courtesy John Schneider.

civil registration participated in extended maneuvers with the Atlantic fleet beginning in February 1947. Flying from the carrier USS *Franklin D. Roosevelt* during the cruise, Sikorsky's chief test pilot Dimitry "Jimmy" Viner performed aerial photography, transported a doctor for an emergency operation, shuttled contestants for intership boxing matches, and otherwise lent invaluable support.

But it was the way Viner, and Sikorsky pilot Jackson E. Beighle who replaced him later in the cruise, handled real-life emergencies that truly sold Navy personnel on the helicopter. When Lieutenant Commander George R. Stablein crashed while attempting to land aboard the FDR, Viner and Lieutenant Joseph Rullo, a Navy pilot acting as observer, reached the scene moments later. One crewman drowned, but Stablein—who weighed 230 pounds—was successfully plucked from the water using a rescue hoist developed by the Coast Guard. Viner performed four other rescues during this cruise, and Beighle—a former Army helicopter pilot—yet another.

Altogether, this hard-working Sikorsky made 154 flights, many on days when no other aircraft could fly. It delivered mail 98 times, transported 231 passengers ship-to-ship or between sea and shore (including the Honorable John N. Brown, assistant secretary of the Navy for air), landed on a gun turret of the battleship USS *Missouri*, hovered at specified heights and distances to aid in radar calibration, and otherwise demonstrated exceptional value.

By this time, the Navy had reorganized to integrate vertical flight into its operations. Helicopter Development Squadron VX-3 had been created July 1, 1946, at the Brooklyn naval air station to "expedite the evaluation and development of helicopter operating techniques for fleet uses and land-based oper-

ations."[14] Led by Commander Charles E. Houston, VX-3 got under way with ten officers, a hundred men, and a fleet of four HNS-1 and seven HOS-1 helicopters. Of enormous help were the existing helicopter training facilities left behind by the Coast Guard, which had recently relocated its helicopter program to North Carolina.

With considerable help from seasoned USCG instructors, VX-3 personnel developed and instituted a thirty-hour helicopter transition course for Navy fixed-wing pilots. This course was open to rated pilots of other military services as well. The men of VX-3 also helped complete the USCG's 40-by-60-foot platform, which was rigged to roll and pitch so that simulated shipboard landings could be practiced. Aircraft availability was low and accidents were initially frequent, but the unit expanded until it outgrew the limited facilities available at Brooklyn. Accordingly, by the end of 1946 it had relocated to NAS Lakehurst, a base in nearby New Jersey made famous by the 1937 *Hindenburg* dirigible disaster.

As of early 1948, the number of Navy helicopters of all types available to fleet and shore-based units was still under a hundred. At Lakehurst, VX-3 continued to thrive. By the spring of 1948, its sizable fleet of training helicopters was busy preparing HO3S-1 crews for sea duty with fleet units, as well as general transport and rescue duties. The Navy by then had forty-six of these Sikorsky observation helicopters on order. Six VX-3 HRP-1s were also busy training the Marine Corps pilots who would perform the USMC "vertical envelopment" exercise planned for the following year.

Captain Clayton C. "Spud" Marcy, one of the Navy's foremost helicopter experts, had by this time assumed command of VX-3.

Flown by a company test pilot, this Sikorsky s-51
demonstrates newfound capabilities to the U.S.
Navy during Atlantic maneuvers in 1947. Courtesy UTC.

Having learned to fly helicopters under Coast Guard instruction in 1943, Marcy in 1946 wrote specific recommendations for the formation of a squadron to evaluate helicopters and develop techniques for their operational employment. Forwarded to the office of the CNO, this influential letter contributed to the creation of the unit Marcy now commanded.

Executive officer of VX-3 was Commander Maurice Peters. Early in 1948, Peters led a flight of three HO3S-IS on a ten-day flight across the continent that ended at San Diego on February 19. Covering 2,600 miles, the trip took 41 flight hours. This event was the first mass flight across the United States by helicopter. The southerly route taken—with stops at Washington, Memphis, Oklahoma City, El Paso, Tucson, and Phoenix—had been flown solo some weeks earlier by Marcy himself in what is believed to be the first coast-to-coast crossing made by a helicopter.

The excursion to San Diego was not without purpose, for VX-3 was shortly to be split into two parts, with one based there. Disbanded April 1, 1948, the experimental unit was immediately recommissioned as HU-1 and HU-2, the Navy's first operational helicopter utility squadrons. Assigned to the Pacific Fleet, the former moved to NAS Miramar in San Diego under the command of Captain Marcy, who soon turned the squadron over to Commander Charles Houston, VX-3's original commander. The latter unit, led by Commander Peters, remained at NAS Lakehurst to support the Atlantic Fleet. Formation of these squadrons truly marks the formal induction of helicopters into regular U.S. Navy use.

The duties of HU-1 and HU-2 included training helicopter pilots and support personnel, and providing helicopters, crews, and mechanics for sea duty aboard Naval vessels.

If VX-3 had found helicopter availability low, HU-2 at Lakehurst fared little better as it struggled to address a demand for vertical flight that far outstripped supply. The new technology was balky, with short intervals between required rotor, shaft, and transmission overhauls. Fortunately, Lakehurst's excellent aviation overhaul and repair (O&R) depot was available to help the unit's frustrated maintenance personnel.

HU-1 on the West Coast functioned in a similar manner except that basic training was not conducted there. It too met the many challenges of providing helicopters to Navy ships, and keeping them flightworthy during extended cruises. The nearby O&R facility at NAS North Island lent the same essential support to HU-1 that Lakehurst's gave its sister squadron back east.

Working closely with this squadron, and indeed with all military users of its helicopters, Sikorsky Aircraft pursued an aggressive product support program typical of the United Aircraft Corporation. By the time the Korean War began, the Navy and America's other military forces had helicopters providing a level of utility unknown in World War II.

Helicopters operating off ships stationed around the Korean Peninsula proved critical to operations during the war in a variety of ways. One was the rapid airlift of wounded to fully equipped hospital ships floating offshore. Some HU-1 helicopters were also stationed on British carriers, Korean islands, and even small LST landing craft. One HU-1 pilot reportedly managed to evade being shot down and successfully returned to the USS *Valley Forge* after being jumped by three MIG-15 jet fighters.

"If any single type of aircraft has sold itself to the entire Navy and Marine Corps by superior performance in the field," asserted Vice Admiral C. Turner Joy, commander of naval forces in the Far East, "it has been the helicopter."[15] For its part in supporting the Pacific Fleet, HU-1 received a presidential unit citation. The award read:

> For extraordinary heroism in action against enemy aggressor forces in Korea from 3 July 1950 to 27 July 1953. Pioneering in the employment of helicopters under combat conditions, Helicopter Squadron ONE achieved a brilliant record while participating in every battle against the enemy throughout this period. Obliged to develop its own tactics and operational procedures, this resourceful and intrepid squadron spotted and directed naval gunfire in actual combat; spotted and destroyed enemy mines; effected the rescue of 429 persons, many of which rescues were carried out over hostile territory in the face of enemy fire; transported personnel and prodigious amounts of mail and material at sea; relieved destroyers of daylight plane guard duties; and maintained ninety-five percent availability for assigned missions. The courage, ingenuity and inspiring teamwork of the officers and men of Helicopter Squadron ONE were contributing factors in the success of friendly forces in Korea and were in keeping with the highest traditions of the United States Naval Service.[16]

Ironically, the role originally envisioned for Navy helicopters—antisubmarine warfare (ASW)—was among the last to emerge. Developing airborne sonar equipment, perfecting bigger helicopters to carry it, and devising techniques for its employment all conspired to delay this high-priority Bureau of Aeronautics program, which would be conducted by the Naval Air Development Center (NADC) at NAS Johnsville, Pennsylvania.

Driving the program was a growing need for countermeasures to offset advances in submarine technology rendering them harder to detect. ASW helicopters were the logical answer. Faster and more maneuverable than surface vessels, they promised to enlarge the radius of detection considerably. Whereas the background noise made by surface vessels as they passed through the water interfered with their sonar by masking faint echoes, helicopter sonar arrays lowered into the water could detect submarines at greater range because they were interference free.

The first such experiments took place before the end of World War II when the Naval Research Laboratory installed Hayes submarine sound equipment in the XHOS-1 (the Navy's first R-6). With electronic equipment developed by Dr. Harvey C. Hayes, head of the NRL's Sound Division since its formation in 1923, plus a crew of two, this overloaded Coast Guard helicopter stalked an actual submarine from the deck of the USCG cutter *Governor Cobb* off Block Island in Long Island Sound during tests beginning February 14, 1945. Commander Frank Erickson and Lieutenant J.G. Stewart R. Graham took turns at the controls while the NRL's Dr. Jesse L. Coop worked the primitive dipping sonar. These rudimentary efforts validated the concept of helicopter sonar platforms.

Early the following year, the NRL's improved XCF dipping sonar was installed in one of the Coast Guard's first HO2S-1 (R-5) helicopters for a new round of experiments. Graham and his mechanic ferried this machine to Key West in March 1946 for tests with Navy Development Squadron VX-1, which had at its disposal a captured German U-boat to serve as the target. This promising effort came to an abrupt halt three months later when hot, windless conditions robbed the overloaded HO2S of sufficient power to land aboard an LST, causing it to crash off the Florida coast.

Further aerial sonar development by the NADC at Johnsville generated a new round of ASW experiments for VX-1 in 1949. Despite delays stemming from the loss of a Sikorsky HO3S fitted with newly developed AQS-1 sonar, this program was pronounced successful by the CNO, who authorized further developments.

Because of their greater size and relative insensitivity to center-of-gravity changes, two Piasecki HRP-1 tandem-rotor helicopters were detailed to perform the next series of tests. Flown from Lakehurst to NAS Patuxent River in Maryland, these machines were extensively modified and evaluated before being flown to Key West for additional ASW trials. Their fabric covering was stripped at Key West to reduce weight and improve hot-weather performance. A drive system failure caused one of these machines to ditch almost inverted, leading to the installation of flotation bags in its replacement. This latter HRP-1 also ended up in the water because of an engine failure. Both machines were salvaged and returned to the air. Despite these mishaps, the HRPs acquitted themselves fairly well and these pioneering sonar tests were deemed successful.

In a 1949 survey of existing helicopters, meanwhile, the Navy settled on the new Sikorsky S-55 (USAF H-19) as the type best suited for interim ASW use. It therefore placed an order for ten of these machines, which it designated HO4S-1. In anticipation of their delivery in 1951, an accelerated Board of Inspection and Survey Trials evaluation was rushed to completion at NAS

Patuxent River using a borrowed H-19.

At Key West, however, VX-1 found these Sikorskys failed to perform when loaded with Bendix AN/AQS-1 ASW equipment. High density altitudes resulting from the hot Florida weather, and the inability of their buried engines to cool adequately, prompted the Navy in 1950 to trade its HO4S-1s outright for four Marine Corps HRP-1s recently used in the development of vertical-assault tactics at Quantico, Virginia. In Florida, these Piasecki helicopters—like their predecessors—were stripped of their fabric for improved performance, saving some 800 pounds per helicopter. The primitive Bendix dipping sonar, flotation gear, and a 35-gallon auxiliary fuel tank were then installed. Thus modified, these helicopters participated in an extremely significant peacetime submarine hunt.

The quarry—one of the most advanced submarines in the world—was U-2513—an advanced German Type XXI U-boat obtained as war booty by the Allies. Its crew of veteran American, British, and German submariners had every advantage. The performance of their vessel was superior even to that of America's best submarines. Each day the U-boat left Key West to cruise submerged while two, three, or more HRP-1s crewed by USN and RAF pilots attempted to locate it by lowering spherical sonar sensors into the water and "pinging" in concert.

These maneuvers continued into 1951 with no trace of the "enemy" submarine being heard. Week after week the helicopter teams returned crestfallen. They and their skeletal aircraft—derisively dismissed by regular Navy personnel as "flying Brooklyn bridges"— became the brunt of every joke, a laughing stock whose humor was appreciated off base as well as on. The universal consensus was that the U-boat was in little danger of being caught.

Over time, however, the helicopter pilots and Dr. Coop's Bendix-trained sonar operators had perfected their tactics and polished their techniques. After ten weeks this training finally paid off on a Friday that would change the course of Naval operations. Piasecki HRP-1s successfully cornered and "killed" the submarine, pelting its hull with dye-marker bags as it surfaced.

The submarine's crew was quick to proclaim the event a fluke, adding that the helicopters would score no more aerial victories. But the formerly elusive submarine was caught again the following Monday, Tuesday, and Wednesday. On Thursday, the commander in chief of the Atlantic Fleet arrived to see for himself what was being accomplished. His observations prompted him to proclaim the beginning of a new era of military defense. The Navy's vision of helicopter ASW was now an actuality.

Meanwhile, airborne sonar development— spearheaded by John Crowley of BuAer—had progressed sufficiently to warrant procurement of an interim ASW helicopter and initiation of a new helicopter specifically designed for the antisubmarine mission. The Piasecki HUP-1, a compact Navy rescue/ utility helicopter first flown in 1948 as the XHJP-1, was selected to be the interim type on the basis of VX-1's experience, which then favored tandem-rotor machines over single-rotor types.

Bell Aircraft's Helicopter Division in Texas won the design competition for a dedicated ASW aircraft with the ungainly XHSL-1 of 1953, a troubled tandem-rotor machine that would not fulfill Navy hopes. Neither would Piasecki's HUP-1, then the service's standard light utility helicopter, which suffered nagging engine problems. During a tryout with the Atlantic Fleet's LANTFLEX exercise of 1952, it could not hover in place long enough with a pinging sonar array in the water because its engine had been derated to improve reliability.

On the organizational front, the Navy began commissioning antisubmarine helicopter squadrons. The first was HS-1, which like VX-1 was based at Key West. Naval planners now found themselves in the awkward position of having ASW units but no helicopters for them to operate. Luckily, a much-improved version of the H-19 was now flying. A few were made available to Pacific Fleet ASW squadrons HU-2 and HU-4. Variously called the HO4S-2, HO4S-3, and HRS-1, this Sikorsky helicopter proved satisfactory in the ASW role.

Supported by the Naval Electronics Laboratory, these operational units now assumed the lead in refining electronic equipment and developing tactics. Thus, despite its initial failure in this mission, the Sikorsky S-55 became the Navy's first regularly assigned antisubmarine helicopter until the larger and heavier S-58 became available after the Korean War. To better adapt this latter machine to ASW use, the Navy funded an accelerated program that made the S-58 the first instrument flight–approved helicopter in history. The service these hardworking Sikorskys performed assumed greater importance as cold war tensions elevated concerns about nuclear missile–equipped Soviet submarines.

The Korean conflict had also demonstrated the need for helicopters capable of minesweeping. Surface vessels were at risk in the minesweeping role, but helicopters—if their performance was up to the task—could detect mines much more quickly and clear them away without endangering themselves.

These advantages prompted BuAer's Armament Division to investigate whether helicopters could carry and use the tow gear. Doubters observed that helicopters often needed full throttle just to hover. They failed to realize, however, that hovering requires considerably more engine power than forward flight. Once moving, a helicopter exerts a strong pull indeed.

A study performed by Piasecki Helicopters under Navy contract showed that tandem-rotor helicopters generate almost their own weight in drawbar pull. Minesweeping experiments involving HRP-1s at Panama City in 1951–52 confirmed this fact before the program shifted to VX-1 at Key West. Although minesweeping helicopters were not operational before the end of the Korean War, they have since been highly successful in this role.

U.S. COAST GUARD

From the outset, the U.S. Coast Guard followed helicopter development with interest. Charged with patrolling America's waterways and performing maritime rescues, frequently in bad weather and high seas, it stood to benefit greatly from vertical flight capability. Therefore, Coast Guard personnel made frequent visits to the Sikorsky plant at Stratford, Connecticut, to observe progress on the Army's XR-4.

Commanders William J. Kossler and W. A. Burton, the latter commanding officer of the Coast Guard air station at Brooklyn, New York, were among the official observers at a dramatic demonstration staged at Stratford Airport on April 20, 1942. The officers watched with growing excitement as Sikorsky test pilot Les Morris put the XR-4 through a variety of maneuvers. Burton's report reads in part: "The helicopter, in its present stage

of development, has many of the advantages of the blimp and few of the disadvantages. It hovers and maneuvers with more facility in rough air than the blimp. It can land and take off in less space. It does not require a large ground handling crew. It does not need a large hangar. There is sufficient range (about two hours) in this particular model to make its use entirely practical for harbor patrol and other Coast Guard duties."[17]

On the basis of this report, acquisition of several R-4s was proposed by Commander F. A. Leamy, aviation operations officer at USCG headquarters in Washington, D.C. His recommendation was heartily endorsed by Commander Kossler, chief of the Aeronautical Engineering Division, who estimated that three machines and support equipment could be purchased for $250,000.

Vice Admiral R. R. Waesche, commandant of the USCG, was himself a strong advocate of vertical-flight use. In his view, employing helicopters to rescue the crews of ships torpedoed in U.S. coastal waters alone warranted their adoption by the Coast Guard. But he had to consider the risks inherent in committing to this emerging form of flight so early in its development. If Igor Sikorsky's first-generation military helicopter were to fail in Coast Guard service, it would be many years before the USCG could again pursue a vertical-flight program. Accordingly, this first helicopter proposal failed to produce results.

On June 29, 1942, Lieutenant Commander Frank A. Erickson, then attached to the Brooklyn air station, sent a memorandum to his commandant describing a meeting three days earlier with Michael Gluhareff and Igor Sikorsky at the Vought-Sikorsky plant in Connecticut. Since the XR-4 prototype itself was away at Wright Field, he had seen the company's visitor films and been given a detailed briefing. The possibilities of helicopter use left him enthusiastic. "The life saving and law enforcement possibilities of the helicopter have heretofore been especially stressed," he wrote. "However, this machine can fulfill an even more important role . . . providing aerial protection for convoys against submarine action, an important function of Coast Guard aviation."[18]

Erickson went on to describe the larger XR-5, then under development by Sikorsky, five of which "could give far greater protection for a convoy than a similar number of heavier-than-air or lighter-than-air craft." He described possible uses of this more advanced model which Sikorsky estimated would be in production by early the next year.[19] Four-hour patrols with a crew of two, two-way radio, and a 325-pound depth charge were conceivable with the R-5.

Commander Burton, Erickson's commanding officer, concurred in an attached endorsement. "It is urged that particular attention be given to those comments concerning the utility of the helicopter for convoy duty," he wrote. "The Army has demonstrated its belief in the value of helicopters for military use by letting a contract for a number of the present models. It is believed that the helicopter has even greater possibilities for Naval military use. Unfortunately, the Navy has not shown any great enthusiasm for this type aircraft. It is therefore an excellent opportunity for the Coast Guard with a very modest appropriation to initiate and proceed with the Naval development of the helicopter. We should seize this opportunity without delay."[20]

Between the first helicopter procurement proposal and Erickson's memo, U.S. shipping losses had reached crisis proportions. In June 1942 alone, fifty-five merchant ships totaling 289,790 tons—representing 4.5 percent of America's total capacity in vessels of over 1,000 tons—had been sunk. This shocking loss far outstripped the replacement capacity of America's bustling shipyards. The Lend-Lease lifeline to Great Britain, and ultimately U.S. military operations around the world, were in jeopardy.

Waesche thus needed little additional urging when Erickson's historic memo arrived. He immediately created a Coast Guard helicopter program and assigned it high priority. As part of the Navy for the duration, the USCG was legally barred from purchasing helicopters directly; like the Marine Corps, it had to obtain its aircraft through the Bureau of Aeronautics. Therefore, Waesche permitted Kossler to initiate procurement of Sikorsky HNS-1 helicopters through that organization.

As maritime helicopters were clearly needed everywhere that submarines might be encountered, not just in coastal waters where the Coast Guard operated, Waesche also took Burton's suggestion of proposing to the Navy that the Coast Guard pursue seaborne helicopter development on its behalf. When neither this proposal nor Kossler's effort to procure helicopters through BuAer produced results after more than six months, the Coast Guard commandant paid a visit to Admiral Ernest J. King, chief of naval operations and commander in chief of the U.S. Fleet.

Waesche's visit—bolstered by emerging criticism of the Navy's opposition to helicopters—prompted the CNO to launch at long last a Navy helicopter program. King's directive of February 15, 1943, assigned the Coast Guard full responsibility for pioneering maritime helicopter use. At Coast Guard headquarters, Kossler—recently promoted to captain—was assigned to head the program.

Kossler's initial planning was soon largely pre-empted by the chief of the Navy's Bureau of Aeronautics, who announced that BuAer would devise and conduct the maritime-adaption experiments.

The Coast Guard thus found itself with nominal responsibility for a program whose conduct it was denied. The Navy would be using Coast Guard pilots during these experiments, of course. Although both services anticipated an eventual substitution of Navy personnel and equipment, the slow pace of helicopter acceptance by that service made it clear that it would not be soon.

Lieutenant Commander Frank Erickson, meanwhile, had been reassigned as Kossler's assistant in Washington, D.C. From Tillamook, Oregon, the thirty-five-year-old Erickson had graduated from the Coast Guard Academy at New London, Connecticut, in 1931 and had become a Coast Guard aviator in 1935. Kossler soon detached Erickson to the Vought-Sikorsky plant as its USN/USCG military representative. There he learned to fly the YR-4A, thus becoming the first rated helicopter pilot in either of those services. Lieutenant j.g. Steward R. Graham and Ensign Walter C. Bolton soon followed as the next USCG aviators to earn helicopter ratings.

The Combined Board for the Evaluation of the Helicopter in Anti-Submarine Warfare was established by directive of Admiral King in May 1943. At that juncture, the Navy took the official position that to be worthwhile maritime patrol helicopters had to carry two-way radios, instrument flying equipment, life rafts, depth charges, and enough fuel to fly four hours. This clearly exceeded the abilities of the R-4 or R-6, and possibly even those of the R-5. Since the latter two types had not yet even flown, the effect of this Navy stance was to forestall any testing of the HNS (R-4).

To prevent this foot-dragging tactic from undermining the Coast Guard program, Erickson wrote to the board on June 10, 1943. "The usefulness for the helicopter in anti-submarine warfare," he informed its members, "is not as a killer craft but as the eyes and ears of the convoy escorts. The detection of enemy submarines is the greatest problem facing anti-submarine forces. . . . It is not necessary or even desirable that the machines be equipped with the 325-pound depth charges as it would be unsafe to bomb from low altitude when hovering or cruising at low speeds."[21]

AAF Colonel Frank Gregory's two dozen landings aboard the ss *Bunker Hill* on May 7, 1943, helped the Coast Guard by demonstrating the ability of R-4s to operate off moving ships in calm conditions. Because larger vessels pitch, roll, and yaw less in rough seas than small ones, this R-4/HNS was clearly at least suited to aircraft carrier use.

The Navy as yet had no interest in placing helicopters on its carriers, despite the obvious lifesaving potential and minimal cost of such "plane-guard" use. The narrow focus of that service remained only to evaluate their use aboard merchant vessels for submarine protection, as mandated by Congress. Only three years later would a helicopter even accompany a U.S. Navy carrier to sea, and even then its pilot would be a Coast Guard aviator.

Erickson, now a commander, took delivery of the Navy's first HNS on October 16, 1943. He flew this machine to the Coast Guard air station at Floyd Bennett Field to begin a program having two goals. One was to adapt the helicopter to Coast Guard use, since BuAer had assumed control of the maritime helicopter effort. The other was to train pilots and mechanics for the Coast Guard, Navy, and other services. A towering figure in the acceptance and employment of helicopters in the United States, Erickson would through this program pursue truly pioneering development work.

By November 8, two other Navy helicopters had arrived at the air station. On December 1, 1943, this facility in Brooklyn was designated the country's first official helicopter base. Four days later, New York City was visited by its first helicopter when Erickson landed one of his three HNS-1s at the Battery on Manhattan's southern tip to take Rear Admiral Stanley V. Parker, USCG, on an inspection flight of New York Harbor.

Meanwhile, as described earlier, two R-4 helicopters were dispatched on the British merchant vessel *Daghestan* for sea trials amid a fifty-ship convoy bound for England. Lieutenant j.g. Graham and Royal Air Force Flight Lieutenant "Jeep" Cable accomplished one flight each during this passage despite high seas and adverse weather. This voyage proved what everyone already knew: the R-4/HNS series helicopter was not suited to maritime use aboard small ships. Subsequent experiments would concentrate on the R-5 (HO2S) and its improved successor, the S-51 (HO3S).

In the spring of 1945, Erickson and Graham flew from the USCG cutter *Governor Cobb* to hunt submarines with primitive dipping sonar. The first vessel in either the USN or USCG to boast a helipad, the *Cobb* had entered service in the spring of 1944. First operational use of its landing pad took place on June 29 of that year.

Lieutenant Walter Bolton would pilot the HNS, carried to sea by the USS *Midway* early in 1946, the first helicopter ever assigned to operational duty aboard a "flattop." By this time, however, the Navy had qualified helicopter pilots of its own and was finally integrating vertical flight into its operations. With the Coast Guard once again part of the Treasury Department, moreover, the Navy no longer had ready access to USCG personnel and equipment. Bolton's cruise would therefore be the last instance of Coast Guard participation in Navy helicopter evaluations.

The substantial contributions of the U.S. Coast Guard to early helicopter acceptance were not made by fulfilling Navy requirements. Rather, they were the development of lifesaving equipment and techniques perfected by Erickson and his pioneering unit. Efforts to adapt helicopters with litters as aerial ambulances began at the end of 1943. These had hardly begun when Erickson was called upon to perform the first true helicopter mercy mission.

The destroyer USS *Turner* suffered an explosion January 3, 1944, while a short distance offshore. Responding within minutes, Erickson flew to South Ferry to pick up two cases of badly needed plasma, which he raced directly to the hospital at Sandy Hook where the injured sailors had been taken. Reducing the plasma's arrival time from hours to minutes reportedly saved several lives.

The Coast Guard's first HOS-1s arrived at the end of World War II. Neither it nor the HNS-1 lent itself well to carrying stretchers. The best solution—and it was hardly ideal—was to remove the HOS-1's 70-gallon fuel tank and mount two external 33-gallon tanks on each side. A stretcher could then be laid crosswise behind the pilot and copilot, its protruding ends covered with aluminum caps.

Another long-standing Coast Guard development program sought to address the lack of stability of early Sikorskys. "Before any helicopter can be flown automatically, or even be flown manually at night without reference lights or under instrument conditions, it must first be stabilized," observed Erickson, who characterized stability as "the crying need of helicopters today."[22]

One result of this effort was the trial installation of a Sperry autopilot in an HOS-1, but the Sikorsky machine proved too unstable for it to function. Another was a mechanical stabilizer flap for the HOS-1 consisting of airfoils below and behind the rotor. Connected to the nonrotating swashplate to hold it in a given plane with respect to the flight path, this aerodynamic device prevented disturbances originating in the fuselage from being transmitted to the rotor in forward flight. It would cut out entirely at speeds below 35 mph, leaving the helicopter free to hover and land with uncompromised control. This cumbersome invention added weight and drag, however, and by the time it flew in 1948 both Bell and Hiller had developed better ways of imparting stability to helicopters.

Erickson's group even pursued helicopter instrument flight with modest success. Procedures were devised and special instruments were developed in conjunction with the Sperry Gyroscope Company, but the poor endurance and instability of the Coast Guard's Sikorskys limited their suitability to operations in nonvisual flying conditions.

By far the most important development made by Erickson and his team was the rescue hoist. The idea came to Erickson after he read classified reports describing early AAF rescues with R-4s in World War II. In one case, an injured pilot had to walk miles through Japanese-occupied jungle to a sandbar in a river because there was no open ground. In another, a critically injured soldier had to wait three days while others cut down trees to clear a landing area. In either case, a power-operated hoist would have permitted a rescue without the helicopter having to land.

Early in 1944, Erickson described his idea to a half dozen Coast Guard mechanics, one of whom was Aircraft Machinist's Mate 2nd Class Sergei Sikorsky, a son of Igor Sikorsky. Installation of an electric winch hoist on an HNS-1 was completed August 11 and tests began over Jamaica Bay. The tendency of the electric braking mechanism to "creep" or slowly unwind led to substitution of a more satisfactory hydraulic winch.

Coast Guard pilots found the hoist completely satisfactory, but not the HNS, whose marginal performance was at times anemic. One pilot—alone in his helicopter and raising a 170-pound man from a boat—recalled that his desperate efforts to keep from dunking his passenger left his helicopter "straining every rivet and shaking like St. Vitus himself."[23]

The Coast Guard also saw to it that a D-ring was added to the Navy's standard life jacket for quick attachment to hoist cables. At the start of 1945, moreover, a sling harness was developed that could be thrown over a person floating in the water. The rescue harness was demonstrated off Manasquan, New Jersey, on October 3, 1944. Four men were retrieved, one at a time, from life rafts and landed aboard the deck of the Cobb.

The Coast Guard's training program was also successful. USCG personnel had built in a hangar at Floyd Bennett a large simulator that moved realistically in response to control inputs. This helicopter equivalent of the Link Trainer proved useful in helping fixed-wing pilots make the transition to rotary-wing flight. Another example of Coast Guard ingenuity was a moving platform devised for practicing simulated landing on ships. Christened the USS Mal de Mer when unveiled on April 16, 1944, this motorized training aid pitched

Sergei Sikorsky—son of Igor—helped perfect the powered rescue hoist from which he dangles in this 1944 demonstration. Lightweight skids have replaced this USCG HNS-1 helicopter's wheels to save weight. Courtesy UTC.

and rolled like the deck of a real vessel at sea.

By the end of 1944, the Coast Guard had sixty-seven rated helicopter pilots. With enough available for the time being, the pilot training program was shut down on March 7, 1945, although mechanic training continued. In addition to members of their own service, the USCG's busy instructors had trained Navy, British, and even civilian CAA and other personnel at Floyd Bennett Field.

On June 1, 1944, the Royal Helicopter Training Unit was established at Floyd Bennett to take over training of British personnel. It drew heavily from the pioneering Coast Guard program. On July 1, 1946, the U.S. Navy began training its own helicopter pilots and mechanics at the airport, although Erickson's group was no longer there to help. Newly commissioned Helicopter Development Squadron VX-3, whose instructors were graduates of the Coast Guard's helicopter program, took over the training facilities, as described above.

The previous May, Erickson and his growing organization had moved to Coast Guard Air Station Elizabeth City in North Carolina. The new facility offered more room and better flying conditions. Its proximity to the Outer Banks gave the isolated residents of those sparsely inhabited barrier islands access to air rescue services. On June 18, 1946, the USCG helicopter program officially became the Rotary Wing Development Project. By then, it had thirty-one rotorcraft including many S-51s. In 1949 it received its first large helicopters with the arrival of three silver-painted Piasecki HRP-1s. These tandem-rotor machines, the last ones off the HRP-1 assembly line, greatly increased Coast Guard air rescue capabilities. They could, and did, rescue many people at once some 90 miles out to sea.

This move came on the heels of the first Arctic helicopter rescue, a dramatic event that generated worldwide interest. A Royal Canadian Air Force Canso (PBY-5A) experiencing severe icing had gone down in Labrador's snowbound interior April 21, 1945. Two of the nine-man crew had been badly injured when the aircraft crashed into trees. The site was eventually located by air, and rescue attempts were made using ski-equipped Noorduyn Norseman bush planes. Bad weather hindered these efforts and one Norseman crashed while taking off from a frozen lake, adding two more to the number anxiously awaiting help.

A Coast Guard HNS-1 helicopter was disassembled and flown aboard a C-54 transport to Goose Bay, Labrador, where it was quickly reassembled and fueled. The next morning—the last day of April—it flew 150 miles in two hours to a rescue post, and from there the last 35 miles to the crash site, where it began retrieving the marooned men one by one. Its engine froze up during the bitterly cold night and the next day was spent defrosting it with a heater dropped by the RCAF. Successful removal of the last of the marooned airmen was accomplished on May 2. The HNS was then flown home, where it was christened the *Labrador Special*.

Not long after the move to Elizabeth City, a Coast Guard R-6 and R-4 participated in yet another northern rescue. These machines were transported to Newfoundland following the crash of a Sabena DC-4, which went down with forty-four people aboard in deep woods southwest of Gander. On September 26 and 27, they recovered the Belgian airliner's eighteen survivors. Like the previous success, this rescue gave a boost to the Coast Guard helicopter program and vertical flight in general.

Rescues of a more routine nature continued, of course. Early in 1947, the transverse stretcher of the HOS-1 was used for the first time in an actual medical emergency to transport a seventy-eight-year-old Outer Banks woman suffering from abdominal complications to a hospital at Norfolk, Virginia. In another instance, a critical stretcher case was transferred from Cape Hatteras to Elizabeth City on a very black night. The pilots had only the phosphorescent glow of the waves breaking on the beach as their guide. Many downed Navy fliers were also rescued, including one dramatic retrieval from Dismal Swamp.

On July 1, 1948, the Rotary Wing Development Project disbanded and was immediately recommissioned as the Rotary Wing Development Unit under the operational and administrative control of Coast Guard Headquarters. Personnel and equipment previously assigned to the RWDP were reassigned to the RWDU, which remained at Coast Guard Air Station Elizabeth City. Commander Erickson retained command, assisted by Lieutenant Graham as executive officer.

The operational mission of the RWDU was to help foster the development of better rotary-wing aircraft, not just to develop equipment and refine rescue techniques as the RWDP had done. Geared to helping the USCG fulfill its assigned patrol and rescue responsibilities, this ongoing program had already given rise to the development of successful flotation gear, winches, baskets, stretchers, and other lifesaving devices. In the future, it would also help define all-weather helicopters fully suited to the rigorous demands of patrol, rescue, and aerial interdiction.

Throughout the 1940s, the United States Coast Guard had played a significant role in the acceptance and development of vertical flight. It spearheaded the adaption of the

helicopter to maritime use and greatly increased its versatility as a rescue vehicle of unsurpassed capability. If there is an unsung champion of vertical flight, it is the U.S. Coast Guard.

U.S. MARINE CORPS

Although the last of America's military services to adopt the helicopter, the Marine Corps embraced vertical flight quickly and effectively. Lacking any helicopters before 1948, it performed the first helicopter missions in the Korean War, established the first helicopter transport squadron in the world, and introduced the Sikorsky S-55 into combat.

The story of Marine Corps rotary-wing flight begins in May 1932 when the USMC received one of three Pitcairn OP-1 autogiros procured for evaluation by the U.S. Navy a year earlier. The Marines took this rotorcraft to Nicaragua, where on June 28 it joined military exercises being conducted there. After testing it in a variety of roles, the Marine Corps—like the Navy itself—was insufficiently impressed with autogiros to pursue their adoption.

Fourteen years passed before this service again had anything to do with rotary-wing aviation, despite its obvious applicability to their mission of amphibious assault. The reasons were twofold: First, the USMC needed transport helicopters, which were slower to evolve. Second, this service is traditionally dependent on the Navy for aircraft, and the Navy was itself slow to adopt helicopters.

On June 18, 1946, General Alexander A. Vandegrift, commandant of the Marine Corps, officially established his service's helicopter program. Major Armand H. DeLalio, a wartime fighter pilot, became the first

First ordered in 1962, the Sikorsky HH-52A (S-62)
flew in the worst imaginable weather and saved
countless lives during three decades of faithful
USCG service. Courtesy NASM/SI.

Marine aviator to learn to fly helicopters when on August 8 he was assigned to rotary-wing flight training with recently formed Navy Squadron vx-3. As yet, the Marine Corps—the last of America's military services to establish a vertical-flight program—lacked a single helicopter.

The evolution of this program changed radically a month later when Lieutenant General Roy S. Geiger, commander of Fleet Marine Forces, Pacific, observed atomic bomb tests at Bikini atoll in the Marshall Islands. It was instantly clear to the general that the conventional method of landing Marine forces, used successfully in World War II, was imperiled by underwater atomic explosions such as he had just witnessed. An alternative was needed to clustering Navy troop and supply ships just offshore and shuttling troops by landing craft.

General Vandegrift convened a special board to study the problem. On December 16, 1946, this body presented its conclusion: Naval vessels had to remain farther offshore and be well dispersed. Since conventional landing craft, or small boats of any kind, had been rendered too slow and vulnerable, the board further recommended that helicopters be adopted as the conveyance to bring Marine troops ashore.

Of course, no helicopter in existence in 1946 could address this mission. Doubts among board members as to the feasibility of such operations were laid to rest, however, by personal assurances from Igor Sikorsky that machines of sufficient performance and payload would be available in the near future.

The idea had substantial appeal to Marine Corps planners, in large measure because helicopters could overfly exposed beaches to land on strategic high ground farther inland. Many U.S. servicemen had lost their lives get-

ting ashore and consolidating positions during landings at Guadalcanal, Tarawa, Iwo Jima, on the Normandy beachheads, and elsewhere during World War II. The prospect of eliminating such zones of vulnerability prompted Vandegrift to order implementation of an airborne assault helicopter program on December 19, 1946.

Following the training of sufficient pilots and mechanics by vx-3 at NAS Lakehurst, the first Marine Corps helicopter squadron was commissioned December 1, 1947, at Quantico, Virginia. Designated HMX-1, this experimental squadron took delivery of its first two Sikorsky HO3S-1 helicopters January 9, 1948. Four more HO3Ss would arrive before the end of the year. The unit would also receive its first Bell HTL-2 on August 9 and its first Piasecki HRP-1 ten days later. Although of marginal performance by present-day standards, the nine large Piaseckis it eventually received at last made it possible for Marine planners to act out and evaluate their vision of carrier-to-shore aerial troop transport.

Colonel Edward C. Dyer commanded HMX-1 in key USMC training exercises at Quantico during the spring of 1949. Ably assisting him as operations officer was Lieutenant Colonel Keith McKutcheon. Under their leadership, the pioneering USMC unit evaluated a range of helicopter missions that included transporting communications equipment and laying wire, shuttling personnel and supplies, and performing artillery spotting and medical evacuation from the huge military reservation's back country to the base hospital.

It was evident to all concerned that the Piasecki HRP-1 helicopter provided tactical capabilities the Marines had never had before. To show off its newfound aerial capabilities, the service's leaders decided to stage an all-out demonstration. It would be an event that would forever alter military doctrine world-wide.

On May 2, 1949, as President Harry Truman, Secretary of Defense Louis A. Johnson, members of Congress, and high-ranking Pentagon officials looked on, HMX-1's eight HRP-1s transported forty-two fully equipped troops, two 75 mm howitzers and their crews, ammunition, and supplies from a simulated aircraft carrier deck at Quantico's air station ten miles distant to a mock beach landing zone before observation stands. Protected by F4U Corsair fighter planes making simulated strafing runs, the dark blue, banana-shaped Piaseckis swept in at low level behind a smoke screen. Each HRP-1 deposited its load and was back in the air within thirty seconds, heading back to the "carrier" for additional loads.

Under the protective umbrella of fighter-bomber cover, the Marines on the beach began an aggressive assault with howitzers and other weapons. Within fifteen minutes, the eight HRP-1s were back with more troops, a mobile combat control center, and medics who sprang into action. "Wounded" soldiers were treated and quickly loaded aboard the empty helicopters for a speedy return to the presumed medical facilities of the imaginary carrier.

To say that those witnessing the display were profoundly impressed is an understatement. Too many lives had been lost during Allied landings in World War II for this novel manner of bypassing traditional beach defenses to go unappreciated. The USMC concept of vertical envelopment—upon which the Army would later base its similar doctrine of airmobility—had been convincingly demonstrated.

The fundamental mission of HMX-1 was in fact to develop "vertical assault," a catchier name for the new Marine Corps doctrine that soon caught on. With the feasibility of ship-to-shore troop transport now established, military leaders coined the term "triphibious" to describe operations combining ships, helicopters, and troops. Operation Packard II, the first triphibious helicopter operation performed with a real aircraft carrier, took place June 6, 1949. During this exercise, HMX-1's eight HRP-1s flew from the USS *Paulau* to mock combat zones near New River, North Carolina.

Many problems remained to be resolved. For one thing, the USMC's small aircraft carriers—wartime "baby flattop" escort carriers discarded by the Navy—had barely enough space for one company of soldiers per vessel, with no room for supporting artillery, ammunition, or supplies. Like the HRP-1 itself, they were unsuitable for combat duty.

The Marines needed helicopters that could fly faster than the HRP-1 and carry more than eight or ten fully equipped soldiers at a time. The rapidly advancing state-of-the-art in vertical flight would soon satisfy this requirement. As a result, although HRP-1s continued to serve the Navy, Coast Guard, and Marine Corps into the mid-1950s, their days were numbered. The finest hour of this significant early rotorcraft—the world's first production transport helicopter—had in fact been the displays at Quantico and off the *Paulau*. Never again would so many HRP-1s fly at one time.

The personnel of HMX-1 also used their HRP-1s to supplement crash boat operations in the Potomac River near Quantico. These duties—which closely paralleled USN and USCG helicopter use—gave squadron personnel valuable experience with hoists, slings, aerial litters, and other rescue equipment developed by the Coast Guard. But the pri-

(Top) Eight Marine Corps HRP-1s of the HMX-1 squadron take to the air in a profoundly influential May 1949 demonstration of "vertical assault" that would forever alter military tactics. Courtesy Ren Pierpoint.

(Bottom) The HMX-1 "flying bananas" demonstrate the ability of helicopters to overfly heavily defended beaches and land troops and equipment inland. Courtesy John Schneider.

mary mission of the pioneering USMC helicopter unit remained vertical assault.

A plan to parachute Marines in ahead of the helicopters to neutralize ground defenses had to be scrapped because the Key West Accord allowed paratroop operations only from U.S. Air Force aircraft. Consequently, Marine Corps leaders decreed that helicopter assaults would be employed only against lightly held enemy positions. Furthermore, they would use joint USMC and USN air cover. To further minimize losses, Marine helicopter pilots would be trained to come in low and fast to avoid ground fire. Formal statement of this new type of operation appeared in November 1949 with publication by the Marine Corps Schools at Quantico of document PHIB-31, *Amphibious Operations: Employment of Helicopters (Tentative)*.

Operation Packard II had been a success: the Marine Corps' vertical-assault philosophy—its aviation role for many decades to come—had largely been defined. But the historical significance of this nearly forgotten military demonstration far outstrips the shaping of USMC tactics, for Packard II had influenced the much larger U.S. Army. That service—soon to emerge as America's largest user of helicopters—wholeheartedly embraced the Marine Corps' new doctrine. Adapted and refined over the coming years, notably by the French in Algeria, this vertical-envelopment philosophy would underlie U.S. Army helicopter tactics during the Vietnam War, and those of other armies worldwide.

In September 1948, meantime, HMX-1 dispatched a Sikorsky HO3S-1 and a Bell HTL-2 to Camp Lejeune, North Carolina, to train with Marine Division infantry and tanks. These helicopters accompanied them on maneuvers with the Atlantic Fleet beginning in February 1949. That summer, HMX-1 sent an HO3S-1 to Argentina with a Marine landing team assigned to practice cold-weather operations. The most far-flung Marine helicopters, however, were two HO3S-1s assigned to rescue duties at the USMC Air Facility in Tsingtao, China, in the fall of 1948.

On June 3, 1949, the Marine Corps Board recommended that two transport helicopter squadrons be created with twelve helicopters each. The office of the commandant of the USMC continued its efforts to obtain large troop-carrying helicopters. Specifications laid down on June 28, 1950, for a twenty-man assault transport helicopter subsequently became Operation Requirement No. AO-17501. It gave rise to the Sikorsky HR2S-1 (S-56) of late 1953, a giant twin-engine machine capable of carrying thirty-six fully equipped soldiers. A month after the outbreak of war in Korea, the Marine Corps accelerated procurement of Sikorsky HO4S helicopters (company model S-55) under the designation HRS-1 as an interim USMC troop and supply transport helicopter.

When North Korean forces crossed the 38th parallel into the Republic of Korea on June 25, 1950, American troops stationed in that country suddenly found themselves at war. Less than two weeks later, the First Provisional Marine Brigade was ordered to Korea. This force consisted of the 5th Marines, a reinforced infantry regiment, and Marine Aircraft Group 33. The air group, in turn, consisted of three fighter-bomber squadrons and one observation squadron designated VMO-6.

Before shipping out, VMO-6 was augmented with a helicopter detachment consisting of four HO3S helicopters. On August 3, a day after landing at Pusan, one of these machines performed an observation flight over the front

A Marine Corps HO3S-1 performs a medical evacuation early in the Korean War. The arrival of Bell
and Hiller light helicopters relieved these larger
machines for other duties. Courtesy UTC.

lines. This was the first helicopter operation of the Korean War.

On January 15, 1951, HMR-161—history's first helicopter transport squadron—was commissioned at El Toro, California. Following accelerated training, this unit was deployed to Korea on July 1. Its HRS-1s, the first of any service to be used there, arrived early in September amid heavy fighting in the country's mountainous eastern "Punchbowl" sector.

Four more transport squadrons were commissioned before year's end: HMR-261 on April 5, HMR-162 on June 30, HMR-262 on September 1, and HMR-163 on November 15. On July 17, meanwhile, the commandant of the Marine Corps published a concept of future amphibious operations calling for landing and supporting the assault elements of a Marine division. He urged the Navy to undertake a parallel ship-building program in support of the HR2S-1 helicopter then being developed. The chief of naval operations approved this plan August 13.

HRS-1s in Korea proved a tremendous boon to the hard-pressed Marines. One remarkable show of support was Operation Switch on November 11, 1951. A dozen HMR-161 helicopters carried 950 fresh troops of the 2nd Battalion, 5th Marines to Hill 884 to relieve 952 battle-weary members of the 2nd Battalion, 1st Marines. In 262 flights totaling less than a hundred flight hours, the hard-working HRSs completed the exchange in one day.

By now, Marine pilots were also flying Bell HTLs, a type previously used for training. The Army's success using this light helicopter for medical evacuation prompted the Marines to do the same, freeing their larger helicopters for other duties.

Yet another helicopter was used in Korea by the Marines, the Sikorsky HO5S, which entered service in 1952. A military version of the S-52, this type served with VMO-6 although it was not as successful as the smaller HTL.

On January 11, 1952, the office of the commandant of the Marine Corps issued Marine Aviation Plan 1-52, which provided a structure for expansion of the USMC helicopter program. Three Marine Air Groups were approved to encompass existing and future transport helicopter squadrons: HMR-161, HMR-162, and HMR-163 would together form MAG (HR)-16; HMR-261, HMR-262, and a third squadron yet to be created would be MAG (HR)-26; and three entirely new squadrons would become MAG (HR)-36. The new squadrons and the groups themselves would all be commissioned before the end of the year.

Early the following year, moreover, the Marine helicopter program saw twelve CVE-55 and four CVE-105 escort carriers earmarked for extensive conversion. Designated LPHs, these vessels carried HRS and HR2S assault transport helicopters around the world. By the end of the Korean War, therefore, helicopters had become central to the operational and logistical effectiveness of the U.S. Marine Corps.

Helicopters were unarmed in Korea. Marine Corps aviators who were fired upon naturally wished they could shoot back effectively from the air. Seen from helicopters, moreover, enemy tanks and armored vehicles looked like sitting ducks. Like their counterparts in other U.S. and foreign armed services, therefore, they eagerly anticipated the arming of helicopters.

This desire led one stateside Marine Corps test unit to undertake a pioneering helicopter-armament evaluation at Quantico early in 1951. With the cooperation of Bell

Armed with automatic weapons and equipped
with an inflatable rubber raft (foreground), a
Marine reconnaissance team prepares to board a
hoist-equipped HRS-1 for a mission. Courtesy UTC.

Aircraft, a bazooka was lashed to an H-13 and fired several times to check the safety of the installation. The first shot, made from hovering flight, was a bull's-eye.

A resourceful Bell pilot/engineer had borrowed the bazooka with verbal permission but no paperwork from a display near the Pentagon office of the secretary of the Navy. In those prescreening days, he had wrapped it and brought it with him aboard an airliner. At Quantico, he overcame a scarcity of shells—live ammunition having been diverted to Korea—by offering a half case of scotch for each round the Marines could scrounge up.

At high levels, this makeshift effort was viewed as an unauthorized escapade, dashing all hopes for armed USMC helicopters in Korea. Barred outright from performing similar experiments by the Key West Accord, the Army had watched from the sidelines with interest. However, military airpower proponents in all branches of the service knew it was just a matter of time until America's ground forces received the lethal rotorcraft they coveted. The Army and Marines would achieve this goal in the Vietnam War, an exhaustively documented conflict that lies beyond the scope of this appendix.

THE ALGERIAN WAR (1956–60)

In the decade preceding U.S. involvement in Vietnam, the French waged a losing campaign to retain possession of Algeria. Observed worldwide, that conflict further shaped the military helicopter and its employment.

The Korean War demonstrated that helicopters were an intrinsic part of modern warfare. To military strategists, however, Korea raised as many questions as it answered. Should troop and transport helicopters be armed? Or should they be escorted by fixed-wing fighters, or perhaps rotary-wing gunships? What size should helicopters be to best perform their missions, and what configuration and features should they have? What range should they have and how high should they be able to hover? Was blind flying capability for all-weather availability required?

By the mid-1950s, four basic categories of military rotorcraft had emerged: light training and observation helicopters, intermediate-size utility types, transports, and heavy lifters. U.S. military inventories included large numbers of helicopters from at least the first three of these categories, yet it was all too clear that planners in every service did not yet know how best to use their rotorcraft. Everything from proper tactics, to the desirability of specific features, to combat serviceability requirements was clouded by uncertainty. And what should be specified for future military helicopter development? Only a war, it seemed, could provide definitive answers.

The Korean War had ended in 1953, too early in the development of helicopter technology to provide answers to these questions. Concurrent British fighting in Malaya, which continued after the Korean cease fire, shed little additional light on requirements. Therefore, it fell to Algeria's hard-fought campaign in the late 1950s to win its freedom from France—a war involving American rotorcraft but not U.S. forces—to truly provide hard answers. Hugely significant in the annals of rotary-wing flight, this conflict helped define a new generation of transport and gunship helicopters, and the tactics for their use.

In May 1954, Vietnam had wrested its freedom from French forces at Dien Bien Phu. This disaster left France determined not to lose Algeria, the last sizable piece of its shrink-

Combat troops board a French Army H-21 on a
hillside in East Algeria during the late 1950s.
Courtesy John Schneider.

ing empire. When Algerian freedom fighters escalated their guerrilla warfare against French occupation in the mid-1950s, one French government response was to place heavy orders for American military helicopters. The first of these machines entered combat in 1956. Within three years, more than a hundred Vertol H-21s,[24] a comparable number of Sikorsky H-34s, several hundred French and American light utility helicopters, and a variety of fixed-wing aircraft were flying in the Algerian desert.

Shaping this military involvement was internal debate at the highest levels of French government as to which of its armed forces, the Army or the Air Force, should control air assets used in support of ground operations. It was the same issue America's policy makers wrestled with both during and after the formulation of the Key West Accord of 1948. Perhaps reflecting a stalemate, Algeria was divided into two sectors. France's H-34s would serve with the French Air Force (FAF) in the west, whereas its H-21s would join the French Army (FA) in the east.

The results overwhelmingly affirmed the desirability of having ground forces directly command their aviation support. The difference in the two sectors was striking: in the east the helicopters responded almost instantaneously to the evolving battlefield situation; in the west, FA ground commanders had to request helicopter support from FAF command personnel. The latter system introduced additional levels of communication that slowed and garbled the transmission of ground-support requirements, and it shifted the decision-making process to distant personnel unacquainted with real-time battlefield requirements.

With the approval of the French Supreme Command, Vertol's Ren Pierpoint—who had spent nine months flying and helping the French in Algeria—quantified and shared these dramatic findings in presentations he made at more than eighty U.S. and NATO military bases during 1959 and 1960. So persuasive was the evidence he presented that the U.S. Army at last gained full control over all its aerial close-support assets before the Algerian War ended in 1960.

As described earlier in this volume, the benefits of direct aircraft control by ground forces—one of World War II's clearest lessons—had been ignored in the United States for political reasons. Interservice wrangling over missions and responsibilities had denied the U.S. Army its transport helicopters until the early 1950s, and continued to deny it armed helicopters. Just in time for Vietnam, therefore, the Algerian experience cleared the way for the world's largest helicopter operator to control both these categories of rotorcraft.

The Algerian War did not usher new technical features into being. Instead, that conflict hastened the widespread adoption of existing features and capabilities. It showed that armor protection is essential for helicopter crews, that loading doors are needed in both sides of the fuselage, and that a rear loading ramp would be valuable. It also confirmed that helicopter assault troops require specialized training, and that reserve engine power can significantly reduce combat losses. Perhaps most significant, Algeria called for the arming of helicopters by demonstrating the value of suppressive firepower capability during troop landings.

Algeria was one factor that spelled an end to the early phase of military helicopter use worldwide. The other was the advent of turbine power, which transformed the helicopter into a far more capable machine. The lighter weight, greater reliability, and higher power output of turboshaft engines brought about a quantum jump in performance. As a result, the helicopters of the 1960s would be profoundly different from those of the 1950s.

America's subsequent involvement in Vietnam—made memorable by the U.S. Army's almost total reliance on observation, utility, and attack helicopters—would offer convincing proof that rotary-wing technology had come of age. With turbine power and Vietnam, the helicopter—heretofore primarily a lifesaving machine—gained the added capability to efficiently take human life—a long-anticipated transformation that greatly saddened pioneer Igor Sikorsky in his later years.

Appendix B / Early Commercial Helicopter Use

No history of the U.S. helicopter industry would be complete without an examination of early civil helicopter use. Although military requirements have largely shaped the helicopter, the industry's pioneers were inspired by a shared vision of success in the commercial arena.

On August 29, 1944, a Model A-1 helicopter made by the Aeronautical Products Corporation performed what was hailed as the first commercial helicopter operation in the United States. Taking off from an outlying warehouse, this two-seat aircraft delivered a rush order to Filene's Department Store in downtown Boston in just eight minutes.

Aeronautical Products of Detroit was one of an estimated three hundred U.S. companies attempting to develop personal helicopters during or just after World War II. With the race on, the firm resorted to a publicity stunt to demonstrate the possibilities of helicopter use by American businesses. It used the occasion as a forum to announce that it would sell the A-1 for $2,500—the cost of a luxury automobile in the postwar era.

But proclaiming this event a commercial use of helicopters was premature. The A-1, civil registration NX-1270, was a prototype rather than a production vehicle. Licensed by the Civil Aeronautics Authority in the experimental category, it could not legally engage in true commercial operations.

Filene's was equally enthusiastic about helicopters. With shopping malls yet to blight the suburban landscape, and few branch stores in existence, many area residents lived beyond convenient shopping range. As a result, Boston's famous store looked to helicopters as a means to speedily deliver items ordered by telephone. It also hoped privately owned helicopters would bring affluent shoppers from country estates too far away for convenient shopping by car. Helicopters, in short, promised increased sales by bringing goods to more people and more people to the goods.

This two-way concept had evolved the previous year as an Oklahoma department store's promotional tie-in to a local forum on civil aviation in the postwar era. When the popular National Clinic on Domestic Aviation Planning convened in Oklahoma City on November 6, 1943, Kerr's Department Store unveiled its vision of futuristic helicopter shopping.

Much to Kerr's amazement, enthusiasm for the notion quickly spread beyond the city to elicit nationwide interest. In a society then infatuated with the concept of personal flying machines, this retailer's plan would find itself written into urban planning models in cities from coast to coast.

The today-forgotten Aeronautical Products A-1
performed what was incorrectly hailed as the first
U.S. commercial helicopter operation in the summer of 1944. Courtesy NASM/SI.

Filene's, located in the populous Northeast, immediately embraced the Kerr blueprint. Before the end of 1943, it had applied to the Civil Aeronautics Board for a helicopter delivery route. It staged the headline-generating promotion described above the following year, although the war prevented it from acquiring helicopters. Filene's persevered, however, and on January 5, 1947, initiated the world's first helicopter retail parcel delivery service using one of the first Bell Model 47s.

G. Fox & Company, a leading Connecticut retail chain, inaugurated store-to-customer air delivery using Sikorskys early in 1947. Promoting the 100th anniversary of its founding, this store used no less than four s-51s to make deliveries to sixty-six communities.

Bunce Department Store of Middleton, Connecticut, was yet another retailer to undertake store-to-door deliveries. Beginning March 18, 1947, a Sikorsky s-51 piloted by Colonel John J. Sanduski—a noted flier who had performed helicopter rescues during World War II—landed at front doors or in back yards to deliver purchases to customers throughout the county.

As late as October 1952, McCreery's Department Store in New York City staged a helicopter fashion exhibition showing what the well-dressed suburbanite would wear for "copter hops" into the city for shopping, dinner, and perhaps a Broadway show. Behind the mannequins in its Fifth Avenue window, McCreery's displayed a full-scale mockup of a Doman lz-5 Air Taxi helicopter. "In this display," its publicity release stated, "Doman Helicopters, Incorporated, reveals to the fashion world and to the general public the helicopter whose functional beauty of design complements fashions for air travel. Helicopter shopping is only one of the limit-less possibilities envisioned by farseeing enthusiasts."[1]

By the start of the new decade, however, prospects for personal helicopter ownership had diminished nationwide. It was clear in the 1950s that working helicopters were successful only where they demonstrated a clear economic advantage over fixed-wing aviation and ground-based alternatives. Because of their high purchase and operating costs, helicopters generally cannot compete except where their vertical flight ability justifies their employment. They cannot be used interchangeably with airplanes, which combine lower operating costs with higher performance.

These economic constraints continue to limit the use of commercial helicopters, keeping the size of the world fleet small. Each new civil market opened over the years has represented a hard-won victory for the vertical-flight industry. It is hardly surprising that America today chooses not to remember the heady days of 1945 when it confidently expected to see helicopters used as personal conveyances and aerial delivery vans.

The first role working helicopters would assume was agricultural. With no demand to speak of for privately owned machines, Bell scrambled to develop spray bars, hoppers, and other agricultural accessories. Hiller did likewise when its Model 360 (uh-12) reached market in the late 1940s. In contrast, Sikorsky was primarily a military contractor. Although it sold civil versions of its military machines, it did not need to court the agricultural market to survive. Its otherwise excellent s-51 was too heavy and expensive for such use in any event.

Developing dusting and spraying equipment alone did not ensure economic survival.

An entirely new market had to be created. This meant identifying potential users of agricultural helicopters, as well as operators willing to serve them. Very often it was a case of convincing people heretofore perfectly happy without "ag helicopters" that they needed them enough to invest in their purchase. A strong plus in this effort was that rotor downwash—almost 2 million cubic feet of air per minute for the Bell and Hiller machines—ensured better coverage during dusting or spraying than fixed-wing aircraft could provide, since the swirling air coated the bottoms of leaves as well as the tops.

Hiller's proximity to California's bountiful Central Valley—source of much of the nation's farm produce—would be an advantage. But with a more than two-year head start, Bell had already made strong inroads in the West. Its first helicopter dealership was Central Aircraft of Yakima, Washington, a company formed early in 1947 to support pioneering Northwest helicopter operators like Bob Johnson of Missoula, Montana, and Walla Copters of Walla Walla, Washington. Before the end of the year, Central expanded into California with a branch office in San Francisco. Bell was already operating right in Hiller's backyard, therefore, when that latter company entered production.

One noteworthy agricultural helicopter user was the National Cranberry Association, a cooperative of nearly one thousand cranberry growers. The NCA took delivery of the first agricultural Model 47, the *Ocean Sprayer*, early in 1947. This helicopter worked a dramatic improvement in cranberry productivity by reducing the need to walk through the bogs. Its success led to widespread helicopter use in cranberry bogs in Massachusetts, New Jersey, Wisconsin, Oregon, and Washington.

Aside from fertilizing and insect control, helicopters proved valuable in frost damage prevention. Rotor downwash could be used to dispel cold ground-hugging air, raising ambient temperatures by as much as ten degrees. Growers of cherries, dates, and other fruits also found downwash valuable for drying rain-soaked fruit to prevent spoilage from splitting or fermentation, two frequent causes of crop loss.

Commercial helicopter operations were forming across the country, but their number—as well as the number of helicopters they purchased—was surprisingly small. Metropolitan Aviation Corporation at Westchester County Airport took delivery of its first two helicopters in April 1947; it operated these machines from Manhattan's Midtown Skyport, a seaplane base at 23rd Street on the East River. Aerial photography, on-the-spot broadcasting, charter work, and crop dusting in outlying areas—a use threatened by urban sprawl—were the services it offered. Elsewhere in New York State, International Helicopter Transport Company incorporated in Buffalo at the end of 1947, right in Bell's backyard, to engage in crop dusting, photography, and the transportation of passengers into the Canadian wilderness.

South America was another early helicopter market. In June 1947, a C-54 of Flota Aérea Mercante Argentina delivered to Trabajos Aéreos y Representaciones SA (TAYR) of Buenos Aires the first three of eleven agricultural Model 47s. These machines had been rushed from the United States to spray against hordes of locusts. So impressed was the Argentine airline that TAYR became Bell's South American distributor. It would later become a Hiller representative.

The agricultural market bought critically needed time for light helicopter builders until

Aerial agricultural use—the first viable market for commercial helicopters—is represented by this Hiller 360 spraying crops circa 1950. Courtesy Hiller.

other commercial markets could emerge. These included power-line and other patrols, geological survey, aerial photography, and—in a national experiment—helicopter air mail and passenger services.

Of course, plenty of secondary uses for helicopters arose that could not of themselves sustain the industry. Western New York Water Company acquired a Bell 47B on floats to take water samples from Lake Erie early in 1947. The New York Port Authority bought a float-equipped Hiller 360 in 1950 for shuttling people and equipment between terminals, docks, and other facilities. The huge half-million-acre Zaccaweista Ranch in Texas even purchased a Bell in 1952 for cattle drives; this machine reportedly replaced "fifteen to twenty cowboys on good horses."[2]

Some commercial uses were downright frivolous, like a 1953 cellophane tape promotion by the Permacel Tape Corporation. A $10,000 sapphire, diamond, and pearl necklace was taped to the skid gear of a Bell helicopter, which then hovered high above Niagara Falls as another Bell took dramatic photographs demonstrating the holding power of the product. Advertisements in newspapers and magazines and on television kept helicopters before the public, but this high-profile use was misleading, for it suggested that helicopters were more numerous than they in fact were. Such use also served to hide the less glamorous agricultural use that accounted for the bulk of commercial helicopter sales.

Although that use remained the struggling industry's bread and butter, Central Aircraft of Yakima branched out into conducting snow surveys on the eastern flanks of Washington's rugged Cascade Mountains. With rubber pontoons, the helicopter landed at different levels and locations to determine the average snow-pack depth. From this data, geological engineers estimated the amount of spring runoff available for irrigation and other uses. Central's helicopter easily performed this survey in a week, several days less than it had previously taken a dozen men on skis and their support vehicles.

Central and other pioneering operators—notably Helicopter Air Service in the Chicago area—also initiated power-line patrols during 1947. Here was another valuable use of helicopters in rural and mountainous regions. Previously conducted on foot, on horseback, or even by light aircraft, such patrols by helicopter more than paid for themselves through the time and money they saved state governments and regional utilities.

In the fall of 1947, Armstrong-Flint Helicopters of Burbank won a $10,000 contract from the California Department of Water and Power for a four-month power-line patrol test in the rugged High Sierra. This winter test aimed specifically at determining the helicopter's value in locating breaks in power transmission caused by heavy snow, ice, and the trees they felled.

The success of this experiment led Pacific Gas & Electric, the giant San Francisco–based utility, to place contracts with Armstrong-Flint (now relocated to San Fernando) and Helicopter Services of California (Central Aircraft's San Francisco branch) for regular helicopter patrol. With one of the most far-flung hydroelectric systems in existence, connecting fifty-five power plants in the mountains through thousands of miles of power lines to cities and farms in forty-six counties, PG&E would lead the nation's utilities in helicopter use. It would later purchase and operate Hiller helicopters of its own for patrol, snow survey, and other purposes.

Appendix B. Early Commercial Helicopter Use 431

The value of vertical flight is evident in this view of a Bell 47G supporting pipeline construction in mountainous terrain. Courtesy Bell.

Helicopter schools represented another emerging market sector. The first generation of civil helicopter pilots and mechanics generally received their training from the Army Air Forces or the Coast Guard. Shortly after World War II, however, it became evident that this pool of skilled personnel was far too small to support the expected huge public demand for personal helicopters. In fact, this lack loomed as a major crisis threatening to undermine the realization of that cultural dream. After all, private purchasers would need instructors to teach them how to fly their personal helicopters, and service stations would need mechanics to fix these "aerial automobiles."

The schools that sprang up to meet this demand were generally fixed-base operators struggling to provide other helicopter services.[3] Like the civil helicopter manufacturers themselves, they would soon be forced to shift away from training to other commercial uses in order to survive.

Central Aircraft at Yakima was only the fourth civil helicopter school in the United States. The first was Helicopter Air Transport at Camden Airport, New Jersey. Just across the Delaware River from Philadelphia, HAT incorporated in Pennsylvania at the start of 1946 and drew much of its staff from the Delaware Valley's diverse aviation industry. Frank T. Cashman was president and Lou Leavitt was operations manager. A former AAF major whose last military assignment was as chief helicopter instructor at Wright Field, Cashman had set a nonstop helicopter distance record for a flight from Dayton to Boston. Leavitt, of course, was well known in the area as Kellett and Platt-LePage's former test pilot.

HAT's primary helicopter was the Sikorsky s-51, a revised and greatly improved civil version of the wartime AAF's troubled R-5. The first example, fitted with dual controls for training, arrived during August 1946. Overlooked by historians, this machine was significant as the first helicopter to be sold commercially. This honor thus went to Sikorsky even though Bell had received the world's first type certificate for civil helicopter production (Bell's first production machines had gone to the military). Two more s-51s and six two-seat Bell Model 47s followed in the ensuing months.

HAT's fleet also included the Platt-LePage XR-1A. Not flown by the school, this unsuccessful prototype was instead used for promotion. When HAT hosted the Third Annual Forum of the American Helicopter Society in March 1947, for example, the XR-1A served as the official backdrop to photographs taken of attendees. Furthermore, HAT actively publicized the fact that its home base, Camden Airport, had before World War II been the site of the first regularly scheduled commercial rotary-wing aviation in the United States.

HAT's efforts to promote the Delaware Valley as the cradle of U.S. rotary-wing flight—which conveniently ignored the success of Igor Sikorsky in southern New England—were entirely self-serving. Portraying itself as heir to the region's aviation heritage, America's first helicopter school lent itself badly needed credibility as it began operations in the latter part of 1946.

The school's rigorous training curriculum closely resembled the one Cashman had known at Wright Field, and a minimum of 500 fixed-wing flight hours was required of all students. Early on, following an official inspection by representatives of the French Air Ministry, HAT received a key contract to train French helicopter pilots, the first of whom—Jacques Guignard—entered training at the start of 1947.

HAT quickly established itself as America's helicopter training center for international students. By the spring of 1947 it also had students from Argentina, Peru, Ecuador, Canada, and Czechoslovakia. Although instruction was its primary reason for being, it also provided aerial application and a variety of other commercial services. HAT flew the oil industry's first geological surveys in Louisiana with a gravitometer-equipped 47B; it delivered parcels in New England under contract to Filene's Department Store (as described above); and it even helped the New Jersey state police hunt fugitives. Without success, it also petitioned the Civil Aeronautics Board for permission to serve helicopter air mail routes locally and in the Chicago area.

Success seemed certain for HAT, the first, grandest, and most publicized of America's pioneering helicopter schools. In many ways, it carried the standard for the entire civil helicopter industry. It thus came as a shock to the supporters of rotary-wing aviation when chronic undisclosed financial woes forced Helicopter Air Transport to file for bankruptcy October 21, 1947. Amid desperate efforts to reorganize, HAT went out of business when a French student wrecked one of its S-51s in November 1947.

Ironically, HAT's failure stemmed in large part from its selection of Sikorsky S-51s for training. The five-seat military machines were simply too costly for civil use. Other schools that wisely chose the Bell Model 47 were better able to survive, although they too found helicopter instruction at best a marginal operation.

New England Helicopter Service became very busy in the fall of 1947 when veterans became eligible for government benefits under the GI Bill of Rights. In November 1947 alone, the company's Bell 47B flew 123 hours by starting at 7:30 A.M. and flying continuously until sunset, stopping only for refueling every two and a half hours. Students were scheduled back to back, with inspection and adjustment of the helicopter performed in the evening to avoid downtime. That such heavy utilization was necessary indicates how narrow the profit margin was even with the diminutive, two-seat Bell. Still, it sufficed to get a new industry on its feet.

At Niagara Falls, Bell Aircraft helped this process along by opening its own flight and mechanics school in the summer of 1946. The postwar aviation bust, which would dispel hopes for personal helicopter use, was still a year away and hopes ran high at the company. "Already many practical uses for the helicopter have been developed," Larry Bell stated at the school's inauguration. "As soon as they are put into full production, there will be an immediate demand for pilots to fly them. Therefore, it is necessary to see that pilot training parallels helicopter construction."[4]

Training military personnel was not new to the industry, but running a civil training school was. Bell Aircraft's willingness to subsidize this activity was just one of several efforts it made to foster the emerging industry. On May 13, 1949, for example, it formed the California-based Bell Aircraft Supply Corporation (BASCO) with divisions in Burbank, California, and Lafayette, Louisiana. The former provided increased customer support to the West Coast, which led the United States in commercial helicopter use. The latter was created specifically to conduct geophysical and seismic field surveys in Louisiana and Texas, although it extended into Arizona before the end of the year.

Formed in early 1946, Helicopter Air Transport
was the world's first commercial helicopter operator. Its reliance on Sikorsky s-51s—a military
type too costly to operate for commercial success—
forced HAT out of business late the following year.
Courtesy NASM/SI.

The formation of the Oil Exploration Division at Lafayette reflected Bell's market analysis showing the petroleum industry to be a large potential user of helicopters. Instead of waiting for this market to emerge by itself, BASCO set up shop and made its services available to the nation's oil producers for geophysical and seismic surveys, shuttling people to and from offshore oil rigs, and other time-saving uses.

Operating its own products for direct commercial gain was difficult for Bell, which worried about possible antitrust actions and in any event had its hands full building helicopters. It therefore planned from the outset to spin off this successful commercial venture as soon as a suitable operator could be found. When several enterprising oilmen approached with an offer, Bell accepted. It even provided the new company with substantial start-up help.

The result was Petroleum Bell Helicopters, later renamed Petroleum Helicopters, Inc., to accommodate the later acquisition of Sikorsky S-55s and other non-Bell types. One of the great rotary-wing success stories, PHI on the tenth anniversary of its founding by Bell was one of the largest rotary-wing operators in the world. By early 1959 it had forty-five helicopters (two-thirds of which were Bells), sixty pilots, and eighty mechanics; it operated from Alaska to Bolivia; and every month it flew nearly 17,000 passengers the equivalent of six times around the world.

No other manufacturer would go to such lengths to foster a new industry as Bell, which even created the Erie Insurance Company in January 1950 to address the lack of helicopter hull insurance and underwriting services. Not all of these efforts would be successful, as Bell found out when it established a uranium-hunting subsidiary called the Bell Exploration and Development Corporation in 1955. With offices in Fort Worth and Glendale, it employed Model 47Js equipped with scintillometers and other gear to find deposits. Its helicopters also had portable diamond-tipped drills on their landing skids to facilitate taking samples.

The subsidiary had been created to expand an aerial prospecting market dating back to the summer of 1946, when Bell and Canadian geophysicist Hans T. Lundberg teamed up for mineral-finding trials in Canada and Alaska with a preproduction Bell helicopter fitted with a magnetometer. The success of this expedition led to the 1947 sale of two 47s to Lundberg-Ryan Air Explorations, which conducted surveys in Canada, the United States, Mexico, and Venezuela.

If helicopters made good mounts for exotic sensing equipment, they also made excellent platforms for aerial photography. A key early sale in this regard was to the Gannett publishing chain, which owned twenty-one newspapers across the country. Frank Gannett reportedly purchased his company's first helicopter when a friend dropped in for breakfast at the publisher's Rochester, New York, home one day in August 1946. The friend happened to be aviation tycoon Larry Bell, who arrived by chauffeured helicopter at Gannett's front porch.

Gannett took delivery of his first machine the following June and immediately put it to work. So dramatic were the aerial photographs taken from this machine, and so great the public's fascination with them, that Gannett newspapers began pointing out helicopter photography—its own and from other sources—to its readers with a little helicopter silhouette in the corner of the photograph. The famous view of Howard Hughes briefly

The oil industry has traditionally been a major user
of commercial helicopters. This early 1950s photograph shows workers being picked up by a Sikorsky s-55 of Petroleum Helicopters, Inc. Courtesy
NASM/SI.

raising his mammoth *Spruce Goose* off the coastal waters of southern California is just one example of helicopter photojournalism of the period.

Other newspapers were quick to follow Gannett's lead. The *New York Journal American*, one of the city's largest papers, bought a Bell 47B in the spring of 1947 for use by its news bureau. This machine had a radio that allowed reporters to dictate copy while hovering above news stories in the making.

The broadcast media were likewise quick to realize the benefits of vertical flight. Early in 1948, Chicago radio station WMAQ put a radio-equipped helicopter to work providing motorists with rush hour traffic updates every quarter hour, the first such service in history. With the purchase of a Hiller 12-B in February 1954, Seattle's KING-5 became the first television station in the nation to operate its own news helicopter.

If helicopters gave newspaper readers new views of their world, it was not long before they also thrilled movie audiences. As camera platforms, these aircraft revolutionized motion picture photography, picking up where hydraulic camera booms left off with dynamic pans and soaring sweeps. Three men pioneered Hollywood's successful adoption of helicopter photography: former Warner Brothers publicity writer Robert William, veteran cinematographer Paul Ivano, and California helicopter operator Knute Flint.

Movie photography with hand-held cameras had already been performed from helicopters with the standard 16-mm Eymo newsreel camera. Hollywood's large Mitchell feature-film camera, however, had yet to be carried aloft for professional filming. Working by trial and error, these three men devised a way to mount this bulky camera to the right side of an Armstrong-Flint Bell 47B, the door of which had been removed. A tubular external mount provided an unobstructed field of view, while the combination of gyro stabilization and rubber isolation rings guaranteed a rock-steady image free of the normal in-flight vibrations.

A breathtaking demonstration of this new filmmaking tool was prepared for viewing by writers and directors at major studios. The process was first used in the 1948 production *Your Red Wagon* starring Farley Granger and Cathy O'Donnell. In a spectacular opening scene, the camera paces three escaped convicts down a hill and across a field, then executes a reverse zoom into the sky for a panorama unprecedented in the history of filmmaking.

Among the most heart-stopping sequences ever filmed by camera-carrying helicopters, by now considerably refined over William's early effort, is the climax to *Edge of Eternity* (1960). A fight to the death on a cable car high above the Grand Canyon ends with the loser (represented by a dummy) plunging to his death. Veteran helicopter pilot Bill Heartily paced the figure, dropping his Bell 47G-2, its bubble removed for camera use, 1,800 feet to the canyon floor to give movie audiences an unforgettable ride.

A Helicopter Corporation of America pilot, Heartily had evacuated the first casualties from Korea's infamous Pork Chop Hill during that conflict. He was also reportedly the first person to fly a helicopter through the Khyber Pass, and the first to land atop Oregon's 11,245-foot Mount Hood.

It took a rugged breed of pilot to make a living from commercial helicopter use. Forsaking the relative ease of fixed-wing aviation, such fliers—pioneers fully as much as the individuals who created their machines—coaxed an evolving technology to extraordinary

Dean Johnson's Oregon flying service was typical of small helicopter operations around the United States. A Hiller 12-b being prepared for once-a-year duty as Santa's sleigh shares the ramp with other Hillers and Piper Super Cubs. Courtesy Hiller.

lengths doing what until recent times had been utterly impossible. Wandering the globe, they flew to its remotest corners where helicopters were most in demand. The often-dramatic experiences of these forgotten pilots are among the least-told tales of aviation.

An expectation prevailed during the 1940s that commercial helicopters would follow the proven path to success established by fixed-wing aircraft between the world wars. Scheduled service would doubtless be the helicopter's arena of commercial success, beginning—as had the airplane—with air mail deliveries. Government mail subsidies would support such operations until rotary-wing technology had progressed to the point where bigger passenger-carrying helicopters, capable of generating profits without help, could be developed. Mail subsidies would be dispensed with and America would enjoy the benefits of a self-sustaining new transportation industry.

The prospect of vertical-flight aircraft in scheduled commercial service then seemed promising. Air mail helicopters could speed pouches between the roofs of main post offices and outlying branches, waiting airliners, ships at sea, and so on. Larger machines could whisk passengers between downtown heliports and outlying airports. They could also fly short-haul intercity routes without any need of airports. Traffic jams, bridges, and other obstacles to ground transportation would be rendered meaningless.

There was no shortage of interested parties applying to the Civil Aeronautics Board for permission to engage in such operations at the end of World War II. These applicants can be divided into three categories: general speculators, primarily companies already providing some form of ground transportation

service; established fixed-wing airlines; and dedicated helicopter transport companies. Of these, only the last achieved any measure of success in a government-sponsored experiment that ultimately failed.

Beginning in 1945, the CAB received scores of petitions from companies wishing to engage in scheduled and unscheduled commercial helicopter service. The applicants were primarily bus lines, railroads, and even taxicab companies. Because regulatory policy prohibited surface carriers from participating in air transportation, the agency declined to act on the majority of these petitions.

Heated debate ensued over national transportation requirements and the wisdom of excluding surface carriers. Bus companies in particular, including Greyhound, Red Star Way, and the North Little Rock Transportation Company, argued persuasively that air service to outlying areas would be neglected were they excluded from the market. The Washington-based Bus Operators' Association further argued that the roofs of the nation's existing bus terminals were ready-made heliports.

Not to be left out, the railroads also pressured the board for permission to operate helicopters. The first was the Chicago, Burlington and Quincy Railroad, which petitioned in 1945 to use helicopters to connect Rockford, Des Moines, and Peoria with express trains to the West Coast. This company further announced plans to spend $100,000 to construct a new freight and passenger station from which helicopters could operate. Another line requesting permission to operate helicopters was the Baltimore and Annapolis Railroad Company. Its 1952 petition sought to transport passengers, property, and mail along the busy Baltimore, Washington, Wilmington, Philadelphia, and

New York corridor. Before the end of the year, the Baltimore and Ohio Railroad and the Pennsylvania Railroad jointly petitioned the CAB in opposition to the B&ARR request, claiming helicopter use by that railroad would give it an unfair competitive advantage.

The Yellow Cab Company of Cleveland, Ohio, was the first and largest of several taxicab operators to petition the CAB.[5] Its 1945 application sought approval to operate commercial helicopters throughout the greater Chicago, Canton, Akron, and Cleveland area of the Midwest. Yellow's Philadelphia branch filed the following year for similar authority to operate helicopters in its part of the country.

Yellow Cab's lead was soon followed by Boston's Checker Cab and Cambridge Taxi companies, both of which applied for regional helicopter taxi and shuttle services to Logan Airport. With two million people living in eighty-two communities within thirty miles of the city proper, the greater Boston area—New England's most productive industrial center—seemed a promising market for helicopter transportation. By 1947, four more eastern Massachusetts companies had applied to the CAB for permission to operate commercial helicopters: Norseman Air Transport, formed during World War II by returned servicemen to undertake ambitious freight and taxi service from Rhode Island to Canada; Frank P. Hagan of Boston; Arthur A. Fogarty of Springfield; and E. W. Wiggins Airways of Norwood.

Founded as a fixed-base operator in 1930, Wiggins had just received CAB certification as a fixed-wing local-service carrier in June 1946. It was providing scheduled airline services with small twin-engine Cessna T-50 Bobcats—surplus wartime trainer/utility aircraft—when it added its name to the fast-

growing list of hopeful helicopter operators that fall. Wiggins petitioned the CAB for the right to transport passengers, mail, and express goods between the business centers of fifty-three Massachusetts towns and cities, including Boston itself. The following March, Wiggins broadened its application to include routes centered around Westfield, Massachusetts; Hartford and New Haven, Connecticut; Hillsgrove, Rhode Island; and Albany, New York.

Like many CAB applicants, Wiggins entertained visions of providing bus-type helicopter service using machines costing about as much as city buses to purchase and operate. Such helicopters having yet to be developed, the airline began trials with a less expensive alternative, purchasing in 1947 the fifty-seventh Bell Model 47 produced. On April 10, 1953, even as hopes faded for commercial helicopter transportation in the United States, Wiggins took delivery of a second Bell, a 47D-1 that was the thousandth Model 47. It put both these machines to training and other conventional FBO uses.

Ultimately, the CAB passed over Wiggins and other Massachusetts applicants to grant the Skyway Corporation of Providence, Rhode Island, the honor of providing Boston with scheduled commercial helicopter service. In the spring of 1947, Skyway inaugurated regularly scheduled "sky taxi" service between downtown Boston and Logan International Airport. Flights between the one-acre roof of the Motor Mart Garage in Park Square and the airport a mile and a half distant took just 75 seconds. Skyway's shuttle service, which cost $3.00 one way, ran every ten minutes between 10:00 A.M. and 5:30 P.M. Offering convenient parking directly below the improvised heliport, and avoiding the slow bridge traffic across the Charles

River, this popular service was hard to beat. Company President J. Burleigh Cheney entertained visions of providing similar services throughout New England, as had his would-be rival Wiggins, until this short-lived commercial venture proved unprofitable.

Other general applicants petitioning the CAB to operate helicopters around the United States included the Turner Aeronautical Corporation of Indiana, the John Fabick Tractor Company of St. Louis (applying for non-scheduled helicopter service within 100 miles of that city), Van Dyke Taxicab and Transfer in Buffalo, and the Asbury Park–New York Transit Corporation (formed to transport commuters between their New Jersey homes and Manhattan offices). The award for the most ambitious proposal to the CAB certainly went to Wheeling Transportation of Port Newark, New Jersey, which applied for a permanent certificate of franchise of public convenience and necessity permitting it to link New York City, Cleveland, Cincinnati, and points between with vaguely described "giant helicopter-type planes."

The CAB generally reserved its approval for the few dedicated helicopter air carriers selected by the Post Office Department to conduct large-scale experimental operations in selected American cities. However, it did issue a few experimental approvals of its own among the ground carriers described above. These invariably failed because of the unfavorable economics of helicopters in commercial service.

The first of these general approvals came late in 1947 when—after two years of deliberation—the regulatory agency finally granted Yellow Cab permission to operate helicopters between Cleveland's municipal airport and downtown Cleveland, Shaker Square, and Euclid. After seven months of study, the company regretfully announced in the spring of 1948 that it was temporarily shelving its plans to conduct America's first helicopter passenger service. The reason cited was high equipment and operating costs that would render such service uneconomical. One year later, when the Yellow Cab Company finally conceded that its dream of aerial taxicabs was simply not feasible, it permanently relinquished all rights previously conveyed to it under the CAB approval.

Ground operators had seized upon helicopters as aerial buses and taxicabs. In contrast, the nation's air carriers saw them as short-haul airliners. Fixed-wing aircraft were simply not economical on short hops, yet demand for precisely such services existed in many markets. To study such use, United Airlines on July 19, 1946, became the first airline in the United States to apply to the CAB for permission to conduct scheduled passenger flights using helicopters.

United's petition sought to give its home base of Chicago helicopter air mail and passenger services—the latter only if the former proved successful—between Midway Airport, the downtown area, and thirty-two suburban communities. With this in mind, the airline took delivery of a new Sikorsky s-51 helicopter in May 1947. It promptly placed this machine into tests designed to evaluate its operating costs. In the spirit of civic cooperation, the airline also made this machine available at no cost to the Coast Guard, which lacked helicopters for rescue use on the Great Lakes. The test results were so discouraging that United was relieved when the CAB ruled against its request late in 1948. It sold its Sikorsky and dismissed all considerations of helicopter airliners.

United Airlines—the first U.S. air carrier to consider helicopter use—acquired this Sikorsky s-51 for evaluation in May 1947. Courtesy NASM/SI.

In the closing months of 1953, National Airlines added its name to the list of some forty companies of all types then petitioning the CAB for commercial helicopter use. A major operator between New York and Miami, National had already purchased a Sikorsky S-55 for passenger trials that began in Florida on February 1, 1954. Service was provided from Miami to West Palm Beach (with intermediate stops at Miami Beach, Bel Harbour, Hollywood, Fort Lauderdale, Boca Raton, Delray Beach) and back. One-way fares ranged from $5.00 to approximately $30.00. This forgotten service was short lived and National elected not to exercise options on two additional S-55s.

United and National were "trunk" airlines, this term denoting the nation's first-tier carriers. Below them existed a level of "feeder airlines," so called because they served to channel passengers from outlying markets into the high-volume, long-distance route systems of the trunks. Because helicopters were then small, short-range vehicles with performance more closely matching feeder route structures than those of the trunks, it was inevitable that feeder airlines would also evaluate their use. Mohawk and North Central were two such airlines that applied to the CAB in the early-to-mid 1950s for permission to provide commercial helicopter services.

Mohawk provided helicopter passenger service between Newark, New Jersey, and Liberty, New York, a resort area in the Catskill Mountains. Inaugurated June 7, 1954, with a Sikorsky S-55, these short-lived operations quickly showed that a helicopter could not compete with the venerable DC-3. North Central Airlines petitioned the CAB in the opening months of 1955 for permission to operate helicopters between Chicago and Milwaukee. Although it acquired a small

Hiller helicopter for trials, however, it did not engage in scheduled rotary-wing services.

Air cargo operators also took a hard look at vertical flight. Early in 1947, Globe Freight Airline of Hartford, Connecticut, teamed a helicopter with a DC-3 in a three-way experiment. Using an S-51 chartered from Skyway Corporation, Boston's airport shuttle operator, Globe picked up newly hatched chicks at a farm, flew twenty-five miles north to land in the yard of a home where furniture was then loaded, and proceeded six miles west to pick up packages of processed spinach. The Sikorsky then flew to Hartford's Brainard Airport where this mixed consignment was transferred to Globe's DC-3, which was off the ground in minutes. Despite impressive time savings, this experiment showed only too clearly that helicopters were too expensive to make such operations viable.

Had these efforts borne fruit, helicopters would have found America's airspace ready to accommodate them with special procedures and regulations geared to their peculiar abilities and limitations. New rules pertaining specifically to helicopters took effect October 8, 1947, following amendment of Part 60 of the Civil Air Regulations (today the Federal Aviation Regulations) by the Civil Aeronautics Authority. This revision exempted helicopters from minimum altitude restrictions pertaining to airplanes. Under the new rules, helicopter pilots were only required to fly at altitudes permitting them to effect emergency landings without undue hazard to persons or property.

Meanwhile, the Civil Aeronautics Authority (predecessor to today's Federal Aviation Administration) worked closely with manufacturers to develop certification standards for civil helicopters. Existing guidelines then applied only to fixed-wing aircraft. With so

(*Top*) Mohawk Airlines inaugurated scheduled helicopter passenger services with this Sikorsky s-55 in 1954. Courtesy NASM/SI.

(*Bottom*) The Skyway Corporation s-51 delivers cargo to a Globe Freight Airline DC-3 at Boston's Logan International Airport in a 1947 demonstration of coordinated helicopter-airplane use. Courtesy NASM/SI.

many unknowns from the CAA's standpoint, certification of first-generation machines like the civil Bell 47, Sikorsky S-51, and Hiller 360 threatened to stretch out endlessly, becoming so expensive that companies would be forced to drop plans for civil-market production. Fortunately, however, the CAA wisely enlisted the aid of the industry, relying on the helicopter manufacturers to help define test standards and procedures.

Helicopter use also benefited from the scrutiny of President Truman's Air Policy Commission, an official advisory panel convened shortly after World War II. Charged with establishing a basis by which a coherent national aviation policy could be formulated to integrate commercial, military, and private flying, the commission conducted special helicopter hearings during which the views of key rotary-wing industry leaders and experts were solicited.

More support came from state governments and interested organizations, which rallied to the cause. In the early 1950s, the National Association of State Aviation Officials established a helicopter committee to work from within to prompt states to "prepare intelligently and wisely for the widespread operation of helicopters in the future."[6] The Air Transport Association, representing the nation's scheduled air carriers, also formed a helicopter committee about that time to expedite airline adoption of helicopters for scheduled passenger service. Finally, the courts helped define the parameters of helicopter use, since rulings on disputes arising over emerging uses of vertical flight set significant legal precedents.

In short, a quiet yet thoroughgoing reworking of the nation's complex aviation infrastructure to accommodate helicopters had begun around the end of World War II. It

would last approximately a decade. This process had scarcely begun when the U.S. Post Office Department initiated the first of three major experiments in scheduled commercial helicopter operations, all of which would progress from carrying air mail alone to eventually transporting passengers.

On July 6, 1939, a Kellett KD-1 belonging to Eastern Air Lines inaugurated the first scheduled rotary-wing commercial service in history. Flying between the roof of Philadelphia's post office and Camden Airport under government contract, this autogiro shuttled mail during a yearlong experiment to see how practical rotorcraft were in speeding up postal service.

The autogiro was merely an available expedient; what the Post Office Department wanted to use was the helicopter. Under development in the United States and already flying in prototype form in Europe, this invention—like the airplane before it—promised to profoundly accelerate the nation's flow of mail. In those pre-interstate highway system days, helicopters seemed the answer to the aggravating problem of congested and inadequate roads.

Mail flowed constantly into major urban post offices by airplane, train, and ship, only to bog down in its subsequent distribution to outlying post offices for final delivery. Vertical flight was heartily endorsed as the solution to this problem. In fact, America at large confidently expected commercial helicopters to earn their keep transporting both mail *and* passengers.

The military services—America's only helicopter operators at the close of World War II—worked to further this popular vision. As part of National Air Mail Week festivities late in 1946, a Sikorsky of newly commissioned Navy Squadron vx-3 landed at Yonkers on the northern edge of New York City to help celebrate that town's 150th anniversary. Piloted by the squadron's leader, Commander Charles E. Houston, this machine (HOS-1 no. 606) landed on a giant enlargement of a five-cent air mail stamp, where Houston handed a bag of mail to Postmaster William Cronin. In turn, Cronin loaded the bag onto a waiting stage coach for ceremonial transport to the town's post office.

This exchange marked the first preannounced helicopter delivery of nonmilitary mail (albeit by a military machine and pilot) in American history. The publicity it generated helped pave the way for the inauguration less than a year later of America's first true regularly scheduled commercial helicopter air mail service.

This honor fell to Los Angeles Airways, a company formed by California businessmen during World War II. One of many groups across the country vying for this privilege, LAA had been selected by the U.S. Post Office Department to conduct this pioneering service in part because sprawling Los Angeles was an especially promising venue for evaluating the concept.

The country's first experimental demonstration of helicopter air mail delivery had already been staged there under the auspices of the Post Office Department using helicopters provided by the U.S. Army Air Forces. Beginning July 8, 1946, olive-drab Sikorskys of the Air Transport Command's Air Rescue Unit carried mail between thirty-three southern California communities in the greater Los Angeles area on two routes, one inland and the other coastal, as well as between the airport and the main post office downtown.

In 1947 the Civil Aeronautics Board awarded Los Angeles Airways a three-year temporary certificate of public convenience and necessity, authorizing it to transport property and mail by helicopter on three circular routes radiating from Los Angeles International Airport to thirty post offices in the greater city area. Twenty-three would be served in the beginning. The specified routes stretched some two hundred miles to encompass the San Fernando Valley, San Bernardino, and Newport Beach. The government had made it clear that LAA's service would be extended only if the first three years were deemed successful.

On this basis, LAA's two green Sikorsky s-51s inaugurated the nation's first helicopter air mail service October 1, 1947. Film comedian Eddie Cantor, appropriately dressed as a postmaster, presided as the master of ceremonies. Following these lighthearted proceedings, LAA (as the nation's fixed-wing air mail pioneers had done two decades before) went to work. The initial results were gratifying. In its first two months, it carried six million letters. In November alone, it flew 12,642 miles with 56,253 pounds of mail, whose delivery had been accelerated by as much as twenty-four hours.

The company's two hardworking Sikorskys acquitted themselves well, completing 85 percent of their scheduled runs despite winter weather delays. At this juncture, LAA was so sanguine that it announced service extensions to thirteen new communities by January 10. To meet this goal, it ordered four more Sikorskys.

However, the Post Office was troubled by the company's request for an increase in its mail subsidy from $1.00 to $1.15 per mile flown. The government was in no hurry to comply; even at the existing rate, LAA's service seemed inordinately expensive to Post

Office officials, whose funds were being depleted at a rapid rate.

"The cost of the Los Angeles service is $1.00 per mile," Assistant Postmaster General Paul Aiken warned in an address to the helicopter industry in April 1948, "[and] the Post Office considers this high. Part of this high cost can no doubt be attributed to the fact that this is to some extent an experimental route. Application has now been made by the operator of that route for an increase in pay. We realize that the helicopter is an expensive aircraft . . . , but I must warn you that the Department believes that an increased rate may make the service too expensive to justify its continued use."[7]

In the end, however, the increase was granted to accord the experiment every chance of success. The rate hike came as good news to Los Angeles Airways, which was far from recouping its heavy start-up investment or the costs of its ongoing expansion. LAA flew a record 60,000 pounds of mail during the week ending May 8, as much as it had carried during its entire first month the previous October. Its fleet—now numbering five Sikorskys—had inaugurated regularly scheduled night operations May 1, 1948, in order to accommodate the growing volume. Daytime schedules were also expanded, there being twenty-four daily shuttle flights for continuous service from 6 A.M. to 8 P.M. between the airport and the roof of the terminal annex post office.

With the arrival of a sixth helicopter that summer, LAA's monthly total of miles flown reached 35,000, enough to keep a dozen pilots busy. As a result, the government subsidy soared to a yearly $400,000, a figure that sobered even ardent supporters of scheduled commercial helicopter transport. If just one operator could cost so much, they foresaw, the dream of continentwide helicopter mail service—and the helicopter passenger service it was expected to engender—might be prohibitively expensive. Clearly to blame were the helicopter's excessively high operating costs.

Los Angeles Airways celebrated its first anniversary in the fall of 1948. The operator now served forty-four suburbs within a fifty-mile radius of Los Angeles International Airport. Its route system had four segments known as A, B, C, and the Shuttle. The first three were served three times daily, including at night, while the fourth route—the shuttle to the main post office—was served twelve times daily. Logging some 40,000 landings and takeoffs during the previous year, LAA had carried 1,750,000 pounds of mail and parcel post without any severe delays stemming from mechanical troubles. Pound-miles per month escalated dramatically from 60,360 in October 1947 to 273,935 in September 1948.

LAA had done it all with a perfect safety record. With helicopters still a new technology, reliability had been the most worrisome issue. But the workhorse S-51s had been up to the job. Among those on hand to celebrate the achievement were Igor Sikorsky, LAA President Clarence Belinn, and actress Donna Reed, whom some Hollywood publicity flack had proclaimed Miss Helicopter Air Mail.

Just weeks later, ironically, Los Angeles Airways experienced a fatal accident. Harry Slemmons, a twenty-seven-year-old pilot, was killed January 21, 1949, when his S-51 crashed into Macy Street. Slemmons had just departed the post office roof heading for the airport when witnesses observed a flash. The helicopter plummeted to the busy street, snaring a high-tension line on the way. An official investigation revealed that the mail recovered from the wrecked s-51 exceeded the craft's gross weight limitations by 30 percent. To prevent future accidental overloads, an inspector was henceforth required to verify all weights before departure.

Despite this setback, Los Angeles Airways continued to grow. In the spring of 1950, one of its original s-51s (NC-92813) became the first helicopter in the world to log 3,000 flight hours. Two years later, LAA took delivery of the first of a fleet of larger s-55s, planning for it to carry passengers as well as mail.

By this time, two other major American cities enjoyed helicopter mail services, Chicago and New York. Described below, New York's carrier would be the first in the United States to engage in scheduled helicopter passenger service. Concurrently, Great Britain and Europe would also enjoy helicopter mail and passenger services, but they would be conducted by established fixed-wing airlines using helicopters as feeder airliners to bring passengers to major airports.

British European Airways inaugurated England's first helicopter mail service in 1948 using three Sikorsky s-51s and two Bell 47s. On July 1 it became the first carrier in the world to conduct scheduled passenger helicopter services, with Westland-Sikorsky s-51s built under license in England. Discontinued as uneconomical after less than a year, that historic service was followed by other British helicopter services as BEA aggressively championed vertical flight.

Sabena inaugurated the continent's first mail service in the summer of 1950 with two Bell 47s (a third arrived in 1952). The Belgian airline also purchased two Sikorsky s-51s, which it put to spraying use in the Congo under contract to that newly independent country's government. Sabena's strong commitment to helicopters dated back to the 1946 crash of a fully loaded Sabena DC-4 in the snowbound wilds of Newfoundland. A major helicopter rescue operation mounted by the U.S. Army Air Forces had saved the lives of eighteen survivors in a dramatic demonstration of vertical flight that greatly impressed the airline's leaders.

There would, of course, be other scheduled commercial helicopter services beyond America's borders, notably in Australia, Italy, Canada, Colombia, Pakistan, and the former USSR. They lie beyond the scope of this volume, the primary focus of which is the United States.

As in the case of Los Angeles, a limited-duration demonstration of helicopter mail delivery was staged in Chicago before commercial service was inaugurated there. Begun October 1, 1946, and lasting approximately three weeks, this highly publicized event—christened Experiment Chicago by Post Office officials—again made use of helicopters of the Air Rescue Service (as the AFF's Air Rescue Unit was now known). It also employed United Air Lines' s-51, a civilian version of the R-5DS flown by the ARS.

At the eleventh hour, one of the four Army R-5DS failed to show up due to damage suffered in Wilmington, Delaware. Igor Sikorsky, on hand to observe the experiment, saved the day by providing his personal s-51 as a replacement. These three military and two civil machines together provided twice-daily mail service to forty-three regional communities on three separate routes, served in turn for a week each. Ranging north to Waukegan, west to Elgin and Aurora, and south to Joliet, Lansing, and Gary, the helicopters acquitted themselves well. Whether they could do the job economically, however, remained to be seen.

Belgian airline Sabena initiated Europe's first helicopter air mail service with two Bell 47s in 1950.
Courtesy NASM/SI.

In addition to United, eight aviation companies and two bus lines had applied to provide Chicago's commercial helicopter service by the time the CAB opened hearings on the subject in mid-1947. The aerial applicants included fixed-base operators and certificated airlines, the latter camp including Chicago-based Continental Air Transport, Regan Air Services, Chicago Helicopter Air Transport, and Helicopter Air Service; Milwaukee-based Anderson Air Activities; Wisconsin Central Airlines, which would be absorbed by North Central Airlines in the early 1950s; Parks Air Transport, an abortive airline subsidiary of Parks Aeronautical College of East St. Louis; and Helicopter Air Transport, the pioneering New Jersey helicopter school. The busline applicants were Mandel Brothers and Greyhound. A subsidiary of the latter, known as Greyhound Skyways, had already purchased two helicopters for evaluation.

On May 15, 1948, CAB Examiner Ferdinand D. Moran recommended that Helicopter Air Service be awarded a five-year temporary certificate to provide Chicago with helicopter air mail service. HAS had applied for three circular routes and shuttle operations between the municipal airport and main post office, but Moran on his own initiative recommended that the carrier be issued a temporary exemption order permitting it to serve any point at all within a fifty-mile radius of the airport. In urging that the petitions of runners-up United Air Lines and Anderson Air Activities be denied, he noted that "of all the applicants in the proceeding, HAS is the only one which offers the undivided attention of a single management able to devote its energies entirely to the problems and responsibilities of conducting the experiment."[8]

Thomas H. Reidy, president of the front-runner, had indeed confirmed that his pioneering FBO would suspend dusting, spraying, power-line patrol, training, charter, and other commercial helicopter operations were it to win the coveted Post Office contract. Located at Sky Harbor Airport in Northbrook, Illinois, HAS had begun operations with a Bell 47B in April 1947, and proposed flying the mails with six Bells over routes totaling 305 miles. Making every effort to reduce costs from the outset, it further announced that it would employ hovering mail pickups to eliminate the need for constructing landing sites at regional post offices lacking suitable open space.

What tipped the balance in HAS's favor, however, was its choice of Bell helicopters. Since Sikorsky S-51s, which had been developed for military use, were proving too expensive in Los Angeles, planners in Washington, D.C., decided to give the Model 47—history's first civil helicopter—a chance to show what it could do. Accordingly, the CAB adopted Ferdinand Moran's recommendations in full. On November 26, 1948, it awarded Helicopter Air Service, Inc., a five-year temporary certificate of public necessity and convenience to conduct helicopter mail and express operations within a fifty-mile radius of Chicago Municipal Airport.

On August 22, 1949, less than two years after Los Angeles Airways began operations, America's second certificated helicopter carrier inaugurated service in the Chicago area. Six Bells in orange HAS livery began speeding the flow of mail between forty-four communities along three routes, as well as shuttling bags between Midway Airport and the main post office downtown, a nine-minute hop. So successful were these operations that on March 8, 1950, HAS logged its millionth pound of mail and transported a record 12,600 pounds in one day.

On Christmas Eve 1952, the carrier completed 20,000 accident-free flight hours over a total of 1,075,000 miles—equivalent to seventy-three trips around the equator—during which 9,420,000 pounds of mail had been carried. Best of all, it had done it all with a perfect safety record, at half the overall cost of Sikorsky-operators Los Angeles Airways and New York Airways. The only disadvantage of the more economical Bells was their inability to carry more than one-third of the s-51's standard load of 580 pounds of mail.

Even before scheduled commercial helicopter service began in Los Angeles, the Post Office Department conducted a third and final limited-duration "dress rehearsal" of helicopter air mail service in New York City. This preliminary experiment in the nation's largest urban area involved no less than twelve rotorcraft (none of them military), three of which were held in reserve in case others broke down. Lined up at LaGuardia Airport, the seven Sikorskys, four Bells, and one experimental Firestone were gathered from Helicopter Air Transport, Greyhound Skyways, New England Helicopter Service, and directly from the manufacturers (or would-be manufacturer in the case of Firestone, which hoped to stimulate interest in its unwanted prototype).

Early on the morning of January 6, 1947, nine of these helicopters began four days of intensive flying along five routes. Three routes ran north through parts of Westchester County, New York, and Fairfield County, Connecticut; east to Long Island through Nassau and Suffolk Counties; and west across seven densely populated communities in northeastern New Jersey. The remaining two were shuttles between LaGuardia and Newark Airports, and LaGuardia and Floyd Bennett Field.

Of much shorter duration than the other dress rehearsals, this much-publicized precursor to helicopter service was clearly more an exercise in public relations than a true evaluation. Perhaps for this reason, the military had declined to participate. Even so, all flights were on schedule despite bitterly cold weather. With large crowds and a wildly enthusiastic press, the effort was hailed as another triumph for the Post Office Department.

Nevertheless, New Yorkers had to wait the better part of six years for their scheduled helicopter services to begin. In the meantime, they had other chances to indulge the helicopter fever then rampant in the United States. One came the first week in August 1947, when the city staged reportedly the biggest air show in history at newly completed Idlewild Airport in Queens. President Truman himself dedicated this new facility, then the world's largest airport, which supplanted historic Floyd Bennett Field as New York's international gateway. Hundreds of thousands of spectators watched as more than a thousand USAAF aircraft flew overhead in the largest aviation display ever assembled over the United States. It took thirty-five minutes for the "aluminum overcast" to pass by.

Next came a display of civil and military helicopters that included a Sikorsky s-51 and s-52, a tiny tandem JOV-3, a Brantly, a Bell 47, and a Piasecki HRP-1. A real hit with the crowd, this popular demonstration included a simulated rescue by the Navy HRP-1, which lowered a chain ladder to six men sitting in rubber rafts on the ground. Then, in a realistic demonstration of helicopter air mail, a Sikorsky s-51 showed how easily it could pick up and deliver mail pouches wherever there was sufficient clearance for its whirling rotor. This last display prompted newspapers to call for the imme-

Mail bags are loaded aboard a Helicopter Air Service Bell 47 on a Chicago-area rooftop. Courtesy NASM/SI.

diate instigation of such services, which were termed long overdue.

Official approval to provide the greater New York City area with scheduled helicopter service finally came December 5, 1951, when the CAB authorized newly formed New York Airways[9] to conduct passenger, freight, and mail service between downtown Manhattan and its three major regional airports, LaGuardia, Newark, and New York International, as Idlewild was officially called. After one year of operation, NYA was further authorized to expand its services as desired on linear routes extending to suburban communities beyond those airports.

Only two companies had petitioned to serve New York. An appeal by the other applicant delayed formal authorization until March 13, 1952. Another frustrating delay for New York Airways was the virtual monopoly held by the military services on production of the ten-passenger Sikorsky S-55. With America bogged down in a war in Korea, NYA's request to purchase up to ten S-55s had come at a bad time.

The carrier explored the possibility of "borrowing" S-55s. Eager to cultivate a commercial market for its helicopter, Sikorsky negotiated with its military customers on behalf of NYA. In the summer of 1952, wartime production pressures eased sufficiently for arrangements to be made, and New York Airways took delivery of its first S-55.

On October 15, 1952, escorted by two Bells belonging to the New York Police Department and a Sikorsky demonstration helicopter, New York Airways' newly purchased S-55 left its base at LaGuardia for Idlewild. Heavy fog disrupted this maiden run, forcing the aircraft to return to LaGuardia instead of pushing on to Newark. Nevertheless, America now had three commercial helicopter

companies engaged in scheduled mail service.

The helicopter carriers, as these mail-only airlines were known, shared a high dependence on government subsidies that accounted for about 70 percent of their revenues. They did indeed improve mail services in the greater Los Angeles, Chicago, and New York areas, but these improvements came at a higher cost than government planners had ever envisioned. As a result, plans for such service across the continental U.S. were shelved. Only if Los Angeles Airways, Helicopter Air Services, and New York Airways ultimately achieved profitability with little or no government subsidy would other scheduled commercial helicopter services be fostered (although one would flourish for a time without subsidy in the San Francisco area, as described below).

New York Airways extended its mail services to Bridgeport, Connecticut, and intervening communities on December 10, 1952. To further increase revenues, it added express freight services along its route system on January 26, 1953. By this time, its three hardworking Sikorskys were landing eight times daily at New York's airports, with more flights added when interairport night operations were initiated February 16. Then on June 8, NYA instituted twice-daily mail and cargo service to Trenton and many intervening New Jersey communities. All this extra service necessitated the acquisition of two more S-55s by midyear.

On July 8, 1953, an NYA S-55 "Skybus" inaugurated the first scheduled commercial helicopter passenger service in the United States. This helicopter was configured to carry seven passengers, a flight attendant, and mail. At its controls was Captain Jack E. Gallagher, who had piloted NYA's first mail flight nine months earlier. Hired in April

1952 as operations chief, the thirty-four-year-old veteran had previously worked for Republic Aircraft and United Air Lines. As a civilian pilot during World War II, he had flown his company's airliners in globe-girdling cargo operations for the Army Air Forces. In 1948, UAL had sent him to the Sikorsky plant for rotary-wing training during that airline's evaluation of helicopters. Gallagher had been the pilot of UAL's S-51, as described earlier in this appendix.

New York Airways had in fact incorporated expressly to carry passengers. For this reason, it had held out for hard-to-get S-55s instead of initiating mail service with readily available S-51s. More than a promising source of direct revenue in the country's most populous region, passenger operations yielded additional federal assistance because the helicopter transport of people, not just mail, was subsidized.

The government's expectation, of course, was that these services would become self-supporting. Unfortunately, the S-55 was not the machine to make this happen. It was too small, too expensive to operate, and too limited in performance to wean NYA from its heavy reliance on public monies. From the carrier's standpoint, the S-55 was just an interim type to be used until twenty-to-thirty passenger helicopters appeared that could indeed generate profits in an unsubsidized environment.

Even as it took delivery of its first S-55, therefore, NYA initiated discussions with Sikorsky as to its requirements for a next-generation helicopter airliner. The carrier and the manufacturer shared the then-prevalent belief that helicopter operating costs would decrease as rotary-wing technology improved and a large manufacturing base formed. This expectation has yet to be fulfilled.

The public had no inkling that NYA's Sikorsky Skybus was anything but a winning airliner. Nationwide acclaim had greeted the inauguration of these passenger services in New York, thus helping to foster the illusion that helicopters had come of age in the air transport arena.

By the first anniversary of its operations on October 15, 1953, New York Airways had much to celebrate. It had flown 281,000 miles in 4,700 flight hours, during which it had transported 3,112,400 pounds of mail, 102,000 pounds of cargo, and 987 passengers. Its plans for service to a new midtown Manhattan helipad were proceeding well, moreover, and demand for its new passenger service continued to outstrip capacity.

During this period, the helicopter airline had received $1,348,464 in subsidies. Clearly alarmed, the CAB acknowledged its recognition of the "problems inherent in any initial period of operations, plus the problem of instituting the first scheduled passenger service by helicopter [which] tended to increase the initial subsidy requirement." However, the agency went on to warn NYA that its "subsidy requirements should be carefully controlled."[10]

The carrier's management knew that the federal government would eventually move to cut back or eliminate the subsidy if they did not voluntarily reduce their reliance on government funds. However, increasing the revenue base dictated that they expand services and operate more helicopters, all of which would increase demands on the U.S. Treasury. The only hope was for operations to be made profitable before official patience ran out, and that meant replacing the S-55s with more efficient machines. Consequently, efforts were redoubled to secure industry support for development of a larger twin-engine helicopter capable of transporting twenty or more passengers at 125 mph, half again the cruise speed of the lumbering s-55.

It also made sense for the carrier to complete its route structure while subsidization continued at a high level. On August 3, 1954, it inaugurated commuter service on the Trenton, Princeton, New Brunswick, Idlewild, LaGuardia route. On the 30th, it began nighttime passenger operations between the three airports under a special waiver, following eighteen months of safe freight and mail night service on that route. Before the month was out, NYA announced that in October it would extend night passenger service to Trenton and inaugurate day and night passenger service to Bridgeport.

That the flow of public funds to NYA was rapidly increasing did not escape the notice of the CAB. "We consider it timely and desirable to place New York Airways on notice that we expect it to maintain the helicopter experiment within the framework of the [established] subsidy support," the regulatory agency announced in the summer of 1954, again warning that helicopter program payments "must be kept within reasonable bounds."[11]

Across the country, meanwhile, Los Angeles Airways was finally ready to inaugurate passenger service following extensive delays stemming from the crash two years earlier of its first s-55. That long-ordered craft had arrived in the spring of 1952, several months before newcomer New York Airways received its first s-55. After being christened in a formal ceremony on the lawn of the Ambassador Hotel, it had flown back to Los Angeles International, where it dropped off company President Clarence Belinn and his party. Watching their helicopter depart for the company hangars down the field, the group

was horrified to see the Sikorsky's tail rotor fly off. Flames shot from the exhaust of the hapless machine as it spun straight downward into the ground. Fortunately, although the $150,000 s-55 was totally destroyed, pilot Fred Milam and the four other occupants survived.

A service representative dispatched from Sikorsky Aircraft determined that a spring lock had become dislodged from the aircraft's tail rotor shaft. Although the manufacturer took immediate steps to see that the problem never recurred in any s-55, the spectacular crash—and perhaps memories of LAA's fatal 1949 s-51 accident—left Belinn and company cautious about engaging in passenger transport. They therefore elected to wait, carefully observing New York Airways all the while.

The wait ended when Los Angeles Airways inaugurated America's second scheduled helicopter passenger service November 22, 1954. It operated six daily flights between Los Angeles International Airport and Long Beach, timed to match major airline departure and arrival schedules. Additional passenger services between the airport and surrounding communities commenced in the new year.

But for the accident, Los Angeles Airways might have been the second company in the world to inaugurate helicopter passenger service, after British European Airways. But it was not even the third. Sabena claimed that honor less than two months after New York Airways' success. On September 1, 1953, Sabena's first Sikorsky s-55 launched passenger service along the Brussels, Antwerp, and Rotterdam route. Its helicopters soon also connected Brussels to Lille, and later embraced Bonn via Liege, Maastricht, and Cologne. In its first full year of helicopter operations, conducted as in America only under visual conditions, Sabena transported 13,000 passengers on 3,500 scheduled helicopter flights, and 5,000 more travelers on special helicopter charters.

In Chicago, meanwhile, Helicopter Air Services celebrated its fifth full year and 32,000 hours of flight using the same six helicopters it had purchased in 1948, although Bell had upgraded these machines to a newer standard. Despite Midwest weather extremes, HAS had completed 96 percent of its scheduled flights, and its eighteen pilots had carried more than 600 million air mail letters and parcels. Remarkably, this was accomplished without so much as an injury or any damage whatsoever to a helicopter. In part because it took little profit (company payroll rates were half those of LAA and NYA), HAS never lost money serving Chicago and its suburbs.

Upon receipt of revised CAB authority to conduct passenger operations on August 20, 1956, HAS changed its name to Chicago Helicopter Airways. A few weeks later, it took delivery of three seven-passenger Sikorsky S-55s and it placed a further order with Sikorsky for three newer and larger S-58s.

On November 12, 1956, Chicago Helicopter Airways inaugurated passenger service between Midway (formerly Chicago Municipal Airport) and O'Hare International. Charging just $6.00 for the twelve-minute flight (less than the average cab fare), CHA's twenty daily flights were fully booked from the outset. So great was the demand that the carrier doubled its traffic each of the next two years. It soon also expanded passenger service to the Loop (Meigs Field), and eventually provided passenger service north to Winnetka and south to Gary, Indiana.

By the end of its first year of passenger service, Chicago Helicopter Airways had carried a remarkable total of 44,276 passengers. Its fleet of nine helicopters was evenly divided between seven-passenger S-55s, twelve-passenger S-58s, and its remaining mail-and-express Model 47s, some of which had been sold off.

Spurring CHA's remarkably brisk passenger business was an ongoing transfer of fixed-wing airline operations from Midway to O'Hare, Chicago's large new international airport. Formerly Douglas Field, a military base and site of a wartime aircraft factory run by the Douglas Aircraft Company, O'Hare had been turned over to the city of Chicago by the Army Air Forces following World War II. Conversion of this facility, then known by the interim name Orchard Airport, into Chicago's major airline terminus had been delayed by the Korean War, which necessitated a temporary reactivation of its aircraft plant. Consequently, the airlines still used both fields when CHA's shuttle service arrived to help travelers needing to make quick connections between airports.

It came as something of a shock to CHA's management and backers to realize that even booming business could not remove the red ink from company books. In 1957, during which the carrier received $1,091,834 in federal subsidies, it recorded direct revenues of just $344,252 ($276,016 from passenger transport and $68,236 from mail service). The unprofitability of the military-inspired Sikorsky S-55 and S-58 in commercial service had once again been demonstrated.

Nevertheless, CHA bought two Sikorsky S-58cs in the spring of 1959, for a total of five S-58s, and ordered three new twin-turbine S-61s. At this juncture, two factors conspired to put an end to this most successful of America's subsidized helicopter carriers. First, demand for CHA's interairport shuttle services ended when the airlines consolidated passenger operations at O'Hare, leaving Midway with cargo and general aviation operations only (and gave O'Hare the title of world's busiest commercial airport, which Midway had held in earlier times). Second, a new high-speed freeway serving O'Hare opened, undercutting the remaining demand for CHA's passenger services. Chicago Helicopter Airways now slid into irreversible decline.

In the East, meanwhile, New York Airways had taken steps beginning in the early 1950s to reduce dependence on public funds. With little hope of lowering its recurring costs, helicopters being so expensive to fly, it sought to shift part of the financial burden to the private sector, beginning with the major airlines. It signed an agreement with Scandinavian Airlines (SAS) to conduct joint services via combined fares and through booking, a popular convenience from the passengers' standpoint. By 1955, it had secured similar arrangements with most domestic and international carriers.

By this time, NYA offered hourly services between airports. Fares were just $5.00 between LaGuardia and Idlewild, and $10.00 between either of those airports and Newark. In 1956 it carried 43,034 passengers (80 percent more than the previous year) on 800,000 scheduled passenger miles over parts of New York, Connecticut, and New Jersey. In addition to its five S-55s, which now featured floats for added safety, NYA took delivery before year's end of the first of three twelve-passenger S-58s.

By now, NYA also served Manhattan's first heliport, located where West 30th Street met the Hudson River (a NYA S-55 dedicated this facility September 26, 1956). NYA subsequently served even more convenient and lucrative landing sites in Manhattan: the Downtown Heliport, near the foot of Wall Street, and the top of the Pan Am Building. Well remembered today, this last service provided direct access to midtown Manhattan, several subway lines, and train service from Grand Central Station.

With demand for its services continuing to outstrip its capacity, NYA—which had introduced the S-55 and S-58 into commercial service—defected from the Sikorsky fold in 1957 to order ten Vertol fifteen-passenger 44B helicopters. This order was soon reduced to five at a total cost of $2 million plus spares. The first of these tandem-rotor airliners entered service April 21, 1958.

NYA's ridership had more than tripled during 1957 to reach 144,551 passengers by year's end. As a result, even the new Vertols failed to give NYA sufficient seating capacity. At the start of 1959, therefore, the carrier agreed to buy between five and fifteen Fairey Rotodynes from Kaman, the U.S. representative and manufacturing licensee of the Fairey Aviation Company in England. When the sixty-passenger Rotodyne failed to materialize, NYA instead ordered ten turbine-powered Vertol 107s in January 1960. This order was also reduced to five before the first example was delivered. The capable but costly 107s—civil versions of the successful H-46 military transport helicopter—entered service July 1, 1962, by which time NYA was serving New York's major airports every half hour.

Sikorsky Aircraft also had military-inspired turbine helicopters that it hoped to sell commercially. The first to become available was the twelve-passenger S-62, a new boat-hulled rotorcraft based on the S-55. The second was the twenty-five-passenger twin-turbine S-61, also boat-hulled. The cost of these new-generation helicopters was high, but the revenue-generating power of their greater seating capacities rekindled hopes of commercial via-

(*Top*) Helicopter shuttle hops between Midway and O'Hare airports cost $6.00 aboard this Chicago Helicopter Airlines s-55 in 1956. Courtesy NASM/SI.

(*Bottom*) In the early 1960s, New York Airways served the New York area's major jetports every half hour with turbine-powered Boeing-Vertol 107s. Courtesy John Schneider.

bility. Both turbine power and amphibious fuselages were strong selling points from a safety standpoint. The former improved reliability while the latter permitted low-altitude operations over rivers, where helicopter noise was less objectionable.

Los Angeles Airways became the first of the world's scheduled helicopter airlines to upgrade to turbine power with an agreement at the start of 1959 to purchase two Sikorsky s-62s. Although civil certification of both the helicopter and its T58 engine delayed inauguration of s-62 service until December 21, 1960, LAA nevertheless initiated its turbine helicopter service a year and a half before NYA.

The s-62 proved so successful that it gave rise to California's second scheduled commercial helicopter service. Incorporated January 6, 1961, San Francisco & Oakland Helicopter Airlines began operations June 1 with two s-62s leased from the manufacturer. Linking downtown San Francisco, Oakland, and Berkeley with the Bay Area's two major airports, this carrier managed to purchase three s-62s of its own by early 1963, by which time it was making nearly one hundred scheduled flights per day. More remarkable still, SFO managed to stay in business with no federal subsidies.

Meanwhile, payments to the nation's other helicopter carriers continued to soar. With endless warnings from the CAB having had no effect, a Congress strongly opposed to artificial subsidies set a cap of $6 million in total annual payments in 1961. At the end of 1964, it lowered this limit to $4.3 million.

By then the government had given America's first three commercial helicopter carriers a dozen years to succeed—more than enough time, Congress concluded. That a fourth carrier had arisen by itself to operate profitably without any subsidy further suggested that federal assistance was neither essential nor desirable. Accordingly, helicopter carrier subsidies were eliminated April 11, 1965.

The first helicopter carrier to fail was troubled Chicago Helicopter Airways. Forced to defer receiving its turbine-powered s-61s in 1962, it continued passenger services with a piston-powered fleet. With the rug now pulled out from under it, this airline had to cease operations on the last day of 1965.

Meanwhile, Los Angeles Airways had inaugurated the world's first multiturbine-engine helicopter passenger services with the new Sikorsky s-61L on March 1, 1962. Comparable in passenger capacity and performance to a DC-3, although far more expensive to operate, the s-61—which was capable of instrument flight—nevertheless offered adequate economics that promised to reduce LAA's chronic dependence on subsidies. However, the s-61's appalling safety record would ironically help destroy the helicopter-airliner market that Sikorsky ardently hoped to dominate.

The summary cancellation of subsidies in 1965 was little short of catastrophic for Los Angeles Airways, which survived temporarily only by surrendering its autonomy to two trunk lines. As endorsed by the CAB, American Airlines and United Air Lines were together allowed to acquire control of LAA through equal shares of a $3.2 million loan.

On May 22, 1968, the tail of an LAA s-61 separated in flight, killing twenty-three passengers and the crew. Less than three months later, on August 14, a second s-61 crash—this one caused by the departure of a rotor blade in flight—claimed the lives of twenty-one passengers plus the crew. Forced to sus-

(Top) The Sikorsky s-61 carried about as many passengers as a DC-3 but was more expensive to operate. Courtesy NASM/SI.

(Bottom) Two fatal Sikorsky s-61L crashes forced Los Angeles Airways out of business in late 1970. Courtesy NASM/SI.

(Top) Wearing Pan American Airways livery, this New York Airways Vertol 107 linked New York's airports with the top of the Pan Am Building in midtown Manhattan. Courtesy John Schneider.

(Bottom) San Francisco & Oakland Helicopter Airlines was the last U.S. airline to operate large helicopters in scheduled passenger service. Courtesy NASM/SI.

pend all service by October 1970, LAA sold its routes and two remaining s-61s to Golden West Airlines the following year for $500,000. In turn, that fixed-wing carrier sold the Sikorskys on the commercial market. It was a tragic end to America's first scheduled commercial helicopter operator.

New York Airways, meanwhile, found progressively more support from the major airlines to offset waning government assistance. Ever mindful of promotion, Pan American Airways had purchased two additional Vertol 107s, which it leased under favorable terms to NYA for use at the New York World's Fair in 1964. Connecticut's United Aircraft Corporation, the parent of Sikorsky Aircraft, also provided NYA with three s-61Ns, a fully amphibious version of the s-61 that NYA introduced into service on special flights to the fairgrounds and back.

Shortly before Congress terminated subsidy payments in April 1965, New York Airways conducted demonstration flights between John F. Kennedy International Airport (Idlewild's new name) and the top of the famous Pan American Building in midtown Manhattan. So promising were these tests that Pan American Airways and Trans-World Airlines bought major interests in NYA. This arrangement provided Pan Am with high-visibility rooftop services that enhanced its prestige, and both airlines got direct helicopter delivery of passengers to their flight ramps at Kennedy, LaGuardia, and Newark. Services from the Manhattan skyscraper commenced December 21, 1965, with seventeen daily round-trips to Kennedy. The seventeen-minute flight cost just $7.00 one way and $10.00 round-trip.

After almost a dozen years of such service, NYA—like LAA—suffered two s-61 accidents that precipitated its demise. On May 16,

1977, as people boarded an NYA s-61L atop the Pan Am Building, a landing gear attach strut failed. The Sikorsky dropped to one side and sheared the ends off its whirling rotor blades, killing four would-be passengers and wounding six others. One blade fragment killed a pedestrian at street level two blocks distant, while another plunged through the window of a neighboring skyscraper without injury to the occupants.

This helicopter had not actually crashed, but the gruesome incident forced an immediate cessation of New York Airway's popular service. Downtown Manhattan was simply too densely inhabited for such operations. Then on April 18, 1979, a second NYA s-61 crashed at Newark Airport, killing three and injuring a dozen more. By then, the major airlines had already concluded that NYA was not worth assisting because its through services had not generated sufficient bookings to be worthwhile. With its support among fixed-wing carriers thus eroded even before the crashes, New York Airways was forced to cease operations in May 1979.

San Francisco & Oakland Helicopter Airlines alone struggled on, albeit in reduced form. Following a bout with Chapter 11 bankruptcy at the start of the 1970s, the once-profitable operator of large helicopter airliners devolved to limited scheduled services with tiny Bell 206 JetRangers.

Even in densely populated Europe with its closely spaced urban centers, passenger helicopter service inevitably declined. Sabena's suspension of helicopter services on November 1, 1966, coincided with the belated post-war resurgence of Lufthansa, which undercut the Belgian carrier's rotary-wing services to Dortmund and other centers in Germany's industrial Ruhr Valley. Services continued elsewhere in the world at the end of the 1960s and into the 1970s—notably in Greenland, Australia, Italy, and Great Britain—but those limited operations were generally confined to extraordinary situations warranting the subsidization of high operating costs.

Thus, despite herculean efforts over more than two decades, commercial helicopter airline operations—much like supersonic air travel—have yet to prove economically viable without heavy subsidization. In retrospect, the grand experiments of the past in scheduled commercial rotary-wing operations can only be viewed as failures.

The niches for commercial rotorcraft are elsewhere. Today, helicopters perform countless duties around the world. Refined and continuously improved, they have become an essential tool in virtually every country. Although the size of civil helicopter fleets remains small because of their cost and complexity, civil helicopters are nonetheless indispensable.

Notes

2 / SIKORSKY

1. Frenchmen may be tempted to award this title to Louis Breguet, and Germans to Heinrich Focke.

2. Better known simply as Vought, this company was formed by onetime race car driver Chance M. Vought, who added his first name to the company's because he believed that having a name starting with a letter late in the alphabet cost him business.

3. Rentschler, with William Boeing, Sr., created the powerful United Aircraft and Transport Corporation.

4. J. P. W. Vest, "Recollections of Igor Sikorsky: A Memoir" (unpublished article in Sikorsky biographical file, National Air and Space Museum, Smithsonian Institution [ca. 1988]), p. 1.

5. Interview with author, March 11, 1990.

6. Sergei I. Sikorsky, "Reflections on a Pioneer," Wings Club's 26th annual General Harold R. Harris "Sight" Lecture, Grand Hyatt Hotel, New York, May 24, 1989. Transcript New York: Wings Club, 1989, p. 13.

7. Memorandum of January 25, 1939, Igor I. Sikorsky to Rensselaer W. Clark, vice president and board member of United Aircraft Corporation and Vought-Sikorsky general manager. United Technologies Corporation Archive, page 3 of document 12, file B-1, inventory number 236.

8. Memorandum of February 21, 1939, Sikorsky to Clark. UTC Archive, page 3 of document 14, file B-1, inv. no. 236.

9. Collective control involves a uniform increase or decrease in the pitch of the blades of the main rotor. Increasing collective pitch (combined with a simultaneous increase in power to maintain rotor RPM) causes the rotor to generate more lift. In this sense, collective is the "vertical control."

Cyclic control is achieved by changing the angle of individual rotor blades as they pass through the same point in their rotation above the helicopter. Pushing the control stick to the left, for example, produces locally increased blade pitch—hence greater aerodynamic lift—where needed to induce a roll to the left. The effect is similar to physically tilting the rotor above the helicopter, although with cyclic control the rotor's plane of rotation remains flat with respect to the helicopter. Cyclic, then, controls the lateral motion of the helicopter.

The cyclic stick is directly in front of the helicopter pilot, while the collective lever is to one side (in most helicopters, it includes a twist-grip throttle). Helicopters also have "rudder pedals"— so called even though helicopters lack rudders— for yaw control; these move the nose left or right by increasing or decreasing the blade pitch—and hence thrust—of the tail rotor, which spins at a constant rate in relation to the main rotor.

10. Frank J. Delear, *Igor Sikorsky: His Three*

Careers in Aviation (New York: Dodd, Mead & Co., 1969), p. 190.

11. *American Helicopter Quarterly* 1, no. 1 (January 1946): 58.

12. The Army's first helicopter had been the large cruciform machine designed by scientist and mathematician George de Bothezat in 1922. Capable only of hovering, this machine was largely unsuccessful (as was a small coaxial helicopter constructed by de Bothezat in 1940).

13. AHQ, p. 58.

14. Sergei Sikorsky, "Reflections on a Pioneer," p. 13.

15. Harold E. Lemont, letter to author, January 6, 1993.

16. Delear, *Igor Sikorsky*, p. 195.

17. Jean Boulet, *History of the Helicopter: As Told By Its Pioneers, 1907–1956*, translated by Claude Dawson (Paris: Éditions France-Empire, 1984), p. 95.

18. Memorandum of May 12, 1942, Eugene E. Wilson, president of UAC, to Igor I. Sikorsky. UTC Archive, page 1 of document 4, file B-1, inv. no. 236.

19. Memorandum of July 17, 1940, Igor I. Sikorsky to C. J. McCarthy. UTC Archive, page 2 of document file B-1, inv. no. 236.

Memo reads: "This aircraft, of a radically novel type, was designed and built within 5 months with practically no outside design information available. The ship has proven to be the most successful direct lift aircraft ever produced in the United States up to the present time. The total expenses covering the engineering, construction, repairs after the accident of December 11, 1939, various refinements and several months of test flying up to July 1, 1940, were about $60,000, which includes complete normal overhead."

20. The designations XR-2 and XR-3 had been assigned to Kellett for autogiro use, since the Dorsey Bill embraced all forms of rotary-wing flight.

21. Lightfoot interview, UTC Archive, p. 72.

22. The center of lift of most cambered airfoils shifts fore or aft depending on the airfoil's angle of attack to the relative wind. However, the center of lift must remain directly below a rotor blade's spar (by which it is connected to the rotor hub); otherwise, there will be a force tending to pitch the blade up or down. Use of symmetrical airfoils solves this problem, for they display a constant center of lift regardless of angle of attack. The cost is loss of efficiency, because symmetrical airfoils generate less lift than do most cambered airfoils.

23. Even weighing the same amount, blades with different longitudinal centers of gravity will not balance on a teeter. Those with proportionately more of their weight near the tip tilt down because they exercise a greater moment (just as sliding a weight tilts a doctor's scale even though the total weight of the scale remains constant).

24. In contrast, helicopter pioneer Frank Piasecki, helped by autogiro engineer Elliot Daland, realized the need for dynamic blade balancing from the outset. His PV-2 of 1943 flew very well.

25. A center of gravity *slightly* ahead of the spar is not undesirable, since it tends to make the rotor blade self-correcting, but one that is too far forward—like an aft center of gravity—is destabilizing.

26. Lightfoot interview, p. 72.

27. Charles Lester Morris, *Pioneering the Helicopter* (New York: McGraw-Hill, 1945), p. 91.

28. In 1943, German submarines were sinking Allied shipping at a rate 2.5 times faster than new ships could be built. Had that rate continued, America's resupply effort would have ended within fourteen months. British Prime Minister Winston Churchill later claimed that the Nazi U-boat menace was the only thing that ever really scared him.

29. Lightfoot interview, p. 132.

30. Although new for Sikorsky, vertically mounting an engine to put its crankshaft in line

with the rotor shaft had been done before, even in the United States. Frank Piasecki's PV-2 and Arthur Young's Bell Model 30—both already in existence—had vertically mounted Franklin engines.

31. Lightfoot interview, p. 119.

32. United Aircraft Corporation Annual Report for 1944 (East Hartford, Connecticut: UAC, 1945), p. 8.

33. The possibility exists that rotary-wing pioneer Gliddan Doman may have provided the inspiration for the S-55, which propelled the Sikorsky company to success. Before the S-55 came into being, Doman—then an employee of Sikorsky Aircraft—had designed a helicopter embodying its winning configuration.

34. Because the Bell HSL-1 had failed to prove satisfactory in the antisubmarine warfare role, the Navy had adapted the workhorse S-58 and had spearheaded its authorization for instrument flight in order to make it compatible with the ASW mission.

35. Sikorsky-licensee SNCASE, developer of the piston-powered Alouette I and turbine-powered Alouette II, in 1957 merged with SNCASO, manufacturer of the tip-powered Djinn pressure-jet helicopter. The resulting company, Sud-Aviation, was itself absorbed into a larger corporate entity with the formation of Aérospatiale in 1969.

On January 14, 1958, the five-passenger Alouette II became the first turbine helicopter to receive CAA production certification. The desire of Republic Aviation on Long Island, New York, to manufacture Alouette IIs under license for U.S. and Canadian markets explains how the French helicopter beat American designs to this unique distinction.

36. A dozen years earlier, when Sikorsky sent a civil-registered S-51 to sea aboard the USS *Franklin Delano Roosevelt* in 1947 to prove to the Navy that it needed helicopters, that aircraft carrier's captain had been none other than J. P. W.

Vest. A career Naval aviator, Vest had earned his wings in 1925.

37. Vest, p. 4.

38. Lightfoot interview, p. 151.

39. The A-model suffix had been reserved for USAF S-61s, which would enter Air Force service as the CH-3B early in 1962.

40. And, of course, the subsequent one-shot Apollo-Soyuz Test Program of 1975 and Skylab missions flown between 1973 and 1979. Both these programs employed Project Apollo hardware.

41. A malfunction of precisely this system, producing a false indication of imminent blade failure, forced a (Marine Corps CH-53) Sea Stallion to set down in the Iranian desert in April 1980. This needless landing contributed to the failure of the Carter administration's ill-fated covert military operation to free fifty-three American hostages being held by Iran following the November 1979 seizure of the U.S. embassy in Tehran.

42. Annual report, United Aircraft Corporation, 1970, p. 4.

43. Ibid., 1985, p. 6.

44. "Sikorsky Aircraft: Yesterday and Today," *Defense* (Redhill, Surrey, UK: International Trade Publications, industry supplement, June 1989), p. 7.

3. / PIASECKI, VERTOL, AND BOEING HELICOPTERS

1. Even as the Wilford Gyroplane flew in Paoli, Arthur M. Young—a native of that Pennsylvania town—was testing his first electrically powered model helicopter. This experimentation culminated a dozen years later in Young's invention of the Bell helicopter.

2. Piasecki interview with author, April 4, 1990. Subsequent quotations of Piasecki in the text are from this interview unless otherwise noted.

3. W. J. Holt, Jr., "He likes to Fly Straight Up," *Saturday Evening Post,* August 11, 1951, p. 33.

4. Ibid.

5. Jean Boulet, *History of the Helicopter: As Told By Its Pioneers, 1907–1956*, translated by Claude Dawson (Paris: Éditions France-Empire, 1984), p. 110.

6. Piasecki interview.

7. Frank Mamrol, interview with author, April 3, 1990.

8. "Ten Years Since PV-2 Made First Flight: Piasecki, Daland, and Meyers Recall Flight," *Tandemeer* (Piasecki Helicopter Corporation newsletter) 7, no. 6 (April 1953): 2.

9. Boulet, *History of the Helicopter*, p. 112.

10. Holt, "He Likes to Fly Straight Up," p. 61.

11. Ibid.

12. *Aero Digest* 43, no. 5 (November 1943): 188.

13. *Aviation* 42, no. 11 (November 1943): 229.

14. Thomas R. Pierpoint, letter to author, May 20, 1990.

15. Holt, "He Likes to Fly Straight Up," p. 61.

16. Piasecki interview.

17. Boulet, *History of the Helicopter*, p. 112.

18. Reflecting the newness of helicopters, this designation departed from standard USN aircraft nomenclature guidelines. Had normal practice been followed, this first Piasecki tandem-rotor prototype would have been christened XHRP-1.

19. Frank Piasecki to author via Thomas R. Pierpoint, October 21, 1991.

20. Ibid.

21. This Navy contract award was engineered by financier Laurance Rockefeller, who served during World War II as a lieutenant commander in the Navy Bureau of Aeronautics in Washington, D.C. Shortly before the war, Rockefeller led the speculative investment groups that established both the Platt-LePage and McDonnell aircraft companies.

22. Kenneth Meenen, interview with author, April 5, 1990.

23. Edward T. Keast, interview with author, April 4, 1990.

24. One commuter who had precisely this reaction was Florence Newell, who would join PHC in 1948. Soon assigned as Frank Piasecki's secretary, "Flossie" Newell Piazza, at the time of this writing, remains his invaluable administrative assistant at the Piasecki Aircraft Corporation in Essington, Pennsylvania.

25. Holt, "He Likes to Fly Straight Up," p. 63.

26. Ibid.

27. Just how much of a role Laurance Rockefeller played in McDonnell's choosing to invest in Platt-LePage and—following the latter's demise—acquiring its assets is subject to speculation. So is his role in the St. Louis company's further decision to develop an unbuilt Platt-Le Page design as the XHJD-1, which then won a contract from the Navy's Bureau of Aeronautics, with which Rockefeller maintained close ties.

28. *Tandemeer* (Piasecki Helicopter Corporation newsletter) 1, no. 5 (December 1946): 1.

29. Pierpoint to author, May 20, 1990.

30. Handwritten draft, interoffice memorandum, T. R. Pierpoint and W. G. Knapp to W. Guzewicz, Piasecki Helicopter Corporation, January 30, 1947, pp. 5–6. (Pierpoint collection).

31. *American Helicopter* 7, no. 8 (July 1947): 39.

32. Piasecki Helicopter Corporation Annual Report for 1947, p. 6.

33. There was no "XH-21" because this USAF helicopter was not a new design. It was an improved version of the HRP-3 which Piasecki Helicopters had proposed to the Navy.

34. *Field Notes*, American Helicopter Society, November 1947, pp. 17 and 30.

35. The change in designation prefix from PV to PD reflected the absence of Harold Venzie, who departed shortly before P-V Engineering won its key Navy helicopter contract in 1944. Standing for Piasecki-Daland, this new prefix would give way to PH for Piasecki Helicopters about 1950.

36. This progression explains the strong resem-

blance between the rotor heads of the PV-2 and the Hughes 269/TH-55 light piston helicopter.

37. Memorandum, "Summary of Discrepancies Noted During Recent Operations with HRP-1 Helicopters," T. R. Pierpoint to F. N. Piasecki, Piasecki Helicopter Corporation, August 13, 1948, p. 3.

38. Supplied by the U.S. under the Mutual Defense Assistance Program, these French machines —then comprising the bulk of the French Navy's vertical-flight capability—would be used in the Mediterranean in training and utility roles, and in antisubmarine warfare trials. Arriving before the cease-fire in Indochina, these HUP-2s would also participate in France's losing effort to retain that region as a territorial possession.

39. The HRP-2 gave rise to the H-21. In November 1949 a ten-man USAF evaluation team visited Piasecki and other companies, looking for a manufacturer to build the Air Force an arctic rescue helicopter. Although the HRP-2 lacked sufficient performance to fulfill this requirement, it struck the team as the most promising design. On its recommendation, Piasecki was awarded the H-21 contract.

40. Meenen interview.

41. Among others who shared Piasecki's vision of interchangeable underbody pods was Igor Sikorsky, who refined the concept in the S-60 and applied it in operational service in Vietnam in the S-64 Skycrane. However, the popular detachable-pod concept never really caught on.

42. The Curtiss-Wright Corporation itself would contribute to U.S. rotary-wing development by sponsoring an aeronautical research laboratory at Cornell University. Among the pioneering helicopter studies made at this upper New York State facility were investigations into fiberglass rotor blades, ground resonance, rotor vibration isolation systems, and governors for use with turboshaft engines. Curtiss-Wright, whose interest in

vertical flight began in the 1920s with sponsorship of the unsuccessful Curtiss-Bleeker helicopter, would develop and test two tiltrotor VTOL prototypes shortly before its demise in the 1960s.

43. John Schneider, "The Evolution of the Tilt Rotor," *Boeing News, Philadelphia Edition* 42, no. 7 (September 30, 1988): 4.

44. Pierpoint letter to author, June 8, 1991.

45. *Operations Research Study to Determine Optimum Transport Helicopter Characteristics for Military Assault Operations in Algeria*, Vertol Aircraft Corporation Report R-120, April 11, 1957, p. iv.

46. David Anderton and Jay Miller, *Boeing Helicopters CH-47 Chinook*, Aerofax Minigraph 27, Arlington, Texas, 1989, p. 2.

47. Lee Douglas, interview with author, April 8, 1990.

48. One early Chinook shook so badly, despite all efforts by the company to tame it, that the Army finally gave up and reassigned it for ground training.

49. Flown in 1970, the Model 347 also featured retractable landing gear and was tested with a tilting wing.

50. Once costs absorbed by the parent Boeing Company are factored in, it becomes evident that the Philadelphia division has rarely been profitable. In this regard, Boeing Helicopters resembles its traditional rival Sikorsky, which has generally not contributed to the profitability of its corporate parent, United Technologies.

4 / BELL HELICOPTER

1. Bartram Kelley, transcribed interview with author, January 25, 1990.

2. Arthur M. Young, *The Bell Notes: A Journey from Physics to Metaphysics* (New York: Delacorte Press/Seymour Lawrence, 1979), p. 11.

3. Ibid., p. 12.

4. Ibid.

5. Richard S. Tipton, *They Filled the Skies* (Fort

Worth: Bell Helicopter Textron, fourth printing, 1989), p. 3.

6. Ibid.

7. Coincidentally, Harvey Gaylord—who would rise to lead Bell's helicopter division in Texas ten years later—also joined Bell Aircraft on this date.

8. Kelley interview, p. 14.

9. Tipton, *They Filled the Skies*, p. 4.

10. Young, *Bell Notes*, p. 15.

11. Arthur Young, transcribed interview with author, January 5, 1990, p. 10.

12. Donald J. Norton, *Larry: A Biography of Lawrence D. Bell* (Chicago: Nelson-Hall, 1981), p. 157.

13. Tipton, *They Filled the Skies*, p. 8.

14. Ibid., p. 22.

15. Quoted to author by Joseph Mashman, December 17, 1989.

16. Kelley interview, p. 1.

17. Tipton, *They Filled the Skies*, p. 10.

18. Young interview, p. 27.

19. Kelley interview, p. 30.

20. Young interview, pp. 21–22.

21. Young, *Bell Notes*, p. 20. *Birth of the Bell Helicopter*, videotape narrated by Bartram Kelley (Fort Worth: Bell Helicopter Textron/Bartram Kelley, 1977). Mashman interview, p. 20.

22. Young, *Bell Notes*, p. 20.

23. Mashman interview, pp. 17–18.

24. Ibid., p. 13.

25. Ibid., pp. 13–14.

26. Young, *Bell Notes*, p. 21.

27. Young interview, p. 18.

28. Tipton, *They Filled the Skies*, p. 18.

29. Norton, *Larry*, pp. 159–60.

30. Tipton, *They Filled the Skies*, p. 15.

31. *American Helicopter* 8, no. 10 (September 1947): 44.

32. Performed by a Model 47B in February 1948, this rescue closely paralleled the March 1945 retrieval of two stranded fishermen by Floyd Carlson in the third Bell Model 30 prototype (described earlier in this chapter).

33. Norton, *Larry*, p. 160.

34. One day before receiving the Collier Trophy, Larry Bell was awarded the Certificate of Merit by President Harry Truman.

35. Wheelabrator was not acquired outright, unlike other Bell subsidiaries. Bell Aircraft initially gained a controlling interest, which it held until June 27, 1954, when it took full possession by acquiring the Indiana company's outstanding shares.

36. *American Helicopter* 12, no. 10 (September 1948): 25.

37. Doyle O. Hickey, "The Helicopter's Role in the Armed Forces: In the Army Field Forces," *American Helicopter* 44, no. 5 (April 1956): 15.

38. Hans Weichsel, Jr., interview with author, May 17, 1990.

39. The stockpiled engines also expedited fulfillment of rival builder Hiller's Korean War production. Larry Bell made many of these power plants available to the government for use in Hiller H-23 medical evacuation helicopters.

40. As quoted by Joe Mashman, interview with author, January 26, 1990.

41. Norton, *Larry*, p. 165.

42. Ibid.

43. *Bell Helicopter News* 10, no. 5 (December 8, 1961): 5.

44. *Bell Aircraft News, Texas Edition* 2, no. 14 (March 26, 1954): 5.

45. BAN 1, no. 1 (September 26, 1952): 1.

46. Norton, *Larry*, p. 168.

47. James C. Fuller, interview with author, May 17, 1990.

48. Jan Drees, letter to author, April 27, 1992.

49. BAN, *Texas Edition* 3, no. 2 (October 8, 1954): 2.

50. Fuller interview.

51. *American Helicopter* 45, no. 1 (December 1956): 8 and 22.

52. BHN 5, no. 22 (July 19, 1957): 1.

53. BAN, *Texas Edition* 3, no. 14 (April 8, 1955): 1.

54. The XH-40 started life as the Model 212. This company designation lasted only until mid-June 1955, when what would be the Huey was redesignated the Model 204. The number 212 would later be reused.

55. BAN, *Texas Edition* 5, no. 4 (November 9, 1956): 2.

56. The prefix HU, denoting a utility helicopter, was reversed to UH on September 18, 1962, during a revision of U.S. military designations to create a single nomenclature for all branches of the American armed forces.

57. The Agusta Group—a European manufacturer dating back to Italian aviation pioneer Giovanni Agusta in 1907—has license-built Bell, Sikorsky, and Boeing Vertol helicopters in addition to producing its own designs.

58. BHN 11, no. 14 (April 12, 1963): 1.

59. BHN 9, no. 20 (July 7, 1961): 1.

60. Testimony and accounts of Hughes's LOH subversion are to be found in *Review of Army Procurement of Light Observation Helicopters*, Subcommittee for Special Investigations, Committee on Armed Services, House of Representatives, 90th Congress, 1st sess. (Washington, D.C.: Government Printing Office, 1967); Donald L. Barlett and James B. Steele, *Empire: The Life, Legend, and Madness of Howard Hughes* (New York: W. W. Norton, 1979); and Jay P. Spenser, *Vertical Challenge: The Hiller Aircraft Story* (Seattle: University of Washington Press, 1992).

61. John W. Olcott, "The Making of a Classic," *Business and Commercial Aviation* 38, no. 7 (July 1986): 43.

62. Kenneth Peoples, *Bell AH-1 Cobra Variants* (Arlington, Texas: Aerofax, 1988), p. 2. The reader is also directed to other Aerofax publications for highly detailed and accurate technical descriptions of major helicopter programs.

63. Major Department of Defense production contracts generally make provision for independent research and development (IR&D). Amounting to 2 or 3 percent of total contracted value, such funds may be put to whatever R&D use the manufacturer wants.

64. Drees, letter to author, April 27, 1992.

65. Charles Seibel, interview with author, May 14, 1990.

66. Weichsel interview.

67. Seibel interview.

68. BHN 10, no. 7 (January 5, 1962): 1.

69. *An Exhibition of Innovation*, promotional booklet (Fort Worth: Bell Helicopter Textron, [1985]), p. 19.

5 / HILLER AIRCRAFT

1. Hiller to author, August 26, 1990.

2. Hiller, transcribed interview, June 2–4, 1988, p. 7.

3. Ibid., p. 10.

4. Hal Risdon, "Hiller—Boy Aero Wizard," *Flying Aces*, March 1945, p. 33.

5. Page Mill Road is today the heart of Silicon Valley. On the exact spot in a field where the J-5 first flew stands the headquarters of the Hewlett-Packard Corporation.

6. Hiller interview, p. 59.

7. Ibid.

8. Scholer Bangs, "Hiller Copter Has Built-In Stability," *Aviation Week*, December 15, 1947.

9. Ibid.

10. Hiller interview, p. 66.

11. William Flynn, "Helicopters Are Easy: Look Ma, I'm Hovering," *San Francisco Chronicle*, no date [1947].

12. Model 12 production shifted from Hiller Aircraft in California to Fairchild Hiller in Maryland in the 1960s. Subsequently built elsewhere, notably in Washington State, intermittent 12E production continues to the time of this writing.

13. As observed by retired Bell Vice President Joe Mashman, "The Hiller aircraft always outper-

formed us. We were always behind them." A noted helicopter authority, Mashman joined Bell in 1943 and subsequently logged more than 16,000 hours of rotary-wing time in all makes and models of helicopters. Interview with author, January 26, 1990.

14. Three Navy helicopters had already accomplished this feat in February 1948.

15. "Helicopter Unable to Help Injured Lad," no source [August 3, 1949]; reproduced by Hiller Helicopters in promotional compilation of rescue clippings.

16. "'Copter Rescues Injured Boy," *San Francisco News*, August 4, 1949, p. 1.

17. Interview with author, p. 53.

18. Valérie André, *Madame le Général* (Paris: Librairie Académique Perrin, 1988), p. 138.

19. John F. Straubel, "Sample Chapter Four," manuscript portion of proposed Hiller history, Hiller Museum archives, p. 31.

20. "Hiller Unveils New Jet Helicopter," Hiller Helicopters press release, February 27, 1951.

21. Straubel, "Sample Chapter Four," p. 33.

22. Hiller interview, p. 129.

23. Ibid.

24. Promotional leaflet, "Marines' XROE-1 Rotorcycle," Hiller Helicopters, 2 pages [1957].

25. Delford M. Smith to Robert Wagner, 1989.

26. Ibid.

27. Everett L. Barrick, telephone interview with author, November 14, 1989.

28. Smith to Wagner, 1989.

29. G. F. Champlin, "Hiller Predicts Sales Increase," *American Helicopter*, April 1960, p. 6.

30. Interview with author, June 3, 1988, p. 52.

31. "'High' Records Set Over Rockies," *Ag-Pilot International*, June 1983, p. 47.

32. "Hiller Graphic: Vertical Flight News Pictorial," Hiller Aircraft pamphlet promoting Model Ten99 [1961], p. 2.

33. LOH Hearings, testimony of Stanley Hiller, Jr., January 27, 1967, p. 173.

34. More properly called the Senate Special Committee to Investigate the National Defense Program, this body—nicknamed the Truman Committee, after its first chairman—came into being in 1941. Having sped America's wartime mobilization and saved billions of tax dollars, the Truman Committee was in decline and mopping up by the time Senator Owen Brewster, its fourth and last chairman, took on Howard Hughes in 1947. The committee disbanded the following year.

35. Hiller to author, May 20, 1989.

36. Report, technical evaluation of LOH proposals, U.S. Navy, as quoted by Donald L. Barlett and James B. Steele in *Empire: The Life, Legend, and Madness of Howard Hughes* (New York: W. W. Norton, 1979), p. 352.

37. LOH Hearings, testimony of Stanley Hiller, Jr., January 27, 1967, p. 173.

38. The Hughes 269's rotor and dynamic components borrowed heavily from the small, experimental McCulloch MC-4 tandem helicopter, to which Hughes had acquired the rights. It, in turn, was a revised version of the Helicopter Engineering and Research Corporation JOV-3, a 1948 helicopter incorporating rotor technology borrowed from the Piasecki PV-2 of 1943.

39. LOH Hearings, testimony of Alfred B. Fitt, January 25, 1967, p. 8.

40. Ibid., testimony of General Herbert B. Powell, May 24, 1967, p. 561.

41. Ibid., testimony of Lieutenant Colonel Samuel R. Boyer, p. 557.

42. Ibid., p. 554.

43. Ibid., testimony of Donald Armstrong, p. 511.

44. Ibid., statement of Honorable Porter Hardy, Jr., p. 42.

45. Stanley Hiller, interview with author, May 5, 1990.

46. Ibid.

APPENDIX A / EARLY MILITARY
HELICOPTER USE

1. The Engineering Division was created by act of Congress in 1917 to probe the limits of aviation technologies in support of the nation's fledgling Air Service. So successful was it that McCook—whose functions were later transferred to nearby Wright Field, and later still to Edwards Air Force Base in California—is an unsung birthplace of American air power.

2. Lt. Col. Edgar C. Wood, "The Army Helicopter: Past, Present, and Future," *Journal of the American Helicopter Society* 1, no. 1 (January 1956): 88.

3. *United States Statutes at Large*, vol. 52, 75th Congress, 3rd sess., June 30, 1938, H.R. 10605, Public, No. 787, Chapter 852 (Washington, D.C.: U.S. Government Printing Office, 1939), p. 1255.

4. It may seem surprising that an Army captain held such an important post. In the interwar period, however, promotion was slow and officers often retired after full careers as captains or majors.

5. James Thomas, "Operation Garrigus," *American Helicopter*, September 1947, p. 6.

6. Cold weather tests were also performed atop Mount Washington, the highest peak in the White Mountains of New Hampshire, during the winter of 1944–45. These tests revealed that icing of rotor head controls, rather than rotor blades, was the true hazard in arctic helicopter operations. As a result, the Piasecki/Vertol H-21 of the 1950s—whose development was fostered by the USAF for Distant Early Warning (DEW) Line use in the far north—featured spinners and boots to protect its rotor head from control loss due to icing.

7. Between World War II and the Korean War, the French initiated the world's first routine combat rescue and evacuation operations in Indochina with American-built Hiller helicopters beginning in 1949.

8. After the AAF became the separate USAF, the U.S. Army had no mechanism for direct aircraft procurement. For a dozen years, it procured military aircraft through the Navy or the Air Force. An expedient alternative available to all branches of the military was "off-the-shelf procurement," or direct purchase of CAA/FAA-approved civil aircraft.

9. *Bell Aircraft News, Texas Edition* 1, no. 4 (November 7, 1952): 2.

10. *BAN, Texas Edition* 1, no. 26 (September 11, 1953): 1.

11. J. F. Farley, "The Helicopter's Role in the Armed Forces: In the Coast Guard," *American Helicopter* 13, no. 2 (January 1949): 20.

12. "The Piasecki Story of Vertical Lift: Pioneers in Progress for Over Forty Years" (Essington, Penn.: Piasecki Aircraft Corporation, ca. 1982), p. 4.

13. The HTK-1 was the least successful of these primary trainer/light utility machines, with just thirty being procured in 1950. The Kaman K-225 would also fail on the commercial market, unlike the Bell and Hiller machines.

14. "First Helicopter Squadron Formed," *American Helicopter*, September 1946, p. 48.

15. "A History of Achievement: U.S. Navy and Sikorsky Aircraft" (Stratford, Conn.: Sikorsky Aircraft, 1975), p. 2.

16. William G. Knapp, "Helicopters in Naval Aviation," *Journal of the American Helicopter Society* 1, no. 1 (January 1956): 100.

17. Farley, "Helicopter's Role," p. 18.

18. Erickson to Waesche, "Helicopters for Coast Guard Use," memorandum dated June 29, 1942, p. 1. United Technology Archives.

19. In fact, Sikorsky's estimate was optimistic: as described in Part 1, the XR-5 prototype would not fly until August 1943, and wartime production of the type would be greatly hampered by chronic technical problems.

20. Burton to Waesche, "Helicopters for Coast Guard Use, 1st Endorsement," June 30, 1942. United Technology Archives.

21. Farley, "Helicopter's Role," p. 19.

22. Frank Erickson, "U.S. Coast Guard Helicopter Stabilizer," *American Helicopter* 48, August, p. 59.

23. Thomas, "Operation Garrigus," p. 25.

24. The Piasecki Helicopter Corporation became the Vertol Aircraft Corporation in 1956.

APPENDIX B / EARLY COMMERCIAL HELICOPTER USE

1. News brief, *American Helicopter* 28, no. 12 (November 1952): 18.

2. *Bell Aircraft News, Texas Edition* 1, no. 1 (September 26, 1952): 2.

3. Fixed-base operators (FBOS) are airport-based businesses providing a variety of services to aircraft owners, often including fueling, sales, leasing, charters, rentals, maintenance, and training.

4. "Bell Starts 'Copter School,'" *American Helicopter*, September 1946, p. 25.

5. The Yellow Cab Company had an interest in aviation going back fully twenty years. In 1925 it had acquired and modified designer Giuseppe Bellanca's first cabin monoplane, the C.F. of 1922, and had evaluated its use as a "Yellow Aircab."

6. News brief, *American Helicopter* 19, no. 2 (January 1953): 19.

7. "The Helicopter in the Post Office Department," *American Helicopter*, March 1949, p. 18.

8. Ferdinand D. Moran, news brief, *American Helicopter*, June 1948, p. 17.

9. This helicopter carrier was actually the second airline to be called New York Airways. The first began operations in 1930 using Ford, Fokker, and Sikorsky aircraft before being absorbed by Eastern Airlines.

10. News brief, *American Helicopter*, April 1954, p. 3.

11. Ibid., August 1954, p. 4.

Bibliography

André, Valérie. *Ici, Ventilateur!* Paris: Calman-Lévy, 1954.

———. *Madame le Général.* Paris: Librairie Académique Perrin, 1988.

Apostolo, Giorgio. *The Illustrated Encyclopedia of Helicopters.* New York: Bonanza, 1984.

Army Aviation; Modernization Strategy Needs to Be Reassessed: Report to Congressional Requesters. U.S. General Accounting Office. Report No. GAO/NSIAD-95-9. Washington, D.C.: Government Printing Office (G.P.O.), 1994.

Bain, Edward Ustick. *S-O-S Helicopter.* Chicago: A. Whitman, 1947.

Baldwin, William Lee. *The Impact of Department of Defense Procurement on Competition in Commercial Markets: Case Studies of the Electronics and Helicopter Industries.* Office of Policy Planning, U.S. Federal Trade Commission. Washington, D.C.: Government Printing Office, 1980.

Boulet, Jean. *History of the Helicopter: As Told by Its Pioneers, 1907–1956.* Paris. Editions France-Empire, 1984.

Bracke, Albert. *Les Hélicoptères Paul Cornu.* Paris: F.-L. Vivien, 1908.

Bradin, James W. *From Hot Air to Hell Fire: The Story of Army Attack Aviation.* Novato, California: Presidio, 1994.

Branch, Melville Campbell. *Urban Air Traffic and City Planning: Case Study of Los Angeles County.* Design Environmental Planning Series. New York: Praeger, 1973.

Brie, R. A. C. *A History of British Rotorcraft, 1866–1965.* Yeovil, England: Westland Helicopters, 1968.

Brown, Eric M. *The Helicopter in Civil Operations.* New York: Van Nostrand Reinhold, 1981.

Colby, Carroll B. *Helicopters to the Rescue: How the Amazing "Whirly-Birds" Do the Impossible.* New York: Coward-McCann, 1958.

Cooke, David Coxe. *Helicopters That Made History.* New York: Putnam, 1964.

Davis, Ann N., and Robert A. Richardson. *The Helicopter: Its Importance to Commerce and the Public.* Washington, D.C.: Helicopter Association of America, 1978.

Debay, Yves, and Lindsay Peacock. *Heliborne: USMC Helicopter Assault.* Osceola, Wisconsin: Motorbooks International Division, Chronicle Publishing, 1993.

de la Cierva, Juan. "The Development of the Autogiro." *Journal of the Royal Aeronautical Society,* January 1926, pp. 8–29.

———. "The Autogiro." *Journal of the Royal Aeronautical Society,* November 1930, pp. 902–21.

———. "New Developments of the Autogiro." *Journal of the Royal Aeronautical Society,* December 1935, pp. 1125–43.

———. *Wings of Tomorrow: The Story of the Autogiro.* New York: Brewer, Warren and Putnam, 1931.

Diliberto, Stephen Peter, and Alexander A. Nikolsky. *Notes on Helicopter Design Theory: A Series* of Lectures Delivered March–April 1944 at Princeton University. Princeton: Princeton University Press, 1944.

Dorland, Peter, and James Nanney. *Dust Off: Army Aeromedical Evacuation in Vietnam*. Washington, D.C.: U.S. Army Center of Military History, 1982.

Everett-Heath, John. *Helicopters in Combat: The First Fifty Years*. London: Arms and Armour, 1992.

———. *Military Helicopters*. Land Warfare Series, vol. 6. London: Brassey's, 1990.

Examination of Rental Charges for Commercial Use of Government-Owned Facilities Furnished to Bell Helicopter Corporation. U.S. General Accounting Office. Washington, D.C.: Government Printing Office, 1959.

Fails, William R. *Marines and Helicopters, 1962–1973*. Upland, Pennsylvania: Diane Publishing, 1955.

Fay, John. *The Helicopter: History, Piloting and How It Flies*. New York: Hippocrene, 1987.

The First Commercial Helicopter Flight in the World as Sponsored by Filene's. William Filene's and Sons Department Store. Boston: no publisher (Library of Congress call no. TL716.F5), 1944.

Floherty, John Joseph, and Mike McGrady. *Whirling Wings: The Story of the Helicopter*. Philadelphia: Lippincott, 1961.

Focke, Heinrich. *Neue Wege der Flugtechnik*. Berlin: VDI-Verlag, 1938.

Gablehouse, Charles. *Helicopters and Autogiros: A Chronicle of Rotating-Wing Aircraft*. Philadelphia: Lippincott, 1967.

Gersdorff, Kyrill von, and Kurt Knobling. *Hubschrauber und Tragschrauber: Entwicklungsgeschichte der deutschen Drehflügler von den Anfangen bis zu den internationalen Gemeinschaftsentwicklungen*. Die Deutsche Luftfahrt, vol. 3. Munich: Bernard & Graefe, 1982.

Glines, Carroll V. *Helicopter Rescues*. New York: Four Winds Press, 1966.

Gregory, H. Franklin. *Anything a Horse Can Do: The Story of the Helicopter*. Introduction by Igor Sikorsky. New York: Reynal & Hitchcock, 1944.

Grose, Parlee Clyde. *The Problem of Vertical Flight*. McComb, Ohio: General Publishing Company, 1931.

Gunston, Bill. *Helicopters of the World*. Combat Aircraft Library. New York: Crescent, 1983.

———. *An Illustrated Guide to Military Helicopters*. Battlefield Weapons System and Technology Series. London: Brassey's Defense, 1985.

Harvey, J. Darrel. *The Helicopter Market of the United States*. Mass Market Survey, no. 1. Chicago: Land-Air, 1952.

The Helicopter and Its Commercial Applications. Washington, D.C.: Atlantic Airlines, Inc., 1947.

Helicopters in Korea, 1 July 1951–31 August 1953. Final draft of Far East Command Study ST55-170. Fort Eustis, Virginia: U.S. Army Transportation School, 1955.

House, David J. *An Introduction to Helicopter Operations Offshore*. Herefordshire, United Kingdom: Oilfield Publications, 1992 (U.S. publication, Tallahassee, Florida: AM Educational Publishing, 1993).

Jarolimek, Anton. *Über Luftschrauben und Schraubenflieger*. Vienna: Verlag des Österreichischen Flugtechnischen Vereines, 1909.

Lambermont, Paul, with Anthony Price. *Helicopters and Autogiros of the World*. Foreword by Igor Sikorsky. London: Cassell & Company, 1958.

Lamé, Maurice Luc Valère. *Le vol vertical et la sustentation indépendante: Hélicoptères, gyroptères, avions-hélicoptères*. Paris: Libraire de la Vie Technique et Industrielle, 1926.

———. *Le vol vertical: Théorie générale des Hélicoptères; les appareils à voilures tournantes de leurs origines à 1934*. Paris: E. Blondel La Rougery, 1934.

LePage, W. Lawrence. *Growing Up with Aviation*. Pittsburgh: Dorrance Publishing, 1981.

Local Service Air Transportation and Metropolitan Helicopter Services: A Study of Two of the Newer Elements of the Air Transportation Industry from the Investment Banking Viewpoint. Investment Bankers Association of America, and American Securities Committee. No place or publisher (Library of Congress call no. TL726.2.15), 1954.

Lopez, Donald S., ed. Vertical Flight: The Age of the Helicopter. Washington, D.C.: Smithsonian Institution Press, 1984.

Lukins, A. H. Modern European Helicopters. Oxford: G. Ronald, 1952.

Major Weapons Programs Oversight. Hearing Before the Subcommittee on Oversight and Investigations of the Committee on Energy and Commerce, House of Representatives, 102nd Congress, First Session, October 3, 1991 (McDonnell Douglas AH-64 Apache). Washington, D.C.: Government Printing Office, 1992.

McDonald, John J. Flying the Helicopter. Blue Ridge Summit, Pennsylvania: Tab Books, 1981.

Montross, Lynn. Cavalry of the Sky: The Story of U.S. Marine Combat Helicopters. New York: Harper and Brothers, 1954.

Moore, Oliver W. Initial Study of Helicopters. Cleveland: Cab Research Bureau and Post-War Planning Committee of the National Association of Taxicab Owners, 1944.

Morris, Charles Lester. Pioneering the Helicopter. New York: McGraw-Hill, 1945.

Munson, Kenneth. Helicopters and Other Rotorcraft Since 1907. Rev. ed. London: Blandford Press, 1973.

O'Leary, Michael, and John Guilmartin, Jr. The Illustrated History of Helicopters in the Vietnam War. The Illustrated History of the Vietnam War. Bearsville, New York: Rufus Publications, 1988.

Pelletier, Alain J. Bell Aircraft Since 1935. Annapolis: Naval Institute Press, 1992.

"The Piasecki Story of Vertical Lift: Pioneers in Progress for Over Forty Years." Lakehurst, New Jersey: Piasecki Aircraft Corporation, 1967.

Pitcairn, Harold F. "The Autogiro: Its Characteristics and Accomplishments." Annual Report to the Board of Regents of the Smithsonian Institution, 1930.

Polmar, Normal, and Floyd D. Kennedy, Jr. Military Helicopters of the World: Military Rotary-Wing Aircraft Since 1907. Annapolis: Naval Institute Press, 1981.

Prewitt, Richard Hickman. Report on Helicopter Development in Germany, May 1945. New York, 1945.

Prouty, Raymond W. Practical Helicopter Aerodynamics. Peoria, Illinois: PJS, 1982.

Rawlins, Eugene W., and William J. Sambito. Marines and Helicopters. Washington, D.C.: U.S. Marine Corps, 1976.

Riddle, Donald H. The Truman Committee: A Study in Congressional Responsibility. New Brunswick, New Jersey: Rutgers University Press, 1964.

Ross, Frank (Xavier). Flying Windmills: The Story of the Helicopter. New York: Lothrop, Lee & Shepard, 1953.

Smith, Frank Kingston. Legacy of Wings: The Story of Harold F. Pitcairn. New York: Jason Aronson, 1985.

Spenser, Jay P. Vertical Challenge: The Hiller Aircraft Story. Seattle: University of Washington Press, 1992.

Stein, Joe. Lift. Zig Zag, Oregon: Zig Zag Papers, 1985.

Taylor, John W. R. Helicopters and VTOL Aircraft. Garden City, New York: Doubleday, 1968.

Taylor, Michael J. H. Jane's Pocket Book, 20 Helicopters. London: Mcdonald and Jane's, 1978.

Tolson, John J. Airmobility, 1961–1971. Vietnam Studies. Washington, D.C.: U.S. Department of the Army, 1973.

Townson, George. Autogiro: The Story of the "Windmill Plane." Fallbrook, California: Aero Publishers, 1985.

Transportation by Helicopter, 1955–1975: A Study of Its Potential in the New Jersey–New York Metropolitan Area. New York: Aviation Department, Port Authority of New York, 1952.

The U.S. Helicopter Industry: Its Development, World Market, and Foreign Competition: An Ad Hoc Study Project of the Aviation Division, Aerospace Technical Council, Aerospace Industries Association of America. Washington, D.C.: AIAA, 1983.

Vallier, Emmanuel. *Notes sur la dynamique de l'aéroplane.* Paris: Dunod, 1905.

Wagner, Adolf. *Die richtigste Luftschraubenform in ihrer Anwendung als Trag-und Triebschraube bei Luftschiffen (Schraubenfliegern).* No place, self-published (printed in Frankfurt by C. E. Schock), 1909.

Williams, Samuel Clay. *Report on the Helicopter: The Helicopter and Its Role as a Transport Vehicle.* New York: Brundage, Story, and Rose, 1955.

Winson, Jonathan. *Motion of an Unarticulated Helicopter Blade with Application to the Problem of Vibration of the Rigid Rotor Helicopter.* Pasadena, California, 1916.

Wragg, David W. *Helicopters at War: A Pictorial History.* New York: St. Martin's Press, 1983.

Young, Arthur M. *The Bell Notes: A Journey from Physics to Metaphysics.* New York: Delacorte Press/Seymour Lawrence, 1979.

Index

Joy, C. Turner, 403

Kaadtmann, Roger, 244
Kaiser, Henry J., 292, 297, 298
Kaiser Shipyards, 285, 295
Kalista, Cliff, 269
Kaman, Charles, 49
Kaman Helicopters, 68, 69, 152, 167, 239, 257, 326, 333, 375, 458
—HTK-1 (K-225), 398
—HU2K/UH-2 Seasprite, 68, 152, 257, 272
Kauffman, Virgil, 100
Kawasaki Heavy Industries, 171
Keast, Edward, 128
Kellett, Wallace W., 95
Kellett Aircraft Corporation, 28, 64, 95, 96, 97, 100, 101, 102, 148, 151, 302, 334, 379, 381, 433
—KD-1, 96, 98, 446
—XR-8, 10, 160, 381
—XR-10, 148, 381
Kelley, Bartram, 184, 193–209 passim, 211, 236, 239, 244, 252, 262, 265, 269, 270, 384
Kelley, Frank H. "Bud," 196, 239
Kerr's Department Store, 426
Kesling, Paul, 264
Keystone Aircraft, 94, 102
Keystone Helicopters, 261
Key West Accord, 267, 342, 384–85, 386, 388, 393, 418, 422, 424
King, Ernest J., 394, 396, 407, 408
KING-5, Seattle, 438
Klemin, Alexander, 100–101, 121
KLM Nordzee Helikopters, 72
Knapp, William G., 136, 138, 139, 143
Korean War, 57, 154–55, 159, 215, 231–32, 237, 242, 324, 326, 328, 330, 331, 385–93, 402, 403, 405, 406, 413, 418–20, 438
Kossler, William J., 31, 406, 407, 408
Kozloski, Frank, 103, 104, 145

Labensky, Boris P., 22
LaGuardia, Fiorello, 210

LaJudice, Frank, 236
Lakehurst Naval Air Station, New Jersey, 141, 400, 402, 404, 415
Lalli, Philomena, 106, 112
LAMPS (Light Airborne Multi-Purpose System), 86, 91, 178
Langley Research Center, Virginia, 120, 297. See also NACA; NASA
Larson, Agnew, 95
Laterite (abrasive grit in Vietnam), 80, 171
Launoy, 4
LaVassar, Leonard, 143, 155, 169, 223
Leach, Bertram G., 356
Leamy, F. A., 406
Lear Aircraft, 151
Leavitt, Lou, 96, 102–3, 119, 160, 433
Lemont, Harold E., Jr., 18, 34, 302
LePage, W. Laurence, 95, 101, 102, 186
Lewis, A. W., 289, 292
LH Program, 93, 177, 278. See also Sikorsky-Boeing RAH-66
Library of Congress, 183
Lichten, Robert, 255, 262, 269
Lightfoot, Ralph, 37, 39–40, 42, 46, 49, 66, 67, 80
Light Observation Helicopter (LOH), 262–65, 267, 357, 360, 362–71
Lindbergh, Charles A., 12, 15, 31, 36, 77, 183
Liquidometer, 303
Little, Royal, 261
Lockheed Aircraft, 192, 268, 273, 331, 362
—AH-56 Cheyenne, 268, 272, 273
—CL-475, 268
Loewy, Raymond, 211
Los Angeles Airways, 49, 59, 70, 72, 76, 447, 448, 449, 452, 454, 456, 460
Lovett, Leland P., 394–95
Luckett, Link, 354–56
Ludington, Nicholas, 133, 154
Lufthansa, 463
Luke, Butch, 196, 239
Lundberg, Hans T., 436

Peterson, Frank W., 43, 303, 304, 306, 318, 337

Peterson, Harold, 155, 157

Petroleum Bell Helicopters, 225, 242, 436

Petroleum Helicopters (PHI), 72, 225, 247, 436, 437

Pettit, Smith D., 302

Philadelphia Navy Yard, 191

Phoenix Conversion, Hiller 12E, 359

Piasecki, Emilia, 100

Piasecki, Frank, 3, 94, 95, 96–162 passim, 180, 182, 198, 231, 283, 300, 373, 379, 397

Piasecki, Nikodem, 96

Piasecki Aircraft, 160

—16H, 272

Piasecki Helicopters, 3, 43, 94, 133–62 passim, 223, 231, 239, 283, 309, 384, 406. *See also* Boeing Helicopters; Boeing Vertol; Vertol

—PV-1, 105

—PV-2, 94, 105, 106–11, 112–17, 118–19, 122, 123, 130, 131, 136, 154, 160, 198, 397

—PV-3, 122, 131. *See also* Piasecki XHRP-X; XHRP-1; HRP

—XHRP-X *Dogship*, 122–24, 125–33 passim, 136, 141, 145, 154, 160, 397

—XHRP-1, 131, 133–38, 139, 397

—HRP-1 Rescuer, 43, 53, 59, 128, 131, 138, 141–143, 145, 147–48, 162, 398, 400, 404, 406, 412, 415, 416–18, 452

—HRP-2, 148–50, 155

—H-16 Transporter/Turbo-Transporter, 139, 143, 148, 155, 157, 381, 386

—H-21 Work Horse, 143, 155, 157, 159, 162, 164, 165, 390, 424

—XHJP-1, 53, 138, 143, 145, 150–51, 228, 405. *See also* HUP; H-25

—HUP Retriever, 59–60, 138, 151–52, 155, 167, 390, 405. *See also* Piasecki XHJP-1; H-25 Mule

—H-25 Mule, 139, 152, 390. *See also* Piasecki HUP

—PV-11. *See* HERC JOV-3

—XR-16. *See* Piasecki H-16

Pierpoint, Thomas R., 136, 138, 147, 148, 162, 164, 166, 167, 180, 384, 424

Pinilla, Gustavo Rojas, 245

Pitcairn, Harold F., 95

Pitcairn-Cierva Autogiro Company, 28, 95, 96, 97, 101, 102, 379

—OP-1, 413

Pitcairn-Larson Autogiro Company, 379

Platt, Haviland, 95, 101, 186, 187

Platt-LePage Aircraft, 28, 36, 101, 111–12, 121, 124, 133, 160, 379, 381, 433

—XR-1, 28, 95, 101, 103, 121, 125, 191, 378, 379

—XR-1A, 111–12, 124, 160, 379, 433

Plenefisch, Adolph, 22

Polytechnic Institute of Kiev, 14

Post Office Department, 17, 378, 446, 447, 452

Pozda, John, 196

Pratt & Whitney, 17, 18, 22

Prewitt, Richard, 95, 101, 151

Prewitt Aircraft, 151

Pride, A. M., 141

Princeton University, 183, 232

Propeller Laboratory, Wright Field, 383–84, 433

Purdue University, 159

P-V Engineering Forum, 43, 103–33 passim, 154, 182, 397. *See also* Piasecki Helicopters

Quantico Marine Base, 141, 148, 231, 415, 416, 420, 422

Quinlan, Bill, 251, 272, 274

Radio City Music Hall, 51

Ray, James G., 111

Raymond, Arthur, 31

Reconstruction Finance Corporation, 139

Red Star Way, 440

Reed, Donna, 448

Reed Tool, 370

Regan Air Services, 451

Reidy, Thomas H., 451

Reitsch, Hanna, 12